Interest in regional integration has recently revived in both developed and developing countries. The United States has responded to the lack of progress in the Uruguay Round of the GATT by pursuing bilateral trade negotiations with Canada and Mexico, while the developing countries' trade liberalisations of the 1980s have prompted them to re-evaluate the potential benefits of regional integration. The tendency for the world trading system to divide into three blocs – the European Community, the Americas and East Asia – is providing their members with guaranteed access to large markets, but non-member countries will suffer from the loss of access and there is an increasing risk of trade wars.

In this book, derived from a conference organised jointly by the World Bank and CEPR in April 1992, leading international experts assess the renewed attractiveness of regional integration to individual countries, the types of integration that are suitable to various circumstances, the conditions necessary to their success, and the relationship between regionalism and multilateral free trade.

New dimensions in regional integration

The World Bank

The World Bank is an international organisation whose primary objective is to help raise standards of living in developing countries by channelling financial resources to them from developed countries. In addition to its lending operations, the Bank engages in policy dialogue with its developing member countries and plays an active part in stimulating the kind of debate, of which this conference is an example, that helps shape development policy. The opinions expressed in this volume are those of the authors and not those of the World Bank.

Centre for Economic Policy Research

The Centre for Economic Policy Research is a network of more than 180 Research Fellows, based primarily in European universities. The Centre coordinates its Fellows' research activities and communicates their results to the public and private sectors. CEPR is an entrepreneur, developing research initiatives with the producers, consumers and sponsors of research. Established in 1983, CEPR is already a European economics research organisation with uniquely wide-ranging scope and activities.

CEPR is a registered educational charity. Grants from the Leverhulme Trust, the Esmée Fairbairn Charitable Trust, the Baring Foundation, the Bank of England and Citibank provide institutional finance. The ESRC supports the Centre's dissemination programme and, with the Nuffield Foundation, its programme of research workshops. None of these organisations gives prior review to the Centre's publications or necessarily endorses the views expressed therein.

The Centre is pluralist and non-partisan, bringing economic research to bear on the analysis of medium- and long-run policy questions. CEPR research may include views on policy, but the Executive Committee of the Centre does not give prior review to its publications and the Centre takes no institutional policy positions. The opinions expressed in this volume are those of the authors and not those of the Centre for Economic Policy Research.

Executive Committee

Chairman
Anthony Loehnis

Vice-Chairmen
Guillermo de la Dehesa
Adam Ridley

Giorgio Basevi
Honor Chapman
Sheila Drew Smith
Jacob Frenkel
Sarah Hogg

Otmar Issing
Mervyn King
Peter Middleton
Mario Sarcinelli
Alasdair Smith

Officers

Director
Richard Portes

Deputy Director
Stephen Yeo

Director of Finance and Research Administration
Wendy Thompson

22 December 1992

New dimensions in regional integration

Edited by

JAIME DE MELO

and

ARVIND PANAGARIYA

CAMBRIDGE
UNIVERSITY PRESS

Published by the Press Syndicate of the University of Cambridge
The Pitt Building, Trumpington Street, Cambridge CB2 1RP
40 West 20th Street, New York, NY 10011-4211, USA
10 Stamford Road, Oakleigh, Melbourne 3166, Australia

© Centre for Economic Policy Research 1993

First published 1993
First paperback edition 1995

Printed in Great Britain by Athenæum Press Ltd, Gateshead, Tyne & Wear

A catalogue record for this book is available from the British Library

Library of Congress cataloguing in publication data

New dimensions in regional integration / edited by Jaime de Melo
and Arvind Panagariya.
    p.   cm.
Includes index.
ISBN 0 521 44431 4
1. International economic integration – Congresses.
2. Regionalism Congresses.
3. Commercial policy – Congresses.
4. Free trade – Congresses.
5. International economic integration – Case studies – Congresses.
I. De Melo, Jaime.   II. Panagariya, Arvind.
HF1418.5.N48   1993
337.1–dc20   93–9818   CIP

ISBN 0 521 44431 4 hardback
ISBN 0 521 55668 6 paperback

CE

To R.E.W. Macght and C.J. Rich

To my father, B.L. Panagariya and mother, M.K. Panagariya

Contents

PART TWO: COUNTRY ISSUES

Figures

Tables

xvii

Preface

This volume is the outcome of a World Bank–CEPR conference held at the World Bank, Washington DC, on 2–3 April 1992. Partial funding for the conference was provided by the Research Administration of the World Bank under RPO 677-12. The support is gratefully acknowledged.

We owe special thanks to Ghislaine Bayard, Karla Cabana and Rebecca Sugui for a flawless administration of the conference. The large number of congratulatory messages we received after the conference were testimony to the superb organisation they carried out and to their untiring contribution to activities related to the production of the volume on the Western side of the Atlantic.

The editing, coordination and production of the volume have been carried out on the Eastern side of the Atlantic at CEPR. David Guthrie and Kate Millward were most effective at ensuring that authors (including the usually delinquent editors) delivered their manuscripts and revisions on time. Barbara Docherty, as Production Editor, was swift and thorough in editing the manuscripts.

Finally, we wish to thank Francis Ng of the World Bank for his superb statistical assistance on a number of chapters in the volume.

December 1992

Jaime de Melo
World Bank and University of Geneva

Arvind Panagariya
World Bank and University of Maryland

Foreword

The World Bank and the Centre for Economic Policy Research share the objective of promoting economic analysis with policy applications. A dominant concern in the current policy debate is whether the 'new' regionalism in trade policy can lead to a more integrated world economy. Will the regional approach promote world-wide economic integration? Or will it work at cross purposes with the more traditional multilateral approach? Are the resources needed successfully to complete the Uruguay Round being diverted into the negotiation of regional arrangements? Is the recent surge in regional arrangements leading to a world of a few trading blocs that will make the negotiation of future reductions in trade barriers easier? Is it likely that a world organised around trading blocs will entail a significant problem of market access for countries left out?

This volume is the outcome of the first collaboration between the World Bank and CEPR. It brings answers to these leading policy issues and advances the debate on the implications of the new regionalism for the world trading system. The contributions to the debate by eminent economists, many involved in policy making, address the choices facing a country that must choose between unilateral trade liberalisation that would be extended to all its trading partners but might be more difficult to implement domestically, and a trade liberalisation that is extended only to its regional partners, but that is more likely to have domestic support.

The volume also reviews the experience with all the major integration arrangements and discusses the prospects for new integration arrangements, including the Middle East and Eastern Europe. It will assist academics and policy makers in designing an efficient world trading system. We are therefore very pleased that Jaime de Melo and Arvind Panagariya have so successfully put together this conference and resulting volume.

December 1992

Richard Portes
Director
Centre for Economic Policy Research

Lawrence H. Summers
Vice-President, Development
Economics, and Chief Economist
The World Bank

Acknowledgements

The editors and publisher wish to thank the following for permission to reproduce copyright material.

International Organization, for Figure 2.2, from E. Mansfield, 'The Concentration of Capabilities and International Trade' (1992).
League of Nations, for Figure 4.1, from G. Haberler, *Quantitative Trade Controls: Their Causes and Nature* (1943), for Table 4.3, from *Report on Exchange Control* (1938), and for Table 4.4, from *Review of World Trade, 1938* (1939).
United Nations, for Figure 7.1, from 'Economic Survey, 1989/90' (UNECE, 1990).
European Economy, for Figure 7.2, from 'International Trade of the European Communities' (CEC, 1990).
Federal Reserve Bank of Kansas City, for Table 3.1, from L. Summers, 'The Move to Free Trade Zones: Comment', Federal Reserve Bank of Kansas City, *Review* (1991).
Macmillan, for Table 4.2, from H. Liepmann, *Tariff Levels and the Economic Unity of Europe* (1938).
Institute for International Economics, for Table 5.1, from J.J. Schott (ed.), *Free Trade Areas and U.S. Trade Policy* (1989) and for total trade figures in Table 9.2, from P. Wonnacott and M. Lutz, 'Is There a Case for Free Trade Areas?', in Schott (ed.) (1989).
IMF, for Table 7.1, from 'The Common Agricultural Policy of the European Community' (1988), and for data in Tables 8.2–8.3, 9.8 and 9.11, from *Directions of Trade*, various issues.
The World Bank, for data in Tables 8.1–8.3, from *World Development Report* (1991) and *World Bank Atlas* (1990); for data in Tables 9.4 and 9.5, from J. Nogués and S. Gulati, 'Economic Policies and Performance under Alternative Trade Regimes' (1992); for data in Tables 13.1, 13.2 and 13.5, from *World Development Indicators* (1991), in Tables 13.1–13.4, from

Human Development Report (1991), in Table 13.1, from *World Bank Atlas* (1991), in Table 13.5, from *World Debt Tables* (1991–2) and in Table 13.10, from *World Development Report* (1982).

Overseas Development Council, for data in Table 9.9, from R. Bouzas, 'A U.S.–MERCOSUR Free Trade Area' (1991).

Journal of Commerce (Poland), for data in Table 10.6.

Report on Eastern Europe, for data in Table 10.6, from P. Dobrowski, 'East European Trade, Part II: Creative East Bloc Solutions' (1991).

University of Chicago Press, for data in Table 12.1, from P. Petri, 'The East Asian Trading Bloc: An Analytical History', in J. Frankel (ed.), *U.S. and Japan in Pacific Asia* (forthcoming).

Bank of Israel, *Annual Report*, for data in Table 13.4 (1988) and Table 13.5 (1989).

MIT Press, for data in Table 13.7, from N. Choucri, 'Asians in the Arab World: Labor Migration and Public Policy' (1983).

OECD, for data in Tables 13.9 and 13.10, from *Development Co-Operation* (1990).

List of conference participants

Richard Baldwin   *Graduate Institute of International Studies, Geneva, and CEPR*
Robert Baldwin   *University of Wisconsin*
Jean Baneth   *World Bank*
Elliot Berg   *Development Alternative Inc.*
Jagdish Bhagwati   *Columbia University*
Nancy M. Birdsall   *World Bank*
Richard Blackhurst   *GATT*
Christopher Bliss   *Nuffield College, Oxford, and CEPR*
Josef Brada   *Arizona State University*
Christopher Clague   *University of Maryland*
Fernando Clavijo   *Economic Advisor to the President of Mexico*
Richard Cooper   *Harvard University*
Max Corden   *Johns Hopkins University*
Rudiger Dornbusch   *MIT and CEPR*
Barry Eichengreen   *University of California at Berkeley and CEPR*
Ronald Findlay   *Columbia University*
Michael Finger   *World Bank*
Stanley Fischer   *MIT*
Faezeh Foroutan   *World Bank*
Alan Gelb   *World Bank*
Enzo Grilli   *World Bank*
Robert Hudec   *Minnesota Law School*
Ishrat Husain   *World Bank*
Shahid Husain   *World Bank*
Douglas Irwin   *University of Chicago*
Ronald Jones   *University of Rochester*
Ravi Kanbur   *World Bank and CEPR*
Paul Krugman   *MIT and CEPR*
Ulrich Lächler   *World Bank*

Johannes F. Linn   *World Bank*
Jaime de Melo   *World Bank, Université de Genève and CEPR*
Constantine Michalopoulos   *World Bank*
Michael Mussa   *IMF*
Julio Nogués   *World Bank*
Gábor Oblath   *Kopint Datorg Institute for Economic and Market Research and Informatics, Budapest*
Mancur Olson   *University of Maryland*
Arvind Panagariya   *World Bank and University of Maryland*
Hugh Patrick   *Columbia University*
Rosalinda Quintanilla   *World Bank*
Dani Rodrik   *Harvard University and CEPR*
Bruce Ross-Larson   *World Bank*
André Sapir   *Commission of the European Communities, Université Libre de Bruxelles and CEPR*
Gary Saxonhouse   *University of Michigan*
Jesús Seade   *Mexican Ambassador to the GATT*
T.N. Srinivasan   *Yale University*
Lawrence Summers   *World Bank and Harvard University*
Vinod Thomas   *World Bank*
John Whalley   *University of Western Ontario*
L. Alan Winters   *University of Birmingham and CEPR*

Part One

SYSTEMIC ISSUES

1 Introduction

JAIME DE MELO and
ARVIND PANAGARIYA

The cornerstone of the post-World War II world trading system is the most favoured nation (MFN) clause that underlies all GATT-negotiated reductions in tariffs. Through the MFN clause, non-discrimination creates global order out of an essentially mercantilist system. Most importantly perhaps from the standpoint of lesser nations with little bargaining power, through the application of the MFN clause, purely bilateral bargains negotiated under the auspices of the GATT become available to all. Enormous progress towards global free trade has been made under this non-discriminatory approach to tariff reductions. For example, between the opening of the first round of multilateral talks in Geneva in 1947 and the close of the Tokyo round in 1979, the average US tariff had declined by nearly 92 percent. On the eve of the Uruguay round in 1987, the average tariff for the United States was 4.9 percent, for the European Community it was 6.0 percent, and for Japan it was 5.4 percent.

This long period of progressive trade liberalisation also witnessed two waves – waves because they came suddenly, and the first one at least, foundered – of regional trading arrangements. The first came during the early 1960s. Under the impetus of the European Common Market, regionalism spread throughout Africa, Latin America and other parts of the developing world. The United States was then a hegemon and a staunch supporter of multilateralism. Regionalism then came to a halt during much of the 1970s.

The second wave started in the middle 1980s. This time around, the United States was a major player. Following the negotiation of bilateral free-trade areas (FTAs) with Israel and Canada, the United States launched a proposal for a hemispheric FTA with the Enterprise for the Americas Initiative (EAI). And, most recently, the United States initialled the agreement for the North American Free-Trade Area (NAFTA) with Canada and Mexico. At the same time, European integration spread with the Southern (Greece, Portugal and Spain) and the Northern enlargements

3

(Norway and Sweden). More recently, the European Community has negotiated the Europe Agreements with Czechoslovakia, Hungary and Poland. Last but not least, a single market is about to be formed in Europe with 'EC 92'.

Likewise, throughout Africa, Asia, Latin America, and the Middle East, old arrangements are being revived and new ones created. A new lease on life has been given to the Central American Common Market (CACM) and to the Association for South East Asian Nations (ASEAN) with calls for the establishment of a Common Market and an FTA, respectively. And in the Southern cone of Latin America, the Southern Common Market (MERCOSUR) is to establish a Common Market between Argentina, Brazil, Paraguay, and Uruguay.

Because under regionalism preferences are extended only to partners, it is discriminatory. At the same time it represents a move towards freer trade among partners. Is this approach then a complement to multilateralism? Or is it a substitute for multilateralism that may well take the world economy away from the promised (and perhaps tortuous!) path of global free trade? Yet again, given the recent deadlocks in multilateral negotiations, isn't regionalism accelerating the transition towards global free trade? How have arrangements during the first wave of regionalism turned out, and what are the lessons for the new ones?

Is the world evolving towards trading blocs: one around the United States encompassing the Americas, another around the European Community encompassing most of Europe, and a third around Japan including most of Asia? To many observers, this is indeed the case and the issue is then whether such a move should be welcomed. Those who answer in the affirmative feel that the blocs will speed up the progress towards global free trade as negotiations would be better carried out among a few blocs than within the large membership of the GATT. Those opposed fear that trading blocs might turn inward and erect high barriers against non-members. There is also the issue of small countries left out of blocs. Will the GATT and the international trading system protect them sufficiently? And if not, what measures should be taken to strengthen the multilateral institutions so that the interests of the weaker nations are protected? These are some of the questions addressed by the distinguished contributors to this volume.

In this chapter, we introduce the themes addressed in the volume. Where should one start? One natural organising principle would be to start with the basic propositions of the economics of Customs Unions (CUs) and then to discuss the experience of past regional arrangements in that light. Another would be to start with a presentation of Article XXIV of the GATT which sanctions FTAs and CUs and then to discuss the first and second waves of regionalism. Instead, we prefer to discuss first the second wave of regionalism and the concomitant rise of trading blocs. This choice reflects the strong feeling shared by many that trading blocs are in the making and that this new wave of regionalism is here to stay.

In section 1, we review the causes behind the rise of trading blocs, why they are here to stay, and then turn to a brief discussion of the economics of trading blocs. We close with a summary of the lessons of history offered by the trading blocs in the 1860s and the 1930s. In section 2, we ask whether the first wave of regionalism achieved its goals, the discussion centring around the propositions derived from the theory of FTAs and CUs. The 'new' regionalism – a term we use to distinguish it from the first wave of regionalism – occupies section 3. Central to this discussion is that the new initiatives go beyond the extension of trade preferences to institutional aspects, and that the second wave of regionalism is occurring in a very different world-trading environment than the first. Finally section 4 returns to a discussion of the implications of the 'new' regionalism for countries with little bargaining power. At issue is how best these less powerful countries can protect their interests, and the role of multilateralism in protecting them.

1   Regionalism and (versus?) multilateralism

1.1   Revival of regionalism: why?

How do we explain the current revival of regionalism around the world? In Chapter 2, Jagdish Bhagwati argues that the single most important reason why regionalism is making a comeback and is likely to be more durable than the first round is the conversion of the United States. The first round failed principally because the United States was firmly committed to the multilateral approach and did not endorse the regional approach except in the case of the European Community.[1] Even there, it saw and subsequently used regionalism as an instrument to promote multilateralism. An organised Western Europe under the leadership of the European Community facilitated the GATT-led multilateral negotiations.

Unfortunately, this has changed in recent years. Disappointed by a lack of progress at the GATT negotiations, the United States has decided to switch course and gone on to conclude first the Canada–US Free-Trade Agreement (CUSTA) and is now going ahead with the North American Free-Trade Agreement (NAFTA). The United States has also announced its intention to negotiate free-trade agreements with groups of other Latin American countries under the EAI. Alongside this, the European Community has continued to widen and deepen its integration. These developments have, in turn, led other countries to reconsider the regional option. East Asia, in particular, is beginning to fear that a regional bloc there may be the only way to meet the challenge posed by developments in the Americas and Europe. Even developing countries are beginning to fear that their access to world markets may be curtailed considerably if trading blocs become a reality and they are left out.

A key reason for the United States' conversion to regionalism is the slow progress at the GATT. But why is it that the GATT negotiations are having less success in recent years than in the past? In Chapter 3, Paul Krugman offers four reasons. First, the number of players participating in the process has grown large which makes negotiations difficult and free-rider problem harder to handle. Second, the character of protection has changed. The presence of voluntary export restraints (VERs), anti-dumping (AD) mechanisms, and other forms of administered protection make the negotiating space vastly more complicated than it was in the past. Third, the decline in US dominance has made it more difficult to run the system. Finally, institutional differences among major countries make negotiations more complicated. Pointing to Japan, Krugman argues that with markets in that country 'governed by informal understandings and cartels', offers of tariff concessions by it are not the same as similar offers by the United States 'with its free-wheeling markets'.

1.2   The welfare economics of trading blocs

Given that the current round or regionalism is here to stay and that the possibility of the world dividing into three blocs cannot be ruled out, we must ask how these developments are likely to impact the welfare of the world, and of individual participants. The traditional answer to this question is provided by Viner (1950) who introduced the highly influential concepts of 'trade creation' and 'trade diversion'. To understand this, suppose that starting with a non-discriminatory tariff on all trading partners, the United States forms a FTA with Mexico. Suppose further that shoes are produced under constant costs everywhere and that the FTA results in the United States importing shoes from Mexico. Is this change for the better or worse? The answer, reasoned Viner, depends on who is the pre-FTA supplier of shoes. If the United States produced its own shoes in the initial equilibrium, it must do so at a higher cost than Mexico. In this case, the FTA shifts shoe production from a higher- to a lower-cost source and is trade creating; welfare of the union and of the world rises. If, on the other hand, the United States initially imports shoes from another country, say, the Republic of Korea, that country must be a lower-cost producer of shoes than Mexico. In this case, the FTA causes shoe production to shift from a lower- to a higher-cost source. There is trade diversion and the welfare of the union and the world declines. In this example, trade creation is accompanied by no change in trade with the rest of the world but increased trade between partners; the world as a whole moves closer to free trade. By contrast, trade diversion is accompanied by increased trade within the union at the expense of trade with the rest of the world; national protection is extended to the regional level and the world as a whole moves away from free trade. Traditionally, those who associate regionalism largely with trade creation consider it a positive force and those who think the reverse fear that it will be detrimental to the world trading system.

Today, the issue of regionalism has become more complex. For one thing, regional schemes cannot be considered in isolation as Viner assumed. With blocs forming almost simultaneously around the world, we must take into account the interaction effects as well as possible strategic behaviour among nations. More importantly, as Bhagwati emphasises, the static impact effect is only a part of the story. We must also pay attention to the dynamic time-path question: even if a particular regional scheme moves the world towards freer trade, over time it may result in a more protectionist world, and vice versa.

Turning first to the impact effect, we have Krugman's now familiar model of trading blocs. He considers a symmetric world in which there is a large number of identical countries. Individuals consume a differentiated good with many potential varieties. Each nation specialises completely in one variety and imports all the other varieties. At one extreme, with as many blocs as there are countries, each bloc is too small to have any market power. Therefore, Nash tariffs are zero and competitive behaviour maximises world welfare. At the other extreme, with one trading bloc, there are once again no trade restrictions and welfare is maximised. In between, welfare is lower. Starting with one bloc, if we divide the world into two blocs of equal size, each bloc exercises monopoly power over its products and imposes a Nash tariff on imports from its rival. There is trade diversion and each bloc suffers a loss of welfare. Next, suppose we divide the world into three equal blocs. This leads to only one-third rather than half of the goods being subject to free trade and there is further trade diversion. But the reduced size of each bloc also reduces its market power and the Nash tariff declines. This generates a trade-creation effect. With both trade diversion and trade creation taking place simultaneously, welfare may now rise or fall. As the number of blocs rises, the Nash tariff continues to decline and at some point must become sufficiently small to yield a larger trade-creation than trade-diversion effect. The critical question is the number of blocs at which this turning point obtains.

Surprisingly, Krugman finds that for a variety of parameters, the number of blocs for which a declining welfare begins to rise again is three! Taken seriously, this implies that the number of blocs into which the world is most likely to divide – three – minimises welfare. This finding remains robust to alternative tariff-formation processes.

In his Discussion, T.N. Srinivasan contends that Krugman's model 'comes uncomfortably close to being "theory without relevance"'. Among other things, Srinivasan suggests that the strong symmetry assumed by Krugman is devoid of reality. He then provides an alternative model which allows for both symmetric and asymmetric blocs and shows that in general there is no necessary relationship between the number of blocs and welfare. To illustrate his point, suppose there are two goods, 1 and 2, and labour is the only factor of production. Assume there are n identical countries with comparative advantage in good 1 and another n identical countries having a comparative advantage in good 2. Then if we divide the world into two blocs each consisting of n identical countries, welfare will be below the level attained under free trade. By contrast, if two blocs are formed by including $n/2$ countries of each type in each bloc, the outcome coincides with free trade without any trade between the blocs. Indeed we can form anywhere between 1 and n blocs with each bloc having half of the countries of one type and half of the other type and the outcome will coincide with the free-trade equilibrium. There is no necessary relationship between the *number* of blocs and welfare: the same number of blocs may yield different levels of welfare and different numbers of blocs may be associated with the same level of welfare. Drawing upon the work of Deardorff and Stern, Ronald Jones makes a similar point in his Discussion.

Results of his elegant model notwithstanding, Krugman admits that the real world is not symmetric and that, in practice, countries engaging in free-trade agreements have more in common with one another than with other countries. These countries are 'natural' trading partners in that they already trade intensively with each other. Citing evidence provided by Lawrence Summers, he concludes that within North America and within Europe trade is influenced heavily by geographic proximity and that a move to FTAs in these regions is unlikely to reduce welfare. Because intra-trade among countries of these regions is already substantial, trade-creation effects of regional integration are likely to dominate trade-diverting effects. Bhagwati disagrees, and notes that this argument is based on incorrect premises. First, citing Lipsey, he argues that the premise that an FTA is more likely to create trade the larger the ratio of a country's foreign trade with the partner relative to outside countries is incorrect. Second, there is no necessity that geographically proximate countries trade more intensely than distant countries even after we control for economic size. Africa and South Asia export 95 percent of their goods outside their own regions.

From the viewpoint of the world trading system, more critical than static effects are the dynamic time-path implications of the regional approach. Here divisions among economists are even deeper. Summers (1991) argues that the world is likely to move toward global free trade far more rapidly if the number of negotiating parties is reduced to three via bloc formation. Currently, with 105 parties negotiating at the GATT, the free-rider problem makes a substantive agreement unlikely. The flip side of the argument, however, is that large blocs also have greater market power and, in the absence of cooperation, will impose higher tariffs on each other. Taking this latter view, Bhagwati notes that larger countries often tend to be more inward-looking than smaller countries. Once a bloc is large enough, the need to be open to extra-bloc countries is reduced. Bhagwati is also sceptical of the argument, made by regionalists, that the regional approach is quicker and more certain. Depending on the relative power of different interest groups, trading blocs may turn inward over time. Interest groups within the bloc may take the view that the bloc's markets belong to them and resist extra-bloc liberalisation. Illustrative of this is the statement by the EC Commissioner for Foreign Relations Willy de Clerq, quoted by Alan Winters in Chapter 7, 'We are not building a single market in order to turn it over to hungry foreigners'.

Turning to evidence, Bhagwati argues that while the first round of regionalism was essentially a failure except in Europe, the GATT successfully oversaw the dismantling of prewar tariffs in the OECD countries. As for speed, it has taken even the European Community – the best example of regionalism – almost four decades to start talking about a single market. In agriculture, the European Community has ended up becoming an instrument for extending national protection to the regional level.

1.3   Prewar historical experiences

Can we learn something about the relative effectiveness of multilateralism and regionalism in promoting free trade from pre-World War II experiences? In Chapter 4, Douglas Irwin begins by noting that the general endorsement of the multilateral approach in the GATT owes much to the relatively free trade during the second half of the 19th century induced by a network of treaties containing the MFN clause. By the same token, the lukewarm reception for bilateral agreements is deeply influenced by the experience of the interwar period when discriminatory trade blocs and protectionist bilateral arrangements sharply contracted world trade.

After a careful look at history, Irwin finds – rather surprisingly – that the drive for an open trade regime in the late 19th century came from the *bilateral* Anglo–French commercial treaty of 1860. Britain adopted the unconditional MFN clause so that its tariff reductions to France became automatically available to all its trading partners. France adopted the conditional MFN whereby its tariff reductions were available to any country willing to sign a treaty similar to the Anglo–French treaty with it while the higher tariffs applied to all other nations. Other European states quickly followed suit. To seek lower tariffs for their goods, they concluded agreements with France, Britain, and each other. Thus, a bilateral agreement led to dozens of agreements culminating in the creation of a free multilateral trading system. By 1908, France had MFN agreements with 20 countries, Britain with 46, and Germany with 30.

The regime brought into existence by bilateral treaties ended abruptly in August 1914 with the outbreak of World War I. Trade restrictions of all kinds proliferated. After the end of the war, the progressive bilateralism of the 19th century was abandoned and a number of *multilateral* conferences were sponsored during 1920s to restore the unconditional MFN first. These were broadly a failure and with the advent of the Depression, a destructive bilateralism emerged. A malfunctioning international monetary system gave rise to the worst kind of bureaucratic control of trade flows. Import quotas, exchange control and tariffs were used simultaneously to eliminate all bilateral trade imbalances.

From these historical episodes, Irwin concludes that history does not provide a clear guide to policies which lead to a better world trading system. 'Multilateral cooperation on trade policy is not necessary either for the liberalisation of trade policy or for the prevention of illiberal trade policies. Multilateralism was not a feature of the 19th century, whereas multilateral talks were repeatedly held to no avail in the 1920s and 1930s. Similarly, bilateral trade policies cannot be uniquely praised or condemned. A progressive bilateralism flourished in the 19th century, . . . At the same time, pernicious bilateralism that emerged [in the interwar period] . . . prompted the bureaucratic allocation of import quotas and foreign exchange to eliminate all bilateral payments imbalances'.

1.4   Reforming the rules of the game

Whether good or bad, if regionalism is here to stay, perhaps the most fruitful task for us is to reform the rules of the game in such a way that they complement rather than substitute for the multilateral approach. Three suggestions have been made. First, Bhagwati suggests that regionalism be open-ended, the kind William Brock propagated. Brock, as the

United States Trade Representative, had offered an FTA to Egypt and ASEAN at the same time that he offered it to Israel. Indeed, Brock was willing to negotiate an FTA with any government interested in it. In his Round Table Discussion, Cooper makes the same point in a broader context. Recognising that with over 100 contracting parties, the MFN-based multilateral negotiations may well impede rather than foster liberalisation, he suggests reverting to a conditional MFN. This will entail forming clubs with open membership such that any nation willing to adhere to club rules can join but no nation is obliged to do so. Second, Article XXIV of the GATT should be reformed to allow only CUs. Because CUs require a common external tariff (CET) and most countries' tariffs are GATT-bound, this will force each tariff down to the lowest level prevailing in a member country. There will be minimal trade diversion and the overall change will, likely, be towards freer world trade. Finally, the GATT Articles VI and XIX dealing with AD actions and VERs, respectively, should be strengthened. This is necessary to ensure that regional arrangements which start out as trade creating on balance do not become trade diverting *ex post*. For example when, in a given industry, the least efficient partner's producers are threatened by a more efficient partner, the former is likely to react by subjecting the most efficient outside suppliers to AD actions or VERs. To minimise this type of trade diversion, Bhagwati suggests tightening the criteria, in Article VI, for employing AD actions and eliminating VERs from Article XIX.

1.5 Can it be done?

In Chapter 5, Michael Finger provides a rather pessimistic view of the GATT's ability to enforce its rules in general, and those in Article XXIV in particular. Despite numerous regional arrangements around the world that violated the basic provisions of Article XXIV, the GATT has not censured a single arrangement as being incompatible with its standards. This casts a shadow of doubt on whether the suggestions for reform mentioned in the previous paragraph can serve any purpose beyond the creation of more unenforceable rules. Discussing Finger, Robert Hudec provides a more optimistic assessment of the contribution of the GATT Articles. He argues that the GATT's ability to regulate governments' decisions *after* they have been taken is limited because these decisions require extensive bargaining and are difficult to reopen. The GATT's influence on regional arrangements must therefore come *during* negotiations for regional arrangements. Here, at least in the case of developed-country regional arrangements, EC, EFTA, EEC–EFTA and CUSTA, Hudec finds 'plenty of anecdotal evidence testifying that the diplomats negotiating each of these agreements were operating under instructions to make maximum efforts to comply with GATT rules'. So, there is after all hope that reforming the GATT rules may yield real results.

2   The experience with regional integration

2.1   Intra-regional trade

Regional arrangements fall under two broad categories. First, those that have modest aims at integration and seek only either a preferential trading arrangement (PTA) – lower tariffs on imports from the partners than from the rest of the world – or an FTA – which involves zero tariffs among partners and positive, but not necessarily identical, tariffs with the rest of the world. Second, those that aim at 'deep' integration with either a CU – which imposes a CET by partner countries – or a Common Market as in the single market that is to be established by the European Community with the so-called four freedoms – movements for labour, firms, services, and capital. In any event, whatever the ultimate goal of a regional arrangement, increased intra-regional trade ranks high among the priorities. It is also the yardstick to measure how deep integration actually is.

Table 1.1 displays all the regional arrangements for which the share of intra-regional exports in total exports is at least 4 percent and sustained over time. This is a modest cut-off point. Four facts stand out. First, only five among the many South–South arrangements signed during the 1960s appear in the table, whereas all the arrangements among developed countries qualify for inclusion. Second, among the South–South arrangements, only the CACM registered a noticeable, though temporary, increase in intra-regional exports. Interestingly, from the standpoint of implementation, the CACM was just about the only South–South arrangement which implemented tariff cuts across the board rather than on a piecemeal basis by choosing a list of products exempted from tariff reductions. But even this sharp increase in intra-regional trade was not long-lived as the debt crisis of the 1980s brought back the application of quantitative restrictions (QRs) to improve the balance of payments and contributed to the decline by half in intra-regional trade. Third, in contrast, all North–North arrangements reveal much higher shares of intra-regional exports, with the European Community displaying a particularly large increase in intra-regional trade after the signing of the Treaty of Rome. Finally, there is a sharp difference between the evolution of world trade shares in the North–North and South–South arrangements: the former increased their share in world exports while the latter

Table 1.1. *Regional trading schemes: intra-regional exports and world exports*

	Founded	1960 IR[a]	1970 IR	1975 IR	1980 IR	1985 – IR	1990 IR
ANZCERTA[b]	1983	5.7	6.1	6.2	6.4	7.0	7.6
		(2.4)[c]	(2.1)	(1.7)	(1.4)	(1.6)	(1.5)
EC	1957	34.5	51.0	50.0	54.0	54.5	60.4
		(24.9)	(39.0)	(35.9)	(34.9)	(35.6)	(41.4)
EFTA	1960	21.1	28.0	35.2	32.6	31.2	28.2
		(14.9)	(14.9)	(6.3)	(6.1)	(6.3)	(6.8)
Canada–US FTA	1989	26.5	32.8	30.6	26.5	38.0	34.0
		(21.9)	(20.5)	(16.8)	(15.1)	(16.7)	(15.8)
ASEAN	1967	4.4	20.7	15.9	16.9	18.4	18.6
		(2.6)	(2.1)	(2.6)	(3.7)	(3.9)	(4.3)
ANDEAN PACT	1969	0.7	2.0	3.7	3.8	3.4	4.6
		(2.9)	(1.6)	(1.6)	(1.6)	(1.2)	(0.9)
CACM	1961	7.0	25.7	23.3	24.1	14.7	14.8
		(0.4)	(0.4)	(0.3)	(0.2)	(0.2)	(0.1)
LAFTA/LAIA	1960/80	7.9	9.9	13.6	13.7	8.3	10.6
		(6.0)	(4.4)	(3.5)	(4.2)	(4.7)	(3.4)
ECOWAS	1975	n.a.	3.0	4.2	3.5	5.3	6.0
		n.a.	(1.0)	(1.4)	(1.7)	(1.1)	(0.6)
PTA	1987	n.a.	8.4	9.4	8.9	7.0	8.5
		n.a.	(1.1)	(0.5)	(0.4)	(0.3)	(0.2)

[a] Intra-regional trade measured by share of intra-regional exports in total exports.
[b] Definitions of regional integration schemes are ANZCERTA – Australia–New Zealand Closer Economic Relations Trade Agreement; EC – European Community; EFTA – European Free-Trade Area; ASEAN – Association of South East Asian Nations; CACM – Central American Common Market; LAFTA/LAIA – Latin American Integration Association; ECOWAS – Economics Community of West African States; PTA – Preferential Trade Area for Eastern and Southern Africa.
[c] Share of RI scheme in total world exports in parenthesis.
n.a. Not available
Source: IMF, *Direction of Trade*, various years.

usually experienced a decline. As explained below, an increase in intra-regional trade accompanied by an increase in world export share is not enough to draw firm conclusions, but at least it suggests that North–North arrangements had an impact on the pattern of trade.

2.2   The ambiguous economics of FTAs

Unfortunately, one cannot go much further with the statistics in Table 1.1. In particular, one cannot infer from an increase in intra-regional exports that the members' welfare has gone up. In Chapter 6, de Melo, Panagariya and Rodrik explore the conditions under which an FTA is likely to raise members' welfare. Starting with the proverbial three-country, two-good case, they note that if the partners import the same good initially, they will import it from the non-partner so that an FTA will leave the pattern of trade unchanged. This scenario where nothing happens with an FTA explains pretty well the outcome of Table 1.1 for the regional arrangements in Africa in particular. In Chapter 8, Foroutan notes that there is very limited trade potential among Sub-Saharan African (SSA) countries as the bulk of their trade is based on factor endowments. These being similar, there is very little scope for trade, and Foroutan concludes that 'the limited extent of intra-industry trade cannot be attributed to the "failure" of integration schemes, but rather to their ineffectiveness'.

The ambiguity of FTAs starts with the more substantive case where the partners do not import the same good. Then in the simplest case where imports are available at constant costs, the formation of the FTA has two effects: the elimination of a distortion at the border with the partner, and a loss of tariff revenue as the imports are now purchased duty-free from the partner. There is therefore ambiguity for the welfare effect of an FTA, although several commonsense propositions can be derived on the conditions under which an FTA is likely to raise rather than lower members' welfare. Perhaps the most relevant case examined by de Melo, Panagariya and Rodrik is that of designing a welfare-improving FTA in the presence of QRs, a case that prevails in virtually all South–South integration arrangements. In the spirit of Kemp and Wan (1976), they show that if post-FTA trade restrictions leave their trade with the outside world unaffected, the joint welfare of partners improves.

Ambiguity also extends to the comparison of an FTA with unilateral trade liberalisation (UTL). Following up on the discussion in section 2, suppose that the world divides into three trading blocs, each with free trade inside the bloc and high tariffs with the outside world. What should the developing countries outside the blocs do: liberalise unilaterally or join one of the blocs? Clearly, join one of the blocs if the barriers to external trade erected by the blocs are high enough.

2.3   South–South integration

The review of integration efforts in Africa and Latin America in Chapters 8 and 9 reveals that, in general, the treaties sanctioning these arrangements remained a dead letter. More often than not, the treaties were not implemented. And when there was implementation, the terms proved to be too ambitious for the members' limited administrative capacities. It proved extremely difficult to devise equitable compensation schemes that did not nullify the intent of integration in the first place.

A typical example is the ambitious Treaty of Brazzaville that called for the formation of a CU and full monetary integration for the former French Central African countries. In the end, the CET was *de facto* abandoned, and free trade was extended only to a limited range of industrial products. Worse, as documented by Foroutan, a complex system of compensation schemes was implemented both to compensate for the loss of tariff revenues resulting from intra-regional trade, and for the 'cost' of trade creation. Community-financed development projects were promoted according to complicated formulae that were tailored to the protection needs of the poorest members and the financing was raised through a highly distortionary and unpredictable tax (the Taxe de Coopération Regionale). Though compensation was less prevalent in the case of Latin American regional arrangements, Nogués and Quintanilla in Chapter 9 report arbitrariness in the limited implementation of industrial development projects.

In the case of trade integration among members of the Council for Mutual Economic Assistance (CMEA) countries, much more trade occurred than would be suggested by comparative advantage. The welfare losses from trade integration and other forms of cooperation were likely to be larger. In Chapter 10, Josef Brada suggests that trade diversion occurred not only because of considerable differences in resource endowments and levels of development, but also because none of the members (including the Soviet Union) were low-cost suppliers of industrial goods.

Were there any notable successes in these regional arrangements? On purely economic grounds, no. But there was some limited cooperation in the form of joint projects as in the successful Beira project in the Southern African Coordinating conference, and the relative stability brought about by monetary integration in the CFA Franc zone. Yet, these examples of cooperation are few, and it is likely that political and cultural differences as well as the prospects of small benefits from economic integration all contributed to the limited cooperation among South–South arrangements.

In the final analysis, until recently, South–South regional arrangements were used to promote an import-substitution industrialisation strategy. It is now widely accepted that this strategy was the wrong one and that South–South regional arrangements were a contributing factor, even if the scope for diversionary trade was often small. At the same time, they contributed to the distraction of policy thinking from the needed UTL which would have had large pay-offs since trade restrictions of developed countries were falling.

2.4 North–North integration

Here, low transport costs, large markets among partners, and the large scope for variety-producing specialisation among partners considerably raised the potential for economic benefits from integration. Furthermore, relatively similar levels of development and intra- rather than inter-industry specialisation considerably reduced the need for compensation. This applies as much to the EFTA as to the European Community, both of which fully liberalised trade among partners while simultaneously substantially reducing their overall level of protection through participation in several rounds of multilateral trade negotiations. And when one considers the added benefits from reduced political tensions and the strategic advantages of size in trade negotiations, there is no doubt that North–North integration was immensely successful.

But what would have happened without the 'deep' integration given that multilateralism was pushing the world towards greater market integration? We will never know. However, in Chapter 7, Alan Winters suggests that European Community integration was not an unmitigated success, a view that is strongly challenged by André Sapir in his Discussion. Winters argues that not only did the European Community bring with it the very costly Common Agricultural Policy (CAP) that is now proving so difficult to dismantle, but that the EC Commission has often 'communitarised' its members' restrictive policies, as for instance in the case of VERs on imports of Japanese autos. Also, the European Community has suffered from the 'restaurant bill' problem, as each member has often been successful in having the Commission add its restrictive measure to those that are adopted at the Community level. He also notes that the European Community has been increasing its use of non-tariff barriers relatively more rapidly than other countries. He is also sceptical of the net impact of successive enlargements on the acceding countries, as they have had to join a club with existing rules and a tradition of what he calls 'managed liberalism'. Newcomers could not modify community rules.

In his Discussion, André Sapir reaches diametrically opposite conclusions. To him European Community integration has been overwhelmingly successful, and he points out that countries like Sweden and Switzerland that did not join the European Community had even more restrictive agricultural policies. He also notes that the second (Southern) enlargement was strongly liberalising for the newcomers, as Greece, Spain, and Portugal all had higher tariffs than the CET.

3 The new regionalism and new initiatives

3.1 Institutional dimensions

The bulk of the literature on regional arrangements has emphasised the effects of adopting preferential tariff concessions. This emphasis reflected the negotiations that were carried out during the first wave of regionalism. Now that world-wide protection has been greatly reduced, the nature of tariff reductions is no longer an overriding concern. Negotiations for 'EC 92' dealt with harmonisation of a wide range of policies that would eliminate remaining market segmentation, and much of the discussions in the recently initialled NAFTA agreement concerned establishing common legislation or standards, as in the case of labour and environmental standards. In any event, the second wave of regionalism has an added focus on coordination at the institutional level, as it is increasingly recognised that regional integration goes beyond trade in goods, services, and factors.

The implications of having to adopt common institutions when there is deep integration or when partners with very different institutions integrate – as in the case of NAFTA and the recent Europe Agreements – are explored by de Melo, Panagariya and Rodrik in Chapter 6. Recognising that any regional arrangement worth its name entails the imposition of some common rules of conduct and is often used to commit to desirable policies, they explore within the framework of the rules-versus-discretion literature the channels through which the adoption of regional institutions can alter economic outcomes. They adopt a setup in which non-cooperative lobbies influence policy decisions at the national level. (The assumption of non-cooperation by lobbies across countries is questioned by Ronald Findlay in his Discussion and by Winters in his discussion of the behaviour of lobbies in the European Community.)

Within that non-cooperative setup, they show that a regional arrangement with a larger political community dilutes the role of politically important groups which may enhance economic efficiency, and that if a negotiation of a regional arrangement opens the possibility for setting up a new institutional forum, the resulting greater flexibility in institutional design may also increase economic efficiency. Their analysis also shows that when members have different objectives and preferences, compromise will have an ambiguous effect on economic efficiency, and reaching an agreement will be more difficult. This leads them to conclude that the conditions for meaningful North–South integration were not met until recently because of large differences in objectives. Now, there is evidence of convergence in economic objectives reflected in the greater outward-orientation of Southern states, suggesting that the road is open for meaningful North–South integration.

3.2   North–South integration

The Europe Agreements signed with Czechoslovakia, Hungary, and Poland, the preferences accorded to the Mediterranean states through the Mediterranean agreements, and the recent US initiatives all involve arrangements between countries with substantially different income *per capita* levels. In the case of the Mediterranean states, benefits for the Southern states came from preferential market access to the EC market. But in all the other cases, a key perceived benefit was the cementing of recent reforms and economic institutions (including democracy for the East European states).

In Chapter 11, John Whalley analyses the rationale for Mexican integration with the United States. The broader benefits for the Mexicans are difficult to measure since they are mostly institutional: binding the recent trade liberalisation initiatives, and added pressure for sound macroeconomic policies. From a trade perspective, given the low levels of protection for manufactures in both countries, the main benefit for the Mexicans is one of a safe haven in case the world turns into trading blocs, and of less harsh treatment in the case of AD and countervailing duty (CVD) actions initiated by the United States. At the same time, he notes that some components of the agreement, such as the purchase of US automotive parts have the potential for being strongly diversionary as American car manufacturers are seeking high domestic content requirements that would prevent transhipment through Mexico.

Besides the systemic issues raised above in section 2, what are the objectives and benefits for the Northern partners? The objectives are mostly non-economic, so the benefits are harder to evaluate. Whalley and Winters emphatically state that containment of migration is the main objective. Subsidiary objectives are extending the sphere of political influence, and the adoption of institutions by Southern partners (e.g., environmental protection legislation).

Will North–South regional agreements be successful? Although this question is not directly addressed, the chapters in the volume suggest several lessons. First, the new initiatives, unlike the old ones – such as the Lomé convention – are reciprocal so the opportunity for the accedant countries to maintain high protection barriers is avoided. Second, the experience of the European Community shows that the adoption of common rules (institutions) is not easy to achieve. Third, substantial compensation was a key to the success of the second (Southern) EC enlargement. Compensation turned out to be an unsurmountable barrier for South–South integration. It could still foil the success of new initiatives if the need for some redistribution is not directly addressed.

3.3   New initiatives: Middle East, East Asia and Eastern Europe

Though not yet concretised, new initiatives are on the table in every region of the world. Perhaps the most interesting are those in East Asia, a region that had been spared from the first wave of regional integration (ASEAN focused mostly on political and security issues). In Chapter 12, Gary Saxonhouse looks into the new initiatives in the region. First, based on econometric estimates, he concludes that there is no evident bias in the pattern of East Asian trade – as for instance there was in the case of CMEA trade. Second, he draws on the results of pricing equations of Japanese firms suggesting the presence of strategic behaviour to argue that there is scope for a beneficial reduction in intra-regional trade barriers. At the same time, the strong opposition from the United States to the recent initiatives around an East Asian Economic Group (EAEG) suggest that perhaps regional cooperation will have more success on a Pacific-wide basis. Nonetheless, Saxonhouse concludes that the rapid growth in intra-regional Asian trade, the revival of ASEAN calling for the establishment of an FTA within fifteen years, and the successful Shenzen Free Trade Zone between Hong Kong and Guandong Province in PRC all suggest that there could be trade-creating effects from region-wide liberalisation.

Prospects for regional integration in the Middle East are reviewed by Stanley Fischer in Chapter 13. Here economic attributes of the countries in the region substantially limit the scope for trade-creating effects and Fischer concludes that 'There is no realistic prospect of Middle East-wide regional integration on either the NAFTA or EC models in the near future'. However, even though there is the possibility of free-trade agreements among a subset of countries, any resulting benefits would at most be small. The more promising – but perhaps difficult to achieve – integration would be cooperation in functional areas such as water management, and agreements on the creation of regional infrastructure. Fischer also points out that any regional cooperation would have the added benefit of reducing the region's high level of military expenditures.

In the rapidly changing economic and political scene in Eastern Europe, economic disintegration has considerably blurred any assessment of future prospects. In Chapter 10, Brada argues that, although the collapse of CMEA trade owed more to the illiquidity and collapse of the Soviet economy than to the ending of the CMEA trading system, it is a move in the right direction. He observes that 'monetary and economic disunion may prove more beneficial than misguided efforts to preserve a domestic market that, in fact, was no market at all'. Alan Gelb and Gábor Oblath in their Discussions, while agreeing that the move is in the right direction, argue that it is too rapid. They suggest that one should consider temporary measures to arrest the collapse in intra-regional trade during the transition to market-oriented economies.

4   Concluding remarks: the new regionalism and smaller countries

A priori, it is difficult to predict whether the current bilateralism will help the cause of multilateralism as in the second half of the 19th century, or prove pernicious as in the 1920s and 1930s. We can, however, take steps to maximise the benefits and minimise the damage from it. As suggested by Bhagwati and Cooper, a key to preserving the openness of the world trading system while pursuing the regional approach is to ensure that membership of regional arrangements is kept open via the application of a conditional MFN. This is not an easy task and, according to Winters, quite an unrealistic hope. The European Community has not been, and will not be, an open club; expansion of membership will continue to be as carefully 'managed' as in the past. The message then is that regionalism is as likely to be as destructive of an open global trading system as it is likely to be a positive force.

In the meantime, what are the options of smaller countries who do not have a great deal of bargaining power to open the markets for their goods under the auspices of the GATT? As far as South–South integration is concerned, there is no future in it. In the Round Table Discussion, Corden puts it succinctly: 'It is far better for Argentina to go for the world markets – i.e., to liberalise unilaterally and in non-discriminatory fashion, as she has been doing – than just go for the Brazilian market. Brazil has the largest economy in the Third World and yet it is smaller than Canada's . . . And this applies even more to Brazil'.

As regards North–South or North–North integration, the regional approach is likely to be justifiably attractive to small countries; rising uncertainties with respect to the openness of the world trading system will induce them to look to regionalism as an instrument of ensuring future market access. As Whalley notes, traditionally, small countries have been staunchest advocates of non-discriminatory trade rules. Yet, in the case of CUSTA and NAFTA, it is the smaller countries (i.e., Canada and Mexico) which have been the initiators of regional arrangements. Whalley views this as a vote of no confidence by smaller countries in the present trading system's ability to protect their interest: 'What they have sought have been safe-haven agreements with larger trading powers, seen by them as helping them avoid being sideswiped by protectionist barrier increases by their larger trading partners even if directed at other countries [United States against Japan, for instance]'.

NOTE

1 During 1960s, proposals were made to create a North *Atlantic* Free Trade Area extending all the way to Great Britain, but the United States was quick to reject them.

REFERENCES

Kemp, M.C. and H. Wan (1976) 'An Elementary Proposition Concerning the Formation of Customs Unions', *Journal of International Economics*, **6** (February) pp. 95–8.

Summers, L.H. (1991) 'Regionalism and the World Trading System', in L.H. Summers, *Policy Implications of Trade and Currency Zones*, Federal Reserve Bank of Kansas City, Wyoming, M-295–303.

Viner, J. (1950) *The Customs Union Issue*, New York: Carnegie Endowment for International Peace.

2 Regionalism and multilateralism: an overview

JAGDISH BHAGWATI

The question of 'regionalism', defined broadly as preferential trade agreements among a subset of nations, is a longstanding one. As with all great issues, economists have long been divided on the wisdom of such arrangements. So have policymakers.

While this may not be evident to the many economists who are not inhibited by lack of comparative advantage from pronouncing on these matters, and whose pronouncements are a testimony to the enduring value of the theory of comparative advantage, preferential trade arrangements were debated by economists, as such, during the very formation of the General Agreement on Tariffs and Trade (GATT). The context, of course, was the difference between the British, led by Keynes, who were devoted to the continuation of the discrimination in Britain's favour through Imperial Preference, and the Americans, with Cordell Hull to the fore, who were strongly opposed, and embraced multilateralism and most favoured nation status (MFN) instead. Keynes, quite characteristically, at first denounced the American attachment to non-discrimination in trade and then later, when the British had virtually capitulated, celebrated its virtues with equal passion. I will juxtapose the two positions in Keynes' inimitable words, quoted in Bhagwati (1991a):

> My strong reaction against the word 'discrimination' is the result of feeling so passionately that our hands must be free . . . [T]he word calls up and must call up . . . all the old lumber, most-favored-nation clause and all the rest which was a notorious failure and made such a hash of the old world. We know also that it won't work. It is the clutch of the dead, or at least the moribund, hand.

> [The proposed policies] aim, above all, at the restoration of multilateral trade . . . the bias of the policies before you is against bilateral barter and every kind of discriminatory practice. The separate blocs and all the friction and loss of friendship they must bring with them are expedients to which one may be driven in a hostile world where trade has ceased

over wide areas to be cooperative and peaceful and where are forgotten the healthy rules of mutual advantage and equal treatment. But it is surely crazy to prefer that.

Closer to our times, the question of customs unions (CUs) and free-trade areas (FTAs), both permitted under GATT Article XXIV, became a major topic of theoretical research. The focus, however, since Jacob Viner's (1950) classic treatment, distinguishing between trade diversion and trade creation, was on showing that CUs and FTAs were not necessarily welfare-improving, either for member countries or for world welfare: in other words, the case for preferential trade arrangements was different from the case for free trade for all. The latter, enshrined in Adam Smith and Ricardo, and rigorously proved later by Samuelson (1939), Kemp (1972), and Grandmont and McFadden (1972), is a first-best case. The former, by contrast, reflects second-best considerations and was argued by Lipsey and Lancaster (1956–7), Lipsey (1957), Meade (1956), Johnson (1958a, 1958b) and others.[1]

But if the main focus of these analyses was on disabusing the faith in regionalism as being desirable (on static immediate-impact grounds) by analogy with the different and legitimate case for multilateralism (in the sense of free or freer trade for all), and thus could be seen as reinforcing the case for multilateralism, the effect could also go the other way, and did at times. One could thus argue, from the opposite counterfactual, that if you believed that regionalism, in being discriminatory, was necessarily inferior to non-discriminatory reduction of trade barriers, then this too was wrong. Ironically, in view of the later shift of his views to multilateralism and free trade, reflecting perhaps the changed intellectual environment in Cambridge and Chicago and also further reflection, it is interesting to quote Johnson (1967, pp. 163–4) in the context of proposals for trade preferences, for and among developing countries, for manufactured goods:

> Both proposals violate the non-discrimination principle of the General Agreement on Tariffs and Trade and the GATT ban on new preferential arrangements other than customs unions and free trade areas embracing the bulk of the trade of the participating countries. This, however, does not mean that the proposed trading arrangements would necessarily be economically disadvantageous. The postwar development of the theory of customs unions and of commercial policy changes, culminating in the theory of second best has shown that in a tariff-ridden world economy there is no a priori reason for believing that nondiscrimination among import sources is economically superior to discriminatory trading arrangements. It has demonstrated also that the question of whether a discriminatory tariff reduction improves or worsens the efficiency and economic welfare of the countries involved and the world as a whole depends on the empirical circumstances of the particular case.

> Both the theory of second best and modern welfare economics (as well as ordinary common sense) indicate that policy changes that secure desirable results in terms of income distribution or other objectives at the cost of reduced economic efficiency may constitute improvements on a balance of gain and loss, and may legitimately be recommended if no more efficient method of achieving the same objectives is feasible or acceptable.

In fact, Johnson was an active proponent of NAFTA, an acronym which then stood for the North *Atlantic* Free-Trade Area (inclusive of the United Kingdom) rather than for the present North *American* Free-Trade Area which is predicated on a conceptually narrower, geographically-defined regional basis. As it happened, the concept of NAFTA failed to get off the ground, though the ideas concerning regional blocs and trading arrangements remained seductive through much of the 1960s, only to be abandoned thereafter until the recent 1980s' revival.

The recent revival of regionalism, which I describe as the 'Second Regionalism' in contrast to, and because it is a sequel to, the 'First Regionalism' of the 1960s, raises several of the old issues anew. But the historically changed situation which has resurrected regionalism equally provides the context in which it must be analysed, raising several new issues.

In this chapter, I address these manifold questions, dividing the analysis into a discussion of six areas:

- Article XXIV of the GATT, which sanctions CUs and FTAs (section 1);
- the 'First Regionalism', briefly reviewing the factors that led to it and the reasons why, in the end, it failed (section 2);
- the 'Second Regionalism', the reasons for its revival and its differential prospects (section 3);
- the key issues that this renewed regionalism raises, distinguishing among two main questions (section 4);
- the first, relating to the static impact effect of regional trade blocs (section 5);
- the second, concerning the dynamic time-path that regionalism offers, in itself and *vis-à-vis* multilateralism when the objective is to reach (non-discriminatory) free trade for all, so that one asks 'whether multilateralism is the best way to get to multilateralism', therefore distinguishing between 'process multilateralism' and 'outcome multilateralism' (section 6).

In the light of this analysis, I conclude by examining the current US trade-policy shift to regionalism and arguing for a change in its focus from 'piecemeal' to 'programmatic' regionalism, less antithetical to reaching the 'outcome-multilateralism' objective of eventual free trade for all (section 7). Some final observations conclude the chapter (section 8).

1   Article XXIV of the GATT: rationale

The principle of non-discrimination is central to the final conception of the GATT, signed on 30 October 1947 by representatives from 23 countries in Geneva. Article I embodies the strong support for non-discrimination, requiring (unconditional) MFN for all GATT members.

Aside from 'grandfathering' provisions, the only significant exception to MFN is made in Article XXIV, which permits CUs and FTAs and therefore sanctions preferential trade-barrier reductions among a subset of GATT members, as long as they go all the way to elimination.[2]

It is an intriguing question as to why Article XXIV was accepted, and it is a question that also has significance for some of the issues raised by the 'Second Regionalism'. It is a bit odd that an exception to MFN should be allowed as long as it is total (going all the way to 100 percent) rather than partial (say, 20 percent preference for one's favoured friends): it is as if your cardinal told you that petting is more morally reprehensible than sleeping around. In fact the post-Vinerian theory of preferential trade areas suggests that 100 percent preferences are less likely to increase welfare than partial preferences.[3]

The rationale for Article XXIV's inclusion in the GATT must therefore be explained in other ways. Perhaps there was an inchoate, if strong, feeling that integration with 100 percent preferences was somehow special and consonant with the objective on multilateralism. Thus, Dam (1970, pp. 274–5) quotes the prominent US official Clair Wilcox as follows:

> A Custom union (with 100% preferences) creates a wider trading area, removes obstacles to competition, makes possible a more economic allocation of resources and thus operates to increase production and raise planes of living. A preferential system (less than 100%) on the other hand, retains internal barriers, obstructs economy in production, and restrains the growth of income and demand . . . A customs union is conducive to the expansion of trade on a basis of multilateralism and nondiscrimination; a preferential system is not.

Wilcox's statement was little more than assertion, however. But the rationale for inclusion of Article XXIV in the GATT appears to have been threefold, as follows:

● Full integration on trade, that is, going all the way down to freedom of trade flows among any subset of GATT members, would have to be allowed since it created an important element of single-nation characteristics (such as virtual freedom of trade and factor movements) among these nations, and implied that the resulting quasi-national status following from such integration in trade legitimated the exception to MFN obligation toward other GATT members.

- The fact that the exception would be permitted only for the extremely difficult case where all trade barriers would need to come down seemed to preclude the possibility that all kinds of preferential arrangements would break out, returning the world to the fragmented, discriminatory bilateralism-infested situation of the 1930s.

- One could also think of Article XXIV as permitting a supplemental, practical route to the universal free trade that GATT favoured as the ultimate goal, with the general negotiations during the many Rounds leading to a dismantling of trade barriers on a GATT-wide basis while deeper integration would be achieved simultaneously within those areas where politics permitted faster movement to free trade under a strategy of full and time-bound commitment. This is an argument that is not at centre stage: is regionalism truly a building, rather than a stumbling, bloc towards multilateral free trade for all: in other words, will it fragment, or integrate, the world economy?

The clear determination of 100 percent preferences as compatible with multilateralism and non-discrimination, and the equally firm view that anything less was not, meant that when Article XXIV was drafted, its principal objective was to close all possible loopholes by which it could degenerate into a justification for preferential arrangements of less than 100 percent; paragraphs 4–10 of Article XXIV were written precisely for this purpose. But, as is now commonly conceded, their inherent ambiguity and the political pressures for approval of substantial regional groupings of preferences of less than 100 percent have combined to frustrate the full import of the original desire to sanction only 100 percent preferences.

This tension between intention and reality has a direct bearing on the important question of strengthening Article XXIV today beyond even what its original drafters intended. I will therefore sketch briefly the important respects in which the original intention of Article XXIV was reasonably clear but was occasionally violated in spirit, to the point where the great expert on GATT law, Professor John Jackson, has gone so far as to observe that the accommodation of the European Common Market's imperfect union in disregard of the legal requirements of Article XXIV was the beginning of the breakdown of the GATT's legal discipline, which we now seek to repair.[4] Two issues suffice to demonstrate this contention.

First, in regard to the elimination of internal barriers down to 100 percent, there was enough scope within the language of Article XXIV, paragraph 8, for its intent to be successfully avoided. Ambiguities could be exploited on two main fronts.

The first ambiguity lay in the directive that 'duties and other restrictive regulations on commerce' were (with specified exceptions permitted under Articles XI, XII, XIII, XIV, and XX) to be 'eliminated with respect to substantially all the trade between the constituent territories'. Skilful lawyers and representatives of governments could work wonders with the concept of 'substantially all the trade', and then, even if a percentage cutoff point was accepted for this purpose (for example, 75 percent of all initial trade), important issues remained ambiguous, such as whether across-the-board (75 percent) cut on everything were required or whether substantial sectors could be left out altogether from the scope of the cuts – the latter being evidently at variance with the intent of those who favoured (100 percent) CUs but opposed (less than 100 percent) preferential arrangements. With both interpretations possible, sectorally non-uniform preferential arrangements could evidently not effectively be ruled out.

An ambiguity of equal importance arose in regard to the problem of the speed with which the '100 percent preferences' would be implemented. Evidently, if they were stretched out over very long periods, one was *de facto* sanctioning 'less than 100 percent' preferential arrangements. In GATT jargon, this was the problem of 'interim arrangements'. Paragraph 5 therefore addressed this issue, requiring 'a plan and schedule', and asking for the CU or FTA to be fully consummated 'within a reasonable length of time'. Paragraph 7, in turn, laid down specific procedures for such interim arrangements to be approved. Needless to say, this nonetheless left the door open for substantial laxity in conception and execution of the CUs and FTAs under Article XXIV.

Dam's (1970, p. 290) overall judgement of the outcome is perhaps too harsh, but is certainly in the ballpark:

> The record is not comforting . . . Perhaps only one of the more than one dozen regional arrangements that have come before the GATT complied fully with Article XXIV criteria. That was the recent United Kingdom/Ireland Free-Trade Area, and even in that case certain doubts were expressed before the working party. In some cases, the regional arrangements were very wide off the mark. The European Coal and Steel Community, covering only two major product lines, could not even qualify for the special regional-arrangement waiver of Article XXIV: 10 but required a general waiver under Article XXV:5. The New Zealand/Australia Free-Trade Agreement, although not purportedly an example of 'functional integration', provided for the liberalization of an even smaller percentage of intermember trade. A strong tendency has also been manifested for interim agreements to provide for an even longer transitional period and to contain increasingly fewer detailed

commitments for eventual completion of the customs union or free-trade area.

2   The 'First Regionalism': failure in the 1960s

In any event, one can correctly assert (based on the acceptance of Article XXIV into the GATT) that regionalism, in the shape of (100 percent) CUs and FTAs, was not generally considered, by the architects of the GATT or by the United States, which was the chief proponent of multilateralism and non-discrimination, as antithetical to the GATT and to these principles.

1. Nonetheless, the United States, long suspicious of discriminatory trade arrangements, restrained itself from resorting to Article XXIV. The formation of the European Community in 1958 marked a partial watershed. The United States puts its shoulder to the wheel and saw the Common Market through, negotiating around the different hoops of Article XXIV, emasculating the Article somewhat so as to seek GATT approval of an imperfect union (especially in regard to discriminatory preferences for the eighteen ex-colonies in Africa that the Europeans insisted on retaining, requiring therefore a waiver of GATT rules), all in the cause of what it saw as a *politically* beneficial union of the original six nations that formed the Community. But despite the enthusiasm of many to follow the European Community with a NAFTA, and even a Pacific Free-Trade Area (PAFTA), centred on the United States, nothing came of it: the United States remained indifferent to such notions.[5]

2. There was an outbreak of FTA proposals in the developing countries as well. While stimulated by the European examples, they were motivated by the altogether different economic rationale formulated by Cooper and Massell (1965a, 1965b), Johnson (1965) and Bhagwati (1968). This was that, given any targeted level of import-substituting industrialisation, the developing countries with their small markets could reduce the cost of this industrialisation by exploiting economies of scale through preferential opening of markets with one another.[6] By the end of the 1960s, however, the attempts at forming regional FTAs and CUs along these lines had also collapsed. The problem was that, rather than use trade liberalisation and hence prices to guide industry allocation, the developing countries attempting such unions sought to allocate industries by bureaucratic negotiation and to tie trade to such allocations, putting the cart before the horse and killing the forward motion.

Thus, while the world was indeed filled with proposals for NAFTA, PAFTA, LAFTA (the Latin American Free-Trade Area, replaced by

LAIA, the Latin American Integration Agreement, in 1980), and ever more in the 1960s, until one could be forgiven for imagining that a veritable chemical revolution had broken out, regionalism had virtually died by the end of the decade, except for the original European Community and EFTA.

3 The 'Second Regionalism': revival in the 1980s

But regionalism (i.e., preferential trade liberalisation) is now back. Those who do not know the history of the 'First Regionalism' are doomed to extrapolate from the current political ferment in favour of FTAs and CUs and assume uncritically that regionalism is here to stay. Those who know the history may make the reverse mistake of thinking that regionalism will again fail. I believe that careful analysis of the causes of the resurrection of regionalism suggests that regionalism this time is likely to endure.

The main driving force for regionalism today is the conversion of the United States, hitherto an abstaining party, to Article XXIV. Beginning with the FTA with Israel (a reflection of the special relationship between the two nations and hence of little general value), the FTA with Canada marked a distinct change. Now the NAFTA is being negotiated with Mexico, and the Enterprise for the Americas' Initiative (EAI) envisages more FTAs with the nations of South America, with Chile at the head of the line (see chapter 9 in this volume).

The conversion of the United States is of major significance. As the key defender of multilateralism through the postwar years, its decision now to travel the regional route (in the geographical *and* the preferential senses simultaneously) tilts the balance of forces at the margin away from multilateralism to regionalism. This shift has taken place in the context of an anti-multilateralist ethos that has reflected alternative but nonetheless eventually reinforcing views:

- The 'Memorial Drive' school[7] holds that the GATT is dead (Thurow: Davos) or that the GATT should be killed (Dornbusch).[8] Regionalism is then presented in effect as an *alternative* to multilateralism. This school, aptly named in view of its funereal approach to multilateralism, has influence in Democratic circles and plays to the prejudices that one finds in Congressional circles that mistakenly identify multilateralism with America's postwar altruism and regionalism (with its connotation of 'exploiting our own markets for ourselves') with the presumed current necessity finally to 'look after one's interests'.
- An alternative view is that regionalism is a useful *supplement*, not an alternative, to multilateralism. 'We are walking on only two legs' is

the popular argument. That we may wind up walking on all fours is ignored.

- It is also often asserted that regionalism will not merely supplement multilateralism. It will also *accelerate* the multilateral process: the threat of going (unilateral and) regional will produce multilateral agreements that may otherwise be held up. (However, this may be an optimistic view since threats that have to be implemented and repeatedly made, as has been the case with US regionalism, are not efficient threats; and they change external perceptions about what US trade policy priorities are, quite regardless of what the United States asserts to be its true intentions. In fact, the taking of two roads simultaneously can affect adversely the travel down one, as I argue below at length.)

- The panic over the continuing payments deficit has also fed demands for 'quick' results on trade (although the two issues are broadly delinkable: payments surpluses and deficits are macroeconomic phenomena that are not influenced in any predictable way by trade policy changes whose impact on the difference between domestic savings and investment, if any, can come in different ways that can go in opposing directions). Associated with this has been impatience with the pace of the multilateral trade-negotiating process and the *non sequitur* (examined below) that regionalism necessarily works faster.

- In addition, 'Europe 1992' and the impending integration of Eastern Europe into the European Community have reinforced, as the formation of the Common Market did with many three decades ago, those in North America who feel that a countervailing bloc must be formed there as well. Indeed, the fear that European investments would be diverted to Eastern Europe, once it is integrated with the European Community, was cited by President Salinas of Mexico as a factor decisively pushing him toward the Mexico–US FTA: this would, he felt, enable Mexico to get the investment needed from America and Japan.

- There are strong non-economic, political and cultural factors also driving Mexico toward an FTA with its northern neighbour. Just as the Turks since Ataturk have tried to seek a European rather than an Arab (or Islamic) identity, the Mexicans clearly now seek an American future rather than one with their southern neighbours. The Hispanic (economic) destiny that many in America fear from illegal immigration and integration with Mexico has its flip side in the American (economic) destiny that Mexico's reforming elite, trained in the top universities in the United States, hope for.

- The offer in June 1990 by President Bush to get more nations from

South America to join the United States in an FTA, as part of a general package of economic initiatives to assist these nations, reflects the compulsions that the debt crisis there imposes on American policy to respond in a regional framework to ensure that this crisis remains manageable and does not engulf the United States, whose banks are principally endangered by it.

- Then again, the response of South American nations to the prospect of FTAs with NAFTA, and in some cases with one another first and then joining up with NAFTA, has been enthusiastic. This time around, the prospects are better than in the 1960s. Quite simply, there is now a marked shift in economic thinking towards trade liberalisation and market forces. The macroeconomic crisis of the 1980s has fed the movement to microeconomic reforms, much as it is currently doing in India. The changed economic and political attitudes are comforting to those of us who went into the trenches to fight these battles as early as the 1960s. It is also amusing to see those who dismissed our arguments as 'reactionary' or 'ideological' then, now embracing these ideas and policies and the leaders who are implementing them, with no apologies to us and with a facade of independently-obtained wisdom. But, frankly, it is good to have them finally on the right side; and it is good to have been in the right.
- Finally, the conjunction of the two dramatic events, 'Europe 1992' and the US–Canada FTA, even though fortuitous and prompted by different motivations and historical circumstances, certainly has created a sense elsewhere that regionalism is the order of the day, and that others must follow suit. In the Far East, for instance, there has been a sense that a Japan-centred regional bloc may be necessary in a bloc-infested world, and Malaysia has actively sought a Japan-centred Asian bloc to rival and confront the US-led Americas bloc.

4 Regionalism versus multilateralism: key questions

I suspect therefore that the 'Second Regionalism' will endure: it shows many signs of strength and few points of vulnerability. But if so, those of us who see virtue in a rule-based, open and multilateral trading system must ask searching questions as to its compatibility with such discriminatory trading arrangements. In particular, two major questions must be answered:

- Is the immediate impact effect of such preferential trade blocs, whether CUs or FTAs, to reduce rather than increase world welfare?
- Regardless of the immediate impact effect, will regionalism lead to

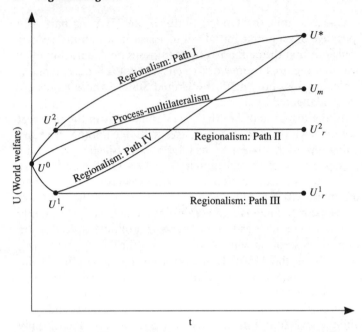

Figure 2.1   Regionalism and welfare: static impact versus dynamic time-path issue
Note: Regionalism may improve welfare immediately, from U^0 to U^2_r or (because of net trade diversion) reduce it to U^1_r. The time-path with regionalism, in either case, could be stagnant (Paths II and III), implying a fragmentation of the world economy through no further expansion of the initial trade bloc. Otherwise, it could lead (Paths I and IV) to multilateral free trade for all at U^* through continued expansion and coagulation of blocs. Under process-multilateralism, the time-path may fail to reach U^* and instead fall short at U_m because of free-rider problems. Otherwise, it may overcome them and reach U^*. As argued in the text, the regionalism and the process-multilateralism paths are interdependent, e.g. the simultaneous pursuit of both processes will affect the path and outcome of either.

non-discriminatory multilateral free trade for all, through continued expansion of the regional blocs until universal free trade is reached, or will it fragment the world economy? And will, in any event, such a dynamic time-path show that regionalism will get us closer to the *goal* of multilateral free trade for all than multilateralism as the *process* of trade negotiation will?

In terms of Figure 2.1, starting from the initial U^0 level of world welfare with trade barriers in place, and with multilateral free trade for all implying maximal welfare at U^*, the two questions can be readily illustrated:

- Will the static immediate impact effect of a regional bloc be to *reduce* welfare to U_r^1 or to increase it to U_r^2?
- Will the dynamic time-path be to reach $U*$ through continued coagulation of blocs or will it lead to fragmentation of the world economy and lead, say, to continued stagnation of welfare at U_r^1 or U_r^2, each in turn *lower* than U_m, reached (with all the greater free-rider difficulties) through the multilateral process or will the multilateral process in fact override the free-rider problem and achieve $U*$ and dominate the regionalist outcomes?

I shall now treat each of these two important, and distinct (if at times analytically interrelated), questions in turn.

5   The static impact-effect question

The question of the static impact effect of preferential trade arrangements such as FTAs and CUs is, quite simply, the question raised by Viner (1950): would not such discriminatory arrangements be trade-diverting rather than trade-creating?[9]

It is important to raise this question because, as Viner taught us, FTAs and CUs are two-faced: they liberalise trade (among members), but they also protect (against outsiders). The important issue therefore is: which aspect of an FTA or a CU is dominant? Or, to put it in the economist's language: is a particular FTA or CU trade-diverting (that is, taking trade away from efficient outside suppliers and giving it to inefficient member countries) or trade-creating (that is, generating trade from one more efficient member at the expense of another less efficient member)?

Sadly, one might have scanned the leading articles, the editorials, and the Congressional testimony when the renewal of fast-track authority for the extension of NAFTA to Mexico was being debated in 1991, looking for references to trade diversion – and find scarcely any. Astonishingly, it was not just the politicians and lawyers for Mexico's lobby who equated the FTA with (non-discriminatory) free trade; reputed economists did so too.[10]

What can we say about this issue? In particular, what can we propose to ensure that, if CUs and FTAs are to flourish, they do not become trade-diversionary? Article XXIV's injunction not to raise the CU's or the FTA's average external tariff can be interpreted as a precaution against trade diversion and harm to outside GATT members, though (as argued below) this is not a satisfactory way to do it.

In essence, there are three approaches to containing the fallout of trade diversion from CUs and FTAs.

5.1   Converting preferential CUs and FTAs into (geographically) regional blocs

It is occasionally argued that we should encourage geographically proximate countries to form CUs and FTAs, discouraging geographically distant countries from doing so since the latter would be more likely to be trade-diverting.[11] This is a misguided prescription in my view, for several reasons.

To see this, it must be first appreciated that it rests on a syllogism. The first premise is that a CU or FTA is more likely to create trade and thus raise welfare, given a country's volume of international trade, the higher is the proportion of trade with the country's CU or FTA partners and the lower is this proportion with the non-member countries. The second premise is that countries sharing borders, or closer geographically to one another, have higher proportions of trade with one another than countries further apart do.

The first premise is, of course, well known to trade economists from the early post-Vinerian theory, as developed by Lipsey (1958). But Lipsey's argument focuses on the relative sizes of imports from each source *vis-à-vis* expenditure on domestic goods as the key and decisive factor in determining the size of losses and gains from the preferential cuts in trade barriers.[12]

While the likelihood argument is valid within the Lipsey model, it must be noted that it is only that. Thus, for specific CUs and FTAs, the *actual* welfare effects will depend, not merely on the trade and expenditure shares *à la* Lipsey but also on the *substitution* at the margin between commodities. Thus, for instance, the substitution between non-member goods and domestic goods may be very high, so that the costs of discrimination would tend to be high as well, *ceteris paribus*. In short, it is important to guess at substitution elasticities among goods *as well as* trade shares, with and between members and non-members of CUs and FTAs, to arrive at a better picture of the likely effects of *specific* CUs and FTAs that may be proposed.

As for the second premise, I have problems with this too, as a policy guideline. If I had access to captive research assistance and funds, I could examine whether, for all conceivable combinations of countries and distances among them, and for several different time periods, the premise is valid. I do not, so I must rely on casual empiricism and *a priori* arguments. Compare, for instance, the trade throughout the 1960s between India and Pakistan with that between India and the United Kingdom or the then USSR. The former trade has been smaller than the latter. Borders can breed hostility and undermine trade, just as alliances among distant countries with shared causes can promote trade (Gowa and Mansfield, 1991). The flag follows trade; and trade equally follows the flag which, at least in the 19th-century European expansion, was not directly across the European nations' borders. Again, even if the premise is statistically valid for any set of observations, it may be a result of trade diversion itself: proximity may have led to preferential grant of concessions such as OAP and GSP at the expense of countries elsewhere.

In short, prescriptions to confine CUs and FTAs only to geographically proximate countries are not defensible because both premises have problems: the former is, at best, a likelihood proposition that should not be applied to specific situations where the welfare impact depends critically on other variables as well, whereas the latter does not have a firm empirical or conceptual basis.

But possibly the most damaging criticism that one can make of such a prescription is that it concentrates, at best, on the static impact-effect question and ignores the more important dynamic time-path question. By prescribing that we must rule out 'distant' country unions, as between the United States and Israel and Chile, we would make the CUs and FTAs more exclusive and less open to new members, undercutting the objective of moving speedily towards the shared objective of (non-discriminatory) multilateral free trade for all. That would be tragic indeed.

5.2 Designing disciplines to minimise trade diversion

A different, and my preferred, approach is not to pretend to find rules of thumb to exclude CUs and FTAs 'likely' to be trade-diversionary, but rather to examine the different ways in which trade diversion could arise and then to establish disciplines that would minimise its incidence.

5.2.1 Article XXIV In a sense, Article XXIV (paragraph 5) seeks to do this by requiring that CUs, which must have a common external tariff, should ensure that this common tariff 'shall not on the whole be higher or more restrictive than the general incidence of the duties and regulations of commerce applicable ... prior to the formation of such a union'. For FTAs, the rule is that the 'duties and other regulations of commerce' are not to be 'higher or more restrictive' than those previously in effect.

Evidently, when tariffs change, as in CUs, and some increase and others fall, the scope for skulduggery arises again, since Article XXIV leaves the matter wholly ambiguous. As Dam (1970, p. 217) has noted:

> these ambiguities plagued the review by the CONTRACTING PARTIES to the EEC Treaty of Rome – The Six, having used an

arithmetic average, refused to discuss the best method of calculation, because in their view paragraph 5 did not require any special method.

Besides, it is evident to trade economists that maintaining external tariffs unchanged is, in any event, not the same as eliminating trade diversion. What *can* be said is that, the lower the external barriers, the less is the scope for diverting efficient foreign supplies to member countries. A desirable discipline to impose on CUs and FTAs would thus be to require, for Article XXIV sanction, that one price to be paid must be the simultaneous reduction of the external tariff (implicit and explicit), *pro rata* to the progressive elimination of internal trade barriers.

Possible ways of ensuring this may be indirect disciplines. One way would be to modify Article XXIV to rule out FTAs with diverse tariffs by members[13] and to permit only CUs with common external tariffs (CETs). With most tariffs bound, this would ensure that for the most part a substantial downward shift in tariffs would be a consequence – that, say, Argentina or Brazil would be lowering her trade barriers, *not* that the United States would be raising hers. Since regionalism is probably going to be a matter of low trade barrier hubs such as the United States and Japan, joining with their respective regional spokes, this insistence on CUs could perhaps produce excellent results.

An alternative, and surer, way would be to insist on CUs but also write into Article XXIV the requirement that the *lowest* tariff of any union member on an item *before* the union must be part of the CET of the union.

5.2.2   Articles VI and XIX: AD and VERs   But none of this is enough today. For the trade economists who work in a sustained way on the problems of the world trading system are aware that protection today takes the form of unfair capture of fair trade mechanisms such as anti-dumping (AD) actions and of voluntary export restraints (VERs); countries today thus have access to selective and elastic instruments of protection.[14] Given this reality, even the modification of Article XXIV, to ensure that the external (implicit and explicit) tariff barriers come down as a price for CUs to be allowed under GATT rules, will leave open a gaping hole that would be tantamount to an open invitation to trade diversion by these preferential arrangements. In fact, trade creation can degenerate rapidly into trade diversion, when AD actions and VERs are freely used.

Imagine that the United States begins to eliminate (by outcompeting) an inefficient Mexican industry once the FTA goes into effect. Even though the most efficient producer is Taiwan, if the next efficient United States outcompetes the least efficient Mexico, that would be desirable trade creation (though the best course would be free trade so that Taiwan would take more of the Mexican market instead).

But what would the Mexicans be likely to do? They would probably start AD actions against Taiwan, which would lead to reduced imports from Taiwan as the imports from the United States increased, leaving the Mexican production relatively unaffected: trade diversion from Taiwan to the United States would have occurred. Similarly, the effect of Mexican competition against the United States could well be that the United States would start AD actions and even VERs against Taiwan.

My belief that FTAs will lead to considerable trade diversion (because of modern methods of protection, which are inherently selective and can be captured readily for protectionist purposes) is one that may have been borne out in the European Community. It is well known that the European Community has used AD actions and VERs profusely to erect 'Fortress Europe' against the Far East. Cannot much of this be a trade-diverting policy in response to the intensification of internal competition among the member states of the European Community?[15]

Two conclusions follow: (1) If inherently discriminatory regionalism is to flourish, as seems likely, then we need greater discipline for AD actions and VERs; Article VI needs reform and Article XIX needs compliance alongside the elimination of VERs (as the Dunkel draft on the MTN recommends). (2) This also implies that regionalism means, not the redundancy of the GATT, but the need for a stronger GATT. Those who think of the two as alternatives are prisoners of defunct modes of thinking, based on the days when protection was a different beast.

5.2.3 Judging trade diversion case by case   While the foregoing analysis embraces a set of policy-framework and incentive-creating reforms to minimise trade diversion, an alternative approach to the problem could be in terms of a case-by-case approach where the approval by the GATT of a proposed CU or FTA would depend on the evaluation of its trade-creating and trade-diverting effects and the requirement that the net anticipated effect be trade-creating.

McMillan (1991) has argued this in an ingenious paper[16] which proposes a simple test of admissibility: 'does the bloc result in less trade between member countries and outsider countries?'. Based on the welfare economics of CU theory, this is an aggregative test and therefore has some obvious analytical problems. It is also subject to the problem of computing plausible trade outcomes. It is hard enough to apply it *ex post*; *ex ante*, as a test of admissibility, I see little prospect of its being effectively used to exclude any proposed CU or FTA.

Its main merit is its apparent simplicity and its better grounding in economic theory. I therefore endorse the advisability of *some* version of the McMillan test replacing in Article XXIV the current requirement not to raise the average external tariff. But I see it as doing little *in practice* to avoid trade diversion. For this, we will have to rely on changing the incentive structure, including through suitable constraints imposed by stricter discipline on selective and elastic targeting of foreign suppliers. The issue of constraining trade diversion from proliferating preferential groupings is so important that it may not be a bad idea to *combine* the proposals made by McMillan and myself, rather than to treat them as alternatives.

6   The dynamic time-path question

The question of the dynamic time-path is particularly difficult: it is almost virgin territory.

Perhaps the theoretical approach to CU theory that appears to be most relevant to this problem is that of Kemp and Wan (1976). In contrast to the Vinerian approach, Kemp and Wan make the external tariff structure endogenously determined for the CU such that it improves the CU members' welfare while maintaining the outsiders' welfare unchanged. This restores the pre-Vinerian intuition that a CU should be welfare-improving. The problem with the operational significance of the Kemp–Wan argument is that it really is an existence argument, without any structure being put on it within the context of a specific model so that we can develop intuition about what the external tariff structure for such a Kemp–Wan CU would be.[17] But that *any* subset of countries *could* form an unambiguously (world) welfare-improving union is definitely established by Kemp and Wan.

This also implies that the time-path to U^* in Figure 2.1, achieved under multilateral free trade as the *optimum optimorum*, can be made monotonic.[18] But what it does *not* say is that the union will necessarily expand and, if so, in a monotonically welfare-improving manner. For *that* answer, we must turn to the *incentive structure* that any CU provides to relevant 'groups' for further expansion of the CU.

The incentives in question need not be *economic* incentives. In fact, it is hard to imagine that the arbitrary groupings of countries that seek FTAs and CUs are dependent on economic arguments as their key determinants. Often, politics seems to drive these choices of partners, as in the case of the European Community, and now in the case of FTAs throughout the Americas. This also accounts for the occasional non-regionally proximate choices of partners in such blocs: e.g., the United States and Israel, and Pakistan, Iran and Turkey in the early 1960s. But that economic factors contribute to the incentives for such blocs to be formed is not implausible. Thus, for instance, Edward Mansfield, a

Columbia University political scientist, has suggested that trade blocs will tend to be formed by security-driven allies because the gains from trade from them will accrue to friends rather than foes.[19]

A meaningful examination of the incentives to form and to expand trade blocs will therefore have to be in the new and growing field of political economy–theoretic analysis. I believe that the models within which we investigate these issues will have to distinguish among at least three kinds of 'agents', which I will detail below with illustrations of the kinds of arguments which we would find relevant:

- *Governments of member countries:* whether a CU will expand or not will depend partly on the willingness of the CU authorities to do so. This will be affected by ideas and ideology. Here I worry that CUs will be under pressure *not* to expand because one possible reaction to a CU will be: 'we are already a large market, so what do we really stand to gain by going through the hassle of adding more members?'. This is what I call the 'Our Market Is Large Enough' syndrome. I think, as Martin Wolf has often noted, that large countries tend to be more inward-looking for precisely this type of reason.

  In addition, the expansion of the CU to include any specific set of outside countries will imply differential aggregate-welfare effects for current members, implying in turn differential incentives for member countries for and against the expansion.[20] In this context, a CU (which generally includes transfers among members) may be more expansionary (*à la* Kemp–Wan argumentation) than an FTA, though a CU that simultaneously seeks *political* integration may be less willing to expand.

- *Interest groups in member countries:* We need also to consider how interest groups, who lobby for or against CU expansion, will behave. Again, since CUs are a balance of trade-creating and trade-protecting forces, it is possible that the protectionists who profit from the diversion of trade away from efficient suppliers abroad to themselves will line up against CU expansion to include those suppliers. The problem then will be the 'These Are Our Markets' syndrome.

  This syndrome is not absent from the NAFTA scene, as many leader articles and media quote from business groups testified during the fast-track renewal. In fact, this syndrome was also present in the Eastman Kodak pamphlet (Dornbusch *et al.*, 1989) that I cited earlier. It is also a sentiment that was beautifully expressed by Signor Agnelli of Fiat: 'The single market must first offer an advantage to European companies. This is a message we must insist on without hesitation'.[21] It is, of course, fine for Signor Agnelli to express such sentiments: after all, Fiat has run for years, not on gas, but on VERs against the Japanese. But should economists also embrace such sentiments?

● *Interest groups and governments of outside countries:* The third set of 'agents' has to be the outside countries. Here, the example of a CU may lead others to emulate and seek entry. Otherwise, the fear of trade diversion may also induce outsiders to seek entry: Irwin's marvellous study on the historical experience with trade liberalisation in the 19th century (1992) shows that the Anglo–French Treaty may well have served this purpose. If so, this acts as an incentive to expand the CU.

This is clearly an uncharted area that is evidently the most interesting for further analysis.[22] I might add just one empirical–econometric study, by Mansfield (1992), which takes trade data for 1850–1965, estimates an index of 'power distribution' (reflecting, among other things, trade blocs and economic power distribution) and comes up with Figure 2.2. When power was centred in hegemons, during periods of British and American hegemony, and when there was 'anarchy', the world economy was relatively liberalised (in the sense that global exports : GDP ratio was high); when there were a few middle-sized powers, as could happen with trade blocs, the result was a smaller ratio of trade to GDP (Figure 2.2).

If Mansfield's analysis is accepted, and if it is considered to be a reasonable approximation to the question whether CUs will have expansionist or protectionist outlooks (mapping perhaps also into their attitudes to CU expansion or stagnation), then the presumption would be that historical experience suggests that trade blocs will fragment the world economy, not go on to unify it. Of course, history does not always repeat itself. But Mansfield's work certainly suggests caution in place of the gung-ho regionalism that has been urged by the Memorial Drive School.

To conclude, consider the following popular assertions by the regionalists:

● regionalism is quicker;
● regionalism is more efficient; and
● regionalism is more certain.

6.1   Is regionalism quicker?

The regionalists claim that the GATT is the 'General Agreement to Talk and Talk', whereas regionalism proceeds quicker. But is this really so?

(1) Historically, at least, the 'First Regionalism' failed whereas the GATT oversaw the effective dismantling of prewar tariffs in the

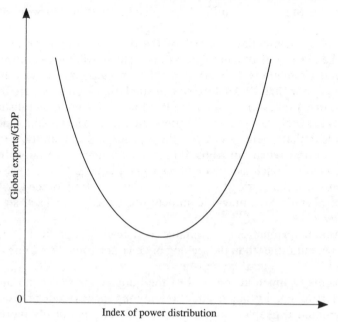

Figure 2.2   Concentration of power in the world and global exports
Source: Mansfield (1992)

OECD countries and the enlargement of disciplines over NTBs at the Tokyo Round and beyond. A little caution, to say the least, is necessary before celebrating regionalism's quickfootedness.

(2) For those who believe that regionalism offers a quick route to effective trade liberalisation, Dam's analysis quoted above needs renewed attention. There is a world of difference between announcing an FTA or a CU and its implementation, and the comparison is not pleasing if you are in the regional camp.

(3) As for speed, even the best example of regionalism, the European Community, started almost four decades ago (1957) and is now into 1992. The 'transition' has not therefore been instantaneous any more than negotiated reductions of trade barriers under the GATT Rounds. And this, too, despite the enormous political support for a united Europe.

(4) Take agriculture. The record of regional trade blocs dealing with agricultural trade liberalisation is either non-existent or dismal; the CAP is not exactly the European Community's crowning achievement. In fact, if it were not for multilateralism (i.e., the Uruguay Round and the coalition of the Cairns Group that crystallised

around the MTN), it is difficult to imagine that the process of unravelling the CAP could even have begun.

(5) The (actual or potential) exercise of the regional option can also affect the efficacy of the multilateral one. The unwillingness of the European Community to start the MTN in 1982 and its largely reactive, rather than leadership, role at the Uruguay Round, are in some degree a reflection of its being less hungry for multilateralism given its internal market size and preoccupations. Then again, is it not evident that, were it not for the European Community, the capacity of the French (for whose political predicament one can only have sympathy, much as one deplores its consequence for the willingness to liberalise agriculture) to slow down the reform of the CAP and the liberalisation of world agriculture would have been significantly less?

(6) Moreover, if regionalism is available as a realistic option, it will encourage exit rather than the seeking of voice and even the manifestation of loyalty to multilateralism:

- This may happen at the level of the bureaucrats who wind up preferring small-group negotiations among friends (code phrase: 'like-minded people') to the intellectually and politically more demanding business of negotiating with and for the larger community of trading nations.

- Or else it may happen that, just as public choice theory à la Olson tells us in regard to the diffusion of consumer losses and concentration of producer gains that favour protectionist outcomes, the proponents of regionalism tend to be better focused and mobilised (they are often regional 'experts' and partisans who ally themselves with the preferred policy options of the countries whose FTA cause they support), whereas the support for multilateralism is often more diffused and less politically effective and therefore takes second place when regionalism is on the political scene.

- Then again, regionalism may appeal to politicians since it translates more easily into votes: the wooing of the Hispanic voters, by urging them to identify with the FTA, was quite evident during the renewal of the fast-track authority in 1991 for the NAFTA negotiations with Mexico.

- The support of business groups for multilateralism may also erode with regional alternatives because of two different reasons: (i) If one can get a deal regionally, where one may have a 'great deal of trade', then one may forget about the multilateral arena. Thus, if Canada could get the United States to agree to a fairer operation of the unfair trade mechanisms (a matter on which many Canadians today feel they were mistaken, with Prime Minister Mulroney and Mr Riesman talking about Americans being 'thugs' or like 'third world dictators'[23]), why bother to fight the battles at the Uruguay Round where the powerful American manufacturing lobbies, zeroing in with the European Community against the Far East, seek instead to weaken the GATT rules? (ii) Again, one may get better protectionist, trade-diversionary deals for oneself in a preferential arrangement than in the non-discriminatory world of the GATT: e.g., Mexico's textile interests should benefit in the NAFTA relative to Caribbean and other external competitors in the US market, weakening the Mexican incentive to push for reform in the MFA forthwith.

(7) Finally, it is true that the free-rider problem looks difficult as the number of GATT members increases steadily. Yet recent theoretical work on GATT-style trade negotiations (Ludema, 1991) suggests that the free-rider problem may not be an effective barrier to freeing trade. Moreover, as Finger (1979) has pointed out, and as experience of inadequate GSP concessions underlines, developing countries have not been able to free-ride as much as their exemption from reciprocity under Special & Differential (S & D) treatment would imply: the trade concessions on commodities of interest to them have not gone as far as the concessions on commodities of interest to other GATT members without such an exemption. (Unconditional) MFN does not work in practice as well as it should from the free-riders' perspective.

6.2   Is regionalism more efficient?

Occasionally, one finds the regionalists arguing that regionalism is also more *efficient*: it produces *better* results. A typical argument is that, as part of the NAFTA negotiations, Mexico has accepted virtually all the US demands on intellectual property (IP) protection. A story, told in developing country circles, serves to probe this assertion critically: Ambassador Carla Hills was on a tour of South America, extolling the virtues of Mexico's 'capitulation'. At a dinner in her honour in Caracas, she apparently claimed: 'Mexico now has world-class IP legislation'. At this point, President Carlos Peretz supposedly turned to his left and remarked: 'But Mexico does not have a world-class parliament'.

The true moral of the story, however, is that, as part of the bilateral *quid pro quos* in an FTA or a CU, weak states may agree to specific demands of strong states,[24] in ways that are not exactly *optimal* from the viewpoint of the economic efficiency of the world trading system. In turn, however, these concessions can distort the outcome of the multilateral negotiations.

This may well have happened with TRIPs and TRIMs at the Uruguay Round.[25] As is now widely conceded among economists, the case for TRIPs for instance is *not* similar to the case for free trade: there is no presumption of mutual gain, world welfare itself may be reduced by any or more IP protection, and there is little empirical support for the view that 'inadequate' IP protection impedes the creation of new technical knowledge significantly.[26] Yet the use of US muscle, unilaterally through 'Special 301' actions, and the playing of the regional card through the NAFTA carrot for Mexico, have put TRIPs squarely and effectively into the MTN.

Again, a distorting impact on the multilateral trade rule from NAFTA negotiations can be feared from the fact that, as a price for the latter to be accepted by the Congress during the delicate renewal of fast-track authority, the US Administration had to accept demands for harmonisation in environment and labour standards by Mexico towards US standards. In political circles this effectively linked the case for free trade with the demands for 'level playing fields' or fair trade (extremely widely interpreted),[27] legitimating these demands and weakening the ability of economists and of governments negotiating at the GATT (multilaterally for arm's length free trade) to resist this illegitimate constraint on freeing trade.[28]

6.3 Is regionalism more certain?

Much has been made, in the Mexican context, of the argument that the FTA will make trade liberalisation irreversible. But something needs to be added here:

- GATT also creates commitments: tariffs are bound. (This does not apply to concessions made under conditionality, of course, by the IMF or the IBRD.) Mexico *is* a member, if recent, of the GATT.
- Recall Dam (quoted above): Article XXIV is so full of holes in its discipline that almost anything goes. Reductions of trade barriers can be slowed down, as 'circumstances' require, other bindings can be torn up by mutual consent (an easier task when there are only a few members in the bloc but more difficult under the GATT), etc.
- Recall, too, that regional agreements have failed (LAFTA) and stagnated (ASEAN) as well. The current mood in Canada over NAFTA is sour and the MTN looks better in consequence.[29] The sense, however,

that the United States has let Canada down and failed to live by the spirit of the FTA agreements will probably not endure. But who knows?

7 The United States: from 'piecemeal' to 'programmatic' regionalism

Let me conclude by considering more specifically the US shift to regionalism for the Americas in the perspective of the objective of arriving at (non-discriminatory) free trade for all.

US regionalism, when presided over by Ambassador William Brock, then the US Trade Representative, was *not* geographically-circumscribed regionalism. Rather, it was truly open-ended. Brock was known to have offered an FTA to Egypt (along with the one to Israel) and to the ASEAN countries; indeed, he would have offered it to the moon and Mars if only life had been discovered there with a government in place to negotiate with. This regionalism was evidently motivated by a vision, even if flawed,[30] that saw regionalism as clearly the route to multilateralism: it would go on expanding, eventually embracing many, preferably all.

By contrast, today's regionalism, confined to the Americas by President Bush's men, lacks the 'vision thing'. In fact, when allied with Secretary Baker's recently reported admonition to the Japanese not to encourage an Asian trade bloc, as suggested by Malaysia as a necessary response to the European Community and US regionalism, the US policy appears to Asia also to be self-contradictory and self-serving: 'regional blocs are good for us but not for you'. And it simply won't wash, though Japan, fearing further bashing, will be deterred for a while.

If America's regionalism is not to turn into a piecemeal, world trading system-fragmenting force, it is necessary to give to it a programmatic, world trade system unifying format and agenda. One possibility is to encourage, not discourage, Japan to line up the Asian countries (all the way to the Indian subcontinent) into an AFTA, with the US lining up the South Americans into the NAFTA, on a schedule, say, of 10 years. Then, Japan and the United States, the two 'hubs', would meet and coalesce into a larger FTA at that point,[31] finally negotiating with the European Community and its associate countries to arrive at the Grand Finale of multilateral free trade for all in Geneva.

Only such 'programmatic' regionalism, in one of several possible variants, would ensure that US regionalism was not perceived by Asia to be hostile and fragmenting.[32] It alone would make regionalism less harmful to the MTN and the GATT and more supportive of the cause of multilateral free trade for all.

8   Concluding remarks

The question of regionalism is thus both a difficult and delicate one. Only time will tell whether the revival of regionalism since the 1980s will have been a sanguine and benign development or a malign force that will serve to undermine the widely-shared objective of multilateral free trade for all.

My judgement is that the revival of regionalism is unfortunate. But, given its political appeal and its likely spread, I believe that it is important to contain and shape it in the ways sketched here so that it becomes maximally useful and minimally damaging, and consonant with the objectives of arriving at multilateral free trade for all.

NOTES

This chapter reflects my personal views and bears no relationship to my position as Economic Policy Adviser to the Director-General, GATT. Thanks are due to Robert Baldwin, James Benedict, Richard Blackhurst, Christopher Bliss, Don Davis, Sunil Gulati, Douglas Irwin, John McMillan, Arvind Panagariya, T.N. Srinivasan and John Whalley for helpful conversations and suggestions.

1 The Vinerian approach to customs union theory has been carried forward by others more recently, chiefly by Berglas (1979) and Corden (1976). In addition, three alternative theoretical approaches can be distinguished: by Kemp and Wan (1976): by Cooper and Massell (1965a, 1965b), Johnson (1965) and Bhagwati (1968); and by Brecher and Bhagwati (1981). All four approaches are distinguished and discussed in the graduate textbook by Bhagwati and Srinivasan (1983, Chapter 27) and in Bhagwati (1991a). Each is touched upon later in this chapter.

2 Two points should be noted. First, there is a difference between intention and reality: as argued below, the Article XXIV-sanctioned FTAs and CUs have never gone 'all the way'. Second, GATT's MFN is universal only for its members, so it falls short of total universalism. but the important point to remember is that the GATT is open to membership to all who meet the criteria for admission, and has generally been inclusive rather than exclusive.

3 Of course, this theory developed *after* the incorporation of Article XXIV into the GATT. So its inconsistency with Article XXIV, on its own terms, is perhaps only an amusing observation. Note, however, that James Meade was a main actor in both. The argument is developed in two alternative ways in Lipsey (1960, p. 507) and in Johnson (1967, p. 203).

4 A substantially improved and more effectively functioning dispute settlement mechanism, aimed at restoring GATT's legal discipline, is an important part of the 1992 'Dunkel draft' of what the Uruguay Round should conclude.

5 Japan in fact, appears to have probed the possibility of going into such an arrangement with the United States as one of its partners in the 1960s but to no avail.

6 The question of 'multilateralism' versus 'regionalism' surfaced at a different level even within this preferential trade liberalisation among the developing countries. Thus, in the early 1960s, we were discussing whether the Cooper–

Massell–Johnson–Bhagwati argument should not be considered on a G-77-wide basis rather than for much smaller groups of developing countries. This was the main issue before a 1962 UNCTAD Expert Group in New York, of which I was a member, which met over three weeks to draft the recommendation that preferential trade liberalisation among the developing countries be 'multilateral', i.e., G-77-wide, rather than narrowly focused. Unfortunately, the preferential arrangements that were contemplated took the latter, narrower focus.

7 The MIT Economics Department is at 50 Memorial Drive in Cambridge, Massachusetts. I obviously exclude the diaspora, including myself! If the views expressed with Dornbusch in an Eastman Kodak publication (Dornbusch *et al.*, 1989) are a guide, Krugman may hold one of the positions described above. This pamphlet makes somewhat odd and untenable statements about what the GATT does and does not do. Cf. Finger's (1989) rather blunt analysis of these assertions in *The World Economy* and my own complaints about the confusions following from loose writing on trade-policy issues, and the resulting prostitution of an important debate, in Bhagwati (1991b). Whether the Memorial Drive school has by now under fire shifted its anti-multilateral stance and joined the more common view that regionalism is a useful supplement, not an alternative, to multilateralism is anyone's guess, given the conflicting reports one hears of its many oral pronouncements on the lecture circuit from its peripatetic members. But if it truly has abandoned its early vitriolic anti-GATT position, I would be delighted in its demise.

8 I rely upon oral presentation at the 1988 annual meeting of the American Enterprise Institute in Washington, DC.

9 Defined in Vinerian fashion, a trade-diverting FTA can still improve a member country's welfare but will generally harm outside countries. The focus below is on the impact on others, as is presumably the intention also of Article XXIV's injunction not to raise the average external tariff.

10 Aside from obfuscating the distinction between preferential and non-discriminatory trade liberalisation, the pro-FTA economists got carried away by the 'battle for Mexico'. Thus, while it is perfectly possible for Mexico to gain much while the United States gains little, a *Wall Street Journal* article by Dornbusch (1991) argued that trade with Mexico was already largely free because of OAP provisions and the GSP (so that the union fears of job losses, etc. were exaggerated), and simultaneously that Mexico would achieve prosperity thanks to the FTA. It is, of course, possible to argue each position separately in the 'segmented markets' of Mexico City and Washington, DC, turning arguments on their head as necessary for one's case. But it takes *chutzpah* to make the contradictory arguments in the same article.

11 I must confess that I had not come across this prescription earlier. But in a report in the *Economic Focus* column in *The Economist* in 1991, of a Jackson Hole Conference on FTAs, it was attributed to Paul Krugman and Lawrence Summers.

12 See Lipsey (1960, pp. 507–8): 'As far as the prices of the goods from a country's union partner are concerned, they are brought into equality with rates of transformation *vis-à-vis* domestic goods, but they are moved away from equality with rates of transformation *vis-à-vis* imports from the outside world. These imports from the union partner are thus involved in both a gain and a loss and their size is *per se* unimportant; what matters is the relation

between imports from the outside world and expenditure on domestic commodities: the larger are purchases of domestic commodities and the smaller are purchases from the outside world, the more likely is it that the union will bring gain. Consider a simple example in which a country purchases from its union partner only eggs while it purchases from the outside world only shoes, all other commodities being produced and consumed at home. Now when the union is formed the "correct" price ratio (i.e., the one which conforms with the real rate of transformation) between eggs and shoes will be disturbed but, on the other hand, eggs will be brought into the 'correct' price relationship with all other commodities – bacon, butter, cheese, meat, etc., and in these circumstances a customs union is very likely to bring gain, for the loss in distorting the price ratio between eggs and shoes will be small relative to the gain in establishing the correct price ratio between eggs and all other commodities. Now, however, let us reverse the position of domestic trade and imports from the outside world, making shoes the only commodity produced and consumed at home, eggs still being imported from the union partner, while everything else is now bought from the outside world. In these circumstances the customs union is most likely to bring a loss; the gains in establishing the correct price ratio between eggs and shoes are indeed likely to be very small compared with the losses of distorting the price ratio between eggs and all other commodities.'

13 In any event, by encouraging rules of origin because the trade-barrier walls everywhere are not equally high, FTAs encourage in turn the bureaucratic-cum-industry capture of the essentially arbitrary 'local content' rules for protectionist purposes.

14 VERs are evidently selective by countries; AD actions are selective down to the level of the firm, as Brian Hindley has often noted.

15 Brian Hindley and Patrick Messerlin are investigating this hypothesis for the GATT Secretariat as part of a set of studies to support the 1992 GATT *Annual Report* on *Regionalism and Multilateralism*, following the 1991 *Annual Report* on *Trade and the Environment*.

16 This paper has also been commissioned by the GATT Secretariat for its 1992 *Annual Report*.

17 Christopher Bliss (1990) has recently made a valuable stab at this problem.

18 Such time-paths are clearly not unique. Thus, for instance, any number of such paths could be generated by relaxing the requirement that, at each stage, the non-union outside countries be left only as well off as before the new expansion of the CU.

19 This argument is being investigated in Mansfield's forthcoming paper for the 1992 GATT *Annual Report*.

20 This analysis must use the Brecher and Bhagwati (1981) approach to theorising about CUs since it relates to analysing the effects of changes in domestic and external policies and parameters on the distribution of income and welfare among member states.

21 Quoted by Wolf (1989).

22 Again, at the instance of the GATT secretariat, this question will be investigated in depth for the 1992 GATT *Annual Report*, by Bernhart Hoekman with Michael Leidy, and by Edward Mansfield.

23 Those who think that much of Japan-bashing is not prejudiced may want to think about the differential and exaggerated reaction in the United States to

the far more innocuous remarks of Prime Minister Miyazawa and Speaker Sakarauchi.

24 In Mexico's case, President Salinas's political stake in getting an FTA with the United States is vastly disproportionate to President Bush's.

25 TRIPs are trade-related IP provisions and TRIMs are trade-related investment measures. The weakness of the case for their inclusion in the GATT, at least in the forms canvassed by many lobbies, is discussed in Bhagwati (1991a).

26 It is not surprising therefore that the spokesman for TRIPs have shifted from utilitarian methods of argumentation to 'rights': they talk now of 'theft' and 'piracy'.

27 That the environmental and labour standards' negotiations in NAFTA will be 'parallel' rather than 'integrated' is of no consequence, any more than running the services negotiations parallel to other negotiations at the Uruguay Round has been.

28 The danger posed by the proliferating demands for 'level playing fields' or fair trade, chiefly in the United States but elsewhere too, is extremely serious. It is analysed, and the theoretical questions raised by it are noted, in Bhagwati (1992). The environment issue, in particular, has been discussed in this context in the 1991 GATT *Annual Report*.

29 Whalley's splendid study of the US–Canada FTA (1992) supports the sceptical views that I have advanced of the prospect and wisdom of the 'Second Regionalism'.

30 For reasons that I have already indicated above, regionalism is not quite the benign trade policy that it is now popularly believed to be.

31 This would require discarding the extreme Japanophobia that characterises the so-called 'revisionists' who are really 'regressionists' twice over: they use simple-minded regressions to condemn Japan for its 'closed markets' (e.g., that Japan's manufactures' import share is stagnant and/or low compared to others') and they also wish to return the United States to the Japan-bashing of the prewar period that had given way to sense and sensitivity in the postwar years; cf. Bhagwati (1991a).

32 Saxonhouse's excellent study (1992) only complements and underlines what I argue here. I should add that while the United States signals a world trading system fragmenting message to Asia through NAFTA, Mexico by contrast signals a pro-world trade message. In joining in free trade with the colossus to its north, President Salinas boldly and effectively tells the developing countries that free trade is good and not to be feared.

REFERENCES

Berglas, E. (1979) 'Preferential Trading Theory: The *n* Commodity Case', *Journal of Political Economy*, **87**, pp. 315–31.

Bhagwati, J.N. (1968) 'Trade Liberalization Among LDCs, Trade Theory and GATT Rules', in J.N. Wolfe (ed.), *Value, Capital, and Growth: Papers in Honour of Sir John Hicks*, Oxford: Oxford University.

(1991a) *The World Trading System at Risk*, Princeton: Princeton University Press and Harvester Wheatsheaf.

(1991b) 'Revealing Talk on Trade', *The American Enterprise*, **2(6)**, pp. 72–8.

(1992) 'Fair Trade, Reciprocity and Harmonization: The New Challenge to the Theory and Policy of Free Trade', Columbia University, Economics Department, *Discussion Paper Series*, **604** (April).

Bhagwati, J.N. and T.N. Srinivasan (1983) *Lectures on International Trade*, Cambridge, Mass.: MIT Press.

Bliss, C. (1990) 'The Optimal External Tariff in an Enlarging Customs Union', CEPR, *Discussion Paper*, 368 (February), London: CEPR.

Brecher, R. and J.N. Bhagwati (1981) 'Foreign Ownership and the Theory of Trade and Welfare', *Journal of Political Economy*, **89(3)**, pp. 497–512.

Cooper, C.A. and B.F. Massell (1965a) 'A New Look at Customs Union Theory', *The Economic Journal*, **75**, pp. 742–7.

(1965b) 'Towards a General Theory of Customs Unions for Developing Countries', *Journal of Political Economy*, **73(5)**, pp. 461–76.

Corden, W.M. (1976) 'Customs Union Theory and the Nonuniformity of Tariffs', *Journal of International Economics*, **61(1)**, pp. 99–107.

Dam, K. (1970) *The GATT: Law and International Economic Organization*, Chicago: University of Chicago Press.

Dornbusch, R. (1991) 'If Mexico Prospers, So Will We', *The Wall Street Journal* (April 11) Op.-Ed. section.

Dornbusch, R. *et al.* (1989) *Meeting World Challenges: United States Manufacturing in the 1990s*, Rochester, NY: pamphlet issued by the Eastman Kodak company.

The Economist (1991) Economics Focus column (July).

Finger, J.M. (1979) 'Trade Liberalization: A Public Choice Perspective', in R.C. Amachen, G. Haberler and T. Willett (eds), *Challenges to a Liberal International Economic Order*, Washington, DC: American Enterprise Institute.

(1989) 'Picturing America's Future: Kodak's Solution of American Trade Exposure', *The World Economy*, **12(3)**, pp. 377–80.

Gowa, J. and E. Mansfield (1991) 'Allies, Adversaries, and International Trade', paper presented to the American Political Science Association Meetings, Washington, DC (mimeo).

Grandmont, J.M. and D. McFadden (1972) 'A Technical Note on Classical Gains from Trade', *Journal of International Economics*, **2**, pp. 109–25.

Irwin, D. (1992) 'Multilateral and Bilateral Trade Policies in the World Trading System: An Historical Perspective', Chapter 4 in this volume.

Johnson, H.G. (1958a) 'The Gains from Free Trade with Europe: An Estimate', *Manchester School of Economic and Social Studies*.

(1958b) 'The Economics Gains from Free Trade with Europe', *Three Banks Review*.

(1965) 'An Economic Theory of Protectionism, Tariff Bargaining, and the Formation of Customs Unions', *Journal of Political Economy*, **73** (June), pp. 256–83.

(1967) *Economic Policies Toward Less Developed Countries*, Washington, DC: Brookings Institution.

Kemp, M.C. (1972) 'The Gains from International Trade', *The Economic Journal*, **72**, pp. 803–19.

Kemp, M.C. and H. Wan (1976) 'An Elementary Proposition Concerning the Formation of Customs Unions', *Journal of International Economics*, **6** (February), pp. 95–8.

Lipsey, R.G. (1957) 'The Theory of Customs Unions: Trade Diversion and Welfare', *Economica*, **24**, pp. 40–6.

(1958) 'The Theory of Customs Unions: A General Equilibrium Analysis', University of London, Ph.D. thesis.

(1960) 'The Theory of Customs Unions: A General Survey', *The Economic Journal*, **70**, pp. 498–513.

Lipsey, R.G. and K.J. Lancaster (1956–7) 'The General Theory of Second Best', *Review of Economic Studies*, **24**, pp. 33–49.

Ludema, R. (1991) 'International Trade Bargaining and the Most Favoured Nation Clause', *Economics and Politics*, **3(1)**, pp. 1–41.

Mansfield, E. (1992) 'The Concentration of Capabilities and International Trade', *International Organization* (forthcoming).

McMillan, J. (1991) 'Do Trade Blocs Foster Open Trade?', University of California at San Diego (mimeo).

Meade, J.E. (1956) *The Theory of Customs Unions*, Amsterdam: North-Holland.

Samuelson, P.A. (1939) 'The Gains from International Trade', *Canadian Journal of Economics and Political Science*, **5(2)**, pp. 195–205.

Saxonhouse, G.R. (1992) 'Trading Blocs and East Asia', Chapter 12 in this volume.

Viner, J. (1950) *The Customs Union Issue*, New York: Carnegie Endowment for International Peace.

Whalley, J. (1992) 'Regional Trade Arrangements in North America: CUSTA and NAFTA', Chapter 11 in this volume.

Wolf, M. (1989) 'European Community 1992: The Lure of the *Chasse Gardée*', *The World Economy*, **12(3)**, pp. 373–6.

Discussion

ROBERT BALDWIN

Jagdish Bhagwati in Chapter 2 provides a very perceptive analysis of the possible conflicting and complementary relationships between regionalism and multilateralism. I shall focus on a few of the points he raises, and elaborate somewhat on them.

I want to comment first on the political economy motivations for forming trading blocs. As we know, political as well as economic goals played a major role in the formation of the European Community (EC), and remain today. The founders of the Community believed that, by increasing the degree of economic interdependence among members, both the democratic political institutions and the market-oriented economic institutions of these countries would be strengthened and the likelihood of future military conflicts thereby reduced.

Such political economy motivations have remained an important feature of the Community and are crucial in explaining its success, and especially the continuing expansionary efforts. We saw the importance of these motivations in the decision to bring Spain into the Community as quickly as possible. Economic objections to early membership were swept aside by the argument that it was necessary to move quickly to strengthen the new democratic and market-oriented government of Spain. The rapid merging of East and West Germany is another example where political considerations dominated what was perceived to be the optimum economic pace of integration.

In my view, the political arguments for trading blocs do have strong merits in some instances and the resulting benefits easily dominate economic considerations. In moving from a democracy to an authoritarian form of government, it is generally necessary for the new leaders to bribe key economic groups into accepting the new order by directing significant economic rents to these groups. The use of inward-looking trade policies has been an important means of creating these rents. Consequently, integrating a newly formed democratic country into a major trading bloc eliminates this means of undermining democratic institutions and, instead, creates rents that strengthen both democratic and free-market institutions.

It should be noted that multilateral liberalisation can also help to strengthen market-oriented economic institutions as well as democratic political institutions. The one-sided trade liberalisation undertaken by the United States after World War II had these effects. However, such effects can be focused in a stronger manner on specific countries by using regional arrangements rather than the multilateral approach.

Most of the other trading blocs created in the 1950s and 1960s involved developing countries who were motivated mainly by economic rather than by political objectives. This was, in my view, a major reason for their failure. The formation of a trading bloc can bring appreciable collective economic gains to countries with a relatively low level of manufacturing activity, but there is likely to be a serious problem associated with the distribution of these gains among the members. At early stages of industrialisation the most advanced country in the group tends to benefit significantly, but some of the smaller members are likely to lose absolutely in the integration process. Bhagwati argues that the free-trade areas formed in this period failed because they attempted to allocate industries among the members by bureaucratic negotiations rather than through the market system. This is correct, but the basic problem that led to these negotiations was the realisation that the benefits would be distributed very unevenly if the market alone were used as the allocative mechanism.

Since the GATT was established in 1947, the US government has accepted the legitimacy of the political arguments for trade blocs. As Bhagwati points out, this is the main reason why the United States supported the creation of the European Common Market and helped it gain GATT approval. The American government adopted a tolerant but sceptical view toward other economic unions not based on strong political ties and, until recent years, rejected offers for US participation in such arrangements.

This position changed significantly in the 1980s, however, first with the US-sponsored Caribbean Basin Initiative, followed by the US–Israel Free Trade Agreement, the US–Canadian Free Trade Agreement, and now the North American Free Trade Agreement (NAFTA), involving Canada, Mexico, and the United States. This policy shift is part of a much more general change in US trade policy that, in addition to a new willingness to participate in free-trade blocs, includes an increased willingness to use non-tariff measures to restrict imports, a much more vigorous enforcement of the so-called 'unfair' trade laws, and the adoption of an aggressive unilateral approach to opening foreign markets. These policies are, in turn, related to the increased foreign competition faced by such politically powerful import-competing industries as textiles and apparel, steel and automobiles and in such export-oriented sectors as computer chips and other high technology items.

Basically, US political and economic leaders have blamed others for these pressures to adjust rather than face up squarely to the need to shift resources to different economic activities. Adopting an aggressive market-opening policy under section 301 of US trade law, tightening the unfair trade laws, introducing import restrictions outside of the GATT framework, and being more receptive to negotiating free trade agreements are all efforts aimed both to bring pressure on GATT members to change the rules as the United States wishes and to explore whether the country can do better outside of the GATT multilateral framework. An interesting feedback from the stricter enforcement of the anti-dumping (AD) and countervailing duty (CD) laws and more aggressive use of section 301 is that a number of countries now want to join the United States in a free-trade agreement in the hope that these laws will then not be used as extensively against them.

How successful these policies turn out to be will play an important role in determining the extent to which the United States emphasises regional versus multilateral approaches in its future trade policies. We must remember that foreign policy objectives were decisive in shaping the liberal trade policies promoted by the United States for many years after World War II. These objectives are no longer pressing ones; moreover, the ideological commitment to liberal trade policies has weakened greatly so that trade policy is now largely shaped by domestic economic considerations.

While the vigorous pursuit of regional arrangements seems unlikely on the part of the United States, an outcome that is not at all unlikely, provided there is no significant change in the GATT system, is a gradual drift toward the expansion of the North American regional bloc to include a number of other Latin American countries. This would be driven by pressures from these countries to tap into the US market and the absence of any compelling reason on the United States' part why it should not go along with the enlargements. Still another factor that might drive expansion of an American-centred bloc would be the growing influence of the European Community in trade, macroeconomic and foreign policy matters. US political and economic leaders may adopt the view that it is necessary to expand such a bloc in order to match the increasing political and economic power of the Community.

The likelihood of the extension of trading blocs in the world economy, especially an American-centred bloc, would be greatly reduced, in my view, if there were basic changes in the way the GATT is now operating. For the last 20 years the GATT has attempted to deal with the non-tariff measures that distort trade by writing new rules or codes of good conduct. While these codes have merit, GATT operations have tended to ignore the other activity of the organisation that made it so successful in the postwar period, namely, actual negotiations to reduce trade distortions such as tariffs. Unfortunately, the view gained credence in the early 1970s that negotiations to reduce non-tariff barriers were not feasible; it was only possible to write codes about how countries should behave with respect to these barriers. The outcome has been a serious weakening of the multilateral trading system. Since the GATT did not undertake such negotiations, larger countries such as the United States and the Community took the task on themselves and used various unilateral pressures to achieve their goals.

The way to move the setting of trade policy back toward a multilateral approach is not so much by tightening the rules to prevent certain types of policies but by channeling the bilateral negotiations that have resulted in these policies through a GATT-sponsored negotiating framework. Specifically, negotiations between the United States and other countries or between the Community and other nations over such matters as subsidies, government purchasing policy, intellectual property rights, discriminatory standards, quantitative restrictions (QRs), and so forth should be conducted under the auspices of the GATT.

RICHARD BLACKHURST

To begin, let me say that I like Bhagwati's Chapter 2 very much, which perhaps is not surprising considering its strong support for multilateralism and the GATT system. Second, I have little to add to the discussion in sections 1 and 2; they provide a good overview of GATT's Article XXIV, including how countries have used, and abused, it. These sections also put the current interest in regional integration into postwar perspective.

Section 3 includes one of the chapter's most important propositions: 'that regionalism this time is likely to endure' (p. 29). While I do not necessarily disagree with this proposition, I think the arguments for it are not quite as one-sided as a reader might guess from the chapter. We read on page 29, for example:

> The conversion of the United States is of major significance. As the key defender of multilateralism through the postwar years, its decision now to travel the regional route (in the geographical *and* the preferential senses simultaneously) tilts the balance of forces . . . away from multilateralism to regionalism.

I believe that this understates the commitment of the US administration to a successful Uruguay Round. A review of some of the current troubles plaguing a number of actual and proposed regional groupings would also contribute to a more balanced perspective on the outlook for regional economic integration.

In section 5 the chapter raises the issue of designing disciplines to minimise trade diversion from regional economic integration. One option involves reforming Article XXIV. This may in fact be a useful approach, but it needs to be examined in conjunction with the problem of countries' *compliance* with the rules in Article XXIV. Compliance has arguably been a serious problem;[1] if it remains a problem, then simply reforming Article XXIV may not accomplish very much.

One of the chapter's most important parts is that in which Bhagwati raises the issue of the interaction between current usage of anti-dumping (AD) provisions and voluntary export restraints (VERs) on the one hand, and regional integration (RI) on the other, and how this interaction increases the risk of trade diversion. I strongly endorse Bhagwati's conclusion that if regionalism is destined to flourish, this will strengthen both the need for greater discipline over AD actions and VERs (mainly to safeguard the interests of third countries), and more generally the need for a strong GATT.

My main comment on section 5 is that it would be interesting to expand the discussion to include trade in commercial services. There are at least two important differences in the case of traded services:

(1) Policies governing trade in services are not yet subject to multilateral rules, but will be if the Uruguay Round succeeds. Clearly the scope for taking trade-diverting policy decisions in the course of negotiating an integration agreement is much greater in the absence of multilateral rules.

(2) Barriers to trade in services generally do not take the form of border measures, and factor flows tend to be more important than is the case with goods. The implications of these differences for the analysis of trade creation and trade diversion in services trade is an area which needs to be examined in more detail.

As regards the discussion of the 'dynamic time-path' in section 6, the future of regional integration arrangements will depend in part on their ability to deal more effectively, than either unilateral or multilateral approaches, with emerging policy issues. Thus we need to ask two related questions:

(1) What are the likely key trade issues for the 1990s (besides regionalisation)? Candidates include the interaction between trade and environment, the integration of former centrally planned economies (CPEs) and highly protected LDCs into the world market, international competition policies as they interact with trade and trade rules, and likely pressures for regulatory harmonisation of other economic and social policies.

(2) Does regional economic integration have a comparative advantage in dealing with any or all of these issues?

Another interesting aspect of the time-path issue – beyond the scope of the present chapter, but nonetheless worth noting – are the implications of regional economic integration for the monetary fiscal, and exchange rate policies of the members. For example, suppose regional economic integration tends to result in improved macroeconomic policies, which in turn improve the economic performance of the countries involved, making it easier to sell *multilateral* trade liberalisation to politically important domestic groups?

My final comment is that I found that reading the chapter strengthened my view that the fundamental issue in this area is not regionalism versus multilateralism, but rather interventionism versus liberalism. In other words, the fact that regional economic integration can be either support-ive of or antagonistic toward the multilateral trading system, depending on the details, suggests that regional economic integration *per se* is not the basic issue.

If we can get governments to commit themselves in the Uruguay Round to improved market access and reduced government intervention in agriculture, textiles, steel, and other goods and services, it is likely that the world trading system has little to fear from regional integration. In contrast, if governments cannot bring themselves to reduce intervention and increase market access, we may see a spread of inward-looking trading blocs, but they would be simply the manifestation of a much more basic problem.

NOTES

The analysis, conclusions, and opinions in this Discussion are my own, and do not necessarily reflect the views of the GATT Secretariat.

1 One of the 15 proposals for action put forward in the Leutwiler Report (1985) reads: 'The Rules permitting customs unions and free-trade areas have been distorted and abused. To prevent further erosion of the multilateral trading system, they need to be clarified and tightened up'.

REFERENCE

Leutwiler, F. *et al.* (1985) *Trade Policies for a Better Future*, Geneva: GATT (March).

3 Regionalism versus multilateralism: analytical notes

PAUL KRUGMAN

With the Uruguay Round still (at the time of writing) on the brink, with growing tensions between the United States and Japan, and with growing support in the United States for a more or less aggressive industrial policy, it is evident that the GATT-centred system of multilateral trade relations is in considerable trouble. At the same time, regional trading arrangements such as 'EC 1992' and the North American Free-Trade Area (NAFTA) have appeared to be the cutting edge of whatever success-ful international negotiations have taken place. This apparent shift away from globalism to localism has created severe ambivalence among policy intellectuals. Should the rise of regional trading arrangements be wel-comed, as a step on the road that will ultimately reinforce global free trade? Or should regional trading blocs be condemned, as institutions that undermine the multilateral system? Or, yet again, should they perhaps be accepted more or less grudgingly, as the best option we are likely to get in an age of diminished expectations?

This ambivalence, and the striking extent to which reasonable analysts find themselves in sharp disagreement, are not surprising. The issue of multilateralism versus regionalism is a difficult one to get one's arms around, on at least two levels. First, even in narrowly economic terms it is a tricky area: after all, it was precisely in the context of preferential trading arrangements that the byzantine complexities of the second best were first discovered.

Second, the real issues cannot be viewed as narrowly economic. Inter-national trading regimes are essentially devices of political economy; they are intended at least as much to protect nations from their own interest groups as they are to protect nations from each other. Any discussion of the international trading system necessarily thus involves an attempt to discuss not what policy ought to be, but what it actually will be under various rules of the game. And the science of politics is, if possible, even less developed than that of economics.

In this realm of foggy discussion it is natural for economists to grab hold of any analytical tools they can find, even if they are ill-adapted to the work at hand. In an earlier paper (Krugman, 1991a), I offered a simple framework for thinking about the effects of the consolidation of a world of many nations into a smaller number of trading blocs. That framework (briefly reproduced in the Appendix to this chapter, see pp. 75–78) had some merit as a concise way of thinking about the issues of trade creation and diversion, but was grossly unrealistic in its description of the trade-policy process. Nonetheless, it was one of the few games in town – at the very least, it offered a language for talking about the issue – and plunged me into the debate. In a follow-up paper (Krugman, 1991b) I used the original model as stiffening for a broader and looser analytical argument, which was in turn used to give some intellectual credibility to a largely model-free discussion of the political economy of trade. That paper proved startlingly controversial, to an extent that was bound to worry an economist who knew that he was speculating well beyond his analytical base.

The problem, of course, is that in spite of decades of intense research into the normative economics of trade policy, there are no widely accepted positive models of policy formation. And the multilateral–regional debate hinges crucially on how the institutions of the trading system will affect not just the consequences of given trade policies, but the choices by governments of what policies actually to adopt.

The purpose of this chapter is obviously not to propose a general theory of the political economy of trade policy – not only do I not have such a theory, I have no idea even where to start.[1] Instead, it offers a set of partial analyses that try to move the discussion of the trading bloc issue a little closer to giving a realistic account of trade policy, and thus a better account of the likely economic effects.

The chapter is in five sections. Section 1 reviews briefly the simple trading-bloc model originally developed in Krugman (1991a), then argues that its main *economic* conclusions are not too sensitive to the outrageously unrealistic trade-policy process that that paper assumed. Section 2 offers a stab at a more realistic description of unilateral trade-policy formation, based on the idea that governments maximise 'weighted social welfare', and tries to relate this description to the issues raised earlier. Section 3 turns to bargaining and international negotiations. Finally, section 4 combines the pieces to offer a loose second cut at the multilateralism–regionalism issue. Section 5 draws some summary conclusions.

1 The narrow economics of trading blocs

The pure economic theory of trading blocs is essentially part of the broader theory of preferential trading arrangements. This theory has been extensively studied. Unfortunately, it is a subject of inherent complexity and ambiguity; theory *per se* identifies the main forces at work, but offers few presumptions about what is likely to happen in practice. To make any headway, one must either get into detailed empirical work, or make strategic simplifications and stylisations that one hopes do not lead one too far astray. Obviously detailed empirical work is the right approach, but will not be followed in this chapter. Instead, I continue to use the stylised approach from Krugman (1991a).

1.1   A political economy model (Krugman, 1991a)

In my initial trading-bloc model I tried to cut through the complexities of second-best analysis with a highly stylised model of a world economy. The structure of this world economy was as follows:

(1)   The world was assumed to consist of a large number of small geographical units ('provinces'), each specialised in the production of a distinct good.
(2)   The products of all provinces were assumed to enter symmetrically into world demand, with a constant elasticity of substitution σ between any two such products.
(3)   The world was assumed to be organised into B trading blocs of equal economic size, with free trade within each bloc and an *ad valorem* tariff rate t charged by each bloc on imports.
(4)   The blocs were assumed to set tariffs non-cooperatively, in order to maximise welfare.

The unrealism of this setup is obvious. Yet it had the virtue of offering a simple way to think about regionalism versus multilateralism. One could envision a move to regional trading blocs as involving a reduction in B. In the model, such a reduction in B leads to a mixture of trade creation and trade diversion. Trade creation occurs because a larger share of world trade takes place within blocs, and hence free from tariffs. Trade diversion occurs for two reasons. First, at any given tariff rate, enlarging blocs will lead to some diversion of trade that would otherwise take place between provinces in different blocs. Second, given the policy assumption (4), larger blocs, which have more market power, have an incentive to levy higher tariffs than small blocs; so as B falls, trade between blocs becomes less free.

Because of the mix of trade creation and diversion, consolidation into a smaller number of blocs has an ambiguous effect on welfare. Somewhat surprisingly, the best outcomes are with either very few or very many trading blocs. The intuition for the desirability of few blocs is obvious: when there is only one bloc, the world has achieved free trade. The converse case is perhaps less obvious: when there are many small players, each has limited market power and thus sets tariffs low – and imports are so large a share of consumption that a flat tariff has little distortive effect in any case. The worst case turns out to be for intermediate numbers of blocs, where potential inter-bloc trade is important yet tariffs distort it significantly.

The startling result is numerical: for a wide range of elasticities of substitution σ, the welfare-minimising number of blocs is three.

What is wrong with this model? The economic assumptions are grossly unrealistic, especially the absence of any structure of natural trading relations that defines natural blocs; we return to this point below. Even worse, however, is the description of trade politics embodied in assumption (4). Whatever it is that countries do when they set trade policy, they certainly do not choose the tariff level that satisfies the optimal tariff criterion. Even in Krugman (1991b), the problems with this assumption were acknowledged: 'This setup is clearly both too cynical and not cynical enough about the political economy of trade. The internal politics of trade are not nearly this benign: governments do not simply (or ever) maximize the welfare of their citizens. At the same time, the external politics of trade show far more cooperation than this'.

In fact, the numerical results themselves are a dead giveaway that the description of politics is very wrong. For any reasonable elasticity of substitution, the model predicts tariff rates that are far higher than what large industrial countries, which are presumably the ones with the most market power, impose in fact.

But do the conclusions about the shape of the relationship between the number of blocs and world welfare hinge crucially on the unrealism of the assumed trade-policy process? In fact, they do not.

1.2 Robustness of the economics to policy description

The surprise of the basic trading-bloc model is its assertion that welfare is U-shaped in the number of trading blocs, and that welfare is minimised for a small number of blocs – which suggests that current trends could indeed be adverse.

The question is whether this result depends crucially on the political piece of the model. That is, does it depend crucially on (i) the very high tariff rates predicted by the model, and (ii) the tendency of larger blocs to impose high tariffs?

One might already have guessed that (ii) was not very important to the results from the charts presented in Krugman (1991a). It turned out that predicted tariff rates did not, in fact, rise very much with reductions in B.

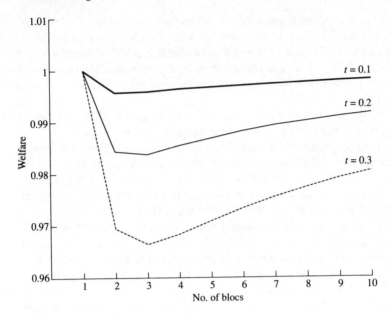

Figure 3.1   Number of blocs and welfare

The reason was basically that sufficient trade diversion takes place as *B*
falls that the share of a typical bloc in foreign markets does not rise much –
for example, when we move from a four-bloc to a three-bloc world,
interbloc trade falls so much that each of the three blocs has only a slightly
higher share in the external market, and hence faces only a slightly lower
elasticity of demand, than each of the previous four blocs. This suggests
that trade diversion at a *constant* tariff rate is doing most of the work.

The easy way to confirm this hunch is to examine how welfare varies with
B when one holds tariffs constant at much lower, more realistic levels.
That is, we abandon assumption (4) and replace it with the simple
assumption that all blocs maintain a common external tariff at the rate *t*,
whatever the number of blocs. It is possible to show (see Krugman, 1991a)
that if we normalise so that world welfare is 1 under global free trade,
welfare with *B* blocs charging a tariff rate *t* is

$$U = \left[\frac{B}{(1 + t)^{\sigma} + B - 1} \right] [(1 - B^{-1}) + B^{-1}(1 + t)^{\sigma - 1}]^{\frac{\sigma}{\sigma - 1}}. \qquad (1)$$

Figure 3.1 shows calculations of (1) for an elasticity of substitution of 4
(which implies optimal tariff rates of more than 35 percent), varying *B*
while holding *t* at 0.1, 0.2 and 0.3. The U-shape appears in spite of the lack

of an endogenous tariff rate. Indeed, for the higher tariff rates world welfare continues to be minimised at $B = 3$, although at a 10 percent tariff the pessimum moves to two blocs.

The moral of this exercise is that the basic story about potential losses from consolidation into a limited number of trade blocs is not dependent on the specific model of tariff determination laid out in earlier papers. We may note also that this means that focusing on policy changes as a result of bloc formation may be missing the point. For example, suppose we ask whether NAFTA will hurt world trade. The participants may pledge solemnly not to raise external barriers, and may even honour that pledge. Nonetheless, this model suggests that the net effect is still one of trade diversion that could easily outweigh trade creation.

What could invalidate the story? The question is how the tariff rate depends on B. If the tariff rate rises as B falls, as in the case where t is set non-cooperatively to maximise bloc welfare, then the story is simply reinforced. In order to change the story sharply, one must offer a reason why a reduction in the number of blocs might actually lead each bloc to adopt lower rather than higher external tariffs.

We will turn to (crude) models of policy below. First, however, it is necessary to repeat a caveat that plays a key role in any attempt at realistic discussion: the importance of natural trading relations.

1.3 The 'natural' trading-bloc issue

If transportation and communication costs lead to a strong tendency of countries to trade with their neighbours, and if free-trade areas (FTAs) are to be formed among such good neighbours, then the likelihood that consolidation into a few large trading blocs will reduce world welfare is much less than suggested by Figure 3.1. The reason is straightforward: the gains from freeing intra-regional trade will be larger, and the costs of reducing interregional trade smaller, than the geography-free story suggests.

Imagine, for example, a world of four countries, which may potentially consolidate into two trading blocs. Suppose that these countries are all symmetric, and that external tariffs are fixed at 10 percent. Then two blocs is the number that minimises world welfare, and hence this consolidation will be harmful. Suppose, however, that each pair of countries is on a different continent, and that intercontinental transport costs are sufficiently high that the bulk of trade would be between continental neighbours even in the absence of tariffs. Then the right way to think about the formation of continental FTAs is not as a movement from four to two, but as a movement of each continent from two to one – which is beneficial, not harmful.

Table 3.1. *Regional trading patterns*
Ratio of export share to share of gross product, 1989

	Importer					
Exporter	US	Canada	Other Americas	Japan	Developing Asia	EC
United States	—	5.2	1.3	1.1	1.7	0.6
Canada	2.9	—	0.4	0.6	0.6	0.4
Other Americas	1.5	0.6	2.0	0.6	0.5	0.5
Japan	1.1	0.9	0.5	—	3.1	0.5
Developing Asia	0.8	0.5	0.2	1.5	3.3	0.5
EC	0.3	0.3	0.3	0.3	0.5	2.5

Source: Summers (1991).

In practice the sets of countries that are now engaging in FTAs are indeed 'natural' trading partners, who would have done much of their trade with one another even in the absence of special arrangements. A crude but indicative measure of the extent to which countries are especially significant trading partners is to compare their current trade patterns (in a world of fairly low trade barriers) with 'geographically neutral' trade, in which country B's share of A's exports is equal to B's share of gross world product outside of A.

Lawrence Summers (1991) has calculated the ratio of actual trade shares to those that geographically neutral trade would predict for major industrial countries; I reproduce his results in Table 3.1. They show that within North America, and especially within Europe, trade is much more intense than geographic neutrality would predict. The Western Pacific is less clearly a natural bloc than either of these, perhaps fitting its dubious status as a political reality as well.

In my policy discussion (Krugman, 1991b), I argued that this correlation between the lines of emerging FTAs and those of natural trading blocs implied that the move to free-trade zones is unlikely to reduce world welfare – that the main concern ought to be not global efficiency, but the problems of small economies that find themselves caught out in the cold. This issue will not be pursued in this chapter, however, which focuses more on the analytical issues than the practical ones.

The point of this section has been that the economic analysis of trade creation versus trade diversion in a simple trading-bloc model is not dependent on taking the assumption of optimal tariff warfare literally. But this still leaves open the question of how to think about what does determine policy.

2 Modelling trade policy

It is one of the well-known ironies of international trade theory that the only intellectually sound basis for a tariff, the terms of trade argument, plays virtually no role in actual policy discussion – even though most empirical estimates suggest that for large countries the unilaterally optimal tariff rates are startlingly high.[2]

Nor do modern, 'strategic trade' arguments play much role. Even in the midst of widespread concern about technology and new calls for a sophisticated industrial policy, when George Bush went to Japan to demand market access he declared the purpose of his trip to be 'jobs, jobs, jobs' – and focused the political weight of his demands not on likely candidates for external economies but simply on politically visible sectors.

I have tried to summarise the apparent preferences of governments by a set of rules which can be described as 'Gatt-think' (Krugman, 1991b). The essence of these rules is a desire for exports, an abhorrence of imports, but a willingness to trade off increased imports in some sectors for increased exports in others. This summary may or may not be helpful as a way to organise discussion; but in any case it does not lead on to any modelling. In this section I offer a crude further step that may prove usefully suggestive, particularly when (in section 3) we try to apply it to the issue of bargaining in trade.

2.1 An approach to trade policy

It is obvious that governments act as if they care more about the interests of producers – import-competing or exporting – than they do about consumers. This concern may in turn be rationalised as the result of the superior organisation of producers, which enables them to influence government behaviour through, say, campaign contributions. And the superior organisation of producers itself may be modelled as resulting from the role of political activity as a public good, which is more easily provided by small concentrated groups of producers than by large diffuse groups of consumers.

Modelling all these levels explicitly is, however, a difficult task.[3] We do not have clear models either of how organised groups influence policy or of how groups get organised. Eventually we will have to devise such models. Meanwhile, however, we need a shortcut.

One such shortcut is simply to take the preference of the government for producer interests as a given. This is the 'weighted social welfare' approach.[4] It has the disadvantage of telling us nothing about where the weights come from, but it can still give us some insights about trade-policy setting.

Consider, then, a country that is setting policy in a single market (an extension to a crude version of general equilibrium is considered below). In this market, there is an upward-sloping domestic supply curve $S(p)$, where p is the internal price of the good. There is also a downward-sloping domestic demand curve $D(p)$. Imports are available at a price p^*, which we take for the moment as given (i.e., we assume away any domestic market power). The internal price is related to the external price by the relationship

$$p = p^*(1 + t) \tag{2}$$

where t is the *ad valorem* tariff rate.

There are three key quantities here: producer surplus, consumer surplus, and tariff revenue. The two surpluses can most easily be defined in differential form, since the constants of integration are arbitrary:

$$d(PS) = S \, dp. \tag{3}$$

$$d(CS) = -D \, dp. \tag{4}$$

And revenue is simply

$$R = p^* t(D - S) = p^* t M. \tag{5}$$

Suppose the government were to choose t so as to maximise the sum of producer surplus, consumer surplus, and revenue. It is straightforward to show that the optimal value of t would be zero: in the absence of market power the government would choose free trade.

What we will assume instead is that the government has a preference for producer interests. Specifically, the government's objective function is

$$V = (1 + \pi)PS + CS + R. \tag{6}$$

In this function, π represents the premium placed on producer interests. The function may equivalently, and usefully, be written

$$V = [PS + CS + R] + \pi PS \tag{7}$$

where the term on the left-hand side represents 'welfare', and the term on the right-hand side represents the extra preference the government gives to producers.

2.2   Implications of preference for producers

The conditions for maximising government behaviour may be seen by considering Figure 3.2. In Figure 3.2, we show a position in which there is some initial positive tariff t, and the effects of a small increase dt in that tariff.

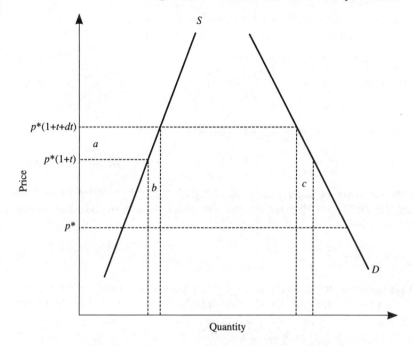

Figure 3.2 Tariff equilibrium when government favours producer interests

First, ignore the preference for producers and consider the effect of a tariff increase on welfare. A tariff increase worsens both the production distortion and the consumption distortion. The increase in the production distortion is shown in Figure 3.2 as the area b; it is equal to

$$tp^* dS = tp^* S' dp. \tag{8}$$

The increase in the consumption distortion is shown in the figure as the area c; it is equal to

$$- tp^* dD = - tp^* D' dp. \tag{9}$$

These two areas measure the decline in social welfare $PS + CS + R$. The government is not, however, maximising social welfare; against these losses it sets the premium it places on benefits to producers. These benefits are equal to π times the area shown in Figure 3.2 as a; they are equal to

$$\pi S dp. \tag{10}$$

Suppose that t is a V-maximising tariff. Then it must be the case that a small increase in t has a zero impact on the government's objective function, i.e., the weighted extra payoff to producers must just offset the increase in distortions. So for an equilibrium tariff we must have

$$\pi S dp = - t p^* (D' - S') dp. \tag{11}$$

Define the following:

$$\mu = M/S \tag{12}$$

as the ratio of imports to domestic production, and

$$\epsilon = - \frac{\partial M}{\partial p} \frac{p}{M} \tag{13}$$

as the elasticity of import demand. Then after some rearranging we find that the tariff rate that maximises the government's objective function must satisfy

$$\frac{t}{(1 + t)} = \frac{\pi}{\epsilon \mu}. \tag{14}$$

This equation contains endogenous variables on the right- as well as the left-hand side. Nonetheless, it offers a rather neat summary of the forces that should determine how much protection a given industry receives. It says that tariffs will be high in industries whose producers command an especially large premium in the government's welfare function (surprise), in industries which have a low elasticity of import demand (so that the distortionary costs of protection are less), or industries in which imports are low relative to domestic production (so a tariff is effective at transferring income to producers).

2.3   Relationship to previous analysis

Suppose that a relationship like (14), rather than optimal tariff-setting in the public interest, actually determines protection. How does the trading-bloc model of section 1 above hold up?

The key question is how tariffs will vary with the number of trading blocs. Recall that the basic story of trade creation versus trade diversion went through even with fixed tariffs – the rising tariffs that resulted from a reduction in the number of blocs in the original version of the model turned out not to be necessary. So what we need to ask is whether external tariffs will either rise, or at any rate not fall, as blocs become fewer in number.

We can take the preference for producers π as fixed, less out of conviction than as an application of what one of my colleagues calls the 'principle of insignificant reason'. The elasticity of import demand represents a more problematic variable. But there is a clear presumption that a larger bloc will, on average, have a smaller import share, other things being equal – that the ratio of imports to domestic production, both overall and industry by industry, will normally be lower in a large country or trading area than in a small one. And this will tend to imply that *if countries set tariffs unilaterally*, large economic units will be more protectionist than small.

This proposition cannot be tested by looking at modern industrial nations, which have operated under a regime of negotiated tariffs since the 1940s. In the pre-1939 era, however, a crude comparison does suggest that rates of protection were positively correlated with economic size. In particular, as Bairoch (forthcoming) points out, the United States, the largest economy even in the early 20th century, was notably more protectionist than any other major nation. Arguably it has also been the case that large developing countries such as Brazil and India have generally had higher rates of protection than smaller nations.

Thinking of tariff rates as set more with a view toward political pressure than as maximising national welfare does not thus, at first blush, invalidate the proposition that a move toward fewer, larger trading areas may well produce large trade diversion. This conclusion depends, however, on the assumption that tariff rates are set non-cooperatively – an assumption that was true before 1914 but has not (we hope!) been true under the GATT. So we need to turn next to the effects of negotiation on tariff-setting.

3　Negotiation and protection

US protectionism actually peaked with the Smoot–Hawley tariff, and began a 45-year decline during the 1930s. The basic pattern was already visible during the Roosevelt years: the United States would offer nations increased access to the US market in sectors in which we had a comparative disadvantage, in return for reciprocal access in sectors in which we had the advantage. The political economy of this method was apparent: it set the interests of US exporters as a counterweight to import-competing industries.

Trade negotiations have been highly successful in reducing trade barriers. So to make sense of actual trade policy it is necessary to think in terms of a bargaining process in which there is linkage both across industries and between the trade policies of different nations.

3.1　Justifying partial equilibrium

As soon as we introduce multiple-industry complications, we must deal with general equilibrium. Yet full general equilibrium concerns do not seem to be of the essence in understanding trade negotiations, and are certainly not uppermost in the mind of, say, Carla Hills. So in this subsection I introduce a somewhat artificial framework that is formally general equilibrium in nature but can continue to be discussed using partial equilibrium techniques.[5]

This setup is as follows: in each of two countries, we suppose that $n + 1$ goods are produced. One of these goods, call it K, is a 'residual' good: it plays a special role in both consumption and production. Utility is separable among the goods and linear in K:

$$U = K + \Sigma_i f_i(C_i) \tag{15}$$

where C_i is consumption of good i, and $f_i' > 0, f_i'' < 0$.

Production has a similar structure. There is an intersectorally mobile factor of production, labour, which can be used in all sectors. Labour is the only factor of production in K, so that there are constant returns in that sector:

$$Q_K = L_K. \tag{16}$$

In each of the n other sectors, however, there is a specific factor as well. This gives rise to diminishing returns with respect to labour:

$$Q_i = g_i(L_i) \qquad g_i' > 0, g_i'' < 0 \tag{17}$$

for all i.

The behaviour of this model is obvious. Demand for each of the n non-residual goods depends only on the price of that good relative to the residual good. Supply of each of the non-residual goods similarly depends on the price of the good relative to labour, or equivalently relative to the residual good.

Suppose that there are two countries that share this production and demand structure, and that all goods are tradeable. Under free trade, market equilibrium for the n non-residual goods can be determined in partial equilibrium fashion. In effect, we can draw back-to-back supply–demand diagrams, and set one country's excess supply equal to the other country's excess demand industry by industry. The residual sector's market must then clear because of Walras's Law.

A system of tariffs is also easy to introduce, as long as we maintain free trade in the residual good. Again, we simply do partial equilibrium good by good.[6]

What we have done with this setup, then, is rationalise (justify is too strong a word) the partial equilibrium approach used to discuss trade policy above. The main qualification is that even in the partial setting there will now necessarily be some market power on the part of the

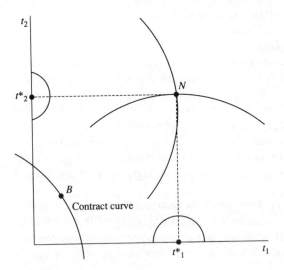

Figure 3.3 **Tariff bargaining**

protecting nation in each industry, so that there is a terms of trade motive as well as a weighted social welfare motive for protection. Basically, however, we have now given ourselves licence to use the partial analysis in the context of multiple industry trade negotiations.

3.2 Trade bargaining

Imagine that there are two countries and two non-residual industries. We suppose that under free trade each country would be an importer in one of these industries, and that each has a politically optimal tariff that it would choose in that industry if acting independently.[7]

Let t_1 be the tariff charged by the first country, and t_2 the tariff charged by the second. We can then illustrate the situation with Figure 3.3. The tariff rates t_1^* and t_2^* are the individual optima; a few contour lines are sketched in. These contour lines reflect the fact that an increase in either country's tariff hurts the other government's objective function, both by reducing welfare and additionally by hurting exporting producers.

If the two countries set tariffs non-cooperatively, the outcome will be at point N. But as is evident from Figure 3.3, both governments prefer points to the southwest – again, this is both because they care to some extent about national welfare, and because they want to provide benefits to domestic producers.

An efficient bargain B will lie somewhere on the contract curve between the two governments, and will involve a reduction in both tariff rates from the non-cooperative outcome.

The interesting thing about this result is that it does not depend at all on the assumption that governments are maximising national welfare. If π were zero – if governments were not subject to interest group pressures – the contract curve would pass through the origin. In that case, free trade would be an efficient bargain from the governments' point of view (although not necessarily the bargain at which they would arrive). But international negotiation will lead toward free trade, even if not necessarily all the way, even if governments are strongly affected by interest group politics.

Trade bargaining in this description is characterised by a Prisoners' Dilemma. This dilemma arises in part from the terms of trade effect of conventional optimal tariff analysis, but also (and presumably in practice mostly) from the effect of each country's tariffs on the other country's producer interests.

Because of the Prisoners' Dilemma characteristic of trade negotiations, we can now invoke all the usual folk theorems of repeated games to help us think about the possibilities and difficulties of reaching cooperative solutions. Trade liberalisation must be supported by the belief of countries that if they cheat they will lose from the subsequent collapse of the cooperative outcome. And to make this sanction effective, countries must be able to observe each others' trade policies, and must find each others' promises credible.

To make any sense of the issue of regionalism versus multilateralism, we need to think in terms of how the range of countries included in negotiations affects the likelihood that the conditions for successfully achieving cooperation will be met.

4   Regionalism, multilateralism, and bargaining

At this point we turn to the weakest part of the discussion. To talk seriously about trade negotiations, we need to take an already loose analysis of trade bargaining between a pair of countries and try to apply it to multicountry issues. Obviously this discussion cannot be more than speculative. Indeed, for the most part I will simply state issues and a few hypotheses.

There are, I would argue, two basic issues. First, other things being equal, will the formation of regional trading blocs within a multilateral system tend to lead to lower or higher barriers to trade between blocs? Second, is the rise of regional trading blocs a second-best solution to the breakdown of a multilateral system?

4.1 Consequences of regional blocs

In section 1 of this chapter, I showed that consolidation of the world into a small number of trading blocs was likely, with unchanged external tariffs, to produce more trade diversion than creation – with the important practical caveat that to the extent that the blocs followed the lines of natural trading areas, the effect was likely to be more favourable. If blocs set trade policies non-cooperatively, consolidation will normally lead to higher external trade barriers, reinforcing the likelihood of adverse effects. But what if trade policies are set through negotiation?

Once upon a time, European nations came to multilateral negotiations as individual negotiators; now they come as a bloc. Does this make them more or less able and/or willing to compromise?

The answer seems to be that it can cut either way. On one side, consolidation into regional blocs could make it more likely that negotiated agreements would be reached simply because there were fewer players. A world trading system effectively run by a G-3 of NAFTA, the European Community, and Japan poses many fewer problems of free-riding than one in which France or Italy are free to make independent demands and cheat on their own.

On the other side, as argued in section 2 of this chapter, large blocs would in the absence of cooperation tend to impose higher tariffs than small players, i.e., their temptation to protect is higher. At the same time, in the realistic case where blocs follow natural geographic lines, a collapse of free trade to non-cooperative tariff-setting will probably do less harm if nations are organised into a few blocs – and therefore the prospect of such a collapse is less of a deterrent to cheating. So a consolidation into large trading blocs could undermine the sustainability of a cooperative international system.

All of this needs some careful modelling. But, overall, the answer seems to be definitely ambiguous. Regional trading arrangements could work either for or against global free trade.

4.2 Forces for regionalism

In some sense, the question of whether regional trading arrangements are good or bad is a moot point. There is nobody who is in a position to decree regional blocs either into or out of existence. So we need to ask why such blocs are in fact emerging.

This come down to asking why nations may feel that they are able to negotiate more at a regional than at a global level. Or to put it more pessimistically, what are the problems of the GATT that lead countries to turn to their neighbourhood instead?

I would list four reasons, all of them tied to the Prisoners' Dilemma sketched out above.

First, there is the sheer number of participants in the multilateral negotiations. As a practical matter, this changes the character of negotiations. In the early, highly productive GATT rounds, the relatively small number of players were able essentially to carry on parallel bilateral negotiations, something like playing a game of Risk. By the time of the Kennedy Round, the numbers were too great, and it was necessary to resort to formulaic tariff reductions, which inevitably find it harder to strike the right political balance. Also, once there are many players the threat that cheating will bring down the system becomes less credible – will the GATT really collapse because, say, Thailand fails to honour its rules?

Second, the changing character of trade restrictions makes monitoring increasingly difficult. The rise of the New Protectionism of voluntary export restraints (VERs), orderly marketing agreements (OMAs), etc. has been massively documented; it represents both exogenous bureaucratic creativity and an end run around negotiated tariff reductions. What it does is to make the negotiation space vastly more complicated than indicated in Figure 3.3, and to make monitoring of adherence extremely difficult.

Third, the decline in the relative dominance of the United States has probably made the system more difficult to run. The political theory of 'hegemonic stability' – essentially, the view that some dominant power must be there to enforce the rules of a cooperative game – is not as well founded in theory as one might suppose. Nor is it universally accepted even among political scientists. But it is certainly reasonable to argue that a dominant America, preoccupied with trade as a binding agent in a political and military struggle, may have helped the GATT to work better a generation ago than it does now.

Finally, institutional differences among major countries pose problems for the system. (This means Japan.) The reason is not that there are no gains from trade between countries with different institutions. It is that at least a shared understanding is necessary to overcome the Prisoners' Dilemma. Suppose that a tariff reduction in country A, with its free-wheeling markets, really does open access to those markets; while a tariff reduction in Country J, whose markets are governed by informal under-standings and cartels, does little to open the gates. Then unless J can find something else to offer, the trade-bargaining game between the countries will break down. It may well be the case that A's welfare would be higher if it ignored this problem and simply pursued unilateral free trade. But as the GATT process itself recognises, governments do not maximise national welfare, and a successful trade regime must build on the motives governments actually have, not the ones we wish they did have.

Regional trading arrangements offer an opportunity to reconstitute the bargaining process at a level where all of these problems can be diminished. They involve smaller groups of nations; they can (as in 'EC 92') involve what Robert Lawrence has called 'deep integration', which essentially removes borders and thus the possibility of creative protectionism. Because the numbers are small, the problem of finding a hegemon is pretty much eliminated. And regional trading blocs, at least so far, avoid including nations with institutional differences large enough to undermine faith in the process.

5   Summary conclusions

We can pose two questions about the role of regional trading blocs. The normative question is, will the formation of such blocs lead to trade creation or to trade diversion? The answer is clear: more research is needed. Small numbers tend to make cooperative solutions more likely; ability of players to fare well if bargaining fails make such solutions less likely; both effects are at work.

The positive question is whether there are deep-seated reasons for a move toward regional trading blocs. Although the discussion here is loose and speculative, I would argue that the answer is yes: for a mix of reasons, the ability to support a cooperative solution at the multilateral level is declining, while at the regional level it remains fairly strong.

Appendix: a basic trading-bloc model

This Appendix briefly restates the simple trading-bloc model of Krugman (1991a).

We imagine a world whose basic units are geographic units that we will refer to as 'provinces'. There are a large number N of such provinces in the world. A country in general consists of a large number of provinces. For the analysis here, however, we ignore the country level, focusing instead on 'trading blocs' that contain a number of countries and hence a larger number of provinces. There will be assumed to be $B < N$ trading blocs in the world. They are symmetric, each containing N/B provinces (with the problem of whole numbers ignored). In this simplified world, the issues of free-trade zones reduces to the following: how does world welfare depend on B?

Each province produces a single good that is an imperfect substitute for the products of all other provinces. We choose units so that each province produces one unit of its own good, and assume that all provincial goods enter symmetrically into demand, with a constant elasticity of substitution between any pair of goods. Thus everyone in the world has tastes represented by the CES utility function

$$U = [\Sigma_{i=1}^{N} c_i^{\theta}]^{1/\theta} \qquad (A1)$$

where c_i is consumption of the good of province i, and the elasticity of substitution between any pair of products is

$$\sigma = \frac{1}{1 - \theta}. \qquad (A2)$$

A trading bloc is a group of provinces with internal free trade and a common external *ad valorem* tariff. We ignore the realistic politics of trade policy, and simply assume that each bloc sets a tariff that maximises welfare, taking the policies of other trading blocs as given. This is a standard problem in international economics: the optimal tariff for a bloc is

$$t^* = \frac{1}{\epsilon - 1} \qquad (A3)$$

where ϵ is the elasticity of demand for the bloc's exports.

In a symmetric equilibrium in which all blocs charge the same tariff rate, it is possible to show that (see Krugman, 1991a)

$$\epsilon = s + (1 - s)\sigma \qquad (A4)$$

where s is the share of each bloc in the rest of the world's income measured at world prices. The optimal tariff is therefore

$$t^* = \frac{1}{(1 - s)(\sigma - 1)}. \qquad (A5)$$

It is apparent from (A5) that the larger the share of each bloc's exports in the income of the world outside the bloc, the higher will be the level of tariffs on intra-bloc trade. This immediately suggests that a consolidation of the world into fewer, larger blocs will lead to higher barriers on interbloc trade.

One cannot quite stop here, however, because the share of each bloc in the rest of the world's spending depends both on the number of blocs and on the world-wide level of tariffs. Again after some algebra it is possible to show that this share equals

$$s = \frac{1}{(1 + t)^\sigma + B + 1} \tag{A6}$$

so that the share of each bloc's exports in the rest of the world's income is decreasing in both the tariff rate and the number of blocs.

Equations (A5) and (A6) simultaneously determine the tariff rate and the export share for a given number of blocs B.

It is straightforward to show that a reduction in the number of blocs will lead to a rise in both s and t.

Clearly this change will reduce the volume of trade between any two provinces that are in different blocs. Even at an unchanged tariff, the removal of trade barriers between members of the expanded bloc would divert some trade that would otherwise have taken place between blocs. This trade diversion would be reinforced by the rise in the tariff rate.

We now turn to welfare. Given the utility function (A1), it is possible to calculate the welfare of a representative province as a function of the total number of provinces N, the number of blocs B, and the tariff rate t on interbloc trade. Since N plays no role in the analysis, we can simplify matters somewhat by normalising N to equal 1. Again after considerable algebra, given in Krugman (1991a), we find that the utility of a representative province is

$$U = \left[\frac{B}{(1 + t)^\sigma + B - 1}\right][(1 - B^{-1}) + B^{-1}(1 + t)^{\sigma\theta}]^{1/\theta} \tag{A7}$$

If trade were free, this would imply a utility of 1. Since the tariff rate t is also a function of B, we can use (A5), (A6) and (A7) together to determine how world welfare varies with the number of trading blocs.

The easiest way to proceed at this point is to solve the model numerically. This grossly oversimplified model has only two parameters, the number of trading blocs and the elasticity of substitution between any pair of provinces; it is therefore straightforward to solve first for tariffs as a function of B given several possible values of the elasticity, and then to calculate the implied effect on world welfare. In Krugman (1991a) the values of ϵ considered are 2, 4, and 10.

Several points about the results are worth noting. First, the relationship between tariff rates and the number of blocs is fairly flat. The reason is that when there are fewer blocs, trade diversion tends to reduce interbloc trade, and thus leads to less of a rise in each bloc's share of external markets than one might have expected. Second, except in the case of an implausibly high elasticity of demand, predicted tariff rates are much higher than one actually observes among advanced nations. This is not an artifact of the economic model: virtually all calculations suggest that unilateral optimum tariff rates are very high. What it tells us, therefore, is that actual trade relationships among advanced countries are far more cooperative than envisaged here.

Finally, welfare calculations yield a striking result. World welfare is of course maximised when there is only one bloc, in other words, global free trade. As suggested informally in the text, however, the relationship between welfare and the number of trading blocs is not monotonic but U-shaped: world welfare reaches a minimum when there are a few large blocs, and would be higher if there were more blocs, each with less market power.

But where is the minimum? For the full range of elasticities considered, world welfare is minimised when there are three blocs.

NOTES

1 Grossman and Helpman (1992) are currently engaged in a line of research that seems extremely promising; some of the discussion in this chapter was inspired by initial presentations of their work – although little of the flavour of their elegant analysis will seep through, and I of course bear all responsibility for any foolishness.
2 For example, Whalley (1985) estimates that in an 'optimal tariff' war among major world trading areas, the tariff rate levied by the United States would be approximately 150 percent.
3 As mentioned above, Grossman and Helpman have made some important progress toward modelling the process by which organised groups exert influence.
4 Richard Baldwin has proposed using this approach for normative analysis of trade policy, and has proposed a catchy name: 'politically realistic objective functions', or PROFs.
5 This framework was originally introduced by Samuelson (1964) in an attempt to psychoanalyse conventional views about the transfer problem. In his version the residual good, described below, was assumed to be non-traded. The version with a traded residual good has been part of the oral tradition in trade for some time, but as far as I know the recent work of Grossman and Helpman represents its first systematic application.
6 This partial approach can be badly misleading in one respect: it misses general equilibrium terms of trade effects. For example, suppose that a country imposes a tariff in an industry in which it has very little monopsony power. Does this tariff improve the terms of trade? One is tempted to say no; yet the tariff will pull resources out of other industries, which will include export sectors in which the country may have substantial market power. The assumption of a linear residual sector sterilises all such effects, but in reality they may be quite important.
7 This politically optimal tariff now combines the terms of trade and weighted social welfare motives.

REFERENCES

Bairoch, P. (forthcoming) *Myths and Realities of Economic History*, London: Harvester Wheatsheaf.

Grossman, G. and E. Helpman (1992) 'Protection for Sale', Princeton University (mimeo).

Krugman, P. (1991a) 'Is Bilateralism Bad?', in E. Helpman and A. Razin (eds), *International Trade and Trade Policy*, Cambridge, Mass.: MIT Press.

(1991b) 'The Move to Free Trade Zones', Federal Reserve Bank of Kansas City, *Review* (December).

Samuelson, P. (1964) 'Theoretical Notes on Trade Problems', *Review of Economics and Statistics*, **46**, pp. 145–54.

Summers, L. (1991) 'The Move to Free Trade Zones: Comment', Federal Reserve Bank of Kansas City, *Review* (December).

Whalley, J. (1985) *Trade Liberalization among Major World Trading Areas*, Cambridge, Mass.: MIT Press.

Discussion

RONALD W. JONES

In the title of Paul Krugman's stimulating paper I would have been tempted to replace 'versus' connecting 'regionalism' and 'multilateralism' with an 'and'. Herein, I think, hangs a tale. Those who view the emergence of regional efforts to establish free-trading areas, especially in Europe and North America, as a threat to the more than forty years of efforts of GATT to lower trade barriers on a multilateral basis are driven to compare the benefits of multilateralism with the potential or actual welfare-reducing possibilities of discriminatory regional arrangements. To my knowledge few economists would do an 180° turn on the comparison to argue that regional efforts raise welfare whereas multilateral reductions in trade impediments lower real incomes. 'Regionalism and multilateralism' reflects a different point of view: in today's world regionalism and multilateralism can coexist. Indeed, given the strong inclinations of certain regions to pursue closer economic associations among small groups of countries, there is an even more important role for GATT and international consultations to ensure that trading blocs join others in a multilateral effort to reduce obstacles to trade. Choosing between the two is not the option.

Krugman's Chapter 3 is based on a paper that is the third of a sequence inaugurated at a conference in Tel Aviv in 1989 (Krugman, 1991a). In that paper the Krugman touch is well illustrated by his analysis of the effect on world welfare of a systematic joining of countries into trading blocs, with each such bloc imposing an optimal tariff on imports. As the number of blocs decreases (with each getting larger), so does world welfare, with such welfare racing a minimum when there are three such blocs. Further bloc formation raises welfare until world free trade is reached. This model is summarised by Krugman in the paper prepared for the Kansas City Fed's conference on trade and currency zones in Wyoming in August 1991 (Krugman, 1991b), and, as well, serves as a central core of reference for his discussion in Chapter 3 here. The earlier papers seem to have encouraged strong reaction – from Fred C. Bergsten at the Kansas City Fed meeting and, at a 'Conference on Analytical and Negotiating Issues in the Global Trading System' held at the University of Michigan in the autumn of 1991, from Alan Deardorff and Robert Stern (1991). As I read these reactions I must admit to being puzzled, for in the end they seem to agree with Krugman that regional efforts are a fact of life but that there is still a useful role to be played by GATT.[1] Admittedly, Krugman's enthusiasm for a multilateral approach to supplant regional efforts at integration is weaker than that of his critics, but it is hard to see that he is 'soft' on regionalism when it is his model that is most forceful in pointing out the damaging effects of having a few large trading blocs.

Deardorff and Stern engage in model-building in an attempt to counter this Krugman conclusion. They claim that Krugman's assumptions are crucial to his results: trade is of the 'intra-industry' variety wherein each country specialises in a different commodity and all commodities have the same degree of substitutability with each other in consumer preferences. When countries form trading blocs and remove barriers to trade within a bloc, demand is 'diverted' from inter-bloc trade, and this leads to a loss of welfare. This welfare loss dominates in the welfare calculation until the number of blocs is reduced to three. Different assumptions are used by Deardorff and Stern: trade takes place in homogeneous products among countries which share the same technology but have different factor endowments – Heckscher–Ohlin trade. The most simple Deardorff–Stern example envisages two types of countries, with a pair of countries of each type. If two blocs are formed, each combining a country of each type, all the benefits of a move to free trade are achieved at the two-bloc level. In more general settings, with equal-probability draws to form trading blocs, Deardorff and Stern argue that in their framework as the number of blocs diminishes (with each bloc becoming larger) world welfare increases monotonically. The U-shaped welfare contour in Krugman's model is not inevitable.

Both the Krugman core model and the Deardorff and Stern analysis are characterised by a high degree of symmetry in production structure and taste patterns: countries are like billiard balls, with random and symmetric groupings into trading blocs. However, in discussing his own model, Krugman introduces two important asymmetries. First, if bloc formation takes place only in a subset of countries, say the more developed nations of Europe, North America, and perhaps Asia, other regions (Latin America, Australia, Africa) may suffer from the diversion of trade flows. Furthermore, as Chapter 8 has made clear, regional attempts at bloc formation among small less developed countries (LDCs) often seem inward-looking – trying to get local production started to service the bloc market instead of seeking possible scale advantages in gearing production for the world market. Secondly, some countries are more likely to form 'natural' trading blocs than others, with a key role played by transport costs. And, since trade is heavier within these blocs, Krugman argues that regionalism leads to increases in world welfare. Indeed, the two principal free-trade areas, in Europe and in North America, do seem 'natural' in this respect, although the motivation for bloc formation may lie elsewhere. This is a theme I wish to emphasise in my own remarks.

Countries typically exhibit ambivalence about pursuing a more open trade stance. As classical trade theory suggests, a nation may increase its gains from trade by enlarging the scope of markets in which trade is allowed. However, special groups within the economy may be hurt by such a process. Rent-seeking behaviour is commonplace and may serve to block the pursuit of more open trading opportunities. But another inhibiting factor is in operation. More open markets imply less local or national control over the economy, and countries may be reluctant to surrender what they perceive to be elements of sovereignty. Binding trade agreements limit the range of options a country can pursue in the face of changing markets and technologies, although the experience with non-tariff barriers in the past two decades has revealed an ingenuity in circumventing these trade agreements. The point I wish to stress is that in reaching for further gains from trade countries may be willing to enter into regional arrangements with 'like-minded' neighbours, whereas a crippling reluctance may be shown to enter into wide multilateral agreements.[2] Transport costs may well enter into the calculations, but other characteristics may be just as important, e.g. expectations that one's trading partners will tend to want regulations and arrangements fairly consistent with what is desired at home. Countries are countries for a reason, and extending the boundaries of trading blocs may be easier on a selective basis grounded in a mutually shared set of interests than in a wide multilateral fashion.[3] A joint pattern of regional and multilateral arrangements may press countries further down the path towards free trade than reliance solely upon the latter.

The argument whereby countries may be more receptive to regional groupings than to multilateral arrangements is strengthened to the extent that trading arrangements encompass not only markets for final consumer goods but also services and international movements of labour and capital. Few developed countries would be willing to tolerate on a worldwide basis, say, the extent of labour mobility characteristic of countries of the European Community. An insistence that arrangements be made only on a multilateral basis under the aegis of the GATT may result in less trade or factor mobility than if regional associations are tolerated or even welcomed. This still leaves a role for GATT to provide a framework within which reductions in trade barriers among blocs and individual countries can be negotiated. I do not view as 'unnatural' a world in which any individual is free to trade in some items in a world arena, in others within a trading bloc, and in still others in a national area with, indeed, some provisions affecting trade, such as taxes, varying from state to state or province to province. A political fact of life is that individuals wish to form coalitions, countries, and trading blocs – but with countries and regions of their choice. A GATT-type umbrella encouraging more open trading possibilities among trading blocs while still allowing scope for trading preferences within blocs or countries may not only be a more realistic alternative to a pure multilateral trading system, but one which brings the world closer to free trade.

I wish to conclude with a few remarks on the uses of simple general equilibrium models to capture what Krugman refers to as multiple-industry complications in trade negotiations. The specific factors model has proved useful in the analysis of effective protection where applied work is based on fairly extensive disaggregation of a country's economy. It is this model that Krugman describes in his justification of partial equilibrium analysis with a 'residual' good. This good is typically taken to be labour (or leisure), but a commodity that uses only labour as an input could be chosen instead if, as Krugman desires, this commodity is traded on world markets. However, as Krugman notes, such an assumption rules out the phenomenon whereby a country's tariff may alter its terms of trade, since the wage rate and all other commodity prices are nailed down. Only rents in the protected sector rise. One can easily escape from this bind by dispensing with trade for such a 'residual' good and allowing a tariff to raise the wage rate, pulling labour away from all other sectors.

This is a simple and useful model, but as just described substitutability is everywhere prevalent. The same is true of Krugman's demand assumption – a price rise would deflect demand onto all other commodities. A richer model allows for complementarities as well, which is a phenomenon which may be of relevance in the analysis of trading blocs. Over twenty years ago Fred Gruen and Max Corden (1970) described a simplified Australian-type economy in which a tariff worsened the terms of trade. A tariff-induced price rise for textiles, say, might attract labour from agriculture, in which grain and wool compete for land use. The loss of labour might cause a Rybczynski-like expansion of land-intensive wool output at given prices, resulting in an eventual fall in the world price of wool.[4] Thus a trading bloc whose formation favours some bloc industries may also encourage an expansion of other traded sectors. Such a trading bloc need not improve its terms of trade *vis-à-vis* the rest of the world.

The possibility that bloc formation may lead to increased demand for the products of countries outside the bloc is perhaps enhanced if account is taken of the high proportion of trade represented by raw materials, intermediate goods and other middle products. Expansion of protected activities within the bloc can easily spill over to world markets for inputs required by these activities, just as income gains for bloc countries can spill over to enhance demand for a wider range of commodities and factors. As Krugman notes in the introduction to his chapter, the formal analysis of multilateralism and regionalism is fraught with difficulties, and a richer set of models of the simple general equilibrium type serves to underscore the ambiguity possible in such comparisons. So let me end where I started by suggesting that the most likely future scenario makes room both for regional groupings and for multilateral efforts to mitigate the potential damage which such distortions to world trade may introduce. And the importance of multilateral GATT negotiations increases the more important regional blocs become.

NOTES

1 Bergsten does disagree with Krugman in forecasting a more successful conclusion to the Uruguay Round talks as well as downplaying the importance of transport costs in encouraging Krugman's 'natural trading areas'.
2 Do neighbours make good friends or enemies? Here some time perspective is desirable – consider France and Germany in the 1930s. Some trading blocs may be advocated primarily to avoid military conflict. Perhaps the lessons of history hold out hope for Middle Eastern arrangements (see Chapter 13 in this volume).
3 The focus on extending the reach of trading blocs may seem out of place in some areas of the world today where *dis*integration of previous national groupings is under way.
4 A formal general equilibrium framework in which complementarities of this type are explored is found in Jones and Marjit (1992).

REFERENCES

Deardorff, Alan and Robert Stern (1991) 'Multilateral Trade Negotiations and Preferential Trading Arrangements', unpublished paper.

Gruen, Fred and W. Max Corden (1970) 'A Tariff that Worsens the Terms of Trade', in T.A. McDougall and R.H. Snape (eds), *Studies in International Economics: Monash Conference Papers*, Amsterdam: North Holland.

Jones, Ronald and Sugata Marjit (1992) 'International Trade and Endogenous Production Structures', in W. Neuefiend and R. Riezman (eds), *Economic Theory and International Trade: Essays in Honor of J. Trout Rader*, Berlin: Springer-Verlag.

Krugman, Paul (1991a) 'Is Bilateralism Bad?', Chapter 1 in E. Helpman and A. Razin (eds), *International Trade and Trade Policy*, Cambridge, Mass.: MIT Press.

(1991b) 'The Move Toward Free Trade Zones', Federal Reserve Bank of Kansas City, *Policy Implications of Trade and Currency Zones*.

T.N. SRINIVASAN

Jagdish Bhagwati, reflecting his frustration with what he obviously considers to be ill-informed and ill-considered criticisms of the GATT,[1] has identified and christened the 'Memorial Drive' School of the Massachusetts Institute of Technology as a major source of the 'funereal' pronouncements inimical to multilateralism (Chapter 2 in this volume). I am sure that, in so criticising the school, he did not mean to disparage their many dazzling analytical contributions.

Among the members of this funeral school, Paul Krugman stands out for his analytical eminence. He was the first to perceive the possibility of intellectual arbitrage between the returns that the Dixit–Stiglitz (1977) model had in the theory of industrial organisation and the returns it could achieve in the theory of international trade. As they say, the rest is history! While economists of my generation continue to insist that many of the worthwhile elements of the new trade theory pioneered by Krugman also existed in the traditional theory in more relevant forms, it would be churlish not to recognise the rapidly growing influence of the new theory among the best and brightest of young trade theorists.

In a celebrated review, the late Tjalling Koopmans once criticised the NBER's business cycle research as 'measurement without theory' (Koopmans, 1947). I am afraid that Krugman's modelling in his Chapter 3 comes uncomfortably close to being 'theory without relevance' for discussing many of the important issues of multilateralism versus regionalism. Many of these issues are considered in other chapters in this volume and also by Fred Bergsten (1991) in discussing Krugman (1991). (Before I list some of them, let me dissociate myself from one of Bergsten's recommendations, namely a global system managed by the three rogue elephants of the world trading system, Europe, Japan and the United States.) Krugman's model is not of much help for thinking through the complex issue of complementarity or contradiction between the regional and multilateral approaches to the ultimate Nirvana of global free trade. Even if regionalism does not jeopardise the ultimate goal and even accelerates the time schedule to reach it, it could involve a short-run cost that might be substantial as compared to an albeit slower progress through multilateralism.[2] This and other issues related in an essential way with the transition path to the ultimate steady state are not addressed by Krugman's model since it is static, or at best describes a steady state.

The critical issue of the instrumental use of unilateralism and regionalism in achieving global free trade is not modelled. In plain language, is the threat to go regional a credible one in supporting a multilateral equilibrium? Of course, excellent theorist as he is, Krugman surely would be able to come up with an infinitely repeated game for which global free trade is the cooperative (multilateral) equilibrium but which is supported by a trigger strategy based on the threat to revert to unilateralism or regionalism if anyone deviates. This is not the occasion for a critique of the repeated game approach to trade negotiations; suffice it to say that I find it implausible as a tool for analysing the problems at hand. I would argue that the use of threats such as moves towards regional or bilateral arrangements or, even worse, the uses of unilateral measures, such as the noxious 'Special 301' provision of the US 1988 omnibus Trade and Competitiveness Act, ostensibly to force markets open, are unlikely to promote a well-designed multilateral system (Bhagwati and Patrick, 1991; Sykes, 1991). Such a system would be rule-based, transparent, and effective in ensuring that rules are observed. Its processes would not only be fair but also seen as fair by the participants, large and small, in sharp contrast to a system that depends on threats and the exercise of economic and political muscle.

Krugman mentions that the political economy considerations are perhaps more salient than the economics of trading blocs. I agree. He models such considerations by introducing producer interests directly into the objective function of the government. It seems to me that this ignores the fact that interest groups use resources in an attempt to have their interests represented in public policymaking. To a significant degree such lobbying or influence purchasing divert resources away from productive activities. A model that ignores such wasteful use of resources is likely to be misleading, both in its description of the process of policymaking and in its appraisal of the social welfare consequences of the resulting policies.

Let me now turn to the analytics of Krugman's model. In the model all 'provinces' are identical in every respect and trading blocs are formed by combining such 'provinces' into two or more groups of equal size in terms of number of 'provinces' included in a group. As is to be expected, global free trade (which can be described equivalently as a world without blocs or as a world with just one bloc) *maximises* global welfare. The number of blocs that *minimises* global welfare turns out to be small, namely, two or three. I suspect that the strong symmetry assumptions of the model in large part explain this unambiguous outcome.[3] This can be seen by considering a model which, in contrast, builds in significant asymmetries between provinces.

Consider a *two-goods-one-factor* Ricardian model with a *continuum of provinces* that is analogous to the *two-province-one-factor* model with a *continuum of goods* that was used effectively to analyse several interesting issues by Dornbusch, Fischer and Samuelson (1977). I will make a specific assumption about the distribution of factor endowments among provinces to facilitate my analysis. This is not an innocuous assumption, but then what is the fun in modelling, if one can't choose one's own assumptions? It is too bad for the real world if it does not fit my assumptions!

Each province in my model can produce two goods – good 1 using one unit of labour per unit of the good and good 2 using a units of labour per unit of the good. Countries are indexed by a and the distribution of provinces with respect to a is uniform with the support $[1 - \lambda, 1 + \lambda]$ where λ lies strictly between zero and one. The labour endowment of country a is $\bar{L}(a)$ where $\bar{L}(a) = a$ if $1 - \lambda \leq a \leq 1$ and $\bar{L}(a) = 1$ if $1 \leq a \leq 1 + \lambda$. Each province has the same Cobb–Douglas utility function with equal expenditure shares of the two commodities.

Suppose all these atomistic provinces follow a free-trade policy. It is clear that if p^* is the equilibrium relative price of good 2 in terms of good 1, then provinces with $a < p^*$ will specialise in good 2 and those with $a > p^*$ will specialise in good 1. Countries with $a = p^*$ can produce either good in equilibrium but since their 'measure' is zero, their production choices have no influence in determining aggregate outputs. However for concreteness let me assume that they specialise in good 1. It is easy to show that $p^* = 1$ is the equilibrium price. With $p^* = 1$, a province with $a < 1$ produces $\bar{L}(a)/a = 1$ unit of good 2 and consumes $1/2$ units of each good.[4] A province with $a \geq 1$ produces $\bar{L}(a) = 1$ unit of good 1 and consumes $1/2$ units of each good. Thus world output of good 1

$$= \frac{1}{2\lambda} \int_1^{1+\lambda} 1 \, da = \tfrac{1}{2}.$$

World consumption of good 1

$$= \frac{1}{2\lambda} \int_{1-\lambda}^{1+\lambda} \tfrac{1}{2} da = \tfrac{1}{2}.$$

Hence the market for good 1 clears and by Walras' law the market for good 2 clears as well. Thus $p^* = 1$ is the equilibrium price. Each country achieves a welfare level of $(1/2)^{1/2}(1/2)^{1/2} = 1/2$ in equilibrium and with a utilitarian welfare function global welfare is also $1/2$.

Let me turn to equilibria with trading blocs. First consider the case where the provinces are grouped into two trading blocs of equal size in terms of number of provinces with their composition as follows:

Bloc I: Provinces with *either* $1 - \lambda \leq a \leq 1 - \lambda + \epsilon$
         or $1 + \lambda - \epsilon \leq 1 + \lambda$
Bloc II: Provinces with $1 - \lambda + \epsilon < a < 1 + \lambda - \epsilon$

The proportion of provinces in Bloc I is 2ϵ and that in Bloc II is $2(\lambda - \epsilon)$. By setting $\epsilon = \lambda/2$, one can make the two blocs to be of equal size.

It is straightforward to see that the autarky equilibrium price in Bloc II is 1. With a little bit of work it can be shown that the autarky price in Bloc I is also 1, with provinces with $1 - \lambda \leq a \leq 1 - \lambda + \epsilon$ producing 1 unit of good 1 and consuming half a unit of each good, and provinces with $1 + \lambda - \epsilon \leq a \leq 1 + \lambda$ producing 1 unit of good 2 and consuming half a unit of each good. With autarky price being the same in the two blocs, there is no incentive for *interbloc trade* and all trade is *intra-bloc trade*. Thus trade diversion is complete relative to global free trade. Yet the welfare level of each province in this two-bloc equilibrium is the same as in the global free-trade equilibrium. Of course global welfare is the same as well.

Let me now change the composition of the two blocs as follows:

Bloc I: Provinces with $1 - \lambda \leq a \leq 1$
Bloc II: Provinces with $1 < a \leq 1 + \lambda$

Once again the blocs are of equal size. However the autarky prices in the two blocs are no longer the same! In Bloc I the autarky price p_A^1 will lie between $1 - \lambda$ and 1 and can be shown to be the unique positive solution to the following equation:

$$p^l_A = \tfrac{1}{2} \frac{1 - (p^l_A)^2}{p^l_A - (1 - \lambda)} \quad \text{or} \quad p^l_A = [(1 - \lambda) + [(1 - \lambda)^2 + 3]^{1/2}]/3$$

Similarly in Bloc I the autarky price p^{ll}_A will lie between 1 and $(1 + \lambda)$ and can be shown to be the unique solution to the equation

$$\log p^{ll}_A = \left(\frac{1 - \lambda - p^{ll}_A}{p^{ll}_A} \right)$$

Now $p^{ll}_A > p^l_A$ and there is incentive for interbloc trade. Of course if there is *free interbloc trade* the equilibrium price will once again settle at 1 with Bloc I specialising in good 2 and Bloc II specialising in good 1. But now there could be *restricted* trade with each bloc imposing a tariff.

One can easily work out the implications of increasing the number of blocs to any arbitrary number. For example, let there be n blocs. Let bloc j consist of province with *a* *either* in the interval $(1 - \lambda + j\epsilon, 1 - \lambda + (j + 1)\epsilon)$ *or* in the interval $(1 + \lambda - (j + 1)\epsilon, 1 + \lambda - j\epsilon)$ for values of $j = 0, 1, 2, \ldots (n - 2)$ and the nth bloc consists of provinces with a in the interval $(1 - \lambda + (n - 1)\epsilon, 1 + \lambda - (n - 1)\epsilon)$. The size of each of the first $(n - 1)$ blocs is 2ϵ and the size of the nth bloc is $2[\lambda - (n - 1)\epsilon]$. By setting $\epsilon = \lambda/n$ one can set all blocs to be of the same size. It is easy to see that the autarky equilibrium price in each bloc is 1 so that there is no incentive for interbloc trade. But even with complete trade diversion, welfare of each province enjoys the same welfare as in global free trade. It is also easy to put together n blocs of equal size such that there is an incentive for interbloc trade and by imposing tariffs on such trade, each bloc would end up with lower welfare than under free trade.

The point of this exercise should now be obvious: once asymmetry is introduced in some form it no longer makes sense to talk of the monotonicity or otherwise of global welfare as the number of blocs changes. Alas, the world other than that of 'new' trade theorists and the single representative-consumer cult of macroeconomists is one of heterogeneity and asymmetry!

NOTES

I thank Jagdish Bhagwati for his valuable suggestions on an earlier draft of this Discussion.

1 Pursuing what he has called the Dracula Principle – 'expose evil to sunlight to destroy it' – he has identified several such pronouncements (Bhagwati, 1991, Appendix I).

2 These questions, including the impact of regionalism on the social efficiency of the agreements reached multilaterally, are discussed by Bhagwati in Chapter 2 above.

3 Deardorff and Stern (1991) also make the point using a Heckscher–Ohlin model.

4 To be precise, one should say that the *density of output* rather than *output* of good 2 at $a < 1$ is $\bar{L}(a)/a = 1$, etc.

REFERENCES

Bergsten, F. (1991) 'Commentary – The Move to Free Trade Zones', by Paul Krugman, in 'Policy Implications of Trade and Currency Zones', Symposium sponsored by the Federal Reserve Bank of Kansas City, pp. 43–58.
Bhagwati, Jagdish (1991) *The World Trading System at Risk*, Princeton: Princeton University Press.
   (1992) 'Regionalism and Multilateralism: An Overview', Chapter 2 in this volume.
Bhagwati, Jagdish and Hugh Patrick (eds) (1991) *Aggressive Unilateralism*, Ann Arbor: Michigan University Press.
Deardorff, A. and R. Stern (1991) 'Multilateral Trade Negotiations and Preferential Trading Arrangements', mimeo.
Dixit, Avinash K. and Joseph Stiglitz (1977) 'Monopolistic Competition and Optimum Product Diversity', *American Economic Review*, **67**, pp. 297–308.
Dornbusch, R., S. Fischer and P.A. Samuelson (1977) 'Comparative Advantage, Trade and Payments in a Ricardian Model With a Continuum of Goods', *American Economic Review*, **67(5)**, pp. 823–39.
Koopmans, T.C. (1947) 'Measurement Without Theory', *Review of Economics and Statistics*, **29**, pp. 161–72.
Krugman, P. (1991) 'The Move to Free Trade Zones', Federal Reserve Bank of Kansas City, *Economic Review*, **76(6)** (November–December) pp. 5–25.
Sykes, Alan O. (1991) 'The Carrot vs. the Stick in International Commercial Relations: A Strategic Analysis of Section 301', mimeo.

4 Multilateral and bilateral trade policies in the world trading system: an historical perspective

DOUGLAS A. IRWIN

1 Introduction

Events of the past two decades have generated increasing concern about the direction of the world trading system. While the General Agreement on Tariffs and Trade (GATT) helped orchestrate the substantial reduction in tariffs after World War II, the multilateral approach to trade liberalisation has encountered difficulty in stemming the proliferation of non-tariff trade barriers and in extending international rules to new areas of trade. Meanwhile, the appearance of bilateral or regional trade arrangements in Europe, the Americas, and elsewhere provides an alternative track for expediting trade reform, but also risks deteriorating into exclusionary, trade-diverting blocs that possibly may bring harm to world welfare.

The loss of momentum in the multilateral system and the movement toward bilateral agreements have sparked renewed debate over the relative merits of the two approaches to trade liberalisation.[1] This chapter aims to provide some historical insight into this debate by examining whether multilateral or bilateral trade policies have been more effective in promoting trade reforms in the past. How has trade liberalisation been achieved in the past, and which types of policies have proved constructive or detrimental to multilateral cooperation on trade policy? Throughout the chapter the focus will be almost exclusively on trade policies in Europe, not only because Europe accounted for the bulk of international trade during these periods but because trade policies set much of the agenda for the rest of the world.

Historical analysis is useful for a related reason. Because most economists and policy analysts agree that multilateral free trade should be the ultimate objective of international commercial diplomacy, concern is often expressed that bilateral agreements may divert attention away from this goal, and thus substitute for rather than complement efforts at multilateral reform. This deep-seated support for the multilateral framework and critical caution about the bilateral approach is derived in part from a common generalisation about two historical episodes in which international trade policies differed sharply. In the late 19th century, a network of treaties containing the most favoured nation (MFN) clause spurred major tariff reductions in Europe and around the world. These treaties ushered in a harmonious period of multilateral free trade that compares favourably with – and in certain respects was even superior to – the recent GATT era. In the interwar period, by contrast, discriminatory trade blocs and protectionist bilateral arrangements contributed to the severe contraction of world trade that accompanied the Great Depression. The disaster of the interwar period strengthened the resolve of policymakers during World War II to construct a sound multilateral trading system that would prevent any return to discriminatory bilateralism in trade policy.

These two periods have indelibly shaped our ideas about multilateral and bilateral trade policies. The architects of the postwar world trading system, who lived through both periods, concluded that the 19th century exemplified the virtues of non-discriminatory multilateralism and the interwar experience demonstrated the vices of preferential bilateralism. These conclusions continue to underlie the trade-policy debate about whether bilateral or regional agreements contribute to or detract from the ultimate objective of multilateral free trade. In probing these conclusions by focusing on these two key historical episodes, this chapter finds that these generalisations are somewhat inaccurate. The 19th-century liberalisation was attained entirely through bilateral agreements, with an utter absence of multilateral cooperation. In the interwar period, multilateral institutions and negotiations failed to reverse the spread of protectionism and promising bilateral attempts at trade reforms were actually discouraged by these multilateral gatherings.

This chapter first discusses the formation of customs unions (CUs) within a sovereign state as an important prelude to trade negotiations between nations, negotiations that had their European origins in the 1780s. Then the growth, maintenance, and decline of the 19th-century multilateral treaty network is described, along with a comparison of its strengths and weaknesses in relation to the current GATT system. Finally, the contribution of bilateralism to the unravelling of the world economy during the interwar period is analysed, with particular attention being paid to the forms of bilateralism that emerged and the obstacles they posed to multilateral cooperation in trade policy. A conclusion draws together the themes and lessons that emerge from this retrospective look at the world trading system.

2   The origins of European trade liberalisation

Mercantilist trade policies of the 17th and 18th centuries aimed to achieve several objectives, such as an inflow of specie via a balance of trade surplus or a large market share in world trade. The mutually advantageous expansion of trade through tariff reductions was not one of these objectives. The most prominent commercial treaty of the period was based explicitly on mercantilist grounds and gave bilateral trade agreements a poor reputation among economists that has continued to this day. The Methuen treaty between England and Portugal in 1703, granting Portuguese wines preferential access to the English market and English woollens to the Portuguese market, was sought by England to improve its trade balance with a country that had a direct source of bullion through its new world colonies. Adam Smith ridiculed the treaty for encapsulating what he thought was the gross mercantilist error of confounding specie with wealth. David Hume heaped scorn on the treaty on grounds of trade diversion: 'But what have we gained by the bargain? We have lost the French market for our woollen manufactures, and transferred the commerce of wine to Spain and Portugal, where we buy worse liquor at a higher price'. The English classical economists continued this tradition of hostility toward discriminatory or preferential trade arrangements, with J.R. McCulloch calling all treaties of commerce 'radically objectionable'.[2]

While commercial treaties between sovereignties on the treatment of each others' merchants and shipping can be traced back centuries, negotiations over tariffs became a significant feature of the world economy only when full CUs (i.e., internal free trade with a unified external tariff) had been established within the nation-state. Nearly all European states emerged from the medieval period riddled with internal tolls and customs areas that reflected remnants of local power. The centralisation of political control within a given region, however, provided no guarantee that a national CU could be easily or quickly formed. England and Scotland united under a single monarch in 1603, for example, but successive attempts to reach agreement on commercial union failed until the Act of Union in 1707. Although politically unified under the king for centuries, France remained divided – even after several reforms – by 1600 internal tolls and tariffs when the French Revolution enabled their abolition in 1790. At this same time over 1800 customs frontiers littered the various states in central Europe that later comprised Germany. Prussia made incremental moves toward economic union from 1808, culminating in the formation of the Zollverein in 1834 when most German states adopted Prussia's external tariff. Each canton in Switzerland retained tariff autonomy until 1848 and the Italian CU was not completed until the 1860s.[3]

Successful European tariff negotiations also had to wait for an opportune political environment. The Treaty of Utrecht in 1713, for example, governed Anglo–French trade for much of the 18th century, but the important Articles 8 (establishing MFN treatment) and 9 (abolishing prohibitions) were never passed by the British parliament for fear that they would undermine the Methuen treaty and harm the balance of payments. Furthermore, as long as the colonial trade of major European countries was flourishing, there was no pressing need to undertake efforts to expand intra-European trade, which was less complementary and hence more apt to increase import competition and offend domestic producers.

The first real impetus to negotiations on liberalising European trade came with the collapse of colonial trade routes in the 1770s, when Britain and France lost among others their North American colonies. This shock severely affected Britain's trade in particular – export volume fell nearly 20 percent between 1772–3 and 1780–1 – and the share of British exports destined for north-western Europe rose from 15 percent to 28 percent over the same interval (Mitchell, 1988, p. 496). These events naturally shifted British attention to the high tariff barriers impeding trade with the continent. Indeed, writing in 1783 to a government official named William Eden, Adam Smith saw opportunity in the colonial loss: 'By an equality of treatment to all nations, we might soon open a commerce with the neighbouring nations of Europe infinitely more advantageous than that of so distant a country as America' (Ehrman, 1962, p. 202).

Prime Minister William Pitt shared this recognition, and dispatched Eden to conclude treaties of commerce with major European countries. The resulting Anglo–French accord of 1783 involved the elimination of prohibitions and a modest reduction of duties on bilateral trade to eliminate smuggling and raise tariff revenues for both governments. While this agreement ranks among the first significant modern action on mutually advantageous trade liberalisation, Britain's unprecedented attempt at trade negotiations was most notable for its utter failure. From 1785–93, interminable negotiations with Portugal, Spain, Poland, Prussia, and several other important trading partners in Europe (and even Ireland) failed to produce any agreements. European fears of import competition and a variety of political and diplomatic considerations account for this failure. Even the accord with France lasted less than six years as the French revolution led to cross-channel tensions. The subsequent Napoleonic wars severely disrupted European trade for nearly two decades and extinguished any immediate hopes for progress on tariff reform.

2.1 Britain's lead to free trade

The end of European hostilities in 1815 brought a steep fall in agricultural prices as normal commerce resumed. Import protection for agricultural producers was established throughout Europe in response as landowners, not merchants, retained control of economic policy. Yet this only temporarily delayed continuation of the prewar liberalisation effort: despite the passage of the highly protectionist Corn Law of 1815, Britain still recognised the value of foreign markets for its manufactures. With the Reciprocity of Duties Act (1823), the Board of Trade strove to conclude reciprocal agreements with foreign governments for MFN treatment of goods and shipping. Although several such agreements were signed, they did not eliminate prohibitions or reduce tariffs, and were therefore of limited consequence. Tariffs were later the subject of what proved to be unsuccessful negotiation. Britain deliberately maintained high tariffs on sugar, coffee, wines, and spirits for bargaining purposes, but all to no avail. In 1836 Britain offered to abolish its timber duties for Prussia in exchange for lower tariffs on British textiles, but Prussia held out for a reduction of the Corn Laws and no agreement was reached.

Efforts at reciprocal tariff reductions thus failed in the 1830s and 1840s, just as they had in the 1780s and 1790s.[4] As Brown (1958, p. 132) put it, 'the drive to open markets in the countries of western Europe for British industry, and particularly in the years 1838–40 the British cotton industry, was uniformly unsuccessful'. Frustration and discouragement with reciprocity accumulated: trade negotiations were 'ever pending, never ending'. This lack of progress set the stage for unilateral tariff reforms in the early 1840s, which culminated in the repeal of the Corn Laws in 1846.[5] As Prime Minister Robert Peel explained that year, 'Wearied with our long and unavailing efforts to enter into satisfactory commercial treaties with other nations, we have resolved at length to consult our own interests, and not to punish those other countries for the wrong they do us in continuing their high duties upon the importation of our products and manufactures, by continuing high duties ourselves'.[6] By adopting unilateral free trade, Britain resolved to forsake the bargaining motive for tariffs henceforth applying its tariff without discrimination, enacting tariff reforms on its own timetable, and leaving other countries free to determine their own tariff policies.

So complete was the conversion to unilateral free trade that treaties came to be viewed as dangerous, as tempting compromise with Britain's principles of non-discrimination and of bargaining abstinence. No longer desirable yet unobtainable, treaties of commerce became entirely disreputable and any effort toward them was dismissed as entirely counterproductive. W.E. Gladstone, the future Prime Minister who served at the Board of Trade during this period, later reflected about the legacy of the 1830s and 1840s, which was

> the period during which England was most actively engaged in the endeavour to negotiate, with the principal states of the civilized world, Treaties for the reciprocal reduction of duties on Imports. The task was supplied on our side with sufficient zeal; *but in every case we failed. I am sorry to add my opinion, that we did more than fail.* The whole operation seemed to place us in a false position. Its tendency was to lead countries to regard with jealousy and suspicion, as boons to foreigners, alterations in their laws, which, though doubtless of advantage to foreigners, would have been of far greater advantage to their own inhabitants (Tooke and Newmarch, 1857, p. 398, emphasis in original).

Foreign countries were unprepared to reduce trade barriers in part because of the suspicion that to do so would be mainly to Britain's advantage.

British policymakers were left to hope that other countries would see the benefits of unilateral free trade and follow Britain's example. In the decade following the repeal of the Corn Laws, Britain's unilateral policy was not an overwhelming success in establishing free trade abroad, although free-trade activism was widespread (see Kindleberger, 1975). Some trade liberalisation occurred in the United States, which passed its most liberal tariff of the *ante bellum* period (timed clearly in conjunction with the Corn Law repeal) in 1846, and in Holland, Switzerland, and Portugal, where tariffs were eased significantly in the early 1850s. But the movement toward free trade did not overtake the rest of Europe until the Anglo–French commercial treaty of 1860, a treaty that heralded the beginning of a liberal international trading order which lasted until the outbreak of World War I in 1914.

2.2 The Anglo–French commercial treaty (1860)

Diplomatic considerations weighed most for both France and Britain in deciding whether to pursue a trade agreement. Tensions were high in Europe – indeed, there was a real possibility of war – as a result of France's opposition to Austria's influence in Italy. Domestic political and economic factors generally ran against such an agreement. Though the French emperor Napoleon III had initiated some tariff reforms in the 1850s, he worried about reducing tariffs too much and offending protectionist interests in the legislature. Britain was also somewhat reluctant to pursue an agreement as that would violate its policy of unilateral free trade. But both governments saw a commercial treaty as a way of defusing tensions and improving diplomatic relations, and an agreement was quickly reached.

There was one important political economy reason for pursuing an agreement as well. Though abandoning its policy against bargaining over tariffs, Britain had a rare opportunity to provide a mechanism that would enable the French emperor to circumvent domestic protectionist interests. Unlike the strong support for free trade in the British parliament, the French legislature overrepresented import-competing interests that wholly opposed lower tariffs. Although the legislature was responsible for all tariff legislation, Napoleon III had the authority under the constitution of 1851 to sign foreign treaties without legislative approval. Consequently he embodied the tariff changes in a diplomatic accord with Britain.[7]

According to the terms of the treaty, France abolished all prohibitions and imposed specific duties not exceeding 30 percent *ad valorem*, or 25 percent after 1865, although in practice most duties were set at 10–15 percent (Ashley, 1926, pp. 299–300). Britain cut the number of dutiable goods from 419 to 48 and reduced the wine tariff. The treaty was subject to renewal after 10 years, and either party could withdraw from the agreement after giving a year's notice. Perhaps the most important element of the treaty was Article V of the complementary convention, which stated: 'Each of the contracting powers engages to extend to the other any favor, any privilege or diminution of tariff which either of them may grant to a third power in regard to the importation of goods whether mentioned or not mentioned in the treaty of 23d of January, 1860' (US Tariff Commission, 1919, p. 395). Inclusion of the MFN clause eliminated the need for renegotiation in the event that either country lowered tariffs with a third country and automatically preserved non-discriminatory access of both countries in each other's markets. The unconditional MFN clause became the linchpin of the 19th-century commercial treaty network.

3   The 19th-century open trading regime

The systemic effects of the Anglo–French treaty were of much greater significance than its importance to either country alone. The treaty sparked a spectacular movement toward the liberalisation of world trade, the initial impetus for which was the trade diversion that promised to accompany the integration of Europe's two largest economies. While Britain insisted on making its own tariff reductions applicable to all nations, France lowered its import duties on British goods only, adopting a two-tiered tariff system of 'autonomous' tariff rates for MFN countries and higher 'conventional' rates for others. Only Britain benefited from the new lower rates and other countries were left at a substantial disadvantage in exporting to the large French market.

As other European states quickly sought agreements with France to secure equal treatment for their own goods, the Anglo–French treaty – which began as a purely bilateral arrangement without abiding support in either country – rapidly cascaded into a series of bilateral trade agreements, all linked by the inclusion of an unconditional MFN clause. France extended the unconditional MFN trade network by concluding commercial treaties with Belgium in 1861, the Zollverein in 1862 (effective in 1865), Italy in 1863, Switzerland in 1864, Sweden, Norway, Spain, and the Netherlands in 1865, and Austria in 1866. These agreements entailed significant new tariff reductions for those joining the arrangement, and the unconditional MFN clause proved to be a remarkably efficient instrument that encouraged other countries to join and also receive MFN treatment. The increase in treaty participants extended the coverage of low tariffs to virtually all of Europe.[8]

What triggered the swift acceptance of a new, low-tariff regime in Europe? Some bargaining models suggest that free-rider and other problems create difficulties in sustaining trade liberalisation under the MFN clause.[9] But in this period when MFN treatment was *sought* by most countries in Europe, the clause propelled trade liberalisation and acted as a strong inducement for others to join the treaty network, thereby building the number of treaty participants. Once Britain and France initiated the move to lower tariffs, the smaller countries of Europe clearly had an economic interest in obtaining equal treatment in the French market. The addition of the Zollverein, where a mix of political and economic motives were present, built particular momentum to the Europe-wide movement and added further incentives for other European states to join the chain of unconditional MFN treaties.[10] Britain, Belgium, Italy and others then signed agreements with the Zollverein in 1865 to receive MFN treatment.

Thus, through a variety of fortuitous circumstances, a single bilateral agreement to reduce tariffs blossomed into dozens of bilateral accords, resulting in an effectively multilateral arrangement under which international trade entered an unprecedentedly liberal era. Under the treaty arrangement, tariffs were generally set at about 8–15 percent with a maximum of 25 percent (Liepmann, 1938, p. 369). Bairoch (1989) suggests that the period of free trade in Europe peaked from 1866 to 1877, although not just this narrow window but much of the half-century to 1914 was marked by low government barriers to trade. At the start of 1908, Britain had MFN agreements with forty-six countries, Germany with thirty countries, and France with over twenty countries (Hornbeck, 1910, p.57).

It is important to note that diplomatic objectives and tariff-bargaining were not the sole impetus behind European trade liberalisation. Additional unilateral reforms by Britain resulted in essentially four items taxed for revenue purposes (i.e., tariffs as the application of domestic excise duties to comparable imports) by the 1880s. Internal free-trade interests prompted Germany to enact substantial tariff reforms independently of treaty obligations when the Reichstag voted in 1873 to eliminate virtually all import tariffs by 1877 and to reduce those on textiles substantially. Consequently, tariffs on chemicals were eliminated at the beginning of the 1870s and all tariffs on grains and iron products (except fine iron goods) were to be phased out by the end of the decade (Ashley, 1926, p. 40). The same was true to varying degrees in other countries, even if protection was not entirely erased across Europe.

Even the colonies were brought into the liberal trading order. In the 19th century, the developing countries of today were, for the most part, colonies of the major European countries, each traditionally maintaining reciprocal preferences for each other's goods. In the mid-1840s and 1850s, Britain eliminated all tariff preferences for colonial supplies of timber, sugar, and other raw materials and also granted tariff autonomy to its self-governing colonies, allowing them to abolish preferences that favoured British manufactures. In dependencies such as India, Britain maintained a non-discriminatory 'open-door' policy of applying the same low tariffs on foreign and British goods.[11]

In the trade treaties signed after 1860, the MFN clause was widely interpreted to include colonial trade and open-door policies were practised by other countries.[12] French colonies adopted the same tariff code as France, thus completing a full CU. German, Belgian, and Dutch colonies operated with low, non-discriminatory tariffs. At the Conference of Berlin in 1885, the European powers established that all colonies in central Africa would be open to trade with any country on the same terms, and this practice was maintained elsewhere to a remarkable degree. The European powers also took active steps to open up new regions to international trade on a non-discriminatory basis, often using military power to force autarkic countries to trade and fixing their tariffs at low levels. China lost its tariff autonomy with the Treaty of Nanking of 1842, which set its import duties at 5 percent *ad valorem* for over fifty years, and Japan faced similar externally-imposed constraints on its tariffs after 1858.[13]

3.1   The 19th-century treaty system and the GATT

The 19th-century treaty system invites comparison with the post-World War II trade regime led by the GATT. The main features of the two

Table 4.1. *Features of two world trade regimes*

	The 19th-century regime (c. 1860–1914)	The GATT system (c. 1947–)
Underlying principle	Unconditional MFN treatment for treaty signatories	Unconditional MFN treatment for member states
Coverage	Effectively multilateral via bilateral treaties	Multilateral agreement
Terms of accord	Often subject to renewal after 10 years	Life of agreement
Permissible methods of protection	Tariffs only (*de facto*)	Tariffs only (*de jure*)
Restrictions on tariff level	Generally unrestricted	Bounded by agreement
Institutional basis	None	The GATT
Countervailing and anti-dumping duties	Virtually non-existent	Permissible under Article VI
Preferential arrangements	Presumption against as violation of MFN	Permissible under criteria in Article XXIV

regimes are compared in Table 4.1. A key similarity between the 19th-century order and the postwar GATT system is the principle of non-discrimination through the use of the MFN clause in its unexceptional and unconditional formulation. In the 19th century, MFN treatment would be granted to all countries with which an MFN agreement had been signed, and not just countries explicitly named in the treaties, as had been earlier practice. The MFN clause was also unconditional, meaning that the lowest available tariff would be applied automatically without requiring reciprocal concessions. The MFN clause ensured that all countries participating in the treaty network would continue to receive the best available tariff treatment, even if other countries engaged in further tariff reductions. Either an exceptional or a conditional interpretation would have slowed the initial advance of trade liberalisation by complication or extending the process of negotiation, although it is less clear that MFN was useful in sustaining lower tariffs. The unconditional form of the MFN clause became so well established that, despite the growth of protectionist pressures after the late 1870s, the conditional interpretation was not adopted. As with the treaty network, the GATT is based on the similar rule of granting unconditional MFN treatment to member states.

The treaty system also had significant weaknesses *vis-à-vis* the GATT. After the initial tariff cuts embodied in the agreements of the 1860s had formed the core of the 19th-century treaty arrangement, further progress on tariff reductions was not guaranteed. Most of the commercial treaties after this initial negotiating period ensured only non-discriminatory tariff treatment and did not place any limit on tariff rates, leaving each country free to set their tariffs without an effective external constraint on tariff behaviour. Nor was there any commitment to ensure progress toward even lower tariffs. In addition, the treaties were subject to periodic renewal and set to expire with regularity. The GATT, by contrast, established a contract in perpetuity that fixes and binds tariffs at a low level for the life of the agreement and provides for trade negotiating rounds. In principle the GATT also details a mechanism for compensation to penalise countries that nullify tariff obligations. At least in the 19th century, tariffs – with very few exceptions – were the only major government policy impeding international trade. While this has been legally true under the GATT, quantitative restrictions (QRs), orderly marketing arrangements (OMAs), and voluntary trade restraints (VTRs) continued to exist outside of the GATT's purview. It could have been that tariff flexibility in the 19th century enabled countries to avoid resorting to these more pernicious barriers.

Unlike the GATT which arose as an institution by design, the 19th-century trade regime arose spontaneously from an uncommon confluence of events. Indeed, the 19th-century order was more an informal arrangement than a system. There was no primary sponsor with the economic standing or diplomatic ability or willingness to cajole or manage the arrangement, to punish defectors or free-riders, or to consolidate the abundance of bilateral treaties into a more soundly-based multilateral system. The most obvious candidate to play such a central role, Britain, failed to nurture the treaty network, provided no systemic guidance, and clung to a unilateral, *laissez faire* policy regarding international trade. Soon many of these weaknesses came to the fore.

3.2   The erosion of the liberal economic order

The outbreak of World War I in 1914 ensured that the treaty network never had the chance to break down completely. But tariff rates began to rise and tariff disputes became more frequent after the late 1870s, even if adherence to unconditional MFN remained intact and there was no turn to regional or preferential arrangements.

The general turn to higher tariffs in Europe in the late 1870s can be traced to one key source: the decline in agricultural prices in the late 1860s and into the 1870s, which created difficulties for the liberal trading order just as the oil shocks of 1970s contributed to a revival of protectionist pressures in the postwar period. The extension of railway networks into Russia and the United States brought a flood of cheap grain to Europe: grain imports by Belgium, France, and Germany averaged only 3 percent of domestic production a year in 1862–6, but had climbed to 20 percent by 1876–80 (Bairoch, 1989, p. 47). With Prussia having shifted from a net exporter to a net importer of grains, the 'iron and rye' coalition facilitated passage of the Bismark tariff of 1879 that increased protection to agriculture and, to a lesser extent, manufactures. Other countries, such as France, Belgium, Switzerland, and Sweden, followed with tariff increases in 1880s.

The backsliding in trade policy that followed the decline in agricultural prices was later compounded by a concentration of expiry dates for the European trade treaties. According to Bairoch (1989, p. 54), of the fifty-three treaties with expiry dates in force in 1889, twenty-seven were due to lapse in 1892 and twenty-one by 1895. Renegotiation of these treaties was more contentious than earlier because protectionist pressures were greater. The result was increasing acrimony and even tariff wars after 1885. Tariff wars often originated with a country repudiating a trade agreement to establish higher tariff rates. France and Italy (1888–9), Germany and Russia (1892–4), and France and Switzerland (1892–5) engaged in some of the more disputatious trade wars of the period. In a 'non-system' such as that in the 19th century, the threat of retaliation served as a constraint on domestic discretion in tariff matters and helped to maintain a low tariff equilibrium. But the realisation of retaliation, as during this period, suggests that the threat of retaliation was no longer a sufficient deterrent to ensure continuity of the low-tariff status quo.

Multilateral action was not taken to contain the rise in protectionist pressures. As early as 1875, several British officials sought to persuade their government that a European tariff conference should be convened to stem the growing threat of protectionism. But the government, specifically the first Gladstone Administration, remained firmly opposed to tariff-bargaining and still adhered to unilateral free trade as the basis for its policy (see Gaston, 1987). Britain also had precious few tariffs with which to bargain (the Treasury objected to reducing any revenue duties) and threats to exclude others from its market were not credible and were never made. While perhaps there was little it could do about higher European tariffs, Britain did not even attempt to seize the initiative and seek a multilateral agreement that would freeze tariff levels at existing levels.

The European trade policy environment did deteriorate after 1879, but the extent of the deterioration should not be exaggerated. Capie (1983), for example, suggests that effective rates of tariff protection remained relatively low through the final quarter of the 19th century to 1914. Germany returned to a more liberal policy in the 1890s and, under Chancellor Caprivi, signed several treaties that again reduced tariffs on agricultural goods and textiles. Yet tariffs were now being established for bargaining purposes; according to the US Tariff Commission (1919, p. 467), countries (particularly in central Europe) 'framed their general schedules not with a view to their being made operative but with reference to the advantages which they may offer as a basis for negotiations'. Furthermore, the increased specialisation of tariff categories meant effective tariff discrimination, with maximum advantage given to treaty partners and minimum advantage to other countries despite the MFN clause. The number of items in the German tariff code, for example, rose from 387 in 1879 to 946 in 1906.[14]

In several respects, however, the recent deterioration of the GATT system has been sharper than that of the 19th-century treaties. In the 19th century, unconditional MFN did not give way to regional or colonial preferences, as previously mentioned, and quantitative restrictions or prohibitions did not reemerge. Perhaps more significantly, unlike the present there was no recourse to anti-dumping (AD) actions or countervailing duties (CVDs) despite the appearance of a 'fair trade' movement in Europe in the 1890s (see Viner, 1923). Canada enacted a 'less-than-fair-value' law in 1904 and was soon followed by other self-governing colonies, but such laws were entirely absent in Europe despite increased concern about dumping. In 1892, Belgium was the first European country to institute a CVD law, but few countries followed this practice before 1914. Many commercial treaties of the period contained anti-bounty pledges, but they neither prevented export subsidies (which were uncommon) nor were they enforced. Even the first prominent 'managed trade' issue was resolved in a rare multilateral agreement that achieved a liberal outcome.[15]

The foremost achievement and great success of the 19th-century treaty network was the establishment – through the widespread use of the MFN clause – of non-discrimination as the fundamental principle of European trade policy. This achievement stood as a solid advance over the centuries of discrimination in European markets. In addition, for at least twenty years after 1860 European countries enacted unprecedented tariff reductions. However, the 19th century achieved only part of what might have been hoped for. The lack of binding constraints on tariff levels allowed countries to backslide toward greater protection after 1879. The interwar period would see not only the absence of movement toward this higher objective, but even the substantial loss of the principal 19th-century accomplishment.

4 The interwar trade policy experience

The bilateral treaty regime ended abruptly in August 1914 with the outbreak of World War I. Tariffs, quantitative restrictions, prohibitions, and exchange controls were rapidly instituted around Europe to protect industries associated with national security and to secure foreign exchange for state-determined allocation. At the Allied Economic Conference of 1916, Britain, France, and Italy gave the first indication that the postwar international economic order would not resemble the prewar one. They resolved to cooperate on commercial policy after the war, but hinted at creating trade preferences for Allied countries by ruling out the extension of MFN treatment to Germany and other wartime opponents. The United States – now taking a more prominent role in the world trade arena – opposed any such discrimination and the third of President Wilson's Fourteen Points called for 'the removal so far as possible of all economic barriers and the establishment of an equality of trade conditions among all the nations consenting to the Peace and associating themselves for its maintenance' (League of Nations, 1942, p. 15).

But European countries were ill-inclined, and interwar institutions were ill-equipped, to restore commercial policy to its prewar basis. The Covenant of the League of Nations in 1919 weakened Wilson's call for 'equality' of treatment, insisting in Article 23(e) only upon 'equitable treatment' in trade. And making no provision to ensure the reduction of trade barriers, the Covenant instead invited departures from this course by sanctioning trade controls owing to the 'special necessities' of economic recovery.

To be sure, the depression of economic activity and high rates of unemployment in the early 1920s were scarcely conducive to achieving progress on liberalising European trade policies. But efforts to coordinate the reduction of trade barriers after World War I were slow to get on track: no formal, multilateral action was ever taken to abolish prohibitions, reduce tariffs, or restore the MFN treaty network, and a consensus in favour of serious cooperative action was never achieved. Although most wartime controls were gradually phased out on a unilateral basis, the far-reaching degree of wartime intervention ensured that the pace of liberalisation was slow and uneven and extended well into the 1920s. As late as 1927 the League of Nations was still calling for the eradication of prohibitions and other restrictions that had been instituted during the war.

In instances where strict wartime controls were abolished, other barriers – mainly tariffs – rose to take their place. The United Kingdom, for example, did not return to its prewar free trade policy, but enacted the Safeguarding of Industries Act (1921) to extend wartime tariff protection to scientific instruments and other goods. After President Wilson left office, the United States passed the Fordney–McCumber tariff in 1922 to raise import tariffs substantially. Throughout the 1920s, European countries also took the opportunity to raise tariffs as normal commerce resumed. As Table 4.2 indicates, even by 1927 when many wartime prohibitions and restrictions had been eliminated or scaled back, tariffs – particularly on manufactured goods – were higher than before the war.

The restoration of some degree of economic stability in Europe by around 1925 put efforts to reach a European trade accord on a firmer basis. The World Economic Conference of 1927 called for any action whatsoever – unilateral, bilateral, or collective – to stabilise and then reduce trade barriers and restore the effectiveness of the MFN clause. Though the conference was not an official diplomatic meeting, many governments endorsed its recommendations and it was hailed as a success when several countries abandoned plans to revise their tariff codes. Stabilisation of tariff levels was thought to have been achieved when the number of countries revising their tariffs fell from sixteen in 1926 to five in 1928 (League of Nations, 1942, p. 42). A committee of the League even began considering particular formulae – either specifying maximum tariffs or taking percentage reductions – to be used in multilateral negotiations for tariff reductions on semi-manufactured goods. In addition,

Table 4.2. *Potential tariff^a levels in selected European countries, %, 1913–31*

	Foodstuffs			Manufactures		
	1913	1927	1931	1913	1927	1931
Germany	21.8	27.4	82.5	10.0	19.0	18.3
France	29.3	19.1	53.0	16.3	25.8	29.0
Italy	22.0	24.5	66.0	14.6	28.3	41.8
Belgium	25.5	11.8	23.7	9.5	11.6	13.0
Austria	29.1	16.5	59.5	19.3	21.0	27.7
Yugoslavia	31.6	43.7	75.0	18.0	28.0	32.8

Note:
^{a} The 'potential' tariff level refers to each country's tariff on 144 representative commodities using European-wide trade weights.
Source: Liepmann (1938) p. 413.

the MFN treaty network showed faint signs of resurrection. The failure of the United States to join the League of Nations was compensated in part by its adoption of the unconditional interpretation of the MFN clause in 1922. France readopted the MFN clause when signing a trade agreement with Germany in 1927, and the number of countries linked by commercial treaties rose from thirty in 1927 to forty-two in 1928.

Although serious discussion of tariff reductions on either a multilateral or a bilateral basis had yet to be undertaken, the upward drift in tariffs appeared to have been broken and a path to freer trade was emerging. At this point scarcely a decade had passed since the end of the war and continued economic recovery in Europe promised an ever-improving environment for the reform of trade policy. But a year later any hope of progress on trade liberalisation was dashed with the onset of the Great Depression.

4.1 The onset of the depression

The temporary respite from higher tariffs ended in the summer of 1929 when a sharp fall in agricultural prices prompted tariff hikes in Germany, France, Italy, and elsewhere by the year's end. The initial outbreak of protection in response to lower agricultural prices had some similarities with the late 1870s, but the situation deteriorated much more rapidly in the early 1930s. The passage of the Smoot–Hawley tariff in the United

States in June 1930 sparked another round of tariff increases, retaliatory and otherwise, throughout Europe. As the depression deepened, even the United Kingdom imposed emergency duties in late 1931, followed by the general tariff of February 1932. Table 4.2 illustrates how tariffs rose substantially in many other European countries between 1927 and 1931 and were heavily skewed toward protecting agriculture.

The unravelling of the world trade regime after 1929 made the mild erosion in the low-tariff era prior to World War I appear entirely trivial. Widespread deflation, increasing unemployment, and financial crises in the early 1930s landed devastating blows at what remained of the open trading system. Agricultural interests were behind the initial resort to higher tariffs and achieved some sectoral favouritism, but protection arose so rapidly and became so broadly based as the depression spread and deepened that its rise can perhaps be explained only as a desperate attempt to insulate all sectors from falling prices and to stimulate overall economic activity in response to a crisis of major proportions.

And further unlike the period after 1879 when there were no multilateral conferences held or actions taken to resist the tariff increases, the interwar period was replete with meetings and pronouncements reflecting international concern about maintaining open trade, but without any real political resolve to resist growing protectionism in the face of economic collapse. As Gordon (1941, p. 33) put it, 'the complete failure of every attempt to secure multilateral action in the sphere of commercial policy in 1930 and 1931 resulted in large part from the unwillingness of nations to commit themselves to international obligations which would limit their freedom to combat the depression through autonomous measures'. Conferences sponsored by the League of Nations aimed to declare a 'tariff truce' in 1930 and 1931, for example, but failed in part because agricultural states in central and eastern Europe insisted on further protection and demanded preferential treatment for their goods in industrial Europe. As the League of Nations (1942, p. 101) later observed, 'the international conferences unanimously recommended, and the great majority of Governments repeatedly proclaimed their intention to pursue, policies designed to bring about conditions of "freer and more equal trade"; yet never before in history were trade barriers raised so rapidly or discrimination so generally practiced'.

The policy instruments of the 'new protectionism' of the 1930s were blunt: quantitative restrictions, prohibitions, exchange controls, and clearing agreements. State bureaucracies were created to monitor or manage each international transaction, whether financial or merchandise. The market mechanism in international trade was subordinated to state planning and the priority of state requirements; the extent of government regulation of international trade across Europe had perhaps never been so pervasive and detailed. Protectionism consequently became much more entrenched than in the 19th century when only non-discretionary tariff barriers had to be grappled with.

Yet countries varied distinctly in the degree to which they adopted protectionist measures. Just as Eichengreen (1992) describes how the magnitude of a country's macroeconomic difficulties during this period can be linked to its policy toward the gold standard, the stance of a country's commercial policy was also crucially related to its position in the international monetary system. In the early 1930s, deflationary pressures in many countries arose from a loss of foreign exchange or gold reserves. These countries faced a choice between import restrictions or devaluation as a means to stimulate the domestic economy while preserving external balance. The gold-bloc countries led by France clung to the gold standard and strove to maintain their currencies at par. In acceding to the accompanying deflationary pressures, these countries experienced a severe overvaluation of their currencies. This worsened the merchandise trade balance and forced resort to quantitative restrictions and import licensing to stem the further loss of reserves so that gold-standard parity could be maintained and devaluation avoided. By contrast, the sterling-bloc countries led by Britain took their currencies off the gold standard in September 1931. The depreciation of sterling against gold relieved the deflationary pressures arising from the balance of payments, alleviated macroeconomic distress, and consequently tempered the demand for severe import restrictions.

This relationship between direct controls on trade and commitment to the gold standard is illustrated in Figure 4.1. The proportion of total imports (by value) subject to licensing or quota restrictions in 1937 (for countries that maintained freedom in foreign exchange dealings) was highest for the gold-bloc countries – France, Switzerland, the Netherlands, and Belgium. Particularly surprising is the degree to which Switzerland and the Netherlands, traditionally free-trade countries, adopted direct trade controls. By contrast, the sterling-bloc countries – Sweden, the United Kingdom, Norway, and Ireland among them – faced less pressure to institute import restrictions because they opted for exchange rate depreciation. This cross-country pattern of import regulation appears more consistent with trade protection that had its origins in the macroeconomic depression rather than in the lobbying efforts of various interest groups.[16]

A third group of countries, mainly those in central and eastern Europe, curtailed trade directly through stringent controls on foreign exchange transactions. The collapse of international lending by western creditors to

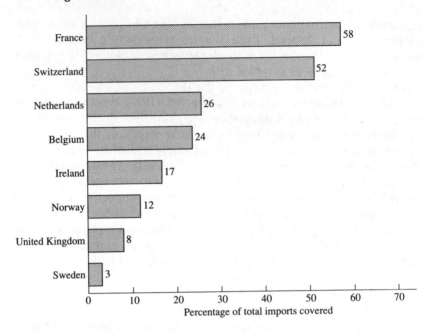

Figure 4.1   Licence or quota restrictions in 1937
Source: Haberler (1943, p. 19)

Germany and eastern Europe after 1929 resulted in severe balance of payments difficulties for these debtors. A financial panic in 1931 prompted Germany to lead these countries to restrict international payments by introducing controls on foreign exchange. Virtually every other east European country, from Poland and the Baltics in the north of Yugoslavia and Greece in the south, followed in rapid succession. Italy and Poland regulated nearly every foreign exchange transaction, while other countries such as Austria, Czechoslovakia, and Greece restricted substantial shares of such transactions (see Haberler, 1943).

While varying in their degree of stringency, these controls choked international trade and were followed by exchange-clearing arrangements aimed at eliminating bilateral trade imbalances and stemming the flight of capital. Clearing agreements were instituted to avoid the use of foreign exchange transactions in international trade to preserve liquidity and reserves. Through the Schacht agreements, Germany took deliberate steps to divert imports from those countries demanding payment in convertible currencies to those accepting German exports as payment, mainly countries in south-eastern Europe and Latin America. In many instances, trade in eastern and central Europe was reduced to barter. In South America, different exchange rates and multiple tariff rates were

Table 4.3. *Share of gold value of world exports, excluding the United States, %, 1931 and 1937*

	1931	1937
Exchange control countries[a]	27.2	22.5
Gold-bloc countries[b]	15.9	12.1
Other countries[c]	56.8	65.4

Notes:
[a] Austria, Bulgaria, Czechoslovakia, Denmark, Estonia, Germany, Greece, Hungary, Italy, Latvia, Lithuania, Poland, Portugal, Roumania, Turkey, Yugoslavia.
[b] France, Belgium, the Netherlands, and Switzerland.
[c] Principally sterling-bloc countries.
Source: League of Nations (1938), p. 30.

used to discriminate against countries with which a country had a trade deficit.

The consequences for world trade of this pattern of restrictions among the exchange control group and the gold- and sterling-bloc countries are not difficult to predict. Table 4.3 shows that the restrictions imposed by the exchange control group were so severe that even the depreciation of their currencies against gold could not stimulate their trade. Their share of world exports fell from 27 percent in 1931, when the controls were largely introduced, to 22 percent in 1937. Gold-bloc countries also saw their share of trade shrink in the face of quantitative restrictions and overvalued currencies. The trade of other countries, mainly the sterling group, accounted for a larger proportion of world trade as exchange rate depreciation boosted trade directly and avoided need for trade restrictions. The share of these countries rose despite 'exchange-dumping' measures, i.e., tariff surcharges to offset exchange rate changes, taken against them by other countries.

In seeking to eliminate all losses of foreign exchange reserves by ensuring balanced trade on a bilateral basis, the exchange control group gave rise to a 'pernicious' bilateralism in trade policy. This bilateralism stifled and diverted trade by bureaucratic fiat. Similarly, the harsh trade measures adopted by the gold-bloc countries were also inherently discriminatory, if not strictly 'bilateral' in nature. However, these policies were rooted in the difficulties of the international monetary system. Countries that opted for exchange rate depreciation did not resort to protectionist trade barriers to the same degree.

To be sure, explicit discrimination through tariff preferences was a feature

Table 4.4. *Shift in trade patterns, 1929–38*

(a) Share of intra-imperial trade, 1929 and 1938, %

		Imports		Exports	
Trade of	Share of	1929	1938	1929	1938
United Kingdom	British Commonwealth, colonies, protectorates	30.2	41.9	44.4	49.9
France	French colonies, protectorates, mandated territories	12.0	27.1	18.8	27.5
Belgium	Belgian Congo	3.9	8.3	2.6	1.9
Netherlands	Overseas territories	5.5	8.8	2.6	1.9
Portugal	Overseas territories	7.9	10.2	12.7	12.2
Italy	Colonies and Ethiopia	0.5	1.8	2.1	3.3

(b) Regional preferences in the trade of Japan and Germany, 1929 and 1938, %

		Imports		Exports	
Trade of	Share of	1929	1938	1929	1938
Japan	Korea, Formosa, Kwantung, Manchuria	20.2	40.6	24.1	54.7
Germany	Six south-eastern European countries and Latin America	16.7	27.6	12.8	24.7

Source: League of Nations (1939) pp. 34–5.

of European trade policies during the 1930s, and this discrimination was heavily slanted toward diverting the source of imports rather than expanding trade overall. The open-door policies of the 19th century were abandoned and forgotten. Britain reinstated limited tariff preferences for the former colonies in 1919, but the Ottawa Agreement of 1932 raised general import duties to establish substantial tariff preferences for goods imported from Commonwealth countries. France and other European countries took similar steps to implement preferences with their colonies and dependencies. Germany and Japan roughly doubled the share of their trade with neighbouring countries that came under their political influence. As shown in Table 4.4, trade patterns shifted dramatically in the decade after 1929 as a result of these actions.

But preferential tariff treatment should hardly have been the major concern of the day. The shift in trade patterns described in Table 4.4 was probably accomplished more through exchange rate agreements, clearing and payments arrangements, bureaucratic allocation of import quotas and the like rather than through tariff preferences. The League of Nations (1942, p. 119) observed that 'effective discrimination by methods which did not violate the letter of the [MFN] clause continued to be widely practiced' throughout the 1930s. Non-tariff restrictions became so far reaching as to render tariffs – even discriminatory tariffs – the least important trade barrier to be surmounted. In an environment of quotas and exchange controls, attempts to reestablish non-discriminatory MFN tariff treatment among major countries were absolutely meaningless. As Nurkse (1944, p. 175) observed, 'Real equality of treatment, aimed at ensuring multilateral trade in accordance with market criteria, is . . . impossible when the control determines not only the purposes, commodities and firms but also the countries to which exchange is allotted.'

Yet the League and other international gatherings during this period constantly emphasised the need to restore MFN treatment in Europe. These efforts were misplaced and probably even counterproductive by harming the chances for trade liberalisation. The instability in the international financial system that bred the use of 'hard core' non-tariff barriers (such as licences, quotas, and exchange controls) was the root source of the protectionist trade policies in the 1930s. Removal of the underlying instability by improving international macroeconomic policy and the 'tariffication' of existing restrictions would have been a more useful allocation of multilateral effort. With an international economic environment so vastly different from that in the 19th century, stress on unconditional MFN in the 1930s stymied what little effective support there was for trade liberalisation. High-tariff countries refused to accept any exception to MFN treatment by others unless they were to be recipients of the lower tariffs. This intransigence over the interpretation of the MFN clause posed a barrier to regional liberalisation that at least would have allowed some countries to end and reverse the upward movements in tariffs. With the benefit of hindsight, even the League of Nations (1942, pp. 119–20) conceded that 'instead of facilitating, the clause tended to obstruct the reduction of tariffs', noting that

> when it became apparent that multilateral negotiations on an almost universal scale were not likely to succeed, certain groups, especially the Oslo group of countries, were anxious to achieve the general objects advocated in international conference within a more restricted area. Had general support of such endeavours been forthcoming, it is possible that the practice of reduction through group agreements might have spread and the groups gradually have extended their size. Such a procedure

> might have been less favourable to world trade as a whole than the rapid conclusion between a large number of countries of bilateral treaties embracing the MFN clause, but not less favourable than the failure to grant concessions owing to the quasi-universal implications of the MFN.

For example, the Second Conference with a View to Concerted Economic Action, in late 1930, recognised that the chances for a multi-lateral agreement did not exist and that bilateral agreement was the only feasible path to liberalisation. But the conference encouraged this path only if tariff reductions from those agreements were extended to others through unconditional MFN treatment. Later, in mid-1932, Belgium, Luxembourg, and the Netherlands signed the Ouchy Convention in which they and any other willing participants agreed to staged tariff reductions amounting to 50 percent of existing tariffs. This could have formed the nucleus of a movement toward freer trade, but Britain and others insisted that the convention would be a violation of the unconditional MFN principle unless the tariff cuts were generalised. This undermined the agreement and the convention never entered into force.

This 'progressive' bilateralism, allowing a subset of countries to expand trade through tariff reductions and thereby giving an incentive for others to follow, was squelched while the 'pernicious' bilateralism of quantita-tive restrictions and bureaucracy-administered exchange controls was allowed to fester unchecked. The result was a sharp reduction in world trade: the volume of trade declined 40 percent from 1929 to 1932, while real world output fell only 20 percent. When economic recovery had gradually been restored by the mid-1930s, the volume of trade lagged severely behind the rebound in income.

4.2   Toward another postwar order

The seeds of more effectual international cooperation were sown in the mid-1930s after the trough in economic activity had passed. Though not of sufficient strength to save the decade of the 1930s, international cooperation, particularly between Britain and the United States, helped set the groundwork for the next postwar international economic order.

The Tripartite Agreement of 1936 was a success in initiating cooperation on financial matters between the United States and western Europe. France, Switzerland, the Netherlands, and Italy finally devalued their currencies against gold, thus enabling the gold-bloc countries to dis-mantle some of their import quotas and licences. The recession of 1937, however, ended this liberalisation of import restrictions.

Of greater significance was the stirring international activism of the United States. Having contributed in no small degree to increased world protection by instituting the Smoot–Hawley tariff in 1930, the United States now played a key role in the Montevideo conference in December 1933 which promised negotiations among western hemisphere republics to reduce tariffs on trade in the Americas. By the Reciprocal Trade Agreements Act of 1934, subsequently renewed in 1937 and 1940, the Congress delegated limited tariff-negotiating powers to the president, enabling him to offer reciprocal concessions amounting to up to a 50 percent reduction in tariffs. The United States had mixed success with the purely bilateral approach to trade liberalisation, although some tangible progress on creating momentum toward lower tariffs was made. By 1938, a full third of American tariffs had been cut by at least 20 percent, and many by the full 40–50 percent, with countries signing agreements with the United States. By 1939, the United States had signed 20 MFN treaties with countries that accounted for 60 percent of its trade. Most notable was the agreement with Britain in 1938 that set the stage for the great Anglo–American cooperation during World War II that eventually led to the Bretton Woods conference in 1944 where the cornerstones for the postwar economic order were established.

While the economic environment for trade liberalisation was improving, if still shaky, after 1934, the political situation in Europe began to deteriorate with the rise of fascism. After the mid-1930s, the League of Nations (1942, p. 149) observed, 'the political foundations for any liberalization of commercial policy had been shattered and the tendencies towards closed economies and rigid state regulation gained impetus from year to year under the exigencies of a near-war economy'.

5   Trade liberalisation in historical perspective

The lessons to be drawn from the trade policy experience of past decades for current concerns about the direction of the world trading system are, unfortunately, somewhat limited. The relative serenity and simplicity of the 19th-century order, with its absence of discrimination, quantitative restrictions, 'fair trade' laws, or industrial policies, cannot be replicated today. And the challenges for trade policy today are nowhere near as urgent as those experienced in the interwar period. Nonetheless, certain themes that have relevance for today's concerns do emerge from this retrospective look at trade policy.

One important lesson about facilitating multilateral free trade is that long periods of macroeconomic stability provide an environment conducive for the adoption of liberal trade policies. That is based on the 19th-century and postwar experiences, a sound international monetary and financial system appears to be a prerequisite for (or at least an important complement to) an open trading system. Major supply disruptions such as large positive or negative price shocks had proved to be detrimental to an open trade regime. The agricultural and raw material price shocks of 1815, 1879, 1929, and 1973 are each associated with an important shift in the direction of world trade policies toward greater protection.[17]

But avoiding macroeconomic difficulties and large price shocks lie outside the realm of what trade policy can achieve. What lessons emerge about the types of policies that change the world trading system for the better? Here again, the trade policy experience of the past 150 years does not provide clear guidance. Multilateral cooperation on trade policy is not necessary either for the liberalisation of trade policy or for the prevention of illiberal trade policies. Multilateralism was not a feature of the 19th century, whereas multilateral talks were repeatedly held in the 1920s and 1930s to no avail. Similarly, bilateral trade policies cannot be uniquely praised or condemned. A progressive bilateralism flourished in the 19th century, with the prospect of trade diversion from the Anglo–French accord of 1860 leading other countries to join and reduce tariffs rather than to retaliate and raise them. In the interwar period, such progressive bilateralism – the sole hope for freer trade – was extinguished in the misplaced desire to restore unconditional MFN treatment first. At the same time, the pernicious bilateralism that emerged was rooted not so much in terms of international trade policy and tariff discrimination as in the malfunction of the international monetary system, which prompted the bureaucratic allocation of import quotas and foreign exchange to eliminate all bilateral payments' imbalances.

Although the complexity of international economic issues was greater in the interwar period than in the 19th century, the number and size distribution of European countries did not change considerably between these periods. Britain provided no leadership on international trade negotiations in the 19th century and it is not clear that the vacuum of leadership in the 1920s and 1930s (on the trade policy front, if not in the international monetary system) was the primary source of the period's failures.

Yet the fact that multilateral cooperation was absent in the 19th century and failed in the interwar period is no excuse to ignore its great success since 1947 and abandon this path to the reform of policy owing to current difficulties. The GATT eliminated the tariffs and the discrimination in international trade that was established in the interwar period, thereby restoring world trade to its pre-World War I basis. To top the 19th-century achievement, the GATT also imposed restrictions on the imposition of new trade barriers, however imperfect those restrictions may be, and set up a dispute settlements mechanism, however weak that mechanism may be, and ensured ongoing liberalisation, however time-consuming and complex these negotiations have become. While there remain major gaps in its effectiveness, notably dispute settlement and the control of fair trade laws, the GATT in principle represents a substantial improvement over the 19th-century treaty network.

As for bilateralism, it is extremely difficult to judge the trade policy environment and to determine whether the regional blocs of today constitute the progressive or the pernicious variety of bilateralism. Fortunately, the trade blocs of today are at least predicated on the notion of reducing barriers among participants and not raising barriers against non-participants. That the EFTA countries seek links with the European Community and that the several South American trading arrangements have as their ultimate aim to join the North American Free Trade Agreement (NAFTA) provides at least one signal that recent regional blocs exhibit the ability to expand membership rather than remain exclusive. If this expansion can be accomplished without harming efforts to strengthen the multilateral GATT approach, then the liberal postwar open trading system will be far from finished.

NOTES

1 Bhagwati (1991) makes a vigorous case for preferring multilateralism, and urges that regional trade agreements be harnessed toward improving the multilateral GATT system. Dornbusch (1990) expresses greater scepticism about the viability of the multilateral approach, and argues that bilateral agreements can restore progress on world trade liberalisation.

2 See O'Brien (1976) for a discussion.

3 Although political union often precedes customs union, the converse is less frequent. According to Viner (1950, p. 96), 'aside from the German Zollverein case, there appear to have been only three instances where substantial tariff unification preceded political union, and in none of these cases can it be held that the tariff unification was in any way responsible for creating a sentiment favorable to political union, or that in any other significant way made a substantial contribution to the eventual realization of political unity'.

4 Britain encountered difficulty in tariff bargaining in part because it refused to grant preferential access to other countries in its own market. Export interests demanded that raw materials, which comprised much of Britain's imports, be obtained at the lowest possible cost, while Richard Cobden (a founder of the Anti-Corn Law League) argued for non-discrimination in trade as fostering international peace. In addition, Britain found no need to strive for preferential access in foreign markets, remaining confident that its comparative advantage in manufactured goods would ensure the success of exporters, provided only that non-discriminatory treatment of its goods abroad was assured.

5 The crisis sparked by the harvest failure in Ireland paved the way for the repeal of the Corn Laws, leaving no time for them to be used as a bargaining tool.

6 Hansard's *Parliamentary Debates* (27 January 1846), p. 601.

7 Commercial agreements in the form of foreign treaties proved useful in circumventing protectionist interests in the legislature throughout Europe. The treaty mechanism allowed European countries to reduce legislative discretion over tariffs far in advance of the United States and thereby liberalise their policies sooner. In the United States, only with the Reciprocal Trade Agreements Act of 1934 were limited tariff-making powers formally delegated from the legislative to the executive branch. In the absence of a pro-trade executive, however, the lack of broadly-based domestic support for trade liberalisation meant the underlying commitment to such reforms was weak. In France, for example, the Anglo–French treaty was weakened and eventually abandoned after Napoleon was replaced in 1870.

8 The only major European state that resisted joining the spate of trade treaties in early 1860s was Russia, which finally acceded in 1874. Britain signed a similar number of agreements to secure the MFN treatment it had already granted to others, though it was unable to sign treaties with Spain and Portugal which demanded preferential treatment. The United States also stood outside of the treaty system and sought (by and large unsuccessfully) preferential trade agreements with Latin America. The United States also held to a conditional MFN policy, wherein reciprocal concessions were required before extending MFN treatment to third countries.

9 See Caplin and Krishna (1988). However, in a more general model Ludema (1991) finds that the MFN clause does not give rise to the free-rider problem because countries will opt to continue rather than conclude the process of negotiations.

10 A change in the Zollverein's tariff required unanimous agreement among members, and Prussian grain producers and western German merchants had long been prevented from enacting lower tariffs by the protectionist states in southern Germany. Prussia also sought to maintain its preeminent status in the Zollverein by excluding its rival Austria. Knowing that the current Zollverein agreements were soon up for renewal, Prussia approached France about a trade pact two days after the signing of the Anglo–French treaty and then committed itself to substantially freer trade by signing an agreement with France in 1861. Prussian leaders reasoned that Austria would have no interest in joining the Zollverein at such low tariff levels, and that the southern German states would have either to endorse the accord and align their tariff with Prussia's or leave the Zollverein. The tactic worked: after sharp resistance, the south German states agreed to stay in the Zollverein, Austria remained outside the agreement, and Prussia achieved greatly enhanced power in the Zollverein. See the discussion in Henderson (1957, 1959).

11 Sometimes it is asserted that there was a 'free-trade imperialism' in China, Argentina, and elsewhere such that the open-door policy was more posture than reality. But Platt (1968a, p. 297) found that 'the range of government action on behalf of overseas trade permitted by the *laissez faire* tradition of the time was extraordinarily narrow; official demands on behalf of British interests overseas never went beyond equal favour and open competition'. High trade volumes between the colonies and the European coloniser could persist not

because of discriminatory government policy, but because of monetary integration, transactions costs (such as telegraph and shipping links), and trade-related foreign direct investment.

12 For a detailed study, see US Tariff Commission (1922).

13 According to Huber (1971), as a result of the forced opening by the West, Japan's terms of trade improved by a factor of three and its national income rose roughly 65 percent in the transition from autarky to free trade.

14 In the German tariff of 1902, according to Platt (1968a, p. 93), there was even a tariff category for 'large dappled mountain cattle or brown cattle, reared at a spot at least 300 meters above sea level, and which have at least one month's grazing each year at a spot at least 800 meters above sea level'.

15 A convention in 1864 among major European powers failed to end the subsidisation of domestic sugar beet producers in many European countries. After removing the sugar tariff in 1874, Britain's colonies complained about competing against subsidised sugar in the British market. Law officers of the Crown ruled in 1880 that CVDs could not be imposed because they would violate the MFN clause of various commercial treaties. The Brussels convention on sugar in 1902 abolished all direct and indirect support for sugar and called for CVDs against countries that continued to subsidise sugar exports. The convention was generally a success, but Britain was so adamant about not violating the MFN clause that it withdrew from the convention in 1912 on the grounds that either quantitative restrictions or CVDs would violate it.

16 See Dornbusch and Frankel (1987). State bureaucracies as interest groups, however, would have a much greater stake in import regulation than in allowing the market to function anonymously through a change in relative prices brought about by a devaluation.

17 It is also instructive to note that the agricultural sector has long been a chronic stumbling block on the path toward free trade. Local 'policies of provision' ensured regional self-sufficiency in the mercantilist period, the Corn Laws hindered trade liberalisation in the aftermath of the Napoleonic Wars, the Russian and American grain shock triggered a move to protection and significantly weakened the 19th-century trading system, acute agricultural distress sparked the return to protection in the 1930s, and, of course, agricultural trade has stubbornly resisted all attempts to be brought under the rules of the GATT.

REFERENCES

Ashley, P. (1926) *Modern Tariff History*, 3rd edn, New York: Dutton.

Bairoch, P. (1989) 'European Trade Policy, 1815–1914', in P. Mathias and S. Pollard (eds), *The Cambridge Economic History of Europe*, vol. viii, *The Industrial Economies: The Development of Economic and Social Policies*, New York: Cambridge University Press, pp. 1–160.

Bhagwati, J. (1991) *The World Trading System at Risk*, Princeton: Princeton University Press and Harvester Wheatsheaf.

Brown, L. (1958) *The Board of Trade and the Free-Trade Movement, 1830–42*, Oxford: Clarendon Press.

Capie, F. (1983) 'Tariff Protection and Economic Performance in the Nineteenth

Century', in J. Black and L.A. Winters (eds), *Policy and Performance in International Trade*, New York: St Martin's Press.

Caplin, A. and K. Krishna (1988) 'Tariffs and the Most-Favored-Nation Clause: A Game Theoretic Approach', *Seoul Journal of Economics*, 1 (September) pp. 267–89.

Dornbusch, R. (1990) 'Policy Options for Freer Trade: The Case for Bilateralism', in R.Z. Lawrence and C.L. Schultz (eds), *American Trade Strategy: Options for the 1990s*, Washington, DC: Brookings Institution.

Dornbusch, R. and J. Frankel (1987) 'Macroeconomics and Protection', in R.M. Stern (ed.), *U.S. Trade Policies in a Changing World Economy*, Cambridge, Mass.: MIT Press.

Ehrman, J. (1962) *The British Government and Commercial Negotiations with Europe, 1783–93*, Cambridge: Cambridge University Press.

Eichengreen, B. (1992) *Golden Fetters: The Gold Standard and the Great Depression, 1919–1939*, New York: Oxford University Press.

Gaston, J. (1987) 'The Free Trade Diplomacy Debate and the Victorian European Common Market Initiative', *Canadian Journal of History*, 22 (April) pp. 59–82.

Gordon, M.S. (1941) *Barriers to World Trade*, New York: Macmillan.

Haberler, G. (1943) *Quantitative Trade Controls: Their Causes and Nature*, Geneva: League of Nations.

Henderson, W.O. (1957) 'A Nineteenth Century Approach to a West European Common Market', *Kyklos*, 10, pp. 448–57.

(1959) *The Zollverein*, Chicago: Quadrangle Books.

Hornbeck, S.K. (1910) 'The Most-Favored-Nation Clause in Commercial Treaties', *Bulletin of the University of Wisconsin*, 343 (February).

Huber, J.R. (1971) 'Effects on Prices of Japan's Entry into World Commerce After 1858', *Journal of Political Economy*, 79 (May/June) pp. 614–28.

Kindleberger, C.P. (1975) 'The Rise of Free Trade in Western Europe', *Journal of Economic History*, 35 (March) pp. 20–55.

League of Nations (1938) *Report on Exchange Controls*, Geneva: League of Nations.

(1939) *Review of World Trade, 1938*, Geneva: League of Nations.

(1942) *Commercial Policy in the Interwar Period: International Proposals and National Policies*, Geneva: League of Nations.

Liepmann, H. (1938) *Tariff Levels and the Economic Unity of Europe*, New York: Macmillan.

Ludema, R.D. (1991) 'International Bargaining and the Most-Favored-Nation Clause', *Economics and Politics*, 3 (March) pp. 1–20.

Mitchell, B.R. (1988) *British Historical Statistics*, New York: Cambridge University Press.

Nurkse, R. (1944) *The International Currency Experience: Lessons of the Inter-War Period*, Geneva: League of Nations.

O'Brien, D.P. (1976) 'Customs Unions: Trade Creation and Trade Diversion in Historical Perspective', *History of Political Economy*, 8 (Winter) pp. 540–63.

Platt, D.M.C. (1968a) 'The Imperialism of Free Trade: Some Reservations', *Economic History Review*, 2nd ser. 21 (August) pp. 296–306.

(1968b) *Finance, Trade and Politics in British Foreign Policy*, Oxford: Clarendon Press.

Tooke, T. and W. Newmarch (1857) *A History of Prices*, 6 vols, London: Longman, Brown, Green, Longmans and Robert.

United States Tariff Commission (1919) *Reciprocity and Commercial Treaties*, Washington, DC: Government Printing Office.

(1922) *Colonial Tariff Policies*, Washington, DC: Government Printing Office.

Viner, J. (1923) *Dumping: A Problem in International Trade*, Chicago: University of Chicago Press.

(1950) *The Customs Union Issue*, New York: Carnegie Endowment for International Peace.

Discussion

BARRY EICHENGREEN

Commenting on Douglas Irwin's papers is no fun. They are historically literate. They are elegantly written. They are carefully argued. They leave the discussant little to say. Chapter 4 here is no exception. In an approach to policy analysis near and dear to my heart, Irwin looks back at previous historical episodes of successful and failed trade liberalisations to see what light they shed on current controversies over how to best achieve an open trading system. The motivation, as the chapter makes clear, derives from the trend in recent years away from the multilateralism of the GATT and toward regional – in some cases, bilateral – trade agreements. At issue is whether bilateralism or multilateralism is more conducive to trade liberalisation, a question upon which Chapter 4 seeks to shed historical light.

If the author strongly endorsed one or the other strategy, it might have been possible for us to engage in an entertaining fight. What he has instead done is to conclude – correctly – that the answer depends on the circumstances. There is good bilateralism and bad bilateralism. Bilateral agreements can be trade-creating or trade-diverting. Bilateral agreements can lead to a cascade of other bilateral agreements and to a general opening of trade, or to retaliation against discrimination and to the fragmentation of trade. Similarly, there is good multilateralism and bad multilateralism. Multilateral negotiations can reduce negotiating costs through economies of scale, or they can divert attention away from potentially beneficial bilateral deals.

History provides, as Irwin notes, examples of all of these cases: of benign bilateralism in the 1860s and pernicious bilateralism in the 1930s; of successful multilateralism in the 1960s and failed multilateralism in the 1920s.

It is hard to quibble with this conclusion. I want to spend the remainder of my time suggesting, however, that the author's conclusion would be more compelling if his chapter addressed four additional issues.

First, some crucial and, at this stage, confusing issues could be greatly clarified if Irwin explicitly specified the bargaining game in which his historical actors are engaged. In particular, it is not obvious from the narrative description that universal use of the unconditional most favoured nation clause (MFN) will necessarily promote liberalisation. Will Country A be more or less inclined to conclude an agreement with Country B which would be advantageous in isolation, if any concessions it grants have also to be extended to Country C? Put in this way, it does not appear that MFN would promote liberalisation on the margin. Clearly, however, Country A also has to worry about how Country C will respond in subsequent negotiations both with it and with Country B. Specifying the game in extensive form would go a long way toward clarifying this and several other aspects of the chapter.

Second, the choice between multilateralism and bilateralism is generally addressed in the chapter taking the constellation of countries as given. There exist notions in both economics and political science suggesting that the outcomes of bargaining games will depend on the balance of large and small players. According to hegemonic stability theories popular in political science, for example, attempts to provide international public goods like a liberal trading system are more likely to be effective when there exists a dominant country in a position to internalise international externalities and to provide the leadership that the provision of public goods requires. Britain is sometimes said to have played this role in supporting the liberal international economic order before World War I, the United States after World War II. This issue is typically couched in terms of whether hegemony is conducive to liberalisation. Here, the issue is different: it is how the presence or absence of a hegemon influences the likely effectiveness of the bilateral and multilateral approaches. In the realm of trade, history suggests a positive association between hegemony and successful multilateralism. The United States was much more dominant after World War II, economically and militarily, than between the wars or than was Britain before World War I. (The chapter notes this in passing, in the section on pp. 112–13 where the liberal trading order of the late 19th century and post-World War II experience with the GATT are compared.) Thus, the only example of successful multilateralism the historical record provides coincides with a period of exceptional economic dominance by a single power. And the growing difficulties of the GATT have coincided, of course, with US relative (I underline 'relative') economic decline.

Why might this be? Simple cartel theory suggests that it is possible to deter defection from a cartel containing many members only when there is a dominant firm capable of acting as enforcer. In its absence, duopolies of, say, neighbouring firms may be the most that monitoring and enforcement capabilities can support. This suggests that the growing prevalence of bilateralism is a corollary of the increasingly multipolar nature of the world economy. Again I emphasise that this is mere theoretical speculation, determining the validity of which requires writing down the model.

Third, I am struck by the secondary role played in the chapter by domestic politics, in particular distributional politics. I can see Irwin grimacing: not only do I want a dynamic game with heterogeneous players, but I want links between strategic behaviour in the international sphere and strategic behaviour among domestic interest groups. To ask for the full model is unrealistic, but let me provide one example of why I think more attention to sectoral considerations is warranted. Anyone who has read Chapter 4 will be struck by the inordinate role played by agriculture. When the 18th-century trend toward trade liberalisation faltered after 1815, falling agricultural prices were to blame. When the trade liberalisation of the second half of the 19th century was reversed, slumping agricultural prices were again responsible. When tariffs went up in the 1920s, agricultural protectionism was again the reason. When trade conflicts break out between the United States, Europe, and Japan in the 1990s, the Common Agricultural Policy (CAP) and Japanese rice are again central issues. For those interested in trade liberalisation, the question is whether the pressure applied by agricultural interests seeking to block it is better deflected through the bilateral or multilateral approach. Casual observation does not provide an obvious answer.

Fourth, and finally, a plea for more extensive and systematic quantification. Let me provide one example. Irwin's discussion of the 1930s suggests that bilateral agreements had significant costs in terms of distorting the pattern of international trade. A paper by Kitson and Solomou (1992) shows, to the contrary, that changes in trade policy in the 1930s did not significantly increase the extent of bilateral settlements. For each of seven countries, Kitson and Solomou construct a time series measure of bilateralism, essentially the Grubel–Lloyd measure of intra-industry trade, except that they fit it to data for countries rather than industries. For the world as a whole, the extent of bilateralism rises slightly after 1929, but insignificantly so. As early as 1932, a trend back toward multilateralism is evident. The only exception to this generalisation is Germany, for obvious reasons. Thus, the notion that trade was heavily distorted in bilateral directions in the 1930s due to the failed multilateralism of the 1920s is not supported by systematic, quantitative evidence. To analyse properly the effects of alternative approaches to trade negotiation in history, we need more evidence of this sort.

So what I have provided is not a set of criticisms but an agenda for research. Alternative approaches to achieving trade liberalisation – and especially the choice between bilateral and multilateral policies – is a fertile area for the application of historical evidence, especially if that history is complemented by the systematic use of theory and quantification.

REFERENCE

Kitson, M. and R. Solomou (1992) 'Bilateralism in the Interwar International Economy', Department of Applied Economics, Cambridge University, mimeo.

MANCUR OLSON

1 A paradox

Since the factual generalisations in Douglas Irwin's Chapter 4 seem to me to be sound, I shall offer an outline of a simple theory to explain his main finding. Irwin finds that the system of relatively free trade in Europe in the half-century before World War I did *not* emerge from any continent-wide agreement, but rather mainly from a series of bilateral treaties. The extent of these bilateral treaties, and the customary provision that each signatory would receive any more favourable treatment its partner later gave to any other country, generated a relatively unprotectionist Europe. There were efforts to work out wide multilateral agreements to combat the extreme protectionism that emerged between World War I and World War II, but these efforts were unsuccessful. Irwin's finding that countries that would not work out a multilateral agreement for an open trading system nonetheless obtained such a system as the largely unintended consequence of a set of individually discriminatory bilateral agreements is paradoxical.

The paradox arises because the same nationalistic self-interest that motivates a country to make a bilateral trade deal with another country in most cases keeps it from making any significant sacrifices to obtain an open world economy. There are more than a hundred countries in the world economy, so let us consider the optimisation problem facing a single country that accounts for, say, 1 percent of world trade. Each country gains from an open world trading system even if its government chooses protection for many of its own industries – it will not want other countries to tax its exports, however much protection it chooses for itself. But while each country gains from free access for its exports to other countries, it can persuade, induce, or force other countries to open up their economies only at a cost.

The country that accounts for 1 percent of world trade will, on average, get only about 1 percent of the gains from a general increase in the openness of the rest of the world economy, but it will normally bear *all* of the costs of whatever it does to bring about a more open world economy. Therefore, a country that accounts for 1 percent of world trade will, on average, gain from allocating resources to make other countries open themselves to multilateral trade only if the world benefit–cost ratio from this resource use is at least a 100:1.

This logic applies not only to conventional resource expenditures, but also to the political costs that the leadership of a country bears in opposing organised interests within its own society that want protection for particular industries. Even if the national political leadership in our typical small country could bring about more freedom of trade in the rest of the world economy by agreeing to open its own economy, the economy over which this leadership presides will obtain only about 1 percent of the benefits, while the leadership will bear the whole political costs of combating the organised protectionists in its own polity. Thus the typical country usually does not have an incentive to use its scarce resources to seek freer trade in the world economy, and its political leaders normally do not have an incentive to work for such a system even if they could obtain it simply by doing away with protection that reduces the real income of their own society.

2   The logic of collective inaction

The difficulties the nations of the world face in obtaining the benefits of free international trade are therefore an illustration of the general difficulties of the voluntary provision of public goods, or more generally of the logic of collective action (Olson, 1965). This logic demonstrates that the likelihood of the voluntary provision of public goods increases monotonically when:

(1)   the number of beneficiaries of a collective good is smaller; or
(2)   the proportion of the benefits of collective action that go to the party
      with the highest absolute demand for the collective good increases.

Condition (1) can be made immediately clear by considering a collective good that involves three countries and supposing for ease of illustration that they are of equal size. Each country will then get a third of the benefits of any amount of the collective good that it provides and this alone will normally motivate some provision. In addition, the small numbers create an incentive for strategic interaction: each country has an incentive to tell each of the other countries that it will provide an additional amount if the others share the marginal costs, but not otherwise. Each of the others can then easily gain by agreeing to such an arrangement, and if they do agree each country then has an incentive to provide more of the collective good. If marginal costs are shared in exactly the same proportion as marginal benefits, the small group will in the aggregate provide a Pareto-efficient quantity of the collective good. When there is a collective good that involves only two parties (or an ordinary two-party trade in private goods), reaping the gains from cooperation is normally even easier than with three parties.

That is why the European countries that did not make any continent-wide multilateral agreement to have free trade nonetheless made a series of bilateral agreements that came close to achieving this objective. If the deal remains totally bilateral, each party reaps the benefits of the concessions it extracts from the other. Each therefore has an incentive to make the concessions of its own that procure the changes it wants in the policies of the other. The two parties have an incentive to continue making bilateral trade concessions until they have maximised their joint gains. Each country also has an incentive to demand that any further concessions its partner might later extend to another country should also be extended to it, and this favours the freer multilateral trade that Irwin shows tended to emerge. Note, on the other hand, that this nice 'externality' also increases the numbers involved and thereby, in one respect, makes it more difficult for the parties to reap all potential joint gains.[1]

3   The hegemonic incentive

Condition (2) can be made clear by supposing that, even if the number of countries that enjoy the collective good is large, one of them may be so much larger and wealthier than the others that it obtains a large part of the total gains from the collective good. When the country with the largest absolute demand for a collective good obtains, say, a third or half of the benefits from the collective good, it has as much unilateral incentive to provide a collective good as a country in a world of two or three countries of equal size would have had. Thus some provision of international public goods can occur, even when the number of beneficiary countries is large, if one country has such a large share of total income that the value of the international public good to it alone is sufficient to make it better off from providing some amount of this public good, even though it must pay the whole cost by itself.

Charles Kindleberger has applied the logic of collective action to explain the workings of the international system in two periods (Kindleberger, 1981). Kindleberger noted that in the years before World War I, when the British Empire covered a fourth of the globe Great Britain, partly by acting as a lender of last resort for the world financial system, provided international collective goods that made the international economy work better. Kindleberger also observed that, in the first decades after World War II, when the United States had perhaps as much as half of the GDP of the non-communist world, it provided, with the Marshall Plan, the Kennedy Round, and other actions, some public goods for the entire international economy. Thus the world works better when there is a 'hegemonic' power – one that finds it in its own self-interest to see that various international collective goods are provided (see Oneal and Elrod, 1989).

Naturally, the incentive a hegemonic power has to provide international collective goods diminishes as it becomes relatively less important in the world economy. In the United States, there has been a conspicuous resurgence of protectionist thinking, and a diminishing willingness of the country to provide foreign aid, as the American economy has come to encompass relatively less of the world economy.

4   Tardy hegemons

Irwin's chapter reminds us that, in spite of multilateral conferences with liberal purposes, there was a huge increase in protectionism in Europe in the years between World Wars I and II. We also know that there was a world-wide depression in this period and no lender of last resort to provide international liquidity that could help financial systems survive even temporary calamities. Irwin concludes that bilateral agreements were unable to cope with the pressures for protectionism that emerged from World War I and the interwar depression. There was also in this period nothing akin to foreign aid, to the Berlin airlift, or to the postwar containment of aggressive dictatorships.

It is now widely agreed that there was no way the problems of the interwar world could have been solved without a major contribution from the United States. Though not then as important relatively as it was in the years just after World War II, the United States was already a huge economy. Yet American policy was isolationist – the United States continued with a policy of non-involvement in Europe that dated back to George Washington. During World War II, there came to be a virtual consensus in the United States, as well as elsewhere, that the United States' isolationism and protectionism had been mistaken. In the language of the present argument, the United States failed to obtain the gains for itself that it could have obtained by taking the lead in seeing that some international collective goods were provided.

There appears to be a parallel between the behaviour of the United States in the 1920s and that of Japan today. The Japanese economy, though only about half as large as that of the United States, is nonetheless a significant fraction of the international economy. In certain areas of international trade and finance, Japan is the leading country. Yet Japan has not been providing leadership in bringing about a more liberal international economy or in the provision of other international public goods.

Why did the United States in the interwar period fail to see the gains to itself from provision of international collective goods? And why does Japan seem to fail to perceive these gains today?

A likely explanation is the slow social learning arising because of the 'rational ignorance' of the typical citizen (Olson, 1982). Information about public affairs is itself a collective good and thus subject to the logic of collective action. If a typical citizen invests a lot of time in studying public affairs, he is not likely to be any better off. The chances that he will change the outcome of the election are miniscule, and if he does he will reap only a minute share of the gains himself. Because of the rational ignorance of the typical citizen, nations are slow learners. Thus neither the United States in the interwar period nor Japan today appear fully to have taken account of the benefits to themselves of the provision of international collective goods.

5   Cooperation by a small number of large countries

The logic offered here suggests that, in the present international situation, where only limited amounts of unilateral provision of international public goods from the United States and Japan can be expected, the only real hope for international public good provision is the cooperation of a *small number* of *large* countries. In the aggregate, the United States, Japan, and the largest countries of Western Europe receive such a large proportion of world income that they will, with marginal cost sharing, internalise most of the gains from a better world order.

NOTE

1 If the concessions that country M extracts from country L also go, by virtue of most favoured nation (MFN) treaties that country L has signed, to countries A through K, then country M does not have an incentive to extract a group-optimal degree of concession from country L, since much of the benefits will go to others.

REFERENCES

Kindleberger, Charles (1981) 'Dominance and Leadership in the International Economy', *International Studies Quarterly*, **5**(2) (June) pp. 242–54.
Olson, Mancur (1965) *The Logic of Collective Action*, Cambridge, Mass.: Harvard University Press.
  (1982) *The Rise and Decline of Nations*, New Haven: Yale University Press.
Oneal, John R. and Mark A. Elrod (1989) 'Nato Burden Sharing and the Forces of Change', *International Studies Quarterly*, **33** (December) pp. 435–56.

5   GATT's influence on regional arrangements

J. MICHAEL FINGER

The World Bank, the International Monetary Fund (IMF), the Organisation for Economic Cooperation and Development (OECD), the General Agreement on Tariffs and Trade (GATT) – they are all in the same business. They try to influence, and sometimes do influence, national choices of policy. But no international organisation has sovereignty over any nation's policy. In the end, a nation's tariff or its import licensing requirement is what that country's government says it is.

Though regional arrangements are coming into fashion (perhaps more rapidly than into function), the GATT will remain the major global steward of commercial policy. Knowing how the GATT has nudged regional arrangements toward good international (multilateral) citizenship in the past is important in judging how it might continue to do so in the future.

But if we ask 'What are the GATT rules about regional arrangements?' we are asking at best only half the question. Equally (or more) important is how the GATT attempts to influence a national government to keep its trade policies in line with the objectives the GATT was created to advance – fewer and less discriminatory trade restrictions.

Section 1 looks at the historical origins of GATT's rules for regional arrangements and then at their substantive content. Sections 2–4 review GATT's experiences with regional arrangements. Section 5 presents some conclusions and policy applications. The key to understanding the lessons these experiences provide is to remember that GATT began as an exchange of market access concessions. Preserving and extending the value of that market access is still the motivating interest for GATT's member countries. The formation of free-trade areas (FTAs) and customs unions (CUs) among the industrialised countries – particularly the European Common Market – significantly compromised the market access of the countries left outside. GATT's rules told outside countries that they must accept the loss of access to markets in EEC member-states

128

that the formation of the European Economic Community would cause, but they were unwilling to do so. But in the end, the outcome was a positive one. GATT procedures for channelling trade conflicts into consultations and negotiations prevented a negative reaction by outside countries, and led eventually to the Common Market agreeing to significant reductions of its external restrictions.

The major lesson for policy is that preserving and extending market access is the driving force behind the GATT. Hindsight suggests that GATT's rules would have been more useful had they provided guidance as to how to rectify the loss of market access to outside countries that is implicit in the formation of a preferential arrangement. The foregoing by countries outside of a regional arrangement of their most-favoured nation (MFN) right should be treated as a concession: the implementation of any regional arrangement should be followed by negotiation between that arrangement and its outside trading partners, with a view to reducing, on an MFN basis, the external barriers of that arrangement.

1   GATT provisions for regional arrangements

To understand how the international community has influenced regional arrangements, it is useful to recall a bit of history. Post-World War II deliberations on institutional arrangements for the world economy were successful in establishing the International Monetary Fund (IMF) and the World Bank. The International Trade Organization (ITO) was to be for trade what the IMF is for monetary–macroeconomic policy, and the World Bank is for development. A *New York Times* editorial of April 1947 expressed well the sentiment of the international community toward the proposed ITO: '[T]he first and most basic requirement was a charter setting forth the general rules under which trade should be conducted among the nations' (April 10 1947, p. 24, column 2).

Though the ITO negotiations to establish international stewardship of the trading system were unsuccessful, the community of nations did reach agreement on a more limited matter. Putting matters of economic principle aside, the international community fell back on the traditional mercantilist perception that a country had to 'buy' access to another country's market by giving up access to its own – i.e., that exports were the gains from trade and imports the cost. They agreed to a package of reciprocal tariff reductions and bindings. The document or contract which gave legal effect to this agreed exchange was labelled the General Agreement on Tariffs and Trade, the GATT.[1]

The GATT has the functional parts of a well-written contract. It specifies what was to be delivered by each party, it specifies circumstances under which a party can go back on the deal (and what compensation that party will then owe others), and what a party can do when it feels that what it has claim to under the contract is not being delivered. More familiar labels for these three parts are (i) exchange of concessions, (ii) exceptions, and (iii) dispute settlement. Provisions for regional arrangements are part of the exceptions – one of the ways to go back on the basic agreement to provide non-discriminatory market access.

1.1   The exception for regional arrangements

Because regional arrangements have been a part of international commerce for a long time, provisions for such arrangements have a long history of inclusion in commercial treaties. Viner (1950) lists, for example, the 'Iberian clause' in a 1893 commercial treaty between Spain and Portugal that provided for reciprocal free entry, and the 'Cuban Clause' in trade treaties between the United States and Cuba from 1903 until the early 1950s (see also Chapter 3 in this volume).

The argument for including in GATT provisions for regional arrangements was, in large part, the reality that such arrangements existed and would probably continue to be a part of international commercial arrangements.[2] At the time the GATT was negotiated, Belgium and the Netherlands were discussing joining together in a CU. There are also statements from developing country delegates explaining the utility of CUs for development purposes, i.e., among countries each of whose market was too small to allow development of industry (United Nations, 1946a, p. 9).

The downside of this was that allowance for regional arrangements would constitute an exception to the MFN obligation. At a practical level, the United States saw the MFN obligation as a major tool for forcing the end of metropole–colony preferential arrangements, particularly Commonwealth preferences (Jackson, 1969, p. 576). At a more abstract level, the MFN obligation played a critical role in taming the mercantilist dynamics on which the GATT is built into a liberal, global system. As Martin Wolf (1988, pp. 72–3) lucidly states the matter:

> Nondiscrimination is . . . central to a system whose principal technique of liberalization is reciprocity and whose principal sanction is retaliation. It is nondiscrimination that creates a global order out of an essentially mercantilist system. By virtue of nondiscrimination purely bilateral bargains become available to all participants, even those with little effective capacity to negotiate. Furthermore, the commitment to nondiscrimination puts the retaliatory power of the strong behind the complaints of the weak.

The last sentence in this passage brings out a point that is often over-looked: MFN is important not just to assure that benefits of reducing old restrictions are shared around, it is also a critical discipline on countries' creating new ones. A country will be much more hesitant if its new trade restriction must be applied to imports from *all* sources (i.e., MFN), and thus arouse the threat of retaliation from all of them. Without the MFN constraint, the restricting country could pick off the more dynamic exporters, perhaps making allies rather than enemies of other exporters.

For immediate and for longer-term considerations, then, it was impor-tant that provisions allowing regional arrangements should not provide an avenue for fragmenting the trading system.

1.2 Substantive requirements

The language of GATT Article XXIV, paragraph 5, that permits regional arrangements is as follows:[3]

> The provisions of this Agreement shall not prevent . . . the formation of a customs union or of a free trade area or the adoption of an interim agree-ment necessary for the formation of a customs union or a free trade area.

The substantive qualifications are these:

1a For a CU, 'the [common] duties and other regulations of commerce shall not on the whole be higher or more restrictive than the general incidence of . . . [those] applicable in the constituent territories prior to the formation of . . . or the adoption of such interim agreement' (paragraph 5).

1b For a FTA 'the [individual] duties and other regulations of com-merce shall not be higher or more restrictive than the corresponding duties and other regulations of commerce existing . . . prior to' (paragraph 5).

2. Paragraph 8 specifies that 'duties and other restrictive regulations of commerce (except, where necessary, those permitted under Articles . . .) are eliminated with respect to substantially all the trade between the constituent territories' in products originating in these territories.

3. Creation of the union or area can come in stages, if an interim agreement includes *a plan and schedule* for forming it.[4]

1.3 Enforcement processes

Rules are one thing; convincing countries to keep their policies in line with them is another. What provisions does the GATT make for seeing that countries honour these specifications when they form a CU or an FTA?

Paragraph 7 of Article XXIV sets out notification requirements. The first subparagraph requires that any contracting party:

- 'deciding to enter into a customs union or a free trade area, or an interim agreement leading to [such] . . .
- shall promptly notify the contracting parties . . .
- shall make available to them such information'.

The next subparagraph provides for the Contracting Parties to review the submitted plan and schedule, and to consult with the parties to the proposed arrangement. If the Contracting Parties find that the agreement will not create or lead to a CU or a FTA within GATT's specifications,

- 'the CONTRACTING PARTIES shall make recommendations . . .
- the parties shall not maintain or put into force . . . such agreement if they are not willing to modify it in accordance with these recommendations'.

There is also provision that any substantial change in the plan and schedule of agreement be notified, reviewed, etc.

Another 'what to do about it' provision relates to a tariff rate being increased when a CU is formed. Suppose Germany's tariff on bicycles is 5 percent and France's is 15 percent, both rates bound under the GATT. When the two countries form a CU, the common tariff rate becomes 10 percent. In this instance, Article XXIV, paragraph 6 provides that the 'modification' provisions of Article XXVIII are applicable.

Article XXVIII provides that a bound rate may be raised under certain circumstances through negotiation with exporting countries, and that if, say, Germany raises its tariff rate on one product, exporters have a right to compensatory reductions of the German tariff on other products. Article XXIV, paragraph 6 provides that when a CU is formed, exporting countries may ask for these compensation negotiations. Paragraph 6 also modifies the specification of when the exporters may ask for compensation. In our example, the reduction of the French tariff on bicycles is to be taken into account as compensation for the German increase.

If review by the Contracting Parties ruled that a proposed CU or an FTA did not meet GATT's criteria, the countries proposing it would be forbidden from putting it into force. Their options would include the following:[5]

- they could modify their agreement,
- they could withdraw from the GATT,
- they could attempt to convince the contracting Parties to accept by

two-thirds majority vote (i.e., under Article XXIV, paragraph 10) an agreement not entirely within the specifications of the other paragraphs of Article XXIV, or try to obtain a waiver under Article XXV.

If the parties to the regional agreement chose to go ahead without adjusting to the problems pointed out by the Contracting Parties, they would risk the following actions by other GATT members:

- they might be expelled from the GATT,
- other countries, after going through the GATT dispute settlement process, might retaliate.

1.4   The logic of GATT's rules for regional arrangements

What is the logic of these rules? Are they designed to isolate economically sensible departures from non-discrimination, to limit the degree or amount of discrimination that countries put into effect, or what?

1.4.1 Not trade creation – trade diversion   Jacob Viner introduced the concepts of trade creation and trade diversion in his book, *The Customs Union Issue*. The book was published in 1950, well after the GATT negotiations were completed, so it should come as no surprise that GATT's criteria are not the equivalent of saying that regional arrangements are to be judged against the normative standard from which Viner derived his concepts. For example, in Chapter 2 of his examination of the European Common Market, the legal scholar Allen (1960) points out that trade diversion as well as trade creation are clearly compatible with GATT's criteria for an allowable regional arrangement. The concepts, however, soon came into wide use in legal analysis – as well as, of course, in economic analysis. To Dam (1963), for example, trade creation and trade diversion provided a standard for evaluating not only regional agreements, but for evaluating the GATT itself. To Dam, failure of GATT's criteria to rule out a trade-diverting regional arrangement (the Latin American Free-Trade Area, or LAFTA, see below) was reason enough to set aside these criteria.

1.4.2 The GATT- standard 'Yes, but . . .' rule   The exception GATT makes to its general principles in allowing regional arrangements is similar to its other exceptions. For example, the safeguards exception (Article XIX) provides that a country may impose a restriction against imports, but only if those imports cause or threaten serious injury to domestic production.

Provisions for regional arrangements are an exception, not to the GATT principle that trade restrictions should go down, but to the principle that they should be non-discriminatory. Article XXIV provides that import restrictions may be discriminatory, but only when there is big-time discrimination: the countries who discriminate in favour of one another must *eliminate* (not just reduce) *all* restrictions on *substantially all* trade among themselves.

The idea behind allowing only big-time discrimination is to rule out discrimination as an instrument of everyday commercial policy. As explained in the quote from Martin Wolf above, such piecemeal discrimination would make impossible the maintenance of a liberal trading system.

1.4.3 Outside countries must accept the loss   A second dimension of Article XXIV is addressed more to 'third countries', countries that remain outside of a regional arrangement. Discriminatory trade liberalisation, the drafters of the GATT understood, would often displace the exports of outside countries. Does GATT tell outside countries that they must accept that loss of trade, (market access) without compensation? The answer Article XXIV provides is 'Yes'. Paragraph 5 requires that the tariffs of a FTA shall not be higher, and its other regulations not more restrictive, than those of its constituent territories. Likewise the common external tariff of a CU shall not, on the whole, be higher or more restrictive than those of its constituent territories. Implicitly, if the tariffs and non-tariff barriers (NTBs) of an FTA or a CU are no higher than the (previous) restrictions of its constituent territories outside countries have no basis for claiming a loss of benefits.[6]

2   Overall applications

Table 5.1 provides a summary tabulation of regional arrangements that have come under GATT scrutiny. Schott's (1989) listing, on which Table 5.1 is based, covers only arrangements on which a GATT Working Party has completed a report. It does not provide a count of regional arrangements: some arrangements may not have been submitted to GATT for review, in other cases (e.g., creation of the EEC) GATT may have reviewed an arrangement more than once.

According to Schott, the GATT has never censured an agreement as being incompatible with its standards – and only four arrangements have been formally declared to be compatible: the South Africa–Rhodesia CU, the Nicaragua–El Salvador free trade agreement, Nicaraguan participation in the Central American Common Market (CACM) and the Caribbean Community and Common Market (CARICOM) (see Chapter 9 below).

Table 5.1. *Reviews by the GATT of regional arrangements*

Description of arrangement		Number	%
European Community is a party		42	59
(a) Creation of the Economic Community	2		
(b) Agreements with European countries that have not become members	6		
(c) Agreements with countries that have become members (including accessions)	8		
(d) Associations, agreements and conventions with developing countries	26		
European Free Trade Association, creation and expansions		4	6
Other arrangements among developed countries (e.g., Australia–New Zealand)		5	7
Arrangements among developing countries		12	17
Developing–developed (not EEC) country arrangements (e.g., US–Israel)		2	3
Arrangements between Finland and Eastern European Countries		6	8
Totals		71	100

Source: Tabulated from Schott (ed.) (1989) pp. 376–83.

Of the seventy-one reviews tabulated, well more than half (forty-two) involved the European Community in some way. The Community has free trade agreements (that exclude most agricultural goods) with other Western European countries and an extensive array of associations, agreements and conventions with developing countries.

Regional arrangements among developing countries make up a second large group. In the following sections I will examine how GATT reviewed the formation of the EEC, how it reviewed several of the Community's arrangements with developing countries, and how it reviewed arrangements among developing countries.

3   The European Economic Community (EEC)

The Treaty of Rome, signed on 25 March 1957, marked the beginning of the EEC. The Treaty provided a plan and a twelve-year schedule for eliminating tariffs and quantitative restrictions on internal trade. There was, however, provision for backsliding, and special status for France's special import taxes. Agricultural products were to be included in the common market, but under special rules for coordinating national farm programmes.

The plan for eliminating restrictions on internal trade left certain matters to be worked out. The common tariff rate on any good would, in principle, be the average of the rates charged on that good by the six countries making up the community. But there were lists of products to be excepted from this principle. As to quantiative restrictions (QRs) on imports from outside the Six, the Treaty called for elimination by the end of the twelve-year transition period of all the national restrictions existing when the Treaty was signed. Members could apply no new ones beyond those permitted under decisions of the Organisation for European Economic Cooperation (OEEC).

The overseas territories of the member-states were to be 'associated' with the EEC. The commercial part of this association would involve preferential tariff reductions by the EEC and by each associate, and likewise preferential increases of import quotas. The overseas territories would not be expected to relax import restrictions needed to develop their industries.

3.1   Review by the GATT

Reviewing the EEC presented an enormous issue for the GATT. In Hudec's words (1975, pp. 195–6):

> Although the substance of the rules made sense when applied to the EEC, the very size and importance of the EEC adventure make it unrealistic to expect that permission for its existence had to depend upon conformity with these rules. The EEC was the cornerstone of a new North Atlantic foreign policy, as important as the GATT itself.

Negotiating the Rome Treaty had been a difficult task for the member states, and they would have been reluctant to open its provisions for renegotiation, especially for renegotiation to accommodate the demands of an outside party.

The GATT had up to this time rigorously reviewed proposals for regional arrangements. The European Coal and Steel Community (ECSC), made up of the same member-states as the EEC Six, had been voted a formal GATT waiver, a waiver whose conditions were so strenuous that, according to Patterson (1966, p. 129), they 'virtually modified the Treaty'. And the contracting parties had rigorously monitored the ECSC member-states' behaviour against the terms of the waiver.

But the EEC member-states dug in their heels: 'There can ... be no question either of a readjustment of the Treaty or of any of its provisions, or of waivers or of subjecting the Six to special controls' (quoted by Patterson, 1966, p. 157).

This time the GATT blinked: '[T]he Committee felt that it would be more fruitful if attention could be directed to specific and practical problems, leaving aside for the time being questions of law and debates about the compatibility of the Rome Treaty with Article XXIV of the General Agreement' (GATT, 1959, p. 70).

Putting aside the formal review of the Rome Treaty did not mean an end of contracting parties' attempts to influence the trade policies of the EEC. Negotiation would eventually bring the EEC to make adjustments on trade in manufactured goods that its outside trading partners would consider satisfactory. But, as everyone knows, EEC agricultural policy continues to be a problem.

3.2   Industrial goods

The US government's attitude toward the creation of the EEC – as had been its attitude toward the formation of the ECSC – was strongly favourable. At the beginning, the US position focused on establishing political cohesion and military strength in western Europe: the commercial dimension of the EEC and the ECSC were less important. But other western European countries, countries that traded extensively with the Six, pushed hard to defend their commercial interests.

Legal debate under Article XXVIII over who had claim to what compensation for construction of the common external tariff went on for two years, and was inconclusive (Hudec, 1975, p. 199). The 'practical' strategy that eventually took over was to leave the legal issues in abeyance and deal with the height of the common tariff at a new round of multilateral negotiations. The Dillon Round (1960–1) achieved little, but at the Kennedy Round (1964–7) industrial countries agreed to tariff reductions of about one-third of the initial level on about one-third of their total or two-thirds of their dutiable imports. After the Kennedy Round the EEC negotiated free-trade agreements on industrial goods with nearly all of the other western European countries. It is fair to say that by the mid-1970s the height of the EEC's common tariff on industrial goods was a minor issue in international trade, even to exporters who remained outside of the EEC's extensive network of preferential arrangements.[7]

3.3   Trade in agricultural goods

At the time the GATT was completed, countries were unwilling to commit themselves to removing all restrictions on agricultural trade. The

GATT allows quantitative restrictions on agricultural imports, but governments are required to restrict domestic production to the same extent that they restrict imports. Governments, however, found even this permissive rule impossible to honour. The first major break with the rule was the waiver voted for US agricultural policy in 1955, but European agricultural policies soon became equally troublesome.

The Rome Treaty included trade in agricultural goods in the common market that was to be created. The Treaty also provided for the establishment of a common agricultural policy among the member-states, but it did not specify the mechanics for this agricultural policy. As the policy developed, an important element in it became the establishment of minimum prices for agricultural products, to be maintained by government purchases and by variable levies on imports, these levies equal to the difference between the world price and the politically established internal price. Countries exporting agricultural products feared that implementation would compromise their access to the EEC market, even lead to EEC surpluses that would compete in third markets.

Negotiation was made difficult by the EEC's unwillingness to modify its internal programme. Furthermore, the basic instruments of the EEC's policy were the internal prices and the arrangements for financing them. Negotiating trade policy with outside countries was therefore cumbersome – the focal dimensions of these negotiations, trade policies, were not the focal dimensions of the emerging EEC policy.

At the Kennedy Round, agricultural products were excluded from the across-the-board approach used on industrial goods. The EEC offered at the Round a proposal that could be described as a multilateral version of its minimum price scheme. The proposal gained too little support to be accepted, and in the end hardly any reduction of restrictions on temperate zone agricultural products was agreed.

In later negotiations, the United States pressed the EEC to bind their variable levies to specified ceilings. When this yielded nothing the United States shifted to pressing the EEC to agree to minimum quantities it would import from the United States (Hudec, 1975, p. 202). This was, for example, the strategy the United States followed when Spain and Portugal acceded to the Community.

On agricultural trade, exporting countries have not been satisfied with the compensation and adjustment the EEC has been willing to provide. There have been twenty-five GATT panels on EEC agriculture: more than on any other issue (GATT, 1989); the United States has been the complainant in twelve of these. Likewise, EEC agriculture has been a frequent target of Special '301' cases, all to minimal effect (Office of the US Trade

Representative, 1991). And the Uruguay Round, under way since the Fall of 1987, has made little progress. In sum, all the king's horses and all the king's men have not been able to bring GATT's liberal trade objectives to bear on world agricultural trade.

4   Developing countries in regional arrangements

Many of the regional arrangements that have been brought to GATT for review have included developing countries as parties. Of these, a large fraction are associations or agreements between the EEC and one or a group of developing countries.

4.1   Developing countries associated with the EEC

The Rome Treaty provided for a special arrangement to be created between the EEC and all non-European territories enjoying a special relationship with one of the Six when the Rome Treaty was signed. Imports into the Six from these territories would be duty free. The associated territories would, in turn, treat imports from any one of the Six the same as imports from the mother country[8] (Patterson, 1966, p. 233). Such arrangements would not come into place immediately, they would be worked out and implemented over time.

The EEC made hardly a gesture to defend the resulting arrangements as consistent with the GATT. When first challenged on the matter, spokespersons for the EEC explained that these arrangements were put in place to comply with a UN resolution asking the richer countries to help the less fortunate to prosper.

To the extent that EEC spokespersons did take up the accord of these arrangements with the GATT, their response can be better described as legalistic than as legal. For example, to demonstrate that an agreement between the EEC and certain African countries did include removal of all trade restrictions on substantially all of trade, the EEC considered the convention of association with eighteen African and Malagasy territories as, legally speaking, eighteen FTAs, each with the six EEC member states and one of the territories as the constituents (GATT, 1966, p. 101). No doubt, in each of these, trade among the Six made up 'substantially all' of internal trade.

The EEC was not alone in this casualness toward GATT's standards for the regional agreement involving developing countries. The idea that trade rules that applied to developed countries should not apply to developing countries was gaining increasing importance in the GATT.

This view, applied by members of a GATT Working Party that examined the EEC association agreements with African and Malagasy states, produced the following conclusion:

> Some members of the Working Party took the view that the question of the Convention's consistency with Article XXIV was scarcely relevant since the Article had, in their view, never been meant to apply to free-trade or customs unions arrangements between developed and less-developed countries. In their view, among other things, it was inconsistent with the development of thinking on the question of reciprocity that less-developed countries should have to give preferential access to their markets in return for securing preferences in the markets of developed countries (GATT, 1966, pp. 105–6).

4.2   The import-substitution model of development as GATT policy

The import-substitution theory of economic development was gaining increasing strength within the GATT. Consequently, the following two guidelines became increasingly influential:

(1)   import restrictions were an important instrument of economic development, hence developing countries should be excused from the GATT's disciplines against their use; and

(2)   the developed countries were pressed to take 'affirmative action' that would help the developing countries: provide unreciprocated reductions – and even preferential reductions – of import restrictions on products of export interest to developing countries.[9]

The acceptance of the EEC's arrangements with developing countries was one demonstration of the strength of this view of trade's role in development. GATT approval of arrangements among developing countries was another.

The idea that developing countries should be given licence to restrict imports was more than a part of the reigning theory of economic development: it was a part of the mercantilist ethic on which the GATT was built. Within this ethic, each country views imports as the costs of trade, exports as the gain. But for all countries to be able to export, all would have to be willing to import, hence the idea of each country accepting an obligation not to restrict imports amounts to the ethical proposition of individual sacrifice for the common good. Within this ethical perspective, it is difficult to ask the weaker members of the group to accept the same level of responsibility as the stronger.

Hudec (1987) in his interpretation of the role of developing countries in the GATT, brings out this factor: 'It is very difficult to convene an enterprise involving rich and poor without having some welfare dimension to the work . . . [The] inability to resist this need to "give something" has been a constant factor in the dynamics of GATT legal policy' (1987, p. 16). Hudec also points out that bending to developing countries' pressure for a dispensation from GATT legal obligations has a venal as well as an ethical attraction: it is cheaper than bending to their pressures for resource transfers.

In the view of another eminent legal scholar, Jackson (1969, p. 591), the permissive view the Contracting Parties took of protectionist preferential arrangements amounted to, in effect, amending the GATT to include an ITO provision that would have allowed developing countries to exchange tariff preferences:

> Although the Havana Charter's special article for developing countries' regional agreements was not incorporated into GATT, in practice it appears that the essence of its provisions may have been followed in GATT.

The following two examples document the point.

4.2.1 Latin American Free-Trade Area (LAFTA) The Montevideo Treaty, signed in February 1960, was designed explicitly to provide infant industry protection and 'complementary industrialisation' within the area it covered. Competition within the region was to be avoided, the regional character of the plan was justified as necessary to allow the necessary economies of scale.[10] Hudec (1975, p. 205) sums up its arrangements as follows:

> It was typical of most developing country agreements in two respects. First, it did not even approach the [GATT] requirement of total integration. Second, it was frankly protectionist in tone, for the whole theory of developing country integration was aimed at finding larger sheltered markets for infant industry development.

The GATT's conclusion, however, was that 'the CONTRACTING PARTIES feel that there remain some questions of a legal and administrative nature . . . [and] . . . do not at this juncture find it appropriate to make recommendations to the parties to the Treaty'. The Contracting Parties go on to say that the conclusion does not prevent the parties to the Montevideo Treaty from proceeding with application of it, nor does it prejudice the rights of outside countries to recourse under GATT against actions the parties to the Montevideo Treaty taken under the Treaty (GATT, 1961, pp. 21–2).

4.2.2 Agreement on ASEAN Preferential Trading Arrangements A GATT Working Party was established in November 1977 to examine the provisions of the Agreement on ASEAN Preferential Trading

Arrangements. The agreement provided the framework for a system of preferential trading arrangements involving (1) long-term quantity contracts, (2) purchase finance supported at preferential interest rates, (3) preferences in government procurement, (4) preferential tariffs, and (5) preferential non-tariff barriers.

The agreement itself provided only a framework for exchanging preferences on any of these instruments: there was no plan or schedule, but by the time the Working Party was established, the member countries had agreed to two batches of tariff concessions, covering a total of 826 items (out of the tens of thousands in the tariff nomenclatures of the participating countries).

The decision taken by the Contracting Parties noted that (the words in italics are quoted from the decision, as reported in GATT, 1978, pp. 225–6) because:

> (1) the parties to the agreement had good intentions – *intended to promote economic development through a continuous process of trade expansion among member countries of ASEAN without raising barriers to the trade of other contracting parties,*
> (2) the parties promised to be cooperative – *are prepared . . . to consider the possibility of participating in mutually beneficial trading arrangements with other developing countries,* and
> (3) were not really doing anything anti-GATT – *the Agreement should not constitute an impediment to the reduction or elimination of tariffs and other trade barriers on a most-favored-nation basis,*
> *the CONTRACTING PARTIES decide that:*
> *Notwithstanding the provisions of Article I of the General Agreement the participating contracting parties may implement the agreement in accordance with the conditions and procedures set out hereunder.*

The conditions were that the ASEAN parties continue to have good intentions – *any preferential treatment . . . be designed to facilitate trade between the participating States and not to raise barriers to the trade of other contracting parties* – that they notify the Contracting Parties of their policy actions, and they consult with any contracting party which considers that a benefit to it is being unduly impaired. As to procedures, the Contracting Parties would review (biennially), could recommend . . . .

In sum, no substantive limits were placed on what the ASEAN countries might agree.

5   Conclusions and policy applications

The bulk of GATT's stewardship over regional arrangements is made up of its experiences with the European Common Market and with regional arrangements among developing countries. Neither of these experiences have been supportive of a rule-based, multilateral system. GATT's reviews of developing countries' regional arrangements have been an important part of, in effect, amending GATT to remove all discipline against developing countries' trade restrictions.

The EEC is, arguably, as consistent as is practically possible with Article XXIV's requirements. If we ignore agriculture, the EEC has removed all restrictions (or will have, when 'Europe 92' is completed) on substantially all of internal trade. When the Common Market came into being, the major pressure to break GATT rules came not from the countries that formed the Common Market, but from the countries that were on the outside. Although Article XXIV instructs them to accept their implicit loss of access to the markets of the EEC member-states, they would not accept this loss, and pressed the EEC to make amends. Their sense of a right to the market access they had bargained for in previous GATT tariff conferences was stronger than their sense of obligation to obey the rule in Article XXIV that was in conflict with this instinct. (The GATT began, remember, as an exchange of market access – the ITO negotiations over the rules of commercial policy led to no agreement.)[11]

Responding to such pressures the EEC, at the Kennedy and Tokyo Rounds agreed to significant non-discriminatory reductions of its external tariff on industrial goods. But the EEC went on to take care of the market access concerns of its western European neighbours by negotiating a series of discriminatory arrangements with them; to carry over previous relationships between its member-states and their former colonies through another series of discriminatory arrangements.

Mercantilist respect for a market access bargain obviously weighed in. But systematic concern – concern to preserve the dimension of trade relations that turns these mercantilist bargains into a global system – seems not to have been there. Hudec (1972, p. 1362) after reviewing the discriminatory arrangements negotiated by the EEC, concluded

> The seeming collapse of the MFN rule is probably the single most important cause of the present day pessimism about the GATT substantive rules. It [this collapse] is also the largest obstacle to renegotiation [of GATT rules generally], for no other rules could have much impact if the EEC practice were generalized.

When the issue was EEC trade in agricultural products, GATT started to fight the right fight – for liberal, non-discriminatory policies. The United States, in particular, pressed for MFN bindings on the Community's variable levies. The fight, however, was lost: the weight of the precedent US agricultural policy had earlier set was no doubt important. In turn, the United States would enter into the game in the spirit of which the European countries were playing it for manufactured goods' trade –

asking for preferential assurances that its exports would be maintained. But this, too, came to little. The Community's common agricultural policy continues to be illiberal and destabilising of the GATT system: there have been more GATT disputes over EC agricultural policies than over any other issue (GATT, 1989).

GATT's record with regional arrangements is not, however, as bleak as the above paragraphs might suggest. In 1957, European unification was seen as 'the only means of restoring Europe to a position of power that will enable it to survive in freedom' (*New York Times*, March 26 1957, p. 32); thirty-five years later, we know that Europe has survived, in prosperity as well as in freedom. And it would be hard to argue other than that the rest of the world is better off because of the Community. Breaking a GATT rule in order to allow the rest of the world to press the EEC for a better bargain for outsiders seems a trivial matter.

Another positive note is that the experience of Japan and the Asian NICs has discredited the import-substitution model among developing countries. There is thus less likelihood that developing countries will want to organise regional arrangements that are inward-looking. Indeed, a significant part of Mexico's motivation to form an FTA with Canada and the United States is to solidify against domestic reaction its own unilateral turn toward openness.

As to lessons for policy, one obvious one is that the procedures Article XXIV outlines for GATT to review and influence regional arrangements as they are being implemented have proved difficult to use. This is not surprising: one of the arguments for regional arrangements is that it is often easier for a few countries than for many to reach agreement. The challenge is to preserve the rights of outside countries against the discriminatory effects of the newly created regional arrangement. One way to do this is to make explicit what the Swedish representative argued about the ECSC: that the foregoing by outside countries of their MFN rights constitutes a concession. Multilateral negotiations, like those that followed the formation of the EEC, might be the best vehicle for cashing in the value of that concession – the lower are trade restrictions, the less consequential is discrimination.

There are other ways to take into account the interests of outsiders, e.g., by removing barriers to their joining the arrangement – following the example of European countries acceding to the EEC, or the US–Canada free trade agreement being superseded by the North American Free-Trade Agreement (NAFTA).

It is easy to think of GATT rules that should be changed: Article VI discipline over anti-dumping (AD) actions and Article XIX discipline over voluntary export restraints (VERs) should be strengthened. It might also be useful, as Jagdish Bhagwati suggests (Chapter 2 in this volume), that countries negotiate CUs and abandon the use of FTAs. The objective, of course, is to change what governments do, not just what is written in the rule book. To the extent, however, that governments see their present practices as defending the market access they have contracted for, they are not likely to agree to such changes.

The international community has long debated if GATT usefulness stems from it being a set of substantive rules or from it being a forum for negotiation. Hudec (1972), arguing the 'substantive rules' side, provides an excellent statement of the debate. Using Hudec's language (his paper is titled 'GATT or GABB? The Future Design of the General Agreement on Tariffs and Trade'), I insist that GATT's influence on the EEC is a victory for GABB. Hudec might agree. In 1972 (p. 1377), he was concerned that 'in some areas, the conditions which permitted successful implementation of the original GATT design may have disappeared entirely. In many other areas, conditions are at best uncertain. It is quite possible, therefore, that GABB may turn out to be the only realistic answer in many parts of GATT's original domain'.

There is, however, an important and positive lesson in GATT's experiences with regional arrangements. The lesson is that the value of the market access that countries have bargained for is a powerful motivator for GATT's procedures. The instinct of countries, when the value of the market it has bargained for is compromised, is to bargain that value back again. Mercantilist self-interest, channelled through GATT's procedures for consultations, negotiations, peer reviews, etc. has proved to be an effective guard against the abuses of discrimination. The international community can thus take a relaxed attitude toward regional arrangements. Any arrangement that clearly removes trade restrictions deserves the benefit of the doubt. But countries that negotiate regional arrangements must be prepared to negotiate the discriminatory arrangements with their outside trading partners.

A second, perhaps more academic, finding is that it may not be useful to negotiate rules too far ahead of the problems they are intended to resolve. The international community's best minds put together the Article XXIV rules for regional arrangements, but when actual regional arrangements came along, these rules did not seem relevant. Jackson (1969, p. 588) states the matter diplomatically:

> [T]he basic problem of article XXIV [is] criteria that are so ambiguous or so unrelated to the goals and policies of GATT Contracting Parties that the international community was not prepared to make compliance with the technicalities of Article XXIV the *sine qua non* of eligibility for the exception from other GATT obligations.

This point, too, can be presented in an upbeat way. When push came to shove, GATT did not seem to help: but GABB did.

NOTES

I am grateful for assistance provided by Ms Nellie T. Artis and Ms Sumana Dhar; also for comments and suggestions from Robert E. Hudec, Jean Baneth, and the editors of this volume. I want to thank all of them for their help, without implicating them in any errors that may remain in the chapter.

1 The interpretation summarised here is presented in more detail in Finger (1991a).
2 Continuation of preferential arrangements in existence when the GATT were signed was provided for elsewhere in the agreement.
3 Article I, the article requiring each contracting party to extend MFN treatment to each other contracting party, accepted already existing preferential arrangements, but specified that margins of preference could not be increased.
4 Paragraph 10 provides for approved backsliding on the requirements. It reads 'The CONTRACTING PARTIES may by a two-thirds majority approve proposals which do not fully comply with the requirements . . . provided that such proposals lead to the formation of a customs union or a free-trade area in the sense of this Article'.
5 This discussion is based on Allen (1960, p. 3).
6 There may be some slight basis to argue against this interpretation. In 1952, Norway brought a GATT case against Germany, who had reduced its tariff on sardines imported from Portugal. By art of the German customs nomenclature, sardines imported from Norway were a different tariff category from sardines imported from Portugal, hence Germany's action did not violate its obligation to provide MFN treatment on Norwegian sardines. Nevertheless, a GATT panel found this to be an instance in which Norway's rights and privileges under the GATT had been 'nullified or impaired', even though Germany's action was not a GATT violation. In the end, Germany agreed to similar reductions on other categories of sardines. See Hudec (1972, nn. 97 and 193) for a discussion of the case. During the GATT Working Party review of the ECSC, the Swedish representative argued that the foregoing by countries outside the Community of their MFN right constituted a concession. The point failed to achieve majority approval by the Working Party, but the Working Party agreed that any country might take up the point through normal GATT dispute settlement procedures (GATT, 1953, p. 88). No country has tried to make the case, either against the ECSC or against the later Common Market.
7 Almost two-thirds of manufactured goods' imports by EEC countries come from other EEC member-states. Of the remaining one-third, about one-third comes from other western European countries who enjoy preferential access to the EEC market.
8 The previous arrangements between France and her former colonies were among the preferential arrangements specifically allowed under the annexes to Article I of the GATT.
9 Hudec (1987) provides an excellent depiction of how the import-substitution

view of development worked its way into the GATT legal system. Finger (1991b) contrasts the incorporation of this view into the GATT with the accumulation of evidence favouring the export-led growth model of trade and development.

10 One of the prominent 'vicious circles' of import-substitution theory was that developing countries could not export because their costs were too high, their costs were too high because they could not export and thereby collect the economies of scale that explained the lower costs of industries in the developed countries.

11 Elsewhere (Finger, 1991c), I have argued more generally that GATT rules that helped to implement an agreed trade liberalisation have proved more useful than rules that try to motivate or limit liberalisations.

REFERENCES

Allen, J.J. (1960) *The European Common Market and the GATT*, with a Preface by Heinrich Kronstein, Washington, DC: University Press of Washington.

Dam, K.W. (1963) 'Regional Economic Arrangements and the GATT: The Legacy of a Misconception', *The University of Chicago Law Review*, **30(4)** (Summer) pp. 615–65.

Finger, J.M. (1989) 'Protectionist Rules and Internationalist Discretion in the Making of National Trade Policy', in H.-J. Vosgerau (ed.), *New Institutional Arrangements for the World Economy*, Berlin and Heidelberg, Springer-Verlag, pp. 310–23.

(1991a) 'The GATT as an International Discipline over Trade Restrictions: A Public Choice Perspective' in R. Vaubel and T.D. Willett (eds), *The Political Economy of International Organizations*, Boulder, Col.: Westview Press, pp. 125–41.

(1991b) 'Development Economics and the General Agreement on Tariffs and Trade', in J. de Melo and A. Sapir (eds), *Trade Theory and Economic Reform: North South, and East*, London: Basil Blackwell, pp. 203–33.

(1991c) 'That Old GATT Magic No More Casts Its Spell (How the Uruguay Round Failed)', *Journal of World Trade*, **25(2)** (April) pp. 19–22.

Finger, J.M. and T. Murray (1990) 'Policing Unfair Imports: The United States Example', *Journal of World Trade*, **24(4)** (August) pp. 39–53.

General Agreement on Tariffs and Trade (GATT) (1953) *Basic Instruments and Selected Documents*, 1st Supplement, Geneva: GATT.

(1959) *Basic Instruments and Selected Documents*, 7th Supplement, Geneva: GATT.

(1961) *Basic Instruments and Selected Documents*, 9th Supplement, Geneva: GATT.

(1966) *Basic Instruments and Selected Documents*, 14th Supplement, Geneva: GATT.

(1978) *Basic Instruments and Selected Documents*, 26th Supplement, Geneva: GATT.

(1989) 'GATT Dispute Settlement: Note by the Secretariat', GATT doc. no. MTN.GNG/NG13//W/4/Rev.1, Geneva: GATT.

Hudec, R.E. (1972) 'GATT or GABB? The Future Design of the General Agreement on Tariffs and Trade', *The Yale Law Journal*, **80(7)** (June) pp. 1299–1386.

(1975) *The GATT Legal System and World Trade Diplomacy*, New York: Praeger.

(1987) *Developing Countries in the GATT Legal System*, London: Gower, for the Trade Policy Research Center.

Jackson, J.H. (1969) *World Trade and the Law of GATT*, Charlottesville, Va.: The Michie Co.

(1989) *The World Trading System: Law and Policy of International Economic Relations*, Cambridge, Mass. and London: MIT Press.

Office of the US Trade Representative (1991) 'Section 301 Table of Cases', Washington, DC: Office of the US Trade Representative (August 15 1991) (mimeo).

Patterson, G. (1966) *Discrimination in International Trade: the Policy Issues 1945-1965*, Princeton: Princeton University Press.

Schott, J.J. (ed.) (1989) *Free Trade Areas and U.S. Trade Policy*, Washington, DC: Institute for International Economies.

Tumlir, J. (1985) *Protectionism: Trade Policy in Democratic Societies*, Washington, DC: American Enterprise Institute.

United Nations (1946a) United Nations Economic and Social Council, Preparatory Committee of the International Conference on Trade and Employment, 'Summary Record of Meetings Held on 26 October 1946', Doc. No. E/PC/T/C.II/7, 26 October 1946.

(1946b) United Nations Economic and Social Council, Preparatory Committee of the International Conference on Trade and Employment, 'Summary Record of Meetings Held on 2 November 1946', Doc. No. E/PC/T/C.II/38, 2 November 1946.

Viner, J. (1950) *The Customs Union Issue*, New York: Carnegie Endowment for International Peace.

Wolf, M. (1988) 'An Unholy Alliance: The European Community and Developing Countries in the International Trading System', in L.B.M. Mennes and J. Kol (eds), *European Trade Policies and the Developing World*, London, New York, Sydney: Croom Helm, pp. 31–57.

Discussion

JEAN BANETH

In this Discussion, I shall not contradict anything Finger says in his Chapter 5; I will rather try to build on it and make a few complementary remarks.

Of the numerous regional or, as I prefer to call them, limited-membership, trade agreements concluded since World War II, the European Community alone fully met the formal requirements of GATT Article XXIV; yet none of the others were held up by GATT. These other agreements fall into the following categories:

- The quasi-Community agreements: these bind to each other and to the EC members of the European Free Trade Area (EFTA). These countries generally trade more with the Community than with each other, have effectively eliminated their merchandise trade barriers towards the Community and towards each other in everything but agriculture, and are relatively free traders toward the rest of the world.

- The peri-Community agreements between the Community and developing countries of the (Asia, Pacific and Caribbean) ACP group, of the Mediterranean, and more recently of East Europe. These give free or almost free access to EC markets for non-agricultural goods, and varying degrees of preferential access for agricultural goods. These preferences are applied *de facto* unilaterally for the ACP group, and with various degrees of asymmetry for the others.

- Finally, from the Montevideo Treaty through ASEAN, a host of preferential trading arrangements among developing countries where neither trade nor preferences usually amount to much.

Finger waxes slightly indignant that GATT has never done anything to stop these arrangements. I wish to point to another aspect of GATT's role.

GATT is a treaty and an enforcement mechanism, and Finger is right in that most preferential trade agreements constituted breaches to the treaty, yet remained un-sanctioned: GATT did not enforce the treaty. But GATT is also a negotiating forum, and as such it played its role well. The creation and reinforcement of the Community greatly, and perhaps decisively, contributed to a US desire to reduce trade barriers multilaterally, in the Dillon and Kennedy Rounds. Similarly, when the Community 6 grew to 9, and partially merged with EFTA in a Europe-wide free trade area, major new multilateral trade-barrier reductions occurred in the Tokyo Round. When the Community moved to deepen itself to services trade, services were taken up in the multilateral Uruguay Round, which might still bring results. All these multilateral advances occurred in the GATT, and through the use of its negotiating mechanisms.

The Community was the impulse. Beyond economic reasons, strong political forces had to be brought to bear within its members countries to overcome protectionist resistances to lowering trade barriers. It is symptomatic that in France, which initiated the Coal and Steel Community (ECSC) and, with it, the Common Market process, all economic pressure groups (both business federations and labour unions) were strenuously opposed to it. It is the political wish to build a European federation which would bind Germany to the rest of Europe that overcame this economic resistance. The United States supported the Community at first, for political reasons, though somewhat ambiguously. Yet it rightly wanted to ensure, through multilateral negotiations, that it would not be excluded from Europe. Hence the multilateral trade rounds for which GATT provided an admirable forum and mechanism.

Concerning the second wave of regional agreements signalled by Jagdish Bhagwati in his Chapter 2 above, the wave of the 1990s, the earlier experience provides both an encouragement and a warning. The momentum of regional trade groups and their internal trade liberalisation should constitute strong encouragement for others to seek multilateral trade liberalisation; it thus increases the chances of an ultimate breakthrough in the Uruguay Round. However, if that breakthrough does not come, then the beneficial impacts of past limited-membership trade arrangements will not be replicated.

Other potentially negative factors also appear. The exports of some of the beneficiaries of preferential treatment from the Community, once negligible, have grown; hence their potentially trade-displacing impact has also increased, unless it is offset by renewed multilateral trade liberalisation. The same remark goes with even greater strength for some potential or actual new claimants for entry into preferential systems, Mexico, East Europe, West Asia . . .

In truth the danger of trade diversion (at least for merchandise trade) comes from the possibility that, in order to protect domestic industries or help preferential exporters, or both, selective obstacles might be erected against the non-preferential exporters: say, for instance, that various new 'voluntary' export restraints (VERs) or other non-tariff measures might be opposed to the exports of Hong Kong, or even of India, in order to give enlarged access to Algeria, East Europe or Mexico.

So back to GATT. If multilateral liberalisation proceeds, in particular if the rule of law is tightened to restrict the arbitrary use of non-tariff measures, regional agreements can continue to play a constructive role. If not, the pursuit of regional agreements may well enhance the destructive forces threatening the multilateral trading system.

ROBERT E. HUDEC

Finger's Chapter 5 raises two main issues: (1) To what extent do GATT rules impose the 'right' kind of requirements on regional arrangements? (2) To what extent has GATT succeeded in enforcing its rules pertaining to regional arrangements?

I agree with Finger's general assessment of both issues, and my comments are essentially extensions of these conclusions. To avoid becoming bogged down in arguments about the substance of GATT rules, I shall begin by dealing with the second of these two issues, the issue of enforcement.

1   Enforcement of GATT rules

Finger's Chapter 5 points out that, in all the many review proceedings GATT has conducted to evaluate the GATT consistency of regional arrangements (RAs), GATT has never ruled against a proposed RA, nor has it ever succeeded in requiring any changes in the terms of such proposed agreements. Finger explains the main reasons for this lack of visible effect. For RAs between developing countries, and those between developed and developing countries, the rules of GATT Article XXIV were simply overpowered by a stronger principle – the officially accepted principle known as 'special and differential treatment' which posited, *inter alia*, that discrimination in favour of developing countries was beneficial to their economic development. The power of the latter principle eventually resulted in a *de facto* amendment of GATT in 1979, the adoption of the so-called Enabling Clause granting permanent authority to engage in *ad hoc* discrimination on behalf of developing countries. For RAs between developed countries (EC, EFTA, EC–EFTA and CUSTA, see Chapter 11 in this volume), the lack of visible effect can be ascribed to the fact that these agreements were simply too important to the economic and political life of the member countries to be challenged by GATT once they had been negotiated.

While this is an accurate rendition and explanation of the GATT's record in formal review of RAs, there is a bit more to the story. The enforcement of GATT rules can take place in two settings. One is the formal GATT setting I have been talking about, where national measures are examined by GATT after they have been adopted. This is the enforcement setting we usually look at when examining GATT enforcement, for it is where all the records and documents are generated. The other setting is the process of national decisionmaking – the process that takes place prior to the actual adoption of a measure. Although GATT itself never intervenes at this stage, GATT rules often do exert a major influence on shaping the measure. We all know of instances where GATT rules have been effective at this earlier stage, even if we have few records or documents to prove it.

This earlier stage in the process is particularly important when it comes to RAs. GATT's ability to regulate once governments have decided upon taking a particular measure is tenuous to begin with, because government decisions usually require extensive bargaining that is difficult to reopen. This is especially so when an agreement has already been ratified by legislation in each of the member countries. Reopening the process of decision on such agreements is all but impossible, and it is no surprise that GATT has had such a poor record in regulating RAs after the fact.

Almost by necessity, therefore, GATT influence over the content of RAs must be exercised, if at all, during the earlier stages of decision, when governments are still negotiating the terms of the agreement. GATT has had a limited degree of success in this earlier phase of the process. The success has been confined to the RAs between developed countries – EC, EFTA, EC–EFTA and CUSTA. There is plenty of anecdotal evidence testifying that the diplomats negotiating each of these agreements were operating under instructions to make maximum efforts to comply with GATT rules, and the actual results of these negotiations testify that a quite important degree of GATT compliance was achieved. Except for agriculture, which was excluded from three of these RAs and made worse in the fourth, and except for the EC's relationship with former colonies, the four developed country agreements delivered to GATT were essentially GATT-conforming. To be sure, GATT was unable to do anything further once the agreements were signed and deposited in Geneva for review. The main accomplishment of GATT's after-the-fact review proceedings was merely to create an unpleasant and embarrassing sort of spectacle over allegations of non-compliance, the value of which was mainly to provide government negotiators in the next case with a demonstration of the bad consequences that might follow if GATT rules were not complied with.

For RAs involving developing countries, of course, GATT rules did not have much effect in the national decisionmaking process. The developing country governments involved were generally committed to import-substitution policies, and were interested in RAs only as a way of securing larger protected markets. And far from discouraging this perspective, the

GATT actually reinforced the import-substitution strategy with its endorsement of 'special and differential treatment' for developing countries.

The lesson to be drawn from this enlarged focus is that the place to look when trying to assess the influence of GATT rules in this area is in the internal decisionmaking process that takes place during the negotiation of the agreement. Moreover, the best way to encourage greater adherence to GATT rules is to try to maximise the impact of those rules during this period. GATT traditions prevent conducting a formal GATT review during this pre-agreement stage; GATT never examines measures before they are adopted. But some thought can be given less formal kinds of multilateral surveillance during this earlier period – beginning with greater transparency, and then trying to devise ways of discussing the content of such agreements as it evolves.

With regard to the apparent new round of RAs currently being discussed, it is likely that GATT rules will exert a greater influence over the negotiation of developing country RAs than it has done to date. The underlying policies – both GATT and national – appear to have changed. Although bad ideas like 'special and differential treatment' have a tendency to live on and on, particularly inside international organisations, and although GATT's genuflections toward that particular doctrine are as numerous as ever, there has been a considerable diminution in GATT's commitment to those bad ideas during the last decade. Consequently, GATT is not sending the same wrong message to developing country negotiators this time around – or at least not with the same conviction and unanimity. More important, as several chapters in this volume have already pointed out, many of the developing countries responsible for the current wave of RA negotiations are often hoping to use RA negotiations to 'lock in' recently adopted liberal trade policies – an objective that will be served by the greatest possible compliance with Article XXIV. Thus, this time around we may well see a strong pressure for compliance with Article XXIV from the member developing countries themselves.

2   The substance of the GATT rules

In order to appreciate the full range of policies underlying the rules of GATT Article XXIV, it is useful to make a brief detour to examine the GATT's general policy against discrimination. The important point to be grasped is that, despite the large body of trade-policy writing condemning discrimination in international trade, and despite the large body of GATT propaganda claiming that the MFN obligation is one of the key 'pillars' or 'cornerstones' of the GATT agreement, the actual policy followed by

GATT itself since 1947 has taken a rather open-minded view toward discrimination. GATT has allowed governments to retain colonial preferences, it has allowed them to use discriminatory quantitative restrictions (QRs) for balance of payments reasons, it has accepted a regime of discriminatory QRs for dealing with textiles and, finally, it has accepted a variety of discriminatory trade preferences benefiting developing countries. The GATT's somewhat benign attitude toward RAs is merely one part of this larger tolerance toward departures from MFN in general.

The basis of GATT's rather tolerant attitude, oddly enough, is the success of its multilateral structure. At the risk of oversimplifying, it can be said that the traditional view of MFN as an essential ingredient of a liberal trade regime is a legacy of the world of bilateral trade relations that existed from 1860 to 1939, described so well in Douglas Irwin's Chapter 4 in this volume. When trade relations are entirely bilateral, one's trading partners will always have a network of their own bilateral relations with the rest of the world, and thus will constantly be engaged in entirely separate negotiations with other countries – negotiations that can undermine the commercial value of one's own existing agreements with them. That is exactly what happened during the 1930s, when the world got caught in a continually expanding series of preferential bilateral deals. When bilateralism reigns, the only way to avert such breakdowns is to have a rigorous MFN guarantee covering the entire interlocking network of bilateral trade relationships.

The GATT created a different world. It was a world of multilateral trade relationships, where everyone dealt with everyone else at the same time, and all agreements were locked into a set of permanent rules applicable to all. In this setting, it was possible to make discrimination less destructive. The key was to define the extent of discrimination in advance, and to impose reliable controls against sudden change. To the extent that can be done, discrimination becomes essentially just another form of protection, no more dangerous than a high tariff. The key is to establish multilateral controls that remove – or at least limit – its unpredictability.

The point here is not that GATT has made discrimination something good and desirable. Discrimination is still a trade distortion, and GATT's first priority is still to have no discrimination at all. But GATT has frequently been able to rid discrimination of its most destructive qualities by making it predictable. By doing so, it has probably encouraged more discrimination that would have been tolerable in prewar times.

The rules of GATT Article XXIV pertaining to RAs should be viewed in the context of this overall policy toward discrimination. As Finger's chapter points out, the 'all-or-nothing' requirement in Article XXIV does have an initial effect of producing a no-discrimination outcome for many would-be RAs in which the member countries lack the necessary commitment to go all the way. What I am trying to add to this point is an appreciation of a second dimension to these rules – namely, their effect on predictability. Consider: an RA that meets GATT's rules will have gone to zero restrictions on substantially all trade between members, it will have done so within a reasonable time (no more than ten years, according to the new Uruguay Round gloss on that text), and at the same time it will have been prevented from raising the level of external barriers toward third countries. Once a plan with these elements is actually laid down, there really isn't much more discrimination that can happen. There is simply nowhere to go. That may be a second-best outcome compared to having no discrimination at all, but it is an outcome that makes an important difference. It is an outcome that is considerably less distortive and disruptive than an RA consisting of selective partial preferences that can expand or deepen every year.

A final word is needed on the alternative RA structure just mentioned – RAs consisting of selective partial preferences on just certain products traded between members. Such a structure has been recommended by some critics of the present GATT rules. The critics charge that the present all-or-nothing rules are economically unsound, because they necessarily require trade-diverting preferences as well as trade-creating ones. A better GATT rule, the critics argue, would be a rule limiting RAs to only those preferences that are trade-creating.

In my view there are several arguments against this proposed alternative. First, even supposing such a limitation could be applied and enforced, it would lack predictability, because the 'trade-creating' and 'trade-diverting' categories would constantly change as market forces change. Second, and more important, there are two reasons for believing that such a rule could never be enforced as a practical matter. To begin with, the actual identification of trade-creating preferences is still a pretty conjectural analytic process, and thus is both difficult to do right and even more difficult to supervise with authority. In addition, once governments are allowed to select some products and not others, political forces will inevitably exert enormous pressure to choose trade-diverting preferences first. Trade-diverting preferences are the ones that result in the greatest net political gain for governments; the political gains arise from pleasing local producers who displace third-country producers, while political losses are entirely avoided because third-country producers do not vote.

In sum, while it is possible to think of rules that are theoretically superior to the present GATT rules, as a practical matter the present all-or-nothing rules are in fact quite well directed to the main problems that RAs present.

Part Two

COUNTRY ISSUES

6 The new regionalism: a country perspective

JAIME DE MELO, ARVIND PANAGARIYA
and DANI RODRIK

1 Introduction

Three decades ago, under the impetus of European arrangements, the developing world launched the first wave of regional integration (RI). Free-trade areas (FTAs) and customs unions (CUs) mushroomed in Latin America and Africa. Unfortunately, expectations of economic development through RI were not realised, and two decades later virtually all regional arrangements among developing countries were judged as failures.

By the early 1980s, multilateral tariff cutting by developed countries and unilateral trade liberalisation (UTL) by developing countries had substantially weakened the case for regional arrangements. Yet, paradoxically, it is then that a second round of regionalism got under way. More arrangements (eight) were signed during the 1980s than during the 1960s, and still more (half a dozen or so) are under consideration. The GATT process is running out of steam and many countries are turning back to the bilateral alternative.

From the viewpoint of developing countries, the current regionalism differs from the regionalism of the 1960s in two important respects. First, the regionalism of the 1960s represented an extension of the import-substitution–industrialisation strategy from the national to the regional level and was therefore inward-looking. The current regionalism is by contrast taking place in an environment of outward-oriented policies. Second, in the 1960s, developing countries pursued RI exclusively with other developing countries. Today these countries, especially those in Latin America, have their eyes on integration with large, developed countries.

In this chapter, we review and extend the theory of RI and evaluate empirically its contribution to growth. Our objective is to assess the benefits of RI from the viewpoint of participating countries rather than the world as a whole. In particular, we do not focus on the systemic implications of RI emphasised in Chapters 2–5. A central issue we address is whether the regional approach can accomplish objectives that cannot be accomplished via UTL. We also study the role of economic institutions in the process of regional integration. In analysing these issues, we draw a sharp distinction between the nature of RI today and that in the 1960s.

In section 2, we introduce the conventional welfare economics of RI via freer trade among partner countries. We conclude the section by alluding to the motivations behind current integration efforts which go far beyond trade integration. This theme is developed in greater detail in section 3, where it is formally recognised that integration enforces a certain degree of arbitrage among national institutions. In section 4, we provide an empirical evaluation of past integration schemes. Finally, in section 5, we turn to forward-looking lessons for the 'new' approaches to regionalism.

2   Welfare economics of FTAs

To avoid confusion, we begin by defining the terms 'preferential trading arrangement' (PTA), 'free-trade area' (FTA), 'customs union' (CU), and 'unilateral trade liberalisation' (UTL) precisely. A PTA refers to an arrangement under which partner countries impose lower tariffs on imports from each other than on imports from the outside world. An FTA involves zero tariffs on trade among partner countries but a positive tariff on imports from outside countries. Both PTAs and FTAs allow for different tariffs by partner countries on imports of similar goods from the outside world.[1] A CU is an FTA with a common external tariff (CET) by partner countries. Finally, UTL is defined as a non-discriminatory reduction in trade barriers.

The literature on RI is full of the 'anything may happen' type of results. What we present below is what we regard as helpful insights from the literature.[2] Unless otherwise noted, we assume throughout that the partner countries are small relative to the rest of the world.

In section 2.1, we present the basic Vinerian (1950) analysis and derive conditions under which an FTA is likely to be welfare-improving. In section 2.2, we consider the Kemp–Wan (1976) problem of designing a welfare-improving FTA and apply it to the analysis of FTAs in the presence of quotas. In section 2.3, we address the problem of compensation among union members. In sections 2.4–2.6, we compare FTAs successively to UTL, PTAs and CUs. In comparing FTAs to UTL, we discuss, *inter alia*, the roles of the import-substitution objective, tariff-revenue constraint and economies of scale. In comparing FTAs to PTAs, we show that when chosen correctly the latter are superior, and then proceed to explain why the GATT approach of forbidding PTAs is, nevertheless, sensible. In comparing FTAs to CUs, we pay attention to the rules of origin issue and political economy implications of the two regimes. In section 2.7, we relax the 'small union' assumption and analyse the strategic advantages of an FTA. In section 2.8, we assess explicitly the relevance of RI between developing and developed countries. Finally, in section 2.9, we summarise the main conclusions which follow from the review.

2.1 The basic economics of FTAs

Can an FTA be welfare-improving? Yes, but not always. This is the central point made by Viner in Chapter 4 of his classic work, *The Customs Unions Issue* (1950). Viner introduced the key concepts of trade creation and trade diversion, and concluded that a trade-creating CU is welfare-improving while a trade-diverting CU is welfare-worsening.[3]

In the following, we introduce the conventional analysis of an FTA formally with the help of a two-goods, three-country model. The goods are denoted 1 and 2 and countries A, B and C. A and B are potential partners in an FTA and C represents the outside world. In this setting, there are two possible trade patterns: A and B import the same good or they import different goods.

In the case when A and B import the same good, they will import it from C and there will be no trade between them in the initial equilibrium. Moreover, if the formation of an FTA leaves the tariff on C unchanged, the initial equilibrium will continue to obtain: the FTA will be vacuous. This situation may well describe the reality of some RI schemes in developing countries, particularly Africa. In many of these schemes, the partner countries had very similar patterns of trade and integration attempts had a very limited impact on trade patterns (see Foroutan, 1992, Chapter 8 in this volume).

In the more substantive case when the partner countries import different goods, assume that country A imports good 1 and country B exports it. For now, we concentrate on tariffs levied by country A only. Later we introduce explicitly tariffs in both B and C. In Figure 6.1, $M_1^A M_1^A$ and $E_1^B E_1^B$ are the general equilibrium import demand curve of A and export supply curve of B, respectively. The horizontal line $P^C P^C$ is the relative price at which C is willing to buy and sell good 1 in the world market.

Autarky prices in A and B are given by the respective heights of their curves at their points of origin. Under free trade, the gains from trade are represented by the area under the import demand curve and above the world price for A, and that above the export supply curve and below the

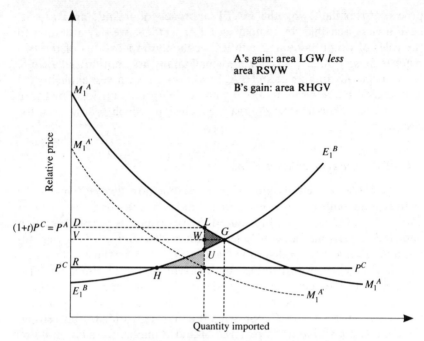

Figure 6.1   Basic analysis of an FTA

world price for B. Given constant costs and free trade in C, it neither gains nor loses from trade.

Assume that initially A levies a non-discriminatory tariff at rate t on imports from B and C. A's import demand curve *as perceived by B and C* is now given by $M_1^{A'} M_1^{A'}$ where the latter lies below $M_1^A M_1^A$ by the amount of tariff per unit. The border price facing A is P^C and total imports are RS (= DL). Of these, RH comes from B and HS from C. Domestic price in A is given by P^A which is the height of the import demand curve as perceived by A's residents. The gains from trade in A are given by area $M_1^A LD$ plus tariff revenue $DRSL$ and those in B by area RHE_1^B.

Now introduce an FTA between A and B. Imports from B are no longer subject to a tariff. As drawn, there is a 'sudden death' of imports from C with all imports 'diverted' to B. The union benefits B both because its terms of trade improve and because its exports expand. The country's net gain equals area $RHGV$. The effect on A is ambiguous in general because, on the one hand, A's terms of trade deteriorate (or equivalently it loses all tariff revenue) while, on the other, the distortion between the domestic and (new) border price is eliminated. The country gains or loses as area

LGW is larger or smaller than the rectangle *RSWV*. As drawn, the country loses. The effect on joint welfare of *A* and *B* is also ambiguous. They benefit jointly if area *LGU* is larger than the vertically shaded area, *HSU* but lose otherwise. As drawn, the union as a whole loses from the FTA.[4] That is to say, *B*'s gains exceed the losses of *A* and it can compensate the latter.[5]

Figure 6.1 has been drawn in such a way that an FTA between *A* and *B* eliminates the imports from *C* entirely. This is done to highlight the point that an FTA will generally generate both positive and negative effects and that the effect on the union's welfare is likely to be ambiguous.[6] If we draw *B*'s export supply curve so that it crosses *A*'s solid curve to the left of point *L*, the FTA does not eliminate imports from *C*. In this case, the internal price facing *A* is unchanged while its terms of trade with *B* deteriorate by the full amount of the tariff. *B*'s share in imports rises but total imports remain unchanged. *A*'s welfare declines because its terms of trade with *B* worsen without any improvement in efficiency; *B*'s welfare rises because its terms of trade improve and exports expand; and the union's welfare declines because over some range imports coming from *B* cost more than *C*'s price and there is no gain in efficiency in *A*.

What factors make the gains from an FTA larger or the losses smaller? If we are willing to restrict ourselves to the case depicted in Figure 6.1 where both positive and negative effects are present, a number of points can be made.[7] First, the higher the initial tariff in a given sector, the larger the favourable effect (area *LUG*) and smaller the unfavourable effect (area *USH*) of the FTA. Second, the lower the post-FTA tariff on extra-union countries the less likely that the lower-priced goods of the latter will be displaced. Third, the higher the tariffs in the outside world on the partner, the larger will be the gain or the smaller the loss. In terms of Figure 6.1, the higher the tariff in *C*, the higher will be P^C facing *A* and *B* and the smaller will be the area *HSU*. Fourth, the greater the complementarity in import demands of *A* and *B*, the larger the gains from FTA. In terms of Figure 6.1, the farther apart are the import demand and export supply curves of *A* and *B*, the larger will be the gains (area *LGW*) and the smaller the losses (area *HSU*).

On this last issue, it is worth noting that at low levels of income, complementarity is more likely to arise between countries that are different in terms of factor endowments and perhaps, therefore, countries with different *per capita* incomes. As we will discuss in section 2.3, this is precisely the condition under which the compensation issue is critical and implementation difficulties most serious. Complementarities among high-income countries are more likely to arise among countries with similar *per capita* incomes. This is because the bulk of high-income countries' trade is

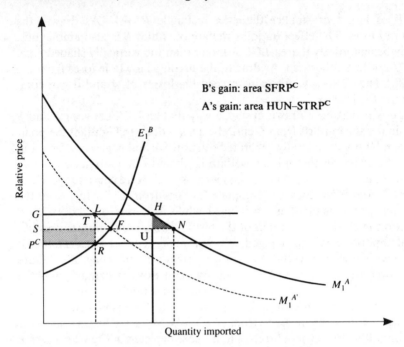

Figure 6.2   An FTA under a QR

of an intra-industry nature which correlates negatively with differences in *per capita* incomes of partner countries.

2.2   Designing a welfare-improving FTA in the presence of QRs

Can a welfare improving FTA always be designed? Yes. This is the essence of the Kemp and Wan (1976) analysis. These authors demonstrate that under very standard assumptions, A and B can adopt a set of CETs which improve their welfare without hurting the outside world. The essential idea is that the common set of tariffs may be chosen in such a way that the external terms of trade and hence the quantities traded with the outside world are unchanged while internal trade is rearranged to maximise the gains from it.

The Kemp–Wan result has important implications for the analysis of FTAs in the presence of quantitative restrictions (QRs). These implications have not been explored in the literature so far and will be considered here briefly. In Figure 6.2, we look at the two-good model. Suppose that initially A restricts its total imports to GH by a global quota.

Assuming that quota licences are auctioned competitively to domestic residents, quantity GL will be imported from B and LH from C. If we now introduce an FTA such that C is subject to a quota at its original level of imports (LH) while imports from B are freed of any restrictions, total imports will expand. Subtracting quantity LH horizontally from $M_1^A M_1^A$ everywhere, we obtain $M_1^{A'} M_1^{A'}$ as the demand curve facing B. This yields SF quantity of imports from B and FN ($= LH$) from C. Once again, as in Figure 6.1, we have a positive effect (HUN) on A due to a reduced gap between the domestic and border prices and a negative effect ($STRP^C$) due to a deterioration in the terms of trade with B. The net welfare effect on A is ambiguous in principle, although as drawn it loses.

Country B necessarily gains in this case. This gain, represented by area $SFRP^C$, is larger than the loss of country A. Therefore, B can compensate A, should it lose from the FTA on balance. The FTA leads to unambiguous benefits for the union as a whole. In the spirit of the Kemp–Wan result, the FTA has not reduced trade with the outside world and has expanded trade between the partners. The outside world's welfare is unaffected so that the FTA improves the world's welfare as well.

2.3   The compensation issue

In the preceding subsections, we have considered RI from the viewpoint of the union as a whole. We implicitly relied on lump sum redistributions between partners to ensure that neither partner loses. In practice, compensation mechanisms are difficult to implement, particularly in developing countries. Because a detailed discussion of the issue is contained in Chapter 8, we confine ourselves here to brief remarks.

Partner countries in integration schemes in developing countries often have very diverse levels of *per capita* incomes. If integration leads to a migration of industries from the poor to the relatively more advanced economies, compensation is essential. In some cases, special funds are created to help the industrial development of the poorest members. The criteria for contributions to and disbursements from these funds often become contentious, leading to very complicated formulas that generally defy economic logic.

In the case of CEAO and UDEAC in Africa (see Chapter 8 below), unions have provided for preferential duties on industrial products based on the protection needs of the poorest of the members. This has resulted in different tariff rates for the import of the same product, depending on the source: the duty is lower on imports coming from the least developed members and higher on others.

2.4   FTA versus UTL

We now consider what is perhaps the strongest criticism of the regional approach from the viewpoint of small economies: an FTA is usually dominated by UTL.

To begin with, observe that in Figure 6.1 country A's welfare is maximised by liberalising its trade unilaterally. That is to say, the FTA with B is welfare-inferior to unilateral free trade. Moreover, the same conditions which make the FTA desirable (e.g., a high initial tariff) make UTL even more desirable. There is thus nothing which B can offer A that the latter cannot get on its own. Why, then, should A bother to enter a bilateral arrangement with B?[8]

A number of complications must be introduced to answer this question. Before we do so, however, it is useful to introduce a dramatic example. Suppose the developed and newly industrialised countries (NICs) are divided into three blocs: north America, western Europe and east Asia. Also suppose that each one of these blocs allows free internal trade but imposes high duties or voluntary export restraints (VERs) on extra-bloc imports. Under these circumstances, will developing countries in Africa, Asia and Latin America benefit more from UTL or from joining one of the blocs? Common sense dictates that the latter option is likely to be welfare-superior even though it involves adopting and maintaining the bloc's barriers to trade with extra-bloc countries. In subsections 2.4.1 and 2.4.2, we develop the argument underlying this example.

2.4.1 Partner-country tariffs   A natural starting point is the introduction of tariffs in B.[9] Figure 6.1 assumes that B is a free trader even before the FTA is formed. This means that B has nothing to offer A as a part of the FTA agreement. In practice, B will have tariffs initially and an FTA will buy A a tariff-free access to B's markets. In terms of Figure 6.1, the deterioration in A's terms of trade which accompanied the FTA need not take place. Indeed, B may end up offering it better terms of trade than C, making the FTA a better option than UTL. It turns out, however, that this cannot happen unless B chooses a suboptimal option for itself.

In Figure 6.3, solid curves show A's general equilibrium demand for imports of good 1 and B's general equilibrium supply of exports of the same good under free trade. The horizontal line gives C's supply price which A and B are too small to influence. Both A and B impose tariffs in the initial equilibrium. The tariff in A causes its import demand *as perceived by B and C* to shift down to the dashed curve. The tariff in B causes its supply of export curve as perceived by A and C to shift up as

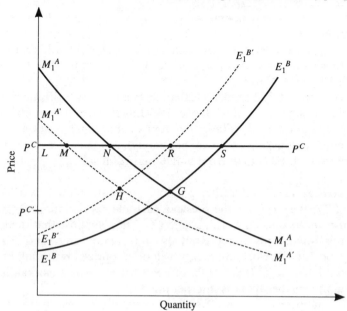

Figure 6.3   FTAs versus UTLs

shown by the upward-sloped dashed curve.[10] In the presence of non-discriminatory tariffs, A and B trade along dashed curves at the price offered by C. A imports ML and B exports RL. It is not necessary for A and B to trade but if they do, B exports up to ML to A and MR to C. Domestic prices in the two countries are given by their respective solid curves. For each country, the gains from trade are measured by the area enclosed by the world price, quantity traded, and its solid curve.

If A now liberalises unilaterally, its imports will rise to LN and its welfare will improve. The critical question is: can A do better by forming an FTA with B? Suppose A and B eliminate tariffs between themselves and impose prohibitive tariffs on C. This will yield G as the equilibrium with A benefiting more than from UTL.

Does this suggest that the FTA in the present case is superior to unilateral free trade? The answer is in the negative. For we have not said anything yet about B's welfare. As is easy to see from Figure 6.3, compared to point G, country B can improve its welfare by liberalising unilaterally and moving to point S. The FTA can be superior only if A can compensate B to ensure the latter the income level at S and still come out ahead relative to unilateral liberalisation. This is impossible, however, since the amount by which A's income at G exceeds its income at N is less than the required compensation by area NGS. Looked at differently, combined gains from trade of A and B under UTL are larger than those under an FTA by area NGS.

The conclusion from this discussion is that partner country tariffs do not negate the overall superiority of UTL over RI. Only if one of the countries – country B in Figure 6.3 – is willing to accept a suboptimal position for some exogenous reasons (e.g., political hegemony), can the other country benefit more from an FTA than from unilateral liberalisation.

2.4.2 Third-country tariffs   Another possible explanation for a preference for an FTA over UTL is the presence of trade restrictions and/or transport costs in the outside world, country C. Thus, suppose that there are tariffs initially in not just A and B but also in C. This means that if C is a buyer of good 1 in the world market, it will offer a price lower than its internal price. Similarly, if C is a seller of good 1 in the world market, it will charge a price higher than its internal price.

In Figure 6.3, suppose now that C's selling price is P^C, its buying price is $P^{C'}$, and its internal price is somewhere in the middle. This means that B no longer has the option of trading at R. Indeed, the terms offered to it by C, $P^{C'}$, are worse than those offered by A. Likewise for A, the terms of trade offered by B are better than those offered by C. The two countries will trade with each other at H. Now if A and B eliminate tariffs on each other, they can trade at G and both do better than if only one of them was to liberalise trade unilaterally. The FTA turns out to be superior to UTL.[11]

An important point to note is that in this example there is no difference between an FTA and complete free trade by A and B. High tariffs in C make that country irrelevant for optimal trade policies in A and B. In order to reach G, A and B do not need any external tariffs. In this sense, the only role of an FTA is to solve the Prisoners' Dilemma for the two countries and bring them to the negotiating table.

A useful application of the example provided in this subsection is that if the world gets divided into inward-looking blocs, UTL will become a less attractive option for the countries outside the bloc than it is today. The countries will then be better off either seeking access to one of the blocs and adopting its trade policy or engaging in RI so as to promote freer trade among themselves.[12] Of course, the current world being quite far from consisting of closed blocs, the example does not justify a preference for RI over UTL.

2.4.3 The import-substitution objective   The most common justification for pursuing RI instead of UTL comes in the form of an implicit or explicit non-economic objective. In the early development literature, industrialisation via import substitution was considered an eminently respectable objective. This, either on grounds of infant industry, 'training ground argument' or other reasons, meant that the option of unilateral free trade was simply not available. Under such circumstances, an FTA which, in the spirit of Kemp and Wan, keeps the imports of industrial goods from country *C* fixed and exploits the gains from specialisation between partner countries is beneficial.[13]

During the 1960s, the import-substitution objective played a key role in the proliferation of RI schemes in the developing world. But the gains from specialisation expected of various schemes were not realised, for reasons we need not go into here. Suffice it to note that today the policy environment has changed dramatically and import substitution as a policy objective has fallen out of favour with policymakers, except perhaps in the early stages of development. This means that an FTA as an alternative to UTL is harder to defend on grounds of import substitution.

2.4.4 The tariff-revenue constraint   Another objective which may preclude free trade as a viable option is the tariff-revenue constraint. In many developing countries, domestic tax machinery is limited and they must rely on trade taxes as the major source of revenue. In this situation, the option of UTL is simply not available, and we can ask whether RI may be a superior option than non-discriminatory tariffs.

For concreteness, assume that *A* and *B* choose their initial revenue-constrained tariffs optimally. With some qualifications, this implies relatively high tariffs on goods with low elasticities of demand. If *A* and *B* now form an FTA, they will have to restrict their tariff structure so as to impose no tariffs on each other's goods. Under standard assumptions, including fixed world prices, this restriction will lead to a lower level of welfare. The same forces which make unilateral free trade superior to an FTA under standard assumptions make non-discriminatory tariffs superior to preferential tariffs in the presence of a revenue constraint.

2.4.5 Economies of scale and product differentiation   During the first wave of RI arrangements, many economists relied on the notion that an FTA could serve as a vehicle for the exploitation of economies of scale. Yet, broadly speaking, scale economies *by themselves* do not make RI superior to UTL.[14] Intuitively, if the minimum cost of production of a good along the long-run average cost curve is below the world price, both potential partners in the FTA should expand production until the marginal cost is less than or equal to the world price. They should then consume domestically as much as is demanded at the world price and export the residual. Goods for which minimum cost is above the world price should not be produced. Unilateral free trade will generally ensure this outcome.

If the case for RI over UTL already exists due to considerations cited in sections 2.4.2 or 2.4.3, scale economies generally make it much stronger. This is perhaps the reason why economies of scale are often a part of the case for an FTA. The point can be illustrated with the help of two examples, of which we develop the first one in detail and refer the reader to Corden (1972) for the second: (i) an import-substitution objective involving a target level of industrial output, as in section 2.4.2; and (ii) tariffs and transportation costs on exports to the outside world which limit access to the latter's market, as in section 2.4.3.

Suppose that both A and B have a target level of aggregate import-competing industrial output. As noted before, starting from a non-discriminatory tariff, the two countries can benefit from an FTA under such circumstances even under constant returns. If scale economies are present, however, the gains from specialisation are likely to be larger. For specialisation in the presence of scale economies yields gains in the form of larger rectangular areas rather than conventional triangular areas. Thus, the case for an FTA is stronger.

The above analysis assumes (implicitly) that products are homogeneous and the scale economies are external to the firm.[15] Suppose now that scale economies are internal to the firm and products are differentiated. These assumptions drive us automatically into the world of imperfect competition, where individual firms are able to exercise market power. In view of market power on the part of firms, potential partners in an FTA cannot be viewed as small in relation to the outside world. Therefore, their optimal tariffs are positive and UTL is non-optimal even in the absence of the import-substitution objective.

Beyond this point, the implications of imperfect competition are rather complex. Depending on the behavioural assumptions, a myriad of models can be constructed.[16] We resist temptation and restrict ourselves to the monopolistic competition model. On balance, the results which emerge from this model are intuitively more plausible than those arising from oligopoly models.[17]

Assume that potential partners consume differentiated goods for which markets are monopolistically competitive and that consumers appreciate variety. Starting from an initial protected equilibrium, formation of an FTA can yield two additional types of gains not available in the conventional models. First, after the FTA is formed, each partner will have tariff-free access to the varieties produced by the other. To the extent that consumers prefer more variety to less, welfare must rise. Second, as the market for each variety is likely to be larger in the post-FTA equilibrium, its scale of operation will expand. Given decreasing costs, this will yield further gains.

Against these gains, we must weigh the losses which are likely to accrue from increased distortion between varieties imported from the partner country and those imported from the outside world. Preferential tariff reduction will reduce imports from the outside world, which is harmful for members of the FTA. Although, in general, the net result is ambiguous, there is a strong presumption that due to decreasing costs welfare will rise. Indeed, if the members freeze their vectors of imports from country C, the FTA will be unambiguously welfare-improving.

Two important policy implications of this analysis may be noted. First, to the extent that intra-industry trade is predominantly among rich countries, these gains are less relevant to FTAs between poor countries. Second, contrary to the results based on models of interindustry trade, similarity among partner countries does not diminish the case for FTAs when potential trade is of the intra-industry variety.

2.5   FTAs versus PTAs

We now show that PTAs can be superior to an FTA. That is to say, partial preferences can yield a better outcome than a 100 percent preference granted under FTAs.

The point is made most easily with the help of a three-good model in which each of A, B, and C exports one good and imports two goods.[18] Goods imported into each country from the other two – say, those into A from B and C – are imperfect substitutes. A and B are small with respect to C so that their terms of trade are fixed. Given symmetry in the trade pattern, we need to consider the effects of a PTA on one partner only, say A. The effects on B are similar.

Denote the goods exported by A, B, and C by 1, 2, and 3, respectively. Assume that initially, A imposes the same *ad valorem* tariff on B and C. That is to say, the initial marginal distortion across B and C is the same. Suppose now that the tariff on B is lowered by a small amount. This will raise imports of good 2 and, given substitutability, lower imports of good 3 and raise exports of good 1. Because exports rise, there is a net expansion of imports, implying that imports of good 2 expand more than the contraction of imports of good 3 at world prices. The initial distortion in the two imports being the same, the gain from increased imports of good 2 is larger than the loss due to reduced imports of good 3. The PTA is welfare-improving.

As we lower the tariff on good 2 further, net imports will continue to expand. But the gain from the expansion of imports of good 2 will be evaluated at the lower tariff than the loss from the contraction of imports of good 3. There is therefore, no guarantee that welfare will continue to rise as we lower the tariff on good 2. Indeed, assuming monotonicity, we can find a critical, second-best optimal tariff at which the gains in good 2 from a small additional reduction in tariff are exactly offset by the losses on good 3. Any reductions beyond this tariff rate will lower welfare. By obvious extension, an FTA which pushes the tariff on good 2 down to 0 will yield a lower welfare than the PTA with the second-best optimum tariff.

This conclusion clearly brings into question the wisdom of the GATT Article XXIV, which prohibits PTAs but permits FTAs and CUs. Viner provided at least two reasons why in practice a 100 percent preference may be superior to something less than that. First, there are likely to be some economies in administrative costs. 'The burden on trade of a customs tariff', Viner reasoned, 'arises . . . also from the costs involved, for exporter and importer, in meeting the customs regulations, and the costs involved, for the tariff-levying government, in administering the customs machinery. These costs are often, in fact, more important than the duties themselves as hindrances to trade'.

A second, and perhaps more important, reason for the preference for an FTA over a PTA is that even though superior PTAs exist, there is no guarantee that those are the ones that will be picked. It is entirely possible, even plausible, that the PTAs that are actually picked are inferior to the FTA. Once again, it is worthwhile to quote Viner (1950, pp. 50–1):

> Customs Union . . . involves across-the-board removal of the duties between the members of the union; since the removal is non-selective by its very nature, the beneficial preferences are established along with the injurious ones, the trade-creating ones along with the trade-diverting ones. Preferential arrangements, on the other hand, can be, and usually are, selective, and it is possible, and in practice probable, that the preferences selected will be predominantly of the trade-diverting or injurious kind.

2.6   FTAs versus CUs

An issue of great significance in the formation of RI schemes is whether the countries should retain their own tariffs (FTA) or erect a CET (CU) on extra-union partners. Economists are divided on this issue.

There are three main arguments given in favour of FTAs. First, they do not result in an increase in tariffs in member countries. By contrast, when a common external tariff is imposed, countries with lower initial tariffs are able to raise their tariffs. This is because Article XXIV requires that the external tariff be no higher than the average of the tariffs in the partner countries prior to the formation of the union. Second, an FTA gives the member countries a greater freedom to pursue their trade-policy reforms. In a CU, more reform-oriented countries may find their hands tied by the agreement to maintain a CET. If lobbies are powerful, the CET may be set at a level high enough to protect producers in the least efficient country in the union. Finally, due to enforcement difficulties under an FTA, the union finds itself importing goods through the border of the country with the lowest tariff. This puts pressure on countries with higher tariff to bring their tariffs down to the level of the least protective country. There are thus dynamic processes at work in favour of ever-declining tariffs under an FTA.

In principle, at least some of these arguments can be turned on their heads. First, if a CU is formed, the least protective country can force the more protective countries to lower their tariffs to its level. This will make the likelihood that integration is welfare-improving higher and result in a lower cost to the rest of the world. Second, in practice, FTAs are accompanied by elaborate rules of origin and content requirement which become powerful instruments of protection. In a CU, such rules are not required. Finally, if protection lobbies are active, their effectiveness may be diluted in a CU since the latter requires union-wide lobbying, whereas under an FTA tariffs are responsive to the lobbying at the national level. In the ultimate, the issue would seem to hinge on whether we can expect institutional arbitrage across countries (in the sense of section 3) to lead to superior outcomes for all, in which case a CU would be preferable. If such arbitrage leads to worse outcomes, then it is better to leave each country with its own external tariffs. Perhaps put differently, if the 'centre' country, when one exists, has a clean trade policy, a CU can be more desirable, since we can expect that region-wide tariff policies will be determined more by this country.

2.7   Strategic advantages of an FTA

Up to this point, we assumed that the union was small in relation to the outside world. We now allow the terms of trade to change and consider the strategic advantages of an FTA for union members. Our discussion is in two parts. First, we summarise the effects resulting directly from the formation of an FTA. Second, we discuss the gains which may arise from increased bargaining power of the union *vis-à-vis* the outside world.

In the two-good model of Figure 6.1, the terms of trade effects of an FTA are straightforward. Suppose that C's supply price is not constant, but increases with quantity. At a constant price of C, formation of an FTA reduces the demand for imports from C. This leads to a decline in C's price. Formation of an FTA improves the union's terms of trade *vis-à-vis* the outside world.[19]

The second type of gain from an FTA can result from increased bargaining power of the union. The terms of trade of union members depend not merely on their external tariffs, but also on tariffs imposed on them by the outside world. To the extent that the level of these tariffs can be influenced through bargaining, an FTA which increases the joint bargaining power of member countries can confer further gains on the latter. Interestingly, unlike the first type of gains, these gains need not come at the expense of the outside world. The union as well as the outside world may benefit from mutual tariff reduction.[20]

Viner provides several examples from history where decisions to forge economic unions were influenced, in part, by expected gains from increased bargaining power with respect to other countries. In the United States, the Articles of Confederation had left each state with its separate tariff. The argument that this put the United States at a disadvantage *vis-à-vis* Britain and other European countries in matters of commercial policy was instrumental in mobilising public opinion in favour of a federal union with a centralised tariff policy. The recent movement for a 'United States of Europe' sprang in large part from the feeling that a European economic union was necessary to deal with a large America.

A case can be made that the existence of the European Community has been instrumental in allowing western European countries to cut out better deals with the United States in bargaining tariff reductions than would have been possible if they had dealt individually with the United States. More recently, the restraint shown by the United States towards the European Community in using 'Super 301' threats is a direct result of the Community's ability to inflict injury on the United States through retaliation. By contrast, the United States has used this instrument with relative ease against individual countries such as Japan, Brazil and India.

The bargaining power of a union is a direct function of its economic size relative to the outside countries with which it must negotiate. In this respect, formation of the European Community did prove beneficial to its member countries. By contrast, economic unions in Africa and Latin America were much too small relative to their counterparts in the developed world (see Chapters 8 by Foroutan and 9 by Nogués and Quintanilla in this volume). As a result, any expectations of these countries regarding benefits from joint negotiations with the United States and the European Community were bound to result in disappointment.

2.8   Implications for efficiency

The above discussions give some clues about the likely effects of RI arrangements. First, countries with high barriers to trade (e.g., India) are likely to benefit most from UTL. The gains from such liberalisation are likely to be much bigger than those from FTAs. Only if the world is divided into closed trading blocs is RI a superior option. Second, in the absence of closed trading blocs, the case for FTAs must be based on an exogenous objective such as import-substitution industrialisation. Third, economies of scale by themselves do not provide a reason for justifying RI over UTL. If there are other reasons for a preference for RI, however, economies of scale can reinforce them. Fourth, RI among low-income, developing countries is unlikely to yield major gains. This is because either these countries import very similar goods from developed countries or because differences in income levels among them lead to very diverse distribution of gains. In the former case, gains from specialisation between partner countries are limited while in the latter case compensation schemes which emerge are highly distortionary. Fifth, similarity in *per capita* incomes reinforces the gains from RI among developed countries. Sixth, *a priori*, it is not clear whether an FTA is superior to a CU. Much depends on how these are implemented. Finally, the larger an FTA, the greater the strategic advantages. For instance, the European Community has been generally insulated from the US 'Super 301' threats while countries such as Japan, India and Brazil have had to face them.

As a prelude to section 3, nothing has been said explicitly so far about North–South integration, which has been gaining popularity in recent years, e.g., Mexico and the United States. Countries engaged in this type of integration have relatively free trade regimes (the average Mexican tariff is 9 percent). The gains for a developing country from integration with a rich country go beyond the trade efficiency gains discussed here. First, should the world get divided into inward-looking blocs, such integration guarantees future access to a large market.[21] With this large market, the competitive pressure to ensure efficiency and availability of new technology is also guaranteed. Second, such integration involving international obligations ensures that the country's reforms will not be reversed. This is critical for the credibility of the country's policies. Finally, as a part of the integration effort, the country may be able to import pro-growth economic institutions (e.g., more liberal labour markets, stable macroeconomic policies, etc.) of the developed country. We now proceed to develop this last point in greater detail.

3   Institutional dimensions of RI

The implications of RI go beyond trade in goods, services, and factors. Almost by definition, any regional arrangement worth its name entails the imposition of some common rules of conduct on the countries entering the arrangement and a set of reciprocal commitments and obligations. RI thereby enforces a certain degree of arbitrage among national institutions, just as it brings about arbitrage in markets for goods and services. The importance of this political dimension of RI may well exceed that of the more direct implications having to do with trade flows.

That the effects of RI can extend beyond trade has long been recognised. More than two decades ago, Hirschman (1971, p. 22) argued that surrendering autonomy to supranational authorities had both costs and benefits for governments:

> [C]ommon markets would not only provide preferential treatment for the industrialists of the participating countries; for these mutual arrangements to be durable, monetary and foreign exchange policies would have to become more uniform and stable than they have been; and such a development would be even more important than the customs preferences themselves in promoting exports from the common market countries, not only to each other, but also to third countries. It is, however, precisely the prospect of less freedom of movement in monetary and foreign exchange policies which makes national governments so skittish about entering effective common market commitments.

The issues go well beyond monetary and foreign exchange policies, and skittishness about losing autonomy is not confined to them alone. RI can also serve as a conduit for industrial policies, environmental preferences, social and welfare policies, and so on.

If the cost of integration is reduced autonomy, the benefit (as Hirschman suggests) may be superior economic outcomes. Much of the recent trend towards RI can be understood as reflecting the desire of certain countries to 'borrow' or 'import' desirable institutions from their neighbours. A central aim of the exchange rate mechanism (ERM) of the European Community was to enhance the credibility of anti-inflationary policies by effectively surrendering monetary autonomy to the Bundesbank. By entering a quasi-irrevocable arrangement in the context of the North American Free-Trade Area (NAFTA), the Mexican government is as anxious to cement its new, open trade policies as it is to obtain specific trade privileges via the arrangement.[22] In both cases, RI is used to commit to desirable policies in a context where discretion is feared to produce suboptimal results.

The literature on rules versus discretion provides the natural reference point for evaluating such institutional implications (see Fischer, 1990, for a survey). However, we should be clear that membership in an RI scheme does not purchase commitment in any direct way. The arrangements that occur in practice rarely involve the complete subordination of a member's preferences to exogenous rules or to the preferences of another member. We will highlight here three other channels through which regional institutions can alter economic outcomes.

(a) *The preference-dilution effect:* Irrespective of the institutional setup, a regional arrangement implies a larger political community and hence a smaller role in determining policy for politically important groups in each of the countries. This renders decisionmaking less responsive to factional interests, and may thereby enhance efficiency.

(b) *The preference-asymmetry effect:* Unless members have identical economic structures and preferences, policymaking at the regional level will have to compromise over the perceived needs of different countries. Somewhat paradoxically, the compromise solution may present a more efficient outcome for some members than could be obtained in the absence of integration. For others, the compromise solution may be worse.

(c) *The institutional-design effect:* Within established nation-states, policymakers have to live with the inherited institutional setting. But when a regional institution is set up from scratch, it may be possible to optimise in the choice of certain institutional dimensions in a way that would not normally be possible in the domestic context. This greater flexibility in institutional design may enhance efficiency in all members.

3.1 An exploratory model

To make these arguments more concrete and to draw some implications, we now turn to a simple model. As in the literature on rules versus discretion, our focus is on the interaction between governments and their private sectors, and the changes in this interaction that would follow from integration. We develop the case of a single country first, and then turn to the case where two countries become integrated.

We suppose that government behaviour can be summarised by a

quadratic-loss objective function which allows for both an economic motive and a non-economic ('political') motive:

$$G = - [(\bar{g} - g)^2 + \gamma(\theta - g)^2].$$ (1)

The government's choice variable is denoted by g. It represents government intervention on some relevant policy dimension (e.g., trade protection, industrial subsidies, aggregate demand-management policies, etc.). The optimal level of g in a strictly economic sense is given by $\bar{g}$. Hence, the first term in (1) captures a purely economic motive in government decisionmaking. In addition, we suppose that the government also comes under pressure to intervene on account of political motives, represented here by the second term in (1). Politically powerful groups in the private sector have a most preferred level of intervention given by θ. The second term captures the idea that the government pays a penalty whenever g diverges from θ. γ is the relative weight placed by the government on the political motive. We attach no normative importance to this objective function; it is simply meant to characterise government behaviour in a transparent fashion.

The level of θ is endogenous, and is selected by a lobby representing politically active groups in society. These groups derive private benefits from government intervention, but they also bear a cost whenever g diverges from the economically most efficient level. This trade-off is represented by a utility function of the following sort:

$$U = ag - (\theta - \bar{g})^2.$$ (2)

The first term here represents the private benefits of government intervention, while the second term stands for its economy-wide costs. These costs are positive whenever the private-sector lobby expresses a preference for a g that is different from $\bar{g}$, and they are assumed to be partly internalised by the lobbying group.

The game proceeds as follows. In the first stage, the private-sector lobby announces θ, its most preferred level of government intervention, taking into account how the government will respond to this announcement. In the second stage, the government determines its optimal level of g, taking θ as given. As we shall see, in this sequence the government suffers a loss in welfare from being unable to precommit to a specified level of g in advance of the political process.

We solve the second stage of the game first. Maximising (1) with respect to g yields:

$$g = (1 + \gamma)^{-1}(\bar{g} + \gamma\theta) \equiv g(\theta).$$ (3)

This is the government's best-response function with respect to θ. In the first stage of the game, the lobby in turn maximises (2) subject to (3). The solution is:

$$\theta = \bar{g} + a\gamma/2(1 + \gamma), \tag{4}$$

which is larger than $\bar{g}$ as long as $a > 0$. Substituting this back in (3), we get the equilibrium level of government intervention:

$$g = \bar{g} + (a/2)[\gamma/(1 + \gamma)^2]. \tag{5}$$

Hence g exceeds $\bar{g}$ as long as a and γ are both positive. There is therefore more intervention than is economically desirable. We can also show that:

$$(\theta - g) = (a/2)[\gamma/(1 + \gamma)^2] > 0, \tag{6}$$

which implies that the government chooses to moderate the lobby's demands. For future reference, we substitute (5)–(6) in (1) to express the value taken by the government's objective function in the non-integrated equilibrium:

$$G_N = - (a^2/4)[\gamma/(1 + \gamma)]^3. \tag{7}$$

By being responsive to political pressure, the government suffers a cost. To see that this cost originates from the specific timing of moves adopted here, suppose that we reverse the order of moves. Now the government can precommit to a specific level of g. Since the lobby moves second, it must take g as given. In view of (2), its optimal θ is then equal to $\bar{g}$. In turn, the government can maximise (1) by setting $g = \bar{g}$. Hence, when the government can precommit, its objective function attains its bliss point (of zero). We can interpret this framework also in terms of time-inconsistency: the government's optimal *ex ante* policy diverges from its optimal *ex post* policy. We note that the private-sector lobby is the beneficiary of this time-inconsistency, as it attains a higher level of utility when the government cannot precommit than when it can.

3.2   Modelling RI

We now turn to the case where two countries decide to integrate. We model this integration by requiring that the level of government intervention be the same in the two economies. We suppose that the two countries differ only with respect to the economically desirable level of intervention. Hence, the foreign government's objective function is given by:

$$G^* = - [(\bar{g}^* - g^*)^2 + \gamma(\theta^* - g^*)^2], \tag{8}$$

while the private-sector lobby in the foreign country maximises:

$$U^* = ag^* - (\theta^* - \bar{g}^*)^2. \tag{9}$$

Note that a and γ are common to the two countries.

How is decisionmaking accomplished at the regional level? It is natural to think that the regional institution will maximise an objective function that has the same structure as the ones in the two countries:

$$G_r = - [(\bar{g}_r - g)^2 + \gamma(\theta_r - g)^2], \tag{10}$$

where the subscript r refers to the regional institution. To save on notation, we do not subscript g, as this is now common to both countries – it may stand, for example, for the CET. As this expression makes clear, there are basically two issues here: first, given that $\bar{g}$ and $\bar{g}^*$ differ, what objective does the centre see itself as fulfilling (i.e., what is $\bar{g}_r$)? Second, as the respective lobbying demands θ and θ^* may in principle differ also, how does the regional institution 'aggregate' these preferences (i.e., what is the relationship between θ and θ^*, on the one hand, and θ_r, on the other)? We make what seems to be the neutral assumption by equating $\bar{g}_r$ and θ_r to the averages of the preferences in the two countries. That is,

$$\bar{g}_r = \tfrac{1}{2}(\bar{g} + \bar{g}^*) \tag{11}$$

$$\theta_r = \tfrac{1}{2}(\theta + \theta^*). \tag{12}$$

Note that having the regional institution maximise the sum of the two governments' objective functions would yield equivalent results to the approach taken here.[23]

Now we can solve for the outcome of the game under RI once again by working backwards. The regional institution's best-response function is:

$$g = (1 + \gamma)^{-1}(\bar{g}_r + \gamma\theta_r) \equiv g(\theta_r). \tag{13}$$

The national lobbies in turn maximise their objective functions, internalising this best-response function, but taking the actions of the other lobby as given. Using (12), this yields:

$$\theta = \bar{g} + a\gamma/4(1 + \gamma) \quad \text{and} \quad \theta^* = \bar{g}^* + a\gamma/4(1 + \gamma). \tag{14}$$

By comparing (14) with (4), we can see that RI moderates the national lobbies' demands for intervention. The reason is simple: each lobby now has a smaller impact on decisionmaking, as the central institution has to contend with not one but two groups clamouring for attention. Since the marginal benefits of lobbying have gone down, the groups rationally choose to do less of it.[24] This is the preference-dilution effect mentioned above.

That larger political communities may be less susceptible to harmful factionalism is in fact an old insight. This was one of the main arguments used in *The Federalist Papers* in support of a 'well-constructed Union' of American states. As James Madison argued, individual factions could well come to dominate the political agenda in small political communities, but they would be unlikely to do so in a federal setup where they would have to contend with many more pressure groups:

> The smaller the society, the fewer probably will be the distinct parties and interests composing it; the fewer the distinct parties and interests, the more frequently will a majority be found of the same party; and the smaller the number of individuals composing a majority, and the smaller the compass within which they are placed, the more easily will they concert and execute their plans of oppression. Extend the sphere, and you take in a greater variety of parties and interests; you make it less probable that a majority of the whole will have a common motive to invade the rights of other citizens; or if such a common motive exists, it will be more difficult for all who feel it to discover their own strength and to act in unison with each other (Hamilton et al., 1981 [1787], p. 22)

However, note that 0 and 0^* also depend on $\bar{g}$ and $\bar{g}^*$, respectively, so that the overall pressure for intervention may not be reduced for both countries simultaneously. Combining (12) and (14),

$$0_r = \bar{g}_r + a\gamma/4(1 + \gamma) = \tfrac{1}{2}(\bar{g} + \bar{g}^*) + a\gamma/4(1 + \gamma). \qquad (15)$$

On account of the second term, each of the two countries experiences a reduction of lobbying (cf. (4)). But the effect of the first term works differently for the two countries. This is the preference-asymmetry effect mentioned above. If $\bar{g} > \bar{g}^*$, the home country gets an additional reduction in lobbying from regional integration, while the foreign country gets an offsetting increase. Using (14), we can now state the equilibrium level of intervention in the union:

$$g = \tfrac{1}{2}(\bar{g} + \bar{g}^*) + (a/4)[\gamma/(1 + \gamma)]^2. \qquad (16)$$

Comparing this with (5), we can see that the direction of change in g after integration depends on the relative magnitudes of the preference-dilution and preference-asymmetry effects. The first effect pulls g down in both countries, while the second effect reduces g in one country but increases it in the other.

Now we are ready to evaluate the consequences of integration for each of the two countries. We will do this from two different perspectives, and ask in turn: (i) does integration lead to more efficient outcomes from a strictly economic standpoint? and (ii) does integration make each of the governments better off in terms of their own objective functions, including their political motives?

3.3 Economic consequences of RI

The economic evaluation hinges on whether integration helps close the gap between the economically desirable levels of government intervention and the actual levels chosen in equilibrium. That is, we need to check whether $(\bar{g} - g)^2$ and $(\bar{g}^* - g^*)^2$ are smaller under integration. Let us denote the economic component of the government's objective function by $\bar{G}$ and use the subscripts N and I to refer to the non-integrated and integrated cases respectively. Then:

$$\bar{G}_N = \bar{G}_N^* = -(\bar{g} - g)^2|_N = -(a^2/4)[\gamma/(1 + \gamma)]^4, \qquad (17)$$

$$\bar{G}_I = -(\bar{g} - g)^2|_I = -\{\tfrac{1}{2}(\bar{g} - \bar{g}^*) - (a/4)[\gamma/(1 + \gamma)]^2\}^2 \qquad (18)$$

$$\bar{G}_I^* = -(\bar{g}^* - g)^2|_I = -\{\tfrac{1}{2}(\bar{g}^* - \bar{g}) - (a/4)[\gamma/(1 + \gamma)]^2\}^2. \qquad (19)$$

(Asterisks denote the foreign country as before.)

Consider first the case where $(\bar{g} - \bar{g}^*) = 0$, that is when the two countries are identical. By inspection, we can see that in that case $\bar{G}_N = \bar{G}_N^* < \bar{G}_I = \bar{G}_I^*$. This is due entirely to the preference-dilution effect, and represents the beneficial economic consequence of a larger political union. This effect operates for both countries. When $(\bar{g} - \bar{g}^*) \neq 0$, on the other hand, the preference-asymmetry effect comes into play. For 'small' differences, this effect benefits the country with the larger level of economically desirable intervention. The reason is as follows. In the absence of integration, government intervention is overprovided in both countries. Under integration, the preference-asymmetry effects works to reduce g in the country with the higher level of desirable interventions, and to increase it in the other country. Given the initial distortion, this benefits the first country and hurts the second. For a 'large' divergence between $\bar{g}$ and $\bar{g}^*$, however, *both* countries are made worse off by integration.

Finally, note an important implication. As the number of countries entering an arrangement increases, the condition that each must be made better off becomes more and more stringent, as long as the countries are not identical. Hence the relatively small number of participants is one significant advantage of regionalism over multilateralism.[25]

We have assumed so far that the regional institution selects as its target for intervention the simple average of the two countries' targets (i.e., $\bar{g}_r = \tfrac{1}{2}(\bar{g} + \bar{g}^*)$). As discussed above, this creates a positive externality for the high-intervention country and a negative externality for the low-intervention country. Now suppose that the regional institution can be designed in a manner that would maximise the joint economic benefits to the two countries. In terms of the present framework, this would allow us to select the weighting of the two countries' economic targets in an optimal manner. That is, through weighted voting or other means, the regional institution's objective function could be altered to the benefit of both economies. Hence we now assume that the countries could jointly commit to an institutional setup at the regional level, even though they cannot commit to particular policies, once the institutions are in place. The fact that these institutions are being set up from scratch may enable such institutional engineering at the international level when they are ruled out domestically.

The analysis proceeds as before, except that the game is now in three stages, with the first stage of the game consisting of choosing the weighting scheme that determines the importance to be attached by the regional institutions to each country's bliss point. It can be shown (see de Melo, Panagariya and Rodrik, 1992) that the institutional design question will result in putting a larger weight on the low-intervention country's preferences.

3.4 Political consequences of RI

Our framework suggests that political considerations and the constraints placed by private-sector lobbying activities should be taken into account in evaluating the benefits of RI. For the same reasons, political considerations should also weigh heavily in the determination of when countries are likely to enter regional arrangements.

The maximised values of G and G^* in the absence of integration are:

$$G_N = G_N^* = - (a^2/4)[\gamma/(1 + \gamma)]^3,\tag{20}$$

Using (14) and (16), we obtain the analogous expression under integration:

$$G_I = G_I^* = - \{[(1 + \gamma)/4](\bar{g} - \bar{g}^*)^2 + (a^2/16)[\gamma/(1 + \gamma)]^3\}.\tag{21}$$

Consider first the case where the two countries are identical and $\bar{g} = \bar{g}^*$. In this case, integration is unambiguously beneficial. This derives entirely from the preference-dilution effect discussed above. Integration reduces the influence of the national lobby, and allows the government to get closer to achieving its dual objectives. When $\bar{g} \neq \bar{g}^*$, on the other hand, the benefits of integration are unambiguously reduced for both partners. The reason is that any economic gains from preference asymmetry are offset by political losses arising from a wider gap between the national lobby's preferences (θ and θ^*) and the common level of intervention. This captures the political cost of giving up national autonomy: while economic performance may be improved, this comes at the cost of a reduction in the government's ability to satisfy politically important groups' demands. On balance, asymmetry hurts. A comparison of (20) and (21) makes clear that RI would not pay for either government when $\bar{g}$ and $\bar{g}^*$ are too far apart.

To summarise, RI entails a commitment to abide by supranational rules. However, since these rules are endogenous and chosen by governments themselves, there is no real sense in which integration can solve the dynamic-inconsistency problems that afflict policymaking. What integration can do, as this framework has highlighted, is to alter the parameters of the situation in certain ways to alleviate the costs of dynamic inconsistency. Hence RI can help governments achieve superior outcomes, even when integration does not involve specific commitments either to other partners' policies or to arbitrarily selected policies. Under certain conditions, the arbitraging of institutions across national borders can be mutually beneficial. But regional partners have to cross a threshold of similarity before integration can become beneficial in this institutional sense and, as argued by Winters (1992, Chapter 7 in this volume), the adoption of common policies and common rules become additional objectives in their own right.[26]

4   Growth effects of RI schemes

The institutional considerations discussed above suggest that successful RI schemes benefit from a convergence in objectives, from having few partners, and from the willingness of countries to surrender some national autonomy and to commit to supranational rules. If these institutional considerations are met, it is likely that dynamic gains, reflected in higher growth, will be reaped. We have not referred above to the 'dynamic' effects, not only because they are rarely addressed in empirical work[27], but also because, like scale efficiency effects, they are not particular to RI arrangements. However these effects, though difficult to identify, are in practice likely to be more important than the static efficiency effects alluded to above. On macroeconomic grounds 'good' policy coordination and less instability is likely to raise long-run growth. In past RI schemes, the benefits of coordination through delegation to supranational bodies was largely absent from developing country arrangements because of a combination of conflicting objectives (e.g., in Africa) and weak central institutions. On the other hand, such benefits were apparent in the European Community (see Foroutan, 1992 and Winters, 1992, Chapters 8 and 7 in this volume).

The most often cited dynamic effects are spillover effects and moving down learning curves. For example, technological diffusion is more likely to be rapid if increased competition from trade puts pressures on domestic firms to adopt these new technologies. An enlarged market also increases the stimulus for investment to take advantage of the enlarged market and to meet the expanding competition. Reduced barriers to trade would thus provide another strong impetus to the convergence predictions of neo-classical growth theory based on diminishing returns. On Gershenkro-nian grounds, one would argue that this catchup effect would be stronger for developing countries provided, of course, that few impediments exist on the importation of technology from developed countries. Since such barriers were erected rather than removed as they were part ˜of the inward-looking development strategy, this dynamic effect was not exploited to its full potential for former developing country RI schemes.

Perhaps the most important potential dynamic benefit for developing RI schemes comes from economic cooperation in areas where significant externalities and public goods (education, research and development, infrastructure, environment) exist. Of course, cooperation can take many different forms ranging from the simple exchange of information through the provision of joint training facilities to the mutual recognition and adoption of rules and regulations, to the implementation of joint policies and the establishment of joint institutions with quasi-legislative powers. Given the general lack of institutional development when the early RI schemes were implemented in the early 1960s, it would appear that the potential for gains even from limited regional cooperation would be great.

Is there any evidence of positive dynamic effects from RI? In other work (de Melo, Montenegro and Panagariya, 1992) we look for the evidence by fitting a simple growth equation to a cross-section of 101 countries stratified into a group of OECD developed (23) and developing (78) countries. We test for the eventual influence of belonging to an RI scheme by the inclusion of a dummy variable. The model is estimated over the period 1960–85 and by subperiods (1960–72 and 1973–85). Besides invest-ment, the explanatory variables include initial *per capita* income and an estimate of the stock of human capital.

We tested for the effects of RI by including dummy variables for the following arrangements (years of implementation in parenthesis): (i) among developed countries, EC (1960) and EFTA (1960); (ii) among developing countries CACM (1960), LAFTA (1960, replaced by LAIA in 1980), SACU (1969) and CEAO (1974) (see Chapters 8 and 9 below). Among the latter group, SACU (Botswana, Lesotho, South Africa and Swaziland) is an example of a North–South RI scheme and CEAO which includes former French colonies are also part of a monetary union since they are all members of the CFA zone.[28]

Three results stand out. First, with one exception,[29] none of the integra-tion dummies was significant. Insofar as splitting the sample controls for some of the effects of omitted variables, which would capture the effects of RI, belonging to an RI had no apparent effect on long-run growth. There was apparently no effect of membership, even for developed countries when the sample was split into two subperiods: 1960–72 and 1973–85. To some extent this should not come as a surprise since trade liberalisation was being carried out multilaterally and benefits were therefore being spread fairly evenly. There is thus no apparent effect of membership in terms of higher growth even for the European Community, EFTA and CACM during the 1960s when intra-regional trade was growing rapidly.

The second result is that splitting the sample into developed and developing country groups reveals an interesting difference in the role of investment and education in explaining growth. Investment has the expected positive (and statistically significant) sign for both groups and both periods, but the human capital variable, though of the right positive sign, is significant only for the developing country group. This result has two interesting interpretations. First, as emphasised by the 'new' growth literature, human capital is a contributing factor to growth for poor countries. Second, as emphasised in the institutional analysis, and in the literature emphasising cooperation, there would appear to be benefits from institution-building and joint training. This aspect of integration, largely neglected during the first wave of RI arrangements, would appear to promise benefits.

Third, initial *per capita* income enters with a negative and statistically significant sign for all regressions except for developed countries during 1973–85. This corroborates findings in the growth literature (e.g. Barro, 1991). From the point of view of RI arrangements this result, which supports the catchup hypothesis of neoclassical growth theory, suggests that the new form of North–South RI is promising for developing country members.

The first result, however, invites a note of caution in interpreting the no-effect results on growth. It could be argued that some of the regressors are correlated with the dummy variable controlling for RI membership – for example, the investment share in GDP could be higher among RI countries because of the positive effect of membership on the macro and institutional environment. In particular, it was found that the investment rate in the European Community, and especially in EFTA, was significantly higher (about 5 percentage points) than for other developed countries until 1973. This significantly higher investment rate is consistent with the positive effects that one would expect from effective integration among institutions and also corresponded to the period when the liberalisation policies were strongest and the European Community's relative growth performance was strongest. While this result is not strong evidence of 'dynamic' effects of RI, it suggests the possibility of an association between comprehensive RI and growth. Interestingly, the same increased investment effect also accompanied the announcement of NAFTA negotiations in Mexico (see Whalley, 1992, Chapter 11 in this volume).

5   Conclusions

Where do we stand? The evidence discussed in section 4 supports earlier findings that countries involved in RI schemes did not fare any better than comparators. But, then, neither was their performance any worse. The outcome was thus quite consistent with the theoretical discussion in section 2, which demonstrated that conflicting factors determine the efficiency consequences of RI arrangements. However, history will not repeat itself as circumstances today are quite different from those prevailing during the first wave of RI arrangements: fewer trade restrictions, an agenda in most RI arrangements that extends beyond the measures considered under the GATT, and a new form of integration involving reciprocal arrangements between developed and developing partners. On the whole, our conclusion is that, under today's circumstances, the new form of arrangement is likely to result in a more favourable outcome for RI schemes if real authority is delegated to well-designed regional institutions that do more than respond to pressure groups, which is a big 'if'.

What the discussion in section 3 showed is that regional partners have to cross a threshold of similarity in their economic objectives before such partial surrender of national autonomy can be mutually beneficial. This has apparently occurred. The political benefits of RI are maximised by integrating with countries that are as similar as possible in their objectives. But from an economic perspective, as discussed in section 3, there is an optimal degree of dissimilarity: Mexico hopes to benefit from NAFTA precisely because standards of government intervention and private property are much more stringent in the United States (and Canada) than they are in Mexico. Normally, these benefits are one-sided: continuing the example, US (and Canadian) institutions may well be contaminated by the less advantageous Mexican institutions. But as we have discussed, the economic benefits of dissimilarity can be shared by all parties provided the common institutions are designed in a way that weights the objective functions of each country appropriately. Hence ability to mould regional institutions from scratch is an important determinant of the gains from integration. However, as the experience of the European Community suggests, regional institutions should resist communitarising restrictive unilateral actions by members, and the necessary pragmatic approach to negotiating changes should avoid excessive compliance with provisions catering to sectional interests.

Looking ahead, the lessons are:

(1) If the current trend of unilateral liberalisation continues, integration is less likely to have negative efficiency effects and can help cement hard-fought reductions in protection.

(2) By including on their agenda areas not covered by multilateral negotiation, such as standards and government procurement, RI arrangements can serve as a catalyst in the pursuit of removing market fragmentations.

(3) Integration can confer substantial institutional benefits, but only if real authority is delegated to central institutions. As long as multi-lateral institutions are weak, and regional arrangements allow for a greater surrender of national autonomy, regionalism may paradox-ically remain attractive to reforming governments. However, strengthened multilateral institutions will provide greater benefits than regional ones as they will present a larger political community and a greater scope for the preference-dilution effect.

(4) To benefit from integration, some convergence in national economic objectives is necessary. This explains why the prospect of integration with rich neighbours was so unattractive to developing countries when they still believed in import substitution, and why it has become more desirable as they have opened up their economies. It also explains why multilateral institutions may be inherently more difficult to sustain than regional institutions in light of the under-lying diversity of national interests.

(5) However, too much convergence may undercut the economic gains from integration. This explains why developing countries currently stand to benefit least (in economic terms, at least) by integrating with other developing countries with similarly unsettled domestic insti-tutions.

(6) The benefits of integration are greater the higher the possibility of shaping the institutions that go along with it in an economically desirable way. Recent regional attempts perhaps offer an additional degree of freedom in this regard compared to existing multilateral institutions.

NOTES

The authors are grateful to Sumana Dhar, Claudio Montenegro, and Francis Ng for superb assistance, and to conference participants for helpful comments.
1 This means that transshipment rules are necessary to prevent imports of high-tariff countries from being channelled via low-tariff countries in the area.
2 In addition to the literature cited later, important contributions include

Corden (1968, 1970, 1972, 1976), Kemp (1969), Lipsey (1957, 1960, 1970), Riezman (1979) and Vanek (1964). Two excellent surveys of the literature are Corden (1984) and Lloyd (1983).

3 According to Viner, trade creation occurs when the formation of an FTA or a CU leads to a switching of imports from a high-cost source to a low-cost source. Analogously, trade diversion occurs when imports switch from a low-cost source to a high-cost source. Subsequent authors noted crucial limitations of Viner's conclusion and demonstrated that in general trade diversion need not be welfare-worsening and trade creation need not be welfare-improving. The concepts have remained highly influential in policy debates, however, and authors have continued to equate trade creation with welfare improvement and trade diversion with welfare deterioration.

4 In terms of Viner's terminology, the FTA just described is trade-diverting. Yet the net effect of it on welfare is ambiguous. This is the point made in the post-Viner literature alluded to in n. 2.

5 As we will argue later, this is easier said than done. In practice, compensation schemes can turn even a welfare-enhancing FTA into a disaster.

6 In section 2.5, we will see that once we recognise that the imports from B and C are *imperfect* substitutes, the positive and negative effects emerge without elimination of trade with C. Figure 6.1 also provides a less extreme representation of the standard Vinerian analysis in which the supply curves of both B and C are horizontal.

7 In the case described in the previous paragraph, the FTA is unambiguously welfare-worsening. It is therefore not of much interest from a policy perspective.

8 This was the issue raised Cooper and Massell (1965a) and Johnson (1965), and also discussed by Berglas (1979) and Robson (1980).

9 The following discussion draws heavily upon Wonnacott and Wonnacott (1981). Also see Berglas (1983) and Wonnacott and Wonnacott (1984) in this context.

10 By the Lerner Symmetry Theorem, the tariff on good 2 by B is equivalent to an export tax on good 1 at the same time. The tariff in B therefore implies an upward shift in its export supply curve.

11 As Wonnacott and Wonnacott (1981) show, elimination of trade with C is not necessary to generate this result. What is critical is that the good imported by C before the FTA be different than that after it.

12 Although we did not formally consider the option of accession to a bloc, it is clear from Figure 6.3 that if the internal price of C is above point G, B will be better off acceding to C than forming an FTA with A.

13 This was the main thrust of the analyses in Cooper and Massell (1965b) and Johnson (1965).

14 See Bhagwati (1968, 1990) in this context.

15 Strictly speaking, the externality implies that if the equilibrium is incompletely specialised, some intervention will be desirable and complete free trade will not be locally optimal. In the discussion just presented, we have ignored this complication.

16 The literature on imperfect competition and FTAs is almost non-existent. Therefore, the best we can do is infer such implications from the models addressing national trade policies in the presence of imperfect competition. Unfortunately, even here the results depend crucially on the specific structure of the model.

17 For examples of monopolistic competition, see Helpman (1981) and Krugman (1980).
18 This model is due to Meade (1956).
19 In models with three or more goods, the terms of trade effects are more complicated and less clear cut, although the presumption is that the union's terms of trade will improve upon the formation of an FTA. Thus, in Meade's model, as each partner country reduces its tariff on imports from the other, given substitutability, the demand for imports from the outside world declines. The union's terms of trade with respect to the outside world improve.
20 This is, of course, a scenario in which FTAs serve as stepping stones to multilateral free trade.
21 The importance of gaining market access is also stressed by Winters (1992, Chapter 7 in this volume) in his discussion of successive enlargements of the European Community.
22 'NAFTA is important to Mexico in itself . . . But it is still more important as a symbolic guarantee of the nature of the changes in the Mexican economy. Since the mid-1980s, when President Miguel de la Madrid took Mexico into GATT and slashed tariffs, its technocrats have used one word to describe the changes: "irreversible"'. A free-trade agreement would, they hoped, prove the point. 'The hard decisions . . . were taken before Mr. Salinas was publicly convinced of the case for free trade with Canada and the United States. But by signalling that within ten years he wants borderless trade within North America, he is telling both Mexico's once inefficient industries and the outside world that there really is no going back' (*The Economist*, 14 December 1991, p. 20).
23 That is because the simple sum of the objective functions differs from expression (9) only by terms that are constant from the perspective of the regional institution. Consequently, the first-order conditions are identical in the two cases.
24 A couple of things could work against this in practice. First, political groups may form transnational alliances. But even if they do, larger groups will probably suffer more from free-rider problems and from diversity of interests. Second, regional institutions may somehow turn out to be more receptive to pressure than the national institutions. This problem can be alleviated by careful institutional design (see below).
25 The advantage of a relatively small number of participants in a world of trading blocs is also made by Mancur Olson in his Discussion of Irwin (1992, Chapter 4 in this volume).
26 On the difficult role and mixed outcome of supranational institutions to help establish a common market in the European Community, see section 4 of Winters (1992, Chapter 7 in this volume).
27 Oft-cited studies of the dynamic effects are Cline (1978) for the CACM and Baldwin (1991) for the effects of 'Europe 1992' on EC growth.
28 Other RI schemes that were not included either did not have a long enough existence (e.g., SADC, the Canada–US FTA, etc.) or did not achieve much by way of integration.
29 The only exception is the significant effect for the dummy variable for SACU (which is entered for Botswana, Lesotho and Swaziland) for the period 1960–72. SACU is a highly integrated RI in existence since 1910 and the members' relation to South Africa is much like that of Liechtenstein to Austria or of Monaco to France.

REFERENCES

Baldwin, R. (1991) 'EMS Credibility: Discussion', *Economic Policy: A European Forum*, pp. 89–91.

Barro, R. (1991) 'Economic Growth in a Cross-Section of Countries, *Quarterly Journal of Economics*, **106**, pp. 407–43.

Berglas, E. (1979) 'Preferential Trading Theory: The *n* Commodity Case', *Journal of Political Economy*, **87**, pp. 315–31.

(1983) 'The Case for Unilateral Tariff Reductions: Foreign Tariffs Rediscovered', *American Economic Review*, **73**, pp. 1141–2.

Bhagwati, J. (1968) 'Trade Liberalization Among LDCs, Trade Theory and GATT Rules', in J.N. Wolfe (ed.), *Value, Capital and Growth: Essays in Honour of Sir John Hicks*, Oxford: Oxford University Press.

(1990) 'Departures from Multilateralism: Regionalism and Aggressive Unilateralism', *The Economic Journal*, **100**, pp. 1304–17.

Chenery, H. and M. Syrquin (1975) *Patterns of Development: 1950–1970*, Oxford: Oxford University Press.

Cline, W.R. (1978) 'Benefits and Costs of Economic Integration in Central America', in W.R. Cline and C. Delgado (eds), *Economic Integration in Central America*, Washington, DC: Brookings Institution.

Cooper, C.A. and B.F. Massell (1965a) 'A New Look at Customs Union Theory', *The Economic Journal*, **75**, pp. 742–7.

(1965b) 'Toward a General Theory of Customs Unions for Developing Countries', *Journal of Political Economy*, **73(5)**, pp. 461–76.

Corden, W.M. (1968) 'Customs Union Theory', unpublished manuscript.

(1970) 'The Efficiency Effects of Trade and Protection', in I.A. McDougall and R.H. Snape (eds), *Studies in International Economics: Monash Conference Papers*, Amsterdam: North-Holland.

(1972) 'Economies of Scale and Customs Union Theory', *Journal of Political Economy*, **80**, pp. 465–75.

(1976) 'Customs Union Theory and Nonuniformity of Tariffs', *Journal of International Economics*, **6(1)**, pp. 99–107.

(1984) 'Normative Theory of International Trade', Chapter 2 in R.W. Jones and P.B. Kenen (eds), *Handbook of International Economics*, Amsterdam: North-Holland.

Fischer, S. (1990) 'Rules versus Discretion in Monetary Policy', in B.M. Friedman and F.H. Hahn (eds), *Handbook of Monetary Economics*, vol. II, Amsterdam: North-Holland.

Foroutan, F. (1992) 'Regional Integration in Sub-Saharan Africa: Past Experience and Future Prospects', Chapter 8 in this volume.

Greenaway, D. (1989) 'Regional Trading Arrangements and Intra-Industry Trade', in D. Greenaway *et al.* (eds), *Economic Aspects of Regional Trading Arrangements*, New York: New York University Press.

Hamilton, A., J. Madison and J. Jay (1981 [1787]), *The Federalist Papers*, **10**, ed. Roy P. Fairfield, 2nd edn, Baltimore and London: Johns Hopkins University Press.

Helpman, E. (1981) 'International Trade in the Presence of Product Differentiation, Economies of Scale and Monopolistic Competition: A Chamberlin–Heckscher–Ohlin Approach', *Journal of International Economics*, **11(3)**, pp. 305–40.

Hirschman, A. (1971) *A Bias for Hope*, New Haven and London: Yale University Press.
Irwin, D. (1992) 'Multilateral and Bilateral Trade Policies in the World Trading System: An Historical Perspective', Chapter 4 in this volume.
Johnson, H.G. (1965) 'An Economic Theory of Protection, Tariff Bargaining, and the Formation of Customs Unions', *Journal of Political Economy*, **73** (June) pp. 256–83.
Kemp, M.C. (1969) *A Contribution to the General Equilibrium Theory of Preferential Trading*, Amsterdam: North-Holland.
Kemp, M.C. and H.Y. Wan, Jr (1976) 'An Elementary Proposition Concerning the Formation of Customs Unions', *Journal of International Economics*, **6** (February) pp. 95–8.
Kowalczyk, C. (1990) 'Welfare and Customs Unions', *NBER Working Paper*, **3476**, Cambridge, Mass.: NBER.
Krugman, P. (1980) 'Scale Economies, Product Differentiation, and the Pattern of Trade', *American Economic Review*, **70**, pp. 950–9.
Lachler, U. (1989) 'Regional Integration and Economic Development', Industry and Energy Department, *Working Paper*, **14**, Washington, DC: World Bank.
Lipsey, R.G. (1957) 'The Theory of Customs Unions: Trade Diversion and Welfare', *Economica*, **24**, pp. 40–6.
(1960) 'The Theory of Customs Unions: A General Survey', *The Economic Journal*, **70**, pp. 498–513.
(1970) *The Theory of Customs Unions: A General Equilibrium Analysis*, London: Weidenfeld & Nicolson.
Lloyd, P.J. (1982) '3 × 3 Theory of Customs Unions', *Journal of International Economics*, **12**, pp. 41–63.
Meade, J.E. (1956) *The Theory of Customs Unions*, Amsterdam: North-Holland.
Melo, J. de, C. Montenegro and A. Panagariya (1992) 'Regional Integration Old and New: Issues and Evidence', Washington, DC: World Bank (mimeo).
Melo, J. de, A. Panagariya and D. Rodrik (1992) 'Regional Integration: An Analytical and Empirical Overview', Washington, DC: World Bank (mimeo).
Nogués, J. and R. Quintanilla (1992) 'Latin America's Integration and the Multilateral Trading System', Chapter 9 in this volume.
Riezman, R. (1979) 'A 3 × 3 Model of Customs Unions', *Journal of International Economics*, **72**, pp. 820–9.
Robson, P. (1980) *The Economics of International Integration*, London and Boston: George Allen & Unwin.
Summers, R. and A. Heston (1988) 'A New Set of International Comparisons of Real Product Prices and Price Levels: Estimates for 130 Countries', *Review of Income and Wealth*, **34(1)**, pp. 1–25.
Vanek, J. (1964) 'Unilateral Trade Liberalization and Global World Income', *Quarterly Journal of Economics*, **78**, pp. 139–47.
Viner, J. (1950) The Customs Union Issue, New York: Carnegie Endowment for International Peace.
Whalley, J. (1992) 'Regional Trade Arrangements in North America: CUSTA and NAFTA', Chapter 11 in this volume.
Winters, L.A. (1992) 'The European Community: A Case of Successful Integration?', Chapter 7 in this volume.
Wonnacott, P. and R. Wonnacott (1981) 'Is Unilateral Tariff Reduction Prefer-

able to a Customs Union? The Curious Case of the Missing Foreign Tariff',
  American Economic Review, **71** (September) pp. 704–41.
  (1984) 'How General is the Case for Unilateral Tariff Reduction?', *American
  Economic Review*, **74**, p. 491.

Discussion

RONALD FINDLAY

De Melo, Panagariya and Rodrik's Chapter 6 serves admirably to
provide the intellectual background to the pressing issues of regional
integration (RI) to which it is devoted. Starting with the celebrated work
of Viner (1950) on the 'customs union issue' the last four decades have
seen an extensive body of research on the theory and experience of
'partial' or 'limited' free trade on a 'preferential' basis. This literature is
lucidly surveyed in section 2 of the chapter. Section 3, which is the most
original, opens up some very interesting and novel issues concerned with
the institutional dimensions of RI. Section 4 presents new empirical
results on evaluating the growth effects of several RI efforts. Altogether
this is an extremely meaty and substantive study, not so much one chapter
by three authors as one chapter by each of three authors, skilfully blended
together. Its value to the profession, in my opinion, will not be confined to
the participants of the CEPR/World Bank conference alone.

  My comments will be in three parts. The first will be addressed to the
survey of the literature in section 2 of the chapter. The second will be
concerned with the political economy issues raised by section 3 on the
institutional dimensions of RI arrangements. The last will consist of some
observations on the broader themes of RI and trade policy raised in this
and other chapters in the volume.

1   The literature survey

By its very nature the analysis of preferential trading agreements falls into
the domain of the 'theory of the second best', and as such one has to be
aware at the outset that general propositions are going to be very hard to

come by. Even such a master as Max Corden inquires plaintively (1984, p. 113), 'Once one goes beyond very simple models, how is one to sort out this complex subject?'

The solution that Corden adopts, and in which he is followed by the authors of Chapter 6, is to begin chronologically with Viner's contribution followed by consideration of a three-country, two-good model, most fully expounded by Vanek (1965). The authors present a very lucid graphical exposition of the main results of this strand of the literature. The problem, however, as they very clearly point out, is that the two-good structure forces some very artificial asymmetries between the two countries that form the union in relation to their trade with the third country, the 'outsider'.

Call the partners A and B and the outsider C, and let the two goods be X and Y. Suppose both A and B export X, while C exports Y. Then both A and B will trade *only* with C and not with each other, so that a union between them would be vacuous. But if A exports X, and B and C export Y, then only A trades with C, while A and B of course trade with each other. It is shown that in the case of production with increasing marginal cost, A *must* lose and B *must* gain when a union is formed and that B's gain is *less* than A's loss, so that the welfare is lower in the union as a whole, while trade is diverted away from C, who therefore also stands to lose.

Symmetry with respect to both partners in their relations to the rest of the world requires at least a three-good model, in which each country exports one of the goods to the other two, a model due originally to Meade (1956). Here again the authors give a very good summary of the results, showing the key role of substitutability between the three goods in consumption.

Such divergent results varying sharply from model to model with changes in assumptions is of course profoundly unsettling, particularly to non-specialists. As mentioned earlier, this is in a sense unavoidable, given the 'second-best' character of the problems in this field. There is one result, however, that is very general and simple at the same time, due to Kemp and Wan (1976), which tends to restore one's faith in the usefulness of theory for economic policy. I would start from this fundamental proposition, since it serves to confirm the widespread intuition that it must be possible to improve matters by successive 'piecemeal' reforms without necessarily having to go all the way at once to the unattainable 'Holy Grail' of universal free trade.

Start with any number of countries and goods and tariffs so that trade is initially as distorted as one can imagine. Suppose now that a subset of the countries form a customs union, i.e., establish free trade between themselves and some common external tariff (CET) with respect to the rest of the world. Kemp and Wan show that it is always possible to raise the welfare of every member of the union, while leaving welfare in the rest of the world unchanged if (a) the CET is set in such a way as to leave the preunion prices facing the rest of the world unchanged so that their excess-demand vector for goods from the union is unchanged and (b) lump sum taxes and transfers between the members of the union are possible.

The proof is an almost immediate consequence of the fundamental theorem of welfare economics. Given the production-possibility sets of the union members and the preunion excess-demand vector of the rest of the world, resources can be allocated within the union in a Pareto-efficient way, equating marginal rates of transformation in production to marginal rates of substitution in consumption throughout the union. The difference between the price vector common to all union members and the preunion world price vector is the necessary CET. Real income is increased within the union as a whole, and thus for each member with lump sum taxes and transfers available for redistributive purposes, while welfare in the rest of the world is unchanged. It is easy to see that the initial union can be progressively expanded, raising the welfare of each member monotonically, until the 'Holy Grail' of universal free trade is reached.

The importance of this Kemp–Wan result is that it demonstrates the fact that aside from difficulties of implementation due to lack of sufficient information and so on, the reason why partial movements towards free trade fail to secure general approval is the essentially *political* one of inability to agree on an appropriate CET and internal taxes and transfers that could bring about a Pareto-improvement in world welfare.

In section 2.4 the authors discuss the question of why 'small' open economies should bother to join preferential trading areas when they could, in principle, maximise their own welfare by unilateral trade liberalisation (UTL). An extensive literature has grown up around this apparent paradox, that the authors summarise and comment upon. It seems to me, however, that the apparent paradox is a pseudo-paradox, an artificial problem that does not seem to require all the attention lavished upon it.

If the developing economy in question is truly 'small', in the analytical sense of trade theory, that it can buy and sell all it wants of any good at exogenous world prices, then it is true that it will be best off with no tariffs at all. However, even 'small' developing countries in the ordinary sense of small, i.e., population and area, are not often in this position, since they may face discriminatory quotas for such primary products as sugar or peanuts, or for labour-intensive manufactured products such as textiles and footwear. Hence countries that are 'small' in this latter everyday sense might reasonably choose to join preferential trading agreements, trading off the restrictive effects of common tariffs against the advantage of market access for their exports within the union. It seems to me that there is therefore no real paradox at all.

In the longer version of their paper presented at the conference, the authors also deal with the important question of international factor mobility and RI. Drawing upon an important study by Wooton (1988), it should be noted that the usual presumption that economists have in favour of factor mobility needs to be modified when the stimulus to mobility comes from such distortionary incentives as protective tariffs. Thus suppose we have a free-trade area (FTA) with a higher tariff on capital-intensive imports, common to both partners, in one country as compared with the other. Make the standard two-good, two-factor Hechscher–Ohlin model assumptions. If capital is *fully* mobile between the partners it will flow into the higher-tariff country, raising the output of the capital-intensive importable and lowering the output of the labour-intensive exportable. In the low-tariff country the opposite effects will occur and will continue until the country is completely specialised on the labour-intensive export with the return to capital equalised with the higher-tariff country that remains diversified, but with a shift towards the capital-intensive importable.

The effects on welfare will be strongly positive for the capital-exporting partner since it enjoys both a higher return to capital (at the expense of its partner) and the elimination of its inefficient protected sector and replacement with more exports to the rest of the world. The higher-tariff partner, however, loses on both counts. I conjecture that the loss to the latter outweighs the gain to the former.

Another possibility, however, is that technology for the capital-intensive, possibly 'high-tech' good is backward within the union relative to the outside world. Direct foreign investment into the high-tariff country from outside could be conducive to transfer of technology leading to productivity gains in the long run. In this case the 'de-industrialised' low-tariff country, that enjoys immediate static gains at the expense of its partner, might conceivably end up losing in the long run.

Migration of labour is an even more important and sensitive issue in relation to regional integration. As in the case of the US–Mexico proposals, trade preferences may be seen by the higher-income partner as a substitute for socially undesirable labour inflows from the poorer partner. 'Non-economic' factors are clearly at work and an integration of the extensive literature on the economics of racial discrimination with that of trade theory should be a promising field for further research.

2   Political economy issues

As I stated at the beginning, I find section 3 on 'institutional dimensions of RI' the most original part of the chapter, concerned with the most difficult but potentially most rewarding issues. Somewhat to my surprise, however, I found the approach taken in this section to these issues not the most natural or fruitful way to proceed, at least to my taste. The approach that is chosen is the 'rules versus discretion' literature of macroeconomics, in which a national 'government' confronts a single unified national 'private sector'. The authors' extension is to two such sets of decision-makers, blended together to form a 'regional' entity.

The view of the authors, for which the authority of James Madison in *The Federalist Papers*, 10 is cited, is that the larger regional association 'dilutes' the mischief that any single national 'faction' or 'interest group' can inflict, so that 'these United States' or whatever the larger entity is, is less splintered by special interests than any one of the constituent states. But is this necessarily so? What about the possibility of wider coalitions forming that have more power to inflict mischief together in the wider union than their component factions could in isolation? Is 'fortress Europe' necessarily unlikely or improbable?

An obvious and realistic example of greater potential mischief the wider is the policymaking entity is provided by the familiar 'economies of scale' argument for protecting industry in developing countries. The limited size of the individual national markets serves to restrain national industrial lobbies but the prospect of a regional market can win support for protection at the higher level.

The approach that I would prefer is an extension of the literature on the political economy of trade policy, in which instruments such as tariff levels are derived endogenously to RI. It seems to me that much interesting work could be done in this area, taking into account how governments and interest groups interact at the regional level, within a general equilibrium model of the economy that contains an endogenous model of the political process determining the nature and magnitude of various policy parameters.

3   On the broader themes of regional integration

The most important issue with which the chapters in this volume are concerned is, of course, whether the regional approach to free trade will be complementary to, or potentially in conflict with, the global approach as represented by GATT. While there is no necessary conflict in principle, I agree with the view that there is the possibility of regionalism undermining the steady progress toward global free trade that we have experienced over the last four decades.

The remarkable progress that we have seen was due to the rapid growth of the Western and, later, the Far Eastern economies, on the one hand, and, to the commitment and drive of the United States concerning the ideal of trade liberalisation, combined with its 'hegemonic' geopolitical and economic power on the other. Within this framework the European Community maintained a strong outward orientation, and Japan, the newly industrialising Far Eastern economies and many developing countries benefited enormously.

At the moment, however, the world economy is not just suffering from a temporary recession, but the engines of productivity growth appeared to have slowed down in the dominant economies. Most importantly the United States has also had its confident hegemonic position eroded, largely by Japanese competition in electronics, automobiles, and other manufacturing sectors. The countries with the most to gain by universal free trade, such as Japan and Korea, are instead unprepared to expose their inefficient agricultural sectors to international competition, while the Community is also unable to persuade its farming lobbies to have their subsidies reduced. Against this background it is not difficult to imagine the European Community and NAFTA (see Chapter 11 below) becoming increasingly protectionist towards Japan and the East Asian NICs, as well as towards agricultural exports from Australia and New Zealand. I hope that the contrary view, so confidently expressed in this volume, will turn out to be correct.

REFERENCES

Corden, W.M. (1984) 'Normative Theory of International Trade', Chapter 2 in R.W. Jones and P.B. Kenen (eds), *Handbook of International Economies*, Amsterdam: North-Holland.
Kemp, M.C. and H.Y. Wan Jr (1976) 'An Elementary Proposition Concerning the Formation of Customs Unions', in M.C. Kemp, *Three Topics in the Theory of International Trade*, Amsterdam: North-Holland.
Meade, J.E. (1956) *Theory of Customs Unions*, Amsterdam: North-Holland.

Vanek, J. (1965) *General Equilibrium of International Discrimination: The Case of Customs Unions*, Cambridge, Mass.: Harvard University Press.
Viner, J. (1950) *The Customs Union Issue*, New York: Carnegie Endowment for International Peace.
Wooton, J.F. (1988) 'Towards a Common Market: Factor Mobility in a Customs Union', *Canadian Journal of Economics*, 00, pp. 525–38.

CONSTANTINE MICHALOPOULOS

Chapter 6 is a wide-ranging study and there is much in it with which I agree; but there are also a number of areas that raise some concern.

First, there is the review of the familiar trade literature. Too little time is devoted to confronting the theory with the reality; and the reality today is that trade agreements are less about tariff preferences and more about gaining security of access and overcoming or diluting non-tariff barriers. The authors recognise this, but still devote too large a portion of the chapter to details on tariffs.

Even within the tariff argument some issues are not settled. In section 2.5 we are told that a free-trade area (FTA) in theory is not superior to a more limited preferential trading arrangement (PTA); the authors recognise that in practice the chosen PTAs can be inferior to an FTA, thereby confirming the wisdom of the GATT. The latter is a conclusion with which I agree. But if it is so, what are we to conclude about the theory? Is it wrong? Why? The explanation of course is simple: irrespective of the theory, in practice, the product-by-product approach is based on trying to promote particular exports through trade diversion. No producer/exporter wishes to enter a preferential scheme because of the trade-creation aspects of the scheme.

The chapter correctly raises in section 2.4.4 the revenue aspect of the tariff as an important issue for regional integration among developing countries which are dependent on tariffs for a significant portion of total revenues. This is a critical issue for some of the Central American countries now considering somehow linking to NAFTA (see Chapter 11 below). Chapter 6 suggests that if they reduce tariffs with each other they would have to raise tariffs to the rest of the world if they have no other revenue-raising instruments. Clearly, in the long run, the correct answer is that they should raise revenues through other means.

Perhaps the most interesting point in section 2 relates to trading blocs and unilateral liberalisation. The chapter argues that beyond a certain point it might be advantageous to join an FTA rather than liberalise unilaterally. But here, as well as elsewhere, the chapter conditions the argument on the existence of 'appropriate compensation' mechanisms: it would be nice if some examples were given of plausible mechanisms which could be instituted.

The exploratory model in section 3 reaches some useful conclusions: integration can help by diluting the influence of nationally important political groups which support policies inimical to efficiency, but it can also extend the influence of one lobby – e.g., farmers in France – to other countries; and establishing new regional institutions can be of importance in promoting efficiency-enhancing policies in all countries. But the benefits are likely to be greater the more similar the partners are. None of these conclusions are objectionable. I do worry about two things in practice: in recent periods, with few exceptions, new regional integration (RI) arrangements have tended to have few institutional structures; and increasing consideration is being given to integration among unequal partners.

The latter issue is of importance not only in NAFTA and Mexico, but also in many other developing countries in Latin America – and among the states of the former USSR. It is an issue not adequately explored in the literature in general and in the chapter. Is size and level of development an important determinant of the distribution of benefits from RI? And if so what compensation mechanisms are appropriate and feasible? Are phasing-in mechanisms needed?

Let me turn next to the empirical section 4, which tries to assess the growth effects of regional integration. The results leave me very cold. The conclusion that in the simple growth model none of the unexplained variation can be attributed to membership in a RI scheme is plausible for the developing countries; they did little integrating anyway. I seriously doubt that such a simple model can come to grips with the complex interactions between integration and growth in the European Community. In any case, in this instance I would have wanted to ask the very difficult counterfactual question: would the twelve countries in the Community have done better individually? I personally doubt it very much.

Let me say a word on the chapter's conclusions: I agree that the past is not necessarily a good guide for the future. However, as in the past, there will always be regional arrangements coexisting within a global system.

The question is one of balance and how to shape regional efforts to be supportive of multilateralism.

It seems to me that how you look at regionalism also depends on where you sit: if you are the United States or your concern is about the trading system, one has to wonder whether regionalism promotes a more efficient global system. If you are a developing country, however, with limited global influence, FTAs can be helpful in particular settings, especially in the presence of trading blocs and the limited capacity of the GATT to move multilateral trade liberalisation forward.

I would like to conclude by pointing to two areas in which additional work is needed. First, as trade economists, we have a tendency to focus too much on trade. Success in trade integration requires coordination in other areas as well, especially in macro policy, which has not been the focus of developing countries considering integration arrangements. Second, we need to analyse more carefully what kind of arrangements are appropriate for developing countries that are considering integration with developed countries; and more broadly, whether and how to facilitate integration among unequals.

7 The European Community: a case of successful integration?

L. ALAN WINTERS

1 Introduction

In a volume such as this, the European Communities are taken as something of an exemplar. This chapter asks what light their experience of economic integration sheds on the organisation of other integration schemes, and on the process of integration in general. Section 2 ponders the success of the Community. That it has survived, expanded and deepened, and that its members have experienced great improvements in material well-being since its foundation, are obvious, and so it has clearly had a good measure of success. I argue, however, that questions about EC economic performance must at least be raised before taking it as the model for future integration: its macroeconomic performance has been mixed; it has, in some regards, turned in on itself; and it has fallen behind comparable countries technologically.

Section 3 notes that while the extension of trade preferences to non-member countries has reduced some trade barriers, it has done so in ways that sometimes reduce the beneficial effects of liberalism, and which have permitted the Community to slow down its integration with the rest of the world. I also argue that while enlargement – the admission of new full members – has reduced world protectionism, even it has an element of 'managed liberalism' about it, which reduces somewhat the competitive benefits of market opening. Section 4 considers how other policies have contributed to integration Community-style; one set of policies – the so-called 'four freedoms' (of movement for labour, firms, services and capital) – aims to extend the customs union (CU) into a common market. The other set – the fiscal transfers and the common sectoral policies, rules, economic and social policy – have essentially been props to the common market, easing adjustment, promoting equity and preventing the national abuse of other policies. Only recently, with the Single Market Initiative, '1992' for short, have the majority of these policies been developed beyond this essentially defensive role.[1]

Since the chapter is concerned with the *ex post* appraisal of EC experience and with drawing lessons for other groups, I concentrate on the early stages of EC integration, for which evidence is available. Hence I have little to say about '1992' *per se*, which is not yet achieved, and nothing about monetary union, political union and the Maastricht Treaty, which have yet to be implemented.[2]

2   Measures of success: inward- versus outward-looking integration

The European Communities is the largest and is frequently cited as the most successful regional economic integration scheme in the world. Its success in terms of institutional survival and growth – both widening and deepening – are indeed impressive, and it is also true that the period of its existence has witnessed very significant economic advance. In 1991, after four years of relative economic buoyancy it would have been easy to conclude that the Community's economic success was clearcut, but it is worth recalling that attitudes in the early and mid-1980s were different (Pelkmans and Winters, 1988, Chapter 1). This section, therefore, casts a cautionary and currently unfashionable eye over some of the evidence of EC economic performance.

After thirty-five years, it is impossible to construct formal *anti-mondes* against which to measure EC performance – indeed, it is hard even to conceive of such *anti-mondes*. Hence the analysis is rather informal and impressionistic. However, the conclusion, which I would characterise in the traditional phrase from school reports – 'adequate but should try harder' – is fairly robust. My reservation is that in some dimensions EC integration has been inward-looking, and that this has been to the detriment of both the Community itself and the rest of the world.

While I acknowledge the Community's considerable achievements, the present enthusiasm for regional integration means that such reservations must be examined. Moreover, the political constraints which have moulded EC integration evolve through time, and one of the best lubricants for that evolution is to recognise the economic burdens that they impose.[3] An economic appraisal of the Community's recent performance is thus useful both for the Community itself and for potential emulators.

2.1   Macroeconomic indicators

The Community's GDP growth has been above average, with the current twelve members – EC(12) – increasing their share of world GDP from 22.5 percent in 1965 to 23.5 percent in 1989, and the original six – EC(6) – from 15.9 percent to 17.0 percent (World Bank, 1991). Moreover, this period has been one of generally high economic growth in the industrial world, so the performance has also been good by historical standards. Whether it has been as good as it might have been, however, it less clear. De Melo, Panagariya and Rodrik in Chapter 6 find no evidence of significant EC growth effects in a cross-country regression exercise, and although EC growth has been good relative to that of the United States, and about equal to that of the EFTA countries, it has clearly lagged behind that in Japan and the NICs.[4] EC unemployment has remained persistently high since rising in the late 1970s, while that in the United States has fallen from high levels and that in Japan and EFTA has remained relatively low (CEC, 1991a). Similarly the Community has been less able to control inflation and nominal unit labour costs over the last two decades than other major economies (CEC, 1991a).

None of these statistics proves failure: there are always factors specific to particular economies, and it is difficult to know how members would have fared outside the Community. But the data suggest that one would need to work hard to maintain that the Community had significantly improved macroeconomic performance.

2.2   Regional disparities

The other important dimension of income in the Community is regional and national differences – the issue of so-called cohesion. While not part of the Treaty of Rome, the Community has long sought to narrow regional income differences, implicitly through the operation of the common market and explicitly through regional policy. In this regard it has been rather successful. Molle (1990) reports the Theil index of regional disparity in GDP per head as declining from 0.124 in 1950 and 0.102 in 1960 to 0.071 in 1985. Around 80 percent of the regional differences are explained by national differences, which suggests that reducing the latter offers the key to future progress. The narrowing of differentials – which has continued since 1985 (CEC, 1991a) – is a sign of increasing integration; moreover, the oft-expressed political will to ensure that it continues indicates the Community's intention not to allow integration to be undermined by distributional struggles.

2.3   Inward- or outward-looking integration?

The strongest indicator of integration within the Community is the substantial re-orientations of trade that followed the creation of the Community or new members' accessions. For example, in 1960 trade between the EC(12) countries accounted for 6 percent of their GDP, whereas by 1990 it accounted for 13.8 percent, while trade with the rest of

Table 7.1. *Self-sufficiency in EC agriculture[a], %, 1960–4 and 1985*

	1960–4	1985
Cereals	84	127
White sugar	99	132
Butter	100	113
Meat	98	102
Wine	94	112

Note: [a] EC (10).
Source: IMF (1988).

the world remained steady at 8.7 percent of GDP for exports and about 9.8 percent for imports (CEC, 1991a). For new members the figures are even more dramatic. The UK's exports of goods to EC(12) countries rose from 5.1 percent of GDP in 1970 to 9.7 percent in 1990 while extra-EC exports fell from 10.5 percent to 8.6 percent. UK inter-EC imports moved from 5.1 percent to 11.4 percent while extra-EC imports fell from 12.3 percent to 10.8 percent over the same periods (CEC, 1991a).

At face value, these data suggest that EC integration has proceeded well, but partly at the expense of integration with the rest of the world. To explore this hypothesis it is useful to disaggregate the data into agriculture, other primary goods and manufactures.

Other primary goods are mostly fuels – specifically oil – imports of which range between 35 percent of total imports in 1980 and 11 percent in 1988. Since oil imports come mostly from outside the Community, the recorded rises in extra-EC trade in the mid-1970s and early 1980s, and their subsequent reversal, are largely determined by oil prices, and hence owe nothing to the existence of the Community.

The story on agriculture, on the other hand, does owe a substantial amount to the existence of the Community. The political significance of the Common Agricultural Policy (CAP) in the formation of the Community is widely recognised, but I note here its distortionary effects and catastrophic effects on EC trade with the rest of the world. The CAP is fiercely protectionist, enshrines the principle of Community preference and relies on subsidised exports to dispose of surplus produce. Table 7.1 reports EC self-sufficiency – the ratio of production to consumption – for various commodities: all show an increase since the early 1960s and most show a switch from net imports to net exports. Comparing 1964–70 with 1985, the EC(10)'s share of total OECD agricultural imports fell from 60 per cent to 55 percent, while its share of exports rose from 45 percent to 50 percent. Little of this seems likely to be due to 'natural' changes in comparative advantage.

In 1989 the gross transfers entailed by EC agricultural intervention were some ECU 40 billion from taxpayers and ECU 49 billion from consumers (OECD, 1990). Much of this was wasted in the process, but the total production subsidy equivalent to farmers was ECU 48 billion, accounting for 38 percent of the value of production. Such policies impose significant welfare losses on the Community: Martin *et al.* (1990), for example, put the cost at over 1.5 percent of total EC real income in 1986–8. The CAP also hits other food exporters, especially countries such as Argentina, Australia and New Zealand, and bears much responsibility for the current parlous state of the Uruguay Round.

Turning to manufactures, Balassa (1975) suggests that much of the increase in intra-trade following the formation of the Community was trade creation and was thus welfare-improving. Similarly, Winters (1987) finds a predominance of creation over diversion in the United Kingdom's accession to the Community. Overall EC openness has increased, the share of extra-EC imports of manufactures in GDP growing from around 5 percent in 1963 to around 7 percent in 1985–8 (CEC, 1991a).

Jacquemin and Sapir (1988a) provide an industry-level analysis of manufactured trade shares over 1973–82. In France, Italy and Germany, the rapid increases in the intra-EC share of total imports over the 1960s abated in the early 1970s and finally reversed in the late 1970s. The reversal represents increasing EC openness and might be taken as a healthy development. Rather, however, it tended to be interpreted officially as a problem – as indicating that the steam was running out of EC integration and reflecting long-term structural weaknesses (Jacquemin and Sapir, 1988b). As Jacquemin and Sapir write, the 'apparent loss of competitiveness [suggested by falling intra-EC shares] prompted efforts towards freeing the internal market from enduring non-tariff barriers'.

Unfortunately the response at an industry level was less constructive. The constantly rising shares of intra-EC imports in agricultural and food products were, to my knowledge, never officially identified as a problem, while the industrial sectors in which falling shares were concentrated – motor vehicles, radio and TV sets, office machinery and data processing equipment, and other machinery – were among the areas of most active and restrictive EC trade policy in the 1980s: see for example, the dumping actions in mechanical engineering and consumers' electronics, and the voluntary export restraints (VERs) in machinery, household appliances and motor vehicles (GATT, 1991).

Thus, while 'Fortress Europe' is plainly a misrepresentation of EC policy, there has at times been an inward-looking strand to the EC perception of integration characterised, for example, by Commissioner for Foreign Relations Willy de Clerq's outburst 'we are not building a single market in order to turn it over to hungry foreigners'. Moreover, while every nation has its protectionists, I suspect that an organisation designed to promote mutual market penetration, and whose yardstick is 'integration', is particularly prone to such perceptions.

Consider next trade policy. Although average tariffs have fallen over the last three decades, the Community has had increasing resort to non-tariff barriers (NTBs). A crude indication of this may be seen in the coverage ratios for NTBs reported by Laird and Yeats (1988) for 1966 and 1986. Coverage ratios report the percentage of a country's imports falling in trade headings subject to one or more NTBs; they record the existence of NTBs not their severity, and do that only imperfectly – see, for example, Nogués, Olechowski and Winters (1986), and Laird and Yeats (1990). Nevertheless, they contain some information, especially in their changes over time.

The growth of EC non-tariff protection in manufactures is remarkable. The coverage of NTBs has increased five-fold, taking the Community from a relatively liberal base (10 percent) in 1966, to approximately the same coverage as the United States and Japan (56 percent) in 1986. Much of this increase has been in the form of discriminatory restrictions against Far Eastern producers, which have been excused (but not justified) as a response to dumping. The data for all commodities show the EC-10 now leading the way: 54 percent compared with 45 percent in the United States and 43 percent in Japan. In part, the growth from 21 percent in 1966 reflects the extension of the CAP, both in product coverage and to new member states; it also, however, reflects the heavy protection of other primary sectors such as coal (see Weiss *et al.*, 1988). The growing coverage of NTBs suggests an EC resistance to change which has almost certainly curtailed economic growth. Some market challenges are met not by swift contraction and industrial restructuring, but by defensive restrictions which substitute prolonged and probably incomplete adjustment.[5]

Further evidence of EC resistance to change is found in the proportion of GDP devoted to subsidies. Again there are statistical difficulties over the data but the relativities are probably robust: in the Community the proportions in 1985 were Italy 3.4 percent, France 3.0 percent, Germany 2.0 percent and United Kingdom 2.2 percent, compared with 1.2 percent in Japan and 0.6 percent in the United States (Kelly *et al.*, 1988). Some subsidies are given to emerging sectors – e.g., Airbus – but the bulk of them go towards resisting changes in traditional sectors. Over 1986–8 state aid was distributed as follows (CEC, 1991b): agriculture/fisheries 13 percent, coal 16 percent, transport (mainly railways) 30 percent, and

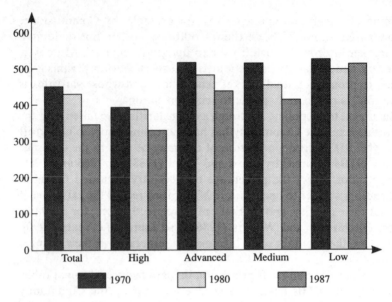

Figure 7.1   Share in world exports of four classes of engineering goods, parts per thousand
Source: Based on UNECE (1990)

manufacturing 41 percent, of which regional aid absorbed 15 percent, steel and shipbuilding 4 percent, and export subsidies (proportionately greatest in Greece and Ireland) 4 percent. The only conceivably progressive aids were to 'other sectors' (mainly motor vehicles) 8 percent, R & D 4 percent and small and medium-sized enterprises (SMEs), 3 percent.

2.4   Technological leadership

The use of protection to avoid industrial restructuring has almost certainly contributed to Europe's falling behind the United States and Japan in hi-tech goods. Figures 7.1 and 7.2 offer graphic illustration of this. Figure 7.1, based on UNECE (1990), examines shares in world exports of four classes of engineering goods; the different levels of sophistication are defined in terms of R & D inputs. The EC(9)'s share of world engineering markets has fallen from 45 percent in 1970 to 35 percent in 1985, which is not surprising given the advances occurring elsewhere in the world. But it is both surprising and significant that the decline is concentrated in the more sophisticated goods and that, indeed, the Community has increased its share of the least technical engineering exports.

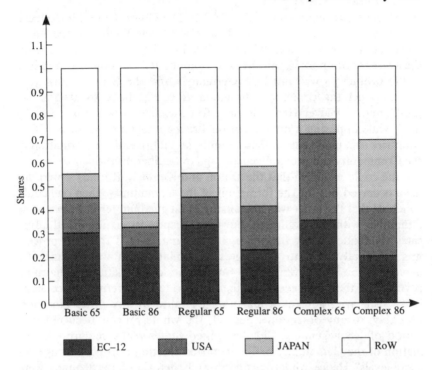

Figure 7.2   Shares of world exports of manufacturing, by degree of processing, 1965–86
Source: Based on CEC (1990)

Figure 7.1 is based on CEC (1990), which breaks trade into six commodity categories, three based on primary goods and three groups of industrial products – 'basic', 'more elaborate' and 'complex'. Between 1965 and 1986 the Community's share of world exports increased in the less processed primary sectors, was static in highly processed primary goods and fell in industrial products. Figure 7.2 shows that the fall was greatest in complex goods.[6]

2.5   Integration and protection

How has the Community affected the general level of trade restrictions in the world? At its simplest, the creation of the Community reduced average tariffs in Italy and France and raised them in Germany and the Benelux countries, and probably had relatively little effect overall. Having encouraged the formation of the Community for political reasons, the United States then sought to ameliorate its discriminatory effects by negotiating reciprocal tariff reductions in the GATT. The Dillon Round introduced minor reductions and when the Community was finally persuaded to enter the Kennedy Round (Curzon, 1965) further negotiations brought the average cut up to 35 percent. The Community's willingness to reduce tariffs probably owed much to Germany's and the Benelux countries' desire to get the common external tariff (CET) back to around the pre-Community level. Hence the net effect was to leave their rates broadly level while imposing a double cut on France and Italy. Morever, other countries also made cuts in these rounds, so that overall the formation of the Community did probably encourage trade liberalisation.

If one could establish that the Dillon and Kennedy Rounds would not have occurred but for the formation of the Community, then one could conclude that the latter was liberalising in the medium term. I have some difficulties with this argument, however, despite its distinguished advocates (Hufbauer, 1990; Lawrence, 1991). First, even if true, the process was essentially akin to the aggressive unilateralism we all currently deplore in the United States: the Community did something to harm its partners (in their own eyes) and then moderated it in return for concessions. Such an argument would not generalise to any other bloc nor, probably, to any other time. Second, the whole process occurred in a period of US hegemony: did the United States really require the formation of the Community before it started twisting European arms over tariff levels? Hence while the timing and rhetoric of the Rounds were driven by the Community, the substance was not necessarily so. Third, although the Community liberalised on average, its more liberal economies hardly did at all. That is, the Community probably constrained German and Dutch liberalism both in the 1960s and later. It is not self-evident that this was a good bargain for the rest of the world. Fourth, since agriculture played such an important and delicate role in the formation of the Community, it is not surprising that the Community resisted that sector's inclusion in the negotiations. But the fact that it got away with this (because the United States refused the *'montant de soutien'* offer) reinforced agricultural protectionism throughout the world and made it doubly difficult to negotiate in future rounds.

Turning to the contemporary situation, it is even more difficult to identify the Community's effects on the world trading system. On one hand, the Community's size has probably constrained the United States' use of 'Super 301' and anti-dumping actions (ADs) against it, although because this might merely deflect US protectionist pressure onto weaker partners, it does not imply that US policy is necessarily more liberal overall as a result. On the other hand, simple theory suggests that the Community's optimum tariff would exceed those of its twelve member states if they operated in isolation. Moreover, EC size might encourage US retaliation: by being *potentially* more threatening if it should act agressively, the Community may encourage the United States to pre-empt more vigorously than if Europe were just a collection of smaller states. Thus, for example, the United States cereal export enhancement scheme is a strategic response to the CAP, and would almost certainly be different if European agricultural policy were solely a national affair. Indeed, such fears may partly explain the current interest in regionalism: countries desire the apparent security of belonging to a bloc in case their partners turn away from them into their own blocs.

2.6 Political economy

De Melo, Panagariya and Rodrik suggest in Chapter 6 that preference dilution could reduce protectionist pressure, and hence protection, in a larger group. But their model is very particular in assuming that groups in different member countries have conflicting rather than reinforcing interests, in ignoring the creation of log-rolling coalitions between protectionist groups, and in not allowing for 'anti-protectionist' lobbying. Dilution could fragment the opposition to protection more than the demand for it, and hence reduce liberalism.[7]

De Melo, Panagariya and Rodrik also introduce 'preference asymmetry'. This, too, can increase protectionism: while the Community undoubtedly constrains some protective policies, it is also a safe bet that without the Community, the United Kingdom and Germany would not have footwear protection today, that UK agricultural protection would be lower, that Denmark would not have an arrangement on Japanese cars, etc. Given that policy emerges from bargaining between national governments and that, even for countries, production is more concentrated than consumption, it is easy to see how 'committee universalism' will lead to coalitions imposing excessive protection (Shepsle and Weingast, 1981).

Turning to the policymakers themselves, I fear that the current ambivalence towards international trade arises from too fixed a vision of the importance of intra-EC trade. Unlike policymakers in unitary states, where the dichotomy is between home and foreign suppliers and the objections to promoting the former artificially are well known, EC policymakers – both national and Community – can shelter in an intermediate space. They can believe themselves to be not opposed to imports *per se*, because they are happy to stimulate intra-EC trade, while being unwilling to grasp the nettle of genuinely foreign, i.e. extra-EC, competitiveness. In this regard I note Jacquemin and Sapir's conclusion (1991) that extra-EC imports constrain EC firms' price–cost markups, whereas intra-EC imports apparently have no such effects. This suggests that it is easier to make tacit, or even unconscious, market arrangements within the Community than with firms outside it.

3   Managed liberalism: enlargement and preferences

The Community has been unique among integration schemes in the way in which it has extended its influence geographically. This section considers this process and explores the pressures for, and consequences of, such extension. I define 'extension' to include not only the accession of new members, but also the preferential trading arrangements and association agreements concluded with other partners. The Europe Agreements negotiated recently with certain Eastern European countries (see section 3.2 below) provide a good illustration of EC expansion; they display a measure of 'managed liberalism' – a desire to open markets in a fashion that restricts the resulting shocks.

3.1   Enlargement

Enlargement – the accession of new members – has been a major feature of the Community from its inception. Article 237 provides the legal framework for it – unanimous agreement among existing members – and convention has dictated that, although accession is preceded by extended negotiation, the Community makes no compromises on the application of its fundamental policies. The rejection of the United Kingdom's first request for accession, which featured demands for reductions in the common external tariff (CET) and agricultural liberalisation, illustrates this well. Accession is very much more the process of joining an existing club than the creation of a new CU. Negotiation concerns issues such as the period of transition, political representation, and financial contributions and transfers, but there are no concessions over, for example, competition policy, environmental standards, or social legislation.

UK accession, coupled with that of Ireland and Denmark, reflected a desire to join a potentially important political bloc, but it also reflected two economic pressures. First, market access: the United Kingdom was concerned at the potential losses in being excluded from a dynamic market, while the others feared the trade diversion, especially in agriculture, that would result from UK accession. Second, the United Kingdom sought the stimulating effects of increased industrial competition. It could, of course, have obtained these through unilateral free trade, but that might have involved too much of a good thing and would perhaps, for that reason, not have been an entirely credible threat to inefficient British producers. The Community provided an attractive half-way house: its competition policy and internal free trade appeared to preclude major backsliding, but its pragmatism in the application of these policies, its tradition of managing internal trade frictions and its secure outer frontier of protection all appeared to provide a welcome safety net.

One might detect similar motives in the Scandinavian countries' present discussions about accession (see Norman, 1991). Norway and Sweden have rather liberal trade policies in industrial goods, but not in services and agriculture.[8] Accession to the Community would impose and under-pin a mild liberalisation in both sectors, but in a much more manageable fashion than entirely free trade.

The second, or Southern, enlargement had different origins from the first. Greece, Portugal and Spain were all relatively poor countries with newly established democracies. Accession offered them a means of secur-ing these political gains by increasing the costs of defection and by introducing an external authority which could take some of the 'heat' for unpopular policies. They were also attracted by the negotiated transfers from the European Regional Development Fund and the European Social Fund, and sought the enhanced credibility that commitment to the Community lent their proposed changes in economic regime. Finally, of course, the Community offered an attractive market for many of their labour-intensive and agricultural exports, especially if they could main-tain EC external protection. Winters (1992a) shows the market gains for these countries in footwear, while Greece's initial opposition to Iberian accession and Iberia's current hostility to liberalising the Multi-Fibre Arrangement (MFA) and to the Europe Agreements with Czecho-slovakia, Hungary and Poland (CHP) illustrate the latter issue.[9]

The attractions of the Southern accession to the Community (by now the EC-9) were essentially political – securing democracy for both altruistic and pragmatic reasons, the latter having to do with stability along their borders and in their sphere of influence. The potential market gains – e.g., disposing of grains in Spain and Portugal – were positive but probably not very significant. It is also possible that the Community felt that its international legitimacy would suffer if it excluded aspiring neighbouring economies, especially if this caused them apparent losses of export sales.

The aspirants to membership over the last decade fall into two groups: the EFTA countries and the Mediterranean ones. There has been little progress over the latter group, but the EFTAns seem to pose relatively few difficulties: the political issue of neutrality has been dissolved and the potential differences over fisheries and regional policies look resolvable.[10] These economies are similar to the richer EC members; their accession offers the Community markets in agriculture and services, greater integration in industrial products through labour mobility and direct investment, potential budget contributions, and the consolidation of a genuinely pan-European bloc.

The advantages of accession to the EFTAns are considerable. I have already mentioned the liberalisation of services and agriculture, and this is supplemented by the fear that investment will be diverted from EFTA to the Community, and their potential loss of sales in the Community (a major market for them) as '1992' boosts EC competitiveness: the difference due to being in or out of the Community could be as much as 3½ percent of expenditure on tradeable goods.[11]

What lessons does EC enlargement have for other regional integration (RI) schemes? First, it suggests that unreality of the proposal that the GATT should require integration schemes to be freely open to any country that is prepared to abide by their rules. Existing members are affected by accession not only through their trade, but also via explicit and implicity budgetary transfers and shifts in the balance of political power.

Second, the willingness of the EC-9 to make budgetary transfers to the Southern accedants clearly smoothed their path in. Transfers were not the only perceived long-term benefit to the new members, but the transfer mechanism – small as it is compared with those in federal and unitary states – was essential to the running of the Community once the Southern accession had occurred. Distribution is a major factor in EC decision-making, but the express willingness to address it constitutionally prevents it from becoming an impassible barrier to progress (see section 4.2 below).

Third, the need for accedants to adopt the CET and other EC external policies affects the aggregate level of protection. The impact effect of Iberian accession was to lower the accedants' external protection almost across the board. The impact of the first enlargement was less clearcut, however: while UK average manufactured tariffs fell (see Han and Liesner, 1971), agriculture became more restricted. Similarly, if Sweden and Norway accede their reduced protection in services and agriculture will be offset by greater restrictions on many industrial products. Thus while accession has not raised external protection relative to preintegration days, there is nothing inevitable in the notion that enlargement reduces protectionism.

Fourth, accession offers the new members more credible steps towards liberal policies than would unilateral action. The latter is a more extreme policy less easily controlled by governments without undermining its credibility. Accession, on the other hand, offers security in that major problems are negotiated and bargained over, and although the resultant erosions of liberalism are frequent, they are finite and controlled largely by external agents (Brussels). Hence major shocks can be ameliorated without suggesting a complete reversal of the accedant's liberalising policy. If other means of establishing credibility were available, accession would lose some of its charm.

Fifth, accession guarantees fairer treatment for the accedant's exports to the Community. In particular, they become subject to competition rather than dumping policy: both constrain predatory behaviour but the latter is open to huge abuse. Similarly accession offers some influence over standards, regulations, etc. Where the existing union is a major market – e.g., as the Community is for EFTA – these factors can be important. The *quid pro quo* for these concessions by the union is the need for the accedent to adopt common policies, which will often constrain their competitiveness and comparative advantage.

3.2   Trade preferences

The Community is also unusual in the extent and complexity of its preferential trading arrangements. It is a confirmed advocate of such arrangements, seeing them as a legitimate tool of policy, especially for relations with neighbouring countries (Luyten, 1989). At present the Community maintains five broad sets of preferences, although within the groups there are several subdivisions (see World Bank, 1987, box 9.2). The arrangements reflect different objectives, but all have at least some trade effects.

The *General System of Preference* (GSP) offers concessions to most developing countries; it parallels policies in other industrial countries; and is basically part of a global system (see Langhammer and Sapir, 1987). The *Lomé Convention* essentially continues EC members' colonial links for altruistic reasons, to boost markets and to maintain a sphere of influence. It offers unilateral preferences to the developing country signatories, but also helps to boost EC exports through elements such as the aid flows and commodity stabilisation finance (see Wang and Winters, 1991).

The free-trade arrangements with the *EFTA* countries arose because the United Kingdom was a major and open market for these countries' exports in 1973; the sudden application of the CET to such trade would have damaged EFTA economically and the Community politically. The Community also saw the arrangements as part of Europe's 'vocation to unify' (Luyten, 1989).

The twelve *Mediterranean* agreements are heterogeneous: all offer concessionary access to EC markets, most include technical assistance and aid clauses, but only those with the more developed partners require any reciprocal market access concessions. In the main they stem from the desire to bind the Mediterranean region into the EC sphere of influence, while simultaneously managing its trade and controlling the pressure for heavy immigration. The agreements also help to diffuse criticism over market access – especially in agriculture, in which some EC concessions are made.

The various pressures towards preferential trade and eventual full enlargement are well illustrated by the Community's recent *Europe Agreements* negotiated with Czecho-slovakia, Hungary and Poland (CHP). The Community had a strong political concern about stability on its borders, especially noting the importance of migration in forcing the pace of German unification. It also clearly felt a strong duty and desire to succour its neighbours and to preserve their fragile democracies. Both EC officials and the newly formed governments in the East saw close association with the Community as the means to this end. The Community also saw Eastern Europe as an issue on which it could legitimately exercise leadership on a world scale (in the Group of 24), which further encouraged active involvement.

Unfortunately the strong political incentives towards eastwards integration were subverted by entrenched economic interests in the Community. The market opening has been delayed and is subject to a number of (potential) restrictions. Indeed, one of the tests of the Community's commitment to liberal policy will be how it interprets and operates the Europe Agreements. Based on Winters (1992b), the principal components of the agreements are that:

- CHP must open their markets within ten years to EC goods – implicitly preferentially, and in one clause explicitly so if CHP maintain any import restrictions;
- the Community will open its 'non-sensitive' markets virtually immediately, but for 'sensitive' industrial markets the abolition of tariffs and quantitative restrictions (QRs) will take from four to six years;
- the Community will offer concessions, but nothing like free trade, on agriculture;
- CHP must adopt EC competition policy within three years, its intellectual property policy within five, and make best endeavours to approximate its other laws to EC standards. Environmental protection – an agreed priority between CHP and the Community – is to converge to EC standards;
- despite the adoption of EC competition policy, CHP goods will still be subject to the Community's anti-dumping policy;
- there are no special provisions for the mobility of ordinary workers, although *de facto* the mobility of the highly skilled is likely to occur;

- there are strong provisions to encourage and protect EC direct investment in CHP – for example, commitments over the flows of funds for repatriating profits and disinvestment, and rules of origin that require non-EC-owned firms in CHP to have 60 percent local content before their exports to the EC qualify for trade concessions.

In summary, the Europe Agreements seem intent on obtaining markets and production facilities in CHP, on managing access to EC markets both directly and indirectly by imposing the EC commercial environment on CHP and, above all, on avoiding serious levels of migration. The Agreements foresee the possibility of eventual EC membership for CHP, so it is sensible to adopt EC institutions in the long run. But membership is a long way off and in the meantime it is difficult not to see in the Agreements a degree of 'managed liberalism'.

The Community's preferential arrangements differ in three major respects from genuine enlargement. First, they exclude migration. The Community has a profound desire to avoid major immigration; by offering selected market access it attempts to relieve the pressure of immigration, while avoiding the worst adjustment pressures on industry through the careful selection of sectors to liberalise and the maintenance of safeguards and anti-dumping policies. Second, although preferences often involve transfers to the non-EC partners they are relatively small and fixed unilaterally by the Community. Members, on the other hand, negotiate transfers mutually on a more generous scale. The third difference lies in trade policy: enlargement entails reciprocal trade policy changes – usually requiring tariff reductions by accedants on their imports from both EC and non-EC countries. Preferences, on the other hand, entail no changes in tariffs on extra-EC trade and, for developing countries, none on imports from the Community. Thus in the past enlargement has been a stronger liberalising force than preferences.

3.3 'Managed Liberalism'

'Managed liberalism' is perhaps the principal feature of EC preferences, but it is also present in genuine enlargement. The Community exploits the weakness of GATT Article XXIV's injunction that preferences must cover substantially all trade and foresee the abolition of intra-area tariffs to protect particular sectors from competition. On accession, it addresses non-members' worries about market shares by bringing partners into the club; but it does so on its own terms and, by imposing its own standards and legislation, in a fashion that mitigates at least some of the competitive pressures on existing members. Managed liberalism is a substitute for genuine liberalisation, but a poor one because it typically attenuates competition in precisely those sectors which are most in need of improved efficiency.

4. Beyond the CU

The second unique feature of the European Communities as an integration scheme is the extent to which it has carried integration beyond mere trade preferences. The Treaty of Rome devotes considerable space to 'The Customs Union', which entails free trade internally and a CET, but supplements and supports it by a series of other policies. This section considers the role of these additional policies in fostering integration. The provisions for factor mobility are additional to those establishing the CU, and are necessary to the establishment of a Common Market – a CU with factor mobility – which was always part of the original conception. I shall argue, however, that the other additions – common policies and common rules – are best seen, at least in the past, as necessary props for the common market rather than as additional objectives in their own right. Only recently have they shown signs of evolving from defensive measures into practical steps towards genuine economic union.

4.1 Commercial policy

The Customs Union title of the Treaty of Rome dealt only with tariffs, but in the 1950s QRs were equally important and it was plain that these must not be allowed to undermine the CU. Hence the same title also called for the abolition of QRs on the flow of domestically-produced goods between members which, with a few exceptions, was achieved without great difficulty. QRs on imports from outside the Community, however, were dealt with elsewhere in the Treaty (under Economic Policy), even though uniformity in this respect would appear to be a necessary part of a CU. They were subject to much weaker provisions for harmonisation than internal QRs, with the result that Brussels has only gradually wrested control of these instruments from the national capitals. Even in the 1990s a few national QRs still exist (see GATT, 1991) supported by internal QRs on third-country goods to prevent trade deflection.

The struggle over commercial policy has, I believe, had some unfortunate consequences for EC trade policy. For example, the EC restrictions on imports of Japanese VCRs in 1983 (see Greenaway and Hindley, 1985) arose from a desire to 'communitarise' unilateral French action against Japan and to avert the threat of it against Germany. Similarly, the official sanctioning of the French and Italian national QRs on footwear from Korea and Taiwan in 1988, followed by their conversion into EC-wide QRs in 1990, reflected Brussels' desire first to capture trade policy and then to harmonise it, even though the resulting policy imposes widespread costs (see Winters, 1992a). Vehicle imports reflect a similar phenomenon, with Brussels unable or unwilling to prevent national import policies which segment the common market (see, for example, de Melo and Messerlin, 1988; Smith and Venables, 1990), but then willing to take them over in the name of Community policy.

These incidents reflect the need for a CU to cover the whole of trade policy from the start. Although, as a result of '1992', the EC is now approaching a genuinely common trade policy, the thirty-five-year transition has been far from smooth and efficient.

4.2 Transfers and cohesion

While liberal trade is generally welfare-improving in aggregate it cannot be guaranteed to be so for every agent involved. Hence many have argued that a long-lived integration scheme must have provision for internal transfers. These might be desired for genuinely alturistic reasons, but in terms of 'Realpolitik' they are necessary in order to defuse distributional struggles. Such conflicts and the difficulty of devising satisfactory compensation schemes led to the collapse of most regional integration schemes among developing countries (see, e.g., Foroutan, Chapter 8 in this volume). Even in less extreme circumstances the inability to separate resource allocation and distributional outcomes can lead to substantial inefficiency in the former. This is particularly so where, as in the Community, unanimity or near-unanimity is required for action.[12]

The Community has long espoused adjustment assistance and income convergence as policy objectives, but it created effective policy tools only in 1972, when the European Social Fund was supplemented by a Regional Development Fund. The latter was explicitly compensatory, responding to UK fears about its declining regions. Further cohesion funds were earmarked in the mid-1980s as a means of encouraging Irish support for the Single European Act, and of smoothing Iberian accession.

There is no doubt about the political importance of the cohesion policies, and little doubt that they distribute resources in roughly the right direction (see Molle, 1990 and Franzmeyer et al., 1991). Whether they are very significant economically, however, is less obvious. The Community's budget is so small relative to those of unitary states' governments that the feasible redistribution is severely limited. Thus in 1990 the budgets for Social Policy and Regional Policy were ECU 3.3 billion and ECU 4.8

billion respectively – approximately 8 percent and 11 percent of the full EC budget and 0.07 percent and 0.10 percent of GDP (Franzmeyer *et al.*, 1991). Molle (1990), summarising various studies of regional policy, concludes that the latter has, so far, been of limited importance.

4.3   The Common Market

The Treaty of Rome explicitly seeks to establish a 'Common Market', which it interprets as a CU plus the free mobility of workers, establishment, services and capital. The Treaty made general provisions in these areas, intending that the details should be determined subsequently by legislation and directives. Progress has been patchy in achieving the so-called 'four freedoms', but it illustrates two important features of the Community's success.

First, since 1965, when the French boycotted Community institutions for six months, the concept of integration has not been seriously challenged by member governments; but in return there has been great pragmatism over the selection of which elements of integration to promote and about how to promote them: national sensitivities have been well regarded, and EC legislation abounds with derogations, long transitional periods, and lax enforcements. The Community has elevated the politics of compromise to previously unknown levels; while this has permitted gradual progress and secured the fundamental institutions of the Community, it has generated some pretty undesirable policy packages. It has also generated the need for periodic consolidations, of which '1992' is the latest example: its objective in many areas is merely to apply to the 1957 Treaty more effectively.

Second, the Treaty of Rome promotes the four freedoms mainly on the basis of *national treatment* – the requirement that member-states do not discriminate against residents of other members in the application of *their own* laws on labour, services and capital. This has then been supplemented by moves effectively to harmonise national standards by *mutual recognition* – the requirement that if a standard or qualification meets one member's criteria it should be seemed acceptable by other members. Together, these have been expected to initiate a period of *competition among rules*, whereby those member-states retaining rules which are unfavourable to their firms or consumers come under pressure to reform them, thus inducing a convergence within the Community around relatively attractive rules. The importance of this approach is that it threatens national sovereignty much less directly than does central rulemaking. In this way it reduces political frictions, allows greater progress over the long term[13] and aids convergence towards the more liberal rules.[14]

It is clear that the four freedoms have increased the degree of integration within the Community, but it is hard to argue that they have been indispensable to its success. Wage rates have converged somewhat across the Community (Molle, 1990; Norman, 1991), but that could as easily reflect trade as migration. Indeed, the evidence suggests that migration fell once trade became more fully integrated. Moreover, internal migration flows are not very large: only around half a million workers from the three Southern accedents work elsewhere in the Community. Similarly for firms: foreign direct investment flows between members are significant but are smaller than flows with third countries. The other two freedoms are even less well developed. Since 1980 financial and portfolio capital mobility has increased substantially for some member countries, but mainly as part of a general liberalisation. Service mobility – the right to sell services in one member-state while based in another – has made little headway. '1992' and the moves towards monetary union have now, however, started to make significant progress in these last two areas.

4.4 Common sectoral policies

The Treaties of Paris and Rome obliged the Community to pursue common policies in three sectors: agriculture (including fisheries), transport, and energy. Such common policies entail integration beyond the realms of a Common Market and, at least in the case of agriculture, have provided important political cement for the creation of the European Communities. Unfortunately, however, from an economic perspective, by enshrining interventionary policies in the Community's constitution, they have been either ineffective or positively harmful.

The European Coal and Steel Community (ECSC), founded in 1952, sought to ensure non-discriminatory supplies of coal throughout the Community, but in keeping with the interventionism of the day, allowed both price and production controls. The latter have since been used extensively to support the coal sector, leaving it one of the most distorted sectors in the 1980s.

Agriculture was a key sector in the postwar European economies and was heavily supported by national governments. In order that national differences in this support did not distort competition in the common market a common policy was required, and it was naturally very interventionist. Price support policies for supply-elastic goods contain the seeds of their own downfall, but in the Community it was doubly difficult to control them. First, the CAP established a new bureaucracy and was for many years the most tangible of Brussels' bureaucratic achievements.[15]

Second, the details of the CAP – specifically the levels of the intervention prices – are fixed in the Agricultural Council and are subject to the 'restaurant bill' problem. The costs of agricultural support are aggregated over the Community and then divided between members more or less proportionately to GDP. Hence each member country has a short-term interest in seeking price increases for any product in which its share of EC production exceeds its share of GDP. Add to this the Community's style of consensus politics and the natural tendencies of committees towards universalism (Shepsle and Weingast, 1981) and the outcome is strong pressure for agricultural prices to rise. Only the severest budgetary pressure seems able to control them.

In 1957 internal transport was also extensively controlled in all member-states, and it was feared that the controls could undermine the common market by substituting discriminatory transportation tariffs for trade policy. Hence Treaty Articles expressly forbid either using transport rates to support or protect manufacturing or the application of different transport rates to exports and imports of the same good over the same route. The Treaty also, however, legitimised and reinforced national policies by implicitly recognising their primacy until a common policy was evolved and by failing to provide the means for doing the latter. Thus, for example, railway prices are determined by governments, road haulage is restricted by quotas and inland shipping operates market sharing agreements (see Molle, 1990 for details).

Transport has been the subject of several competition policy actions, and some of the worst excesses in road haulage have been tackled by the '1992' programme. Nevertheless it and the CAP offer important lessons in the establishment of the institutions of integration. Explicit mention in the Treaty – especially of any policy prescriptions – legitimises one particular constellation of policies, affirming a sort of 'right' to the benefits it provides. The absence of an exit mechanism, coupled with the Community's pragmatic bargaining approach to policymaking, puts huge pressure on member governments to agree, and because change requires complete or near unanimity, the legitimised status quo becomes a very likely outcome in any policy debate (see Scharpf, 1988). Moreover, under such circumstances any change that can be negotiated tends to be an agglomeration of specific provisions catering to the various interests represented in the decision body, reinforcing the 'restaurant bill' and universalist effects noted above, and because EC decision bodies comprise the representatives of national governments rather than of legislatures or electorates, bureaucratic interests get a very high weight in this process. The result, illustrated by the common policies, is stasis; reform becomes almost impossible except in deep crises which make the status quo infeasible.

The experience of the common policies also suggests the dangers inherent in the establishment of powerful sectoral bureaucracies and in the tendency to identify a particular policy with the integration process itself. Finally observe that, in all three cases, the common policies arose from a need to restrain national policies in order to preserve the common market in goods. The problem was, in effect, the existing regulation: integration is likely to be more successful if it is accompanied by liberalisation, as in the '1992' initiative.

4.5   Common rules and economic policy

The wish to support the common market is even more evident in the Community's common rules. Articles 85–94 of the Treaty of Rome define competition policy in terms of situations that are incompatible with the common market. This aims to prevent collusion, the abuse of a dominant position, intra-EC dumping, and state aids, and initially considered these phenomena only to the extent that they distorted internal competition. The policy is designed to remove the excuse that trade policy was necessary because of unfair practices elsewhere in the Community, by promising to treat the unfairness directly. '1992' foresees the effective extension of EC competition policy to transport and finance, and has introduced new merger regulations. While it is natural that an economic union should have a common competition policy, the recent changes may also be thought of as a means of levelling the playing field in support of the greater market opening associated with '1992'. While competition policy has clearly not eliminated all state aids, it has diffused many potential conflicts and has imposed some control over private anti-competitive behaviour. In this, it has probably been rather an important part of the integration process.

Closely related to common rules is the operation of general economic and social policy, originally defined in terms of balance of payments policy, commercial policy, labour law and a catch-all chapter on conjunctural policy. Yet again support for the common market underpins the balance of payments chapter – the need to guarantee the payments flows deriving from other aspects of integration – but in this case further mutual liberalisation and policy coordination was called for and, at least since 1978, achieved. Indeed the fruits of such cooperation are evident in the current push towards monetary and political union. Hence in the very long run these Articles – and their extension beyond the common market – may turn out to have been among the most significant of the Treaty, but they contain few lessons for other groups which do not intend to progress so far along the path of integration.

Common policies are not absolutely necessary to the creation of a CU but, like the provision for compensatory transfers, they probably significantly aid progress in that direction. They remove bones of contention – or rather offer common solutions to them – a job which, in their absence, would have to be done by intergovernmental disputes' procedures, which are more confrontational and divisive. To progress further to a common market, however, almost certainly does require common policies in order to 'level the playing field', for no member is likely to accept factor mobility if policies for competition and labour can vary substantially across the union. The relevance of EC experience in these dimensions is thus limited to those groups which intend, or have taken, effective steps towards deeper integration.

5   Conclusion

EC integration has been rather special. It arose from a sense of mission far beyond the attainment of mere economic benefits. It explicitly sought to go beyond trade preferences to a common market and laid the ground for even deeper integration, as the 'additional' policies and the institutional framework show. The mission continues today and has resulted in a pragmatic attitude towards deepening integration in which (virtually) every partner is brought along, and in which preserving the fact of integration has been as important as its content. This has led to a good deal of untidiness and also to some unfortunate policy, but it has kept the show on the road until such time as a more coherent and tidier policy can be devised. In this regard '1992' has been important. It has implemented many of the intentions of 1957 in a more consistent way than heretofore, and extended integration to new areas such as services, standards and qualifications. It has, more or less, completed the common market and in so doing has provided a considerable economic stimulus even well before the date 1992. More recent developments – European Monetary Union (EMU) and the Maastricht Treaty – go beyond the common market but are too recent to be the source of lessons for others.

What are the main lessons for other schemes? First, political commitment is necessary: the deeper the integration, the greater the required commitment. Second, an explicit commitment to redistribution is useful, even if it is on a small scale. Third, there is a danger of becoming inward-looking, and doing so is harmful. Fourth, the free internal circulation of goods benefits from, and possibly requires, supporting policies designed to prevent or settle disputes. Fifth, pragmatism is probably the only way of proceeding, at least in the early stages: national governments have to be brought along at every step.

NOTES

This chapter is partly based on work conducted under the CEPR's programme 'The International Trade Consequences of "1992"', which was funded by the Community's Stimulation Programme in Economic Science, the Department of Trade and Industry and the Foreign and Commonwealth Office, and on a project funded by the Economic and Social Research Council (grant R000231932). I am grateful to both. I am also very grateful to the editors, the participants of the conference and to Carl Hamilton, Jacques Pelkmans, John Redmond, André Sapir, Helen Wallace and Zhen Kun Wang who put so much effort into commenting on and improving my first draft. I also thank Tina Attwell and Maureen Hyde for typing. None of these people is to be held responsible for the chapter's remaining shortcomings.

1 See Pelkmans and Winters (1988) for a discussion of the policies and economics of '1992'.
2 I have no space to describe the history or institutions of EC integration (see, for example, Swann, 1988 or Molle, 1990) but I must note that the Community springs from the internationalist sentiment of the immediate postwar era. Its major objective was to prevent a future Franco–German war, and it received strong support from the United States for that reason. Hence there has always been more to EC integration than the mere calculation of economic gains and losses. It is also space, not a lack of importance, which precludes discussing the EMS.
3 This fact is well illustrated by the Community's own promotion of '1992': despite its political overtones, it was presented almost entirely in terms of economic gains.
4 Of course much of the latter's growth has represented catch-up, and equally obviously failure to achieve the highest growth rates in the world hardly constitutes evidence of EC economic failure. But the constant European worry about Japanese and NIC technology and competitiveness suggests that the Europeans themselves see these countries as valid yardsticks for EC performance.
5 It is the change in protection, not the level, that affects the growth. It is also worth noting that protection does decline in some sectors, e.g., textiles and clothing (see Hamilton, 1990).
6 One could argue about the precise definition of hi-tech industry, but the basic message of the figures is robust and has been replicated by other researchers (e.g., OECD, 1986 and Dosi, Pavitt and Soete, 1991). CEC (1990) itself offers further evidence on individual industries.
7 For example, suppose that each EC member country had an agricultural sector plus a manufacturing industry different from that of all its neighbours. In isolation, each manufacturing industry might be able to control its agricultural sector's protectionist proclivities, but the combined agriculture might dominate any individual manufacturing industry.
8 Sweden is attempting a unilateral agricultural reform.
9 The long transitional periods negotiated for Iberian accession have been argued to constrain the speed of liberalisation with Eastern Europe, because it would not be right that the latter have more liberal access to other EC markets than the former, even temporarily. This is sometimes said to explain the Spanish position.

10 The Scandinavians use state aids to support the populations in their rural northern areas, but these areas are far too rich to be covered by the regional exemption to the ban on state aids under Article 92.3 of the Treaty of Rome.

11 Haaland and Norman's (1992) general equilibrium simulation model, with five country blocs, thirteen commodities and Cournot oligopoly in most industrial sectors, suggests that '1992' could reduce EFTA's real income by half of 1 percent of their expenditure on tradeable goods. '1992' markets has its greatest effects on skill-intensive and imperfectly competitive sectors – those in which significant rents can be earned. As EC output expands and prices fall in these sectors, EFTA producers, who are already relatively efficient but who receive no *added stimulus* from '1992', lose sales and rents. If, on the other hand, EFTA joins and becomes fully integrated with the Community, in the senses that neither EC nor EFTA firms can price discriminate between EC and EFTA markets and that EFTA adopts all the EC's pro-competitiveness '1992' policies, then EFTA real incomes rise by about 3 percent of tradeables' expenditure. The European Economic Area (EEA) offers some of these benefits: but it does not cover agriculture, external trade policy, taxation and some competition policy; it offers almost no say in EC policy; and it is more easily dissolved than full membership.

12 Scharpf (1988) discusses the way such factors distort political processes.

13 EC attempts at central rulemaking have frequently been tortuous and inconclusive.

14 It must, of course, be recognised that unfettered competition between rules can lead to suboptimal outcomes, such as the underprovision of public goods as members compete to lower taxes. This is more than de Melo, Panagariya and Rodrik's preference asymmetry (see Chapter 6 in this volume): the final outcome could be far different from the mean of the individual countries' preferences.

15 Until 1980 attacking the CAP was equated with attacking European integration, and even now the policy appears virtually immune to fundamental reform and quite beyond rational discussion in fora such as the GATT. As at May 1992 the Uruguay Round remains snagged mainly on agriculture and the reform plans proposed by Commissioner MacSharry have been diluted so far as to be insufficient to cure the problems of overproduction and waste.

REFERENCES

Balassa, B. (1975) *European Economic Integration*, Amsterdam: North-Holland.

Commission for the European Communities (CEC) (1990) 'International Trade of the European Communities', *European Economy*, 39.

  (1991a) 'Annual Economic Report 1991–92', *European Economy*, **50** (December).

  (1991b) 'Fair Competition in the Internal Market: Community State Aid Policy', *European Economy*, **48** (September).

Curzon, V. (1965) *Multilateral Commercial Diplomacy*, London: Michael Joseph.

Dosi, G., K. Pavitt and L. Soete (1990) *The Economics of Technical Change and International Trade*, London: Harvester Wheatsheaf.

Franzmeyer, F. *et al.* (1991) 'The Regional Impact of Community Policies',

Regional Policy and Transport Paper, **17**, Luxembourg: The European Parliament.

GATT (1991) *Trade Policy Review: European Communities, Vol I and II*, Geneva: GATT.

Greenaway, D. and B. Hindley (1985) *What Britain Pays for Voluntary Export Restraints, Thames Essay*, **43**, London: Trade Policy Research Centre.

Haaland, J.I. and V.D. Norman (1992) 'Global Production Effects of European Integration', Chapter 3 in Winters (ed.) (1991) pp. 67–88.

Hamilton, C.B. (1990) 'The Nordic EFTA Countries' Options: Community Membership or a Permanent EFTA-Accord', Chapter 4 in *EFTA Countries in a Changing Europe*, Geneva: EFTA.

Han, S.S. and H.H. Liesner (1971) 'Britain and the Common Market: The Effect of Entry on the Pattern of Manufacturing Production', Department of Applied Economics, *Occasional Paper*, **27**, Cambridge University Press.

Hufbauer, G.C. (ed.) (1990) *Europe 1992: An American Perspective*, Washington, DC: Brookings Institution.

IMF (1988) 'The Common Agricultural Policy of the European Community', *Occasional Paper*, **62**, Washington, DC: IMF.

Jacquemin, A. and A. Sapir (1988a) 'European Integration of World Integration?', *Weltwirtschaftliches Archiv*, **124**, pp. 127–39.

(1988b) 'International Trade and Integration of the European Community: An Econometric Analysis', *European Economic Review*, **32**, pp. 1439–50.

(1991) 'Competition and Imports in the European Market', Chapter 5 in Winters and Venables (eds) (1991) pp. 82–91.

Kelly, M. *et al.* (1988) 'Issues and Developments in International Trade Policy', *Occasional Paper*, **63**, Washington, DC: IMF.

Laird, S. and A. Yeats (1988) 'Trends in Non-tariff Barriers of Developed Countries 1966–1986', *PPR Working Paper*, **WPS 137**, Washington, DC: World Bank.

(1990) *Quantitative Methods for Trade Barrier Analysis*, London: Macmillan.

Langhammer, R.J. and A. Sapir (1987) *Economic Impact of Generalized Tariff Preferences*, Aldershot: Gower.

Lawrence, R.Z. (1991) 'Emerging Regional Arrangements: Building Blocks or Stumbling Blocks?', Chapter 2 in O'Brien (ed.) (1991) pp. 23–35.

Luyten, P. (1989) 'Multilateralism vs Preferential Bilateralism: A European View', Chapter 11 in Schott (ed.) (1989) pp. 271–9.

Martin, J.P. *et al.* (1990) 'Economy-wide Effects of Agricultural Policies in OECD Countries: Simulation Results with WALRAS', *OECD Economic Studies*, **13**, pp. 131–72.

Melo, J. de and P. Messerlin (1988) 'Price, Quality and Welfare Effects of European VERs on Japanese Autos', *European Economic Review*, **32**, pp. 1527–46.

Molle, W. (1990) *The Economics of European Integration*, Aldershot: Dartmouth.

Nogués, J., A. Olechowski and L.A. Winters (1986) 'The Extent of Industrial Countries' Non-tariff Barriers to Trade', *World Bank Economic Review*, **1**, pp. 181–99.

Norman, V.D. (1991) '1992 and EFTA', Chapter 7 in Winters and Venables (eds) (1991) pp. 120–39.

O'Brien, R. (ed.) (1991) *Finance and the International Economy, Number 5*, Oxford: Oxford University Press for American Express.

OECD (1986) 'R & D Invention and Competitiveness', *OECD Science and Technology Indicators*, **2**, Paris: OECD.

(1990) *Agricultural Policies, Markets and Trade*, Paris: OECD.

Pelkmans, J. and L.A. Winters (1988) *Europe's Domestic Market, Chatham House Paper*, **43**, London: Royal Institute for International Affairs.

Scharpf, F.W. (1988) 'The Joint-decision Trap: Lessons from German Federalism and European Integration', *Public Administration*, **66**, pp. 239–78.

Schott, J.J. (ed.) (1989) *Free Trade Areas and U.S. Trade Policy*, Washington, DC: Institute for International Economics.

Shepsle, K.A. and B.R. Weingast (1981) 'Political Preferences for the Pork Barrel: A Generalisation', *American Journal of Political Science*, **25**, pp. 96–111.

Smith, A. and A.J. Venables (1990) 'Automobiles . . .', Chapter 3 in Hufbauer (ed.) (1990) pp. 119–58.

Swann, D. (1988) *The Economics of the Common Market*, 7th edn, Harmondsworth: Penguin.

United Nations Economic Commission for Europe (UNECE) (1990) 'Economic Survey, 1989/90', Geneva: UNECE.

Wang, Z.K. and L.A. Winters (1991) 'The Trading Potential of Eastern Europe', CEPR, Discussion Paper, **610** (November). London: Centre for Economic Policy Research.

Weiss, F.D. *et al.* (1988) *Trade Policy in West Germany*, Tübingen, J.C.B. Mohr.

Winters, L.A. (1987) 'Britain in Europe: A Survey of Quantitative Trade Studies', *Journal of Common Market Studies*, **25**, pp. 315–35.

(1991) *International Economics*, 4th edn, London: Harper-Collins.

(1992a) 'Integration, Trade Policy and European Footwear Trade', Chapter 7 in Winters (ed.) (1992) pp. 175–209.

(1992b) 'The Europe Agreements: A Missed Opportunity', University of Birmingham (mimeo).

Winters, L.A. (ed.) (1992) *Trade Flows and Trade Policy After '1992'*, London: Cambridge University Press.

Winters, L.A. and A.J. Venables (eds) (1991) *European Integration: Trade and Industry*, London: Cambridge University Press.

World Bank (1987) *The World Development Report 1987*, Washington, DC: World Bank.

(1991) *The World Development Report 1991*, Washington, DC: World Bank.

Discussion

RAVI KANBUR

Chapter 7 is a useful survey of the history of EC integration and the issues to which it gives rise. I want to pick up on Winters' argument where he leaves it in section 4.4 – that is, the interaction between integration in the movement of goods and factors, and other instruments of policy such as taxes and regulations. Winters rightly identifies two views on these. One is that after integration, competition over rules and policies, e.g., over tax rates or over environmental and other regulations, will resolve any problems and will in fact lead to convergence of policies. The second view is that supranational intervention is needed to regulate this competition – for example, through explicit harmonisation of policies.

I want to evaluate these two views using a framework that Keen and I have developed for looking at tax competition between countries that differ in economic size (1991), and which he, Sweder van Wijnbergen and I have applied to environmental regulation competition (1992). In such a setting, the amount of tax base that the small country attracts by undercutting is that much greater; thus, in the equilibrium of the revenue-maximising Nash game, the small country will undercut the larger country. The greater the size differential, the greater will be the incentive to undercut, and the lower will be the resulting tax rates, or the more lax will be the regulation, depending on which instrument is in play. In this setting, anything that makes the movement of tax base across boundaries easier will increase the wastefulness of the competition for tax base through use of other instruments. It can also be shown that the increase in wastefulness is greater, the greater is the disparity in economic size between the two countries.

In this setting, the view that competition among rules and policies of different countries will take care of divergences in tax rates and regulations as integration proceeds is somewhat beside the point. It is not the divergence *per se*, but the wastefulness of competition that is important. Hence the standard response of 'harmonisation' is also inappropriate. It can be shown that the key is minimum tax or standards agreements, and that harmonisation efforts are bound to flounder.

If, as seems to be argued in this chapter, there is convergence in incomes and structure in the Community, then that part of wasteful competition which is exacerbated by size divergences may well be relieved. However, the analysis gives little comfort to those assessing the consequences of integration in Africa, where economic size disparities (e.g., between Nigeria and the other ECOWAS states, see Chapter 8 below) are considerable, and are likely to sharpen the problem of wasteful competition in attracting tax bases. The question of institutions that can design and enforce policy cooperation then becomes even more important.

REFERENCES

Kanbur, R. and M. Keen (1991) 'Tax Competition and Tax Cooperation When Countries Differ in Size', World Bank, *PRE Working Paper*, **738**, revised version forthcoming in *American Economic Review*.
Kanbur, R., M. Keen and S. van Wijnbergen (1992) 'Environmental Regulation, International Competition and Direct Foreign Investment'.

ANDRÉ SAPIR

This volume seeks to examine the consequences of regional integration (RI) schemes among industrial nations (North–North) for the countries which are the World Bank's clients, and it aims at making recommendations to these countries as to whether they should form similar schemes either on their own (South–South) or with industrial nations (North–South). On both counts, the European Community deserves close scrutiny. Not only is it the main example of North–North (NN) integration, but it is also – since the accession to membership of Greece, Portugal, and Spain – the only existing case of North–South (NS) integration. In this respect, Winters' Chapter 7 constitutes a central contribution. It provides an assessment of EC integration in general and draws some lessons on the NS aspect of EC integration.

I had major objections with the draft of the paper presented at the Conference. These stemmed from its assessment of EC integration. Winters then claimed that, although 'the EC has survived and expanded, . . . its economic success is less clear . . . [since it] has tended to turn in on itself and to lag behind at least some parts of the world economy'. At first glance, it appears that Winters' revised version has taken on board many of my earlier comments. Although this provides, undoubtedly, some satisfaction, it also makes my task of discussant very difficult. Upon closer examination, however, I find that not all reasons for my earlier dissatisfaction have disappeared. In fact, Winters seems to have changed his mind rather than his heart about EC integration. The giveaway comes in the discussion about whether the Community has been inward- or outward-looking: 'while every nation has its protectionists, *I suspect* that an organisation designed to promote mutual market penetration, and whose yardstick is "integration", is particularly prone to such perceptions' (p. 207, emphasis added). My comments focus on sections 2 and 3 of the chapter which provide, respectively, an assessment of EC integration and a discussion of enlargement and preferences.

1   Assessment of EC integration

Winters qualifies the Community's record on economic integration as 'adequate but should try harder' (p. 203). His reservation about EC integration stems from an 'informal and impressionistic' (p. 203) analysis of

EC trade policy which produces two contentions. First the Community has become increasingly protectionist. Second, the process of EC integration (particularly its decisionmaking procedures) is inherently biased toward protectionist outcomes. Let me examine both arguments in turn.

It is argued that, although tariffs have gradually come down over the past thirty years, the Community has increasingly resorted to non-tariff barriers (NTBs). Although this may be true, it does not follow, as implied by Winters, that levels of EC external protection have generally increased. In fact, the contrary probably holds. This can be seen by decomposing EC expenditure on apparent consumption into three shares: domestic production (net of exports), intra-EC imports and extra-EC imports. Computations by Sapir (forthcoming) for the period 1980–91 shows that, for total processed products, the share of consumption from domestic suppliers has steadily declined (from 67 to 56 percent), while the share supplied by EC partners *and* non-EC partners have both risen (from 19 to 25 percent and from 14 to 19 percent, respectively). This situation of 'double (i.e., internal and external) trade creation' is likely to reflect a lowering in average external protection for total processed products. The opposite holds, however, for the subcategory of processed agricultural products. Here, the share of consumption supplied by extra-EC partners has actually declined (from 7 to 6 percent), presumably as a result of increased protection in temperate agriculture afforded by the common agricultural policy (CAP).

Winters' second allegation is that a coalition of states with a common external trade policy, like the Community, will automatically favour protectionist outcomes. Clearly, theory is of little help in such matters since models could be constructed to confirm or reject this proposition. Rather, given the second-best nature of the problem, we must look for empirical evidence. Winters has clearly in mind the 'fiercely protectionist' CAP (p. 205). Although there is no denying that levels of external protection have been high under the CAP, one cannot be sure that they would have been lower in the absence of the Community (here the United Kingdom is, probably, an exception). The example of Switzerland and the Nordic countries, which protect their agriculture even more than the Community, suggests that the answer is not as evident as Winters would have us believe.

On the other hand, Winters strongly doubts that, in the absence of EC integration, most European nations would have maintained higher rates of external protection. His view runs counter the majority opinion. For instance, Gary Hufbauer (1990, p. 5) states that 'France and Italy, in particular, would have strongly resisted making any trade concessions in the 1960s, and Germany would not have made trade concessions in isolation from its continental partners'. Patrick Messerlin (1992, p. 159) also notes that the 'first impact of the Treaty of Rome was to impose . . . [a] macroeconomic environment [which] allowed the progressive opening of the French economy . . . As a result, the protection granted to the French manufacturing sector vis-à-vis both the Community and the rest of the world . . . decreased during the 1960s'.

2   Enlargement and preferential trading arrangements

Winters is also critical of EC 'extension', which covers enlargement as well as preferential trading arrangements. He argues that such extension 'displays a measure of "managed liberalism" – a desire to open markets in a fashion that restricts the resulting shocks' (p. 212). Although the Community has extended both Northwards and Southwards, I shall confine my comments to the latter.

Viewed from the perspective of NS integration, there is a fundamental difference between enlargement and preferential trading arrangements. Enlargement implies two-way trade liberalisation, while preferential treatment means only one-way liberalisation.

The second, or Southern, enlargement resulted in the Community opening up to Greece, Portugal and Spain, and these countries opening up to the Community. But because the Community is a customs union (CU) (rather than a free-trade area (FTA)) and the existing members were relatively large compared to the new entrants, it meant that the Southern members had to adopt the Common External Tariff (CET), which was substantially more liberal than their own tariff schedule (except for agricultural products). The enlargement led, therefore, to the liberalisation of previously highly protected countries and to trade creation (except in agriculture, where it produced mainly trade diversion). Although Winters now recognises this important point, he claims that accession may nonetheless hurt new entrants as it 'will often constrain their competitiveness and comparative advantage' (p. 215). I am dumbfounded.

Conversely, preferential schemes – such as the arrangements with the Mediterranean countries and the African, Caribbean and Pacific (ACP) states – have provided selected developing countries with free (or nearly free) access to the EC market, without any liberalisation on their part. One-way preferential arrangements have, therefore, wasted an opportunity to liberalise highly protected nations and resulted in trade-diverting rents that have proved difficult to eliminate.

3   Conclusion

My assessment of the impact of EC integration differs substantially from that of Winters. Whereas he feels that the Community may have succumbed to the 'danger of becoming inward-looking' (p. 206), I see a process of RI having led to substantial multilateral liberalisation, beyond what could have happened without the Community. Thus, I share the sentiment expressed by Bob Lawrence (1991): 'The postwar experience of the EC is heartening. Increasing European integration after the Treaty of Rome was quite compatible with the lowering of Europe's external barriers.' At the same time, however, I see two dark clouds in the blue sky of European integration. The first is the CAP and its large costs to citizens both inside and outside the Community. The other is the policy of one-way preferential arrangements which may have both weakened the GATT system and created costly vested interests against trade liberalisation.

As far as NS integration is concerned, I draw two lessons from the EC experience. First, a customs union (like the Community) is preferable to an FTA (like NAFTA, the North American Free-Trade Agreement) when it comes to NS integration, because the former forces the South to adopt the North's (usually liberal) CET whereas the latter preserves the South's (usually protectionist) tariff schedule *vis-à-vis* third countries. Second, to be successful NS integration requires (efficient) transfers from the North to the South. Today, such transfers account for 25 percent of the EC budget and represent a large proportion of Southern Europe's investment in physical infrastructure.

NOTE

Views expressed here are the author's own and not those of the EC Commission.

REFERENCES

Hufbauer, G.C. (1990) 'An overview', in G.C. Hufbauer (ed.), *Europe 1992: An American Perspective*, Washington, DC: Brookings Institution.

Lawrence, R.Z. (1991) 'Emerging regional arrangements; building block or stumbling block?' (June) (mimeo).

Messerlin, P. (1992) 'Trade policies in France', in D. Salvatore (ed.), *National Trade Policies*, Handbook of Comparative Economic Policies, vol. 2, New York: Greenwood Press.

Sapir, A. (forthcoming) 'Regional integration in Europe', *Economic Journal*.

8 Regional integration in Sub-Saharan Africa: past experience and future prospects

FAEZEH FOROUTAN

1 Introduction

In the past three decades, a great number of broadly defined regional integration (RI) schemes have been adopted by all countries in Sub-Saharan Africa (SSA).[1] According to some accounts, there are currently over thirty Inter-Governmental Organisations (IGOs) in West Africa alone. The aims of RI schemes in SSA have ranged from limited cooperation among neighbouring countries in specific areas to the creation of an African Common Market. However, within all of SSA, there are at present no more than seven or eight IGOs that aim specifically at fully-fledged economic integration.

The appeal of some form of RI in SSA is almost intuitive. The SSA countries are very small in economic terms. In 1989, the Gross National Product (GNP) of all SSA countries put together was approximately equal to that of Belgium. They are also among the poorest in the world, with a *per capita* GNP of $340 in 1989 (see Table 8.1), and are very poorly endowed with human and physical capital. Common sense thus dictates that for countries with such characteristics it is economically justified to integrate their markets. Imagine subdividing Belgium into forty-something independent countries, each with its own isolated goods and factor markets, a different public administration, currency, language, fiscal and monetary authorities, army, plus a very inefficient intercountry transportation network. Economists would contend that the welfare of individuals would surely be reduced.

Why, despite the strong common sense appeal of this argument, has RI in SSA so far failed? Does this failure imply that RI as a model of development is harmful or, at best, ineffective for SSA and should be abandoned altogether, even as regionalism in the world appears to be gaining ground against multilateralism?

The objective of this chapter is precisely to address these issues. To do

Table 8.1. *Some economic indicators for SSA,[a] 1989 unless otherwise indicated*

Country	GDP $US million	GDP Annual growth rate 1980–9 (%)	Population 1000	Population Annual growth rate 1980–9 (%)	GNP per capita $US	GNP per capita Annual growth rate 1980–9 (%)
West Africa						
ECOWAS						
CEAO						
Benin	1600	1.8	4593	3.2	380	1.8
Burkina Faso	2460	5.0	8776	2.6	310	2.3
Côte d'Ivoire	7170	1.2	11713	4.0	790	− 3.0
Mali	2080	3.8	8212	2.5	260	1.0
Mauritania	910	1.4	1954	2.6	490	− 2.2
Niger, The	2040	− 1.6	7479	3.5	290	− 5.0
Senegal	4660	3.1	7211	3.0	650	0.0
MRU						
Guinea	2750	—	5547	2.5	430	—
Liberia	—	—	2475	3.1	—	—
Sierra Leone	890	0.6	4040	2.4	200	− 3.2
OTHER ECOWAS						
Cape Verde	281	5.8	369	2.5	760	3.2
Gambia, The	196	2.2	848	3.3	230	− 1.0
Ghana	5260	2.8	14425	3.4	380	− 0.8
Guinea Bissau	173	3.4	960	1.9	180	1.5
Nigeria	28920	− 0.4	113665	3.3	250	− 3.6
Togo	1340	1.4	3507	3.5	390	− 2.4

Table 8.1. (*cont.*)

Country	GDP $US million	GDP Annual growth rate 1980–9 (%)	Population 1000	Population Annual growth rate 1980–9 (%)	GNP per capita $US	GNP per capita Annual growth rate 1980–9 (%)
Central Africa						
UDEAC						
Cameroon	11 080	3.2	11 554	3.2	1010	0.7
CAR	1050	1.4	2951	2.7	390	– 1.5
Chad	1020	6.5	5537	2.4	190	3.9
Congo	2270	3.9	2208	3.4	930	0.1
Equ. Guinea	149	—	334	5.1	430	—
Gabon	3060	1.0	1105	3.7	2770	– 2.6
CEPGL						
Burundi	960	4.3	5299	2.9	220	1.6
Rwanda	2170	1.5	6893	3.3	310	– 1.9
Zaire	9610	1.9	34 442	3.1	260	– 1.6
OTHER CEN. AFR.						
São Tomé & Prin.	43	– 2.8	122	3.0	360	– 5.7
East and Southern Africa						
PTA						
Angola	7720	—	9694	2.5	620	—
Burundi	960	4.3	5299	2.9	220	1.6
Comoros	209	3.1	459	3.7	460	– 0.6

Djibuti	—	—	410	3.5	n.a.	n.a.
Ethiopia	5420	1.9	48861	2.9	120	− 1.1
Kenya	7130	4.1	23277	3.8	380	0.4
Lesotho	340	3.7	1722	2.7	470	− 0.5
Malawi	1410	2.7	8230	3.4	180	− 0.1
Mauritius	1740	5.9	1062	1.0	1950	5.3
Mozambique	1100	− 1.4	15357	2.7	80	− 6.0
Rwanda	2170	1.5	6893	3.3	310	− 1.9
Swaziland	683	4.1	761	3.4	900	0.6
Somalia	1090	3.0	6089	3.0	170	− 1.3
Sudan	—	1.1	24423	3.0	—	− 1.8
Uganda	4460	2.5	16772	3.2	250	− 1.0
Tanzania	2540	2.6	25627	3.5	120	− 1.6
Zambia	4700	0.8	7837	3.7	390	− 3.8
Zimbabwe	5250	2.7	9567	3.6	640	− 0.8
SADCC						
Angola	7720	—	9694	2.5	620	—
Botswana	2500	11.3	1217	3.4	1600	6.7
Lesotho	340	3.7	1722	2.7	470	− 0.5
Malawi	1410	2.7	8230	3.4	180	− 0.1
Mozambique	1100	− 1.4	15357	2.7	80	− 6.0
Namibia	—	—	—	—	—	—
Swaziland	683	4.1	761	3.4	900	0.6
Tanzania	2540	2.6	25627	3.5	120	− 1.6
Zambia	4700	0.8	7837	3.7	390	− 3.8
Zimbabwe	5250	2.7	9567	3.6	640	− 0.8
SACU						
Botswana	2500	11.3	1217	3.4	1600	6.7

Table 8.1. (*cont.*)

Country	GDP		Population		GNP *per capita*	
	$US million	Annual growth rate 1980–9 (%)	1000	Annual growth rate 1980–9 (%)	$US	Annual growth rate 1980–9 (%)
Lesotho	340	3.7	1722	2.7	470	− 0.5
Namibia	—	—	—	—	—	—
Swaziland	683	4.1	761	3.4	900	0.6
South Africa	80 370	1.5	34 925	2.4	2460	− 0.8
Other East & South Africa						
Madagascar	2280	0.8	11 174	2.8	230	− 2.6
Seychelle	285	2.5	68	0.9	4170	1.7
Total SSA	171k	2.1	480k	3.2	340	− 1.2

Note: [a] SSA is uniformly defined to exclude South Africa.
Source: World Bank: *World Development Report* (1991) and *World Bank Atlas* (1990).

so, five types of integration are defined: goods market or trade integration; labour market integration; capital market integration; monetary integration; and integration of government activity and regulation, alternatively known as cooperation. With the first three types of integration, barriers to the free movement of goods, services and factors of production (labour and capital) are removed *vis-à-vis* partners so that the regional market is effectively unified. Monetary integration, at least in the context of SSA, has implied the adoption of a common currency, a common central monetary authority, and the surrender of national autonomy in the field of monetary and exchange rate policy. Regulation and government activity integration implies adoption of similar tax and investment codes, harmonisation of administrative and bureaucratic rules, creation of joint administration such as a common customs administration, creation of common infrastructure and the provision of common services, such as a common civil aviation, multinational universities and research centres, and the like.

In the specific context of SSA, this classification of integration is preferable to the classical taxonomy of regional arrangements (free trade area, customs unions (CUs), common markets, and so on) because it allows each of these possible cases of integration to occur in conjunction with, or separately from, the others. For example, in SSA, monetary union in the CFA Franc Zone, exists without an effective integration of goods and factors markets. In the classical taxonomy, monetary integration would naturally come as the last step towards the creation of an economic union.

This chapter focuses mainly on trade integration, not because other forms of integration are unimportant but because they are more fully discussed in other chapters in this volume or, as with labour market integration, remain rather distant goals.

The fundamental conclusion of the chapter is that the structural characteristics of the SSA economies, the pursuit of import-substitution policies, and the very uneven distribution of costs and benefits of integration arising from economic differences among the partner countries, have thus far prevented any meaningful trade integration in SSA. Moreover, as the experience of the former Eastern European bloc suggests, there is no theoretical and empirical reason to believe that an import-substituting trade-integration strategy, even when successfully implemented, would have been welfare-improving. Other forms of integration, especially government activity and regulation integration, as well as trade integration when pursued as a complement rather than as substitute for global trade liberalisation, may nevertheless help the SSA economies to overcome the current economic impasse by providing an enabling environment to those SSA producers that begin competing in world markets. However, to the extent that the structural characteristics of SSA countries and their economic differences can change only very gradually, complete trade and labour market integration remain at this point a medium- to long-term objective.

The chapter is organised as follows. Section 2 provides a brief history of the most important current RI schemes in SSA, and describes their aims and achievements. Sections 3 and 4 evaluate the experience of SSA with trade and other types of integration and attempt to identify the causes of failure of most RI schemes in the subregion. The chapter concludes with section 5, which examines the implications for SSA of 'Europe 1992' and other such continental-wide RI schemes in the world that may represent a *de facto* demise of multilateralism.

2   RI schemes in SSA

At present, there are some seven or eight groupings in SSA that aim at fully-fledged integration. Some of these groupings date back to the colonial era. However, most integration schemes were adopted after independence during the period that runs from the late 1960s to the early 1980s. In many instances, the groupings comprised countries which had shared colonial ties to the same foreign power because the colonial ties had created a host of common institutions, a common official language, and a common currency. In other instances, the regional groupings, notably the larger ones, were more in line with the geographic proximity of the member countries.

A brief review follows of the major groupings in West, Central, East and Southern Africa. The aim is to highlight the historic circumstances that gave rise to the various groupings, the economic characteristics of the participating countries, and the objectives and achievements of the various groupings (see Table 8.2 for a summary).

2.1   West Africa[2]

There are currently three important regional groupings in West Africa: The Economic Community of Western African States (ECOWAS), the Communauté Economique de l'Afrique de l'Ouest (CEAO) and the Mano River Union (MRU). A fourth RI scheme, the Sene–Gambian Federation, between the republics of Senegal and the Gambia, ended in acrimony in 1989.

2.1.1 ECOWAS   This was formally founded in 1975, but the original idea of a community embracing all of Western Africa dates back to the mid-1960s. The idea was promoted particularly by Nigeria out of the

Table 8.2. General characteristics, objectives and achievements of regional groupings in SSA,[a] 1989 unless otherwise indicated

Name of regional grouping	Date created	No. of members	Total population (million)	Total GNP ($ billion)	Per capita GNP ($US)	Degree of openness ((X + M)/GNP)	Trade with SSA as % of total exports		Objectives	Achievements
							1980	1990		
West Africa										
ECOWAS	1975	16	195	64	326	50	3.6	6.4	Intra-group trade liberalization by 1989; introduction of a CET by 1994; free labor movement; fiscal and monetary harmonization; cooperation	Trade liberalization not yet achieved; CET does not exist; labour movement restricted; fiscal and monetary harmonization far away; limited cooperation in other areas
CEAO	1973	7	50	24	476	46	13.2	15.0	Trade integration and removal of all barriers by early 1990s; CET; monetary union; free labor and capital mobility	Monetary union since 1948; free capital mobility, labor mobility limited. CET not effective; partial preference granted to manufacturing goods: NTBs widespread
MRU	1980	3	12	4	335	46	0.9	2.9	Establishment of a CU	No progress
Central Africa										
UDEAC	1976	6	24	19	806	42	2.1	5.9	Complete trade integration monetary union, CET; free labor and capital movement	Monetary union since 1948; free capital mobility; partial tariff concessions to partners on manufactured goods; CET *de facto* non-existent

Table 8.2. (*cont.*)

Name of regional grouping	Date created	No. of members	Total population (million)	Total GNP ($ billion)	*Per capita* GNP ($US)	Degree of openness $((X + M)/GNP)$	Trade with SSA as % of total exports 1980	1990	Objectives	Achievements
CEPGL[b]	1982	3	47	12	260	28	4.1	7.6	CU and free labor movement; cooperation	Negligible progress in liberalizing intra-group trade; some joint projects
East and Southern Africa										
PTA	1981	18	212	58	274	40	8.4	7.6	Free trade area; complete trade liberalization by year 2000	Partial tariff concessions to partners on a limited number of goods
SADCC[b]	1980	10	80	25	311	55	3.5	6.3	Cooperation, joint projects in transport, communication, agriculture, industry, and energy	Largely successful in achieving its goals
SACU[b]	1910	5	39	89	2294	54	n.a.	n.a.	CU; capital and labor market integration; CET	All objectives achieved
Total SSA		47	480	162	340	43	2.8	6.0		

Notes:

[a] SSA is uniformly defined to exclude South Africa.

[b] Data for SADCC and SACU exclude Namibia.

Source: World Bank: *World Bank Atlas* (1990) and *World Development Report* (1991); IMF: *Directions of Trade*, various issues; discussion in the text.

conviction that a broader community would help her reduce dependence on oil and increase her influence in a French-dominated region. Anticipating the prospect of expanded markets and the opportunity to compete on more favourable terms with multinational corporations, West African private business enterprises, especially the Nigerian ones, also provided strong support to the creation of ECOWAS.[3]

With sixteen members, all the countries in Western Africa, an estimated total GNP of $64 billion and a population of 195 million in 1989, a wealth of mineral resources and a vast variety of agricultural products, ECOWAS is the largest and the most diversified economic community in SSA. Nonetheless, it is poor and economically underdeveloped. The average GNP *per capita* in 1989 was only $326 and economic activity concentrates heavily on extractive industry and agriculture for exports. For example, fourteen out of the sixteen ECOWAS countries derive over 60 percent of their export revenues from just one or two commodities. Despite these common characteristics, the ECOWAS members are more different than similar. The most striking example is provided by Nigeria, whose population and GNP are roughly equal to that of the other fifteen members put together.

The economic differences among ECOWAS members are exacerbated by cultural, historical and political disparities. Historic ties to different colonial powers have given rise to three official languages, English, French and Portuguese, different currencies, fiscal codes and public administration structures and practices. Additionally, the relations between the countries are marked by long-standing territorial disputes and political rivalries. Added to this catalogue of woes is the extreme political instability in most ECOWAS countries which has caused frequent and violent changes in political leadership.[4]

The ECOWAS Treaty of 1975 envisaged the creation of a common market among member countries with a phased reduction of tariffs and non-tariff barriers on products of community origin until their complete elimination for all categories of goods and all countries by 1989; the establishment of a common external tariff (CET) by 1994; fiscal and monetary harmonisation; and close cooperation in all areas of economic activity. In addition, at the Dakar meeting of 1979, ECOWAS members agreed to allow 'free movement of persons' and to establish a common defence pact. Finally, the Fund for Cooperation, Compensation and Development (FCCD), was supposed to alleviate the negative impact of integration and tariff preferences on the least developed members.

To date, after seventeen years since the creation of ECOWAS, none of the above goals have been met. Trade liberalisation and the establishment of a CET are yet to be implemented; the expulsion of foreign workers from Nigeria in 1983 and 1985 proved the political impossibility of removing restrictions on labour movement; and the contributions to and outlays from the FCCD are subject to eternal controversy.

The poverty of ECOWAS members, the undiversified structure of their economies, the economic, cultural, political and ideological differences among them as well as political instability of many member countries explain why the ECOWAS Treaty has remained a dead letter.

2.1.2 CEAO This represents the third attempt by the West African states that belonged to the former federation of French Western Africa to maintain the arrangements for monetary and economic cooperation which were established during the colonial era. Despite past failures in creating a CU, the member states preserved their monetary union by adhering to the CFA Franc Zone. The desire of France to preserve its influence in the subregion and to counter the growing power of Nigeria played a crucial role in the maintenance of monetary and economic ties. CEAO was founded in 1973 by the Treaty of Abidjan and comprises seven members: Burkina Faso, Côte d'Ivoire, Mali, Mauritania, Niger, Senegal, and Benin, which became a member in 1984. All of the member countries except for Mauritania also belong to the West African Monetary Union (UMOA) and to ECOWAS.

The CEAO countries are characterised by varying degrees of economic development, with Côte d'Ivoire and Senegal representing the relatively industrialised poles of the group. Because the economic imbalances among the CEAO members had been the major cause of the dissolution of the earlier initiatives, the Treaty of Abidjan embodied specific measures to attenuate such imbalances by directly assisting the economic development of the poorest countries within the groups. The Community Development Fund was created to compensate member countries for the loss of tariff revenues arising from tariff preferences to partners, while the Solidarity Fund, largely financed by Côte d'Ivoire and Senegal, was established to finance development projects in the most depressed regions. Moreover, the structure of tariff preferences to partners was tailored to accommodate the request for higher protection by the least developed countries. These measures did have some success in promoting intra-group trade and factor mobility, both of which are high by SSA standards. However, as I shall discuss later, they also contributed to the creation of an extraordinarily distorted structure of incentives. Moreover, intra-CEAO trade in goods and factor services is far from being free of restrictions and a common external protection policy is yet to be formulated.

2.1.3 MRU This was founded in 1973 by Liberia and Sierra Leone; Guinea joined in 1980. The Union's objectives included the expansion of trade among member countries through the elimination of existing barriers; the creation of a common protection policy *vis-à-vis* the rest of the world; and the promotion of economic cooperation. Although in theory intra-MRU trade is tariff-free and a CET is established, trade among member states remains restricted by pervasive non-tariff and tariff-equivalent barriers. Moreover, despite the lack of marked differences among the members that is often a distinguishing feature of the larger organisations in the subregion, progress towards integration and intra-regional trade has been slowed down by political unrest in Liberia and by the lack of complementarity among the partners' production structures.[5]

2.2 Central Africa[6]

The Customs and Economic Union of Central Africa (*UDEAC*), represents the continuation of long-standing tradition of cooperation among the former French Central African countries. UDEAC was formally created in 1973 with the Treaty of Brazzaville and comprises six members: Cameroon, Central African Republic or CAR, Chad, Congo, Gabon, and Equatorial Guinea. The latter, a former Spanish colony, acceded to the union in 1985.

The original Treaty of Brazzaville envisaged a customs and monetary union with the complete removal of internal tariffs and non-tariff trade barriers and the establishment of a CET and common customs administration for trade with the rest of the world. However, the Treaty was extensively revised in 1974. This caused the *de facto* abolition of the CET and the common customs administration while intra-union trade in manufactured goods was restricted to those produced by firms enjoying the privileges of the so-called Taxe Unique (TU) system. As will be shown later, the direct result of the TU system has been a structure of tariff preferences that varies with firm, product, country of origin and country of destination. As in CEAO, this structure of tariff preferences has proved to be both highly distortionary and a major obstacle towards any meaningful integration of member countries' goods markets.

In terms of *per capita* income, UDEAC is the second richest grouping in SSA. However, considerable differences exist among member countries. Cameroon is a semi-industrialised country where manufacturing accounts for 14 percent of GDP. Congo and Gabon rely heavily on petroleum extraction. By SSA standards, all three countries have high levels of *per capita* incomes. On the other hand, CAR, Chad and Equatorial Guinea rely heavily on agriculture and are among the poorest nations in the subregion.

A second economic grouping in Central Africa is the Economic Community of the Countries of the Great Lakes (*CEPGL*) which comprises the former Belgian protectorates of Burundi, Rwanda and Zaire. CEPGL was founded in 1976 with support from the United Nations which had unsuccessfully tried to keep Burundi and Rwanda as one political unit. CEPGL's objectives were to remove all barriers to the free movement of goods and people among the member countries and to undertake joint development projects financed through contributions by member countries and by foreign donors. As the insignificant share of intra-group in total trade reveals (Table 8.3), no progress towards trade liberalisation and factor mobility has yet been achieved. The lack of progress is largely due to disparity among the Community members, with Zaire being the largest of the three. Moreover, Burundi and Rwanda also belong to the Preferential Trade Area for Eastern and Southern African States (PTA, see section 2.3.1 below) with whom they conduct the greatest part of their African trade.

2.3   East and Southern Africa[7]

There are presently three important regional groupings in East and Southern Africa: the Preferential Trade Area for Eastern and Southern African States (PTA), the Southern African Development Coordination Conference (SADCC), and the Southern African Customs Union (SACU).

2.3.1 PTA   This was formally founded in 1981, under the auspices of the UN Economic Commission for Africa (ECA) and comprises eighteen countries.[8] For several years, the ECA has been actively promoting regionalism in Africa as the only viable strategy for the continent's development. According to ECA's view, regional groupings in Africa should comprise a large number of states in order to provide sufficiently large markets for the creation of industries that would gradually substitute imports and promote Africa's self-sufficiency. According to this view, no more than four such regional groupings should exist in Africa: North, West, Central, and South and East. Thus PTA, like its counterpart in Western Africa, ECOWAS, received the active support of the ECA.

The PTA Treaty explicitly recognised the establishment of an economic community as its ultimate goal. The creation of a preferential trade area was to be considered as only a first step towards that goal. Initially, a

Table 8.3. *Comparison between some characteristics of SSA^a grouping and some other regional groupings in the world, 1970–90*

Name of grouping	Average intra-group trade imbalance index[b]		GNP per capita in 1989 US$			Share of manuf. in GDP in 1989			Share of intra-group export trade in total exports				
	1980	1990	Min	Max	Min as % of max	Min	Max	Min as % of max	1970	1975	1980	1985	1990
SSA groupings													
ECOWAS	52	54	180	790	23	3	20	15	2.9	4.0	3.5	5.3	5.7
CEAO	66	68	290	790	37	5	20	20	6.3	12.7	8.9	8.7	10.5
MRU	100	26	200	430	46	3	6	50	0.2	0.4	0.5	0.4	0.1
UDEAC	99	92	190	2270	7	0	16	0	4.8	2.7	1.6	1.9	3.0
CEPGL	33	18	220	310	67	10	15	66	0.4	0.3	0.1	0.8	0.2
PTA	59	47	80	1950	4	4	25	16	8.0	9.3	7.6	5.5	5.9
SADCC[c]	31	57	80	1600	5	4	24	17	2.6	3.7	2.1	3.9	4.8
SACU[c]	n.a.	n.a.	470	2470	19	4	24	17	n.a.	n.a.	n.a.	n.a.	n.a.
Other groupings													
LAFTA/LAIA	16	17	600	2620	23	16	35	46	10.1	13.4	13.0	8.0	10.6
CACM	21	20	250	1790	14	14	27	62	26.2	23.4	25.4	15.5	14.2
NAFTA[d]	6	5	1990	21100	9	13	17	76	36.3	35.0	33.6	39.7	41.5

Table 8.3. (cont.)

Name of grouping	Average intra-group trade imbalance index[b]		GNP per capita in 1989 US$			Share of manuf. in GDP in 1989			Share of intra-group export trade in total exports				
	1980	1990	Min	Max	Min as % of max	Min	Max	Min as % of max	1970	1975	1980	1985	1990
ASEAN	13	23	490	10450	5	17	26	65	14.8	11.2	18.3	18.4	18.5
EEC[e]	6	8	4300	20800	20	18	32	56	53.2	52.5	55.7	54.7	60.6

Notes:
[a] SSA is uniformly defined to exclude South Africa.
[b] The index for individual countries is calculated as total exports to the group – total imports from the group expressed as a percentage of trade with the group. The average for the group is a weighted average of each member country's index where weights are equal to the sum of the share of exports and imports.
[c] Data for SADCC and SACU exclude Namibia.
[d] Canada, Mexico, United States.
[e] The average trade imbalance index for EC(6) in 1958, when the European Community was formed, was equal to 8. The 1980 and 1990 data refer to EC(12). Data on the share of manufacturing excludes Ireland.

Source: IMF: Directions of Trade, various issues; World Bank: World Development Report (1991); World Bank Atlas (1990); UN: ComTrade data base; author's estimates.

Common list of 212 categories of goods were selected for preferential treatment within the subregion. The original intention was gradually to expand the list to comprise all goods of PTA origin. Customs duties on the goods in the list were to be reduced by 25 percent every two years until their complete elimination by 1992. The negotiations, however, got bogged down on such matters as what goods to include in the list, how to define the rules of origin, and how to create compensatory mechanisms for those members that would suffer revenue losses. As a result, the target date for effective liberalisation shifted to the year 2000, and even that appears to be optimistic.

Essentially, the lack of progress with intra-group trade liberalisation in PTA is due to the same factors that have slowed it down in ECOWAS. Although in economic terms PTA is the second largest grouping in SSA, all of its members except for Zimbabwe and Kenya, the two relatively diversified economies, are poor and highly dependent on one or two commodities for their export revenues. The ensuing lack of complementarity and the uneven distribution of benefits have thus far stalled all efforts towards any meaningful and effective integration.

2.3.2 SADCC This was formally created in April 1980. The core states of SADCC comprise the frontline states – Angola, Botswana, Mozambique, Tanzania, Zambia and Zimbabwe – as well as the four other majority-ruled states in the region, Lesotho, Malawi, Swaziland and Namibia. The latter joined the organisation in 1990, immediately after independence.

SADCC's principal objective was to promote cooperation among its member-states in order to lessen their economic dependence on the Republic of South Africa. Thus, from the very beginning, the architects of SADCC decided to reject the idea of a CU and concentrate their efforts on the more modest goal of economic cooperation. Similarly, they avoided the establishment of a highly centralised and expensive bureaucracy by creating a small secretariat with limited coordination duties while leaving the responsibility for various sectors to the member-states.

From the beginning of its foundation until the late 1980s, SADCC states and their infrastructure were targeted for destabilisation by South Africa. Despite its heavy cost, the destabilisation attempt by South Africa had two favourable side effects. First, it increased the cohesion of the SADCC states. Second, it prompted more aid and sympathy toward SADCC from the international community than would otherwise have been forthcoming. Financial assistance to SADCC was considered as a 'positive alternative' to economic sanctions against Pretoria. Thus by 1988, the international community had provided over $3 billion in financing for

SADCC projects which represented over 90 percent of the cost of the projects approved.

At the outset, transportation and communication were considered as priority sectors by SADCC and absorbed the lion's share of all SADCC projects and investments. The most successful and well-known SADCC transportation project has been the development of the Beira corridor. The Beira corridor is a 300 km strip running from Beira on the coast of Mozambique to the border of Zimbabwe and containing Beira port, a railway, a road, an oil pipeline, an electricity line and a number of development projects. The Beira Project has brought about a significant decrease in Zimbabwe's use of South African ports; the cooperation between Mozambique and Zimbabwe to protect the corridor from attack by South African-backed guerrillas; the repopulation of the port and a return of the private businesses thanks to improved security. In other sectors, such as energy, agriculture and industry, SADCC has not been able to replicate its success with the Beira project in terms either of cooperation among members, or between these and the donors.

On the whole despite, or maybe thanks to, its limited aims, SADCC has been considered by many inside and outside the region as a successful example of RI to emulate elsewhere in SSA.

2.3.3 SACU This is the oldest and most functional CU in SSA and comprises South Africa and the so-called BLS states, Botswana, Lesotho, and Swaziland. After independence, Namibia also formally joined the union in 1990. The union was created in 1910, soon after the Republic of South Africa was formally created as an independent state, and the new union itself replaced an older one which had been in existence since 1889. The main feature of SACU is the overwhelming dominance of South Africa over the other three members which are exceedingly small and relative to South Africa are more or less comparable with Liechtenstein to Switzerland or San Marino to Italy.

Goods and factors markets are well integrated within SACU, and there is a CET and a common excise tax, the proceeds of which are paid into a Consolidated Revenue Fund. The revenues are then shared by the union members in proportion to their share in total trade. Under the 1969 revenue-sharing formulas, the BLS states receive from the Fund more than their contributions to the Fund as compensation for leaving trade, industry and fiscal decisions entirely to South Africa. All SACU members except Botswana are also members of the Rand Monetary Area, with the central bank of South Africa acting as the central bank of the Area as a whole. The union does not have any institutional structure such as a secretariat; there is only a functional Commission which meets once a year to consider any issues.

With the political events in South Africa, there is a strong feeling that SACU may not survive in its present form, either in terms of membership or in terms of trade and monetary arrangements.

3   Evaluation of SSA's experience with trade integration

In section 2, I analysed the most significant regional groupings in SSA. It was seen that with the exception of SADCC, every one of the existing groupings explicitly aims at goods market integration. However, despite the proliferation of multilateral institutions, treaties' protocols and resolutions, none of the groupings besides SACU has achieved any noticeable degree of integration in their goods markets. The evidence is provided by the small share of intra-group trade in total trade. Table 8.3 contains data on the share of intra-group trade in SSA as well as some other regional groupings in the world. The data reveal that the share of intra-group trade in almost all SSA groupings is not only very small compared to other groupings, but also stagnant over time.[9]

Since the data show the share of intra-group trade in SSA since 1970 (i.e., before any of the major groupings in SSA were formed), it is possible to detect whether the formation of a group exercised any impact on the member countries' trade with each other. The data indicate that for the majority of the groupings in SSA, such an impact was practically non-existent or negligible. For example in MRU, UDEAC, CEPGL and PTA, the share of intra-group trade between 1970 and 1990 remains either stagnant or actually falls. For other groups where the share increases, the increase is little reason for jubilation since in most cases it reflects the terms of trade effect. Because intra-SSA exports are mainly composed of manufactures whereas SSA exports to the rest of the world are principally composed of primary commodities, the worsening of the SSA countries' terms of trade with the rest of the world tends to overestimate the share of intra-group trade based on export value data. A good example is provided by ECOWAS, where the rising share of intra-group trade between 1980 and 1990 is very much linked to the fall in oil prices over the same period which caused Nigerian and ECOWAS dollar exports to the world to decline by 47 and 35 percent respectively. In comparison, during the same period, the Community's and NAFTA's (North American Free-Trade Area) total exports increased almost two-fold. Even in the case of CEAO, the initial favourable impact of the union on intra-group trade appears to have faded away since 1975, when intra-CEAO trade share reached its peak.

In sum, if intra-group as a proportion of total trade is a good indicator of trade integration, it can be concluded that trade integration in SSA has failed. The reason is either because these countries have not removed the barriers that divide their markets into isolated units, or that they do not fulfil the conditions for greater exchange even though all barriers to intra-group trade had been removed. In this section, it will be seen that both explanations are relevant. Let us first examine the limited trade potential explanation.

3.1   Limited trade potential

It should be obvious that simply signing a treaty to remove barriers to trade does not have any effect on the intra-group trade if the prospective partners do not demand each others' exports. In this context, the only effect of integration would be indirect and related to the new level of protection of the group towards the outside world compared to the level of protection in each country prior to integration.[10] Disregarding this effect and abstracting from intra-industry trade, in a two-good model, trade integration will have the usual trade-creation/trade-diversion effects when the prospective partners each have comparative advantage in the production and export of a different good while both goods are consumed by all countries. In other words, the difference in partners' factor endowments makes them natural trading partners.

When the possibility of product differentiation and intra-industry trade is allowed, then two countries could have 'similar' and indeed identical factor endowments, yet trade with each other. In this case the entire trade is of intra-industrial nature.[11] The essence of this discussion is that trade integration among SSA countries could be effective if they satisfy the condition for intra- or interindustry trade. If these conditions are not satisfied, then the limited extent of intra-SSA trade cannot be attributed to the 'failure' of integration schemes, but rather to their ineffectiveness.

In a recent study, Foroutan and Pritchett (forthcoming) try to test precisely for any possible gap between the potential and the actual trade among SSA countries. They apply a gravity model to a cross-section of fifty-four low- and middle-income countries, which includes nineteen SSA countries, in order to estimate intra-SSA trade potential. The gravity model posits that the volume of trade between any pair of countries is a function of their trade potential and their mutual trade attraction. A country's trade potential depends on its size (GDP), its factor endowment, its level of economic development, its geographic characteristics, and other similar factors. The trade attraction between two countries is affected negatively by such factors as the distance between the two, and by policy and political barriers to trade. It is positively affected by cultural and historic ties or by the existence of preferential trade arrangements.

Foroutan and Pritchett estimate an extended gravity equation to determine whether intra-SSA trade is less than expected. They adopt two approaches. In the first, all SSA countries are included in the sample but two dummy variables are included to test for differences in the determination of intra-SSA trade. The first dummy variable is equal to 1 if the reporting country is in SSA and zero otherwise. This variable tests the hypothesis that trade barriers in SSA are on average higher than in the other countries in the sample. The second dummy variable is 1 if both the reporting and the partner countries are in SSA and zero otherwise. The coefficient of this variable is negative if intra-SSA trade is too little, given its determinants. The estimation results show that the coefficient of the first dummy variable is negative and statistically significant, while that on the second is positive but not significant. In other words although SSA countries trade on average too little with the world as a whole, their bilateral trade flows do not fall below what the model predicts.

In the second approach, the gravity model is estimated without the SSA countries in the sample. The estimated coefficients from this model are then used along with the values of the independent variables to predict the bilateral trade flows of SSA with each of the ninety-five partners. This approach implies that bilateral trade flows in SSA are determined exactly as in the other low-income countries. If intra-SSA trade were low for reasons particular to the subregion, the model would predict higher trade shares than those actually observed. The results indicate that this is not the case. For all SSA countries in the sample, the predicted mean or median trade share is practically identical to the actual share.

These results are hardly surprising given the low level of income of SSA countries and the preponderance of primary, resource-based commodities in their outputs and foreign trade. However, the story does not end here. First, Foroutan and Pritchett's results do not exclude the possibility of a higher intra-SSA trade were the SSA countries to remove trade barriers among themselves but not with the Rest of the World (ROW), although whether such a course of action is desirable or not is an entirely different question. In fact, their results indicate that among the three integration schemes that were fully functional during the period under consideration (1980–2, i.e., CEAO, ECOWAS and UDEAC), the first did have a positive and statistically significant impact on intra-SSA trade.[12] Second, to say that based upon the *current* patterns of production and demand the SSA countries are not natural partners is to ignore one of the most fundamental longer-term objectives in the mind of most African scholars and politicians of trade integration: to alter the existing pattern of production by taking advantage, for example, of a larger market in order to create new industries or to expand the output of the existing ones.[13] Thus, despite the limited trade potential of SSA countries with each other at the time many of the RI schemes were conceived, it is not unrealistic to think that they would have been better integrated had they truly removed trade barriers among themselves.

3.2   Failed intra-regional trade liberalisation

Now let us analyse why these barriers have proved to be so hard to remove. It will be seen that import-substitution policies, tariff-revenue constraint, and the skewed distribution of costs and benefits of integration arising from the extreme economic differences among SSA countries are the strongest explanatory variables.

3.2.1 Import substitution   Past import-substitution policies in the majority of SSA countries not only directly contrasted trade liberalisation in general and intra-regional import liberalisation in particular, but to the extent that they contributed to the macroeconomic imbalances, they also indirectly contributed to the maintenance of intra-regional trade barriers. Import-substitution policies often led to the creation of inefficient industries behind high protective barriers and overvalued exchange rates that would allow intermediate and capital goods prices to be kept artificially low. As devaluation was resisted because of its potential short-term contractionary and inflationary effects, trade liberalisation, including intra-regional trade liberalisation, became even less viable as an objective.

3.2.2 Revenue constraint   Since the pioneering work of Viner (1950), it has been shown that whatever advantages trade integration may bring to individual partners when their initial tariffs are explicitly taken into account, under most circumstances unilateral trade liberalisation remains the superior alternative for the group as a whole. This conclusion, however, assumes that tariff revenues do not really matter. Given the importance of tariff revenues in the budgets of SSA governments,[14] free trade is hardly a short- or even medium-term option for the majority of SSA countries.

If free trade is ruled out altogether, then the alternative for SSA countries is between a discriminatory tariff structure and a non-discriminatory tariff structure. The former grants tariff exemptions/reductions to certain partners, and the latter does not.

From the traditional theory of integration it is known that static welfare gains from integration are likely to be maximised when, on balance, trade creation exceeds trade diversion.[15] Tariff-revenue constraint does not change this fundamental conclusion of the theory since trade diversion magnifies the revenue losses. However, revenue constraint clashes with the very conditions that minimise the likelihood of trade diversion: that is, that the prospective partners trade relatively substantially with each other before integration and that they do not raise their trade barriers *vis-à-vis* the rest of the world after integration.[16] Two reasons account for this.

First, the more the potential partners trade with each other, the higher the proportion of revenues they derive from such trade and, hence, the more difficult it becomes to give it up. Second, any preference-induced tariff-revenue loss may actually necessitate a further increase in tariffs against the outside world to raise the fixed amount of revenue, thereby enhancing the trade-diverting effect of trade integration. In addition, to the extent that the presence of a revenue constraint makes it more difficult to work out a proper compensation scheme from the gainers to the losers of an integrative scheme, it further complicates the attainment of true integration.

In sum, while the analysis in section 3.1 showed that SSA countries are not natural trading partners and thus do not fulfil the condition for trade creation, in this section the analysis shows that the presence of a revenue constraint is likely to make trade integration in SSA both more difficult to achieve and/or more trade-diverting than otherwise.

3.2.3 Skewed distribution of benefits The role of the distributional aspects of integration in easing or resisting intra-regional trade liberalisation emerges most clearly from the literature in defence of RI. It is important to review this literature briefly. The purpose here is neither to provide an exhaustive list of arguments for trade integration nor to evaluate their theoretical and empirical merits.[17] Rather, for the most relevant arguments in favour of integration, the discussion that follows focuses on the conditions that ought to be satisfied for the theoretical advantages of regional trade integration to occur. It will be seen that the foremost condition is that the gains and losses from integration be evenly distributed among potential partners, or that a workable transfer mechanism be instituted whereby the net gainers compensate the net losers. After briefly discussing the principal arguments for integration, it is argued that SSA countries do not satisfy the conditions for an equitable distribution of net gains, nor have they been able to find a workable and non-distortionary compensation mechanism.

Three arguments in defence of trade integration are considered. The first argument, which is particularly important in the light of the historical experience of SSA, is essentially an argument for collective import substitution and is based upon the explicit recognition of the value that developing countries attach to industrialisation (Johnson, 1965; Cooper and Massell, 1965). Trade integration in this context is welfare-improving, because it lowers the cost of import substitution that each potential partner would in any case pursue individually in the absence of integration. Joint import substitution is less costly than individual import substitution, because it offers the opportunity of industry swapping among the partners whereby each partner specialises in the production of goods for which it has the greatest comparative advantage.

Whatever the relative theoretical and empirical merits of import substitution, an essential condition for the realisation of a cohesive and lasting trade integration is that the prospective partners be similar, in the sense that they 'are at the same stage of economic development'.[18] This maximises the likelihood that all partners expand at least some industrial activity for which they enjoy a comparative advantage *vis-à-vis* the rest of the group. If this condition is not satisfied and if the preference for industry is strong enough in all countries involved, it may not be possible to work out any compensation scheme that may make all parties better off; complete trade integration may not then be feasible.

A second argument in defence of trade integration is based on the explicit recognition of scale economies together with some other circumstances (e.g., transportation costs or domestic market distortions), which explains why scale economies are not exploited by simply expanding exports (i.e., integrating with the world market) (Corden, 1972; Pearson and Ingram, 1980). Although the small economic size of SSA cautions against attaching too great an importance to scale economies as an argument for trade integration, they may be empirically significant for some industries. For example, Pearson and Ingram show that in a hypothetical CU between Côte d'Ivoire and Ghana substantial welfare gains could accrue to both countries because the union would enable the two to rationalise their joint industrial output by closing down inefficient, duplicate plants while expanding the output of the surviving ones. However, as Pearson and Ingram demonstrate, the likelihood of forming a cohesive and mutually advantageous union increases with the possibility that the potential partners are similar in terms of production cost such that all prospective partners 'can retain and expand some industrial production'.[19]

The third argument in favour of trade integration is based on the explicit recognition of the detrimental effect of protectionist policies in the rest of the world on the terms of trade of a small exporting country.[20] For such a country it may be possible to improve its welfare by trading at better terms with its potential partners in a RI scheme when they remove these barriers than with the rest of the world. This does not imply that for SSA countries the terms of trade argument is highly relevant since their exports are mostly composed of raw materials that face low or zero tariffs in industrialised countries. Nonetheless, it is important to stress that as a result of trade integration, although the partners as a whole may gain, these gains may be distributed very unevenly. Lipsey (1971), for example, discusses several possible outcomes of trade integration in the context of a two-good/three-country model. With more than two goods, it can easily be seen that the likelihood of a more even distribution of gains increases when the prospective partners each have the possibility of expanding some industries and exporting to the other's market (i.e., both partners are diversified).

In sum, whatever the underlying argument for integration, a necessary condition for the realisation of the theoretical gains from integration is that either the partners be similar (i.e., each have something to gain from integration), or that an efficient and equitable compensation mechanism from gainers to losers can be formulated. These are precisely the conditions that are hardly satisfied among any of the existing SSA groupings.

It is not easy to conceive of any single index of similarity. Table 8.3 contains a number of indicators for SSA and contrasts them with other important groupings in the world. The data indicate that for most indicators the SSA have the highest degree of divergence. To begin with, the differences in *per capita* incomes in SSA are enormous. Although such differences also exist among non-SSA groupings, in their case the differences are compensated for by the complementary nature of the economies of the member states.

More important than *per capita* incomes are the differences in the degree of industrialisation of partner countries and their participation in total intra-group trade, given that immediate costs and benefits of integration for a country are proportional to its share in total imports from and total exports to the rest of the group. The data show that compared to other groupings, SSA countries have a very divergent pattern of industrialisation. There is a corresponding variability in individual countries' participation in total intra-group trade. To see this, a trade imbalance index was constructed for each country which expresses the absolute value of its net trade with the group as a percentage of its total trade with the group. The maximum and the minimum values for the index are 100 and zero. If a country exports to (imports from) but does not import from (export to) the group, the index reaches its maximum value of 100. If a country's exports to and imports from the group are balanced, the index reaches its minimum value of zero. A weighted average of individual countries' indexes belonging to a group has been computed for 1980 and 1990, where the weights correspond to one-half of the sum of a country's share in total exports and total imports. Clearly, in both years, the value of the index for all major SSA groupings is very high, far above the value observed for other groupings, and does not diminish over the period considered. The high level of the index for SSA stems from the concentration of exports in one or two relatively industrialised countries which account for the overwhelming share of intra-group industrial output and exports. For example, still in 1990, Côte d'Ivoire accounted for 75 percent of total intra-CEAO exports while it absorbed only 13 percent of total imports; Cameroon had 96 percent of intra-UDEAC exports and only 4 percent of imports; Côte d'Ivoire and Nigeria had respectively 42 and 30 percent of total intra-ECOWAS exports and 18 and 4 percent of imports; Kenya and Zimbabwe accounted for respectively 32 and 27 percent of intra-PTA exports while absorbing only 15 and 7 percent of total imports; and Zimbabwe accounted for 70 percent of intra-SADCC exports and only 13 percent of imports.

The huge imbalance in trade and the degree of industrialisation has two implications for trade integration. First, it benefits disproportionately those countries who happen to have the greatest share of industrial output and intra-regional trade. Second, it justifiably raises concern among the poorest SSA countries that the removal of barriers to trade may cause the migration of the few industries they possess to the industrially more advanced countries, thereby polarising even further the existing uneven pattern of industrial development.[21]

In sum, SSA's import-substitution policies, the revenue constraint, and the unequal distribution of costs and benefits of integration are the principal reason for the limited liberalisation of intra-group trade in industrial products. Where preferences have been granted to partners, these have been negotiated on an *ad hoc*, product-by-product basis and have mostly concerned non-competing goods while duplicate, underutilised plants have been jealously safeguarded. Thus, ironically, all the static and dynamic advantages of trade integration arising from trade creation, the exploitation of scale economies, and enhanced competition have been dissipated. The compensatory mechanisms in place in most SSA groupings have also contributed to this seemingly ironic outcome. This point deserves further attention.

3.2.4 Compensation schemes in SSA regional groupings   Given that the costs and benefits of regional integration are different for different member countries, a successful and lasting integration scheme may require some compensation mechanism (i.e., monetary transfers from net gainers to net losers) in order to assure the latter's continued participation. Because the distribution of costs and benefits of integration in SSA groupings is highly skewed and because intra-SSA trade is largely of the interindustry type and adjustment costs associated with interindustry changes of specialisation are high, the need for compensation is particularly acute in SSA groupings.

Two types of compensation can be conceived. The first is compensation based on the cost of trade diversion. The true justification for fiscal compensation of this sort is the real loss of income that arises from switching from a cheaper to a more expensive source of import supply. In the SSA groupings surveyed here, compensation related to the cost of trade diversion is common and is normally computed on the basis of revenues forgone.

Compensation based on the principle of revenues forgone is distortionary because even assuming that the revenues forgone correctly reflect the cost of trade diversion to the importer so as to leave the importing country indifferent between buying from a partner or from any other source, for the exporter it amounts to subsidising exports to the regional market. Even when an export subsidy may be justified, it is not clear why such an export subsidy should not be generalised and distributed independently of the country of destination.

The second type of compensation is related to the 'cost' of trade creation. This latter cost results from the possible loss of industrial activity if as a result of integration industrial activity migrates from the less developed to the more advanced countries within the grouping. In the context of SSA it has proved exceedingly difficult to devise proper compensation schemes to deal with the trade creation cost of integration. Some groupings in the subregion have created special funds with the aim of directly promoting the industrial development of the poorest member states. The contribution of individual member states are often based on very complicated formulas that have taken a long time to be hammered out, and both the contributions to and outlays from the funds have proved to be a source of ongoing controversy.

In addition to direct, community-financed promotion of development projects in the poorest member countries, the Treaties of CEAO and UDEAC also contain provisions that tailor the preferential custom duties applicable to partners' industrial products to the 'protection needs' of the least advantaged partners. This is the essence of the so-called regimes of the Taxe de Coopération Régionale (TCR) in CEAO and the TU in UDEAC.

Both the Treaty of CEAO and the revised Treaty of UDEAC limit free intra-group trade to resource-based unprocessed commodities. Manufacturing goods that originate in member countries are charged a duty in the form of TCR or TU. Both TCR and/or TU involve the replacement of all import duties on inputs and outputs by a single tax. The eligibility for the single tax as well as the level of the tax is beyond national jurisdictions and is decided by the Council of Ministers in CEAO and by the Secretariat General of UDEAC. The level of both taxes are separately determined for each enterprise, product, country of origin, and country of destination. The motivation behind this *ad hoc* and arbitrary structure of internal trade taxes was to reduce the competitive disadvantage of the least developed members by applying a lower rate of duty on products originating in these countries than on similar products produced elsewhere within the group, and by allowing these countries to apply a higher duty on imports of community origin than the duty applied on the same goods by other importing partners.

Whatever equity purpose the single tax systems of CEAO and UDEAC might have served, they have proved to be exceedingly distortionary because they have created an arbitrary structure of effective protection that does not conform to any economic criterion. Moreover, by allowing artificially high protective barriers for the least viable industries in the most uneconomic location, the single tax system has perpetuated market segmentation and nullified precisely the most important dynamic gains from integration associated with enhanced competition and scale economies.

To recapitulate, this section discussed two sets of reasons why trade integration among SSA countries has failed. First, based upon their current structure of production, the SSA countries are not each others' natural trading partners. Second, if indeed integration could have played a role in changing this structure, it has not succeeded in doing so because the failure to dismantle trade barriers among partners has prevented any meaningful integration of SSA's goods market from taking place. The reason lies mainly with import-substitution policies, revenue constraint, the skewed distribution of net benefits of integration among the partners, and the inadequacy of compensation mechanisms.

4   Other types of integration

In this section the experience of SSA with other types of integration is briefly examined. These include monetary integration, factor market integration, and government activity and regulation integration. As with trade integration, there are two issues involved: first, whether these types of integration are desirable for SSA and second, whether the SSA countries fulfil the conditions for their realisation.

4.1 Monetary integration

Monetary integration has often been claimed as an indispensable tool for promoting intra-SSA trade and an essential ingredient of RI in SSA.[22] The current experience of SSA with monetary integration helps to shed light on whether monetary integration has brought the expected advantages to the member countries, and whether it is an achievable goal any time soon.

Monetary integration in SSA exists only within the Rand and the CFA Franc Zones. However, the latter is of greater interest because it involves a far larger number of countries who are more typical of the region's economies. The CFA Franc Zone comprises fourteen African states and is built around two monetary unions: The West African Monetary Union (UMOA)[23] which includes Togo and all the CEAO members with the exception of Mauritania, and the Union of States belonging to the Banque des Etats d'Afrique Centrale (BEAC) which includes the UDEAC countries. Each union's central bank issues its own currency (CFA franc) which has a fixed parity with the French franc. Although in theory the parity could be revised, in practice it has remained unchanged since 1948. The linkage to the French franc and the complete freedom of foreign exchange operations within the Zone guarantee the convertibility of the CFA franc. The stability of the CFA franc–French franc parity and the convertibility of the CFA franc are maintained through tight monetary rules within the Zone and the mechanism of the operations accounts. The two central banks of the CFA Franc Zone have an operations account with the French Public Treasury where they are required to deposit the bulk of their foreign exchange reserves. These accounts can show a negative balance without a fixed limit, thus guaranteeing the member states of the Zone unlimited access to foreign exchange and the possibility of borrowing from the French Treasury. This has allowed the CFA Franc Zone countries to maintain a fixed parity even in the face of balance of payments difficulties. Despite the possibility of running negative balances in their operations account, monetary restrictions have guaranteed that these accounts have been negative only occasionally and hence the cost to the French Treasury has been quite limited, at least until now.

What has the membership in the CFA Franc Zone implied for the participating countries? Has it helped the process of integration, as was predicted by its proponents? An empirical study[24] based on the comparison of CFA Franc Zone members and a group of other low-income countries which included twenty SSA countries, suggests that membership in the CFA Franc Zone has brought advantages to the participants in terms of lower inflation, higher growth rates, lower debt burden, and strong export performance during the 1970s. However, in the 1980s, changes in the world environment, most notably the debt crisis, the appreciation of the dollar *vis-à-vis* the European currencies and the decline of raw materials prices, meant that the CFA Franc Zone countries, along with most other developing countries, needed to adjust their economies through both expenditure-switching and expenditure-reducing policies. Their inability to alter the exchange rate as a tool to switch expenditure from tradeables to non-tradeables resulted in the burden of adjustment falling disproportionately on expenditure reduction, thereby slowing the growth of exports, investment and income. Moreover, the inability of the CFA Franc Zone countries to change their parity has become a serious obstacle to removing import barriers in these countries either towards the rest of the world or towards their neighbouring countries in SSA. For example, in ECOWAS, the CFA Franc Zone countries have been unable to remove trade barriers *vis-à-vis* non-Zone countries due to the exchange rate misalignment. Additionally, recent real devaluation in other ECOWAS countries, most notably in Nigeria and Ghana, has created serious problems for the Zone countries who have witnessed a surge in their illegal, undeclared imports.

In sum, the experience of SSA countries suggests that monetary integration is a double-edged sword that brings advantages, but which come at a cost. Moreover, the CFA Franc Zone countries have been largely successful in creating a stable and convertible currency due to the French government's backing. Thus, unless a similar arrangement is worked out between the SSA countries on the one hand and a large sponsor (e.g., the European Community) on the other, as has recently been suggested,[25] it is doubtful that monetary integration in SSA would be successfully accomplished in the foreseeable future.

4.2   Factor market integration

At present, the free movement of both labour and capital within various regional groupings in SSA is limited. As far as labour is concerned, there is a fair amount of mobility within certain groupings, most notably SACU and CEAO. However, the international movement of labour generally remains restricted and the legal status of foreign workers is often uncertain and subject to abrupt changes in the host country.

These circumstances are hardly surprising. Even within the European Community, where free movement of labour was incorporated into the Rome Treaty and where the founding members with the exception of Italy were not too dissimilar in economic terms, several restrictions were applied to intra-EC migration in order to prevent the disruptive effects of large movements of people.[26] In SSA, where differences in standards of living are enormous, completely free and unrestricted labour movement appears a remote possibility. The bitter experience of the expulsion of illegal aliens from Nigeria in 1982 and 1985 is just a reminder of the destabilising consequences of a massive movement of people in a short time span.

As far as capital is concerned, relatively free capital movement exists only within the Rand and the CFA Franc Zones. Also, by virtue of convertibility of the Rand and the CFA franc, capital markets in these Zones are practically integrated with the world market.

Free movement of capital and labour within the various regional groupings in SSA has been strongly advocated as an effective way of boosting economic growth by allowing the scarce factors to be employed where they realise the highest return.[27] According to this view, free intra-regional factor movement is also an effective way of attenuating inter-country imbalances and thus minimising the need for compensatory measures because factors of production could migrate from the less developed to the more prosperous areas, and then remit their earnings to the country of origin. Economic theory,[28] however, suggests that free factor mobility when goods trade remains restricted, is not automatically welfare-improving or desirable because of the interaction between goods and factors movement.

For example, Neary (1987) proves that capital mobility increases the welfare cost of tariffs. Johnson (1967) shows that for a small, tariff-distorted country that also imports the capital-intensive good, the importation of capital may be immiserising. The reason is that 'increased capital reallocates production towards the industry using that factor intensively; and if that industry is protected and so wastes resources through excess production costs, the shift . . . involves increased waste of resources, which may more than absorb the increased potential output per head'.[29] The existence of several inefficient, underutilised foreign-owned production plants in SSA that would not survive free market competition suggests that immiserising capital import may be more than an academic curiosity.

4.3 Government activity and regulation integration

It is difficult to define precisely the meaning of this type of integration, which is also referred to as cooperation. It is, however, convenient to define it as broadly as possible to include everything from joint projects, such as the Beira Project in SADCC, to tax harmonisation, harmonisation of public administrative rules, national statistics, health and education standards, transportation policy, or the like.

Government activity and regulation integration as defined above can either be very strong or remain low key, according to the preferences of participating partners. For example, tax harmonisation may be defined as identical unification of both base and rates, or some kind of coordination implying much more variability of national policies, but still aiming towards the higher level of standardisation. However weakly or strongly governments' activities and regulations are integrated, the fact remains that such an integrative effort will greatly assist the cause of market unification at relatively little or no economic cost to the participating countries. Given the miniscule size of most SSA countries, market unification is likely to ease the circulation of information and create an environment more attractive to domestic and foreign investment. Also given the small size of the economies involved, the pay-off to cooperation in realising joint projects is likely to be considerable. The experience of SADCC, often mentioned as the only example of successful integration in SSA, is a good example.

5   Conclusion: what future for RI in SSA?

The analysis to this point has shown that RI in SSA has fundamentally failed to achieve its pre-established goals. The clearest proof of this failure is provided by the abysmal growth performance of the region as a whole. According to the Lagos Plan of Action which was adopted in 1980 by the African Heads of States, RI was supposed to promote 'self-sustaining development and economic growth'.[30] Instead, in the past decade, SSA as a whole has registered the worst economic results of its post-independence history by seeing real incomes of individuals falling at a sustained pace (see Table 8.1) in lieu of growing. Granted, the structural weakness of SSA economies and outside events, especially the collapse of world commodity prices in the 1980s, are partially to be blamed for these disappointing results. However, it remains true that despite great expectations, integration failed to bring any structural changes to SSA's economies that might have lessened their vulnerability to commodity price fluctuations.

What lessons can be derived from this analysis? Does the failure to date imply that RI as a model of development is harmful or infeasible and should be abandoned altogether? What are the implications for SSA of 'Europe 1992' and the *de facto* formation of two more continent-wide trading blocs centred around the United States and Japan? Would the formation of the three trading blocs not imply that Africa must also follow suit and pursue its dreams of an African Economic Community?

Whether RI, especially trade and factor market integration, is good or bad for SSA remains an unanswered question. *Ex ante*, the internal liberalisation of goods and factors movement may be either good or bad, depending on a host of other factors including what happens to external barriers. However, the most meaningful analyses of the costs and benefits of trade integration are normally of an *ex post* character.[31] In the case of SSA, with the possible exception of SACU, such an analysis is impossible because after almost three decades of trials, the SSA markets remain fundamentally isolated. The only *ex post* analysis possible is that of monetary integration and cooperation since concrete examples within SSA do exist. Monetary integration was quite beneficial to the CFA Franc Zone countries until the mid-1980s, when the real appreciation of the CFA franc coupled with the plunge in world prices of primary materials reduced export revenues and slowed income growth. Cooperation, as noted by the experience of SADCC has also been rather successful in realising projects of regional interest and in contributing to the development objectives of the countries involved.

Whether or not trade and factor market integration is a feasible objective, clearly the extreme economic differences among the partners and the ensuing uneven distribution of costs and benefits of integration have been the major obstacle to its realisation. Moreover, the economic differences have been exacerbated by cultural, political, and historic divisions. In the short run, the economic differences are unlikely to disappear whereas recent changes in the world political scene are likely to enhance the move in SSA towards democracy and reduce political conflict in the subregion. Thus, at this stage, it appears unlikely that complete trade and factor market integration is any more feasible today or in the near future than it has been in the past for any of the existing regional groupings. Cooperation, coordination and harmonisation hold greater promise. Moreover, the gradual shift away from past import-substitution policies by a growing number of SSA countries as a direct result of the adoption by these countries of some kind of structural adjustment programme also holds the promise of accelerating the pace of integration in SSA as part of the general trend towards a more liberal and export-oriented economy.

As far as the implications of the *de facto* division of the world into trading blocs is concerned, two types of implications for SSA should be distinguished: one is strategic and the other is economic. A united SSA will be in a strategically superior position to negotiate with the existing or future economic blocs than could any one member country alone. However, as the Lomé negotiations reveal, adherence to an RI scheme is not a necessary condition for obtaining such a united front.

The economic implications of trading blocs, especially 'Europe 1992', for SSA are more crucial and more widely understood. Because for historic, geographic and political reasons, SSA trades far more with Europe than with any other area of the world,[32] the implications of 'Europe 1992' for the subregion are more significant and more carefully studied than the implications of similar existing or to-be-formed trading blocs elsewhere in the world. The general conclusion of most scholars[33] is that the completion of the European Internal Market will not have very significant positive or negative effects on SSA as a whole.

Generally speaking, SSA countries will benefit from the completion of the EC Internal Market principally because of the presumed income growth in the Community in the aftermath of 'Europe 1992'. Higher growth in the European Community is expected to boost SSA's exports of primary goods as well as improving its terms of trade. In addition, coffee and cocoa exports may increase if fiscal harmonisation within the European Community results in the elimination of excise taxes on these commodities in Germany, Denmark and Italy.

The principal source of potential negative impact for SSA is the trade displacement effect. That is, the removal of national restrictions may erode the competitive margin that SSA countries enjoy *vis-à-vis* other exporters to the European Community as a result of preferential access to certain EC markets. For example, in the case of bananas, elimination of national restrictions is expected to cause loss of market share by SSA countries in favour of Latin American countries.

Fundamentally, the impact of 'Europe 1992' on SSA is rather marginal either because of the nature of SSA exports, mostly raw materials, or because of the preferences granted to SSA under the Lomé conventions.[34] Whatever the impact of 'Europe 1992' or other similar trading blocs on SSA, there is again nothing in the analysis so far that may be considered inherently an argument for or against economic integration in SSA. In the long run, the impact of 'Europe 1992' and of other possible trading blocs on SSA countries depends on their own domestic policies. If integration is used as a tool to enable SSA to adopt a credible, outward-oriented economic policy that improves their supply response to outside events, then RI may serve as a stepping stone for SSA producers which begin competing in the world market. If, on the other hand, RI is to be pursued as in the past with import substitution as its foremost aim, then the chances for future success are no better than they have always been: at best, disappointing; at worst, nil.

There are some recent, encouraging signs that RI may indeed be used as such a tool. The example is provided by UDEAC countries which are on the verge of adopting a far-reaching reform of their trade and indirect tax regimes. By exercising peer pressure and by making individual governments' commitment to reform more credible, it appears that with appropriate modifications a RI framework could play an important role in facilitating badly-needed economic reform in UDEAC member-states.

NOTES

I wish to thank Jaime de Melo, Ali Mansoor and Arvind Panagariya for their helpful comments on an earlier draft of this chapter. I also with to thank Francis Ng for valuable research assistance.

1 SSA is defined as comprising all countries in Africa except for the Northern countries of Algeria, Egypt, Morocco and Tunisia. South Africa is also excluded for political reason.
2 For a detailed account of various grouping in West Africa see Arhin (1990), Diouf (1990), Ezenwe (1990), Frimpong-Ansah (1990), Okolo and Wright (1990), Robson (1983), and Thisen (1989). See also Berg et al. (1988) on various grouping in all parts of Africa.
3 Okolo, in Okolo and Wright (1990).
4 For instance, of the seventy-two successful *coups d'etat* in Africa during 1958–89, the majority took place in five of the sixteen ECOWAS member states (see Welsh, 1990, p. 159).
5 For a detailed account of obstacles to economic integration in MRU see Sesay (1990).
6 For details see World Bank (1991).
7 For a detailed account see Economist Intelligence Unit (1989), Hall (1987), Henderson (1985), Martin (1989), Mulaisho (1990), and Wangwe (1990).
8 These are Angola, Burundi, Comoros, Djibouti, Ethiopia, Kenya, Lesotho, Malawi, Mozambique, Mauritius, Rwanda, Somalia, Sudan, Swaziland, Uganda, Tanzania, Zambia and Zimbabwe.
9 It is well-known that much cross-border trade in SSA goes unrecorded. However, in many cases this concerns goods of foreign origin or goods of domestic origin but destined to go to the Rest of the World (ROW). Such trade, which does not qualify as intra-SSA trade, is often caused by the possibility of profitable price arbitrage. Because it is not possible to determine the extent of genuine unrecorded intra-SSA trade, the computations in Tables 8.2 and 8.3 are based solely on official statistics.
10 This case was first discussed in the context of a two-good/three-country model by Vanek (1965) and expanded by Kemp (1969). In a two-good model, all trade is of inter-industrial nature.
11 For an excellent discussion and empirical test of the determinants of intra- and inter-industry trade, see Balassa and Bauwens (1988).
12 The impact of preferential trade arrangements among the sample countries was measured by introducing a dummy variable which is equal to 1 when both the reporter and the partner country share such an arrangement and zero otherwise. Foroutan and Pritchett included seven such dummy variables. Other than for the three trade arrangements in SSA, the other dummy variables were included for ASEAN, LAFTA, CACM, and ACP or Lomé signatory countries. All the preferential trade arrangement dummy variables for non-SSA countries were significant.

13 There is hardly any literature on the issue of trade integration in SSA written by African scholars or any Treaty establishing the current RI schemes in the subregion which does not mention 'self-sufficiency' or increase in the degree of industrialisation and attenuation of the dependence on undiversified exports of raw materials as the most important objective of RI. See, for example, Abegunrin (1990).

14 On average, tariff revenues still account for approximately 40 percent of total government tax revenues in SSA countries, in contrast to a negligible 2 percent in developed economies. See Shalizi and Squire (1989) and Chhibber and Khalilzadeh-Shirazi (1988).

15 For qualifications to this statement see Chapter 6 in this volume.

16 See for example, Johnson (1962, Chapter 3). See also Chapter 6 in this volume.

17 For a comprehensive discussion see Chapter 6 in this volume.

18 Johnson (1962) p. 281.

19 Ibid, p. 1007.

20 See Lipsey (1971) and Wonnacott and Wonnacott (1981).

21 There is of course the possibility that integration, by allowing the exploitation of comparative advantage, also spurs the emergence of new industries in the least developed regions. Which of these opposite effects of integration on industrial development of a country will prevail is ultimately an empirical question. The evidence is mixed. On the one hand, experience suggests that countries that have removed trade barriers and integrated with the world at large have also seen the emergence of solid, competitive industries within their national boundaries. The case of South-East Asian countries is the most revealing example. On the other hand, the persistence of depressed regions within nations or regional groupings such as the Community, suggests that full integration with a geographically limited area (the rest of the nation or the group) may indeed polarise the initial industrial imbalances. For an evaluation of the EC experience see de Grauwe (1991). For an exposition of the US experience see Krugman (1990).

22 See, for example, Frimpong-Ansah (1990).

23 There is a recent proposal to transform UMOA into a fully-fledged economic union. If this proposal is accepted, it would imply a *de facto* demise of CEAO.

24 Devarajan and de Melo (1990).

25 See Guillaumont and Guillaumont (1989).

26 See, for example, Molle (1990, p. 221).

27 See Mansoor *et al.* (1989). They emphasise, however, that free factor movement must occur in the wider context of trade liberalisation.

28 For a more comprehensive discussion see Ruffin (1984) and Wooton (1986). For an excellent summary of the literature see Chapter 6 in this volume.

29 Ibid, p. 153.

30 Lagos Plan of Action, Preamble, Article 3.

31 See El-Agraa (1989).

32 In 1983, the latest date for which data are available, the Community absorbed over 51 percent of all SSA's merchandise exports and accounted for over 65 percent of SSA's total merchandise imports. See Tovias (1990).

33 See, for example, the December 1990 issue of the *Journal of Common Market Studies* dedicated to the implications of 'Europe 1992' for developing countries, especially the article by Stevens. See also Tovias (1990).

34 The Lomé Convention is a comprehensive aid and trade agreement between

the Community and the ACP group of countries. The convention was first signed in 1975 and renewed in 1979, 1984, and 1989. The last renewal, known as Lomé 4, runs for a period of ten years and comprises sixty-eight ACP countries, among whom all of SSA. The trade provisions grant unrestricted access of EC markets for the vast majority of ACP exports. Recognising the problems caused by a heavy debt burden, the volume of aid under Lomé 4 has been substantially increased over the previous arrangements. For a critical evaluation of Lomé 1–3 see Marin (1990). For Lomé 4 see *West Africa* (February 28–March 4 1990) pp. 318–22.

REFERENCES

Abegunrin, O. (1990) *Economic Dependence and Regional Cooperation in Southern Africa*, New York: Edwin Mellen Press.

Arhin, K. (1990) 'Historical Roots of ECOWAS', in K. Arhin (ed.), '*Long Term Perspective Study of Sub-Saharan Africa*', vol. 4, proceedings of a workshop on 'Regional Integration and Cooperation', Washington, DC: World Bank.

Balassa, B. and L. Bauwens (1988) *Changing Trade Patterns in Manufacturing Goods: An Economic Investigation*, Amsterdam: North-Holland.

Berg, E. *et al.* (1988) 'Regional and Economic Development in Sub-Saharan Africa', vol. I and II, a study prepared for the USAID (Alexandria, VA).

Chhibber, A. and J. Khalilzadeh-Shirazi (1988) 'Public Finances in Adjustment Programs', *PPR Working Paper*, **128**, Washington, DC: World Bank.

Cooper, C.A. and B.F. Massell (1965) 'Toward a General Theory of Customs Unions for Developing Countries', *Journal of Political Economy*, **73(5)**, pp. 461–76.

Corden, W.M. (1972) 'Economies of Scale and Customs Union Theory', *Journal of Political Economy*, **80**, pp. 465–75.

Devarajan, S. and J. de Melo (1990) 'Membership in the CFA Zone: Odyssean Journey or Trojan Horse?', *PRE Working Paper*, **428**, Washington, DC: World Bank.

Diouf, M. (1990) 'Evaluation of West African Experiments in Economic Integration', in '*Long Term Perspective Study of Sub-Saharan Africa*'.

Economist Intelligence Unit (1989) *SADCC in the 1990s: Development on the Front Line*, *Special Report*, **1158**, London: Economic Intelligence Unit.

El-Agraa, A.M. (1989] *Theory and Measurement of International Economic Integration*, London: Macmillan.

Ezenwe, U. (1990) 'Evaluating the Performance of West African Integration Movements', in '*Long Term Perspective Study of Sub-Saharan Africa*'.

Foroutan, F. and L. Pritchett (forthcoming) 'Intra-Sub-Saharan African Trade: Is It Too Little?', Washington, DC: World Bank (mimeo).

Frimpong-Ansah, J.H. (1990) 'The Prospects for Monetary Union in Ecowas', in '*Long Term Perspective Study of Sub-Saharan Africa*'.

Grauwe, P. de (1991) 'The 1992 European Integration Program and Regional Development Policies', in J. de Melo and A. Sapir (eds), *Trade Theory and Economic Reform*, Oxford: Basil Blackwell.

Guillaumont, P. and S. Guillaumont (1989) 'The Implication of the European Monetary Union for Africa Countries', *Journal of Common Market Studies*, **28(2)**.

Hall, S. (1987) 'The Preferential Trade Area for Eastern and Southern African States: Strategy Progress, and Problems', *Working Paper*, **453**, Institute for Development Studies, University of Nairobi, Kenya.

Henderson, R.D. (1985) 'The Southern African Customs Union: Politics of Dependence', in R. Onwuka and A. Sesay (eds), *The Future of Regionalism in Africa*, New York: St Martin's Press.

Johnson, H.G. (1962) *Money, Trade and Economic Growth*, Cambridge, Mass.: Harvard University Press.

(1965) 'The Economic Theory of Protectionism, Tariff Bargaining, and the Formation of Customs Unions', *Journal of Political Economy*, **73** (June) pp. 256/83.

(1967) 'The Possibility of Income Losses From Increased Efficiency or Factor Accumulation in the Presence of Tariffs', *The Economic Journal*, **27** (March) pp. 151–4.

Kemp, M.C. (1969) *A Contribution to the General Equilibrium Theory of Preferential Trading*, Amsterdam: North-Holland.

Krugman, P. (1990) 'History and Industry Location: The Case of the Manufacturing Belt', draft seminar paper (May).

Lipsey, R.G. (1971) *The Theory of Customs Unions: A General Equilibrium Analysis*, London: Weidenfeld & Nicolson.

Mansoor, Ali, *et al.* (1989) 'Intra-regional Trade in Sub-Saharan Africa', Report **7685**, Washington, DC: World Bank.

Marin, A. (1990) 'The Lomé Agreement', Chapter 21 in A.M. El-Agraa, (ed.), *The Economics of the European Community*, New York: St Martin Press.

Martin, G. (1989) 'Une Nouvelle Experience d'Integration Régionale en Afrique: La Zone d'Echange Préférentielle des Etas de l'Afrique de l'Est et de l'Afrique Australe', *Africa Development*, **14(1)**, pp. 5–17.

Molle, W. (1990) *The Economics of European Integration*, Aldershot: Dartmouth.

Mulaisho, D.C. (1990) 'SADCC: A New Approach to Integration', in '*Long Term Perspective Study of Sub-Saharan Africa*'.

Neary J.P. (1987) 'Tariffs, Quotas, and VERs With and Without International Mobile Capital', paper presented at the European Economic Association Conference (Copenhagen).

Okolo, J.E. and S. Wright (eds) (1990) *West African Regional Cooperation and Development*, Oxford: Westview Press.

Pearson, S.R. and W.D. Ingram (1980) 'Economies of Scale, Domestic Divergence, and Potential Gains from Economic Integration in Ghana and Ivory Coast', *Journal of Political Economy*, **88**, pp. 994–1008.

Robson, P. (1971) 'Fiscal Compensation and Distribution of Benefits in Economic Groupings of Developing Countries', New York: United Nations.

(1983) *Integration, Development and Equity: Economic Integration in West Africa*, London: Allen & Unwin.

Ruffin, Roy J. (1984) 'International Factor Movements', Chapter 5 in R.W. Jones and P.B. Kenen (eds), *Handbook of International Economics*, Amsterdam: North-Holland.

Sesay, A. (1990) 'Obstacles to Intra-union Trade in the Mano River Union', Chapter 4 in Okolo and Wright (eds), (1990).

Shalizi, Z. and L. Squire (1989) 'Tax Policy in Sub-Saharan Africa: A Framework for Analysis', *PPR Policy and Research Series*, **2**, Washington, DC: World Bank.

Stevens, C. (1990) 'The Impact of Europe 1992 on the Maghreb and Sub-Saharan Africa', *Journal of Common Market Studies*, **29(2)** (December) pp. 217–43.

Thisen, J.K. (1989) 'Alternative Approaches to Economic Integration in Africa', *Africa Development*, **14(1)** pp. 19–60.

Tovias, A. (1990) 'The European Communities' Single Market: The Challenge of 1992 for Sub-Saharan Africa', *World Bank Discussion Paper*, **100**, Washington, DC: World Bank.

Vanek, J. (1965) *General Equilibrium of International Discrimination: The Case of Customs Unions*, Cambridge, Mass.: Harvard University Press.

Viner, J. (1950) *The Customs Union Issue*, New York: Carnegie Endowment for International Peace.

Wangwe, S.M. (1990) 'A Comparative Analysis of the PTA and SADCC Approaches to Regional Economic Integration', in *'Long Term Perspective Study of Sub-Saharan Africa'*.

Welsh, C.E., Jr. (1990) 'The Military Factor in West Africa: Leadership and Regional Development', in Okolo and Wright (eds) (1990).

Wonnacott, P. and R. Wonnacott (1981) 'Is Unilateral Tariff Reduction Preferable to Customs Union? The Curious Case of the Missing Foreign Tariff', *American Economic Review*, **71** (September) pp. 704–14.

Wooton, I. (1986) 'Towards a Common Market: Factor Mobility in a Custom Union', *Working Paper*, **8614C**, Centre for the Study of International Economic Relations, Department of Economics, University of Western Ontario.

World Bank (1991) 'Regional Cooperation for Adjustment: A Program of Trade, Transport and Financial Policy for Member Countries of UDEAC', *Report* **9747-AFR**, Washington, DC: World Bank.

Discussion

CHRISTOPHER BLISS

In a provocative analogy which appears on the first page of her stimulating Chapter 8, Faezeh Foroutan compares Sub-Saharan Africa (SSA) with Belgium, whose 1989 GNP she claims to be approximately equal to the summed GNPs of the SSA countries. 'Imagine subdividing Belgium', she writes, 'into forty-something independent countries, each with its own isolated goods and factor markets'. The force of this extravagant comparison, and its inappropriateness in some respects, almost define the problem which we confront when we think about regional integration in SSA.

A notable difference between the two cases is in size. Belgium is tiny on a world map; Africa is vast. One can drive between any two points in Belgium in a few hours, even if traffic is congested. There are points on the SSA map more accessible to Brussels by air or sea than to populated towns only a few hundred miles away. Africa is poorly integrated as a geographical region, leaving aside the considerable man-created economic barriers. Equally, while Belgium may have more than its share of linguistic and religious divisions by European standards, many African countries, not to speak of African regions, would be happy to swap their fractious tendencies for those of Belgium.

Similarly, Belgium's regions have few comparative advantages of the textbook type *vis-à-vis* other Belgian regions. This is not to say that splitting the country into forty units would be without cost. The costs would be huge – but they would consist predominantly of the unnecessary duplication of activities with scale economies of various kinds. SSA, by contrast, encompasses great diversity, with numerous examples of textbook comparative advantage. These benefits, however, are hard to realise in many cases because of high, or even prohibitive, transport costs.

It is interesting to imagine a free-trade world including a completely unified SSA, with no trade restrictions, common administrative practices, common currency, etc. How much would that SSA trade with itself, what economic regions and patterns would emerge? Is it clear that the big differences such a world would expose would be in Africa's trade and economic relations with the rich industrial countries. Inter-SSA developments would often involve what I shall call semi-tradeable goods and services, where 'semi-tradeable' means imperfectly tradeable, or tradeable only at a high cost. Even the division of labour, orientated to benefit from economies of scale, will often involve semi-tradeability, for without it the world market would define the field for scale economies.

The real world differs from my imagined world in two respects. First SSA is certainly no massive free-market area; but also the rest of the world is far from as open to trade with Africa as one might wish. Trade restrictions push regions in on themselves, and one of the more respectable arguments for the promotion of SSA regional blocs is that such blocs might be able to promote gainful trade to which the world at large would be resistant.

The context of an SSA in a trade-restricted world might give a meaning to the author's discussion of the scope for trade between similar countries, including mention of product differentiation, which it would otherwise lack. Even so, the idea of variety-producing specialisation in SSA subregions lacks plausibility. The scope is too limited and rich-country markets not so severely closed that SSA countries need be forced to such extremely local trade except, again, for semi-tradeables. While the gravity model employed in the chapter confirms that the untapped interregional trade potential of the SSA countries is somewhat limited, it is true to conclude that successful economic integration breeds interdependence and increases the scope for trade.

The application of customs union theory in the chapter is skilful and illuminating. In particular, the association, borrowed from Harry Johnson, between success in economic integration and a sharing of the expansion of industrial activity, is highly pertinent in the SSA context. How is this to be achieved? Two types of difficulty assert themselves, political and economic; and, as typically happens, the two interact.

Politics goes a long way towards explaining how regional integration (RI) initiatives arise, and it accounts for many of the problems which such initiatives encounter. However natural it may seem to an economist that RI should be motivated purely by economic gains, it would be hard to cite an historical example which fitted that pattern. The worst difficulties arise when political forces for union bisect economic rationale, a point which customs union (CU) theory illustrates, and which the mess which is European agricultural policy horribly underlines.

Despite the difficulties of European economic policy, the political push for union has been powerful there, more powerful than is often replicated in Africa, although old colonial patterns sometimes provide a common historical bond. When potential economic gains are unspectacular, as Foroutan argues, the difficulties for RI are apparent.

Political differences translate to administrative tensions inside the union. The chapter considers compensation payments, in parallel with the type employed in classical welfare economics. The objective, neutral and detached civil servant who would have to administer compensation payments provides a service which is scarce in African countries. While compensation payments are an extreme instance, even the channelling of tariff revenues could raise severe problems. Suppose A and B integrate their economies and A has the better port facilities, so that now imports into both A and B all pass through A. Some tariff revenue should be collected in A but transferred to B. Unfortunately B is smaller, less developed and with an inferior educational system, so that officials tend to come from A. I have sketched an integrated region in which political and economic reality may interact to generate serious problems.

The location of industry raises similar issues and comparable problems. Economies of scale inside the plant are likely to require that relatively small economies should not all have plants of every type. So sharing out is indicated if, as seem likely, industrial plants generate external economies and local rents of various kinds. Yet the 'you have this one, now it is your turn' method of dividing plants between regions may run counter to the large economies of conglomeration which occur when plants provide local external economies for other plants. Often the most efficient outcome, and that which the market will tend to select, will involve a high concentration of industrial activity.

We are confronting the possibility that RI might create or sustain regional marginality, a possibility which disturbs some observers of the European Community. Europe has problems which are different from any likely to be encountered in Africa. For instance the wealth and large size imply that there could be big money in compensation and rent-seeking, implying the possibility that some regions may implicitly choose, or have chosen for them, policies which reinforce their economic marginality.

If scepticism concerning SSA RI carries great weight, and the arguments for enhanced trade flows with the rich countries are considerable, the two points can be combined to argue that the most fruitful route for RI may be via the coordination of SSA relations with the rich industrial trade bloc. The development of those relations will often involve negotiation concerning imports from the centre, and for inward investment. The case for coordination of policy in a group of SSA countries will be apparent when one imagines the alternative of a competition to attract inward investment, with different countries offering tax holidays, partial subsidies, etc. Yet our game theory teaches us that the fact that coordination would be mutually gainful does not make it easy to achieve.

ISHRAT HUSAIN

I agree with Foroutan in Chapter 8 that the import-substitution policies and the unequal distribution of costs and benefits of integration are the principal reason for the lack of success in regional integration (RI) in Sub-Saharan Africa (SSA). I also agree that factor mobility in the presence of restricted goods movement is not necessarily and automatically welfare-improving or desirable. Both of these conclusions follow logically from the comparative static framework Foroutan uses for her analysis. I will leave aside the speculative question as to what would happen if we used a dynamic process but I wish to show that, even under the present framework, the story Foroutan tells is only partial.

I do not believe that the African countries trade little among themselves and that they are not natural trading partners. I also do not share the view that differences among them are enormous. Foroutan shows that the differences in *per capita* incomes among countries with lowest and highest incomes in the same regional groupings were 6 to 7 times. If we exclude Mauritius, Botswana, Seychelles, and Gabon whose total population is less than 3 million, the majority of the African countries have *per capita* incomes in the range of $250–$600 and the income differences are less significant than in other regions. Seventeen out of the thirty-nine SSA countries had more than 10 percent of their recorded trade with SSA partners. Seven of these achieved a share of at least 20 percent. The low shares of the largest economies in the region mostly explain the low overall ratio of intra-regional trade.

I would submit that informal integration between countries in the SSA, both in goods and factor markets, is much stronger and robust than any analysis based on simply the official recorded data would tend to suggest. Smuggling, cross-border trade, capital flight, and parallel exchange markets are the most important means of this informal integration in the goods markets. In the factor markets, despite some setbacks such as the expulsion of 1 million Ghanaians from Nigeria in 1983, unrestricted movement of labour especially in the neighbouring countries having common ethnic ties does take place unfettered. There is also evidence of increased monetary dependence through the operation of parallel markets, as is apparent from circulation of CFA currency notes across the markets for the naira.

Although reliable data do not exist, most observers believe that the magnitudes involved in the informal trade flows are more significant than the formal data of intra-regional flows would reveal. To cite one empirical study, the price of cocoa in Ivory Coast affected the quantity of cocoa purchased by Ghana's COCBOD with an elasticity of − 0.12 and the price premium was equal to 667 percent. The quantity smuggled annually was estimated to be around 50,000 tons or $100 million at the then prevailing world prices. This reduced the official foreign exchange earnings of Ghana by one-fourth of the total export receipts. This example illustrates the limitation of any analysis that is based on recorded trade statistics alone, such as the gravity model used by Foroutan.

In the presence of widespread shortages of consumer goods, traders and producers have incentives to smuggle domestic tradeables out to bring back the goods that are in short supply on the domestic market. Import compression or exchange controls also create an incentive for smuggling.

In Niger, Cameroon, Benin, and Chad the price of Nigerian goods, computed as the product of the rural CPI times the black market price between the naira and the CFA franc, turns out to be a good predictor for the price index of rural consumption in these countries. In recent years, the subsidised petroleum and fertiliser prices in Nigeria have enabled these neighbouring countries to reduce their direct imports of petroleum products and fertilisers. The significant depreciation of the Real Effective Exchange Rate (REER) of the naira since 1986 has reversed the flow of goods and opened a booming market for Nigerian textiles even in places as far away as Abidjan.

The non-competitiveness of SSA countries compared to third-party suppliers, the high cost of doing business, the shortage of foreign exchange and credit, the administrative and regulatory constraints, and restrictions on free-trade movements have made flow of goods and factors through the formal trade channels redundant. This set of fundamental problems is responsible for the precipitous decline in the share of SSA in the world markets from 2.4 percent in 1970 to about 1 percent in 1990. Had SSA maintained its 1970 share in world exports, the additional increase in foreign exchange earnings would have been $45 billion in 1990. On the other hand, if all trade barriers on intra-regional trade are removed, the potential for additional trade in SSA would at best amount to $10–12 billion. Africa is still a small economy and its economic size is between Indonesia and Korea and, therefore, regaining its historical share in world markets is not only feasible but also extremely important.

In my view the relative welfare gains from this strategy can far exceed those from extensive economic integration, particularly of the type advocated by a number of enthusiasts of RI. A common customs union (CU) with high common external tariffs (CETs) and high levels of effective protection in the member states enjoying regional preferences would be a recipe for disaster. These attempts would make African production even less competitive by encouraging trade diversion. The main benefits of regional integration would come from the restructuring of African economies that become more flexible and better integrated with the world economy, a dismantling of barriers in goods and factor flows among the neighbouring countries and an improvement in infrastructure, transportation, and telecommunications so that the present transaction costs are reduced and the African products become competitive with those of third-party suppliers.

How can this be achieved? I do not wish to go into the whole litany of measures required to restore competitiveness for African products. Let me just say that the time period for this turnaround is going to be much longer than we had originally anticipated. First, the African economies' main exports are primary commodities and minerals whose demand in the world markets is not as stable as those of manufactured goods, and thus their exposure to fluctuations in the demand and prices for these commodities make them particularly vulnerable. Second, given the deep-rooted nature of initial distortions in these economies and the intensity of other non-price constraints, the supply response to a new configuration of relative prices is likely to be low. Finally, the political changes which are taking place in Africa at present do have a short-term disruptive effect on the level of economic activity.

In sum, the movement towards an efficient integration and expansion of regional markets in Africa would be best served by national policies that liberalise the respective economies and promote competition and efficiency in the domestic product and factor markets.

NOTE

The views expressed are those of the author and should not be attributed to the World Bank, its Board of Directors, its management, or any of its member countries.

9 Latin America's integration and the multilateral trading system

JULIO J. NOGUÉS and
ROSALINDA QUINTANILLA

1 Introduction

This chapter addresses three questions on Latin America's integration efforts: What are the major characteristics of the ongoing integration schemes, and how can they be improved? What integration strategy would provide the greatest economic gains to the region? How can Latin America's integration help to improve the multilateral trading system? Our main conclusion is that since the loss to Latin America from a breakdown of the multilateral trading system will not be compensated by preferential reductions of trade barriers, integration proposals should be liberal and used to reinvigorate the currently strained multilateral trading system.[1] We believe that the broad characteristics of trading arrangements which may enhance economic welfare are that barriers to intratrade should be dismantled and that tariffs and non-tariff barriers (NTBs) with third countries should be significantly reduced; they can be acceded by any country; they support unilateral liberalisation measures by member countries; they avoid using harmonisation of policies such as standards and rules of origin to provide protection; they restrict the group of policies – such as anti-dumping – that have undermined the multilateral trading system; and they support the multilateral trading negotiations (MTNs).

Section 2's main purpose is to present a critical review of Latin America's past integration strategy. Section 3 analyses the effects of Latin America's recent unilateral reforms and the role of the multilateral trading system, and discusses their impact on the integration process. Section 4 analyses the current integration schemes, and addresses the question as to how their potential net benefits can be improved. Main conclusions and policy recommendations are presented in section 5.

278

2   Latin America's past integration strategy

Subsection 2.1 provides a brief discussion of the welfare economics of trade arrangements. It is against this knowledge that we evaluate the soundness of past integration schemes and the main characteristics of the new efforts. This is done in subsection 2.2.

2.1   The welfare economics of trade arrangements

The classical literature on the subject as developed by Viner (1950), Meade (1956) and Lipsey (1960) concludes that a regional arrangement is more likely to be welfare-improving if:

(1)   there is a broad scope for production specialisation among countries within a bloc;
(2)   tariffs and NTBs to intra-trade are substantially reduced;
(3)   tariffs and NTBs with third countries are lower after the formation of the trade agreement.

Regarding the number of countries, two cases are particularly relevant for Latin America. First, consider the 'hub-and-spoke' model of integration (Wonnacott, 1990; Lipsey, 1991) and an expanding agreement. Lipsey (1990) observes that under the hub-and-spoke model, the 'hub' country is likely to attract a more than proportional share of regional investment sensitive to market size since investment in the hub country would have preferential access to all the 'spoke' markets.

Regarding an expanding agreement, Deardorff and Stern (1991), Lipsey (1991) and Nogués (1991) show that universal open entry is a desirable feature since welfare is likely to increase *pari passu* with the number of countries in a trading agreement. At the limit the process approaches world-wide free trade. An expanding agreement also prevents distortions on investment derived from a hub-and-spoke institutional arrangement. Therefore,

(4)   In order to expand the scope of net welfare gains, trading agreements should allow accession by any interested country, regardless of geographical location.

Unilateral trade liberalisation (UTL) is usually not discussed in analysing trade arrangements; this has been an important omission. UTL has been a superior trade strategy for improving growth prospects in developing countries. The experience of the Asian tigers is well known, and in Latin America the performance of Chile is noteworthy. Latin American experience shows that UTL accompanied by supporting macroeconomic policies and an exchange rate regime driven by market forces can significantly improve growth prospects (see section 3 below). Therefore,

(5)   Trading agreements should support member countries to introduce and expand unilateral liberalisation measures.

Support for the MTNs cannot be strong unless the individual integration schemes recognise the policies that have undermined the multilateral trading system, for it is these policies that ultimately help to explain the current rush towards regionalism. Among the most damaging policies we can include the increasing use of unfair trade measures by industrial countries, the expanded nature of the US 'Super 301' provisions and European Community agricultural subsidies (Bhagwati, 1991). Integration schemes that do not reject these policies might fall prey to them and end up providing little economic gains to member countries, to the region and to the international economy. Likewise, interaction schemes should not resort to harmonisation of policies such as standards and rules of origin to protect domestic producers.

(6)   Trading agreements should restrict the use of unfair trade policies, and minimise the protectionist effects of rules of origin, and whatever policies undermine trade competition.

Summing up, the broad characteristics of trading arrangements which may enhance economic welfare are that barriers to intra-trade should be dismantled; tariffs and NTBs with third countries should be significantly reduced; they can be acceded by any country; they support unilateral liberalisation measures by member countries; they avoid using harmonisation of policies such as standards and rules of origin to provide protection; and that they restrict the group of policies – such as anti-dumping (AD) – that have undermined the multilateral trading system, and they support the MTNs.

2.2   Historical overview of Latin America's integration strategy

Scenarios for economic integration in Latin America began to be considered in the late 1940s and early 1950s, though the idea can be traced back to the independence movement in the 19th century. Economic integration post-World War II emerged after several years of negotiating alternative integration schemes (see Vacchio, 1981; Wionczek, 1966). This process culminated in the treaties that created the main regional groupings (see Table 9.2): Latin American Free-Trade Area (LAFTA, February 1960 replaced by LAIA in 1980, see below), the Central American Common Market (CACM, December 1960), the Andean Pact (May

1969), and the Caribbean Community and Common Market (CARICOM, July 1973).

The writings of Dr Raúl Prebisch and the then influential UN Economic Commission for Latin America (ECLA) played a critical role in the process for economic integration (see Prebisch, 1959; ECLA, 1959). They provided a theoretical framework as well as technical support to adopt and implement an integration strategy focused on import-substitution policies at the regional level. The economic rigidities assumed by structuralism were also supported by other influential models such as those developed by Lewis (1954) and Chenery and Strout (1966). These views were accommodated in GATT through the special and differential provisions granted to developing countries (Hudec, 1987). For several decades the internal and external intellectual climate of the region favoured protectionist policies.

The integration process gathered momentum when it became quite clear that the import-substitution strategy implemented at the national level did not solve the foreign exchange constraints of many developing countries. Policymakers concluded that integration and expansion of exports at the regional level economising on foreign exchange were appropriate policies. Each of the Latin American integration programmes extended inward-oriented policies adopted at the national level to their own regional dimension. The characteristics of these Latin American integration programmes are summarised in Table 9.1.

The agreements excluded major trading partners, such as the United States, since an explicit objective was to increase economic interdependence within Latin America and reduce it with respect to the rest of the world. And while the United States supported liberalisation through MTN under GATT, Latin America, as well as other developing countries, were attempting to free-ride the MTNs (see Johnson, 1966; Wolf, 1987).

The strategy towards economic integration led to the adoption of discriminatory practices and elaborate and complex regulations. It also expanded the discretionary powers to those negotiating trade concessions and implementing the agreements (see Balassa, 1966). However, not all the agreements were as discriminatory. The CACM relied more on rules that applied across the board, rules such as a common external tariff (CET) and an important dismantling of barriers to intra-trade. However, the CET was designed to foster regional industrialisation through import substitution (see Saborio and Michalopoulos, 1991). The CACM incentive structure favoured intra-regional trade but its inward orientation limited the growth of extra-regional trade.

This is seen in Table 9.2, which shows the changes in trade ratios (total trade as a percent of GDP) over time. The Andean Pact is perhaps the

Table 9.1. *Latin American integration programmes: objectives and instruments*

Objectives	Instruments
LAFTA/LAIA (12 years to accomplish the objectives)	
* Gradually to eliminate intra-regional trade impediments	* Regional and partial agreements of intra-regional trade impediments
* To expand intra-regional markets	* National and common lists of products
* To promote and regulate intra-regional trade	* Special lists of preferential concessions to lesser developed members
* To promote industrial integration	* Differential treatment across member countries
* To expand investment opportunities of key industries	* Targeting specific industries for preferential treatment
* Fairly to share the benefits of the agreement	* Compensation mechanisms to benefit from non-reciprocal trade concessions
	* The right to withdraw trade concessions when these are related to products produced domestically
CACM (5 years to converge to a common external tariff)	
* To establish a common market	* Immediate elimination of all import duties of Part I products
* To promote and coordinate industrial development	* Providing national treatment to Part I products in the implementation of quality controls (except those related to health, national security, and public safety regulations)
* To cooperate in monetary and financial areas	* Applying most favoured nation (MFN) principle to Part II and III products
* To develop an integrated infrastructure	* Non-discriminatory treatment to producers in the region
* To facilitate intra-regional investment	* Establishment of a common external tariff (CET) for all products except those of Part III
	* Providing national treatment to investors from member countries

Objectives	Instruments
Andean Pact (10 years)	
* To promote balanced and harmonious development through economic integration	* Sectoral Programmes of Industrial Development to create new large-scale key industries
* To programme joint industrial development	* Industrial Rationalisation Programmes to revitalise existing industries
* To coordinate development plans	* Trade Liberalisation Programme to eliminate import duties among member countries
* To harmonise economic and social policies	* Regulating foreign investment to targeted industries and locations
* To establish a common regime, regulate, and direct foreign investment	* Preferential treatment across member countries
* To create preferential margins for member countries	* Industrial programmes targeted to implement import-substitution at the regional level
* To provide preferential treatment for Bolivia and Ecuador	* Lists of products subject to differentiated rules in the elimination of import duties
	* Preferential treatment to products produced by member countries
	* Emphasis in the use of supranational entities to implement the agreement

Sources: Authors' assessment based on texts of trade agreements in INTAL (1986).

Table 9.2. *Changes in trade ratios of regional groupings in Latin America, total trade as a % of combined GDP*

	Intra-regional trade			External trade		
Groupings	Base	Later	1980–90	Base	Later	1980–90
A. Total trade						
Andean Pact[a]	0.5	1.6	1.3	30.8	35.3	30.7
1964–8/1974–8						
CACM[b]	1.8	10.0	6.7	33.4	33.0	36.9
1957–60/1966–70						
LAFTA/LAIA[c]	2.0	1.8	2.6	20.7	15.2	19.1
1956–60/1966–70						
CARICOM[d]	4.7	7.6	5.5	80.4	123.5	103.5
1968–72/1978–82						
EEC9[e]	17.4	24.1	25.1	17.6	23.7	23.7
1968–72/1978–82						
Southeast Asian NICs[f]	3.1	8.7	10.2	55.6	97.7	99.3
1965–9/1978–82						
B. Manufactures						
Andean Pact[a]	0.1	0.5	0.6	10.1	13.1	10.3
1964–8/1974–8						
CACM[b]	n.a.	7.0	4.6	n.a.	15.1	12.6
1957–60/1966–70						
LAFTA/LAIA[c]	n.a.	0.5	1.2	n.a.	5.9	7.7
1956–60/1966–70						
CARICOM[d]	1.9	2.7	2.0	31.8	31.8	25.5
1968–72/1978–82						
EEC9[e]	12.4	16.6	17.8	10.3	14.1	15.4
1968–72/1978–82						
Southeast Asian NICs[f]	2.0	5.5	6.9	39.1	63.9	66.1
1965–9/1978–82						

Notes: Base and later periods are indicated in each group cell, e.g. CACM, 1957–60/1966–70.
[a] Signed on 26 May 1969 by Bolivia, Chile, Colombia, Ecuador, Peru and Venezuela. Chile left the Andean Pact in 1976.
[b] CACM was signed on 13 December 1960 by Costa Rica, El Salvador, Guatemala, Honduras and Nicaragua.
[c] LAFTA was signed on 18 February 1960 by Argentina, Bolivia, Brazil, Chile, Colombia, Ecuador, Mexico, Paraguay, Peru, Uruguay and Venezuela. The Latin American Integration Association (LAIA) replaced LAFTA through the Montevideo Treaty of 1980 (12 August 1980).
[d] CARICOM was signed on 4 July 1973 by Antigua and Barbuda, Bahamas, Barbados, Belize, Dominica, Grenada, Guyana, Jamaica, Monserrat, St Christopher-Nevis, St Lucia, St Vincent and the Grenadines, Trinidad and Tobago.

most sophisticated integration scheme to foster import substitution at the regional level and with the most complex set of regulations to implement the agreement. And it is in the Andean group where intra-trade is and remains the smallest among the regional subgroupings. Likewise, it was mainly during the formative years of LAFTA that regional trade barriers were reduced, but this did not create a significant long-run trend in regional trade (see Table 9.2).

Most of the deadlines stipulated in the agreements were around ten years (with the exception of the CACM which had a five-year framework), but for the most part these were not met. In addition, internal frictions mounted over equitable sharing of benefits and differential treatment to the least developed member countries.

Chile is the only case where the unilateral and liberal economic reforms led her to withdraw from the Andean Pact in October 1976, since the obligations of Chile under the Pact would have otherwise restricted and even prevented the introduction of economic reforms (see Hachette and Rosende, 1991). It was simply impossible to introduce unilateral liberalisation measures such as a reduction in import duties and liberal and non-discriminatory rules for investment and remain a member of the Andean Pact, which maintained high import duties and had a strongly regulated and discriminatory investment code (Behrman, 1976).

The external debt crisis of the early 1980s highlighted the economic vulnerability of countries in the region to changes in the external environment and reinforced the need for inward-oriented integration as they have insisted for nearly three decades. All major regional trading groups made revisions to the original agreements in an effort to revitalise economic integration (IDB/INTAL, 1984).

LAFTA was replaced by LAIA through the Montevideo Treaty of 1980 which provided for a stronger role for partial agreements. In 1983 the Andean Treaty adopted a Reorientation Plan for the Andean Integration process and eight sectoral agreements which led to the Protocol modifying the Cartagena Agreement in 1987. The political frictions among the CACM countries shifted the role of CACM to a forum seeking regional peace, as expressed in the agreements of Esquilpas I (1986) and Esquilpas

Table 9.2. (cont.)
[e] Belgium, Denmark, France, Germany, Ireland, Italy, Netherlands, Luxembourg and United Kingdom.
[f] Hong Kong, Korea, Singapore, and Taiwan.
Sources: Wonnacott and Lutz (1989) for total trade. 1980–90 data and trade in manufacturers are authors' calculations based on DOT, IMF; BESD, The World Bank; and UN ComTrade data bases. INTAL (1986).

II (1987) (IDB/INTAL, 1989). Generally, the 1980s' efforts to revitalise the process of economic integration did not go beyond declaratory statements. However, in 1985 Argentina and Brazil initiated a process of sectoral negotiation which led to seventeen protocols being signed by the end of 1986 and later being ratified without modifications in 1989. These later evolved into the *Mercado Común del Cono Sur* (MERCOSUR).

Yet the external debt crisis and continued economic mismanagement indicated the need for a complete change in development strategy. The persistence of economic stagnation in the region and the contrast with the development of outward-oriented economies emphasised the need for domestic economic reforms. Following the example of Chile, the first to shift during the 1980s were Bolivia and Mexico.

Historical integration schemes in Latin America are in sharp contrast with the economic integration in the European Economic Community and the South East Asian newly industrialised countries (NICs: Korea, Hong Kong, Singapore and Taiwan). The European Community illustrates the process of economic integration formally negotiated as a preferential arrangement while the East Asian NICs illustrates the process *without* a negotiated preferential arrangement.

The major differences in approach were the trade orientation and the role of market mechanisms *vis-à-vis* government interventions (Table 9.3). While in Latin America the integration schemes were inward oriented and fostered regional import-substituting industrialisation by regulating trade and investment flows, the European Community implemented multilateral liberalisation of trade in manufactures under GATT while facilitating intra-regional trade. The South East Asian NICs pursued an outward-oriented strategy and trade liberalisation on a non-preferential basis.

Intra-regional trade patterns indicate that trade expanded much more in the European Community and the South East Asian NICs than in the Latin American regional groupings (see Table 9.2). In addition, the trends of trade ratios indicate that intra-regional and external trade grew more rapidly in the case of the South East Asian NICs (the non-preferential path) than in the European Community (the preferential path). This last observation is particularly important to Latin American countries since, as in the case of the South East Asian NICs and in contrast to the European Community, these countries are pricetakers in the international markets and external trade is much larger than intra-regional trade.

Summing up, when integration programmes began to be signed in the 1960s, the import-substitution strategy was well advanced. Domestic market structures and the interest groups behind them had thus been established and had already captured the process of policymaking. Under

Table 9.3. *Main characteristics of economic integration schemes: Latin America, European Community, and Southeast Asian NICs*

Main characteristics	Latin America	European Community	Southeast Asia
Trade orientation	Inward-oriented	Multilateral liberalisation	Outward-oriented
Mechanism	Negotiated integration	Negotiated integration	Market-led integration
Approach of intra-regional trade liberalisation	Industrial targeting	* Sequencing of across-the-board reduction of trade impediments * Harmonisation of national rules for exceptions	Unilateral trade liberalisation
Trade strategy with non-member countries	Regional import substitution industrialisation	Negotiated liberalism with CET	Market-oriented liberalism
Treatment of member countries	Preferential treatment of least developed member countries	MFN principle	Non-preferential treatment
Main trade objectives	* Regulate trade to foster regional import substitution * Equitable sharing of net benefits	* Facilitate intra-regional trade * Foster conditions for European union	Expansion of international market shares
Institutional framework	No supranational entities with the exception of the Andean Treaty and Clearing House in CACM	With supranational entities	Not applicable

Source: Authors' assessment.

these circumstances, regionalism provided, at most, minimal possibilities for trade creation and greater use of economies of scale (Carnoy, 1970). The approach to economic integration clearly reflects the view that few countries were willing to give up monopoly/oligopoly positions in domestic markets. In fact, the purpose of negotiations was often to avoid disruptions to domestic market structures. At the same time, since the process of import substitution continued at national levels during the 1960s and 1970s, economic losses from trade diversion continued to increase. It is therefore not surprising that intra-regional trade growth in Latin America was much worse than that observed among outward-oriented economies and manufactures in the case of the European Community.

3   The impact of UTL and multilateralism on Latin America

As the 1980s evolved, Latin American countries became increasingly aware of the importance of unilateralism and the multilateral trading system. During the latter part of the 1980s and early 1990s, Latin American countries not only introduced far-reaching unilateral liberalisation measures, but also began to rethink the soundness of their historical ties to the multilateral trading system including its set of rules as well as the MTNs. This reassessment was a natural outcome of the ideological shift in favour of competition that was taking place in the region. The links between unilateral, regional and multilateral liberalisation had consequently become increasingly important. We argue that without far-reaching unilateral liberalisation policies, it is impossible to construct welfare-enhancing integration schemes.

For most of the 1980s, Latin American countries were characterised among other things by inefficient governments, overregulation and a highly protected economy. The dilemma facing the larger economies that could hope to benefit from an MTN was whether to wait (which entails a true cost) or to liberalise unilaterally. Under this situation, a far-reaching unilateral trade liberalisation programme is likely to result in a superior outcome to waiting for the multilateral process.[2] But the pervasiveness of the inward-oriented policies of several decades delayed the undertaking of important unilateral liberalisation measures until the late 1980s and early 1990s. The experience of the 1980s also indicates that commitments to GATT and MTNs help to institutionalise liberal reforms and reduce the scope of policy reversals.

3.1   UTL

The role of unilateralism in re-establishing sustainable growth and improving growth prospects has been realised at a different pace by countries in the region.[3] Chile was the first to introduce a far-reaching unilateral liberalisation programme and the first to benefit from these measures. A profile of trade liberalisation during 1985–90 in Latin America under alternative adjustment policies is summarised in Table 9.4, which shows a classification of trade policies, and Table 9.5, which shows some performance indicators.

By far the most liberal and outward-oriented trade regime was that of Chile, with a low uniform tariff. The distortionary effects of agricultural price bands for a few products subject to variable levies have been limited given their small weight in the Chilean economy, and yet this initial temporary measure to liberalise agriculture is proving to be difficult to dismantle. Chile is followed by Mexico who in spite of significant reductions in trade barriers has maintained some important non-tariff barriers in agriculture and some manufacturing industries. Costa Rica lowered tariffs and maintained export subsidies – the anti-export bias declined, but in a distortionary way. Finally, Argentina and Peru started from a position of very high protection and timidly removed some trade barriers towards the end of the 1980s but have in the 1990s decisively moved significantly closer to a liberal trade regime.

The accompanying policies are classified as being either supportive or unsupportive of more liberal trade regimes. Fiscal policies are considered supportive of liberal trade regimes when government expenditures are declining and the overall budget balance is satisfactory to meet the internal and external obligations of the country. Factor market policies are supportive if they are free from government regulations and provide an environment that enhances efficiency in factor markets. Finally, the real exchange rate is adequate when it supports overall trade growth.

We concluded that among the group of countries reviewed Chile was the only one that resembled quite clearly the type of trade and supporting policies that some economists had been arguing as the best strategy for accelerating exports, inducing investment, reducing unemployment and accelerating *per capita* GDP growth. As indicated in Table 9.5, Chile's performance is far superior to that of the other four countries.

For each performance variable, Table 9.5 has two columns. Except for GDP growth and *per capita* GDP growth, the first column indicates the level of the variable in 1990 and the second shows the country rank according to the proportional change in that variable between 1985 and 1990. These figures show that the improvement of Chile's economic performance has been impressive.[4] Furthermore, there is little doubt that this performance should be attributed primarily to foreign trade activities which between 1985 and 1990 grew at an average annual rate of 15 percent (underlying figures measured in current dollars). Because these activities were undertaken by the private sector, it is not surprising to see

Table 9.4. *Trade and accompanying policies of selected Latin American countries, 1985–90*

| Country | Trade policies | | | | Accompanying policies | | | | |
| | | | | | Fiscal policies | | Factor market policies | | |
	Tariffs	NTBs	Export subsidies	Overall bias of trade regime	Govt. expenditures[a]	Overall balance	Labour	Investment	Real exchange rate
Argentina	High, and variable	Important	Important and slowly declining	Protectionist and inward-oriented	U	U	U	U	U
Chile	Low, uniform and declining	Minimal	Minimal	Competitive and outward-oriented	S	S	S	S	S
Costa Rica	High, variable and slowly declining	Some	Important	Protectionist and declining anti-export bias	U	U	?	U	U
Mexico	Low, variable and declining	Important in some sectors	Minimal	Outward-oriented for most tradables	S	S	?	U	U
Peru	High and variable	Very important	Important	Protectionist and outward-oriented	U	U	U	U	U

Notes: U = unsupportive; S = supportive; ? indicates that we have doubts about the categorisation.
[a] Net of interest payment.
Source: Nogués and Gulati (1992).

Table 9.5. *Economic performance indicators of some Latin American countries, 1985–90*

Country	Trade–output ratio (%) 1990	R[a]	Average annual trade growth (%) 1985–90	R[a]	Investment ratio (%) Private 1990	R[a]	Total 1990	R[a]	Average annual GDP growth (%) 1985–90	R[b]	Per capita GDP growth (%) 1985–90	R[b]	Unemployment (%) 1990	R[a]	Real wages R[a]
Argentina	19	4	5	4	6	5	9	5	− 0.8	4	− 2.2	4	8.6	4	4
Chile	58	1	15	1	16	1	20	1	5.5	1	3.5	1	6.1	2	1
Costa Rica	59	2	10	2	17	3	22	2	4.0	2	− 0.9	2	4.6	3	3
Mexico	23	3	8	3	15	2	18	4	1.3	3	− 1.0	3	2.5	1	2
Peru	19	5	3	5	13	4	17	3	− 1.0	5	− 3.3	5	8[c]	n.a.	5

Notes:
[a] Ranked by proportional changes in the indicated variable between 1985 and 1990.
[b] Ranked by rates of growth during 1985–90.
[c] Data in italics is for 1989.
Source: Nogués and Gulati (1992).

the private investment ratio increasing from 7 percent in 1985 to 16 percent in 1990. As a consequence, the *per capita* GDP growth rate of Chile was one of the best in the region.

Obviously factors other than trade and investment influence economic growth, notably factor accumulation, technology transfer, innovation, entrepreneurship, education and small efficient governments (Barro, 1989) play important roles. The experience of Chile shows that the introduction of appropriate supporting policies, a very open and liberal trade regime, a small and efficient government and efficient factor markets (i.e., elimination of government interventions that prevent clearance in factor markets) result in sustainable GDP growth.[5] Why? Because the significant increase in the degree of competition that these policies entail stimulate several of the growth-inducing factors such as private investment, innovation, entrepreneurship and greater access to international technology. The interaction among these factors then compounds their growth effects.

The policy lesson from the 1980s is that far-reaching trade liberalisation, supported by appropriate accompanying policies, is the most significant goal that developing countries should try to attain. It is with the expectation of replicating the experience of Chile and other countries that an increasing number of Latin American countries have introduced very important unilateral measures. Among the bigger Latin American countries, Argentina, Peru and Venezuela introduced significant measures during the early 1990s. Several smaller economies, notably those in Central America, also introduced important reforms in a short period of time and Brazil is introducing more gradual changes.

We conclude from this review that unilateral reforms are by far the most efficient strategy for improving the region's growth prospects. The most significant challenge of the region's ongoing integration process is whether it will facilitate or hinder these economic reforms. Policymakers should keep in mind that in spite of the unilateral reforms so far introduced, there are significant changes yet to be made. The integration process should not become an obstacle to these necessary changes.

3.2   Multilateralism

As already stated, during the late 1980s and early 1990s Latin American countries introduced important unilateral liberalisation measures and began to rethink the soundness of their historical ties to the multilateral trading system, its set of rules, and the role of MTNs. A liberal multilateral trading system has become increasingly important as the ideological shift in favour of competition has led countries to embrace liberal policies and participate in the Uruguay Round. An increasing number of Latin American countries have become GATT members: Mexico (1986), Bolivia (1989), Costa Rica (1989), Belize (1983), Colombia (1981), Venezuela (1990), El Salvador (1990), Guatemala (1991), Honduras and Paraguay are in the process of negotiating their GATT membership.

Traditionally, acceding to the GATT or being a GATT member did not imply significant obligations to developing countries. But the 1980s were not the 1950s or the 1960s, and industrial countries were not seeking developing countries' membership in the GATT in the context of the cold war (Hudec, 1987). As a consequence, they were no longer eager to let developing countries free-ride the multilateral liberalisation process and they have requested significant concessions during the accession negotiations and in the ongoing Uruguay Round. But for most of the countries that acceded to the GATT during the 1980s, the process of unilateral liberalisation was so far advanced that, generally, these concessions did not add to the reforms which the countries had introduced unilaterally. The main consequence of recent accessions to the GATT have been in using international commitments for making unilateral measures more permanent.

Likewise, as the Uruguay Round evolved, Latin American countries were increasingly willing to offer important concessions. Thus, following the example of Bolivia, Costa Rica and Mexico, several other countries have offered to bind the maximum tariff rate as part of their multilateral negotiation. For example, Argentina, Brazil and Uruguay have offered to bind their maximum tariff at 35 percent. Also, in the last stretch of the Uruguay Round and upon request of some developed partners, several Latin American countries are negotiating market access conditions and a whole range of measures in trade of services.

As section 4 will show, for most of the groupings the share of exports going to non-Latin American markets is relatively high. Latin American countries need to ensure access to these markets and the best way of doing so is by becoming very efficient through unilateral reforms and by supporting the multilateral trading system and the Uruguay Round of trade negotiations.

Political commitment to liberal economic reforms in Latin America has been critical in the process thus far. The economic and ideological shift that has occurred in the last few years in Latin America is without historical precedent. The countries need to continue with these reforms while at the same time developing institutional mechanisms that help to consolidate these changes. One form is by participating actively in the MTNs. Another is by creating liberal integration schemes.

4   Latin America's new integration initiative

Section 4 describes the main characteristics of current integration schemes, excluding LAIA and CARICOM, and discusses some of the policies that could improve their economic outcome. We conclude that Latin America's new integration start could be a very liberal model which would have been impossible to consider without the unilateral reforms introduced in recent years. We first review proposals for integration among Latin American countries, and follow this by an overall assessment of the ongoing process of integration, and end with a review of regional arrangements with the United States.

4.1   Integration among Latin American countries

Subsection 4.1 provides an analysis of three integration proposals – *Mercado Común del Cono Sur* (MERCOSUR), the renewal of the Andean Pact, and the revival of CACM. We review three aspects of these proposals: (1) basic economic indicators of the countries in the group; (2) the economic linkages as measured by intra-export flows; and (3) trade barriers.

4.1.1 MERCOSUR MERCOSUR was created by the *Tratado de Asunción*, signed on 26 March 1991 by Argentina, Brazil, Paraguay and Uruguay, giving a framework to constitute a common market by December 1994. MERCOSUR emerged from a process of sectoral integration initiated by Argentina and Brazil in 1985. These integration efforts were probably motivated by the failures of ECLA and LAIA in expanding intra-trade, the need to expand foreign trade to reduce the external debt burden and the beginning of a democratic era in the region.

Three accords, described in Table 9.6, preceded MERCOSUR. Argentina–Brazil's sectoral approach to integration led to seventeen protocols between 1986 and 1989. These managed trade policies provided restrictive market access in various industries. However, intra-trade expanded only in capital goods (around 50 million dollars in 1986–9) mainly by substituting imports from non-members with more costly Argentina–Brazil production. Their welfare gains, if any, were therefore minimal in this initial stage of integration.

The *Tratado de Integración* of 1989 changed the approach to integration by announcing the creation of a common market by 1998 (see Table 9.6). This treaty reflected the shift from the restrictive policies of the Alfonsín and Sarney governments to a liberal economic strategy supported by the

Table 9.6. *Argentina–Brazil integration process for trade in goods*

Name and year of document	Type of mechanism		Specific objective	Pre-announced timetable
	Automatic	Discretionary		
Acta para la Integración Argentina–Brasileña 1986	No	Yes	CU[a]	No
Tratado de Integración 1989	n.a.	n.a.	Common Market by 1998	No
Acta de Buenos Aires 1990	Yes	No	Common Market by 1994	Yes
Tratado de Asunción 1991	Yes	No	Common Market[b] by 1994	Yes

Notes:
[a] The CU goal was for Protocol No. 1 on capital goods.
[b] Signed also by the Presidents of Paraguay and Uruguay.
n.a.: not available.
Source: Authors' assessment.

political will of the governments headed by Menem and Collor (Nogués and Gulati, 1992). Menem's administration initiated broad economic reforms by undertaking a bold stabilisation programme and trade liberalisation measures, deregulation and one of the most ambitious privatisation programmes in Latin America (Nogués and Scala, 1991). Economic reforms under Collor's administration have been more limited in scope, though significant trade liberalisation measures have been undertaken.

Within a few months of the *Tratado de Integración*, Argentina and Brazil signed the *Acta de Buenos Aires* in July 1990 which moved the creation of the common market to the end of 1994, and established a timetable of objectives through automatic mechanisms (see Table 9.6). It is only at this point that Paraguay and Uruguay joined Argentina and Brazil in this process of integration.

MERCOSUR countries have similar *per capita* incomes, except for Paraguay, but differ significantly in the size of their economies (see Table 9.7). Not surprisingly MERCOSUR is significantly more important for Paraguay and Uruguay than for Argentina and Brazil (see Table 9.8). There are also significant differences in the structure of protection – Argentina has the most liberal trade regime while Brazil has the most restrictive trade regime (see Table 9.9). Paraguay maintains a restrictive trade regime, *de jure*, but most observers argue that the trade regime is, *de facto*, quite liberal because of widespread smuggling.

In principle MERCOSUR is a commitment to trade goods and services free of tariffs and NTBs with factor mobility among member countries. Tariff reductions are automatic according to the timetable given in Table 9.10, starting with the steepest tariff cut and progressing with gradual tariff reductions. However, a CET structure remains to be defined. For the time being, MERCOSUR has announced that its CET will be relatively low and uniform.

In addition to a low and uniform CET, MERCOSUR will need to eliminate NTBs and export subsidies in order to become a liberal trading agreement that expands potential net benefits and avoids internal frictions. Clearly, several member countries will need to accelerate and expand the scope of their unilateral trade liberalisation (UTL) programmes and strengthen their commitment to economic reforms to facilitate the implementation of a liberal MERCOSUR that is also supportive of the multilateral trading system.

4.1.2 The renewal of the Andean Pact   The Andean group contains a wide range of economies in terms of economic size and GDP *per capita* (see Table 9.7). Most of Andean trade is with third countries and the

Table 9.7. *Latin America, economic indicators for regional groups and member countries, 1990*

	MERCOSUR				Andean Pact					CACM				
	ARG	BRA	PRY	URY	BOL	COL	ECU	PER	VEN	CRI	SLV	GTM	HND	NIC[b]
1. GDP $US million	105 498.4	473 689.6	5263.8	8218.3	4482.9	41 122.8	10 875.5	36 548.4	48 273.8	5702.4	5402.2	7632.9	2737.1	3427.7
2. GNP *per capita* ($US)	2400	2680	1110	2560	630	1260	980	1160	2560	1900	1110	900	590	810
3. Trade ($US million)	16 431.1	54 555.0	2271.4	3010.8	1899.1	12 532.4	4767.4	6448.1	23 808.6	3482.4	1949.8	3159.5	2130.3	1047.76
4. Trade output (%)	15.6	11.5	43.2	36.6	42.4	30.5	43.8	17.6	49.3	61.1	36.1	41.4	77.8	30.6
5. Population (million)	32.3	150.4	4.3	3.1	7.2	32.4	10.3	21.7	19.7	2.8	5.2	9.2	5.1	3.5
6. Unemployment rate (%)[a]	8.6	4.3	7.0	9.2	7.0	10.2	14.3[c]	7.9[c]	10.6	5.4	n.a.	14.0	13.8	n.a.
7. Inflation rate (%)	2314.0	2937.8	25.3	112.5	17.3	29.1	48.5	7558.4	40.8	19.0	24.0	41.2	23.3	1011.9

Notes: [a] Preliminary figures of urban unemployment. [b] For 1987 only. [c] For 1989 only.
n.a.: not available.
Argentina (ARG), Brazil (**BRA**), Paraguay (**PRY**), Uruguay (URY), Costa Rica (CRI), El Salvador (SLV), Guatemala (GTM), Honduras (HND), Nicaragua (NIC), Bolivia (BOL), Colombia (COL), Ecuador (ECU), Peru (PER), Venezuela (VEN).
Sources: Authors' calculations based on BESD and IFS, IMF, ECLAC, and PREALC.

Table 9.8. *Latin America, export flows, 1990, ($US million)*

MERCOSUR

Internal trade

	ARG	BRA	PRY	URY	Total	% of total	World total
ARG	0	1422.7	147.4	262.6	1832.7	14.8	12352.6
BRA	660.5	0	277.1	310.5	1248.1	3.9	32114.5
PRY	55.5	312.3	0	11.6	379.4	39.6	958.7
URY	82.1	501.9	15.3	0	599.3	35.4	1693.7

Andean Pact

Internal trade

	BOL	COL	ECU	PER	VEN	Total	% of total	World total
BOL	0	4.7	0.2	49.7	0.4	55.0	5.2	1063.4
COL	3.9	0	37.3	61.8	193.5	296.5	4.5	6631.6
ECU	0.2	46.7	0	93.8	4.6	145.3	5.4	2709.7
PER	19.9	95.0	31.8	0	54.9	201.6	6.2	3276.2
VEN	0.4	302.2	13.0	33.2	0	348.8	2.1	16426.0

CACM

Internal trade

	CRI	SLV	GTM	HND	NIC	Total	% of total	World total
CRI	0	36	52	18	27	134	9.2	1456
SLV	52	0	134	20	4	209	31.7	658
GTM	80	161	0	42	15	297	21.2	1402
HND	2	13	11	0	4	29	3.0	953
NIC	12	10	3	8	0	33	12.1	271

Notes: Argentina (ARG), Bolivia (BOL), Brazil (BRA), Colombia (COL), Costa Rica (CRI), Ecuador (ECU), El Salvador (SLV), Guatemala (GTM), Honduras (HND), Paraguay (PRY), Peru (PER), Venezuela (VEN), Uruguay (URY), Nicaragua (NIC).
Source: Authors' calculations based on IMF, *Direction of Trade*, various issues.

intra-trade ratio is under 6 percent – the smallest among the regional arrangements (see Table 9.8). Andean trade is quite small for several reasons. First, these countries have relatively similar factor endowments, having a high concentration of exports of mineral products, and inward-oriented policies limited the development of exportables. Second,

Table 9.9. *Latin America, trade barriers*

MERCOSUR

	ARG	BRA[a]		PRY	URY
		(1)	(2)		
Average tariff (%)	10	32	14	16	27
Tariff range (%)	0–22	0–85	0.40	n.a.	5–40
NTBs	Few	Some		Abundant but widespread smuggling	Some
Subsidies	Minimum	Important		Important	n.a.

Andean Pact, January 1991

	BOL	ECU	COL	PER	VEN
Average tariff (%)	10	17	24	17	17
Tariff range (%)	5–10	0–50	0–100	5–25	0–50
NTBs	Few		Few	Few	Few
Subsidies	Minimum	Important	Some	Minimum	Some

CACM

	CRI		SLV		GTM		HND		NIC	
	(1)	(2)	(1)	(2)	(1)	(2)	(1)	(2)	(1)	(2)
Average tariff (%)[b]	52	26	48	23	50	25	41	20	54	21
Tariff range (%)[c]	20–70	5–20	5–35	5–20	5–40	5–20	9–50	5–20	5–95	5–20
NTBs	Few		Few		Few		n.a.		Few	
Subsidies	Important		Some		Minimum		n.a.		Important	

Notes:
[a] Column (1) is 1991 and column (2) is preannounced tariff structure.
[b] Column (1) is pre-reform average tariff and column (2) is actual at 1987.
[c] Column (1) is actual at 1991 and column (2) is preannounced tariff range by 1 January 1993.
n.a.: not available.
Sources: Authors' assessments and data from several World Bank Reports and JUNAC and Bouzas (1991).

Table 9.10. *Timetable for tariff reductions of MERCOSUR, %*

30/6/91	31/12/91	30/6/92	31/12/92	30/6/93	31/12/93	30/6/94	31/12/94
47	54	61	68	75	82	89	100

Source: Tratado de Asunción.

transport costs within the region are very high and in general much more expensive than, say, shipping to the United States. And third, producers in the region experience high levels of uncertainty in the application of the complex rules of the Andean Pact (Schuldt and Urriola, 1991).[6]

The Act of La Paz, signed in November 1990 (IV Andean Summit), begins the renewal of the Andean Treaty later reinforced by the Act of Barahona signed in December 1991.[7] These Acts begin to reform the Andean Treaty from its past inward orientation to a relatively more liberal regional arrangement. The Act of La Paz established a free trade zone among Bolivia, Colombia and Venezuela on 1 January 1991, replaced the 1971 Andean investment code by the 1991 code providing national treatment to foreign investment, initiated the elimination of some NTBs such as rules of administered trade, the reserve list (products subject to industrial development programmes), and the exception list (products excluded).

The Act of Barahona established that Ecuador and Peru were to join the Bolivia–Colombia–Venezuela free trade zone on 1 July 1992. It specified a CET structure of 5, 10, 15 and 20 percent for all countries except Bolivia, which will maintain her tariff structure of 5 and 10 percent (effective on 1 January 1992). The CET exceptions (Colombia, Ecuador and Venezuela) are given to agricultural products, automobiles (40 percent tariff ceiling) and products not produced or produced in 'limited' amounts by the Andean countries (0 percent tariff). The CET structure will be maintained until 1 January 1994, when a CET of 5, 10 and 15 percent will be implemented by all Andean members (in early 1992 Peru began negotiations to maintain a more liberal trade regime) and Bolivia maintains her 5 and 10 percent tariff structure.

These arrangements clearly indicate that the extent of UTL has imposed the limits to which each member country has been willing to liberalise trade within the region (see Table 9.9). In terms of economic reforms, Bolivia is by far the most and Ecuador the least advanced. Colombia and Venezuela have requested transitory exemptions for specific protected industries. Peru has initiated economic reforms led by foreign trade liberalisation and is already ahead of most of the Andean countries. In March 1991, Peru adopted two import duties of 15 and 25 percent and plans to implement a flat rate of 15 percent by January 1994. Bolivia and Peru are the main supporters of a liberal approach to economic integration – a low uniform tariff and the elimination of export subsidies and limiting the scope of NTBs.

Empirical evidence clearly indicates that for several decades export subsidies failed to increase exports in Latin American (Nogués, 1990) and that a low uniform tariff, a minimum of NTBs and a supporting macroeconomic environment are far superior to economic privileges granted selectively (Nogués and Gulati, 1992). And yet the renewal of the Andean Treaty remains a compromise of regional interests between the enthusiastic reformers, Bolivia and Peru, and the other relatively more cautious countries.[8] The lack of support for a low uniform tariff and the elimination of export subsidies and NTBs is likely to generate frictions within the Andean group and most certainly limit the Treaty's potential net benefits.

4.1.3 The revival of CACM Foreign trade plays a significant role in the relatively small economies of CACM and their *per capita* income ranges between $590 and $1900 (see Table 9.7). A large ratio of foreign trade with third countries though intra-trade is relatively important for El Salvador and Guatemala (see Table 9.8). The United States is CACM's most important market and traditional exports such as coffee, bananas, sugar, cotton, cardamon, meat and oil represent a large share of total exports.

Broad economic reforms were introduced in the post-debt crisis of the 1980s while countries in the region struggled to contain war and attempted to secure peace. Fiscal and monetary discipline and foreign trade liberalisation are the main components of economic adjustment programmes.

Economic reforms and the need to re-establish peace within and among CACM countries were conducive to the renewal of CACM. During 1989–91 CACM countries set political conditions for peace in the region. The renewal of CACM was initiated with the Declaration of Antigua (June 1990) under this relatively more stable political environment and progressive economic reform. Three subsequent Declarations established an overall framework for the renewal of CACM: Puntarenas (December 1990), San Salvador (June 1991), and Tegucigalpa (1991).

The objectives are: (a) to renew the institutional and legal framework for Central American economic integration; (b) to restore and expand the scope of free trade in Central America;[9] (c) to establish a CET structure of 5, 10, 15 and 20 percent by 31 December 1992; (d) to establish a CET to cover 97 percent of all tariff lines; (e) to permit exceptions to the CET to prevail until 31 December 1994; and (f) to harmonise all other instruments of trade policy such as a common agriculgural policy,[10] rules of origin and anti-dumping (AD) regulations.

UTL measures bring CACM countries closer to the CACM goals (see Table 9.10) and makes the renewal more likely to be sustained as a liberal regional arrangement. However, restrictive rules of origin and the adoption of non-tariff measures such as anti-dumping regulations may limit an otherwise liberal trading regime. In addition, the maintenance of economic reforms by each country – for example, the dismantling of investment and export subsidies in Costa Rica – will play a critical role in avoiding internal frictions. Similarly fiscal and monetary discipline and their consistency with the exchange rate regime are at the core of the process that may facilitate, or their lack otherwise hinder, the renewal of CACM.

4.1.4 The role of Mexico   We briefly now analyse the role of Mexico in the renewal of the processes for economic integration in Latin America, since a detailed discussion of the North American Free-Trade Area (NAFTA) is provided in Whalley (1992, Chapter 11 in this volume).

Mexico's initiative to seek a free-trade agreement with the United States which then evolved into NAFTA could have far-reaching effects in the trading relations with the United States and in the process of economic reforms in Mexico. A liberal free-trade agreement, implemented under stable macroeconomic conditions and with a consistent exchange rate policy, would be a commitment to reduce the uncertainty of market access abroad and the scope of discretionary measures which in turn could, in principle, facilitate the process of economic reform (see Krueger and Quintanilla, 1991).

This initiative has played an important role in the trading relations of Latin America with the United States as well as in the renewal of economic integration among Latin American countries. The Enterprise for the Americas Initiative (EAI) was announced soon after NAFTA and gave preference to negotiating with groups of countries rather than with countries individually. In addition, NAFTA is likely to set a precedent for future free-trade agreements of the EAI. The role of NAFTA in implementing EAI could be even more significant if NAFTA contains an inclusion provision.[11] For other Latin American countries this would be the critical signal that in fact the EAI seeks to liberalise trade across the continent, and eventually with other parts of the world.

Simultaneously, Mexico is expanding her trade consultations with Latin American countries, Europe, and Japan and the Pacific Rim. This reflects a world-wide approach (SECOFI, 1990) to Mexico's trading

Table 9.11. *Export flows among countries signing trade agreements with Mexico, 1990, $US million*

	Exports to Mexico		Exports from Mexico	
	Value	% share of total	Value	% share of total
CACM	78.5	1.7	451.0	1.5
CHIL	72.3	0.8	95.3	0.3
COL	29.8	0.5	113.7	0.4
VEN	79.8	0.5	60.4	0.2

Source: IMF, *Direction of Trade Statistics*, various issues.

arrangements which is seldom appreciated given her strong trading ties with the United States. Mexico has signed a free-trade agreement with Chile (to be completed by 1996), and trade talks under framework agreements for free trade zones are proceeding with Venezuela (to be completed by December 1993), Colombia (to be completed by June 1994), and CACM (to be completed by December 1996). As noted by Schott and Hufbauer (1991), it is likely that for other Latin American countries these agreements are a preamble to an hemispheric free-trade agreement. Note that for these countries trade with Mexico is very small (see Table 9.11).

Regardless of the possible motivations, the world-wide approach to expanding trading ties, places Mexico at an advantage *vis-à-vis* other Latin American countries since NAFTA is likely to be completed under the current fast-track authority (expiring in June 1993). Consequently by the time most other Latin American countries get market access on an equivalent standing, Mexico is likely to have become firmly set in NAFTA markets. The significance of these issues depends to a large extent on the nature and scope finally agreed under NAFTA, the resolution of the Uruguay Round, and whether any hemispheric free-trade area is dominated by liberal trading principles.

4.2   A critical evaluation of Latin America's new integration initiative

Recent proposals for economic integration in Latin America are in sharp contrast to those adopted more than three decades ago. The relatively liberal frameworks for integration in the 1990s which have evolved through the UTL initiated in the 1980s provide a better starting point than the earlier attempts. Likewise their credibility and role in preventing policy reversals rely on further UTL and macroeconomic discipline to consolidate economic reforms. As argued below, entry limitations, a broad scope of interim exceptions, restrictive and distortionary rules of origin, and an uncritical support for unfair trade policies could jeopardise these regional agreements. It could also lay the seeds for reversals in economic reforms.

4.2.1 Entry limitations None of the current proposals for regional arrangements has a universal inclusion clause, such as GATT, that would allow accession by countries willing to subscribe to the regional arrangements. An inclusion clause would not prevent proceeding gradually in defining the scope of the agreements and ensuring their implementation since potential candidates could first be given the status of observers to be incorporated as full members later. Closed membership weakens the multilateral trading system, increases the likelihood that sectoral interests will dominate the nature of the arrangements and motivate responses in kind by other regions which could well be dominated by retaliation.[12]

In the context of Latin America, the potential net benefits of current proposals are quite limited compared to universal open-entry scenarios. First, the scope of intra-regional comparative advantage and consequently of production specialisation is limited compared to the scope of extra-regional specialisation. Second, except for a few cases, intra-regional trade is very small while extra-regional trade is substantial (see Table 9.8). Third, by international standards, regional markets are small. Thus any potential role for economies of scale is unlikely to be an important source of benefits in a closed framework.

Universal open entry would also enhance the credibility that economic reforms in Latin America aim at open and stable economies, provide a broader scope for foreign investment, induce other trading partners such as the United States and the European Community to strengthen their political commitment to a liberal world trading system, and reduce the uncertainty of market access.

4.2.2 Interim exceptions All proposals provide a scope for interim exceptions that favour protected industries, exclude products where regulations prevent market clearing, and allow maintenance of restrictive policies. In some instances, the scope for interim exceptions is too broad; lobbies will use this opportunity to regroup and to raise a strong political opposition, while others will argue that the exceptions imply discriminatory treatment. Limiting the scope of interim exceptions is necessary to ensure credibility that discretionary and frequently unexpected measures by the government are being reduced and to ensure that the proposals liberalise rather than restrict trade.

4.2.3 Rules of origin and structure of CET We remain concerned that rules of origin, in the case of free-trade agreements, and CET structures, in the case of common markets, might eventually become instruments of protection. Rules of origin require minimum local content on goods to benefit from free trade treatment and rules of origin have the similar distorting effects as minimum domestic content requirements. Similarly a CET that is high and with a large variance will distort trade and investment flows, imposing significant domestic resource costs on the economies.

The scope of potential benefits is determined by the scope of production specialisation allowed in the regional arrangement, and consequently on the rules of trade with third countries. Restrictive rules of origin and a protective CET would limit trade with third countries and in turn might significantly limit the scope of net benefits and even reverse part of the benefits from unilateral trade liberalisation.

4.2.4 Scope for unilateral liberalisation measures We want to emphasise the importance of countries continuing to introduce liberalisation measures and firmly setting a liberal trade regime. Yet there are reasons for concern that some policies associated with integration schemes might create obstacles to this goal. Rules of origin is clearly a case in point. Safeguard measures, and the unfair trade policies discussed below, is another. Finally, the emphasis on common markets, unlike FTAs, might put an end to trade liberalisation beyond, say, a maximum tariff rate of around 20 percent. By international standards, this continues to be a high rate and some countries may need, and wish, to reduce the domestic resources costs implied by such protection structure. Trading arrangements should support these countries and provide flexibility for further unilateral liberalisation measures.

4.2.5 Unfair trade policies We have noted that several integration documents provide an unqualified support for the use of protectionist instruments such as measures against unfair trade. These policies, and anti-dumping mechanisms in particular, have become one of the most protectionist instruments undermining a liberal multilateral trading system: Latin American countries know very well how costly the use of anti-dumping measures by other countries have been to them. In spite of this experience, as several countries in the region have proceeded to open their economies, they have been introducing anti-dumping mechanisms, providing a door to protectionist trends that serve sectoral at the expense of national interests. Their use has not yet reached the level observed in industrial countries. Yet some few examples suggest that the little use that has been made of this instrument has entailed social costs (Nogués, 1992).

It is clear that although anti-dumping mechanisms have been sanctioned by the GATT, it does not make them a sensible policy. In fact, they are as costly in much the same way as agricultural protectionism and other policies sanctioned by the GATT. Short of renouncing these policies, with a great benefit to pricetaking countries, they should be modified to make these mechanisms more transparent and participatory of all costs involved, and consequently less biased towards protection (see Finger, 1991).

4.3   US–Latin America regional trading agreements

The EAI was announced by President Bush on 27 June 1990 as a proposal to reinforce market-oriented reforms in Latin America by expanding trade and investment, easing the debt burden and strengthening environmental policies. One track of the EAI covers free-trade agreements preceded by framework agreements, and another track deals with investment, debt and the environment. Here we discuss the issues and processes related to the first track.

The emergence of US regionalism is encouraging regionalism in Latin America, since from the outset as well as in subsequent statements by the United States Trade Representative (USTR), EAI gave preference to negotiating FTAs with groups of countries rather than countries individually (see Bush's speech announcing the EAI, 27 June 1991, USTR testimony before the US Senate of April 1991, and statement before OAS Ministers of October 1991). By the end of 1991 the United States had signed sixteen framework agreements (including Mexico) covering 31 of the 34 Latin American countries (the exceptions are Haiti, Suriname and Cuba) which define the scope of issues and the agenda for binational consultations and corresponding institutional mechanisms. However, only two were signed with country groups – MERCOSUR and CARICOM.

The US administration has also given the initial negotiating FTA objectives under EAI and a list of preconditions. The initial objectives stated are: (1) to eliminate all tariffs and non-tariff barriers on trade according to a specified timetable; (2) to include services; (3) to establish standards for the treatment of investment-eliminating trade-distorting performance requirements; (4) to establish a mechanism for settling disputes about the implementation of the agreement and the treatment of investors; (5) to ensure that intellectual property rights will be protected; (6) to create special provisions for trade and access to natural resources and natural resource-based products; (7) to include technical and security provisions such as rules of origin and rules for standards, public health and safety exceptions, security interest exclusions, safeguards, 'docking' provisions for adding on future free-trade agreements, consultative and dispute settlement procedures; and (8) to establish discipline for specific categories of government actions such as subsidies, state trading, and the use of foreign exchange restrictions and controls.

EAI's preconditions for negotiating free-trade agreements, the so-called 'indicators of readiness' are that a prospective partner must: (1) have the institutional capacity to fulfil the long-term serious commitments involved, and the economic policies required for the success of the free-trade agreement; (2) be committed to a stable macroeconomic environment and market-oriented policies before negotiations begin; (3) be committed to the multilateral trading system (prospective free-trade agreements must be fully consistent with Article XXIV of the GATT);[13] and (4) have demonstrated progress in achieving open trade regimes and be members in good standing with the GATT.

EAI's initial objectives and preconditions reflect the changing nature of US trade policies. While it is clear that for several decades since World War II US trade policies were driven by a rules-oriented approach that aimed at an open world trading system, the strategy has been shifting towards a power-oriented approach to advance national economic objectives very much driven by domestic political pressures of particular economic interests (see Baldwin, 1985; Bhagwati, 1991, Jackson, 1989; Finger and Dhar, 1992).

This probably explains why EAI has been geographically defined and does not seek to discipline the use of unfair trade policies such as anti-dumping and countervailing regulations; these are serious shortcomings of the EAI. Trade preferences under EAI discriminate on a geographical basis rather than on the basis of complying with principles that would expand trade liberalisation beyond what can be achieved under the GATT. These are shortcomings which can still be remedied. Unfair trade measures, particularly anti-dumping, are the new mode of costly protection that emerged in the 1980s. EAI's failure to discipline their use undermines its potential liberalising effects.

There are also sharp contrasts between the processes that led to US free-trade agreements with Israel, Canada, and Mexico and the processes initiated under EAI such as: (1) the circumstances from where the initiatives emerged; (2) the time taken to reach comprehensive framework agreements; and (3) consequently, the process that follows from the framework agreements.

In the cases of Israel, Canada and Mexico, the initiatives have emerged from these countries since the United States signalled its willingness to reach regional arrangements when it found difficulties in initiating a new round of GATT negotiations. It took several years before any of these countries could establish comprehensive framework agreements: nearly three years in the case of Israel (1981–4) and Canada (1983–5) and seven years in the case of Mexico (1982–9).

In contrast, fifteen framework agreements covering 30 Latin American countries were signed within a few months of the EAI announcement. The process from here on will probably proceed at a slower pace. In the cases of Israel, Canada, and Mexico the framework agreements led within a short period of time to formal negotiations under fast-track procedures, and except possibly for Chile, this will not be the case for other countries, since current fast-track procedures expire on 1 June 1993 and precedence is being given to the completion of NAFTA. A free-trade agreement with Chile before the fast-track authority expires is uncertain since it is unclear when NAFTA will be completed and whether NAFTA will contain an inclusion clause making it an expanding agreement to implement EAI.

Finally, the process for a hemispheric free-trade agreement initiated by the EAI remains vulnerable to the issues raised by Wonnacott (1990) and Lipsey (1991) in the 'hub-and-spoke' system. They pointed out that under such a system each country (the spokes) reaching an independent free-trade agreement with the United States (the hub) would benefit from the preferential reduction of trade impediments initially, but the gains to the early spokes would be lower than if there was an expanding agreement. In addition, the hub would probably capture most of the investment driven by market size since the hub would be trading freely with each spoke country while none of the spokes would be trading freely among themselves. In addition, a 'hub-and-spoke system' would be extremely difficult to implement because of the administrative difficulties of different rules of origin and trading rules of free-trade areas (Smith, 1990). To repeat, if NAFTA included an inclusion clause, the risks of expiring fast-track authority and the costs of a 'hub-and-spoke' integration process would be minimised. This is why the inclusion clause is crucial.

It is rather paradoxical that the political battles over the public function of liberal economic policies, won over the last few years in many highly indebted countries in Latin America, are being decided with such hesitation in the industrialised countries. In the process, international trade policies are drifting away from their public function and are increasingly vulnerable to sectoral lobbying seeking economic privileges. The EAI as an idea to develop a more liberal hemispheric trading system opened to *all* countries willing to subscribe to its principles may well represent an opportunity to return trade policies to their public function, particularly disciplining the use of trade remedies. To be sure it will be the political will of the leadership elite in the United States and in Latin America that will ultimately decide whether a truly hemispheric view for a more liberal and non-discriminatory trading area is established or whether the EAI will be driven by mercantilistic and power-oriented forces.

5   Conclusion

Current proposals for economic integration in Latin America are in sharp contrast with those adopted more than three decades ago. Ongoing economic reforms are no longer consistent with inward-oriented policies and the broad scope for government interventions which characterised the integration programmes in the past. Relatively liberal frameworks for integration in the 1990s would not have evolved without the UTL initiated in the 1980s. Indeed further UTL may facilitate, or its lack otherwise hinder, the new process of integration in the region whose potential net benefits should not be overestimated.

Entry limitations, broad scope of interim exceptions, restrictive rules of origin or CET structures, and lack of discipline on the use of unfair trade policies reduce potential net benefits and may even cause reversals in the process of economic reforms. Liberal regional arrangements are critical for Latin American countries since trade with countries outside the region and the hemisphere is substantial. Likewise regional arrangements could, if liberal in nature, help in securing a liberal trading system or alternatively, if discriminatory and restrictive in nature, further undermine the multilateral trading system. Under the current trade and investment links, it should be clear that the loss of Latin America from a breakdown of the multilateral system will not be compensated by economic integration.

We offer two recommendations. First, that proposals for regional arrangements be opened to any country; liberal rules of origin or CET structures be adopted; unfair trade policies be restricted; and interim exceptions be limited by relying on principles that apply across the board. And second, that the process of integration aim at unified trade policy proposals to ensure liberal trade in a multilateral context. The main concern is that several policies of industrial countries are increasingly vulnerable to sectoral interests that seek protection from foreign competition, particularly through unfair trade policies and similar measures. Latin America's experience of lacking a unified approach to the external debt problem of the early 1980s should be avoided in foreign trade policies in the early 1990s. The goal of such a unified approach is a liberal multilateral trading system. It is in the economic interest of the region to have this goal as top priority.

NOTES

The findings, interpretation, and conclusions expressed in this chapter are entirely those of the authors and should not be attributed in any manner to the institutions the authors are associated with. We appreciate the comments from Sunil Gulati, John Nash, Jaime de Melo and Arvind Panagariya. We also appreciate the assistance provided by Francis Ng, María Eugenia Quintero and Mark Fels.

1 Trading arrangements are broadly defined as various types of preferential reduction of trade barriers. A general theoretical framework is provided in Bhagwati (1992) and de Melo, Panagariya and Rodrik (1992, Chapters 2 and 6 in this volume).

2 The cost and benefit of alternative choices is further elaborated in Nogués (1990, 1991).

3 The following draws from Nogués and Gulati (1992). See Michaely, Papageorgiou and Choksi (eds) (1991) for the experiences of foreign trade liberalisation from the early 1960s to the mid-1980s.

4 Over 1985–90 Chile ranks first in terms of improvement in every indicator in Table 9.5 (trade, trade/output, investment GDP, and real wage), while at the same time reducing unemployment the most.

5 Note that growth rates in Costa Rica are unlikely to be sustained over the long run since the economy remains under a relatively distorted environment which implies higher domestic resource costs per unit of growth than under a relatively open and competitive environment.

6 Because of the complexity of the regulations, Andean producers are discouraged from taking advantage of possible benefits of the Pact.

7 See Junta de Acuerdo de Cartagena (1991) for further details of the process.

8 Differences in policy orientation arise not only among countries but also within countries. JUNAC and the Ministries of Industry of Andean countries continue to favour a tariff structure that provides higher effective protection to certain industries while the Ministries of Economy (or Finance) and the Central Banks favour more uniform policies (Abusada, 1991).

9 Belize and Panamá may be joining the CACM group.

10 A common price band for a few but very important agricultural products such as maize, beans and sorghum, has been adopted.

11 A provision that would allow accession by other countries.

12 Bhagwati (1992, Chapter 2 in this volume) provides detailed discussion of these issues.

13 Article XXIV of the GATT has been criticised and suggestions for improving it have been made (see Bhagwati, 1992, Chapter 2 in this volume). This article is not addressed by the Uruguay Round and therefore it will take time to improve it. In the meantime, notification of trade arrangements under Article XXIV is very important for assuring the rest of the world that they are consistent with basic economic principles. The enabling clause under which several trade arrangements have been notified does not provide this assurance.

REFERENCES

Abusada, R. (1991) 'La Integración Andina y la Reforma Comercial', Washington, DC: World Bank (mimeo).

Balassa, B. (1966) 'Integración Regional y Asignación de Recursos en América Latina', *Comercio Exterior*, **17(10)**, pp. 672–85.

Baldwin, R.E. (1985) *The Political Economy of U.S. Import Policy*, Cambridge, Mass.: MIT Press.

Barro, R.J. (1989) 'A Cross-Country Study of Growth, Savings and Government', NBER, *Working Paper*, **2855**.

Behrman, J.R. (1976) *Foreign Trade Regimes and Economic Development: Chile*, NBER, vol. viii, New York.

Bhagwati, J. (1991) *The World Trading System at Risk*, Princeton: Princeton University Press and Harvester Wheatsheaf.

(1992) 'Regionalism and Multilateralism: An Overview', Chapter 2 in this volume.

Bouzas, R. (1991) 'A U.S.–MERCOSUR Free Trade Area', paper presented at a workshop on 'U.S.–Latin American Trade Relations in the 1990s', Overseas Development Council (mimeo).

Carnoy, M. (1970) *The Optimum Location of Specific Industries in LAFTA*, Washington, DC: Brookings Institution.

Chenery, H.B. and A.M. Strout (1966) 'Foreign Assistance and Economic Development', *American Economic Review*, **56(4)** (September) pp. 679–733.

Deardorff, A. and R. Stern (1991) 'Multilateral Trade Negotiations and Preferential Trading Arrangements', unpublished paper.

ECLA (1959) 'Análisis y Proyecciones del Desarrollo Económico', Argentina: Buenos Aires, ECLA.

Finger, J.M. (1991) 'The Meaning of "Unfair" in U.S. Import Policy', *PRE Working Paper*, **745**, Washington, DC: World Bank.

Finger, J.M. and S. Dhar (1992) 'Do Rules Control Power? GATT Articles and Arrangements in the Uruguay Round', *PRE Working Paper*, **818**, Washington, DC: World Bank.

Hachette, D. and F. Rosende (1991) 'Trade Agreements in the Americas: The Case of Chile', LATTP, World Bank (mimeo).

Hudec, R. (1987) *Developing Countries in the GATT Legal System*, London: Gower.

Instituto para la Integración de América Latina (INTAL) (1986) *Ordenamiento Jurídico de la Integración Regional en América Latina* vols. I, II, Buenos Aires: INTAL.

IDB/INTAL (1984) *The Economic Integration Process of Latin America in the 1980s*, Washington, DC: INTAL.

(1989) *The Latin American Integration Process in 1985/1986/1987*, Buenos Aires: INTAL.

Jackson, J.H. (1989) *The World Trading System: Law and Policy of International Economic Relations*, Cambridge, Mass.: MIT Press.

Johnson, H.G. (1966) 'Trade Preferences and Developing Countries', *Lloyds Bank Review*, **80** (April).

Junta de Acuerdo de Cartagena (JUNAC) (1991) 'Profundización de la Integración Andina: Documentos de las Reuniones del Consejo Presidencial Andino en 1989 y 1990', Lima: JUNAC.

Krueger, A.O. and R. Quintanilla (1991) 'Private Sector Perspectives on the Mexican–US Free Trade Agreement', Monterrey, Mexico: Instituto QUANTUM.

Lewis, A. (1954) 'Economic Growth with Unlimited Supply of Labour', *Manchester School*, 22 (May) pp. 131–91.

Lipsey, R.J. (1960) 'The Theory of Customs Unions: A General Survey', *The Economic Journal*, 70, pp. 498–513.

—— (1991) 'Getting There: The Path to an Hemispheric FTA', paper presented at a workshop on 'U.S.–Latin American Trade Relations in the 1990s', Overseas Development Council (mimeo).

Meade, J.E. (1956) *The Theory of Customs Unions*, Amsterdam: North-Holland.

Melo, J. de, A. Panagariya and D. Rodrik (1992) 'The New Regionalism: A Country Perspective', Chapter 6 in this volume.

Michaely, M., D. Papageorgiou and A.M. Choksi (1991) 'Liberalizing Foreign Trade', in D. Papageorgiou, M. Michaely and A.M. Choksi (eds), *Lessons of Experience in the Developing World*, vol. 7, Oxford: Oxford University Press and Cambridge, Mass.: Basil Blackwell.

Nogués, J. (1990) 'The Choice Between the Unilateral and Multilateral Trade Liberalization Strategy', *The World Economy* (March).

—— (1991) 'The Role of Trade Arrangements in the Formation of Developing Countries' Trade Policies', *Journal of World Trade*, 25 (August).

—— (1992) 'El Costo para América Latina de Adoptar Políticas Contra el Comercio Desleal', *Estudios Económicos*, El Colegio de México (forthcoming).

Nogués, J. and S. Gulati (1992) 'Economic Policies and Performance under Alternative Trade Regimes: Latin America During the 80s', LATTP, Regional Studies Program, *Report*, 16 (April) Washington, DC: World Bank.

Nogués, J. and E. Scala (1991) 'The Pro-competition and Growth-oriented Reform Program of Argentina', paper presented at a seminar on 'Latin America's Integration in the World Economy', Washington, DC: Brookings Institution.

Prebisch, R. (1959) 'Commercial Policies in the Developing Economies', *The American Economic Review, Papers and Proceedings* (May).

Saborio, S. and C. Michalopoulos (1991) 'Central America at the Crossroads', paper presented at the Inter-American Dialogue's Project on 'Latin America's Integration in the World Economy', Washington, DC: Brookings Institution.

Schott, J.J. and G.C. Hufbauer (1991) 'Free Trade Areas, the Enterprise for the Americas Initiative, and the Multilateral Trading System: Implications for Latin America', Washington, DC: Institute for International Economics.

Schuldt, J. and R. Urriola (1991) 'Potencial de la cooperación andina: estudio comparativo de casos', in S. Germánico and R. Urriola (eds), *El Fin de las Barreras: Los Empresarios y el Pacto Andino en la Década de los '90*, Caracas, Venezuela: Editorial Nueva Sociedad.

SECOFI (1990) *Las Relaciones Comerciales de México con el Mundo*, Mexico: SECOFI.

Smith, M.G. (1990) 'The Mexico, United States and Canada Trade Talks: Getting Off on the Right Foot', New York: Council on Foreign Relations.

Vacchio, J.M. (1981) *Integración Económica Regional*, Caracas, Universidad Central de Venezuela, Facultad de Ciencias, Jurídicas y Políticas, Imprenta Universitaria.

Viner, J. (1950) *The Customs Union Issue*, New York: Carnegie Endowment for International Peace.

Whalley, J. (1992) 'Regional Trade Arrangements in North America: CUSTA and NAFTA', Chapter 11 in this volume.

Wionczek, M.S. (ed.) (1966) *Latin American Economic Integration: Experiences and Prospects*, New York: Praeger.

Wolf, M. (1987) 'Differential and More Favorable Treatment of Developing Countries and the International Trading System', *The World Bank Economic Review*, Washington, DC: World Bank.

Wonnacott, P. and M. Lutz (1989) 'Is There a Case for Free Trade Areas?', in J.J. Schott (ed.), *Free Trade Areas and U.S. Trade Policy*, Washington, DC: Institute for International Economics.

Wonnacott, R.J. (1990) 'U.S. Hub-and-Spoke Bilaterals and the Multilateral Trading System', C.D. Howe Institute.

Discussion

CHRISTOPHER CLAGUE

Will regional integration (RI) agreements in Latin America promote economic progress among these countries? This question can be split into two parts. Will agreements lead to meaningful economic integration among members, in the sense that market forces will be allowed greater scope: clearly signing agreements does not imply implementation of the envisaged steps. Secondly, if the steps are implemented, what will be the effects on economic progress? Some very tentative remarks on these questions will be offered below. I find myself generally in agreement with Nogués and Quintanilla's policy recommendations in Chapter 9, both with respect to market-friendly development policy and with respect to regional versus unilateral trade reform initiatives. By framing the issues in an explicitly political and strategic context, I intend to add some support to their policy recommendations. Prior to that, it will be useful to make some observations about the reasons for the shift in attitudes toward the market in Latin America and about the importance of trade and trade policy for economic growth.

1   The East Asian experience

The Latin American shift in attitude toward market-oriented development and particularly toward outward-looking trade policies has probably been strongly influenced by the success of the East Asian 'Gang of Four' and the striking contrast of their experiences with that of most of

Latin America. There has been a debate about the sources of East Asian success, with a neoclassical interpretation of Balassa, Krueger, Little, and others emphasising the role of market forces, and a revisionist interpretation of Jones and Sakong, Pack and Westphal, Amsden, and Wade emphasising departures from the market (see Wade, 1990, for a list of sources). Despite differences in viewpoints, there can probably be agreement that these countries have had both effective governments *and* effective markets, and that they have created environments in which individuals have strong incentives to act in socially productive ways. In these countries there are rule-obedient bureaucracies and rule-obedient citizens. The government bureaucracies collect the taxes that are due and provide and maintain public goods. Economic policies are applied with consistency and credibility. Property rights are secure and business agreements are enforced, through reputation mechanisms if not in the courts. As a result of all these factors, there is an environment supportive not merely of static efficient resource allocation but of innovation and technical progress. In short, these countries have created a set of institutions conducive to growth.

How important is trade policy in the whole set of institutions that create an environment conducive to economic growth? I find it hard to imagine that the East Asian countries could have grown anywhere near as fast as they have if external markets had been closed to them or if they had not provided strong incentives for companies to export. But a trade regime conducive to growth seems to be compatible with a certain amount of egregious protectionism and other departures from efficient resource allocation. Japan, Taiwan, and Korea have all developed strong protection of agriculture and according to expert observers there are serious deficiencies in the operation of land markets in these three countries (Anderson and Hayami, 1986, esp. pp. 36–7).

Mancur Olson (1982) has argued that in several historical episodes the creation of unified markets, or what he calls jurisdictional integration, has led to an explosion of growth. These episodes include the formation of the *Zollverein* in Germany, the creation of a unified national market in Meiji Japan, the single market that emerged in the 19th century in the United States, and the trade liberalisation that emerged in postwar Europe. Olson's interpretation of these episodes is that the creation of a much wider market destroyed the protectionist distributional coalitions that had grown up in the smaller markets. Note that each of these episodes is an example of a kind of RI: for the growth spurt to occur, it was not necessary to have free trade with the outside world.

Let us imagine a government team contemplating two different routes to trade reform. The first is to undertake negotiations toward a customs union (CU) with a group of neighbouring countries, while the second is to launch a programme of unilateral trade-barrier reduction on a non-discriminatory basis. Genuine trade reform of either type is likely to impose political costs on the government that outweigh the benefits in the short run. Let us suppose that the two reform programmes are designed to incur the same political costs in the short run. The question then is, which route, the CU or the unilateral liberalisation, is likely to yield greater economic (and therefore political) gains in the future?

It seems to me that there are three reasons why a government interested in long-term growth would tend to prefer the unilateral over the regional liberalisation strategy. First, the unilateral route aims at developing within the country industries and products that are competitive on world markets rather than just on regional markets. To the extent that these efforts are successful, the gains from export expansion are greater, because world markets have much greater capacity to absorb additional exports than do regional markets. Second, in both regional and external markets there is a danger of a protectionist reaction against a successful export expansion, but this danger is probably greater in the regional Latin American market at the present time. In most Latin American countries there is not the popular acceptance of disruption of life resulting from market forces that exists in East Asia and in more developed countries, both because social safety nets are less effective and special interests are more powerful. Third, in Latin America trade liberalisation is normally carried out in conjunction with macroeconomic stabilisation, which is necessary to provide the stable incentives required to induce investment in export activities. Because stabilisation programmes are prone to failure, and such failure is likely to bring the trade reform programme down with it, a regional scheme is more likely to founder than is a unilateral one.

These comments reflecting a strategic preference for unilateral trade liberalisation (UTL) over RI schemes are not inconsistent with the recognition that substantial benefits would probably accrue to jurisdictional integration among Latin American countries. The fact that still greater benefits would flow from multilateral free trade should not obscure the point that there are probably many gains to be realised by opening protected domestic markets to regional competition.

Nogués and Quintanilla state that the Latin American countries are not natural trading partners because they have similar factor endowments. The implication seems to be that there is not much to be gained from the creation of a barrier-free regional market. While it is true that South–South trade is quite small relative to South–North and North–North trade, we really do not know how much trade there would be among neighbouring Latin American countries in the presence of a barrier-free unified market. Much would obviously depend on the developmnent of transport and communications facilities. There is a kind of natural experiment, although I have not seen the relevant data. How much trade is there between provinces of Brazil, or those of some other country, compared to the trade between adjacent countries? With the development of transport and communications facilities, there would seem to be substantial opportunities for trade in goods of quality appropriate to the income levels of the countries, or in what we might call Burenstam-Linder trade. It is important to note that trade does not depend solely on differences in factor endowments. There are differences in relative efficiencies across industries, some of which seem to be related to the overall institutional environment of the country (Clague, 1991) and some of which are simply random deviations in the efficiency of particular industries in particular countries. These differences could contribute to competitive pressures that could stimulate growth.

REFERENCES

Anderson, Kym and Yujiro Hayami (1986) *The Political Economy of Agricultural Protectionism*. Sydney: Allen & Unwin.
Clague, Christopher (1991) 'Factor Proportions, Relative Efficiency, and Developing Countries' Trade', *Journal of Development Economics*, **35**, pp. 357–80.
Olson, Mancur (1982) *The Rise and Decline of Nations*, New Haven: Yale University Press.
Wade, Robert (1990) *Governing the Market*, Princeton: Princeton University Press.

JESÚS SEADE

Chapter 9 is well written and informative, and provides a useful overview of the history and economic rationale of past, present, and prospective regional integration arrangements (RIAs) among the Latin American countries.

As a general comment, I would say that the chapter is by and large an essay on the prescriptive side of these questions – what policies and arrangements ought to look like – from a particular theoretical perspective, without depending much, other than by factual reference, on whether the countries under scrutiny are Latin American or any others. Also, no attempt is made to go much into the positive side – what can be done, or why we observe what we do. Put differently, there is little recognition of the enormous difference it can make to adopt a world, regional, or country perspective in assessing the desirability of a given arrangement. The viewpoint adopted is the second of the options just indicated: regional welfare, interspersed, in the overall conclusions and recommendations, with world welfare. This is no doubt the right guiding principle to have, particularly in a chapter coming from a multilateral agency. But this does not eliminate the need for an assessment of RIAs from an individual country's viewpoint. After all, it is the effect on the welfare of potential members which drives the decisions to form RIAs. In this setting, it is the *differences* in global versus partial evaluations that will reveal any contradictions between RIAs and the multilateral ideal.

One shortcoming is the chapter's exclusive reliance on a static and purely competitive framework in which resources are internationally immobile. For example, there is competition for investment among LDCs. There is also competition among exporters to establish market presence and networks. These and similar motivations of RIAs ought to be recognised – and their differential national versus global welfare implications discussed. In general terms it is reasonable to speculate that national and regional benefits of RIAs will typically exceed global ones.

Now, on the issue of whether or not the RI efforts of the 1960s and 1970s failed because they were not consistent with the requirements of successful schemes, I have a different view. The schemes failed not so much because they did not satisfy those requirements, but because they were put in place when the countries in the region were inward-looking. As import substitution unfolded, almost by definition the scope for integration was limited, and progressively so.

In contrast, it would appear that the present interest in RIAs by Latin American countries is the result not of decisions by governments to create unity, but of their *good reading* of what economic agents and underlying opportunities are pushing for. I refer, specifically, to the effects of, on the one hand, deep liberalisation and market-opening processes that permit the outward-looking RIAs to take hold; and on the other, the expansion of business – through scale and other factors – that requires economic borders to be blurred in various ways so as to permit firms to operate more efficiently across borders and in larger spaces.

Table 9.4 provides useful information and some discussion of the package of trade and other policies – fiscal, factors, and exchange rate – of

Latin American countries. In this regard, no doubt we all can agree, at least in broad terms, on what a 'good' fiscal policy is. The same applies to other accompanying policy areas, such as labour and perhaps investment. But on the exchange rate? No definition is provided of what 'supportive' means here. One is led to assume that the authors simply and unhesitatingly define a 'good' exchange rate as a market-determined one, i.e., a free float or something close to it. Important recent experiences in Latin America do not necessarily support this view. Respectable as such an opinion may be, as presented it appears purely ideological; there is no discussion of different exchange rate doctrines in the chapter.

On the complementarity across key policy areas having strong links with trade policy, one which surely should have been included is *deregulation* (or perhaps regulation) policy. Changes in regulation policy have played a major role in the reinforcement and deepening of reform programmes in many Latin American countries. The regulation framework is indeed closely linked to both trade policy and performance, yet it is not mentioned in the chapter.

As a final comment, I would add that the chapter is as much about free-trade areas (FTAs) and customs unions (CUs), where one has a considerable body of literature on which to build (well reflected in the bibliography, even if references in the text are very sparse), as it is about the political economy of these matters, which is more speculative at this stage. The authors provide a valuable initial treatment in both regards, and it would be nice to see further work by them on these issues.

NOTE

This Discussion is provided by the author in a purely personal capacity, without necessarily reflecting the views of his government or of any other officers of it.

10 Regional integration in Eastern Europe: prospects for integration within the region and with the European Community

JOSEF C. BRADA

1 Introduction

In market economies, regional economic integration is achieved through the selective elimination of barriers against the movement of goods, services and factors of production among the integrating countries. Since private agents undertake the acts that are the subject of integration measures, the causes of integration are transparent and their economic consequences are subject to ready analysis and measurement. Among centrally planned economies (CPEs), such visible incentives to integration were irrelevant because foreign trade was a monopoly of the state, and the state's preferences toward trade with specific partners were implemented by means of administrative measures that were invisible to outsiders. This lack of transparency in the measures for integration among the members of the Council for Mutual Economic Assistance (CMEA) led to considerable confusion and controversy about sources, means and consequences of economic integration among these countries. Thus, now, as these countries face the task of reconsidering economic ties among themselves, and in the case of the former USSR within themselves, the question of which of these past flows of goods and resources ought to be retained and which should be eliminated, as well as the means of doing so, looms large on the agenda of the region's policymakers.

In this chapter, I examine the basis of CMEA integration and its effects on intra-regional trade in order to explain the legacy that it leaves for the region. Important aspects of this legacy include the volume and structure of past trade, as well as the economic benefits that it brought to the region.

The collapse of the CMEA mechanism has faced the region's leaders with the need to re-evaluate and perhaps re-establish economic links among themselves on a new basis. I argue that most proposals for creating formal structures, such as customs or payments unions (CUs or PUs), among those East European countries most advanced in the transition to capitalism are unlikely to yield large benefits. The inclusion of some of the republics of the CIS in such schemes is also not feasible at this time, due to the systemic incompatibility between them and the more reformed economies of East Europe and because of the economic chaos that reigns in the CIS. Moreover, efforts to revive trade between East Europe and the CIS would resurrect many of the inefficiencies that existed in intra-CMEA trade and would expose East European countries to significant financial risks.

Integration of East Europe into the European Community is seen by most East European policymakers as both a more desirable way of expanding the region's trade and as an objective to be sought for a broad range of political and security objectives. Czecho-Slovakia, Hungary and Poland have signed Association Agreements with the Community that envision eventual full membership for these countries in the Community. Nevertheless, there are areas in which conflicts between the Community and these countries will arise in the short run. In the long run, full membership in the Community will depend in part on political and economic progress in East Europe but, perhaps even more, on developments such as the resolution of conflicts surrounding the current GATT negotiations and the enlargement of the Community that are outside East Europe's control.

The fragmentation of the USSR into independent states has hampered economic relations both among the republics and between them and the rest of the world. Given the unsettled nature of monetary arrangements with the CIS, the spectre of hyperinflation and the collapse of production, it is unclear that attempting to create formal mechanisms for promoting trade among the republics is either feasible or desirable at this time.

2   Legacies of the CMEA

The CMEA was founded in 1949, and its integration mechanism consisted of two components. The first of these was a regime for facilitating trade among a group of state-trading countries (Brada, 1988). Trade among members was conducted on the basis of bilateral agreements and cleared, at first through bilateral clearing accounts and later by means of the transferable ruble. With each set of trade negotiations pitting one state monopoly against another, a regime that regularised member behaviour by creating rules regarding pricing, payment, delivery conditions, etc. helped to increase members' confidence in the continuity of their bilateral commercial relations and thus reduced the costs of this cumbersome way of carrying out international trade.

The other component of the CMEA integration mechanism was the effort to promote specialisation in production among CMEA members and to promote technical progress, especially in industry. Specialisation was to be implemented by promoting broad agreement on the pattern of production, and especially of investment, so that a member would be granted a monopoly position in the production of specific products or product lines within the framework of so-called specialisation agreements and longer-term complex programmes.

The former aspect of CMEA integration appears to have been the more successful one, in that the volume of intra-regional trade was greater than it would have been in the absence of the CMEA, thanks to the existence of a regime that reduced the transaction costs of trading among these CPEs (Hewett, 1976; Brada and Mendez, 1985; Biessen, 1991). The second aspect of CMEA integration, the effort to foster specialisation, was less successful. In part, this was due to the fact that all countries sought their 'just' share of specialisation positions without regard to their abilities to develop basic competence in their areas of specialisation. Specialisation thus degenerated into a process of parcelling out new areas of production among all members, often broadening rather than narrowing the range of products produced by any one country.

Viewed in a Vinerian sense, the CMEA probably did not raise members' welfare very much because a good deal of its gross trade creation was the result of trade diversion.[1] Trade diversion was caused by the considerable differences in resource endowments and levels of development among members, and by the fact that none of the smaller and more industrialised East European countries could be viewed as a low-cost supplier of industrial goods, while the USSR, despite its vast natural resources, was not a relatively low-cost supplier of all types of fuels and raw materials.

The CMEA countries may not have chosen to view economic integration in Vinerian terms, that is, as a process to maximise trade creation and minimise trade diversion. In the immediate post-World War II environment, East–West hostility and the Western embargo cut the CMEA countries off from the industrial goods produced in the developed West. Moreover, the leaders of the CMEA countries, imbued with Marxist ideology, no doubt had a more Johnsonian conception of regional economic integration and viewed it more as a vehicle for meeting their desire for industrialisation than as a means of promoting static efficiency.[2]

At first CMEA integration did promote industrialisation in the region, but by the late 1950s and early 1960s conflicts were already evident over the excessive pace and duplicative pattern of industrialisation in less developed East European countries such as Romania. Over time, it became increasingly evident that industrialisation based only on increases in factor inputs rather than on factor productivity could not match industrial progress in developed Western countries, either in terms of the quality and modernity of industrial products or in terms of the ability to master, much less innovate in, new areas of industrial technology. These shortcomings were amply evident in the inability of industrial goods from CMEA countries to penetrate world markets and in the steady decline (and in some cases, retrogression) of total factor productivity growth in the industrial sectors of the CMEA countries (Brada, 1985; Bergson, 1991).

At the same time that the Johnsonian impetus for regional integration was nearing exhaustion, the region's shortcomings in terms of Vinerian considerations were looming increasingly large. The easing of East–West tensions opened the doors to increased East–West trade, thus making the cost of trade diversion toward CMEA producers of machinery and equipment an increasingly real rather than a theoretical burden. The oil price increases of the 1970s intensified the Vinerian strains on CMEA integration and at the same time delayed their resolution. Because the USSR supplied its CMEA partners with virtually all their energy needs and was their primary outlet for manufactures, the run-up in energy prices in the 1970s should have sharply improved the USSR's terms of trade with its CMEA partners. However, because intra-CMEA prices were both fixed for five-year periods and based on past world market prices, the USSR's terms of trade improvement was felt immediately only in its trade with the West; within CMEA, energy prices rose only slowly and gradually. This meant that the costs of CMEA integration rose sharply for the USSR, because it received lower prices for its energy exports to CMEA than it did for its exports to the rest of the world, and because it continued to pay world prices for East European machinery that was not up to world standards (Marrese and Vanous, 1983, 1988).

As energy prices began to rise in intra-CMEA trade, especially after a revision of the pricing formula to allow more rapid price changes, and the USSR reduced its oil deliveries to East Europe, there was little impetus left for CMEA integration beyond old habits and the existence of a huge capital stock and transportation infrastructure that could not easily be adapted to trade with other regions. The collapse of communist rule in Czecho-Slovakia, Hungary and Poland and the decision by those countries to abandon central planning effectively made the CMEA regime irrelevant, since it was institutionally designed to mediate transactions among CPEs, not to facilitate trade between planned and market economies. The desire of these three countries and the USSR to switch intra-CMEA trade to dollar payments and world market prices effectively eliminated any sort of integrative forces in the region's trade and placed it on an equal footing with extra-regional trade. Thus, on 28 September 1991, CMEA's *de facto* demise was recognised as its members formally disbanded the organisation.

3 The aftermath of the collapse of the CMEA

It is widely believed that the collapse of CMEA trade in 1990 and especially in 1991 led to sharp declines in economic activity in East Europe and in the former USSR. Many observers have concluded that a revival of intra-regional trade by means of some substitute for the defunct CMEA is needed in order to raise the volume of intra-East European trade and thus to stimulate economic recovery in the region. Whether steps to revive intra-regional trade by means of integration measures are desirable and feasible depends critically on the economic rationality of the trade that has been eliminated, on the actual relationship between intra-regional and extra-regional trade of the East European countries, and on the sources of the decline in intra-regional trade. If factors other than the lack of an integrating mechanism are at work in reducing intra-regional trade, then policies designed to deal with these factors rather than to strengthen integration will be more appropriate. Moreover, if past intra-regional trade was uneconomically high, then efforts to prevent its decline will be futile and counterproductive.

3.1 A brief history and some statistical issues

The adoption of world market prices and dollar clearing for trade among the CMEA members and the phasing out of the transferable ruble have led to considerable confusion about the geographic distribution of trade of the East European countries and about the evolution of intra-regional trade. In the past, intra-regional trade, measured in transferable rubles, and trade with the rest of the world, measured in dollars, were aggregated using an exchange rate that overvalued the ruble and thus overstated intra-regional trade. Beginning in the late 1980s, the East European countries began to utilise a more realistic cross-rate, effectively devaluing their currencies against the dollar, at least for trade accounting purposes. The implications of such a change in trade accounting practice can be seen in Tables 10.1 and 10.2. The first two columns of Table 10.1 and Table 10.2 show the value of Czecho-Slovak trade calculated at the 'official' exchange rate, which overvalued the transferable ruble, and at the exchange rate of 1 January 1989, which reflected the 'commercial', although not necessarily the equilibrium, values of the dollar and

Table 10.1. *Czecho-Slovak trade with major Western countries, 1988–91, Kcs million*

Country		1988[a]	1988[b]	1989[b]	1990[b]	1991 (Jan–Sept)[b]
Austria	x	4112	11 102	11 830	23 124	15 481
	m	3295	8896	9938	12 717	12 704
FRG	x	7252	19 580	19 931	31 734	41 309
	m	6138	16 573	17 964	27 639	54 559
France	x	1262	3407	3350	4203	4715
	m	1231	3325	3936	5662	5547
Italy	x	1409	3804	3695	5436	7109
	m	1389	3751	4623	6630	9180
UK	x	1687	4553	4731	5862	3834
	m	1634	4413	4396	5521	4340

Notes:
[a] At current exchange rate.
[b] At exchange rate of 1.1.1989.
x: exports.
m: imports.
Sources: Statistická Ročenka (1991); *Statistické Přehled* (1991/12).

transferable ruble.[3] Such a revaluation of the dollar sharply increased the measured volume of East–West trade while leaving intra-regional trade volumes more or less unchanged.

As Czecho-Slovakia, Hungary and Poland liberalised their trade regimes, they devalued their currencies *vis-à-vis* those of the West and revalued *vis-à-vis* the ruble.[4] As a result, the regional distribution of trade of these countries measured in domestic currency or dollars tends to overstate the decline in the share of intra-regional trade in their total trade. The Czecho-Slovak trade data reported in Tables 10.1 and 10.2 go some way toward overcoming this distortion of the trade flows by devaluation *vis-à-vis* the West by reporting trade flows on the basis of a comparable, or constant, set of exchange rates. However, because intra-regional trade went from transferable ruble-denominated and CMEA-determined prices in 1990 to dollar-denominated world market prices in 1991, intra-regional prices evolved differently from world market prices, thus precluding any firm comparison of 1990 and 1991 (Oblath and Tarr, 1992).

The evolution of intra-regional trade can also proceed by examining Table 10.3, on Polish trade, and Table 10.4, on Soviet trade. Polish trade is reported in dollars, and if the transferable ruble rate of 1990 was

Table 10.2. *Czecho-Slovak trade with East European countries, 1988–91, Kcs million*

Country		1988[a]	1988[b]	1989[b]	1990[b]	1991 (Jan–Sept)[b]
Bulgaria	x	4154	5210	4808	2752	1216
	m	4682	5919	5073	3084	1446
GDR	x	13 649	17 190	17 797	—	—
	m	11 705	14 916	14 257	—	—
Hungary	x	7166	9282	10 294	8147	4161
	m	7240	9082	8641	8841	9698
Poland	x	13 747	17 280	18 485	20 370	11 025
	m	13 739	17 238	18 438	13 394	14 762
Romania	x	2995	3762	3561	1732	754
	m	2631	3307	3938	2518	2332
USSR	x	52 023	65 465	63 792	51 410	65 809
	m	57 177	71 924	66 439	54 159	42 919

Notes:
[a] At current exchange rate.
[b] At exchange rate of 1.1.1989.
x: exports.
m: imports.
Sources: Statistická Ročenka (1991); *Statistické Přehled* (1991/12).

Table 10.3. *Polish trade with East European countries, 1990 (Jan–May) and 1991 (Jan–May), $ million*

Country		1990 (Jan–May)	1991 (Jan–May)
Bulgaria	x	49	10
	m	26	13
Czecho-Slovakia	x	201	203
	m	97	115
Hungary	x	42	42
	m	20	30
Romania	x	34	10
	m	9	7
USSR	x	765	487
	m	452	929

x = exports.
m = imports.
Source: Biueletin Statystyczny (1991/6).

Table 10.4. *Soviet foreign trade with East Europe, 1990 (Jan–Jun) and 1991 (Jan–Jun), rubles million*

Country		1990 (Jan–Jun)	1991 (Jan–Jun)	% Δ
Bulgaria	x	4390.0	1306.0	− 70.3
	m	4482.2	1904.7	− 57.5
Czecho-Slovakia	x	4700.2	2732.0	− 41.9
	m	3789.7	2008.1	− 47.0
Hungary	x	2604.4	1578.7	− 39.4
	m	2652.6	1187.0	− 55.3
Poland	x	3783.3	2273.3	− 39.9
	m	6291.6	2101.5	− 66.6
Romania	x	1778.2	820.3	− 53.9
	m	941.2	680.5	− 27.7

Notes:
x = exports.
m = imports.
Source: PlanEcon Reports (10 January 1992) Table 1.

realistic, then the switch to dollar pricing in 1991 ought to have little influence on the 1990–1 comparison. The 1991 figures for Soviet trade in Table 10.4 are according to the PlanEcon Report of 10 January 1992, calculated using an average exchange rate of 1.72 rubles/$. Prior to this time, a different exchange rate, overvaluing transferable ruble trade, was used, but the data in Table 10.4 for 1990 are restated by PlanEcon to be comparable, although the methodology for doing this is not explained.

In sum, there was a decline in intra-regional trade in 1991. While we cannot discern with much certitude what the exact magnitude of this decline was, we can suggest that it was appreciable, in the range of 15–40 percent in real terms. Moreover, there is a clear pattern, with Romanian and Bulgarian trade with the region falling sharply but trade among Poland, Hungary and Czecho-Slovakia holding up at 1990 levels. Soviet trade with East Europe also declined sharply, especially according to Soviet statistics.[5]

3.2   Causes of the decline in trade

3.2.1 Output declines   The OECD estimates that output in the region declined in all countries of the region in 1991; by 20 percent in Bulgaria; 12 percent in Czecho-Slovakia; 7 percent in Hungary; 8 percent in Poland;

Table 10.5. *German trade with East Europe, 1989–91 (Jan–Oct), DM million*

| | German exports by | | | | |
| | Unified Germany | | Territory of former West Germany | | |
Trading partner	1990	1991 (Jan–Oct)	1989	1990	1991 (Jan–Oct)
European state-trading countries	39 203	30 556	24 515	23 458	21 134
Czecho-Slovakia	4429	3882	2734	3080	3326
Hungary	4798	3483	3651	3363	3154
Poland	6566	6902	4470	4691	6034
USSR	20 069	14 539	11 526	10 361	7189

| | German imports by | | | | |
| | Unified Germany | | Territory of former West Germany | | |
	1990	1991 (Jan–Oct)	1989	1990	1991 (Jan–Oct)
European state-trading countries	25 534	27 394	19 243	21 788	21 624
Czecho-Slovakia	3074	4036	2493	2703	3462
Hungary	3553	3480	2687	3254	3267
Poland	5597	5979	3580	5164	5333
USSR	11 698	12 412	8556	9117	8179

Source: Deutsches Bundesbank, *Statistische Beihefte der Deutschen Bundesbank, 1* (January 1992).

9 percent in Romania, and 12.5 percent in the USSR. Such declines in output can be viewed either as a cause or as a consequence of the decline in intra-regional trade. In a number of countries, restrictive monetary and fiscal policies, price reforms and austerity measures reduced effective demand, leading to a decline in production, and thus in incomes and demand for imports. This was most clearly the case in Poland, Hungary and Czecho-Slovakia (Brada and King, 1992). These demand side-induced declines in output and import demand, of course, manifest themselves as declines in exports in other countries, and thus the region

was subject to the workings of the foreign trade multiplier, which served to transmit the deflationary shock to all. In some cases, however, there were supply-side effects as well, with shortages of energy, raw materials and intermediate inputs all playing a role.

3.2.2 German unification   The unification of Germany eliminated an important trading partner for all the East European countries. Table 10.2 gives some testimony of the importance of the former GDR to CMEA trade and Table 10.5 shows the effects of unification on East Europe's trade with the former GDR. It is of particular interest that once trade with the former GDR was placed on a hard currency basis, it declined sharply.

3.3   The special role of the USSR

The USSR was and, in some cases, its successor the CIS remains, the largest trading partner of the East European countries despite the effects of the devaluation of the transferable ruble and the decline in the real volume of CIS trade with the region. It is thus necessary to determine whether this trade has been particularly hard hit by the collapse of the CMEA mechanism or whether other factors are at work.

A large part of the explanation for the USSR's reduced trade with East Europe lies in the attempt to decentralise Soviet trade and switch it to a hard currency basis in a period when the USSR was drifting into insolvency. The decentralisation of Soviet foreign trade began in 1986 with the dismantling of the Ministry of Foreign Trade and the devolution of trading rights to enterprises, associations, and industrial ministries. In 1989 these rights to trade were extended to all Soviet enterprises and to regional bodies, although extensive administrative controls over trade, especially in raw materials, were erected. The units that received trading rights and to cover their own foreign expenditures, which they could do only by retaining some of their export earnings or by obtaining the necessary means of payment from Vnesheconombank, the Soviet foreign trade bank. In 1990 this bank was already experiencing difficulties in meeting its payment obligations to Western firms. Soviet liquidity problems worsened in 1991, culminating with the Vnesheconombank's suspension of business at the end of the year (*Journal of Commerce*, 20 February 1992).

Soviet firms were unable to get the funds necessary for the signing of import contracts, and thus they were unable to import goods from East Europe. East European governments also acted to reduce the risk of non-payment by Soviet importers by imposing quantitative restrictions on exports to the USSR and by levying special surcharges on ruble trade. Finally, there is anecdotal evidence that many East European exports to the USSR went unpaid.[6] Thus, with Soviet authorities prohibiting barter trade, the volume of East European exports to the USSR was sharply reduced in the first half of 1991.

A further source of decline in the USSR's trade with East Europe was the collapse of the Soviet economy, which reduced demand, due both to a real decline in production and to the effects of inflation on consumer purchasing power. Noteworthy is the decline in the production of the USSR's principal export, oil. Soviet oil production peaked at 12.4 million barrels per day in 1988 and then declined to 12.0 million in 1990 and to about 10.2 million in 1991, with end-of-year production reported well under the annual average. Exports of crude oil from Russia, which accounts for the bulk of CIS oil exports, fell by 30–35 percent in 1991.

It is useful to compare the trade consequences of these developments in the USSR for East Europe with the experience of two non-CMEA countries whose trade was previously also conducted on the basis of negotiated prices and clearing arrangements.

3.3.1 Finland Finland had a special trading relationship with the USSR based on a clearing arrangement that obviated the need for hard currency payments between the two countries. This clearing arrangement was abrogated at the request of the USSR in 1990 and replaced with dollar payments at world market prices. In 1991, the value of Finnish exports to the USSR fell by 65 percent and imports from the USSR by 27 percent. There have been admissions on the Soviet side that the move to hard currency payments was largely responsible (*Economist*, 12 October 1991), and efforts are being made to revive trade by means of a new barter arrangement between Finland and the Russian Republic, although the decreased availability of oil for export from Russia, as well as continuing decreases in Russian GNP, are likely to be limiting factors.

3.3.2 India Like Finland, India had traded with the USSR on the basis of negotiated prices and bilateral balancing of trade flows supplemented by technical credits. In 1991 Soviet exports to India failed to reach the agreed levels; crude oil deliveries fell short by 33 percent and ferrous and non-ferrous metals targets were also not met (*Financial Times*, 7 February 1992). Although India acted to reduce its own exports to the USSR, it now holds a technical credit of about $1.2 billion against the CIS, with unclear prospects of how it is to be repaid.

These experiences suggest that the decline in East European exports to the USSR and of Soviet energy exports to them are part of a more general pattern of collapse of Soviet means of payment. In cases such as India, where the USSR could obtain consumer goods on credit, it continued to import, but where hard currency was needed, as in the case of Finland, it reduced its imports. The continued existence of bilateral clearing within the CMEA would therefore have raised the volume of intra-regional exchanges only if the East European countries had been willing to finance large CIS trade deficits through such a mechanism.

3.4   A revival of barter

The Soviet prohibition on barter trade was rescinded in the summer of 1991 for manufactures and, subsequently, by the republics, for all goods. Anecdotal evidence indicates that the ban was never totally effective and that local authorities engaged in illegal barter transactions with East European governments and enterprises, either to maintain traditional trade ties with East European suppliers and customers or to replace deteriorating inter-republican trade within the USSR. With the replacement of Prime Minister Pavlov after the abortive coup in the USSR and the decisive shift of power to the individual republics, there has been an upsurge in formal barter arrangements between them and the East European countries. Available information on these barter arrangements is compiled in Table 10.6.

While such barter arrangements have increased the volume of intra-regional trade, they are unlikely to restore it to its previous levels because they focus on essentials, and thus take the form of Soviet fuels and raw materials for East European food and consumer goods. Exports of machinery and equipment from the CIS have virtually disappeared and East European exports of investment goods have also been hard hit. Also evident from Table 10.6 is the uncertainty of CIS deliveries under the barter arrangements, in part due to production shortfalls in oil and natural gas production and in part in order to obtain terms more favourable than obtained under the original barter negotiation.

3.5   An assessment of the decline in regional trade

The available data suggest that intra-regional trade flows have fallen in real terms by 15–40 percent, with the greatest declines occurring in trade between the former USSR and the rest of East Europe. Within East Europe, trade between Czecho-Slovakia, Hungary and Poland, the most advanced countries both economically and in terms of reform effort, has

Table 10.6. *Barter arrangements between East European countries and the USSR/CIS, 1991–2*

Year	Partners	East European exports	USSR/CIS exports
1991	Bulgaria–USSR	Manufactured goods ($300 million)	Electricity[a]
1992	Bulgaria–Ukraine	Manufactured goods	Electricity
1991	Czecho-Slovakia–USSR	Trolley buses ($200 million), food and consumer goods ($85 million)	Raw materials and manufactures
1991	Czecho-Slovakia–Russia	Grain and meat	Oil
1992	Czecho-Slovakia–Russia	Trucks, food, grain, textiles, shoes	55 million barrels of oil valued at $3.5 billion, of which 15.6 million barrels are covered by barter, the remainder to be paid in convertible currencies
1991	Hungary–Russia	Buses, grain, meat, pharmaceuticals, consumer manufactures ($670 million)	Coal, oil products, wood, tractors, construction materials, fertilisers
1992	Hungary–Russia	Unspecific	Electricity, natural gas, oil (4 million tons)
1991	Poland–Ukraine	Light industrial goods and construction services	Vegetable oil, manganese ore, iron
1991	Poland–Ukraine	Cement	Coal
1991	Poland–Ukraine	Food and farm machinery	Fuel and consumer manufactures

Table 10.6. (*cont.*)

Year	Partners	East European exports	USSR/CIS exports
1992	Poland–Russia	Food ($500 million), medical supplies ($400 million), sulphur (400,000 tons): total value $32.8 billion	Natural gas (8.1 billion m³), oil (4 million tons)[b]

Notes:

[a] Electricity deliveries to Bulgaria were stopped in 1991 to force Bulgaria to deliver goods to Ukraine rather than to Russia and in January 1992 to speed the renegotiation of the barter arrangement.

[b] Natural gas deliveries were halved in January 1992 and Poland was forced to renegotiate the agreement, scaling back natural gas deliveries to 6.6 billion m³.

Sources: Journal of Commerce (21 November 1991); Dobrowski (1991); *Zycie Gospodarcze* (9 February 1992).

held up quite well, especially in the light of declines in economic activity. Trade between them and Bulgaria and Romania has also fallen sharply.

Whether such declines in intra-regional trade are consistent with the elimination of the integrating effects of the CMEA is subject to some controversy. Estimates based on gravity models of trade flows by Brada and Mendez (1985) and Havrylyshyn and Pritchett (1991) suggest that the elimination of CMEA integration should lead to declines of 60–75 percent in intra-regional trade. A study by Wang and Winters (1991), also employing a gravity model, indicates that the difference between reported trade and potential trade in the absence of CMEA is of the order of 50 percent.[7] The collapse of the CMEA mechanism thus appears not to have as great an effect on intra-regional trade as expected, since trade appears to have declined less than these models predict. The resilience of intra-regional trade is all the more striking when the decline in regional incomes is taken into account, since the income elasticity of trade in all three gravity models is greater than 1. Hence, income declines due to deflationary policies and, in the case of Soviet trade, to disruption of the economy, can be seen as being responsible for a large proportion of the real decline in trade.

The decline in intra-regional trade and its partial redirection toward the rest of the world is welfare-improving in the long run if it reduces the level of trade diversion caused by CMEA integration. Whether this is the case is not easy to judge because changes in the commodity pattern of trade are as yet unclear, although preliminary data suggest that, in regional trade, the share of manufactures has dropped in Soviet exports, leaving a greater concentration of fuels and raw materials. Since Soviet manufactures exports to East Europe were 'added on' to Soviet fuel exports in the course of bilateral negotiations, this decline in trade is desirable, as East Europe ought to be able to obtain similar goods for less on world markets. At the same time, East European exports of machinery and equipment of the USSR have declined, perhaps also reflecting the lack of a comparative advantage in this sector relative to that of more developed market economies.

One way of assessing the usefulness of the barter agreements being used to revive intra-regional trade is to inquire whether they correspond to the comparative advantages of the participating countries. One means of making such a judgement is to employ the estimates of Hughes and Hare (1991), who used input–output tables to estimate the value added in industries in Czecho-Slovakia, Hungary and Poland at world market prices. Using their findings to evaluate the desirability of the barter arrangements yields mixed results. For example, foodstuffs are among the items exported by the three East European countries in virtually all their barter deals with the CIS region. Hughes and Hare find that food-processing industries in all three countries tend to have low or even negative value added, suggesting that it makes little economic sense to promote exports of these industries. Polish exports of sulphur and cement also derive from sectors with negative value added. On the other hand, Czecho-Slovak trolley buses, Hungarian pharmaceuticals and buses, and Polish cereal products all come from sectors that are highly profitable at world market prices. Consumer goods cover a broad range of sectors, and Hughes and Hare's results indicate a correspondingly broad range of profitability, or lack thereof, among both sectors and exporting countries. In all, these results suggest that, while barter trade may be a means of saving jobs in East Europe, the economic rationality of some of the resulting trade flows is of questionable long-term value.

4   East Europe's future

4.1   Efforts at regional integration

Czecho-Slovakia, Hungary and Poland have made the greatest progress toward restoring some measure of regional integration, this time based on market principles. The leaders of the three countries have considered the possibility of creating a free-trade area (FTA). This idea, however, has yet to be implemented because of the price distortions that continue to exist in the region; the high, but generally different, rates of inflation in the three countries; and differences in the purchasing power of the countries' currencies. An intimate connection between the three economies could lead one to export its inflation to others; exchange rate adjustments to offset differential rates of inflation would interfere with the use of exchange rate policy to serve as an anchor and as a means of managing trade with the West.

Moreover, the tariff rates of the three countries are quite low, Czecho-Slovakia's averaging about 5 percent *ad valorem* while Poland's were raised from 8 to 16 percent in 1991. Studies of the effects of an FTA raise two concerns. The first is that any increases in trade will increase the output of sectors that are uneconomic in the long run and thus hamper industrial restructuring; the second is that increased trade will impose further unemployment and readjustment costs on all three countries (Foreign Trade Research Institute, 1991, 1992). The three countries have sought to coordinate policies on transportation, communications and finance and the creation of free-trade zones in border areas. Trade liberalisation will also take place on the basis of the bilateral concessions the three countries will make to each other that will be similar to the concessions obtained in the Accords negotiated with the European Community in 1991. Thus quantitative limits will be eliminated and tariffs reduced over a five-year span.

There are proposals for integration between Czecho-Slovakia, Hungary, Poland, and other countries of the region such as Ukraine, Slovenia and Croatia, although the greater progress achieved by the former countries in stabilising their economies, creating functioning markets and forging ties to the West suggests that integrating such heterogeneous economies in a formal framework may prove well-nigh impossible.

4.2   Proposals for a regional payments union

Although the region's leaders have shown little interest in attempting to restore the volume of intra-regional trade by means of some form of a payments union (PU), Western observers have made a number of proposals in that direction. Because the decline in trade is seen as being caused by an inability of the partners to finance trade flows while the decline in demand due to declines in output and demand is not considered an important factor, these proposals seek to develop ways of financing intra-regional trade. Van Brabant (1991) has argued at length for a PU among East European countries as a means of maintaining or reviving regional trade; Havrylyshyn and Williamson (1991) propose a similar payments scheme for the republics of the CIS, conceivably to include the countries of East Europe as well.

Whether such a scheme, based largely on the experience of the European Payments Union (EPU), can increase intra-regional trade is doubtful. It is likely to do so only if the collapse of intra-CMEA trade is due to a lack of financing to settle clearing imbalances among members. As I have suggested above, this assumption is not entirely justifiable except in the trivial sense that some form of financing of potential trade deficits might have kept import demand higher than it was. Whether such a level of credit extension would have been self-sustaining, prudent, or feasible in the long run is unlikely.

The second problem is that there is a serious tension between a PU as a means of preventing trade destruction due to illiquidity and a PU as a means for economic integration. While avoiding the loss of trade and of jobs due to financial constraints is a valid objective, the existence of such a union acts as an integrating force, inducing some members to prefer trade with one another at the expense of trade with the rest of the world. This preference would be felt most by those members least able to compete on world markets and by all members for those goods that they could not sell on world markets. This would serve to replicate the hard goods–soft goods problems of the old CMEA and to hamper the restructuring of the region.

The political feasibility of the scheme is also doubtful. Large debts exist between East Europe and the CIS. While these could be formally kept outside the scope of the PU, as van Brabant suggests, they are nevertheless likely to weigh heavily in any decision to form a union. Another set of obstacles revolves around the emerging conflicts between Russia and the other republics over the role of the central organs inherited by the Russian Republic. The Ukraine already objects to repaying its share of CIS Western debt through the Moscow-based Vnesheconombank, and it and other CIS republics are unlikely to wish to tie their economic fortunes too closely to the Russian Republic.

While the temptation to engineer general solutions to the region's problems is great, it is unlikely that such broad-gauge proposals can be implemented in the near term, and a certain amount of *ad hoc* creativity must be allowed the region's leaders. In the short run, the losses due to unemployment may be greater, but in the long run the prospects for putting the region's trade on a firm footing will also be greater. The most important advice that can be given is that, as prices are rationalised, protectionist policies be eschewed as much as possible.

4.3   East Europe and the European Community

As the role of intra-regional trade has declined, the importance of western Europe and particularly the Community has increased. East European policymakers view trade with the West as a source of economic discipline for their reforming economies, as a spur to greater productivity and efficiency and as the source of the technical know-how, capital and assistance needed to bring prosperity to the region. Moreover, both a desire to re-establish a common European culture and a need to establish new security links oriented the region toward the West. The economic integration of East Europe with the Community would also imply a *de facto* integration among the East European countries through their common participation in the EC integration mechanism, and consequently the pace of integration with the West may also determine the pace of intra-East European integration.

Czecho-Slovakia, Hungary and Poland have proceeded the furthest in their efforts to integrate with the West. By means of long and difficult negotiations they were able to reach agreements with the Community on achieving status as Associate members. The agreements have both political and economic implications. The former stem from the fact that the Accords recognise that the long-term objective of the East Europeans is to achieve full membership in the Community, and from the explicit admission by the Community that these agreements serve as models for agreements to be negotiated with other East European countries as well as with some of the successor republics of the USSR. The economic implications have to do with the expansion of trade and investment flows between the Community and the Associate countries.

Under the agreements, the terms of which are identical for all three countries, the Community will reduce tariffs on its imports of industrial goods during the five years following the signing of the agreements, while the three East European countries will reduce their tariff barriers against Community industrial goods in the following five years.

The negotiations leading up to the Accords were disrupted by three conflicts, all of which reflect problems that have bedevilled the Community in the past and that the Community will have to resolve within a more global context than is afforded by East–West considerations.

The first conflict was over agriculture. In September 1991 France, joined by Ireland and Belgium, vetoed an agreement to increase imports of meat from the three East European countries, leading Poland to withdraw from the negotiations. Given the Community's desire to reach an agreement with the three countries simultaneously, the Polish action had broader implications and led to intense pressure on both France and Poland. In reality, French objections were largely symbolic and intended for domestic political ends, as the measure vetoed would have increased EC quotas for the three countries by 500 tons of beef and 900 tons of lamb. As a compromise, the Community agreed to increase the meat quotas by 10 percent per year for five years; the liberalisation of trade in other agricultural products will begin only in 1995 and will also be phased in over a five-year period. Moreover, it was agreed that the USSR could use 25 percent of a ECU 500 million loan from the Community to purchase meat from the East European countries and that such purchases would count against the EC quota on meat imports from these countries. In the event, even though there was initial Soviet interest in such a triangular transaction, both the loan and East European meat exports have become entangled in the confusion surrounding the dissolution of the USSR.

A second area of disagreement was over textiles, where the Community's less developed members, such as Portugal, expressed concern over East European competition. Consequently, the parties agreed to extend the reduction of EC trade barriers to 1998 and the Community agreed to provide financial assistance to the Portuguese textile industry.

The final area of disagreement was over steel, where France, Spain, Portugal, and Italy raised concerns over the elimination of EC quotas and duties. These countries called for the inclusion of provisions for voluntary export restraints (VERs) for steel and steel products in the Association accords, but the EC Commission rejected this solution. Instead, a safeguard clause permitting individual EC members to reduce steel imports from the Associate countries in case of perceived market disruption was adopted. Eurofer, the trade association of West European steel producers, is reportedly prepared to file complaints against Czecho-Slovakia and Poland and to be contemplating other complaints against dumping by East European steel makers (*International Herald Tribune*, November 15 1991).

The Community's agricultural policy and structural adjustment in sectors such as steel and textiles have long confounded the Community's trade policy. They are unlikely to be resolved in an East–West context because the Community's great negotiating strength *vis-à-vis* the East European countries allows the Community to impose solutions in these areas that do not challenge the foundations of its policies. Whether the Community can continue these tactics while expanding the number of East European Associates is unclear; also difficult to judge is whether the costs of extending the CAP to East Europe in the future could be met by the Community. It is thus likely that some of the issues that most affect East Europe's economic relations with the Community will be determined not in the course of EC–East European negotiations but in international fora such as the GATT or bilateral negotiations between the United States and the Community.

The need to penetrate EC markets has implications for East Europe that include, but go well beyond, the expansion of the volume of commodity trade. All three East European countries are attempting to combat inflation by means of a combination of restrictive monetary policies and tight fiscal policies that call for the government to reduce its budgetary deficit or even to run a surplus. With this sort of a policy stance, these governments cannot stimulate demand by means of variation in government expenditures or in interest rates. The major stimulus to economic growth and the reduction in unemployment must therefore come from the foreign trade sector through an expansion of exports. On the structural side, the better able is East Europe to find markets for its traditional industries, such as steel and textiles, the less will be the need to restructure domestic production. By salvaging some of this old industrial structure, these countries can avoid high levels of unemployment and also reduce their need for capital to build new industries.

All three countries are counting on increased Western investment in their economies to play a major role in privatisation and to bring in new investments combined with Western technology and business expertise. Their attractiveness to Western investors is now not as a potential gateway to the former CMEA market but rather as a base from which to supply West European markets. This is particularly true for Japanese firms since they, more than American and West European firms, are willing to take a long-term view that would be consistent with the gradual elimination of trade barriers between East Europe and the Community. A failure to provide some assurance that these barriers will be reduced would then imply at best a deferral of Western investment in East Europe and at worst its deflection, possibly to the less developed members of the Community, such as Greece, Portugal and Spain.

All three elements have an important time dimension. On the trade front, the East Europeans believe that they must establish a market presence in West Europe as soon as possible. In part, this is because they have seen their share of developed country markets for basic manufactures eroded by newly industrialised countries (NICs), such as Korea and Taiwan. The Community's expansion to include countries such as Portugal, Spain, Greece, and the former GDR, whose level of development and thus export potential is similar to that of East Europe, has intensified this competition for the EC market. The intensification of EC integration through the 'Europe 1992' programme and the potential benefits to East Europe have increased the urgency of becoming part of the integration process from the outset, rather than having to catch up after strong trade and business relationships have been created in the new integrated Western Europe.

While the Association agreements go some way to addressing these issues, the deeper integration of these three East European countries into the Community poses a number of questions. One is whether the Community will in the end be willing to admit more members with relatively low incomes, thus creating greater budgetary strains on the Community. Moreover, economies with large but relatively inefficient agrarian sectors and with a large proportion of industry in sectors such as steel, where the existing EC members continue to face painful restructuring problems of their own, will face difficult adjustments in meeting EC requirements, while at the same time posing adjustment and budgetary problems for the Community. If the East European countries falter either politically or economically, they are also unlikely to be strong candidates for EC membership, if for no other reason than EC fears about inflows of workers or refugees from these countries. Of course, these considerations apply all the more to the less rapidly reforming Bulgaria and Romania and to many of the CIS republics; thus, while EC membership would provide a firm basis for both intra-regional integration and integration with West Europe, it is a relatively distant goal and one whose successful achievement depends on many factors that are outside the control of the East Europeans.

4.4   Jobs versus transformation

The countries of East Europe face a cruel dilemma. Efforts to stimulate intra-regional trade through integration measures face daunting challenges. Integration limited to economies at similar stages of the transformation process provide a relatively small number of integration partners while the expansion of the scope of integration brings in partners whose economic systems may not respond to market-based integration mechanisms or whose financial plight is likely to strain the region's financial mechanisms. Moreover, integration may create jobs only by preserving, or even strengthening, sectors that are uneconomic or uncompetitive in the long run, thus slowing the restructuring of these economies. Integration with the West will yield a more rational economic structure, but in the short run the West is least likely to open its markets in those sectors where East European export potential and domestic unemployment are the greatest. Whether the political systems of East Europe will push policymakers toward short-run or long-run solutions is thus a critical question for the region.

5   Lessons for the CIS[8]

The former USSR could in many ways be viewed as a sort of intra-national CMEA that, unlike the real CMEA, had power to plan both trade flows and the republican pattern of investment and thus specialisation. The Vinerian distortions and Johnsonian elements of CMEA integration were even more pronounced in the case of the USSR than in the CMEA because of the greater power of central authorities to misallocate resources. Measures intended to preserve the existing volume and pattern of inter-republican trade may consequently imply very high costs in the long run. Indeed, monetary and economic disunion may prove more beneficial than misguided efforts to preserve a domestic market that, in fact, was no market at all.

5.1   What are the costs of destroying the internal market of the USSR?

In the USSR, the distribution of productive capacities was not made on the basis of the comparative advantages of various republics in the production of specific goods. Rather, the location of factories was more often based on political considerations or on the basis of developmental objectives that ignored the relative costs of production. Moreover, the industrial structure of the USSR was heavily monopolised, with one or a few factories producing virtually the entire output of the country in many important consumer and industrial products. Finally, despite the USSR's huge size, little thought was given to creating an industrial structure that minimised transportation costs. Indeed, transportation charges were kept artificially low, and the bias toward excessive shipments of goods for long distances was exacerbated by the evaluation of the transportation sector by the ton-miles of traffic generated. Thus, the highly monopolised and regionally dispersed industrial structure of the USSR represents largely the objectives of the planners to create a few large plants in order to facilitate the central planning and allocation of resources, and not a structure that has some economic logic of comparative advantage behind it. The volume of inter-republic trade observed in the USSR is consequently not a useful measure of the economic benefits conferred by the unitary Soviet market; even less so than did all CMEA trade represent mutually beneficial exchanges among members.

This starting point for any efforts to develop an integration mechanism for the CIS republics poses serious problems. To the extent that the pattern of regional specialisation and industrial monopoly requires a relatively high volume of inter-republican trade, disruptions in such trade are likely to be costly. At the same time, such trade can be sustained in the short run only by retaining much of the economic irrationality of the old system. For example, moving toward world market prices for inter-republican trade would create huge windfalls for Russia and a few other resource-rich republics. But if trade is to be sustained on the basis of the ruble, then the deficit republics would be hard put to achieve the surpluses needed to generate increases in their money supplies. On the other hand, if trade continues at arbitrary internal prices that undervalue energy and raw materials, then the suppliers of underpriced goods will face powerful incentives to divert these goods to the world market. Stopping such a diversion of trade would require subsidies and administrative controls that would, in turn, subvert efforts at economic reform.

By allowing CIS republics greater choice between creating their own currencies or remaining in a ruble zone with Russia and between formal trade ties with other republics or the option of a more independent trade policy would enable more progressive republics, including Russia itself, to forge ahead with their own stabilisation and reform programmes without having these undermined by laggard republics. Under such a decentralised system, trade among independent CIS republics would, of course, have to be based on principles of comparative advantage, resulting in pressures to restructure production in each state so as to take international competitiveness into account. This would also mean that international trade with the rest of the world would be placed on an equal footing with trade among the newly independent republics. There would be important advantages to such an arrangement. It would reduce the existing tensions and distortions that result from the internal underpricing of exportables such as fuels, raw materials and foodstuffs. Newly independent republics would have the choice of exporting to each other, or they could direct their exports to world markets, thus ending the implicit subsidisation of some republics by others. Importers in the independent republics, since they would have to pay world market prices for imports regardless of their source, would now be free to make more rational choices between goods from the West and those produced in neighbouring republics.[9] This would be particularly advantageous in those cases where the domestic market is now highly monopolised. Given a few large producers and users of a product, the existing price is more likely to reflect bargaining and pressure than costs of production and usefulness of the product, and critical products are traded at arbitrary prices that satisfy neither sellers nor consumers. By opening up the market through world trade, the monopoly element in pricing would be reduced and more objective economic factors would prevail.

Finally, it is worth bearing in mind that in the long run the volume of trade under this arrangement could far exceed the volume of trade that would be possible under a unitary Soviet market. This is because under present conditions the volume of trade is based on the inter-republican exchange of one or several categories of goods in which the republic has a near-monopoly for those products in which other republics have their near-monopolies. With a wider industrial product profile emerging in each of the newly independent states, there would emerge opportunities for intra-industry trade to supplement the existing inter-industry exchanges. Moreover, the present system of inter-republic trade is collapsing, in part because each republic seeks to exploit its monopoly position, in part because the prices at which they are forced to trade their goods are seen as arbitrary and unfair, and in part because the rubles in which they are paid for their exports are worthless. If each republic were a sovereign state, such a situation would not exist. First, with sovereignty would come the possibilities for importing the monopolised goods from elsewhere or of engaging in import substitution. Prices would have to reflect realistic opportunities faced by these countries on world markets. Moreover, each country would have to either pay for its imports in a convertible currency or maintain the value of its currency in international trade in order to make it acceptable to its trading partners.[10] Many of the current obstacles to regional trade in the CIS would thus be overcome.

5.2   Optimal currency areas versus large markets

The pressure to retain a large and unified market on economic grounds must also be considered in the light of the theory of the optimal currency area. This theory points out that there are benefits to be had from subsuming as much of the market as possible under a common currency since a common currency lowers the transactions cost of exchanges and thus promotes trade and specialisation. Against this consideration one might weigh the fact that a common currency imposes on all its users a common basis or standard for competitiveness. That is to say, if in a country with a single currency there is a region where productivity is lower or costs of production are higher, then this region is likely to suffer unemployment because at the given currency standard it will not be competitive with the rest of the country unless wages are very flexible. The experience of German unification within the framework of a single currency is a clear example of this concept.

It is thus worth examining whether the CIS satisfied the requirements for an optimal currency area. First, there are very significant differences in the level of development and *per capita* income as well as in the distribution of natural resources among the CIS republics. If the CIS were to enter world markets as a single currency area, then its more industrialised regions might prove to be uncompetitive at an exchange rate that also took into account its huge oil exports. The consequence would be a form of 'Dutch disease', with massive unemployment in the industrialised regions. A similar consideration would apply to agriculture. If, however, each republic had its own currency and its own exchange rate, then that rate could be set so as to reflect the country's competitiveness *vis-à-vis* world markets. This might mean that, for example, the national currency of the Baltic states would decline relative to the current value of the ruble to reflect the general uncompetitiveness of the industries of the Baltic region, but the national currency of republics rich in natural resources might appreciate to reflect their strong export position. In any case, each republic could more easily maintain full employment and a balance between imports and exports through its own exchange rate policy.

5.3 Distribution of gains and losses

It should be evident that different republics will emerge from the process of creating independent states in different condition. Some, such as Russia, Ukraine and Khazakhstan, are sufficiently large that most of the benefits of a large internal market will be retained. Others, such as the Baltic states, are so small that they will have no choice but to become very open to international trade or to retain use of the ruble in some form of economic union with Russia. The creation of a number of nations with differing levels of development will also be a spur to the development of the region. Individual countries, by virtue of their policies and management of their economies, will become attractive havens for investment from abroad. Other countries, because of their low level of development, may become eligible for developmental assistance that would not be feasible or consistent with donor guidelines if it were to be directed toward the CIS as a whole.

It is worth noting that there is nothing that would prevent the creation of a regional market that would embrace several independent republics. Russia could become the focus of such a grouping for some small republics whose access to world markets might be limited. However, such trade, and the integration mechanism to support it, must be created after and not as part of the new system of nation-states that is emerging out of the CIS, and should be voluntary rather than imposed by fiat. In view of the difficulties and time it has taken the Community to achieve integration with smaller disparities in the incomes of member countries and with the benefit of functioning markets, and the fact that it has not yet become a single currency area, it is clear that to urge excessively ambitious integration measures on the newly-emerging successor states to the USSR may impose an impossible burden on their economic systems.

5.4   Short-term measures

Proposals to underpin intra-CIS trade by means of a PU are unrealistic in light of the monetary chaos that reigns within, not to mention among, the individual states. The fact that most of the CIS states have failed to remit hard currency to Vnestorgbank to meet the CIS's obligations to Western creditors, despite their having agreed to do so, suggests that efforts to formalise payments among all or many of the CIS republics would be nugatory. Moreover, efforts to create formal structures to underpin CIS trade may hamper the evolution of more informal and limited measures to maintain trade flows. Such less grandiose measures might include bilateral, rather than multilateral, agreements for facilitating barter trade (see Table 10.6), both among enterprises in different republics as well as between republics. Possibly a two-tier system of hard currency clearing for fuels and other goods with ready markets in the West could be supplemented with barter or soft currency trade in manufactured goods that cannot be exported to world markets. Given the differences in foreign trade objectives and progress in stabilisation and reform that are emerging in the region, each republic is likely to seek a different mix of market and non-market mediated trade with its neighbours. The opportunity for a diversity in trade arrangements rather than formal and multi-state trading and payments mechanisms are thus likely to be most suitable for helping intra-CIS trade to survive and for individual CIS members to restructure and reform their economies at a pace that they find acceptable.

NOTES

I am indebted to the American Council of Learned Societies and the RFE/RL Research Institute for support during the period in which this chapter was written. Comments by Alan Gelb, Gábor Oblath, Ben Slay, the editors and participants in seminars at the Czechoslovak Institute for Foreign Affairs, the Osteuropa Institut München and the Second Polish–US Roundtable are gratefully acknowledged.

 1 Viner (1950) viewed economic integration as being based on a calculus of gain, from trade creation due to lower intermember trade barriers, and loss, from trade diversion. The total increase in intra-member trade, the sum of trade creation and trade diversion, is often called 'gross trade creation' which, while easier to measure, provides only ambiguous information about the welfare effects of integration.
 2 Johnson (1965) argued that countries participated in economic integration schemes largely to promote a collective preference for objectives such as industrialisation.
 3 The official rate was about $1.50/transferable ruble; the commercial rate in 1988–9 ranged from $0.70–$0.66/transferable ruble.
 4 For details of trade regime liberalisation, see United Nations Economic Commission for Europe (1991). It is generally accepted that the Czecho-Slovak koruna is undervalued *vis-à-vis* the dollar, and the Polish zloty may also be undervalued.
 5 The evident increase in Czecho-Slovak exports to the USSR in 1991 is alleged to be a statistical aberration, although I have yet to see a convincing explanation for it.
 6 A case in point is that of Polish shipyards. In 1991 the Northern Shipyard in Gdansk built three warships for the USSR, worth $100 million. One was delivered but not paid for, another was seized by shipyard workers before it could be removed, and a third lies incomplete. In Szezecin, Soviet buyers simply failed to claim the vessels for which they had contracted (*Toronto Globe and Mail*, September 30 1991).
 7 Wang and Winters (1991) correctly point out that reported intra-CMEA trade may be biased upwards due to overvaluation of the transferable ruble. Nevertheless, since some of the observed decline in trade reflects the devaluation of the ruble, the actual to predicted ratios they show in their Table 5, are the correct objects of comparison.
 8 This section summarises, in part, suggestions I put forward in greater detail in Brada (1991).
 9 For example, Ukraine has signed an agreement to import oil from Iran. Previously, virtually all of Ukraine's oil came from Russia. Such an excessive dependence on oil suppliers makes little economic or political sense.
10 Thus Khazakhstan's decision to peg its currency to the Deutschemark, if sustainable, may do more to promote the republic's foreign trade than would measures to sustain trade on the basis of a ruble that is increasingly becoming worthless.

REFERENCES

Bergson, A. (1991) 'The USSR Before the Fall: How Poor and Why', *Journal of Economic Perspectives*, **5**(4) (Fall) pp. 29–44.

Biessen, G. (1991) 'Is the Impact of Central Planning on the Levels of Foreign Trade Really Negative?', *Journal of Comparative Economics*, **15**(1) (March).

Brabant, J. van (1991) 'A Central European Payments Union: Technical Aspects', Institute for East–West Security Studies, *Public Policy Paper*, **3**.

Brada, J.C. (1985) 'The Slowdown in Soviet and East European Economic Growth', *Osteuropa Wirtschaft*, **30**(2) (June) pp. 116–20.

(1988) 'Interpreting the Soviet Subsidization of East Europe', *International Organization*, **42**(4) (Autumn).

(1991) 'Ökonomische Kosten und Ökonomischer Nutzen des Zerfalls der UdSSR', *Aktuelle Analysen*, Bundesinstitut für ostwissenschaftliche und internationale Studien (5 September).

Brada, J.C. and A.E. King (1992) 'Is There a *J*-Curve for the Economic Transition from Socialism to Capitalism?', *Economics of Planning*, **25**(1) (1985).

Brada, J.C. and J.A. Mendez (1985) 'Economic Integration among Developed, Developing and Centrally Planned Economies: A Comparative Analysis', *Review of Economics and Statistics*, **67**(4) (November 1991).

Dobrowski, P. (1991) 'East European Trade, Part II: Creative East Bloc Solutions', *Report on Eastern Europe*, **41** (11 October).

Foreign Trade Research Institute (1991) 'Creating a Free Trade Area Czecho-Slovakia–Hungary–Poland: Consequences for the Polish Economy', (Warsaw).

(1992) 'Economic Cooperation among Poland, Czecho-Slovakia and Hungary' (Warsaw).

Havrylyshyn, O. and L. Pritchett (1991) 'Trade Patterns After the Transition', World Bank, *Working Paper*, Washington, DC: World Bank.

Havrylyshyn, O. and J. Williamson (1991) 'From Soviet disUnion to Eastern Economic Community?', Institute for International Economics, *Policy Analyses in International Economics*, **35**.

Hewett, E.A. (1976) 'A Gravity Model of CMEA Trade', in J.C. Brada (ed.), *Quantitative and Analytical Studies in East–West Economic Relations*, Bloomington, Indiana: International Development Research Center, Indiana University.

Hughes, G. and P. Hare (1991) 'Competitiveness and Industrial Restructuring in Czechoslovakia, Hungary and Poland', *European Community*, Special Edition, **2**.

Johnson, H.G. (1965) 'An Economic Theory of Protectionism, Tariff Bargaining, and the Formation of Customs Unions', *Journal of Political Economy*, **73**(3) (June) pp. 256–83.

Marrese, M. and J. Vanous (1983) *Soviet Subsidization of Trade With Eastern Europe – A Soviet Perspective*, Berkeley: Institute of International Studies, University of California.

(1988) 'The Content and Controversy of Soviet Trade Relations With Eastern Europe, 1970–1984', in J.C. Brada, A. Hewett and T.A. Wolf (eds), *Economic Adjustment and Reform in Eastern Europe and the Soviet Union: Essays in Honor of Franklyn D. Holzman*, Durham and London: Duke University Press.

Oblath, G. and D. Tarr (1992) 'The Terms-of-Trade Effects from the Elimination of State Trading in Soviet–Hungarian Trade', *Journal of Comparative Economics*, **16(1)** (March).

United Nations Economic Commission for Europe (UNECE) (1991) (*Reforms in Foreign Economic Relations of Eastern Europe and the Soviet Union*, New York: UNECE.

Viner, J. (1950) *The Customs Union Issue*, New York: Carnegie Endowment for International Peace.

Wang, Z.K. and L.A. Winters (1991) 'The Trading Potential of Eastern Europe', CEPR, *Discussion Paper*, **610** (November), London: Centre for Economic Policy Research.

Discussion

ALAN GELB

Brada has in Chapter 10 provided us with a comprehensive study. It covers East–West, West–East, East–East trade, and both disintegration and integration. It is also a pragmatic and quite sensible chapter, so that (unfortunately from the perspective of a discussant) I must admit to agreeing with a good deal of it, and to finding it very interesting. The basic thrust that CMEA was Vinerian trade-diverting (bad) but that it was viewed in Johnsonian (strategic) terms is surely right. Indeed, it would be hard to find a better example of an 'immizerising empire' than the Russian, with its several layers of subsidies emanating from the core – to energy-poor Soviet states, to still poorer CMEA partners (Mongolia, Cuba and North Korea) and to client developing countries. The distributional effect of these subsidies was superimposed on the systemic inefficiencies characteristic of the Soviet System. A few participants, e.g., Mongolia, may have gained in net terms; Russia – and certainly the East European countries because of their previously developed economies – lost.

Brada is also surely right in concluding that the fall in CMEA trade resulted mostly from the illiquidity and collapse of the Soviet economy rather than simply the end of the CMEA trading system. But then this also implies that, despite the trade-diverting nature of the CMEA, the fall in trade does not necessarily show that the CMEA partners were unable to supply the goods needed by the ex-USSR – given the long-standing problem of dependency created in the CMEA. The gravity model exercises cited by Brada assume marketing and distribution systems well-adapted to 'market' trade patterns, not the specific institutions (e.g., service networks designed for Hungarian buses across the USSR) that existed in 1989. The immediate question is how fast, rather than ultimately how far, intra-CMEA trade 'should' decline. I could believe the gravity models, while at the same time being very concerned at the extent of trade disruption in 1990–2. Brada's chapter is therefore, in my view, too sanguine on the speed of the trade collapse.

Turning now to the CIS, a recent gravity model exercise carried out for the Institute of International Economics suggested that 'normal' trading patterns would show far lower intra-CIS trade levels and greater trade for the CIS as a whole with the rest of the world (with the increase being about equivalent to another Canada in the global trading system). Like Brada's analysis of the CMEA, this suggests relative lack of concern at the sharp fall in inter-CIS–state trade, and no need to institute special mechanisms in an attempt to sustain such trade. While agreeing that the optimal long-run levels of intra-CIS–state trade are surely lower than the ones produced by the old system, we should not be too complacent in the face of a sharp trade collapse. And there may also be good arguments for considering mechanisms temporarily to cushion a sharp fall in intra-CIS trade.

On the first point, there is certainly a constraint on the speed of economic restructuring. Fuzzy though the limit may be, it reflects the social and political constraints to rapid change which, the experience of Eastern Europe suggests, have to be taken seriously. Trade policy is one of several mechanisms for reducing market pressures for restructuring; it may not be attractive, but neither may be the other methods. One can readily imagine scenarios associated with an immediate increase in energy levels to border prices, for example, that would lead to sharp contractions outside the Russian Federation which in turn could impact adversely on Russian industry.

On the second point, measures to sustain trade between the CIS states which are undertaken in a market framework do not necessarily imply a return to the old planned system. For example, if full convertibility is not immediately possible then a currency union-type arrangement, if instituted along lines that have been proposed, would indeed create some preference for intra-CIS trade. But is this such a bad thing relative to the possible alternatives? Certainly it is far from central planning.

I therefore think that Chapter 10 does not adequately address the transit process. We know the starting point and something about the goal in terms of trade and economic restructuring. Is the shortest path always that at the least cost? And even if so, is it politically sustainable?

GÁBOR OBLATH

I consider Josef Brada's excellent Chapter 10 one of the first serious and relevant attempts to interpret the 'post-CMEA condition' and recent changes in trade among east European countries. The analysis is factual, pragmatic and empirically relevant. The strength of Brada's chapter stems from the focus on actual facts and from the attempt to avoid premature judgements and recommendations.

As I understand it, one of the main messages of the chapter is that the task of the West is to draw the countries of this region closer to itself, assisting them in integrating into the multilateral trading system and the European Community, rather than pushing them artificially to re-establish their former ties within the region. Since I basically agree with this conclusion, I should like to treat some current issues on which I have slight disagreements with Brada, elaborate on certain topics raised by him, and add a few further points that may be relevant in the context.

My only objection to Brada's analysis of current problems and prospects of post-CMEA cooperation is related to the lack of a clear distinction among three interrelated, but different, issues and concepts: what is (un)desirable, what is (un)necessary and what is (in)feasible in the short run.

Although trade among CMEA countries was inefficient and there was 'overtrading' among them, I would be reluctant to claim that the sharp fall of intra-regional trade observed in 1991 was desirable either on efficiency grounds, or because it resulted in some sort of a 'normal level' of trade implied by gravity models. Moreover, I see no reason to question that the collapse of intra-regional trade *caused* a substantial drop of production in ex-CMEA countries both directly and indirectly (through the negative multiplier effects of the export decline). However, the chain of causation also ran the other way around, i.e., some of the trade decline is due to the drop in production, and it is certainly not easy to determine the exact magnitude of the output fall resulting from the decline of trade among East European countries. While I do not question the desirability of getting rid of the artificial and distorting elements of the CMEA, for the short run I would favour temporary solutions to slow down the trade decline and to bridge the liquidity problems, *if* any of the temporary arrangements that have been proposed really are feasible.

The point, however, is that where these solutions would be desirable –

i.e., trade between the small Central and Eastern European countries on the one hand and the CIS on the other – they are not feasible, and where feasible they are simply unnecessary. But before explaining this point, I should like to elaborate on the reasons of the trade decline – amounting to more than 50 percent in volume terms – among ex-CMEA countries.

In 1991 at least five distinct factors were at work:

(a)   the economic collapse of the USSR, resulting in short supplies of traditional exports – energy and raw materials – to other East European countries;

(b)   the decline of production in the smaller East European countries as a result of the stabilisation-cum-liberalisation programmes;

(c)   the radical trade liberalisation towards the West in several countries of the region;

(d)   the switch-over from ruble to dollar payments in the trade among countries of the region, leading both to radical changes in relative prices and to liquidity and trade-financing problems for some countries;

(e)   the introduction of customs duties on imports from former CMEA partner countries.

Since (a) and (b) above are self-explanatory, I shall discuss only points (c), (d), and (e).

Trade liberalisation towards the West implied that former importers of ex-CMEA products could turn to Western suppliers. Since the domestic prices of imports from the East increased as a result of the switch-over to dollar payments and the implementation of tariffs among ex-CMEA countries, imports from the West, taking into account the quality differences, tended to be lower-priced than imports from the East. This, in turn, led to a very rapid reversal of the 'trade diversion' discussed in Brada's chapter. But it should be noted that liberalisation of imports contributed not only to the decline of trade within the region, but also to the significant increase of the smaller East European countries' exports to the West.

However, the trade-reducing effects of the switch-over to dollar payments are only partly due to the associated changes in absolute and relative prices; these also stem from liquidity problems of some of the countries concerned, most importantly those of the USSR. The latter consideration drove several observers to recommend some kind of a payments union (PU) for the region. However, as Brada points out by referring to the experience of India (with which the USSR maintained the clearing-currency payments arrangement), given the unwillingness of (ex-)USSR exporters to sell energy and raw materials for any kind of clearing currency, and the propensity of the republics' importers to buy as much as possible in exchange for clearing currency, there is a built-in tendency in such arrangements to accumulate (further) unredeemable claims on the ex-Soviet republics. It is worth mentioning that according to Hungary's experience from 1989 and 1990 (the last two years of ruble trading) political economy considerations also indicate that clearing arrangements should be avoided with partners who cannot, or do not wish to, maintain the balance of trade within the preagreed limits. In such circumstances, the government of the country running an (unredeemable) trade surplus has to restrict its own exports. However, this may turn out to be extremely difficult if pressure groups have vested interests in sustaining exports in the clearing currency. These difficulties are aggravated if the restrictions on exports cause a production decline and increase unemployment.

To sum up: although a case could be made for the temporary mitigation of the negative shock on the output and employment of the smaller ex-CMEA countries deriving from abandoning the ruble payments system, transitional arrangements based on a PU with the republics of the ex-USSR are simply not feasible. Among the more advanced Central and East European countries (Czecho-Slovakia, Hungary, and Poland), a PU would be feasible, but unnecessary.

Finally, let us take a brief look at the proposal for a free-trade area (FTA) within the region. It should be clear from the foregoing that for the time being free trade is relevant only for the three marketised countries. However, present trends in East and Central Europe indicate increasing protectionism within the region.

While there is a political determination to establish an FTA, actual commercial policies do not support this endeavour. Recently, non-tariff barriers (NTBs) have been erected among these countries and there is a danger that while tariffs are eliminated, new quantitative restrictions might more than compensate for the removal of customs duties. Therefore, the movement towards an 'FTA' should be based on policies aiming at getting rid of other barriers to mutual trade as well.

As a final point, I should emphasise that the prospects for the growth of trade within the ex-CMEA region are rather dim. It is through integration into the multilateral trading system and the European Community that these countries may hope to expand trade among each other. This is very well understood and documented by Josef Brada; that is one of the main reasons why I consider his chapter outstanding in the current literature on trade and transition in Eastern Europe.

11 Regional trade arrangements in North America: CUSTA and NAFTA

JOHN WHALLEY

1 Introduction

Since the mid-1980s, both the profile of and the depth of the debate over regional trade arrangements in North America have grown, first with the 1988 Canada–US Free-Trade Agreement (CUSTA), and subsequently with negotiations in the early 1990s between Mexico, Canada and the United States aimed at achieving a three-country North American Free-Trade Agreement (NAFTA).[1] Recently, debate has intensified even further following a wave of proposed Latin and Central American trade arrangements whose objective, in part, is eventually to facilitate an even wider Western Hemispheric Trade Arrangement (WHFTA).[2] These developments are, however, only part of a global trend towards more extensive regional arrangements in the trading system in the 1990s.[3] In Europe it is manifest in the 'Europe 1992' programme, the EC–EFTA pact and other developments; and in Asia it strengthened ASEAN arrangements (AFTA),[4] Australia–New Zealand agreements,[5] and new Japanese regional arrangements.[6]

As elsewhere, the new regional arrangements in North America are driven by a number of factors. A key one is the search for safe-haven trade agreements by smaller countries who now, more than ever before, wish to secure access to the markets of large neighbouring trading partners because of the fear of higher trade barriers in the future. Another is both the frustration felt by larger countries with progress toward new multilateral liberalisation, and their belief that threatening to negotiate, or actually negotiating, regional arrangements on their part may force other reluctant larger powers to make concessions multilaterally. A third is the fact that trade growth between neighbouring countries continues to exceed that of the global economy overall, and that as a result regional trade arrangements are now viewed positively as facilitating growth in the most dynamic portion of world trade.[7] The result has been that earlier

352

regional arrangements already in the trading system have broadened and expanded in coverage over the last five or so years, generating lively debate. Concerns have been raised about regional fragmentation in the trading system on one hand (Bhagwati, 1990), while on the other the new regionalism has been defended as fundamentally trade-creating, and even a potential source of a degree of dynamism in a trading system faced with a frustrated multilateralism (Krugman, 1991a, 1991b).

In this chapter, I discuss the North American regional arrangements, CUSTA and NAFTA, in the context both of these concerns and of the claims made for the new regionalism.[8] The argument I advance is that CUSTA and NAFTA will be likely to prove less important for North American trade and investment flows than is widely thought to be the case, because under these arrangements most existing sectoral protection will remain in place and other liberalisation (largely tariff-based) which will stem from them may not be of an order of magnitude to make a large impact. Instead, it is the exclusionary elements in these agreements against third-country suppliers of inputs and investors in such sectors as autos and apparel, operating through rules of origin, content requirements and other devices, that seem to be a more serious source of concern than the more conventionally debated questions of trade diversion stemming from preferential trade measures at the border.

The chapter makes three main points. The first emphasises the contrast the two agreements represent in terms of their projected and actual impacts on cross-border trade and investment flows. The Canada–US agreement was negotiated against a background of academic studies and government claims showing large trade and welfare gains to follow from its implementation. In the three years since its implementation, growth in Canada–US trade has slowed, claimed increases in net inward foreign investment have not increased to the degree expected, and the agreement has become politically mired in alleged job losses and out-of-country plant relocations. In contrast, even before successful negotiation of a NAFTA, US–Mexico trade had approximately doubled over the last five years, and net inward foreign investment had sharply increased.[9] Strong performance on the trade and investment fronts has thus come across the border without a bilateral agreement rather than across the border with one.

The second point is that, as noted above, the substance of current and prospective North American trade arrangements does not yet seem considerable enough to justify many of the concerns which have been expressed thus far as to their potential adverse effects, both on the system and on excluded countries (in particular, on developing countries). But, equally, attributing either major improvements in economic performance or costly macro adjustments to these agreements seems unfounded. Rather, it is the change in emphasis and the direction of evolution of the system these agreements represent which is the concern, more so than their substance *per se*.

The third point concerns the potential impacts on developing countries. Because the direct effects on trade and investment flows from these arrangements seem small, the impacts of discriminatory reductions in formal trade barriers, and hence concerns over classical trade diversion, seem relatively minor.[10] On the other hand, the danger of entrapment into safe-haven-motivated regional arrangements which contain adverse third-country exclusionary elements may prove to be a more major concern for other countries who would seek to follow the CUSTA/NAFTA route.

One example is the risk in the autos sector that the NAFTA arrangements represent for Mexico: that is, that their effect could be to maintain or create impediments towards inward foreign investment from third countries (Japan) into Mexico for export production, and also to exclude from Mexican markets Japanese transplant production originating in the United States. Another is the pressure from large-country textile producer interests to liberalise in apparel in such ways as to lock the safe-haven-seeking lower-income country into higher cost input supplies (fibres and cloth) from the larger country through complex rules of origin. To the extent that these agreements contain such provisions, they may in the long run pose more of a problem for these developing countries who subsequently attempt to join them than for those who remain outside, insofar as hoped-for benefits are partially (or even wholly) dissipated by exclusionary provisions linked to any new access granted.

2   The substance of the new North American regionalism

2.1   The Canada–US Free-Trade Agreement (CUSTA)

CUSTA, the 1988 Canada–US Free-Trade Agreement (CUSTA) contains twenty-one articles, spans a wide range of issues, and is longer than the General Agreement on Tariffs and Trade (the GATT). It contains a bilaterally agreed elimination of tariffs over ten years[11] (with special arrangements for apparel[12]), a new set of procedures for resolving bilateral disputes concerning countervailing duties (CVD) and anti-dumping duties (ADs), and a series of arrangements and disciplines covering sectoral and other matters (agriculture, energy, autos, investment, services, wine and spirits, procurement, and others).

Despite its length and broad coverage, it is not a trade agreement that is likely to change US–Canada trade flows dramatically, since prior to the agreement trade between Canada and the United States was already largely duty-free or at low duty, and trade barriers in key sectoral areas such as textiles, steel, agriculture, and energy remained largely untouched by the agreement. Before the agreement, the average tariff on Canadian exports to the United States was approximately 1 percent, and nearly 80 percent of Canadian trade with the United States was already duty-free.[13] And while there had been growth in the use of contingent trade measures such as ADs and CVDs, and disciplining these became the major negotiating objective for Canada, their coverage of trade was relatively small.[14]

Chapter I sets out Scopes and Objectives, and Chapter II provides General Definitions. Chapter III lays out rules of origin, rules which may now become even more important in any eventual trilateral arrangement with Mexico. Chapter IV details how various border measures, including tariffs, duty waivers and drawbacks, are to work bilaterally. Article 401 sets out the bilaterally agreed tariff elimination.

Chapter V contains a reaffirmation of the principle of national treatment to bilateral Canada–US trade. Chapter VI discusses technical standards, with most issues in this area being left to an ongoing five- to seven-year negotiation process to follow the 1988 agreement. Chapter VII is a long chapter on agriculture, containing complex formulae but little of substance in terms of new bilateral liberalisation. Chapter VIII covers wine and distilled spirits, primarily setting out disciplines on various domestic arrangements in Canada. Chapter IX (energy) places limits on the use of domestic pricing policies in Canada, and also details security of supply arrangements with a right of first refusal for the United States at the world price on specified amounts of energy in the event of supply shortages.

Chapter X covers trade in autos, grandfathering in arrangements concluded under the 1965 US–Canada Auto Pact, but importantly also tightening earlier domestic content requirements, so that on a comparable basis the early 50 percent Auto Pact rule increases significantly.[15] Chapter XI covers emergency actions, including special bilateral exceptions for any safeguard actions taken under Article XIX of GATT. Chapter XII details limited exceptions for trade in goods from the arrangements in other chapters. Chapter XIII contains provisions relating to government procurement, but importantly does not cover state and provincial governments on the two sides of the border. Chapter XIV on services contains few substantive provisions, grandfathering in all existing service arrangements in both countries, and promising that most favoured nation (MFN) treatment will apply to new service provisions, while at the same time exempting most of the important sectors from even these future arrangements.[16]

Chapter XV covers temporary entry for business persons, with Chapter XVI on investment raising the transaction limit beyond which the screening provisions of Investment Canada are permitted to apply. Chapter XVII contains changes in financial services arrangements on the two sides of the border, covering regulations affecting foreign branch operations, with some changes in cross-border rules on reserves. Chapter XVIII details the institutional provisions of the agreement, including a dispute settlement procedure covering the agreement itself, which operates much like the GATT with panels, a conciliation process, and eventually (if necessary) permitted withdrawals of concessions.[17] Chapter XIX contains new temporary binational dispute settlement provisions covering two areas of ADs and CVDs, pending further agreement on these from a five- to seven-year negotiation process to follow the 1988 agreement. A separate dispute settlement and panel procedure is set out for conflicts over the use of these actions, different from and beyond that contained in Chapter XVIII of the agreement. Chapter XX covers residual provisions and Chapter XXI details various operational provisions, including entry into force, annexes, and other matters.

Thus, beyond a phased bilateral elimination of tariffs, the agreement contains four main sets of provisions. First are new disciplines on (largely Canadian) domestic policies, particularly in the areas of energy and investment, and to a far less reaching extent (in terms of quantitative importance) wines and spirits. Second come two dispute settlement Chapters XVIII and XIX, the latter reflecting the Canadian objective of achieving some new disciplines of US ADs and CVDs. Third come key sectoral Chapters: agriculture and autos. And finally, the agreement contains what, for want of a better term, I would call empty Chapters. These are long and complex Chapters with seemingly little of substance; in this category I would place services, agriculture and procurement.

2.2   The North American Free-Trade Area (NAFTA)[18]

Achieving a North American Free-Trade Agreement (NAFTA) is the current objective of US, Canadian and Mexican trilateral trade negotiations which have been initiated since the conclusion of CUSTA.[19] In the spring of 1991, Congress granted the executive branch negotiating authority for trade negotiations with Mexico, which were trilateralised to include Canada. Negotiations are now in mid-course, with substantial speculation in recent months as to how and when they will conclude.[20]

While in some ways considerably different, these nonetheless have parallels to the Canada–US negotiations which preceded them. The negotiations have largely been driven by the Mexican desire to achieve a trade agreement with the United States following their own unilateral liberalisation begun in 1985, and their entry into GATT in 1986. Mexican objectives seem to reflect their desire to achieve improved and more secure access to the US market to spur growth, their desire to use a trade agreement to underpin domestic policy reform so as to attract inward foreign investment, and their aim of using international treaties as a way of locking in prior domestic policy reforms. A two-track procedure has been used in the negotiations thus far, separating out wider social issues such as environment and workers' rights from more traditional trade issues.[21]

The three-way participation in the negotiation, and the prior existence of CUSTA, both complicate and aid the negotiations. Canada, for instance, seemingly participates with both the defensive interest of protecting and preserving what is seen as beneficial in CUSTA, and the offensive interest of seeking to open up portions of CUSTA whose outcome was not thought satisfactory. Canada also participates so as to be at the table and be clearly informed of what is happening. But Canadian participation is politically important in Mexico, so that Mexican negotiators are not seen to be alone at the table with a large assertive power who could dictate the terms of an agreement.

Having CUSTA as a prior negotiated agreement has given initial focus to the negotiations, since an early question was whether, and how, CUSTA could be trilateralised. However, it quickly became apparent that some of the key Chapters of CUSTA were designed to deal with Canada–US issues which had no Mexican analogue (the wine and spirits Chapter, for instance), while some of the key issues to be discussed with Mexico (environment, labour mobility) had no obvious analogues in CUSTA. Instead, the discussion now is how CUSTA and a NAFTA will coexist – as a core three-way agreement and with separate additional two-country agreements which replace CUSTA, or as a supplementary agreement beyond what is in CUSTA – and with what institutional form (a trilateral trade commission, for instance).

Table 11.1 lists the working groups for the negotiations. These are structured differently from the Canada–US negotiation, with eighteen groups classified under six topic headings. In the conventional trade areas (such as tariffs, agriculture, autos, textiles, ADs and CVDs), it seems likely that negotiations will take similar directions to the CUSTA negotiations, with bilateral tariff liberalisation,[22] and separate sectoral, instrument, and institutional Chapters. Mexico is seeking a quick phase-in of any agreed liberalisation, while the United States is reportedly seeking a fifteen year phase-in.[23]

Autos, textiles, agriculture, and petrochemicals are the sectors where

Table 11.1. *Negotiating groups in the NAFTA negotiations*

---

1 Market access
   (i)   tariffs/non-tarrif barriers
   (ii) rules of origin
   (iii) government procurement
   (iv) agriculture
   (v) autos
   (vi) other industries: textiles, energy

2 Trade rules
   (i)   safeguards
   (ii) subsidies/trade remedies
   (iii) standards – industrial
               – food safety

3 Services
   (i)   principles
   (ii) financial
   (iii) insurance
   (iv) land transportation
   (v) telecommunications
   (vi) other services

4 Investment

5 Intellectual property

6 Dispute settlement

Source: Conversations with Department of External Affairs, Government of Canada, Ottawa (September 1991).

negotiations seem to have been the most intense. Textiles and apparel producers and labour groups have all voiced concerns over threats to their domestic market share from low-wage imports, and fears of Japanese transplant auto production also penetrating US markets from Mexico pervade the US autos sector.

In the tariff and sector negotiations, rules of origin have become a high profile issue. In the automobile sector, requests have already been made by the US auto manufacturers for even higher content provisions than in CUSTA, which if enacted would probably exclude much of the US transplant and Canadian-based production from the Mexican market, and effectively place restrictions on transshipment through Mexico.[24] US auto makers also seem to endorse the maintenance of even stronger domestic content rules in Mexico against third countries which would effectively limit intercontinental auto trade from Mexico, especially from any new Asian transplant operations in Mexico using parts produced outside Mexico. In the textile area, there are US industry proposals that any bilateral tariff and/or quota liberalisation should be subject to stringent rules of origin, with a 100 percent NAFTA content rule applying for each of the fibres, the fabric containing the fibres, and the location of production of garments.[25]

In agriculture, each country has expressed concerns over liberalisation in sensitive products: corn in Mexico, and fruit and vegetables in the United States. The dilemma for Mexico seems to be that to deal with access problems facing the modern horticulture sector potentially large adjustments would need to be undertaken in the traditional component of the sector.[26] Two US industry groups (citrus and tomatoes) have already gone so far as publicly to state their position that these sectors should be off the negotiating table.[27]

Social and non-trade issues have also entered the NAFTA negotiations, a major departure relative to CUSTA. The key areas are environment, workers' rights, drug enforcement, and labour mobility. In the environment area,[28] it has been the concerns of environmental groups in the United States which have propelled the process. They have documented cross-border environmental problems associated with *Maquiladora*[29] production, such as ground water contamination, effluent discharge into border rivers, a high incidence of hepatitis and other diseases in US border towns, and other problems.[30]

Their fear is that increased US–Mexico trade resulting from NAFTA will worsen these problems, and they seek strengthened Mexican environmental standards. But more than this, they seek stronger enforcement of Mexican environmental regulations, perhaps involving some form of new trilateral environmental commission and, if necessary, cross-border inspections. They fear that a cross-border trade agreement could result in a lowering of US environmental standards in some areas, as some claim threatens to happen under CUSTA, notably in the areas of asbestos and pesticide use.[31] These groups also want environmental impact statements to be prepared in the United States to accompany any eventual NAFTA agreement.

Environmental issues in NAFTA have been further elevated by the US use of trade restrictions against tuna imports from Mexico on environmental grounds. A 1991 GATT dispute panel ruled in favour of Mexico and against US import bans required by the 1988 Marine Mammal Protection Act because of allegedly dolphin-unfriendly tuna fishing methods used by Mexican fishermen. While not formally a NAFTA issue, this has made activist NAFTA negotiations in the environmental area seem even more important to those involved in the United States (especially in Congress), while on the other hand elevating concerns outside the United States (including Mexico) over US extra-territoriality.

Linkage between workers' rights and trade in the NAFTA negotiations has focused on alleged production for export in Mexico by child labour, long a concern of advocates of international labour standards in the United States.[32] Drug enforcement issues have come up in the context of proposals linking trade concessions by the United States to agreement by Mexico to allow stronger cross-border enforcement. Labour mobility has been an issue pressed strongly by Mexico, arguing for liberalisation of immigration restrictions against both Mexican permanent and temporary residents in the United States. Mexican negotiators have posed the choice for the United States as being one of either taking more Mexican goods, or suffering more illegal Mexican immigration.

Other regional agreements in Central and Latin America, either currently under discussion or active negotiation, potentially further complicate the NAFTA process since enforcement of rules of origin to prevent transshipment becomes that much more important, as do the issues surrounding eventual third-country accession.[33] The recent Chile–Mexico bilateral agreement is one example, with bilateral elimination of most tariffs and import licences over five years, and a joint reaffirmation of GATT commitments.[34] A similar structure seems likely to result for a bilateral agreement between Venezuela and Mexico. ALADI, an existing agreement from the 1960s, binds Latin and Central American countries not to negotiate discriminatory trade arrangements unless the benefits are extended to all countries in the region, although this agreement has no enforcement mechanism. In addition, other wider developments in the region potentially impinge on the NAFTA negotiations: the Enterprise for the Americas Initiative (EAI) announced by the United States in 1991,[35] which envisages framework negotiations with a number of Latin American countries; the MERCOSUR (Argentina, Brazil, Paraguay, and Uruguay) Common Market Pact of 1990; and the revival of negotiations within the Andean Pact and the Central American Common Market (CACM) (see Chapter 9 above).[36]

In sum, while different from CUSTA in many key respects and while still under negotiation, if concluded, NAFTA seems likely to reflect a similar structure of a bilateral tariff elimination and accompanying sectoral and instrument arrangements. It will probably be less an FTA than a trade agreement, with key sectoral protection left in place or rearranged, and with supplementary agreements covering social issues whose consequences will likely be difficult to evaluate.

3 Assessing the impacts of CUSTA and NAFTA

A variety of effects have been attributed by various authors to either the negotiation or the conclusion of CUSTA and/or NAFTA. These can be grouped under a number of different headings: impacts on trade flows, sectoral impacts (production, adjustment consequences, rationalisation effects),[37] effects on investment flows and associated capital relocation across national borders, domestic labour market and other adjustments, effects on third countries, and long-run welfare effects.[38] While CUSTA has been in operation for only three years, in contrast to NAFTA which is still being negotiated, there are already discernible trends in cross-border trade and investment flows. One can also claim some expectational effects on capital flows following the intiation of NAFTA negotiations.

Somewhat interestingly, the effects that are now being attributed to CUSTA stand in contrast both to the predictions which were made before its negotiation and to the emerging trends in US–Mexico trade and investment even before a conclusion to NAFTA negotiations. Growth rates in Canada–US trade have been lower since CUSTA came into effect, while US–Mexico trade has grown sharply. And inward foreign investment into Mexico has grown sharply, while concerns over de-industrialisation and plant relocation dominate the debate in Canada. Thus, while it may seem paradoxical, lowered trade growth has occurred across the border where trade negotiations have been completed and formal barrier reductions implemented, while elevated growth in trade and foreign investment has occurred across the border where a negotiation is yet to be concluded.

Slowed growth in trade flows between Canada and the United States since the implementation of CUSTA also stands in contrast to some of the strong claims made in Canada before the agreement was concluded. Several studies[39] going back thirty or more years have consistently suggested that significant positive improvements in trade and Canadian welfare would result from free trade with the United States, and that large rationalisation gains in Canadian manufacturing would also follow. Perhaps the most influential of these at the time the agreement was being negotiated was a general equilibrium model-based analysis of the then prospective agreement by Harris (1984), which showed annual real income gains of the order of 9 percent to Canada, an estimate consistent with the earlier and influential calculation by Wonnacott and Wonnacott (1967).[40] Large Canadian export growth to the United States (post-Agreement) of around 90 percent also occurred in their results, with the biggest effect occurring in trade in manufactures. Strikingly, in their analysis, the effect of CUSTA on Canada was to expand rather than to contract previously protected Canadian manufacturing industries by allowing exploitation of economies of scale following the removal of barriers to Canadian exports in United States' markets. Rationalisation and scale economy gains (with nearly 50 percent of firms in Canada disappearing in the Harris–Cox simulations)[41] more than outweighed negative effects for Canadian manufacturing from the removal of protection in Canadian markets. Along with the size of the estimated gains this was a significant argument in convincing a majority of decisionmakers (and eventually Canadian voters in a general election) that endorsing the 1988 Trade Agreement was the way to proceed.

As the document surveying studies of the potential economic impacts of CUSTA produced by the Federal Department of Finance in Canada (1988) indicates, studies surveyed at this time showed a range of long-run annual real income gains to Canada from CUSTA from 0.7–8.9 percent of GNP from general equilibrium models, and around 3 percent from macro models due to productivity and other effects. Gains to the United States, while not reported here, were typically considerably smaller in percentage terms, although still positive.

Table 11.2, however, suggests that these large welfare gains and trade increases have yet to materialise. Canadian exports to the United States in 1990 increased only slightly from 1989 levels (in real terms), and the growth rate of exports post-agreement is below that of the pre-agreement period. Inward foreign investment into Canada from the United States in 1990 in real terms remained below that of 1987 (although not from third countries, see below). Job losses attributed in Canada to the agreement are as high as 250,000.[42]

In defence of the earlier studies which predicted large Canadian gains from a CUSTA, it can be claimed that seemingly anaemic trade and investment performance immediately following the implementation of CUSTA should not be that surprising. The tariff cuts in the agreement are to be implemented over a ten-year period, and hence it is probably still too early to see large positive effects. Furthermore, the recession, high Canadian interest rates, and a strong Canadian dollar have all probably had a larger effect in the shorter term on Canadian trade and investment economic performance than the reduction in trade barriers. However, at the same time earlier model-based analyses of gains from CUSTA may have overestimated the gains, perhaps in part because the reference point chosen was free trade (which CUSTA clearly does not achieve), the barrier reductions assumed were too large,[43] and short-term adjustment costs were not included.

As emphasised above, CUSTA has generated little new liberalisation in

Table 11.2. *US–Canadian trade and investment flows before and after CUSTA, $billion, selected years*

Year	Constant (1985) $ value of Canadian exports to the United States	Constant (1985) $ value of direct investment in Canada from the United States
1975	36.60	51.21
1979	46.86	53.50
1982	45.43	52.70
1985	59.79	59.19
1987	59.81	60.83
1989	67.62	57.56
1990	67.63	60.08
Implied annual percentage growth rates		
1975–87	4.2	1.4
1982–7	5.7	2.9
1987–90	4.1	−0.4

Sources: GATT (1978) Table B: GATT (1982) Table A20; GATT (1986) Table A7; GATT (1988) Table AB7; GATT (1990) Table A7; Statistics Canada (1988) Table 19; Statistics Canada (1990) Table 9; Statistics Canada (1991) Table 10 and p. 15; US Department of Commerce (1991) p. S17.

sectors where liberalisation had previously resisted multilateral GATT disciplines, in particular, in agriculture, textiles/apparel, and steel. Hence the claim that CUSTA is less an FTA than a trade agreement. These sectors seem likely to continue to remain relatively immune to any major direct impact from CUSTA, although at the same time, this immunisation causes problems elsewhere. One example is food processing, with processors in Canada caught between high input costs from protected agricultural inputs, and lower prices for processed products in a more integrated North American market. This has caused a number of food processors to re-examine their strategy, and for those located in Canada to think more in terms of a North American than a Canadian production strategy. Moves towards rationalisation (reducing the number of plants and range of products, but producing larger volumes in remaining plants) have been prominent in this sector.[44]

Effects on the auto and parts sector have also been a topic of discussion in Canada since autos and parts are such a large part of Canada–US manufactures trade. In 1989, exports of manufactures accounted for 70 percent of Canadian exports to the United States, and of this around 50 percent were in autos and parts.[45] In turn, over 60 percent of Canadian exports of manufactures come from Ontario.[46] But while major changes continue to occur in the North American auto industry, they are driven largely by developments outside of the agreement because the earlier arrangements negotiated under the 1965 US–Canada Auto Pact are similar to those in CUSTA. The most important changes tighten the content definition for duty-free trade in autos and parts,[47] and schedulise qualifying plants (preventing successive third-country investment for export under the rules). But growing Japanese transplant production in the United States is taking an ever larger US market share, and is now adversely affecting North American producers whose operations straddle the Canadian and US borders. This, in turn, has hurt the operations of assembly and production plants located in Canada, where concerns over further possible plants closures and relocation to the United States related to Japanese production and trade are strongly argued as the main issues rather than CUSTA-related concerns.

While inward foreign investment from the United States into Canada since CUSTA has been flat, as Table 11.3 indicates, investment from third countries increased significantly between 1987 and 1990. At the time it was negotiated, the claim was made by some Canadian government officials that because CUSTA would provide secure access to the United States market it, in turn, would act as an inducement for new inward foreign investment to Canada from outside the United States (mainly from Japan). It was argued that this would offset the potentially negative effects of US inward investment which had previously come into Canada to produce for the Canadian market behind the Canadian tariff returning to the United States in a free trade environment.

But despite this seemingly occurring, concerns over de-industrialisation and resulting adjustment costs continue to intensify, with claims from the labour groups in Canada of large job losses directly attributable to the trade agreement, especially in Ontario. Concerns in Canada over these adjustment costs stand in sharp contrast to the perception in Mexico that significant job gains in manufacturing will follow from NAFTA due to increases in trade and inward investment flows with the United States.

Assessing the effect of NAFTA on trade and investment flows presents a different problem: namely, that US–Mexican trade growth was so rapid even before an agreement was concluded that other factors (domestic policy reform in Mexico, and elevated Mexican growth rates) seem to dominate what may be the direct effects of a future agreement. Promoters of the agreement can, however, plausibly argue that it has been the prospect of an agreement and its impact on expectations that has helped propel the growth in inward investment that has occurred, particularly

Table 11.3. *Direct investment in Canada from third countries before and after CUSTA, $billion, current and constant prices, selected years*

	Total		From United States		From third countries	
	Current prices	Constant (1985) prices	Current prices	Constant (1985) prices	Current prices	Constant (1985) prices
1985	83.0	74.4	66.0	59.2	17.0	15.2
1987	101.0	85.7	71.6	60.8	29.4	24.9
1990	126.0	95.8	79.0	60.1	47.0	35.7

Sources: Statistics Canada (1988) Table 19, p. 64; Statistics Canada (1990) pp. 15, 17; Statistics Canada (1991) p. 15.

that reflected in the sharp increase following the granting of negotiating authority by the US Congress in 1991.

As Table 11.4 indicates, US–Mexico trade approximately doubled over 1985–90. While it is true that there were some key policy changes affecting trade between the United States and Mexico during these years, such as the effective doubling of major Mexican textile quotas, the fact remains that US–Mexico trade flows have been increasing sharply even before the conclusion of a NAFTA. Much of this growth in trade has come from the *Maquiladoras*,[48] driven in large part by sizeable differences in labour costs between the United States and Mexico, the new-found credibility associated with policy reform in Mexico, and the perceived stability of the wider policy environment. Growth in trade in autos and parts was seen first with engine and parts production and assembly plants locating in the *Maquiladoras*, and more recently with full production facilities. This trade has continued to grow rapidly despite surging Japanese transplant production in the United States, and also despite CUSTA and the absence of a firm trade agreement with Mexico. Trade in consumer electronics from *Maquiladora* assembly operations has also begun to surge, as have exports of apparel (entering the United States under HTS item 9802.00.80[49]).

As with cross-border trade flows, the investment situation could hardly be more different across the two borders. US inward foreign investment into Mexico has sharply increased, particularly in 1990–1. Investment flows in 1992 into Mexico from the United States were approximately 50 percent higher than they were in 1990. In contrast, investment flows from the United States to Canada are flat, and growth rates are down. Concerns over capital flight have become especially dominant in recent

Table 11.4. *US–Mexico trade flows, $ billion, current prices, selected years*

	US imports from Mexico		US exports to Mexico	
	Total	Of which automotive products	Total	Of which automotive products
1980	12.8	0.3	15.1	1.5
1985	19.4	2.8	13.6	2.0
1990	30.2	3.3 (1989)	28.4	2.3 (1989)

Sources: GATT (1990) Tables III.14, and III.15, p. 13; US Department of Commerce (1988) Table 19, p. 113; US Department of Commerce (1991) p. S-17.

Canadian debate, with much talk of de-industrialisation in Canada being triggered by CUSTA, and the awareness by firms located in Canada of the need to pursue a North American rather than simply a Canadian production and marketing strategy.

While more recent, there have also been a number of model-based (primarily general equilibrium) studies of the potential impacts of NAFTA, five of which are presented in a symposium issue of *The World Economy* (January 1992). The results of these studies are summarised in an editorial introduction by Waverman (1992). They show the wage rate as rising in all three countries under a NAFTA. Sobarzo (1992) shows large wage gains to Mexican labour, while, in Brown *et al.* (1992), the US wage rate rises because the improvement in the United States' terms of trade increases the value of US exports. These studies also show the return to capital increasing in all three countries, with the increase in Canada being the smallest.

In the automobile sector, Sobarzo (1992) and Hunter *et al.* (1992) show large output gains for Mexico, while Brown *et al.* and Hunter *et al.* show a slight (0.2–0.5 of 1 percent) decline in US output. Brown *et al.* show the Canadian transport equipment sector as gaining, while Hunter *et al.* find a small reduction in Canadian output. Trela and Whalley (1992) show large increases in both Mexican steel production and Mexican textiles and apparel output and trade under bilateral liberalisation. Trela and Whalley also highlight the potential for a rent transfer effect to occur in favour of the United States in this latter sector, with bilateral or trilateral liberalisation of trade under NAFTA. With binding quotas against third countries, liberalisation towards Mexico lowers prices in the US market and reduces the rent transfers to third countries which accompany MFA quotas.

Generally, the studies show little evidence of significant trade-diversion effects against third countries. Waverman concludes in his summary that increased trade liberalisation in North America would create some trade diversion against the rest of the world, although not large. Losers tend to be outside North America, and an agreement with Mexico, while increasing welfare in all three countries, is not a big source of overall gains (or losses) to the United States and Canada.

These results thus suggest welfare gains for all three countries from NAFTA liberalisation, and most heavily so for Mexico. But at the same time, in coming to this conclusion, they assume complete removal of all border restraints between the three countries. Hence, a difficulty in interpreting them is that they all take free trade, rather than the negotiated outcome which will probably be reflected in NAFTA, as the reference point. They also do not adequately capture a range of other effects: capital relocation and impacts on inward foreign investment, adjustment costs, and others.

Hence, if this is the conclusion from studies of NAFTA which take complete free trade as their reference point, one perhaps seems safe in concluding that the effects of an actual NAFTA agreement will be even smaller. And as emphasised above, the possible exclusionary effects of such possible NAFTA provisions as high content rules in a prospective autos Chapter and rules of origin, especially in the textiles sector, need to be factored in. The prospect of only limited liberalisation in agriculture and difficulties in evaluating any impacts which may follow from the social policy elements in an agreement (such as environment) also make an evaluation of the actual impact of a NAFTA that much harder.

4 Systemic implications of new North American regional trade arrangements

Given the potential impacts of CUSTA and NAFTA, even if the direct effects on trade and investment flows attributable to the agreements do prove to be relatively small, a series of wider issues and questions follows. Those that I discuss in this section relate to the possible implications of these new North American trade agreements for the wider trading system.

Some of the concerns now voiced about these agreements focus not on the direct effects which may follow from having these agreements in place, but rather on whether these developments indicate how the trading system may evolve in the 1990s, and whether this evolution could be adverse, especially for smaller countries. Since Canada is the largest US trading partner and Mexico is now the third largest, some go so far as to suggest that CUSTA and NAFTA provide clear evidence of a strong move towards a tripolar, three-bloc world with regional arrangements centred on the United States, the European Community, and Japan. A series of questions then follows. What exactly are the consequences for developing countries? Should they each try to adhere to at least one of the blocs in case they are left outside the larger global markets altogether? Should they resist this regionalism and, if so, how and with what prospect of success? Should efforts be made within the wider trading system to constrain these new regional arrangements in some way, and if so what form might such efforts take?

But even accepting that this recent lurch towards regionalism is as dramatic as some would claim (which itself is debated), others ask whether it is clear that this new regionalism is good (new liberalisation) or bad (exclusionary), and if so, for whom. Indeed, it is perhaps ironic that Viner's (1950) famous work on whether regionalism in the trading system is good or bad is once again the subject of lively debate. Viner argued that regional trade arrangements may be bad on global efficiency grounds insofar as countries need not buy from their lowest-cost supplier (trade diversion), or good insofar as they create trade between members of an integrating area (trade creation); the net effect either on individual countries or on world welfare is unclear.

Today, one school of thought[50] argues that regional trade arrangements have fostered the most dynamic and rapidly growing part of the global economy: growth in Europe between the integrated members of the European Community, growth between Canada and the United States following the signing of the Canada–US Auto Pact in 1965, and now rapid growth between Mexico and the United States. Trade creation from regional arrangements is thus seen as large and positive.

Moreover, while a true multilateral liberal trading order may be the first-best alternative for the global economy, faced with a seemingly eroding multilateral system which is generating VERs, sectoral derogations in textiles, agriculture, steel and other areas, growing contingent protection under ADs and CVDs, the argument is that second-best arrangements which nonetheless provide continuing forward momentum towards more open trade seem attractive. If regionalism is the form that new openness in trade takes, then regionalism is more desirable than the alternative of a blocked or eroding multilateralism, and is good.

The other school of thought stresses the importance of multilateral trade arrangements and institutions as a bulwark against dark forces which could take the global economy back to the 1930s.[51] This school sees the world headed towards three major trading blocs, each increasingly and aggressively in conflict with each other, generating instability and uncertainty in the trading system, with the result that the probability of major trade conflicts will be increased. In this scenario world economic performance suffers (potentially severely) from the new regionalism, and smaller countries face the prospect of being further excluded from access to any of the larger blocs.

This school thus reiterates the arguments of the past in favour of multilateralism, warning that even though well known, they should not be forgotten. They emphasise how in the negotiation of the GATT in the 1940s, and the subsequent evolution of postwar multilateral institutions, regionalism was viewed as inherently undesirable, since it was inconsistent with the broad principles of the multilateral trading system laid down in 1947. This rule system aspired to two distinct goals: one was to underpin a wider system of international security arrangements and guarantees based on multilateralism, the second was to prevent any return to the events of the 1930s and the trade barrier increases which occurred in the global economy, making the Depression more severe and prolonging it. The point, of course, is that whether one thinks that regionalism in the trading system is good or bad depends upon one's point of reference. Is it an idealised multilateral system of rules and disciplines (the GATT), current arrangements seen as an eroding multilateralism, or the threat of a return to the 1930s?

In asking whether CUSTA and NAFTA are good or bad, one has to ask for whom. Small countries have traditionally been the staunchest advocates of firm multilateral trade arrangements, and especially non-discriminatory trade rules, such as most favoured nation (MFN) status. This has been because they see non-discrimination as enabling them to share in the benefits of trade liberalisation negotiated between other countries, and also insulating them from bilateral pressures to change their policies in ways that larger powers desire.

But perhaps the most remarkable feature of these new regional schemes in North America is that it has been the smaller countries who have been some of the initiators and demanders of them. It was Canada who initiated negotiations on CUSTA, and Mexico on NAFTA. This is, in some ways, the equivalent for the trading system of a smaller country vote of non-confidence in the present multilateral system's ability to protect their interests. What they have sought have been safe-haven agreements with larger trading powers, seen by them as helping them avoid being sideswiped by protectionist barrier increases by their larger trading partners even if directed at other countries (the United States against Japan, for instance). Evaluated against the alternative (being excluded in a world moving towards fortress trading blocs), the arrangements obviously seem good for the smaller countries otherwise they would not seek them. Evaluated against equivalent non-discriminating arrangements they may seem bad, but the issue is whether in the present climate this alternative is attainable. Their current view seems to be that they cannot let the multilateral system do the job; a more activist approach is needed on their part, and the new regionalism is their instrument of choice.

How one sees the broader systemic implications of CUSTA and NAFTA thus follows directly from these considerations. If multilateralism is seen as ineffective, either in generating new market access or in preserving openness in the system, then the pressures on developing countries to seek new alternative bilateral or regional arrangements become that much stronger. Because of this, the regional trade arrangements now taking form in North America are less the outcome of a reciprocal exchange for concessions in a GATT sense than reflecting attempts by smaller countries to secure their access to larger country markets before barriers go up against them and other countries. Hence in CUSTA and NAFTA, both Canada and Mexico have been the demanders driven, in part, by this desire for safe-haven agreements with their largest and dominant trading partner.

North American experience indicates that there is a willingness on the part of the larger country to be accommodative in responding to these initiatives but, and perhaps understandably, at a price. While the large country receives limited direct benefits in a traditional trade-creation sense, it can enlarge its sphere of trade policy influence for subsequent bargaining with other large blocs, and can either discipline annoying domestic policies (as in the Canadian case), or achieve exclusionary arrangements to keep third parties out of the smaller country market (as in the Mexican case). Formal trade diversion may thus be less the issue with these agreements than the terms of entry for those newly seeking safe-haven trade arrangements with larger partners. Countries seeking such agreements must expect to pay a price for being granted this status, a price which may rise if the multilateral system is seen to weaken further. The current stampede of Central and Latin American countries into a search for new regional trade arrangements, and especially new trade arrangements with the United States, may be driven by shared concerns and objectives: fear of a fragmenting multilateral system, fear of exclusion from access to large trading areas, and a sense of opportunity for the larger power. But as the stampede accelerates, so the multilateral system may weaken even further which, in turn, may produce a further escalation in the search for regional arrangements.

The current danger for Mexico in NAFTA is that the price will be paid in the form of adverse exclusionary arrangements which are against the

Mexican national interest, particularly in autos, with potential impediments to third-country inward capital flows and arrangements which effectively reserve the Mexican import market for US suppliers. These imposed higher costs and inefficiencies, in my view, may turn out to be a more important effect of these arrangements for developing countries than formal trade diversion,[52] and importantly affect those entering rather than those excluded from such agreements.

This naturally leads to the issue of whether or not the trading system should, or even can, constrain adverse features of regional trade agreements of the type mentioned above, and should be used to restrain the North American arrangements in some way. One argument is that the trading system (GATT and other global trade rules) should not actively seek to restrain agreements such as CUSTA and NAFTA, because these regional trade agreements are voluntarily entered into by the parties involved, and generally speaking trade is promoted because barriers are lowered and there seem to be no major inconsistencies with Article XXIV of the GATT. This GATT Article has in any case been extremely loose in its application over the postwar years, with little meaningful discipline applied to regional trade arrangements.[53]

The counterargument is that there is a threat of proliferation of regional arrangements in the trading system, with exclusionary arrangements of the type discussed here for North America also evolving further in Europe and the Pacific. The early indications from fledgling Japanese regional trade arrangements, with aid being tied to trade and foreign investment flows as in the Japan–ASEAN arrangement[54] are that such arrangements could evolve further, and even reappear in future EC arrangements with Turkey, North Africa, and other areas.

The result could be that in a fragmented world, smaller developing countries entering into one of these arrangements become excluded from trade opportunities with other larger regions in what becomes an increasingly tripolar world. These negative effects have the potential to retard the growth and development of developing countries, hence the argument that some multilateral attempt be used to restrain them, presumably in the period after the Uruguay Round. This could, for instance, focus on some new effort to clarify Article XXIV through a GATT Understanding on Regional Trade Agreements, which could explicitly set out unacceptable exclusionary features of policy disciplines embodied in new regional agreements. Such an Understanding could be beneficial to larger as well as to smaller powers, since it could help prevent sequential and accelerating exclusion of each other from one another's regional trade arrangements.

The bottom line, however, seems to be that multilateralism and regionalism appear inextricably linked in the system. Future directions for the multilateral system will clearly be affected by how significant regional arrangements such as CUSTA and NAFTA become. But at the same time, the future of these regional arrangements depends on what happens multilaterally. If little is concluded in the Uruguay round over a period of years, we could witness a further and major weakening in the present already eroded multilateral trading system, with the GATT remaining as little more than a legal document, and GATT dispute settlement being ever more weakly applied. The result would probably be that smaller countries, even more than now, would wish to become members of regional arrangements so as to give themselves some degree of security of market access to at least one of the large countries with which they trade. This raises the vista of an eventual 'hub-and-spoke' trading system, with repeated accession of countries to regional arrangements and subsequent concessions undermining the gain of countries who had joined earlier, much as has been suggested in Wonnacott (1991a, 1991b) as a danger for NAFTA and CUSTA.

All in all, then, the medium- to longer-term prospects for developing countries in the face of growing regional arrangements in the trading system seem less good than suggested by the perhaps limited substance of CUSTA and NAFTA as they now stand, which seemingly have only limited direct effects on trade and investment flows. Under the new regionalism, trade barriers may come down and regional trade may grow, but not necessarily in ways which help smaller developing countries that much. And with little leverage in the system and driven by an ever more desperate search for secure access to markets of larger trading partners, their actions may serve to accelerate the drift to regionalism already occurring in the system. Negative consequences could then follow through exclusionary arrangements of the type discussed above for countries subsequently trying to enter such arrangements, even though formal trade diversion from these agreements for countries outside of them remains small. Perhaps a little paradoxically, then, in some ways regional arrangements in the Americas could eventually prove to be more problematic for the countries of Central and Latin America than for the developing countries of Asia and Africa.

NOTES

This chapter draws on material generated from an ongoing project on US–Canada trade supported by the Donner Canadian Foundation, to whom I am grateful for support. I also acknowledge helpful research assistance from Colleen Hamilton and Irene Trela, and discussions with and materials provided by Patrick Low.

1 The CUSTA negotiations began on 23 April 1986, with the granting by the US Congress of fast-track negotiating authority to pursue bilateral negotiations with Canada, and concluded when a document setting out the elements of an Agreement was signed on 4 October 1987 (although, *de facto*, they continued until 2 January 1988, when the agreement was finally signed). Implementing legislation was formally tabled in the Canadian House of Commons and the US Congress in the spring of 1988. The NAFTA negotiations began on 12 June 1991, after Congress granted fast-track negotiating authority in May; authority is to expire in March 1993.

2 See Whalley (1991a) for a discussion of these arrangements and proposals, and how they may or may not eventually integrate into a Western Hemispheric trade pact. The list is long, but includes Mexican and other bilaterals (with Chile, Venezuela, and others), trilateral arrangements (Colombia, Venezuela, Mexico), the Southern Cone MERCOSUR arrangements (Argentina, Brazil, Paraguay, Uruguay), the revivial of Andean Pact negotiations (Bolivia, Columbia, Ecuador, Peru, and Venezuela), new attempts to enlarge the Central American Common Market (Panamanian accession), and explicit country requests for bilateral negotiations with the United States (Costa Rica, Chile).

3 See the recent overview discussion of trading blocs in the system in Schott (1991).

4 As in the recent ASEAN heads of state commitment to achieve an ASEAN FTA (AFTA) within the next fifteen years. See 'ASEAN Free Trade', *Financial Post* (28 January 1992) p. 11.

5 The Australia New Zealand Closer Economic Relations Trade Agreement, which came into force on 1 January 1983, removed bilateral border controls, such as tariffs, import licensing and tariff quotas, under an agreed timetable. In addition, the agreement contained provisions addressing a range of other trade-distorting practices, such as export incentives, government purchasing preferences, standards and trade practices. In 1988 a further package of accelerated arrangements sought free trade in goods by July 1990 (five years ahead of schedule), set out a Protocol on Trade in Services, and detailed plans for harmonisation of business law, quarantine and customs arrangements. See Australia, Department of Foreign Affairs and Trade (1989).

6 Under the 1989 Japan–ASEAN trade understanding, Japan has agreed to provide some $2½ billion of foreign aid to ASEAN through an ASEAN–Japan Development Fund. The Fund is designed to finance joint Japanese–ASEAN ventures, but disbursements are tied to commitments involving imports of components and other inputs from Japan. See Hamilton and Whalley (forthcoming) Chapter 7, Appendix A. See Bollard and Mayes (1991) for a more general recent discussion of regional trade arrangements in the Pacific.

7 See Hamilton and Whalley (forthcoming) Table 2.6, who present data that show the (on average) higher growth rates for trade between large regions and neighbouring smaller trading partners in the 1980s. This has been especially pronounced for trade between Japan and other Pacific Rim countries, and internal EC trade, but is also seen in growing trade between the United States, Mexico, and Canada.

8 I do not discuss other arrangements such as the 1984 Caribbean Basin Initiative (CBI) which also impinge, albeit less importantly, on the performance of the North American economy.

9 In 1991 inward foreign investment into Mexico was a little over $15 billion, up over 50 percent from 1990 ('Increased Investment in Mexico', *Financial Times*, 24 January 1992). Inward foreign investment approximately doubled between 1985 and 1990.

10 My understanding is that Nicaragua has raised concerns over loss in market share for their rock lobster exports to North America due to the Canadian agreement, but outside of this, documented instances of trade diversion from CUSTA seem relatively few.

11 An important further feature of the agreement is the joint commitment to eliminate duty drawbacks covering imports of materials from third countries for bilateral trade as of 1 January 1994. This also applies to autos and parts, and affects Japanese transplant production in Canada shipped to the United States. See Wonnacott (1991b), who emphasises the importance of this provision of the agreement for trade in autos and parts.

12 The agreement establishes a tariff quota for apparel set approximately at 1987 trade levels. Bilateral trade is duty-free up to the quota, but at the MFN rate thereafter. Also, for trade in apparel beyond the tariff quota duty drawbacks are allowed bilaterally (e.g., refund in Canada of Canadian duties on fabric imports from the United States made up into apparel and re-exported to the United States), while they are banned for imported inputs from third countries.

13 See Canada, Department of Finance (1988) p. 57, and Canada, Royal Commission on the Economic Union and Development Prospects for Canada (1985) p. 311.

14 The fraction of Canadian trade covered by such measures in place at the time the agreement was negotiated was around 3 percent of trade in 1986, excluding trade in softwood lumber where a 15 percent Canadian export tax was agreed to by Canada in return for a withdrawal of CVD petitions by the American industry. Also the bilateral use of AD actions (though not CVDs) by Canada was as extensive as by the United States (see the further discussion in Whalley, 1990, p. 125, and Lester and Morehen, 1989).

The sectoral conflicts created by some of the subsidy and dumping issues have nonetheless been sharp, and have seemingly not diminished because of the conclusion of the agreement. A current conflict centres on the pricing policies of Quebec Hydro and the benefits to heavy power users and exporters to the United States. See 'US Moves Threaten Norsk Plant', *Globe and Mail* (February 15 1992) p. B6, which details how Norsk Hydro AS located a plant in Bécancour, Quebec, to sell magnesium to the US market. In December 1991, it was faced with 32.8 percent interim duty after an initial finding of subsidy; and in February 1992 it has been levied with a 32.7 percent provisional anti-dumping duty.

15 Under the new content rule, overhead and other indirect costs are not included in the requirement that 50 percent of the invoice price of a car crossing the border duty-free represents costs incurred in either Canada of the United States (see Canada, Department of External Affairs, 1988a). The 1988 Canadian government annotation of the agreement suggested that the new rule is roughly equivalent to a 70 percent content rule under the previous Auto Pact basis for calculating content.

16 See also the discussion of the treatment of services in CUSTA in Whalley (1991b).

17 Chapter XVIII provides for the settlement of disputes over the interpretation and implementation of the whole agreement. It provides for the establishment of the Canada–US Trade Commission and sets out notification, consultation and binding arbitration panel procedures. Chapter XIX deals with disputes arising from AD and CVD cases. Under Chapter XIX, a binational panel makes determinations as to whether or not an AD/CVD action being taken by either country is compatible with its domestic law. When the agreement was signed in 1988, it was agreed to develop and eventually implement a separate system of AD/CVD arrangements that would simultaneously apply to both countries. This was left to an ongoing five–seven year negotiation process to follow on after the agreement. For more details see Steger (1988) pp. 71–4; Canada, Department of External Affairs (1988a) pp. 484–52; and Anderson and Rugman (1991), who also evaluate the panel findings thus far from disputes dealt with under these two Chapters.

18 Also see the papers on NAFTA in a symposium issue of *The World Economy* (January 1991). These are by Bueno (1991), Hart (1991), Weintraub (1991), Vega (1991), and Wonnacott (1991a, 1991b).

19 An existing 1987 US–Mexico framework understanding and other subsequent accords had already approximately doubled some (but not all) Mexican textile quotas and achieved a degree of bilateral liberalisation in steel. See the discussion of these in Trela and Whalley (1991).

20 The outcome of a two-day Ministerial meeting at Chantilly, Virginia, seems to suggest slowed progress (see 'Free Trade Talks Remain Stalled', *The Financial Post*, February 11 1992, p. 8). According to news reports, US Trade Representative, Carla Hills, indicated that 'we haven't removed any square brackets' from a provisional text, while Canadian Trade Minister, Michael Wilson, identified agriculture, autos, and textiles as key sectors. Mexican Commerce Secretary, Jaime Serra Puche, reportedly emphasised the need for a competitive North American auto industry to emerge from the talks.

21 In order to gain Congressional approval for fast-track negotiating authority for the talks with Mexico, President Bush submitted an 'action plan' to Congress in May 1991. According to this plan, the Administration stated that the Labor Department would sign an agreement with Mexico providing for cooperation on working conditions and child labour. Environmental issues would be negotiated on a parallel track and would deal with air and water pollution, hazardous wastes and spills, pesticides and enforcement. An environmental assessment of the agreement would also be completed. See *Congressional Quarterly* (1991b) p. 1121.

22 Weintraub (1991) reports the average Mexican tariff at 9 percent, suggesting that the further reduction of tariffs to zero will not be traumatic because the more major liberalisation measures were taken between 1985 and 1990. Hart (1991) reports a trade-weighted average Mexican tariff of 8 percent as against current GATT-bound rates for Mexico of 50 percent.

23 'Ministers Talking Trilateral Trade', *Financial Post* (October 26–28 1991) p. 1, and 'Auto Industry Overhaul', *Financial Post* (October 29 1991) p. 5.

   According to the 'action plan' submitted to Congress in May 1991, the longest transition periods will be provided for industries such as fruits and vegetables that would be most threatened by Mexican imports, or those that have been heavily protected in the past. See *Congressional Quarterly* (1991b) p. 1121.

24 See 'Carmakers may face pact changes', *Financial Post* (27 September 1991) p. 3.
25 See a plan along these lines for the treatment of textiles and apparel in NAFTA proposed by the American Textile Manufacturers' Institute (1991).
26 See the discussion of the potential impacts of such liberalisation in Levy and van Wijnbergen (1991).
27 Failing which, increases in temporary entry arrangements which allow low-wage fruit pickers from Mexico to enter and work in parts of the United States on a seasonal basis might be requested by these industries.
28 Also see the discussion in Kelly and Kamp (1991), Leonard and Christensen (1991), Low (1991), and National Wildlife Federation (1990).
29 *Maquiladora* operations are licensed establishments under which imported capital equipment and raw materials for export purposes enter Mexico in bond (effectively duty-free). Initially restricted to a 20 km zone along the US border, since 1972 *Maquiladora* have been approved interior to Mexico, although about 80 percent of *Maquiladora* operations continue to operate within the zone. Exports to the United States qualify for special treatment under HTS subheadings 9802.00.60 and 9802.00.80, with duty being paid only on value added in Mexico. GSP treatment also applies to certain export from *Maquiladora*. Much of the growth of Mexican manufactured exports in recent years has come from *Maquiladora* operations. See USITC (1990) pp. 5–15.
30 See the discussion of these issues in Uimonen and Whalley (1991). In February 1992, USTR and EPA announced an 'Integrated Border Plan' to provide $380 million over two years for an environmental clean-up on the US–Mexican border. Mexico reportedly has committed $460 million over three years. See 'From Fast Track to Back Burners', *The Economist* (29 February 1992) p. 25.
31 See Uimonen and Whalley (1991).
32 See the discussion in Charnovitz (1986) for details.
     See *Congressional Quarterly* (1991b) p. 1121. In the 'action plan' submitted by President Bush to Congress in May 1991, the United States promised that the Labor Department would sign an agreement with the Mexican government providing for cooperation in occupational health and safety, working conditions, child labour and even enforcement of labour standards.
33 Also see the discussion in Nogués and Quintanilla (1992).
34 See 'Chile and Mexico Display the Pioneer Spirit', *Financial Times* (19 September 1991) p. 5.
35 For more details see SELA (1990).
36 Also see the paper by Erzan and Yeats (1992) which suggests that except for Brazil and Mexico, most Latin American economies stand to gain relatively little from bilateral agreements with the United States compared to either what gains may accrue from such schemes to the United States or to the countries in the region, or from regional agreements among themselves.
37 'Rationalisation effects' refer to changes in plant size and number of plants as production is reoriented from servicing the smaller Canadian to the larger US market. See Baldwin and Gorecki (1985) for a survey of Canadian studies of such effects.
38 Also see Thompson's (1991) analysis of stock market effects of the Agreements.
39 These studies date back to Young's (1957) analysis of the gains to Canada from trade liberalisation for the Gordon Royal Commission, taken further in

the pioneering and critically important study of Wonnacott and Wonnacott (1967), which was the first to suggest an annual gain to Canada from Canada–US free trade in the order of 10 percent of GDP. These and successive Canadian studies on potential impacts of Canada–US free trade are summarised in Hill and Whalley (1985) Appendix B.

40 While consistency with the earlier calculation by the Wonnacotts was thought at the time to give this model calculation added credibility, the reduction in Canadian trade barriers in the intervening years, through the Tokyo and Kennedy GATT rounds would, if anything, suggest lower estimates. Subsequent recalculations of these model results with revised trade barrier data by the Canadian Government Department of Finance revealed this to be the case, with the annual gain estimate falling to around 2½ percent of GDP.

41 See Harris (1985) p. 173, Table 8A1.

42 The Job Loss Register of the Canadian Labour Congress details a loss of almost 250,000 jobs since CUSTA came into effect, but importantly attributes the majority of recent job losses in Canadian manufacturing to CUSTA rather than to the recession. The same conclusion emerges from Ontario government data showing that up to two-thirds of all manufacturing job losses since 1989 have been due to plant closures as opposed to more widespread layoffs, double the level of the 1981–2 recession. The Ontario Federation of labour claim a new job loss of 315,000 in manufacturing alone from CUSTA by December 1990, and of 250,000 in Ontario during the eighteen months of January 1989–July 1990. See the background materials for a Donner Canadian Foundation-supported conference on *New Corporate Strategies for a North American Market: The Free Trade Agreement in Practice*, Toronto (2–3 October 1991) London: University of Western Ontario (mimeo).

43 For instance, Harris and Cox (1984) p. 176, in their initial calculations appear to have used estimates of average barriers against US imports (including any VERs in place), and assumed that these applied to trade with Canada. In doing so, they may have overestimated the actual barriers that applied to US–Canada trade, particularly in motor vehicles and parts. One portion of their set of model results (Harris, 1985, Table 8.2, p. 162), while admittedly for multilateral free trade, shows a large (approximately 250 percent) increase in Canadian exports of transport equipment for a free-trade scenario, even though Canada–US trade in this sector was already largely duty-free under the Auto Pact.

44 See 'Campbell Soup ponders pitfalls of free trade pact', *Financial Times* (30 November 1990) p. 7, which suggests that CUSTA has already forced big changes in the operations of the Campbell Soup company in Canada. Internal studies had found that Campbell's best Canadian plants were 30–40 percent less productive than its most efficient US factories. As a result, several production operations were to be transferred south of the border; Campbell's plan was to leave only four plants in Canada, compared to eleven five years earlier. On the other hand, factories producing other product lines were to be expanded in Canada and designed to serve the entire North American market.

45 See GATT (1990) Table A7.

46 See Statistics Canada (1984) Table IV, p. xxvii.

47 But one of the more significant and yet to be resolved disputes concerning the agreement thus far (and not yet before a dispute settlement panel) involves the interpretation of domestic content. One issue concerns content determination

for 'intermediate materials' with Honda shipping engines into Canada cast in a US production facility but containing Japanese components, which on reshipment into the US in assembled cars are treated as non-North American content. Another issue involves exports to the United States from the Cami plant in Ingersoll, Ontario, where interest costs paid to Canadian financial institutions and other indirect production costs are claimed as content to meet the local content test. These issues first came to light through a US Customs Audit in the spring of 1991. The first case involving Honda has generated a ruling by US Customs that the content rules in CUSTA are being violated and that a 2.5 percent duty will be levied. The present issues are whether US Customs will disallow duty-free treatment in the Cami case, and how the Honda case may be dealt with through CUSTA dispute settlement. See 'FTA Arbitration looms: Impasse over Auto Content', *Financial Post* (November 19 1991) p. 5, and 'U.S. Rules Ontario-made Honda Civics subject to Duty', *Globe and Mail* (February 13 1992).

48 Excluding exports of the agricultural, petrochemical, and steel industries which do not qualify under the *Maquiladora* programme, exports from the *Maquiladoras* in 1989 accounted for 78 percent of the remaining (non-agricultural, petrochemical, steel) Mexican export categories to the United States. See USITC (1991) p. xi.

49 Under HTS item 9802.00.80, imported articles assembled wholly or partly with US fabricated components are assessed duty at the US border only on the value added abroad.

50 See Krugman (1991a, 1991b) for instance.

51 See Bhagwati (1990, 1991), who talks of the trading being at risk.

52 As already emphasised above, with CUSTA the direct effects on trade flows between Canada and the United States are themselves currently small, and will probably continue to be, and so formal trade-diversion effects are probably small. But one has to caution that a small percentage effect on large US–Canada trade flows in a particular product category could translate into large percentage effects on a small trade flow in the same category between the United States (or Canada) and a developing country.

53 See the discussion of this point in Hart (1987). This is also reflected in the inconclusive report of the GATT working party on CUSTA (see *GATT Focus*, November/December 1991).

54 See the discussion in Hamilton and Whalley (forthcoming) Chapter 7, Appendix A.

REFERENCES

American Textile Manufacturers' Institute (1991) 'Textile, Apparel Associations Present Plan for North American Free Trade Agreement', *Textile News* (October 24) Washington, DC.

Anderson, A. and A. Rugman (1991) 'A Review of the Dispute Settlement Processes Under the Canada–U.S. Free Trade Agreement and the GATT', *Working Paper*, Toronto: University of Toronto.

Australia, Department of Foreign Affairs and Trade (1989) *The Australia–New Zealand Closer Economic Relations Trade Agreement: Background and Guide to Arrangements Arising from 1988 Review*, Canberra: Department of Foreign Affairs and Trade.

Baldwin, J. and P. Gorecki (1985) 'The Relationship Between Trade and Tariff Patterns and the Efficiency of the Canadian Manufacturing Sector in the 1970s. A Summary', in J. Whalley (ed.), *Canada–United States Free Trade*, volume 11, Research Studies, Royal Commission on the Economic Union and Development Prospects for Canada, Toronto: University of Toronto.

Bhagwati, J. (1990) 'Multilateralism at Risk: The GATT is Dead, Long Live GATT', *The World Economy*, **13(2)** (June) pp. 149–69.

(1991) *The Trade System at Risk*, Princeton: Princeton University Press and Harvester Wheatsheaf.

Bollard, A. and D. Mayes (1991) 'Regionalism and the Pacific Rim', paper prepared for the International Economics Study Group Conference on 'Regionalism and the World Economy', University of Nottingham (13–15 September).

Brown, D.K., A.V. Deardorff and R.M. Stern (1992) 'A North American Free Trade Agreement: Analytical Issues and a Computational Assessment', *The World Economy*, **15(1)** (January) pp. 11–30.

Bueno, G.M. (1991) 'Mexico's Options in Trade Negotiations', *The World Economy*, **14** (March) pp. 67–77.

Canada, Department of External Affairs (1988) *The Canada–U.S. Free Trade Agreement*, Ottawa: Department of External Affairs.

(1988b) *The Canada–U.S. Free Trade Agreement: Synopsis*, Ottawa: Department of External Affairs.

(1988c) *Canada–U.S. Trade Negotiations: A Chronology*, Ottawa: Department of External Affairs.

Canada, Federal Department of Finance (1988) *The Canada–U.S. Free Trade Agreement. An Economic Assessment*, Ottawa: Federal Department of Finance.

Canada, Royal Commission on the Economic Union and Development Prospects for Canada (1985) *Report*, Ottawa: Minister of Supply and Services Canada.

Charnovitz, S. (1986) 'Fair Labor Standards and International Trade', *Journal of World Trade Law*, **20**, pp. 61–78.

Congressional Quarterly (1991a) Weekly Report (February 23 1991) **49(8)**.

(1991b) Weekly Report (May 4 1991) **49(10)**.

Cox, D. and R. Harris (1984) 'A Quantitative Assessment of the Economic Impact on Canada of Sectoral Free Trade with the United States', paper presented at a Macdonald Commission Research Symposium on 'Canada and the Future of the Global Trading System' (24 July) Ottawa.

(1992) 'North American Free Trade and its Implications for Canada: Results from a CGE Model of North American Trade', *The World Economy*, **15(1)** (January) pp. 31–44.

Economic Council of Canada (1987a) 'Impact of Canada–U.S. Free Trade on the Canadian Economy', *Discussion Paper*, **331**.

(1987b) *Reaching Outward*, Twenty-Fourth Annual Review, Ottowa: Minister of Supply and Services Canada.

Erzan, R. and A. Yeats (1992) 'Free Trade Agreements with the United States: What's in it for Latin America?', World Bank, *Working Paper*, **WPS 827**, Washington, DC: World Bank.

GATT (1978) *International Trade 1977/78*, Geneva: GATT.

(1982) *International Trade 1981/82*, Geneva: GATT.

(1986) *International Trade 1985/86*, Geneva: GATT.

(1988) *International Trade 87–88*, volume II, Geneva: GATT.

(1990) *International Trade 89–90*, volume II, Geneva: GATT.

Hamilton, R. and J. Whalley (1985) 'Geographically Discriminatory Trade Arrangements', *Review of Economics and Statistics*, pp. 446–55.

(forthcoming) *Strengthening the Global Trading System After the Uruguay Round*, Washington, DC: Institute for International Economics.

Harris, R.G. (1984) *Trade, Industrial Policy, and Canadian Manufacturing*, Ontario: Economic Council Research Study.

(1985) 'Summary of a Project on the General Equilibrium Evaluation of Canadian Trade Policy', in J. Whalley (ed.), *Canada–United States Free Trade*, volume 11, Research Studies, Royal Commission on the Economic Union and Development Prospects for Canada, Toronto: University of Toronto Press.

Hart, M. (1991) 'North American Free Trade Agreement: The Elements Involved', *The World Economy*, **14** (March) pp. 87–102.

(1987) 'GATT Article XXIV and Canada–United States Trade Negotiations', *Review of International Business Law* (December) pp. 317–55.

Hill, R. and J. Whalley (1985) 'Canada–U.S. Free Trade: An Introduction', in J. Whalley (ed.), *Canada–United States Free Trade*, volume 11, Research Studies, Royal Commission on the Economic Union and Development Prospects for Canada, Toronto: University of Toronto Press.

Hunter, L., J.R. Markusen and T.F. Rutherford (1992) 'US–Mexico Free Trade and the North American Auto Industry: Effects on the Spatial Organization of Production of Finished Autos', *The World Economy*, **15**(1) (January) pp. 65–82.

Informetrica Ltd (1985) *Economic Impacts of Enhanced Bilateral Trade: National and Provincial Results*, Prepared for the Department of External Affairs, Ottawa.

Institute for Policy Analysis (1985) *The Macroeconomic Impacts of Free Trade with the United States: Lessons from the FOCUS–PRISM Models* (by Peter Dungan), University of Toronto, *Working Paper*, **DP 86–86**.

Kelly, M.E. and D. Kamp (1991) 'Mexico–U.S. Free Trade Negotiations and the Environment: Exploring the Issues', *Discussion Paper*, Austin, Texas: Texas Center for Policy Studies.

Krugman, P. (1991a) 'The Move to Free Trade Zones', paper presented at the 1991 Economic Symposium, 'Policy Implications of Trade and Currency Zones', sponsored by the Federal Reserve Bank of Kansas City (22–24 August).

(1991b) 'Is Bilateralism Bad?', in E. Helpman and A. Razin (eds), *International Trade and Trade Policy*, Cambridge, Mass.: MIT Press.

Leonard, R.E. and E. Christensen (1991) 'Economic Effects of a Free Trade Agreement Between Mexico and the United States', testimony on behalf of Community Nutrition Institute before the International Trade Commission, hearing on docket no. 332-307, Washington, DC (April 12).

Lester, J. and T. Morehen (1989) 'Trade Barriers Between Canada and the United States', *Working Paper*, **88-3**, Ottawa: Department of Finance.

Levy, S. and S. van Wijnbergen (1991) 'Transition Problems in Economic Reform: Agriculture in the Mexico–U.S. Free Trade Agreement', draft of a *Working Paper* for the World Bank, Washington, DC: World Bank.

Low, P. (1991) 'Trade Measures and Environmental Quality: The Implications for Mexico's Exports', International Trade Division, Washington, DC: World Bank.

National Wildlife Federation (1990) 'Environmental Concerns Related to a United States–Mexico–Canada Free Trade Agreements', background paper, Washington, DC (November 27).

Nogués, J. and R. Quintanilla (1992) 'Latin America's Integration and the Multilateral Trading System', Chapter 9 in this volume.

Schott, J.J. (1991) 'Trading Blocs and the World Trading System', *The World Economy*, **14(1)** (March) pp. 1–18.

SELA (1990) 'The Bush Enterprise for the America's Initiative: A Preliminary Analysis by the SELA Permanent Secretariat', Caracas (September).

Sobarzo, H.E (1992) 'A General Equilibrium Analysis of the Gains from Trade for the Mexican Economy of a North American Free Trade Agreement', *The World Economy*, **15(1)** (January) pp. 83–100.

Statistics Canada (1984) *Destination of Shipments of Manufacturers*, Catalogue no. 31-530, monthly, Ottawa: Minister of Supply and Services Canada.

(1988) *Canada's International Investment Position 1985*, Ottawa: Minister of Supply and Services Canada.

(1990) *Canada's International Investment Position 1987*, Ottawa: Minister of Supply and Services Canada.

(1991) *Canada's International Investment Position 1988–90*, Ottawa: Minister of Supply and Services Canada.

Steger, D. (1988) *A Concise Guide to the Canada–United States Free Trade Agreement*, Toronto: Carswell.

Thompson, A.J. (1991) 'The Anticipated Sectoral Impact of the Canada–United States Free Trade Agreement: An Event Study Analysis', Toronto: University of Toronto (mimeo).

Trela, I. and J. Whalley (1991) 'Bilateral Negotiations in Quota Restricted Items: U.S. and Mexico in Textiles and Steel', Cambridge, Mass.: National Bureau of Economic Research.

(1992) 'Trade Liberalization in Quota Restricted Items: US and Mexico in Textiles and Steel', *The World Economy*, **15(1)** (January) pp. 45–64.

Uimonen, P. and J. Whalley (1991) 'Trade and Environment', draft, Washington, DC: Institute for International Economics.

US Department of Commerce (1988) '*United States Trade Performance 1987*, Washington, DC.

(1991) *Survey of Current Business*, Washington, DC.

USITC (1990) *Review of Trade and Investment Liberalization Measures by Mexico and Prospects for Future United States–Mexican Relations*, USITC, no. **2275**, Washington, DC.

(1991) *Production Sharing: U.S. Imports Under Harmonized Tariff Schedule Subheadings 9802.00.60 and 9802.00.80, 1986–89*, USITC, no. **2349**, Washington, DC.

Vega, G. (1991) 'Symposium on North American Free Trade', *The World Economy*, **14** (March) pp. 53–5.

Viner, J. (1950) *The Customs Union Issue*, New York: Carnegie Endowment for International Peace.

Waverman, L. (1992) Editorial Introduction to a Mini Symposium on 'Modelling Free Trade in North America', *The World Economy*, **15(1)** (January).

Weintraub, S. (1991) 'Free Trade in North America: Has its Time Come?', *The World Economy*, **14** (March) pp. 57–66.

Whalley, J. (1990) 'Now that the Deal is Over: Canadian Trade Policy Options in the 1990s', *Canadian Public Policy*, **16(2)**, (June).

(1991a) 'CUSTA and NAFTA: Can WHFTA Be Far Behind?', paper presented to the International Economics Study Group meetings, Nottingham (14–15 September 1990) and forthcoming in *Journal of Common Market Studies*.

(1991b) 'Services and the U.S.–Canada Relationship Beyond the FTA', in C. Doran and A.P. Drischler (eds), *The United States, Canada & the World Economy*, Washington, DC: Johns Hopkins Foreign Policy Institute, pp. 45–57.

Wharton Econometrics (1987) 'Canada–U.S. Free Trade: Opportunities, Risks and Prospects', the WEFA Group, Philadelphia: University of Pennsylvania.

Wonnacott, R. (1991a) 'Canada's Role in the U.S.–Mexico Free Trade Negotiations', *The World Economy*, **14(1)** (March) pp. 79–86.

(1991b) 'Mexico and the Canada–U.S. Auto Pact', *The World Economy*, **14** (March) pp. 103–11.

Wonnacott, R. and P. Wonnacott (1967) *Free Trade Between the U.S. and Canada*, Cambridge, Mass.: Harvard University Press.

Young, J. (1957) *Canadian Commercial Policy*, Ottawa: Royal Commission on Canada's Economic Prospects.

Discussion

FERNANDO CLAVIJO

Chapter 11 is well-written, well-balanced, and well-documented. Whalley makes several provocative points, but since they are safely hedged, there is only a limited room for discussion without stepping beyond the scope of the chapter. I therefore divide my comments into two parts, a general comment, followed by two specific points of discussion.

At a general level, Whalley is disappointed with the actual limited outcome of the Canada–US Free-Trade Agreement (CUSTA) compared with the initial expectations and claims of important trade, investment, and welfare gains. However, when appraising the outcome of small Central and South American countries seeking membership in a trade bloc, Whalley succumbs to reality by stating that the bloc might impose such conditions that these countries would end up worse off than countries outside the bloc (e.g., African and Asian countries). In making this assertion, Whalley seems implicitly to be assuming that those countries outside the bloc will be better off because they will operate in a freer trade environment, or at least in a more cooperative negotiating framework. But perhaps the main reason why there has been a global tendency towards regional arrangements in the trading system during the 1990s is precisely the absence of such a free-trade environment in the real world.

I have two specific comments. First, while assessing CUSTA and the likely outcome of the North American Free-Trade Agreements (NAFTA), Whalley stresses the contrast between both agreements in terms of the limited outcome of the former and the strong effects on trade and investment of the latter even before it is ratified. I share some of his views and reasons. However, it seems to me that he is somehow overlooking the difference in factor endowments and therefore the higher complementarity between the United States and Canada on the one hand, and Mexico on the other. In contrast, he seems to have higher expectations in CUSTA's case with similar economies in terms of structure and less difference in factor endowments.

Thus, in assessing CUSTA, I wonder why Whalley is not paying more attention to the question of how trade and investment flows are changing. It is not enough to say that investment flows are lower than prior to the agreement. Which particular sectors have been more affected? What is happening with intra-industry trade and with the expected scale economies and productivity gains? Three years after the agreement, there is data available to allow this type of analysis.

Second, Whalley stresses the higher price that newcomers will have to pay to get into a trade bloc. I wonder why he is not making positive recommendations that will help minimise the effects of uncooperative or coalition behaviour within a trade bloc, in particular, what strategy small countries should follow to minimise being negatively affected when entering it. At the same time, what do big players have to accept and face in terms of adjustment costs? If on the part of big partners, sectors that need serious restructuring remain immune to any major changes, this immunisation will create problems elsewhere, as Whalley correctly points out. As Bhagwati reminds us in Chapter 2 in this volume, the only way small countries will be able to serve their debt is by having better access to big markets for their exports, implying that the cost of restructuring in developed and developing countries needs to be shared. If the whole or most of the adjustment burden cost in a trade bloc falls on developing countries, then we have only to add profit remittances to the item of interest payments on the foreign debt in the balance of payments to see if such a strategy can be sustainable. Of course, if trade flows are not increasing considerably at the same time, investment flows will stop, leading to a worsening situation for the developing countries, and increased difficulties in servicing their external debt.

ULRICH LÄCHLER

The recent resurgence of interest in regional integration (RI) among the Latin American nations may come as somewhat of a surprise in view of the discouraging experiences with such efforts in the past. Earlier integration efforts in the region all either remained inoperative or ultimately failed. The recent integration efforts, exemplified by the prospective North American Free-Trade Agreement (NAFTA), exhibit some fundamental differences from the earlier approaches, however, which has improved their prospects of success. Whereas past integration efforts were based on the pursuit of inward-oriented, trade-diverting industrialisation policies and focused on establishing stronger links exclusively among developing economies, current efforts are being pursued by developing countries that have already embarked on unilateral trade liberalisation (UTL) programmes and aim to promote stronger links with industrialised economies. This change in outlook is particularly true of Mexico. It also characterises the new integration efforts in Central and Latin America. All countries in Central America (including Panama), for example, are currently implementing World Bank-supported structural adjustment programmes, with significant trade liberalisation components. In 1987, only Costa Rica was engaged in such a programme.

Given that the Latin American countries, and Mexico in particular, are already committed to opening up their economies to the rest of the world, what would be the additional gain from negotiating a bilateral trade agreement with the United States? In my reading of his Chapter 11, this is the central question arising from John Whalley's discussion of the prospective trade agreement between Mexico and its two industrialised neighbours to the north.

In seeking to assess the likely impact of NAFTA, the author focuses on Canada's experience after the signing of the 1988 Canada–US Free-Trade Agreement (CUSTA). Although the parameters of NAFTA are still under negotiation, the chapter makes a reasonable case for assuming that the eventual outcome will be similar to CUSTA. That agreement features the bilateral elimination of tariffs in non-sensitive sectors, accompanied by sectoral arrangements that leave unchanged previous protection levels in the sensitive industries (steel, autos, textiles, and agriculture). Wonnacott and Lutz (1989) compared the experience of regions that attempted to integrate on the basis of a selective (product-by-product) tariff-cutting approach to those that relied on an across-the-board trade liberalisation with few exceptions. Their main conclusion was that while the selective approach tends to foster trade diversion, in practice it hardly yields any impact on trade at all. John Whalley's chapter arrives at basically the same conclusion. That is, in the three years since CUSTA was signed, there has been no perceptible increase in trade and investment flows between Canada and the United States, contrary to prior projections, while during the same period these flows have increased sharply between the United States and Mexico in spite of the absence of a formal agreement. Based on this observation, Whalley argues that the immediate impact of NAFTA is likely to remain quite limited.

The Canadian experience with CUSTA during the last three years, however, is of only limited relevance for assessing the impact of a similar trade agreement on Mexico. First, as Whalley notes, the tariff levels between Canada and the United States prior to the agreement were already very low or non-existent. Many of the gains from specialisation and competition, therefore, had already taken place, such that a further elimination of tariffs would have only a marginal impact. Mexico's tariff and non-tariff barriers during the mid-1980s, on the other hand, were substantial, and the subsequent increase in trade largely reflects the UTL measures adopted by Mexico after 1985. Another important feature that distinguishes NAFTA and CUSTA, and serves to explain the divergent Mexican and Canadian experience during the last three years, is the difference in relative factor endowments. The two industrialised economies are much more similar to each other in this respect than either is to Mexico. According to standard Hecksher–Ohlin reasoning, the prospective gains from a reduction in trade barriers are larger the more dissimilar are the two trading partners. This conforms with the observed sharp increase in trade between the United States and Mexico, compared to the recent US–Canadian experience.

The key factor that triggered the increase in US–Mexican trade has been the reduction in Mexico's trade barriers, rather than trade concessions made by the United States. Moreover, if Whalley is correct in conjecturing that the prospective NAFTA will not result in substantial additional concessions by the United States, then I would concur with his assessment that NAFTA is unlikely to yield a substantial impact, *assuming* that Mexico did not reverse its trade liberalisation programme and that the United States did not increase its trade barriers in the absence of an agreement. The most important potential benefit of NAFTA, however, which I think has been underplayed in the chapter, would be its validation of this last premise. NAFTA could help cement the trade reforms already implemented in Mexico by better allowing its policymakers to resist protectionist pressures at home. It could also lock-in Mexico's existing access to the US–Canadian market and make it more difficult to impose arbitrary trade barriers once Mexican imports begin to penetrate; or at least, clarify beforehand the conditions under which countervailing measures would be taken.

Going beyond the issue of NAFTA's impact on the partners to the agreement, Whalley identifies the potential systemic implications of NAFTA as the most important sources of concern from the viewpoint of developing countries. This concern has two aspects: one is the fear that the change in direction toward bilateral trade agreements signalled by the signing of NAFTA could undermine the GATT approach of multilateral trade liberalisation, resulting in an overall welfare loss for the world economy. The other fear is that developing countries might become entrapped through regional trade arrangements featuring tighter rules of origin and local content rules into inefficient trading patterns with the larger trading partners.

With respect to the first concern, it is important to mention from the outset that, in spite of pursuing a bilateral agreement with the United States, Mexico and Central America have not been opposed to GATT, nor have sought to weaken it. This is evidenced by the fact that Mexico and all the Central American countries, except Panama, have recently either joined or are negotiating accession to GATT. (Prior to 1985, only Nicaragua belonged to GATT, as one of its charter members.) Instead, the main motivation for seeking to establish a bilateral agreement with the United States is the desire to extend the gains that are potentially available through the GATT, but which have not been forthcoming in practice due to the slow progress of GATT negotiations. In other words, it mainly reflects an impatience with the slowness of GATT, rather than a rejection of multilateral trade liberalisation principles. The main question, then, is whether such bilateral agreements will further inhibit progress in multilateral negotiations. In this respect, I lean toward greater optimism: to the extent that multilateral negotiations are slowed down by the need to achieve consensus among too many negotiating partners, the creation of larger integrated economies reduces the number of contracting parties, which could facilitate a multilateral consensus.

With respect to the second concern, the potential entrapment into inefficient trading patterns would clearly be a danger if prospective bilateral trade agreements took on the form of inward-oriented customs unions (CUs), involving increased barriers toward non-member imports. Offhand it is difficult to say whether a tightening of local content rules, coupled with a bilateral elimination of tariffs, will result in higher effective protection against third-country imports. This would have to be calculated on an individual basis. My hunch is, however, that so long as the application of tighter local content rules is limited to the sensitive sectors, which each of the bilateral partners is reluctant to liberalise anyway, the dangers of entrapment appear exaggerated. The danger could become more serious if these local content rules are applied in a general, across-the-board fashion, covering substantially all bilateral trade among the contracting partners. Even in this event, however, the problem of resource misallocation would be small if average protection rates *vis-à-vis* third-country imports remain at their currently low levels. The main danger emerges if protection rates are subsequently raised. This would imply the violation of earlier GATT agreements, posing a serious danger indeed.

REFERENCE

Wonnacott, P. and M. Lutz (1989) 'Is There a Case for Free Trade Areas?', in J.J. Schott (ed.), *Free Trade Areas and U.S. Trade Policy*, Washington, DC: Institute for International Economics.

12 Trading blocs and East Asia

GARY R. SAXONHOUSE

At a time when large political and economic agglomerations like the USSR, Yugoslavia and Czecho-Slovakia have broken up, great confidence in strong customs unions (CUs) being the way of everyone's future seems a bit misplaced. Indeed, it is possible to argue that it is the extraordinary success of small East Asian entities like Hong Kong and Singapore within the GATT-governed multilateral trading system that now emboldens Croatians, Azerbaijanis, Latvians and Slovaks to assume that political independence need not mean economic disaster. It is possible to believe that a well-functioning, open multilateral trading system makes continental superpowers that run roughshod over cultural diversity anachronistic. With the multilateral trading system capable of substituting for much of the special economic advantages of large political size, the door might be viewed as potentially open for a plethora of economically viable microstates organised, perhaps in the East Asian image, on the basis of cultural affinity.

While liberal systems could make the world safe for cultural diversity, exclusivity does raise its ugly head. Croatians who believe that the GATT provides the economic charter for their political liberty may be in for a nasty surprise when they negotiate the terms of their access to Europe's so-called Single Market. Of course, it is the new vitality of regional arrangements such as the European Community and the North American Free-Trade Area (NAFTA) and prospective arrangements in East Asia, and not the obsolescence of dinosaurs like the USSR, that provide the context for this chapter.

In section 1 of this chapter, the consequences of trading-bloc formation for countries left outside the bloc will be reviewed. In particular, the case where the formation of such a bloc will leave outsiders worse off will be highlighted. This can happen even without the trading bloc violating Article XXIV of the GATT. Still worse, such blocs can make insiders better off than the case of global free trade. In this situation, side payments apart, insiders will have no incentive to let in additional members, except if the formation of a rival bloc is threatened.

388

The case outlined in section 1 reflects the concerns of the East Asian economies. Trading blocs are being formed elsewhere in the world. Even without violating existing GATT provisions such blocs can lower East Asian welfare. These trading blocs may have no incentive to expand their memberships to include East Asian economies except insofar as they fear provoking the formation of an East Asian trading bloc.

Section 2 reviews the prospects for a regional trade regime in East Asia. Intra-East Asian trade is currently not large by historical standards. Nor does the rapid growth in intra-East Asian trade reflect very much more than the very rapid overall economic growth in this region relative to the rest of the world. Estimation of a bilateral model of intra-industry trade using a factor endowment-based version of the gravity model suggests no East Asian bias in the trading patterns of the leading economies there.

In light of this finding, in section 3, the various proposals for East Asian and Pan-Pacific trading arrangements are discussed. Despite considerable progress on trade liberalisation by many of the East Asian economies over the past two decades, there is some indication that region-wide liberalisation could still be of considerable benefit. Section 4 presents some conclusions.

1   New trading blocs, the consequences for members and non-members and Article XXIV

The economics literature on customs unions has come a considerable way since Haberler, writing in 1936, noted that 'Customs unions are always to be welcomed . . . the economic advantage of customs union can be proved by the Theory of Comparative Cost'.[1] Since Viner, it has been understood that the benefits for members of a trading bloc through trade creation may be less than the costs imposed on non-members through trade diversion.[2] Indeed, many of the benefits of a trading bloc for its members may be gained precisely through a shift in the terms of trade in their favour at the expense of non-members; this can happen even if a trading bloc leaves its protective barriers against non-members unchanged. The very real possibility exists, however, that a newly-formed bloc will attempt to exploit its new-found market power by raising its barriers against non-members and still further improving its terms of trade. Even without assuming such GATT-inconsistent behaviour, in a global economy where not all countries belong to a trading bloc, trading blocs can readily improve member welfare beyond what might be expected with global free trade.

By way of illustration, consider a world whose basic elements are countries. There are n such countries of equal size. Following recent work by Krugman, assume that each country is specialised in the production of a single good that is an imperfect substitute for the products of all other countries.[3] Each of these countries has identical preferences and produces the same number of units of their single good. Unlike Krugman, it is assumed the global economy is divided up between members and non-members of a single trading bloc. All countries impose identical tariffs on the imports of all other countries that trading bloc members allow the free importation of member products.

The interesting question is what happens to bloc member welfare and non-member welfare as the trading bloc members allow the free importation of member products. Welfare can be assessed by considering the value of bloc member output and the value of non-member output respectively, deflated by an index reflecting prices in member and non-member economies. Since countries do not differ except as to membership in the trading bloc, only two prices, P_b, the price of trading bloc member output, and P_f, the price of non-member output, are of any significance. Under these assumptions, real income of trading bloc members and non-members will be given by

$$Y_b = \frac{\bar{s}P_b}{(n-f)P_b + fP_f(1+t)} \tag{1}$$

$$Y_f = \frac{\bar{s}P_f}{(n-f)P_b(1+t) + (f-1)P_f(1+t) + P_f} \tag{2}$$

where

$Y_b \equiv$ real income of bloc member
$Y_f \equiv$ real income of non-bloc member
$n \equiv$ total number of countries
$f \equiv$ number of countries outside bloc
$\bar{s} \equiv$ output.

If the numerator and denominator on the right-hand side of (1) and (2) are divided by the price of bloc member output and the price of non-member output respectively, we get

$$Y_b = \frac{\bar{s}}{(n-f) + f\sigma(1+t)} = \frac{\bar{s}}{n - f[1 - \sigma(1+t)]} \tag{3}$$

$$Y_f = \frac{\bar{s}}{\dfrac{(n-f)(1+t)}{\sigma} + (f-1)(1+t) + 1}$$

$$= \frac{\bar{s}\sigma}{(1+t)[n - f(\sigma - 1)]} \tag{4}$$

where $\sigma \equiv p_f/P_b$.

(3) and (4) make clear that bloc member real income and non-member real income will depend on the relative importance of the bloc member output $(n - f)$ and non-member output (f) in the global market basket and on their relative prices (σ). It is by definition, that as trading bloc size increases the importance of its output in the global market basket increases. This means that assessing what happens to member real income and non-member real income requires looking at σ.

The symmetry in production and preferences among all the economies being analysed here means that each economy will spend an equal share of its income on the goods of every economy except for a correction reflecting relative price differences. Under these demand conditions, as the trading bloc increases in size, the demand for tariff-disadvantaged non-member output will decline relatively and the price of non-member output will fall relative to the price of bloc member output.

The negative relationship between σ and trading-bloc size means that non-member real income will decline as the trading bloc gets larger. As seen from the second and third terms in the denominator of (4), the proportion of non-member expenditure that can take place on non-discriminatory terms is falling (as f declines). By contrast, the proportion of non-member expenditure, which must take place on increasingly unfavourable terms (σ falling) is rising. This is represented by the first term in the denominator of (4).

With non-member real income declining continuously as the trading bloc increases in size, the incentive to join the bloc can be overwhelming. Note, however, that real income per trading bloc member need not increase continuously as the trading bloc increases in size. Increasing the size of the trade bloc is beneficial to members both because it increases the proportion of member incomes that can be spent unburdened by trade restrictions and because it improves member terms of trade with non-members (σ declining). As seen from the denominator of equation (3), if member terms of trade with non-members are already very favourable, the real income gained from expanding the trade bloc may be less than what is lost from having fewer countries outside the trade bloc trading with members on favourable terms. In the absence of side payments, this means that it will not be in the interest of members to expand the size of the trading bloc continuously until the point where global free trade is achieved.

This finding can be made more precise. If β reflects the degree to which each economy adjusts its otherwise equiproportional spending on the goods of every economy to reflect relative price differences, then the price of non-member output to the price of member output, σ, can be given by[4]

$$\sigma = 1 - \frac{n-f-1}{n} \frac{\beta t}{\bar{s}+\beta}. \tag{5}$$

Substituting (5) into (3), trading bloc member income is now a function of trading bloc size

$$Y_b = \frac{\bar{s}}{n-(f+t)\left(\dfrac{n-f-1}{n}\right)\dfrac{\beta t}{s+\beta}-t}. \tag{6}$$

As an example, suppose $s = 1.5$, $t = 0.1$, $n = 20$ and $\beta = 2$. Under these conditions Y_b, the real income for each bloc economy, will reach a maximum when half of all economies are bloc members. After this point, Y_b, real income per member, will decrease monotonically as each new member joins up to and including the point where global free trade is achieved. Beyond $f = 6$, in this example, acting on their own, trading bloc members clearly have no incentive to expand their bloc and move on to free trade. They certainly have no incentive to admit new members on a symmetric basis.[5] This result, which is very robust over a wide variety of parameter values, will hold only so long as outsiders do not organise themselves into a competitive trading bloc.[6]

Nothing in the preceding analysis assumes that the trading bloc will attempt to exploit the growing market power that comes with its increasing size and raise its trade barriers against non-members. Trading bloc members can achieve real income levels better than global free trade and non-members can face continuous declines in real income as the trading bloc expands its membership, even while the trading bloc behaves consistently with GATT Article XXIV and makes no attempt to exploit its increasing market power.

2   The East Asian trade regime

The case just outlined captures many of the concerns of the economies on the Pacific Rim of Asia. Very comprehensive regional trading arrangements have been organised and have been greatly strengthened in North America and in Europe. The possibility that even without raising new barriers at all, the growing role of such blocs in the global economy could lower East Asian welfare is very real. The proliferation of voluntary export restraints (VERs), orderly marketing agreements (OMAs), local content rules, new dumping regulations, and other aggressive unilateral measures against some of these economies suggests that it may even be naive to imagine that the newly-created market power will not be exploited. It may be equally naive to assume that such trading blocs are

Table 12.1. *The importance of trade among Asian countries*

(a) Intra-regional trade (exports plus imports) as a proportion of the region's total trade

	1969	1979	1985	1990
North America	0.379	0.287	0.330	0.313
Western Europe	0.698	0.664	0.654	0.712
East Asia	0.293	0.332	0.363	0.407
Pacific Rim	0.566	0.545	0.643	0.499

(b) Proportion of total trade (exports plus imports) with East Asia, 1990

China	0.59	Korea	0.40
Indonesia	0.60	Malaysia	0.37
Taiwan	0.42	Philippines	0.43
Japan	0.29	Thailand	0.51

Source: Petri (forthcoming).

the necessary waystations to a newly invigorated global trading system. Existing members are likely to be better off in a trading bloc that is exclusive. Under a wide variety of conditions, it may not make sense continuously to expand the size of a trading bloc. In particular, it is not hard to imagine East Asian economies being excluded from European or Western Hemispheric regional trading arrangements.

Exclusive arrangements will be preferred to global free trade by members of regional trading blocs only so long as there remain a non-trivial number of non-members who retain protective barriers against each other as well as against the trading bloc itself. If non-members organise their own rival trading bloc, free trade may once again become a superior outcome for all concerned. It is with this perspective in mind that the prospect of new trading arrangements in East Asia should be examined.

As seen in Table 12.1, intra-regional trade is at present approximately 40 percent of all East Asian trade. This is modest by comparison with Western Europe where intra-regional trade is over 70 percent of total trade, but it is considerably larger than the role played by intra-regional trade in North America. Not only is intra-regional trade more important in East Asia than in North America, its relative importance has been growing rapidly. Twenty years ago intra-regional trade was no more than 30 percent of East Asian trade. By marked contrast, intra-regional trade in North America has actually been declining over the past twenty years. Interestingly, if North America, East Asia, Australia and New Zealand are combined, as in Table 12.1, into a single Pacific Rim grouping, the share of intra-regional trade in its total trade approaches West European levels. And over the past two decades, as over the past decade, intra-Pacific trade has been growing more rapidly than intra-West European trade.

These intra-regional trade trends provide some perspective on East Asia's position in a possibly regionalising global economy. Regional trade is becoming more important for East Asia. This need not reflect increasing isolation at all. Trade with East Asia is not only increasingly important for the East Asian economies themselves, it is also increasingly important for North America and for Europe. This increasing importance of East Asian trade in all regions primarily reflects the rapidly increasing economic weight of East Asia in the global economy.

2.1   Factor endowment-based gravity equations

It may be helpful to examine the issue of regional bias in trade more systematically by estimating a model of bilateral trade. The resulting structure can provide a reference point from which biases in the regional pattern of trade can be identified. The structure which will be estimated is given by

$$X^j_{ik} = \sum_{s=1}^{K} \sum_{r=1}^{K} B_{isr} L_{sj} L_{rk}, \qquad i = 1, \ldots, N \tag{7}$$

and

$$\frac{X^j_{ik}}{\Pi_k} = \sum_{s=1}^{K} B^*_{isr} L_{sj}, \qquad i = 1, \ldots, N \tag{8}$$

where

$X^j_{ik} \equiv$ export of variety j of good i to country k
$\Pi_k \equiv$ GNP of economy k
$L_{sj} \equiv$ endowment of factor of production s in economy j.
$N =$ total number of countries

(7) and (8) are derived from the standard factor endowment-based models of international trade where allowance is made for monopolistic competition. Equation (7) is a factor endowment-based version of the gravity equation, which has been used for years as a framework for estimating bilateral trade relationships.[7] Plausibly it explains bilateral trade flows by the interaction between exporter and importer factor

endowments. Equation (8), which is also closely related to traditional gravity equation formulations, states that an economy's share of its trading partner's market for a particular product is a linear function of its own factor endowments.

The structure embodied in equations (7) and (8) results from relaxing many of the strictest assumptions of the standard international trade models in order to incorporate hitherto neglected phenomena in a bilateral trade model. Still further relaxation is possible. For example, suppose that the assumption of strict factor price equalisation across countries, which is necessary to derive (7) and (8), is dropped. Suppose rather, that international trade equalises factor prices only when factor units are normalised for differences in quantity. For example, observed international differences in the compensation of ostensibly unskilled labour may be accounted for by differences in labour quality.[8] Instead of equations (7) and (8) we get

$$X^j_{ik} = \sum_{s=1}^{K} \sum_{r=1}^{K} B_{isr} a_{sj} a_{rk} L_{sj} L_{rk}, \qquad i = 1, \ldots, N \tag{7'}$$

and

$$\frac{X^j_{ik}}{\Pi_k} = \sum_{s=1}^{K} B^*_{isr} a_{sj} L_{sj}, \tag{8'}$$

where $a_{sj} \equiv$ quality of factors in country j.

2.2   Estimation procedures

Equations (7') and (8') can be estimated for N commodity groups and K countries using cross-country data. For example, the terms a_{sj} are not directly observable but can be estimated from equation (8'). Formally, the estimation of equation (8') with a_{sj} differing across countries and unknown is a multivariate, multiplicative error-in-variable problem. Instrumental variable methods will allow consistent estimation of B^*_{isr}. For any given cross-country sectoral equation, a_{sj} will not be identified. In particular, for the specification adopted in equation (8'), however, at any given time there are N cross-sections that contain the identical independent variables. This circumstance can be exploited to permit consistent estimation of a_{sj}.[9] Since the same error will recur in equation after equation owing to the unobservable quality terms, it is possible to use this recurring error to obtain consistent estimates of the quality terms. These estimates of a_{sj} can then be used to adjust the factor endowment data in equations (7') and (8') to obtain more efficient estimates of B_{isr} and B^*_{isr}.[10]

2.3   Estimation of the trade model

Equations (7') and (8') are estimated with 1985 data taken from the forty-three countries for each of twenty-nine manufacturing sectors.[11] The six factor endowments used in this estimation include directly productive capital, labour, educational attainment, petroleum reserves, arable land, and transport resources.[12] The Heckscher–Ohlin equations (7') and (8') are assumed to hold up to an additive stochastic term.

Unlike the standard Heckscher–Ohlin net trade equations, the dependent variable in these bilateral equations will never be negative, but they will occasionally be zero. As most of the twenty-nine equations to be estimated will contain some zero observations, equations (7') and (8') can be specified as a Tobit model.[13]

Some of the results of estimating equation (7') using the a_s obtained from estimating equation (8) and excluding the East Asian economies from the sample are presented in Tables 12.2 and 12.3. As noted in Table 12.2, twenty-six out of the twenty-nine bilateral trade equations are statistically significant. These results mean that it is possible to get a good explanation of the structure of bilateral trade when full advantage of the many available degrees of freedom is taken by including a large number of cross-country factor endowment interaction terms. Table 12.3 identifies the statistically significant role played by the interaction between exporter and importer factor endowments in explaining bilateral trade flows. The signs of these coefficients will reflect the degree of complementarity or substitutability between the various factors of production and their relative importance in the various sectoral production processes.

2.4   Is there regional bias in East Asian trade?

The results presented in Table 12.2 and 12.3 are obtained by estimating equation (7') without using East Asian observations. Using these estimated structures and introducing East Asian observations, tolerance intervals have been constructed for East Asian regional trade and for East Asian exports to some of their major non-regional trading partners. The constructed tolerance intervals indicate, with a probability of 0.99, that 0.99 of a univariate normal population will be found within the interval. Observed exports are then compared with these tolerance intervals. Observations that fall outside these tolerance intervals are considered evidence of regional bias.[14]

The findings for East Asian intra-regional exports compared with East Asian exports to much of North America and the European Community are striking. East Asian intra-regional exports appear to be well explained

Table 12.2. *The estimation of* $X^k_{ij} = \sum\limits_{s=1}^{K} \sum\limits_{r=1}^{K} B_{isr} a_{sj} a_{sk} L_{sj} L_{rk}$

ISIC #	Sector	R^2	$F(35, 957)$
311	Food Manufacturing	0.334	13.7**
312	Other Food Manufacturing	0.019	0.498
313	Beverage Industries	0.336	13.8**
314	Tobacco Manufactures	0.323	13.0**
321	Textiles	0.195	6.6**
322	Wearing Apparel, except Footwear	0.515	28.5**
323	Leather Products, except Footwear and Apparel	0.538	31.8**
324	Footwear, except Rubber or Plastic	0.515	29.0**
331	Wood and Cork Products, except Furniture	0.197	5.87**
322	Furniture, Fixtures, except Metal	0.266	9.89**
331	Paper and Paper Products	0.592	39.6**
342	Printing, Publishing and Allied Industries	0.454	22.7**
351	Industrial Chemicals	0.505	27.8**
352	Other Chemical Products	0.011	0.331
353	Petroleum Refineries	0.605	41.8**
354	Miscellaneous Products of Petroleum and Coal	0.544	32.6**
355	Rubber Products	0.283	10.8**
356	Plastic Products, n.c.e.	0.013	0.383
361	Pottery, China and Earthenware	0.220	7.7**
362	Glass and Glass Products	0.302	11.8**
369	Other Non-Metallic Mineral Products	0.283	10.8**
371	Iron and Steel Basic Industries	0.491	26.3**
372	Non-Ferrous Metal Basic Industries	0.544	32.6**
381	Fabricated Metal Products, except Machinery and Equipment	0.389	17.4**
382	Machinery, except Electrical	0.331	13.5**
383	Electrical Machinery, Apparatus, Appliances and Supplies	0.174	5.75**
384	Transport Equipment	0.063	1.83**
385	Professional, Scientific Measuring and Control Equipment	0.254	9.29**
390	Other Manufacturing Industries	0.017	0.472

** $\equiv$ Significant at the 0.05 level, $F(35, 957) = 1.43$.

Table 12.3. *Number and sign of significant (0.05) coefficients on factor endowment interaction terms (B_{isr})*

	$CAPITAL_{Exp}$		$LABOR_{Exp}$		$EDUC_{Exp}$		OIL_{Exp}		$TRANS_{Exp}$		$LAND\ ARA_{Exp}$	
	+	−	+	−	+	−	+	−	+	−	+	−
$CAPITAL_{Imp}$	5	17	8	6	10	5	14	6	9	4	14	7
$LABOR_{Imp}$	14	4	5	16	10	8	10	4	6	7	13	8
$EDUC_{Imp}$	15	6	12	11	7	12	11	5	8	3	9	6
OIL_{Imp}	7	7	7	3	9	7	4	14	5	6	7	11
$TRANS_{Imp}$	5	3	6	8	10	14	6	8	10	8	5	6
$LAND\ ARA_{Imp}$	11	5	17	3	12	3	5	12	7	8	8	12

Note: The rows index the factor endowments of importers. The columns index the factor endowments of exports. The cells indicate how many significant coefficients of each sign are found for the associated interaction terms in the twenty-nine estimated equations.

by a factor endowment-based gravity equations. As seen in Table 12.4, out of a total of 2088 trade flows only 325 are outside the tolerance interval. This relatively small number of extreme observations suggests there may be little regional bias in East Asian trade. Neither policy initiatives of one sort or another in Asia, nor very large intra-regional East Asian investment, have resulted in intra-regional distortions in East Asian trade patterns. What is true for the region as a whole is also true at the individual country level. Neither Japan, nor Korea, Taiwan, Hong Kong, Malaysia, the Philippines, Singapore, Thailand, and Indonesia have more than a small number of extreme observations on their intra-regional bilateral trade flows (see Table 12.4).

By comparison, with intra-regional trade, East Asia's extra-regional trade is marked by many observations that fall outside the constructed tolerance intervals. Whereas there are an average of thirty-six extreme observations per intra-regional market, as seen from Table 12.5, for East Asian extra-regional export markets there are more than twice as many extreme observations per market. Ironically, factor endowment-based gravity equations estimated without East Asian data do a much better job in explaining the trade among East Asian economies and overall East Asian trade than they do in explaining the pattern of East Asian trade with non-East Asian trading partners.

The extra-regional biases in East Asian trade are striking. Particularly interesting are the patterns of East Asian exports to the European Community by comparison with East Asian exports to North America. In some 305 instances East Asian exports to the European Community appear lower than what might have been expected given the economic characteristics of the various East Asian economies. In each of these cases actual East Asian exports to the European Community are below the lower limit of the tolerance interval. In only a comparatively few (fifty) cases are actual East Asian exports to EC markets above the upper limit of the tolerance interval. Despite very rapid growth in East Asian exports to the European Community over the past two decades, still greater exports might have been expected.

As with East Asian exports to the European Community, there are also a comparatively large number of extreme observations on East Asian exports to North America. By marked contrast with the extreme observations on East Asian exports to the European Community, the extreme observations on exports to North America are disproportionately above the upper limit of the tolerance interval. While 85 percent of the 355 extreme observations of exports to the European Community are below the lower limit of the tolerance interval, only 19 percent of the 195 extreme observations of exports to North America are below the lower

Table 12.4. *Extreme observations on East Asian intra-regional exports*

	Japan		Korea		Taiwan		Hong Kong		Malaysia		Philipp.		Singap.		Thailand		Indon.	
	+	−	+	−	+	−	+	−	+	−	+	−	+	−	+	−	+	−
Japan	—	—	1	2	1	1	1	—	—	3	2	5	3	1	3	—	—	1
Korea	2	3	—	—	2	1	—	—	4	1	3	3	—	2	2	2	3	1
Taiwan	1	2	—	4	—	—	4	—	3	4	2	2	2	3	1	1	4	2
Hong Kong	3	—	3	3	5	3	—	—	4	2	1	—	3	1	2	3	1	3
Malaysia	2	1	—	2	2	1	1	2	—	—	3	3	3	2	1	4	3	1
Philipp.	2	2	4	1	2	—	3	5	3	1	—	—	3	—	4	5	—	2
Singap.	—	5	1	—	1	4	2	4	4	3	3	2	—	—	2	3	5	1
Thailand	3	1	2	6	3	1	3	5	2	1	2	4	5	4	—	—	4	—
Indon.	3	2	2	—	4	—	3	4	—	7	3	—	6	2	5	3	—	—

Note: The rows index imports. The columns index exports. Each cell indicates the number of extreme observations: (+) indicates overexporting and (−) underexporting. The maximum number of extreme observations for any bilateral pair is 29. The critical value for tolerance interval $T(0.99, 0.99, 957) = 2.51$).

Table 12.5. *Extreme observations on East Asian extra-regional exports*

	Japan		Korea		Taiwan		Hong Kong		Malaysia		Philipp.		Singap.		Thailand		Indon.	
	+	−	+	−	+	−	+	−	+	−	+	−	+	−	+	−	+	−
United States	9	3	11	4	14	6	8	1	12	3	6	—	12	3	7	2	4	1
Canada	11	2	9	4	11	3	12	—	7	1	4	—	9	—	6	—	5	4
W. Germany	—	8	2	12	3	7	4	14	4	10	2	4	2	11	4	6	2	3
Netherl.	1	6	—	4	—	3	2	6	2	7	1	3	1	8	—	2	—	4
United Kingdom	—	3	2	5	—	4	3	7	1	4	—	5	2	5	—	3	—	6
France	—	7	—	8	2	10	1	11	—	8	2	7	—	13	2	8	3	8
Italy	1	13	—	10	1	9	—	13	—	14	—	5	—	11	—	10	—	6

Note: Rows index imports. Columns index exports. Each cell indicates the number of extreme observations: (+) indicates overexporting and (−) underexporting. The maximum number of extreme observations for any bilateral pair is 29. The critical value for tolerance interval $T(0.99, 0.99, 957) = 2.51$.

limit of the tolerance interval. If East Asia exports are less to the European Community than might be expected on the basis of global relationships, it appears to export more to North America than might be expected. While there is no intra-regional trade bias if East Asia is defined as a region, if the region is expanded to include the Pacific Basin, then intra-regional bias does become apparent.

Does Japan play a special role in East Asia? Japan's level of productivity and its industrial skills and experience remain well ahead of even the most rapidly growing economies elsewhere in East Asia. It is hardly surprising that Japan is exporting sophisticated capital goods to its East Asian trading partners, at the same time that it is importing processed raw materials, components and manufactures from them. There is at present little evidence of a regional bias in Japan's relations with the rest of East Asia that goes beyond the existing pattern of East Asian resource endowments. Out of 464 instances of bilateral trade flows between Japan and the other East Asian economies only 62 extreme observations have been uncovered. These divide neatly into 16 cases of Japan overexporting, 16 cases of Japan underexporting, 16 cases of Japan overimporting and finally 14 cases of Japan underimporting.

What is particularly interesting about the regional pattern of Japanese trade is not how it differs from the rest of the countries in East Asia, but rather how similar it is. In common with the rest of the economies in East Asia, Japan exports less to the European Community than might be expected and more to the United States than might otherwise be expected. While the European Community appears to exhibit some negative bias against imports from East Asia and overall North America appears to exhibit considerable bias in favour, Japanese import behaviour, at least insofar as the model estimated here is concerned, appears virtually neutral with respect to the rest of East Asia.

3   Pricing strategies in East Asia

If there is no special intra-regional bias in East Asian trade patterns and if the growth in East Asian intra-regional trade merely reflects the growing global economic importance of East Asia, are regional initiatives superfluous except as a tactical exercise to prevent discrimination and exclusion elsewhere? Not necessarily. The absence of regional bias does not necessarily mean the absence of regional trade barriers. The estimated parameters of equation (7') may embody all manner of protective barriers. The absence of intra-regional bias simply means there is no special discrimination in favour or against East Asian trading partners.[15] This is quite a different matter from concluding, for example, that commodity arbitrage across East Asia is near-perfect. In fact, how integrated are East Asian markets?

One helpful way to examine this issue might be to look at East Asian firms' pricing behaviour across different East Asian markets. Do East Asian firms operate as if East Asia is a single, regional market, or are each of the national markets there treated as if they were separate entities? East Asian firms will treat national markets separately if national barriers exist which make commodity arbitrage ineffective, at least on a regional basis.

East Asian firms' price responses in different markets to exchange rate changes provide a source of data on this issue. If commodity arbitrage is effective, then product prices across the region should be the same after correcting for exchange rates. If commodity arbitrage is ineffective, East Asian firms will face particular demand relationships in each East Asian market. Assuming that the price elasticity of demand varies with prices for these demand relationships, exchange rate movements among the East Asian currencies will change the relative price of a product across East Asian markets. With commodity arbitrage ineffective across markets, even after allowance has been made for lags in adjustment, there is no reason to expect 100 percent pass through of exchange rate changes into product prices across markets. If price elasticity varies directly with price, pass through of exchange rate changes should be less than 100 percent. By contrast, if price elasticity varies inversely with price greater than 100 percent pass through of exchange rate changes could be an equilibrium response.[16]

The preceding analysis suggests that if movements in the real exchange rate between two East Asian economies help to explain the path of relative prices of a particular product across these markets, then the integration of these markets is incomplete. Of course, any study of relative prices of particular products across markets needs to be embedded in a more comprehensive framework which also allows for lags in the adjustment of firm behaviour, cyclical demand factors and cost factors.

While such comprehensive studies remain to be done, results following this approach are available for exporters based in Japan. Table 12.6 lists forty-seven product lines, for which sectoral pass-through equations have been separately estimated for each of six markets including the Republic of Korea, Taiwan, Hong Kong, Singapore, Malaysia and Thailand using data from June 1984 to December 1989.[17] Within the larger group of machinery exports, these products have been chosen on the basis of data availability for all countries in the sample; 276 relative price or pass-through equations have been estimated with the data just outlined. While the results of such estimation are broadly interesting, special interest

Table 12.6. *Japanese capital goods' exports to East Asia (sample)*

Excavators	Knitting machines
Graders	Pumps for liquids
Construction tractors	Air and gas
Shovel trucks	compressors
Lathes	Blowers
NC lathes	Elevators
Drilling machinery	Escalators
Boring machinery	Overhead travelling
NC milling machinery	cranes
Grinding machinery	Winches
NC electric-disch.	Conveyors
machine	Forklift trucks
Machining centres	Ball bearings
Press machines	Roller bearings
Forging machines	Speed changers
Rollers for metal industry	Roller chains
Drills	Copying machines
Milling cutters	Refrigerating machinery
Electric welding machinery	Woodworking machinery
Rectifiers	Printing machinery
Magnetic switches	Centrifugal machinery
Diamond tools	Electric generators
Pneumatic tools	Electric motors
Electric machine tools	Transformers
Spinning machines	Switchboards

focuses in such equations on the coefficients of the real exchange rate. As Table 12.7 indicates, in no less than 207 cases out of a possible total of 272, the coefficient on the level of the real exchange rate is statistically significantly different from zero. Apparently strategic pricing is a pervasive phenomenon. Of particular interest here, Japanese machinery exports exhibit this behaviour in the majority of their Pacific markets. Such behaviour is most pronounced in the Korean market and is practised by Japanese machinery exporters for the vast majority of the capital goods they sell in East Asia. Among types of machinery exports, machinery components, for whatever reason, seem less subject to strategic pricing than the complete machine.

Not all of the 207 statistically significant coefficients on the real exchange rate are positive. In no less than twenty cases this coefficient is negative, illustrating the case where exchange rate changes are more than

Table 12.7. *Statistically significant indication of strategic price-setting in relative price equation*

	Korea	Taiwan	Hong Kong	Singap.	Malaysia	Thailand	Total
Excavators	*	*	|	|	|	*	3
Graders	*	|	|	|	|	*	2
Construction tractors	*	*	*	|	*	*	5
Shovel trucks	*	|	|	|	*	*	3
Lathes	*	*	|	|	|	|	3
NC lathes	*	*	*	*	*	|	5
Drilling machinery	*	*	*	*	|	|	3
Boring machinery	*	*	*	*	*	*	6
NC milling machinery	*	*	*	*	*	*	6
Grinding machinery	*	*	*	*	*	|	5
NC electric-disch. machine	|	|	*	*	|	*	4
Machining centres	*	|	|	|	|	*	6
Press machines	*	*	*	|	*	|	1
Forging machines	*	*	|	|	|	|	4
Rollers for metal industry	*	*	*	*	*	*	5
Drills	*	*	*	*	*	*	5
Milling cutters	*	*	*	*	*	*	6
Electric welding machinery	|	|	*	|	*	|	3
Rectifiers	*	*	*	|	*	*	5
Magnetic switches	*	|	|	|	*	*	5
Diamond tools	*	|	*	*	|	|	3
Pneumatic tools	*	|	*	|	|	*	4
Electric machine tools	*	*	*	*	*	*	6
Spinning machines	*	*	*	*	*	*	6

Table 12.7. (cont.)

	Korea	Taiwan	Hong Kong	Singap.	Malaysia	Thailand	Total
Knitting machines	*	*	*	*	*	*	6
Pumps for liquids	*	*	*	*	*	*	6
Air and gas compressors	*	*	*	—	*	*	5
Blowers	*	*	—	—	—	*	3
Elevators	*	*	*	*	*	*	6
Escalators	*	*	*	*	—	*	5
Overhead travelling cranes	*	*	*	*	*	*	6
Winches	*	*	*	*	—	—	4
Conveyors	*	*	*	—	—	*	4
Forklift trucks	*	*	*	*	*	*	6
Ball bearings	*	*	—	*	*	*	5
Roller bearings	*	*	—	*	*	—	4
Speed changers	*	*	—	—	—	—	2
Roller chains	*	—	—	—	—	—	1
Copying machines	*	*	—	*	—	*	4
Refrigerating machinery	*	*	*	—	*	*	5
Woodworking machinery	*	*	*	*	*	*	6
Printing machinery	*	*	*	*	*	*	6
Centrifugal machinery	*	*	*	—	—	*	4
Electric generators	*	*	*	*	*	*	6
Electric motors	*	*	—	*	—	*	4
Transformers	*	*	—	—	*	*	4
Switchboards	*	*	*	*	*	*	6
	44	39	32	26	30	36	207

Note: Coefficients here are statistically significant at the 0.05 level.

Table 12.8. *Cases of more than full pass through, by country*

Korea	2
Taiwan	—
Hong Kong	4
Singap.	5
Malaysia	3
Thailand	6

passed through into foreign prices. The distribution of such cases by country is given in Table 12.8. These cases typically reflect the very small size of some of the overseas markets being investigated here, and the resulting instability of some of the unit value indexes being used as independent variables.

What is particularly interesting here is not just that Japanese firms practise strategic price-setting behaviour in all their East Asian markets for almost all the capital goods in this sample. Strategic price-setting behaviour varies in a statistically significant way not just across product lines but also across markets. In no less than thirty-five out of forty-seven product lines, the hypothesis that the coefficient on the real exchange rate is the same across geographic markets cannot be accepted. The capital goods for which this is true are listed in Table 12.9. Significant barriers to commodity arbitrage in East Asia appear to exist. Considering the interest in regional trade and investment initiatives in East Asia, further investigation is clearly needed as to why pricing behaviour by exporters of the same machinery should vary so much across geographical markets. Do East Asian firms really have the capacity effectively to segregate proximate markets in Asia in the absence of host government connivance of some sort?

The results on the weakness of commodity arbitrage rest on a very simple model of international price discrimination. The limitations of this model should not be forgotten. The impact of exchange rates on strategic pricing behaviour depends critically on the price discriminator's perception of the shape of the demand function for his product. The model employed here does not contain any explanation as to why this perception should vary from market to market, and across exporters. Oligopoly theory is helpful in explaining such variation;[18] empirical versions of such models, however, are not easily employed across a large number of different product lines and markets.

Even apart from issues of specification, further evidence for other product lines and for firms operating out of other home markets needs to

Table 12.9. *Capital goods for which the coefficient on the real exchange rate is statistically significantly different across East Asia markets*

Construction tractors	Elevators
NC lathes	Escalators
Boring machinery	Overhead travelling cranes
NC milling machinery	Winches
Grinding machinery	Conveyors
NC electric-disch. machine	Forklift trucks
Machining centres	Ball bearings
Forging machines	Roller bearings
Rollers for metal industry	Copying machines
Drills	Refrigerating machinery
Milling cutters	Woodworking machinery
Rectifiers	Printing machinery
Magnetic switches	Centrifugal machinery
Pneumatic tools	Electric generators
Electric machine tools	Electric motors
Knitting machines	Transformers
Pumps for liquids	Switchboards
Air and gas compressors	

be examined. Despite the extraordinary growth in intra-regional trade in East Asia, the price evidence presented suggests the continuing importance of official and non-official barriers to intra-regional trade in East Asia. Are these barriers, however, significantly different from barriers to intra-regional trade in North America or Western Europe? Relative price equations have already been estimated for forty-three of the forty-seven product lines for Japanese firm behaviour in the US and Canadian markets. As seen from Table 12.10, in less than half the cases in either the US and Canadian market is the real exchange rate coefficient statistically significant in the relative price equation. Despite all the complaints about lack of Japanese pass-through exchange rate changes in the North American market, strategic pricing is far less pervasive there than in East Asia. Moreover, as indicated in Table 12.11, while there may be as many as twenty product lines in the sample examined here where US and Canadian firms do not appear well integrated with the rest of the global economy, in only half of these twenty cases do Japanese firms act as if commodity arbitrage were not an easy matter across the Canadian–US border. By comparison with their behaviour in East Asia, Japanese firms appear to treat the Canadian–US market as very well integrated. This is true even for the period before the Canada–US Free-Trade Agreement (CUSTA) was ratified (see Chapter 11 in this volume).

Table 12.10. *Japanese strategic price-setting in North America*

	Canada	United States
Excavators	—	—
Graders	—	—
Construction tractors	*	*
Shovel trucks	—	—
Lathes	—	—
NC lathes	—	*
Drilling machinery	—	—
Boring machinery	*	—
NC milling machinery	*	*
Grinding machinery	*	—
NC electric-disch. machine	—	*
Machining centres	*	*
Press machines	—	—
Forging machines	*	—
Rollers for metal industry	—	*
Drills	*	*
Milling cutters	*	*
Electric welding machinery	—	—
Rectifiers	—	*
Magnetic switches	*	—
Diamond tools	—	—
Pneumatic tools	—	*
Electric machine tools	*	*
Pumps for liquids	*	*
Air and gas compressors	—	—
Blowers	—	—
Escalators	—	*
Winches	—	—
Conveyors	—	*
Forklift trucks	*	*
Ball bearings	*	—
Roller bearings	—	—
Speed changers	—	—
Roller chains	—	—
Copying machines	*	—
Refrigerating machinery	*	*
Woodworking machinery	*	*
Printing machinery	*	*
Centrifugal machinery	—	—
Electric generators	*	—
Electric motors	—	—
Transformers	—	—
Switchboards	*	
	19	20

Note: * ≡ Statistically significant at the 0.05 level.

Table 12.11. *Capital goods for which the coefficient on the real exchange rate is statistically significantly different across US and Canadian markets*

Construction tractors
NC lathes
NC electric-disch. machine
Machining centres
Electric machine tools
Forklift trucks
Copying machines
Printing machinery
Electric generators
Switchboards

4   Regional initiatives in East Asia

Despite the absence of intra-regional bias in East Asian trade, evidence on the ability of East Asian firms to behave as if East Asian markets were substantially segregated from one another does suggest that important barriers to trade remain. Quite apart from the tactical benefits in global negotiations that an East Asian grouping might bring, new East Asia-wide liberalisation could still have substantial trade-creating effects within the region.

It should be no surprise that compared with other regions East Asia has been slow to develop region-wide initiatives. No region has enjoyed the scale of East Asia's economic success over the past two decades. As pointed out earlier, however, East Asia's success has been global in its scope, and the successful East Asian economies have been wary to take steps that might undermine the centrality of the GATT. Great variation across East Asia in both the role the government plays in the economy and in the level of development have also contributed to a dearth of formal regional initiatives. The absence of any identifiable regional bias in East Asian trade also suggests that the absence of formal arrangements in no way masked any kind of informal preferential arrangements. In particular, at least as late as the mid-1980s, there is no evidence at all of a Japanese-led informally organised regional bloc in Asia.

ASEAN, the Association of Southeast Asian Nations, is the oldest and best-known regional grouping in East Asia. While originally focused on political and security issues, this grouping, which includes Brunei, Indonesia, Malaysia, the Philippines, Thailand and Singapore, has always had an economic component. As long ago as 1977, ASEAN negotiated a preferential trade agreement. Unfortunately the amount of trade covered by this agreement has always remained small.

With renewed commitment by the ASEAN member-states to economic liberalisation in early 1992, however, agreement has been reached to transform the old preferential trade agreement into a free-trade area (FTA) over the next fifteen years. How much substance this new agreement will have remains to be seen. Intra-ASEAN trade remains relatively small and the ASEAN economies may be too similar to generate large gains from the projected liberalisation. The removal of intra-ASEAN barriers, however, may aid the region's efforts to attract still more investment.

While ASEAN continues to lack substance as an economic grouping, there are regional arrangements on still a smaller scale in East Asia which have the promise of exerting considerable economic force. The most important of these is the Shenzen Free Trade Zone which ties together Hong Kong and Guandong Province in the PRC. Much of the extraordinary development of this part of China in recent years can be attributed directly to the institution of this trading arrangement.

The great success of the Shenzen Free Trade Zone has triggered proposals to link (1) Singapore, the Johore Province of Malaysia and the Batam Island of Indonesia, (2) China, the Koreas, Eastern Siberia and Western Japan, (3) Japan, Korea and the Coastal Province of China, (4) Hong Kong, Taiwan, China South of Shanghai, (5) Hong Kong, Guangding, Guangxi and Northern Thailand, Laos and Vietnam, (6) Thailand, Cambodia and Southern Vietnam, (7) Myanmar, Thailand and Indochina, and (8) Thailand, Northern Sumatra and Northern Malaysia.[19] While nothing may come of most of these proposals, what is characteristic of almost all of them is the joining together of parts of what were once heavily regulated non-market economies with other areas of East Asia that have long records of economic dynamism.

Notwithstanding the many Asian free trade area proposals made in the image of the Shenzen Free Trade Zone, the most widely discussed proposals are much more comprehensive in scope. The best known of these was made by President Mahathir of Malaysia in 1990 and called for the formation of an East Asian Economic Group (EAEG), consisting of Japan, the East Asian NIEs, China and the other ASEAN economies. Although the precise role that such an economic grouping might play was never set out in detail, it was clear at the outset that EAEG was meant to be the East Asian response to emerging trade blocs in Europe and the Americas. As such, the Mahathir proposal was strongly opposed by the United States, Australia and New Zealand, all of whom wished East Asian regional cooperation undertaken rather in the context of Pacific-wide economic institutions such as APEC (Asia Pacific Economic

Cooperation). Strong pressure from the United States has also led Japan publicly to oppose EAEG. Privately, however, at least some Japanese government officials and business leaders have been more supportive.[20] Indeed, it has been suggested that Japanese encouragement may have prompted Mahathir to make his proposal in the first place.

The opposition to the original Mahathir Plan has led to changes in this proposal. EAEG is now thought of not so much as a formal grouping but rather as a periodic consultative mechanism. Whether this East Asian consultation will deal chiefly with the coordination of East Asian positions on global trade policy or whether it will extend to regional economic integration remains to be seen.

While Mahathir has been seeking an East Asian locus for regional cooperation, Australia, New Zealand and the United States have been stressing regional cooperation on a Pacific-wide basis through the development of APEC. Since 1989, the Foreign Ministers of twelve Pacific Rim countries including Australia, Brunei, Canada, Indonesia, Japan, Korea, Malaysia, New Zealand, the Philippines, Singapore, Thailand and the United States have agreed to meet annually to review issues of mutual interest. More recently, in a precedent-setting arrangement, China, Taiwan and Hong Kong have all been admitted to APEC.

To date, APEC's accomplishments have been extremely limited. The small secretariat that has been established has confined itself almost entirely to regional information exchange and technical cooperation. The annual APEC ministerial meetings have been used primarily as fora where resolutions stressing global economic goals have been framed and endorsed. APEC has yet to deal in a concrete way with any significant regional economic issues. It has yet to sponsor (1) regional economic liberalisation initiatives, or (2) harmonise regional economic policies, or (3) resolve regional economic disputes.

5   Conclusion

Regional initiatives in Europe and North America have triggered considerable interest and concern in the Pacific Basin. New trade initiatives by ASEAN, the Mahathir proposal for an EAEG, the evolving APEC, now with its own secretariat, reflect, at least in part, a reaction to developments elsewhere. This is quite apart from the somewhat more familiar, smaller subregional trading zones, proposals for which are proliferating wherever there is proximity in East Asia. These proposals are not being made in the face of long dormant East Asian economic interaction: quite the contrary. In absolute terms, East Asian regional trade and East Asian cross-investment have grown very rapidly.

In the perspective of these developments this chapter concludes that:

(1) It is certainly possible that trading blocs being formed elsewhere in the world might lower East Asian welfare. This can happen even in the absence of any explicit or implicit effort by these blocs to exploit their market power at the expense of East Asia. These trading blocs may have no incentive to expand their membership to include East Asian economies except insofar as they fear provoking the formation of an East Asian trading bloc. In the presence of a substantial group of disorganised, non-retaliating outsiders, a trading bloc even without violating GATT Article XXIV can achieve outcomes for its members that might be superior to global free trade.

(2) The rapid growth in intra-regional East Asian trade reflects not very much more than the very rapid growth in this region relative to the rest of the world. Estimation of a bilateral model of intra-industry trade using a factor endowment-based version of the gravity model suggests no East Asian bias in the trading pattern of the leading economies there. When the Pacific region is defined to include North America, however, substantial regional bias will probably be present. This reflects the positive bias found in East Asian exports to North America. By contrast, there is a negative bias in East Asian exports to Western Europe. From the perspective of the first section of this chapter, there may be some tactical merit in an East Asian regional trading arrangement, but there is no evidence in the available trade data that this is yet happening.

(3) Despite the absence of intra-regional bias in East Asian exports, evidence that East Asian markets are substantively segregated from one another in ways, for example, that Canadian and US markets are not, does suggest that important barriers to trade remain. While East Asian economies have benefited from substantial liberalisation in recent years, new region-wide liberalisation could still have substantial trade-creating effects within the region. Extra-regional effects remain to be analysed.

NOTES

1 See Haberler (1936).
2 See Viner (1950).
3 See Krugman (1991).
4 This is derived in Saxonhouse (forthcoming).
5 Since global free trade maximises global welfare there will always be some system of side payments which will allow non-members to bribe members into allowing them entry to the trading bloc. The terms of such side payments,

leaving symmetric economies in vastly different circumstances, may make this an unappealing alternative. See Kemp and Wan (1976) pp. 95–7.

6 The structure of the game that might result in this event is analysed empirically in Stoeckel *et al.* (1990), among other places.

7 The model presented here is developed in full detail in Saxonhouse (forthcoming). The model presented is an extension to bilateral trade of earlier work presented in Saxonhouse (1989).

8 This was first pointed out by Leontief (1956) as a possible explanation for the empirical failure of the simple Heckscher–Ohlin model.

9 The approach taken here is analogous to the two-step 'jackknife' procedure first proposed in Guilkey and Schmidt (1973). As an example of the approach taken here, let $a_{sj} = 1 + a'_{sj}$, assuming $E(a'_{sj}) = 0$. Using instrumental variable techniques in the presence of multiplicative errors allows consistent estimates of the B^*_{isr}. Using these estimates, for each economy, an $N(J-1) x1$ vector $[v_i]$ of the net trade residuals can be formed. Consistent estimates of the quality terms can be obtained from

$$(B^*_{isr} L_{sj})' (B^*_{isr} L_{sj})^{-1} (B^*_{isr} L_{sj})' (v_i).$$

10 Following Durbin (1954) and in common with two-stage least squares, the approach taken here uses synthetic instrumental variables. Factor endowments are ordered according to size, and rank is used as an instrument.

11 Since the factor endowment variables in equation (8) explain national development, there is no need to limit the sample used here to just the most advanced economies. This development-related protection is explained by changes in the levels of the factor endowments. Typically, the higher the level of factor endowments, the less the protection. The economies in this sample include Argentina, Australia, Austria, Belgium, Brazil, Chile, Denmark, Finland, France, Germany, Greece, Honduras, Hong Kong, India, Ireland, Italy, Jamaica, Japan, Korea, Malaysia, Malta, Mexico, the Netherlands, New Zealand, Nigeria, Norway, the Philippines, Peru, Portugal, Singapore, Spain, Sri Lanka, Sweden, Switzerland, Taiwan, Thailand, Turkey, Egypt, the United Kingdom, the United States and Yugoslavia.

12 Following the suggestion of Dixit and Norman (1980) transport costs are incorporated in the Heckscher–Ohlin framework by treating them as another factor of production. Transport costs are treated as proportional to the weighted average of country distance from potential trading partners. Countries are weighted in this calculation by their GNPs or GDPs. This particular approach allows the incorporation of transport costs within the bilateral Heckscher–Ohlin framework without abandoning the possibility of factor price equalisation up to some multiplicative constant. This treatment of distance is different from the standard approach in the gravity model where bilateral distortion is used exclusively.

13 The Tobit estimation methods used here for equations (8) and (7') are described in Greene (1981) pp. 505–13, and (1983) pp. 195–212, and Chung and Goldberger (1984) pp. 531–4.

14 See Christ (1966).

15 See Saxonhouse (1983) pp. 259–304.

16 See Marston (1990) pp. 217–37.

17 The work discussed here is presented in full detail in Saxonhouse (forthcoming).

18 See Krugman (1986); Dornbusch (1987) pp. 93–106.
19 Further detail on these proposals can be found in Petri (forthcoming).
20 See Petri (forthcoming).

REFERENCES

Christ, C.F. (1966) *Econometric Models and Methods*, New York: John Wiley; T.N. Srinivasan (1979) 'Tolerance intervals', unpublished ms.
Chung, C. and A.S. Goldberger (1984) 'Proportional Projections on Limited Dependent Variable Models', *Econometrica*, 52 (March).
Dixit, A. and V. Norman (1980) *Theory of International Trade*, Cambridge: Cambridge University Press.
Dornbusch, R. (1987) 'Exchange Rates and Prices', *American Economic Review* (March).
Durbin, J. (1954) 'Errors in Variables', *Review of the International Statistical Institute*, 22.
Greene, W.H. (1981) 'On the Asymptotic Bias of the Ordinary Least Squares Estimation of the Tobit Model', *Econometrica*, 49 (March).
   (1983) 'Estimation of Limited Dependent Variables by Ordinary Least Squares and Method of Moments', *Journal of Econometrics*, 21 (February).
Guilkey, D.K. and P. Schmidt (1973) 'Estimation of Seemingly Unrelated Regressions with Autoregressive Errors', *Journal of the American Statistical Association*, 63 (September).
Haberler, G. (1936) *Theory of International Trade with Applications to Commercial Policy*, London: Macmillan.
Kemp, M. and H. Wan (1976) 'An Elementary Proposition Concerning the Formation of Customs Unions', *Journal of International Economics*, 6 (February) pp. 95–8.
Krugman, P. (1986) 'Pricing to Market when the Exchange Rate Changes', National Bureau of Economic Research, *Working Paper*, 1926 (May).
   (1991) 'Is Bilateralism Bad?', in E. Helpman and A. Razin (eds), *International Trade and Trade Policy*, Cambridge, Mass.: MIT Press.
Leontief, W.W. (1956) 'Factor Proportions and the Structure of American Trade: Further Theoretical and Empirical Analysis', *Review of Economics and Statistics*, 28 (November).
Marston, R. (1990) 'Pricing to Market in Japanese Manufacturing', *Journal of International Economics* (November).
Petri, P. (forthcoming) 'The East Asian Trading Bloc: An Analytical History', in Frankel (ed.) (forthcoming).
Saxonhouse, G.R. (1983) 'The Micro- and Macroeconomics of Foreign Sales to Japan', in W. Cline (ed.), *Trade Policy in the 1980's*, Cambridge, Mass.: MIT Press.
   (1989) 'Differentiated Products, Economies of Scale and Access to the Japanese Market', in R. Feenstra (ed.), *Trade Policies for International Competitiveness*, Chicago: University of Chicago Press for the National Bureau of Economic Research.
   (forthcoming) 'Pricing Strategies and Trading Blocs in East Asia', in J. Frankel (ed.), *U.S. and Japan in Pacific Asia*, Chicago: University of Chicago Press for the National Bureau of Economic Research.

Stoeckel, A. *et al.* (1990) *Western Trading Blocs*, Canberra: Center for International Economics.

Viner, J. (1950) *The Customs Union Issue*, Washington, DC: Carnegie Endowment for International Peace.

Discussion

HUGH PATRICK

Saxonhouse in Chapter 12 examines the economic forces which drive the East Asian economies toward or against the formation of a regional trading bloc. He applies new methodologies to analyse the trade patterns and practices of East Asian market economies (including the ASEAN nations) to ask how economically integrated the region is, whether there are biases within the region beyond the normal economic complementarities of factor endowments and distance which push these economies toward formation of a regional bloc, and implicitly what would be the optimal form of trade arrangements. The bottom line is that the East Asian economies benefit far more from an open global, multilateral trading system than they do from one in which the world is divided into two or three major regional blocs.

Section 1 presents a theoretical model which shows that forming a trade bloc can benefit its members while reducing world GNP, by changing the terms of trade against the unorganised non-members. However, as membership expands, the incremental GNP gain is at some point offset by a reduction in the terms of trade effect, so the bloc is unwilling to take in new members. For the East Asian economies the policy implications of this plausible model are clear: join the newly-forming North American Free-Trade Agreement (NAFTA), or fight it by forming their own bloc.

The most innovative and important part of the chapter is the development and testing of a bilateral trade model to determine whether the existing trade patterns among the East Asian market economies are due essentially to factor endowments and distance (transportation costs), or are driven in addition by some non-economic regional bias. The model is an extension of the Heckscher–Ohlin-style gravity model, based on Saxonhouse's earlier research on trade flows and barriers. One important innovation is the use of tolerance intervals to define what constitute normal trade patterns based on the trading patterns of a large sample of non-East Asian countries. Saxonhouse examines bilateral trade flows for twenty-nine manufacturing sectors to determine whether they can be explained by ordinary economic causes.

The results are striking. While there is a great deal of intra-East Asian trade, some 84 percent of the 2088 product bilateral trade flows are explained by ordinary economic factors. In contrast, there is a much larger proportion of extreme cases in East Asian trade with EC countries and with the United States and Canada. This important result shows that while regional trade is substantial there is no *de facto* regional bloc among the East Asian economies. The number of extreme cases of underexporting in East Asian–European Community trade indicate considerably more bias; some 23 percent of East Asian exports are below the tolerance limit, particularly to Italy and France, which discriminate even more against the Asian NIEs than Japan. In contrast, in one-third of the bilateral trade flows East Asian economies export more than is normal toward the United States and Canada. A useful extension of this analysis would be to estimate North American and European exports to East Asian economies and to each other. Are there biases? In what directions?

I derive several implications from these results. First, there is a great deal of complementarity even in manufacturing among the East Asian economies, reflecting different levels and rates of change in factor endowment. Second, there are few cultural, political or institutional predilections or other non-economic factors substantially biasing the exports of North America and the EC to East Asian economies and, indeed, to each other; regional patterns are based essentially on economic complementarities. Third, if the lower import barriers of the currently less restrictive countries prevail, then East Asian exports to a more integrated European Community will grow to more normal levels as firms are able to penetrate the now more restrictive national markets. Fourth, and in a policy sense the most important, the unusual degree of East Asian penetration of the North American markets – indeed the huge share of the United States in their exports – makes clear why the East Asian economies are so fearful of a restrictive NAFTA arrangement, and especially any extension to the rest of Latin America.

Section 3 of the chapter addresses the degree of integration among the major East Asian market economies, more precisely the extent to which there exists price discrimination among countries and product markets for a sample of Japanese exports – forty-seven capital goods to the four NIEs plus Thailand and Malaysia, and to the United States and Canada. The test examines strategic pricing as measured by the degree, and time lag, of export price changes in response to exchange rate changes. Strategic pricing is defined to mean that the producer raises the foreign price less than the appreciation of the exchange rate, assuming that in these markets for capital goods Japanese firms differentiate products and have some market power.

Note, however, that with strong market power strategic pricing policy would be to pass through exchange rate changes, rather than refraining from raising prices. Saxonhouse examines only price changes, without considering associated changes in export volumes.

Saxonhouse finds that in thirty-five out of forty-six products there are significant East Asian differences in pricing among the importing economies. Japanese firms are able to segment the East Asian markets to which they export; interestingly, he shows this is much less true of exports to the United States and Canada, where markets are considerably more integrated. This is a new avenue of research, and we need further micro analysis to understand more adequately what Japanese firm pricing behaviour is, and what these results imply. To some extent they may represent differences in the location of Japanese multinational corporations, intra-firm trading, and internal transfer pricing.

In terms of economic (and not coincidentally political) relationships East Asia is substantially less institutionalised than other economic regions. It has no OECD; no common market or free-trade area (FTA) of any significance; no major regional political or security alliances. In a very real sense, this lack of institutionalisation reflects the great success of the East Asian economies in taking advantage of the GATT multilateral trading system.

The key issue of East Asian regionalism is a matter of political economy. How can the United States, the Western European nations, and Japan work with each other in reforming and managing an open world economic order? What are the likelihoods and dangers of the formation of three major, inward-looking, regional blocs: the European Community; an extension of NAFTA to encompass the entire Western hemisphere; and the Western Pacific? The basic problem is how to integrate Japan effectively into the decision-making process of the world leadership system. This is difficult because Japanese policymakers have not articulated their vision of a new world economic order, Japan's appropriate role in it, or what measures Japan should take to achieve this role, however defined.

Larry Summers (1991) has suggested that trading blocs are advantageous in facilitating negotiations among three major blocs rather than 153 countries. In contrast, Krugman in Chapter 3 above has argued that three major trading blocs lead to a minimisation of global welfare. The world does not need to be divided in trading blocs to get Japanese, EC, and American policymakers to talk with each other. The existence of such trading blocs would probably hinder the process of discussions and negotiations among the three, because it would lock them into potentially confrontational positions. My concern is that a system of three major trading blocs – the existing European Community, the potential US-led Western hemisphere, and Japan-led East Asia – would promote regional integration but result in global disintegration.

REFERENCE

Summers, L.H. (1991) 'Regionalism and the World Trading System', in L.H. Summers, *Policy Implications of Trade and Currency Zones*, Federal Reserve Bank of Kansas City, Wyoming, M-295–303.

VINOD THOMAS

Saxonhouse has in Chapter 12 given us a valuable study on the implications of trading blocs for East Asia. In one sense this discussion is timely and relevant for policymaking in this part of the world. After all, only as recently as January 1992, the ASEAN economic ministers entered a basic agreement under which Indonesia, Malaysia, the Philippines, Singapore, Thailand and Brunei, with a combined population of 325 million, were to complete a tariff reduction system by the year 2008. This came against the backdrop of the Malaysian proposal for a grouping that would also include Japan, the Asian NIEs, and China, in addition to ASEAN.

But in another important sense, the current interest in trading blocs is ironic and unfortunate. The global trading system, and East Asia's in particular, is more open today than at any time in recent memory. Non-tariff restrictions have declined sharply in East Asia, while tariff levels in economies such as Korea, Malaysia, and Taiwan are approaching 10 percent. More than any other part of the world, this region has taken advantage of global trading opportunities, spurring its economic growth. Exports from East Asia grew at roughly 10 percent annually in the past quarter of a century, contributing to the most rapid economic expansion of any region in history. East Asia's trade expansion has cut across regions: about 12 percent annually during the 1980s with the United States, with the European Community, with South Asia and within East Asia.

In this setting, there is a lot to be said in support of what seems to be the main message of this chapter: despite much recent progress, further region-wide liberalisation could be of particular benefit. But here and elsewhere, the chapter's conclusions need to be clarified. Most importantly, with respect to the last statement of the chapter, is Saxonhouse recommending region-wide internal liberalisation only or region-wide global liberalisation, and if it is the former, why not the latter?

If it is region-wide concerted but non-discriminatory liberalisation, including non-tariff barriers, including services, and including investments, then the conclusion of the chapter would be of tremendous importance, not only for East Asia, but also for the entire world. But even though the bulk of the chapter is devoted to the method of analysis, it is not clear how such a conclusion was reached and, more to the point, how it would be affected by the chosen time periods, country and product samples. To take one example, how would the results change if instead of the number of products, their trade value were the basis for considering the deviations from the predictions of factor endowments?

Before turning to the main findings of the chapter, it is crucial to highlight the socialist and other transitions taking place in East and South Asia, which could qualify anything else one might say on the subject. Despite all the progress, the largest countries in the world, China and India arguably still have about the most protected import regimes. In these countries, as well as in Vietnam, Laos and Cambodia, the question of what arrangements are most likely to generate the political support for trade liberalisation cannot be minimised. It is thus quite conceivable that an argument that trading blocs are not desirable for East Asia is qualified once these cases are considered. On the one side, it is when these cases of strong differences in trade regimes are introduced that possibilities arise of a substantial liberalisation through regional blocs. On the other, the possibilities of trade diversion are also greater once the sharp differences within the larger Asia are considered. But these questions are not addressed in the chapter.

On what is covered in Chapter 12, there seem to be two important policy questions. Is an East Asian bloc the best response to blocs elsewhere that could potentially reduce East Asian welfare? If so, what type of blocs make sense?

One might question whether the empirical results are robust, but the models presented do help to illustrate some key propositions. First, trading blocs can improve member welfare. But, second, if the initial condition is one of high and varying protection within a region, non-member welfare could be reduced from the formation of a bloc. And, third, trading blocs can soon become exclusionary, or the path of blocs does not necessarily lead to global free trade, especially if the blocs are successful. These are propositions debated by Chapters 2 and 3 in this volume with the common ground that their validity depends on the country or regional conditions in question. With East Asia on its way to participating in global free trade, the region would not seem to have an interest in establishing an exclusionary trading bloc, except as a reaction and as a deterrent to bloc formation elsewhere – a main point of the chapter. The argument of the chapter seems to be that the best response of East Asia is to threaten bloc formation elsewhere with its own bloc.

This conclusion deserves scrutiny: why is not the best strategy further progress in East Asia's trade liberalisation multilaterally bringing continued economic strength to the region? Lack of its own regionalism in the past has not hurt East Asia's trade with the European Community with which trade has grown annually at 12 percent in the past decade. Would it be different with other blocs?

If indeed a unification of trade policies in East Asia is the best counterbalance to bloc formations anywhere (because these blocs will realise that free trade with East Asia is better for their welfare), that would be serious policy issue with tremendous political economy implications. It would be crucial to address a number of issues.

- One question is whether an Asian or an East Asian bloc could hurt global welfare. For instance, is trade diversion likely to be serious if India and China, or for that matter Japan or Korea, were to open up only preferentially within Asia?
- A related question is why currently protected Asian countries should open up more within the region than the outside. The past growth in trade of other East Asian countries as well as that of these countries was no more within the region than with the United States or with the European Community. The negative implications of introducing a regional bias for the future could be sizeable.
- A third question is the extent and nature of Asian liberalisation that is yet to be done. The chapter argues that there is no intra-regional bias in East Asian trade, but a pro-US and an anti-Community bias, compared to what one would expect from factor endowments. The lack of bias in observed trade patterns is not equivalent to a lack of

barriers. But it is still surprising that priority is placed in the chapter on lowering intra-regional interventions to trade, against the backdrop of the observation about there being no trade bias within the region. Are there strong intra-industry biases? In fact, would not the observation about the bias with North America support the case for lowering barriers across the Pacific?

- A related question concerns barriers to the flows of services, investment and capital, which are likely to be substantial in Asia. These areas seem to be beyond the scope of the chapter, but might represent more fruitful lines for correcting intra-regional biases.

In conclusion, let me return to the global trends. World-wide trade openness is far greater today than forty years ago. The trend of liberalisation of the last decade is particularly strong in East Asia and the developing countries in general. The strong qualifications to this story are twofold: first there is the opposing trend of the last decade in the industrial world, including the United States, that Robert Baldwin referred to in his Discussion of Chapter 2 (p. 51). Second, the distance to be travelled in many developing countries, including some of the largest ones, is considerable.

In these circumstances, one can make an argument, depending on initial conditions of the region in question, either that: regional blocs may be a bad idea in principle, but good in practice, something Professor Krugman seems to argue in Chapter 3 above. Or that even if it is a good idea in principle, it is likely to be bad in practice, as Professor Bhagwati seems to conclude in Chapter 2 above. In the interest of free trade and prosperity, including in East Asia, a continued drive in multilateralism and unilateralism is the best avenue. But in the face of regionalism and protectionism, continued success with multilateral liberalisation is not assured. Concerted efforts to liberalise in what amounts to regional actions for global openness, as opposed to closed regionalism, including in the area of services and investments, is an idea of considerable appeal in the countries of Asia.

13 Prospects for regional integration in the Middle East

STANLEY FISCHER

The Middle East is the home of three great religions and a host of historic conflicts: between Israel and the Arab countries; between Iran and Iraq; between Iraq and members of the Gulf War coalition: in Lebanon; between religious fundamentalists and secularists; and *sub rosa* between the rich 'have' states of the Gulf and the 'have nots' in most of the rest of the region. The potential for economic integration in the region is inextricably tied up with the resolution of these political conflicts.

Definitions of the Middle East range from the Balkans and Turkey in the north, to Mauritania in the west, Sudan in the south, and Pakistan in the east. Alternative definitions reflect differing emphases on some of the characteristics of countries in the area – Arab, Islamic, and geographic. To focus discussion, I will follow the International Monetary Fund (IMF) in defining the region as consisting of the fifteen countries listed in Table 13.1: the Gulf states and Yemen,[1] Israel and its neighbours, and Libya.[2] For convenience, I shall refer to the Gulf states and Yemen as the Southern ME, and the remaining states as the Northern ME.[3] The Occupied Territories of the West Bank and Gaza are part of the region but are not listed in Table 13.1: their population is about 1.7 million, and *per capita* income is about $1200.

The most significant definitional choices are whether to include Turkey, which has long-standing historic ties with the region, and Iran. Each has a population in excess of 50 million, and each is on the periphery of the region. Turkey is excluded because its interests increasingly focus elsewhere – on Europe, and the former Soviet Central Asian republics. Iran is included because much of its interest does focus on the region, but it too is paying increasing attention to the former Soviet republics. The marginal included country is Libya, which as a member of the Arab Maghreb Union is already part of another regional grouping.

The total population of the fifteen-country region is 184 million. Iran and Egypt, each with more than 50 million people, are the two relative

423

Table 13.1. *Countries of the Middle East, selected indicators*

	Pop. (million) 1989	Per capita income (IBRD) 1989	Per capita income growth 1965–89	Life expectancy 1989	Pop. growth proj. 1989–2000	Adult illiteracy 1985	HDI[a] ×100 1989	GNP rank – HDI rank 1989
Bahrain	0.5	6380		69	2.8	27	81.0	– 21
Egypt	51.0	640	4.2	60	1.8	56	39.4	– 10
Iran	53.3	2530	0.5	63	3.3	49	57.7	– 28
Iraq	18.3	3020[b]		63	3.4	11	58.2	– 44
Israel	4.5	9790	2.7	76	1.8	5	95.0	6
Jordan	3.9	1630	3.0	67	2.8	25	61.4	– 10
Kuwait	2.0	16 160	– 4.0	74	3.1	30	82.7	– 30
Lebanon	2.7	880[b]		66	0.1	23	59.2	5
Libya	4.4	5310	– 3.0	62	3.6	33	66.5	– 41
Oman	1.5	5220	6.4	65	3.9	70	60.4	– 49
Qatar	0.4	15 220		70	3.1	24	81.2	– 26
Saudi Arabia	14.4	6020	2.6	64	3.7	49	69.7	– 37
Syria	12.1	870	3.1	66	3.7	41	68.1	– 4
UAE	1.5	18 410	– 3.1	71	2.3	40	76.7	– 43
Yemen	11.7	600	3.5	52	3.6	80	24.2	– 20

Notes:

[a] HDI ≡ Human Development Index from *HDR* (1991).

[b] Based on estimates for 1988 in *HDR* (1991).

Sources: World Development Indicators (1991); *International Financial Statistics; Human Development Report (HDR)* (1991); *World Bank Atlas* (1991).

population giants.[4] Summing Table 13.1's estimates of dollar income *per capita*, aggregate dollar income of the fifteen countries in 1989 was about $480 billion, a bit below the income of Canada,[5] and accounting for 2.5 percent of global GDP. Because the income of the oil-rich countries fluctuate a great deal, the region has in some years, especially 1980, had a much higher real income;[6] and since the Gulf War, aggregate and *per capita* incomes in the region must be much lower, especially in Iraq, Jordan and Yemen.

In 1989, with average dollar income of $2600, the region as a whole would have been classified by the World Bank as having an upper middle income. However regional income disparities are enormous: for 1989, six of the countries, with a total population of 23 million were classified as high-income; three countries, with a total population of 59 million were classified as upper middle-income; and six, with a total population of 100 million, were lower middle-income. None of the countries in the region falls into the World Bank's low-income category, although Yemen with an average income of $600 *per capita* comes close to the low-income category, which in 1989 ended at $580.

All the high- and upper middle-income countries, with the exception of Israel, are in the Southern ME; all the lower middle-income countries except for Yemen are in the Northern ME. In 1989, the Northern ME had a population of 76 million, with average *per capita* income of $1300, while the average *per capita* income of the 104 million people in the Southern ME (including Yemen) was $3400. Egypt has over two-thirds of the population of the Northern ME; Iran has half the population of the Southern ME.

Income growth in the region over the last twenty-five years has been extremely uneven. According to Table 13.1, *per capita* income in some of the oil-exporting countries has actually declined, which is partly the result of rapid population growth. High rates of population growth are forecast for the rest of this decade for most of the countries in the region. At a growth rate of 3.5 percent per annum – which is not unusual in Table 13.1 – population increases by 41 percent within a decade and doubles in two decades. These extremely rapid rates of population growth will put heavy pressure on both the economic and the political structures in the region.

The region's social and human accomplishments do not yet match its income. Longevity is low and illiteracy is high. The gap can be seen clearly in summary form in the last column of Table 13.1, which compares the rankings of countries by *per capita* (Summers and Heston, 1991) GDP and by their Human Development Indicators (HDIs).[7] Except for Israel and Lebanon, every country in the region is ranked higher by income than by HDI – and some of the gaps are very large. These gaps help define the economic development tasks confronting the region in the coming decade.

The North American Free-Trade Area (NAFTA) and the European Community are the two most prominent current models of regional integration.[8] The models differ both in the extent of their economic integration and in the eventual political objectives associated with the initial steps to economic cooperation. Each creates a free trade area (FTA) among its member countries. Goods and financial markets will be, or are, completely open. Labour flows in NAFTA will continue to be restricted, while they may eventually become more free within the Community. The Community, by contrast with NAFTA, is building a network of supranational institutions to tie the economies and the foreign policies of the member countries together, with the eventual possibility of the creation of a federal Europe. The shift to a single money when it comes will be only the most visible signal of the growing cohesion of the countries of the Community.

There is no realistic prospect of Middle East-wide regional integration on either the NAFTA or EC models in the near future. More limited moves towards economic cooperation in the region can be envisaged. These could take the form of free trade arrangements among subsets of countries,[9] agreements to cooperate in functional areas such as water management, agreements on the creation of regional infrastructure that will facilitate trade within the region, and the creation of regional institutions such as a Middle Eastern Bank for Reconstruction and Development (MEBRD). The goals of economic cooperation are as much political as economic – just as they were when the founders of the Community set up the Coal and Steel Community (ECSC) in the early 1950s.

Proposals for Middle Eastern cooperation have of course to be politically feasible, and that constraint will be taken into account. But it is possible to overemphasise the political constraints. Experience in the last three years – in Eastern Europe and the USSR, in South Africa, and not least in the Arab–Israeli peace talks – proves that what is politically impossible today may be politically inevitable tomorrow.

Background data and information on the structures of the fifteen economies are presented in section 1. In section 2 I outline the economic problems that confront the countries of the region. Section 3 presents data on current levels of trade in goods and factors of production within the region. Potential gains from economic reform and economic cooperation in the region are discussed in section 4. In section 5 I discuss a Middle Eastern Bank for Reconstruction and Development as a possible early confidence- and institution-building step on the road to cooperation among the countries and peoples of the region. Concluding comments are presented in section 6.

Table 13.2. *Economic performance of Middle Eastern countries, 1989*

	GDP growth 1980–9	Inflation 1980–9	Curr. acc./ GDP^d	Govt spend./ GDP	Bud. def./ GDP	Exp./ GDP^a
Egypt	5.4	11.0	− 9.0	40.2	6.9	22
Iran	3.4	13.5	− 1.6	17.5	8.0	10
Israel	3.2	117.1	− 4.7	49.1	3.9	34
Jordan	3.4^c	6.3^c	− 18.0	38.4	9.9	53
Kuwait	0.7	− 2.7	40.4	31.0	− 23.5^b	56
Libya	− 9.9^b	0.2	− 7.8	^{e}	^{e}	^{e}
Oman	12.8	− 6.6	11.0	48.6	9.9	48
Saudi Arabia	− 1.8	− 4.4	− 5.3	^{e}	^{e}	37
Syria	1.6	15.0	− 5.0	26.7	2.5	33
UAE	− 4.5	1.1	9.9	13.0	0.6	55

Notes:
^{a} Exports of goods and non-factor services as a percent of GDP.
^{b} Data from *HDR*, for 1988 or 1980–8.
^{c} Data on Jordanian GDP and inflation, and Omani exports, from *International Financial Statistics*.
^{d} Current account is shown pre-transfers.
^{e} Missing data are not available in the sources consulted.
Sources: World Development Indicators (1991); *Human Development Report* (*HDR*) (1991); *International Financial Statistics*.

1 Background: the economies of the region

The economic fortunes of the region have been driven by the price of oil, labour and remittance flows, aid and capital flows, and of course government economic policies. For most of the countries in the region except Israel, the period between 1973 and 1980 was one of exceptional growth, based either on oil or on transfers from the oil producers. For all countries in the region, except Oman, growth in the 1980s was much slower, with Libya, Saudi Arabia and UAE actually experiencing negative growth between 1980 and 1989 as a result of the decline in the price of oil (see Table 13.2). Oman aside, it was Egypt that continued to maintain rapid growth in the 1980s, though the high rate of population growth meant that *per capita* growth was less impressive.

Inflation rates in the region have been moderate, with none of the countries except Israel experiencing high rates of inflation; nonetheless the double digit inflation in Egypt, Syria and Iran is in the discomfort

Table 13.3. *Middle Eastern countries, military spending/GNP, 1986*

Egypt	8.9
Iran	20.0
Iraq	32.0
Israel	19.2
Jordan	13.8
Kuwait	5.8
Libya	12.0
Oman	27.6
Saudi Arabia	22.7
Syria	14.7
UAE	8.8
Yemen	9.1
Average ME[a]	14.2
Developing countries	5.5
Industrialized countries	5.4

Notes:
[a] Unweighted average, excluding Iran and Iraq.
Sources: Human Development Report (HDR) (1991).

zone. Israeli inflation continues at below 20 percent but has not been reduced to single digits seven years after the 1985 stabilisation. In some cases, inflation has been controlled with the assistance of price controls; in addition, credit controls have been pervasive.

Current account deficits in the Northern ME (except Libya) have been large, and covered by transfers,[10] almost entirely in the case of the Arab countries from Southern ME countries in the region. The current account deficit of Saudi Arabia in 1989 reflects the increase in the level of domestic spending between 1980 and 1989. There is nothing especially surprising in the Saudi deficit: given the instability in the price of oil, and other regional instabilities, the appropriate course is to build up reserves during booms and draw them down during periods of low (relative to trend) export earnings – provided of course that the trends can be identified. The massive Kuwaiti surplus of 1988 must have disappeared in the wake of the Gulf War.

Government spending levels in the region are quite high for the state of development of the economies, except for Syria and UAE. The high spending levels reflect both government redistributive programmes and military spending. Data on military spending as a share of GNP are included in Table 13.3.[11] Even excluding Iran and Iraq, which were at war in 1986, the share of military spending in GNP in the area is nearly 10

Table 13.4. *Middle Eastern countries, public sector spending on health and education/GNP, 1986*

	Health	Educn
Bahrain	2.6	5.4
Egypt	1.1	5.5
Iran	1.4	4.6
Iraq	0.8	3.7
Israel	3.2	7.1
Jordan	2.7	6.5
Kuwait	2.7	5.1
Libya	3.0	10.1
Oman	2.3	5.3
Quatar	NA	5.6
Saudi Arabia	4.0	10.6
Syria	0.4	2.9
UAE	1.0	2.2
Yemen	1.2	5.6
Average ME[a]	2.0	5.8
Developing countries	1.4	3.7

Note:
[a] Unweighted average.
NA   Not available.
Sources: Human Development Report (HDR) (1991); for Israel, *Bank of Israel Annual Report* (1988).

percentage points above the world average. A gradual reduction of Middle Eastern to world levels of military spending would free up enormous amounts to resources for investment in human and physical capital. This would be about $50 billion per annum, well in excess of any estimates of the amount of assistance the much called for and unlikely to happen Marshall Plan for the Middle East could hope to deliver. And since much of military spending is on imports, a cut in military spending would generate balance of payments' support as well – provided that economic assistance is available on the same terms as military assistance.

Although the human capital indicators for the region, such as literacy, are on the whole poor, a massive investment effort has been taking place in Saudi Arabia and Libya (Table 13.4). The Northern ME states in Table 13.4, except Syria, have also been spending significantly on health and education; it is, however, noticable that some of the oil-rich countries have spent relatively little on these social sector investments.

Table 13.5. *Middle Eastern countries, debt and external financing, 1989*

	Debt/ GNP	Debt group	Curr. acc./GDP[a]	Net long-term debt flows/ GDP	Grants/ GDP[c]	FDI/ GDP	ODA/ GNP
Egypt	167	SILIC	− 9.0	2.3	1.6	5.0	4.7
Israel	40		− 4.7		7.1	0[b]	7.1
Jordan	181	MIMIC	− 18.0	20.2	2.6	0	6.3
Syria	169	SIMIC	− 5.0	5.7	0.2	0	1.2
Yemen	69	MIMIC	− 7.3	4.7	1.3	0	

Notes: SILIC ≡ severely indebted low-income country; SIMIC ≡ severely indebted middle-income country; MIMIC ≡ moderately indebted middle-income country.
[a] Current account deficit before official transfers.
[b] This is the net of gross inflows and outflows, each about 1 percent of GNP.
[c] Grants are public sector.
Sources: World Development Indicators (1991); *World Debt Tables* (1991–2); *Bank of Israel Annual Report* (1989); *International Financial Statistics.*

Returning now to Table 13.2, several states in the region had large budget deficits in 1989. At the rates of growth experienced in the region, deficits much in excess of 5 percent of GNP would pose an inflationary and balance of payments' danger, unless there were extensive financial repression. That was indeed the case in Egypt and no doubt also in other deficit countries.

The share of exports in GNP appears high for most Middle Eastern countries. That is obvious for the oil exporters. Raw and processed materials are important also in the case of Jordan. Tourism is an important revenue source for Egypt, Israel, and Jordan.

Data on the structure of production are presented in Table 13.2. Agriculture accounts for a significant share of output only in Iran, Egypt and Syria, with in each case a larger share of the population being involved in agriculture than the share of the sector in GDP. Manufacturing sectors tend to be small, except in Egypt, Jordan and Israel (not shown).[12] Even so, manufacturing accounts for a smaller share of GNP in the Middle East than in developing countries at similar income levels. Several of the economies show high shares of output being generated in the industrial sector, which generally includes extraction and utilities. Employment in these sectors is probably relatively small, and the service sector in the poorer countries of the region is relatively large.

Table 13.5 describes the external financing and debt situations of Egypt, Israel, Jordan, Syria and Yemen, the indebted countries in the Middle East for which debt data are available. Syria and Egypt were each regarded as severely indebted in 1989. Egypt's debt cancellation following the Gulf War would move it into the moderately indebted category. Yemen and Jordan are each moderately indebted, though Jordan's current account deficit is very large. The inflow of long-term in 1989 was unusually large, coming about equally from commercial and (concessional) bilateral sources, with multilateral sources accounting for about $100 million or one-eighth of the long-term flows. Israel's debt situation has improved greatly since its stabilisation programme in 1985, in part because US aid is now on a grant basis. Egypt is the only country in the region to receive significant amounts of foreign direct investment, the annual net flow of which has been sustained at around $1 billion or more since 1985. At more than 3 percent of GDP, this is a large ratio by international standards.

2   The need for reform and reconstruction

The data, particularly on the balance of payments and budget deficits, point to the macroeconomic problems facing many of the economies of the region, particularly those in the Northern ME. But they do not tell the most crucial part of the story, which is that several of the economies are in crisis, and that the declines of the 1980s have become far worse in the early 1990s.[13]

In the Southern ME, Iran, Iraq and Kuwait all face major tasks of reconstruction. Iran has begun to move to deal with these problems, renewing relations with the international financial institutions, and slowly opening up to the outside world. Iraq is still mired in conflict with the rest of the world, has begun postwar reconstruction from its own resources, but still has a long way to go to recover from the effects of the Gulf War. Kuwait is moving ahead slowly, apparently determined not to rely as heavily as in the past on migrant labour, but it seems increasingly doubtful that this intention will be carried out. The future of Yemen's economy depends both on its ability to develop its energy resources, and on the recovery of labour flows from Yemen to the Gulf countries.

The remaining high-income countries of the Southern ME face no major economic crises so long as the oil markets remain reasonably stable, as Saudi Arabia intends they will, and provided their population growth rates start declining. These countries have seen their primary economic goal as being to diversify their economies to reduce their oil dependence. Given Saudi Arabia's position in the world oil markets, diversification is bound to be limited, and should continue to take predominantly the form that it has so far – of developing oil-related industries. The more urgent economic policy task in such an economy is to manage savings and the flows of production and consumption so as to maintain a high and reasonably stable level of consumption: diversification is more a matter of portfolio than of production management. Attempts to go further afield in diversifying production, for instance to develop the Saudi wheat industry, are both extremely expensive and inhibit the development of interregional trade based on comparative advantage.

After the Gulf War, the oil-rich countries are even more aware than they were before of the need for political stability in the region. In the past they have provided large amounts of aid to the poorer Arab countries. By employing migrant workers from the poorer economies (see section 3 below), they have assisted those economies through trade (in factor services) as well as aid. Trade is more likely than aid to lead to constructive long-term relations: if the Gulf countries no longer want to import migrant labour on the scale of the past, they will need to consider increasing their financial investment in the home countries of the migrants, so that capital goes to labour as well as labour coming to capital. This would both require and contribute to greater economic and political stability in the capital-importing countries.[14] Egypt is the only Northern ME country to have received significant amounts of foreign direct investment since the Lebanese Civil War began.

The tasks of reconstruction and reform in the Northern ME countries are as difficult as those in the Southern ME. The Lebanese economy has been devastated in the last fifteen years, and will need large amounts of capital as well as a political settlement and a government if it is to be reconstructed.[15] But the financial service and entrepôt functions that Lebanon served in 1975 have moved elsewhere.[16]

Syria, which had been pursuing an inwardly-oriented development strategy, dependent for military assistance on the USSR, and had stopped servicing its debt to the international institutions, is beginning to open up its economy. It has energy, agriculture, and tourism to develop (see Hilan, 1992), and would benefit from reductions in military spending and from the reductions in bureaucracy and state intervention that would accompany reform.

Jordan's economy suffers from a narrow production base, and from heavy dependence on aid and remittance flows, which have declined in the last year. Jordan is one of the few countries in the region that has traded (goods) significantly with its neighbours, but that trade has been disrupted by the Gulf War. It has run a reasonably open economy, and implemented market-oriented economic reforms with the support of the

IMF, and at some political cost. Nonetheless, the massive economic shocks it has suffered mean that it will need additional aid if further declines in output and income are to be kept to politically acceptable levels.

The Israeli economy has the most sophisticated technological base in the area, and is very open to trade, with exports exceeding 35 percent of GNP and imports exceeding 40 percent of GNP. Israel has free trade agreements with the United States and with the European Community, and it has since its 1985 stabilisation gradually liberalised important branches of the economy, especially the capital markets and foreign exchange transactions. The role of the state in the economy is still excessive; if a much-promised privatisation programme gets under way, Israel will be signalling that it is willing to move away from its previous excessively interventionist policies.

Israel faces the prospect of large-scale immigration in the next few years, and has already received 400,000 Soviet immigrants, almost 10 percent of the population. The absorption of younger immigrants is proceeding reasonably well; that of the older immigrants less well. The flow of immigrants slowed sharply in the first half of 1992, but is likely to revive if US loan guarantees are used productively. Israeli officials believe as many as a million immigrants might eventually arrive from the former USSR.

Israel has since 1973 received significant amounts of US aid; since the mid-1980s, military assistance has been about $1.8 billion a year, and economic assistance $1.2 billion. Israel receives other contributions from abroad of about $1 billion per year.

The Israeli economy has had to develop in essential economic isolation from the region. There is very little direct trade with other countries in the region; some indirect trade has taken place through the West Bank since 1967. Trade with Egypt since 1979 has been largely in oil. The Arab boycott of Israel has helped keep foreign direct investment low.

In the context of the Middle East peace talks, Israel has agreed to increased autonomy for the Palestinians in the Occupied Territories – though much work remains to be done to define and agree on this concept. The economies of the West Bank and Gaza are major suppliers of labour to the Israeli economy, which provides over one-third of the employment in the Occupied Territories; Israel is also the main direct market for exports from the Territories, a phenomenon that results in part from the free trade between Israel and the Territories.[17] The remaining one-third of exports are sent to Jordan. The West Bank and Gaza also provide markets for Israeli exports, but account for only about 3 percent of the Israeli total (Kleiman, 1992).

The future of the economy of the West Bank and Gaza obviously depends on political developments. The West Bank's economic future is bound to be most closely tied to its relations with both Israel and Jordan, the latter serving potentially as a valuable entry point into the rest of the Arab world. But there are competing views among Palestinians of the best development strategy for the economy, with the usual split among those who see the need for import-substituting industrialisation – which could build on the relatively high levels of Palestinian human capital in the region and abroad – and those who want a more open economy.[18] It is essential in this discussion to emphasise that the economy of the Occupied Territories is very small, and that an inward-oriented development strategy is certain to fail.

Egypt's pivotal position in the Middle East has given it the ability to attract sufficient aid to avoid radical economic reforms. But the very favourable debt deal that Egypt received after the Gulf War, conditional on cooperation with the international agencies, and trends that had in any case been visible beforehand, have increased the likelihood that it will carry through a structural reform programme. Reforms started in the middle of 1991, with tariff, exchange rate, interest rate and price adjustments, as well as a change in the law on public enterprises (Handoussa and Shafik, 1992).

With its potentially large markets, favourable geographical position, reasonably high levels of human capital including a large labour force and sophisticated elite, ability to attract foreign capital, and political importance, Egypt has the potential for rapid growth once economic reforms are introduced.[19] Some of Egypt's reluctance to reform stems from its government's concerns over the social consequences of adjustment, reinforced by riots in Egypt in the 1970s, and more recently in Jordan, following price rises that were part of stabilisation and reform plans. The generally increased attention that has been given to protecting the poor in stabilisation and adjustment programmes should help make the adjustments more acceptable. In the case of Egypt, as elsewhere in the region, there is a need to increase the efficiency of large-scale public enterprises, with privatisation the most promising strategy.

Most economies in the Middle East need large-scale reconstruction and reform, with or without regional integration.[20] We turn next to examine the current extent of, and potential for increases in, economic integration in the region.

3   Intra-regional trade

Intra-regional goods trade in the Middle East accounts for only a small proportion of total trade, 6.2 percent in 1983, the last year for which

Table 13.6. *Middle Eastern countries, intra-regional and total trade, 1983,* %

	Total trade/2 (GDP)	Intra-regional/ total trade	Contiguous/ total trade[a]
Bahrain	65.4	50.9	45.6
Egypt	24.0	6.6	5.8
Iran	10.3	0.6	0.5
Iraq	23.3	7.5	7.4
Israel	43.4	0.1	0.1
Jordan	35.3	29.2	25.1
Kuwait	44.9	9.0	5.0
Lebanon	40.1	23.4	1.7[b]
Oman	17.9	25.7	24.0
Qatar	37.6	3.8	3.5
Saudi Arabia	54.0	3.9	3.5
Syria	18.4	22.6	1.7
UAE	16.0	7.7	6.1
Yemen	25.8	22.2	13.2

Notes:
[a] All countries on the Gulf are treated as contiguous; Saudi Arabia and Egypt are contiguous; Lebanon and Egypt are not treated as contiguous in the above calculation.
[b] Lebanese statistics report trade with both Syria and Israel as zero. Data in the table are adjusted by including Syria's reported trade with Lebanon in Lebanon's trade data.
Source: UN ComTrade data base; World Bank for dollar GDP.

complete data for all countries in the region are available.[21] Nor does the picture change when oil trade is excluded: only 6 percent of non-mineral fuel trade is intra-regional.

Table 13.6 presents 1983 trade data. The first column gives the average of the share of exports and imports in GNP.[22] The most striking fact in Table 13.6 is that there is only one country in the region (Bahrain) for which intra-regional trade amounts to as much as 50 percent of trade,[23] and no other country for which as much as 30 percent of trade is intra-regional. As should be expected, the bulk of intra-regional trade is conducted with contiguous states.

The data underlying Table 13.6 are more than usually subject to error. The trade matrix from which the data are derived should be, but is far from, symmetric.[24] Some of the biases in the data would lead to under-statement of the importance of intra-regional trade: first, no trade is reported between Israel and Arab countries, except Egypt, but such trade is reputed to take place; second, trade between Israel and the Occupied Territories can be regarded as intra-regional, but is not recorded as such; third the Iran–Iraq War must have sharply reduced intra-regional trade in 1983, the year to which the data apply; the same holds for the aftermath of the Israeli invasion of Lebanon; and smuggling over the long borders of Middle Eastern states is legendary. In addition, Jordan and Lebanon each traded about 10 percent of GDP within the region in 1983.[25] The fact remains, however, that intra-regional goods' trade in the Middle East is at present at very low levels.

Most strikingly, the general impression conveyed by Table 13.6 is confirmed for each of the ten categories of goods for which trade matrices are available,[26] except mineral fuels. There is no general category of commodities for which intra-Middle Eastern trade is very important.

The question arises of why intra-regional trade is so low. Tariff rates within the region are not generally high; indeed, for members of the Gulf Cooperation Council (GCC)[27] they are practically zero for most goods including food. UNCTAD data suggest that GCC non-tariff barriers are relatively low, while those for the non-oil producing countries of the Middle East (excluding Israel) are high.[28] Intra-regional trade involving potential imports to the GCC must be low primarily because the poorer countries of the Northern ME do not produce the high-quality goods that the richer countries of the Southern ME import, and because from time to time politics interferes with trade. Trade among the Northern ME countries remains at a low level because of the lack of peace and stability in the area, and because tariffs and non-trade barriers are high. But to concentrate on trade in goods is to miss most of the trade flows within the region.

3.1   Trade in labour services

While goods flows within the Middle East are relatively small, labour flows are large – a fact that was brought home by the labour expulsions associated with the Gulf War. Table 13.7 presents data for the early 1980s; no doubt the details would be different in the wake of the Gulf War. According to Table 13.7,[29] 18 percent of the labour force of the exporting countries within the Middle East – Egypt, Jordan, Lebanon, Syria, and Yemen – worked in the Gulf in the early 1980s.[30] Table 13.7 also implies, almost incredibly, that over half the labour force of the eight labour-importing countries of the Middle East – Bahrain, Iraq, Kuwait, Libya, Oman, Qatar, Saudi Arabia, and UAE – came from other countries, including Asian countries.

Table 13.8 presents data on remittance flows to and from countries in the

Table 13.7. *Middle Eastern countries, migrant workers as a proportion of the labour force, early 1980s, 000*

	Exports of migrant workers to Libya and Gulf	Imports of foreign workers	Migrant workers/ labour force (%)	Immigrant workers/ labour force (%)
Bahrain		81	—	59
Egypt	2000		18	—
Iraq		0.8–1 million	—	19–25
Jordan	300	120	67	27
Kuwait		379	—	79
Lebanon	140		20	—
Libya		467	—	51
Oman	50	145	17	49
Qatar		94	—	85
Saudi Arabia		1.1–2 million	—	44–59
Syria	80		3	—
UAE		491	—	89
Yemen	680		24	—

Source: Choucri (1983).

region. These data probably underestimate the extent of remittances. Table 13.8 includes remittance flows to countries outside the region. For Egypt and Jordan, remittances in 1989 accounted for more than 10 percent of GNP, and for all the labour-exporting – and poorer – countries in the region, remittances in 1983 were far larger than intra-regional exports.

Remittances from the Gulf to the Occupied Territories are presumably also large relative to GNP and exports. Aggregate remittances to the recipient countries in the region reached their peak level of $6 billion in 1984, a year in which Egypt received nearly $4 billion, and Jordan over $1.2 billion.

Labour flows thus constitute a more important form of trade within the region than goods' flows. But this trade has been severely reduced by the Gulf War and its attendant political disruptions. There have also been reports that migrant workers have very few rights within host countries, suggesting the need to establish and follow a code of labour conduct.

Table 13.8. *Middle Eastern countries, net worker remittances, 1989, $ million*

	Remittances	Remittances/ GDP (%)	Remittances/ intra- regional exports (1983)
Bahrain	− 199	− 6.4	− 0.22
Egypt	3532	11.2	5.99
Jordan	623	15.9	4.66
Kuwait	− 1300	− 5.5	− 0.64
Libya	− 472	− 2.1	− 400
Oman	− 791	− 10.2	− 2.47
Saudi Arabia	− 8300	− 10.3	− 1.47
Syria	395	3.4	1.90
Yemen	581	7.3	43.82

Note: Data for Middle Eastern countries missing from the table are unavailable.
Source: World Bank.

3.2   Capital flows

Private capital flows within the region take place mainly among the GCC countries, and in the form of foreign direct investment to Egypt. In addition, substantial amounts of aid have flowed from the Gulf states to countries in the Northern ME and Yemen (Tables 13.9 and 13.10). These aid flows were extremely large in 1980 and have declined along with the price of oil and with political disagreements in the area. The aid picture after the Gulf War will look different than it did in 1989, both because some sources have dried up and because Syria has joined the list of recipients.

At the start of the 1990s, the capital-rich countries of the region are in a very different position than they were a decade ago. Then the price of oil was at its peak and they could provide aid on a far larger scale relative to GNP than other rich countries. Now the price of oil is relatively low, the Southern ME is living in the uneasy aftermath of two major wars, the current accounts of all the countries in the Southern ME except Oman are in deficit, and aid will not flow on the scale of the past. Since much of that aid was provided without strings, the decline in aid in the long run is not unmitigatedly bad for the recipient countries.

Table 13.9. *Middle Eastern countries, aid receipts, 1986 and 1989,*
$ million

	1986		1989	
	Arab bilateral	Total ODA	Arab bilateral	Total ODA
Egypt	54	1716	− 15	1578
Israel		1937		1200
Jordan	433	564	134	280
Lebanon	27	62	4	132
Syria	632	728	0	139
Yemen	107	329	34	338

Note: Data for Middle Eastern countries missing from the table are unavailable.
Source: OECD, *Development Co-Operation* (1990) (DAC Report).

Table 13.10. *Concessional assistance, by Middle Eastern Arab countries,*
selected years, $ million

	Commitments 1989	Net disbursements			% of GNP	
		1980[a]	1986	1989	1980	1989
Kuwait	98	1140	715	169	4.18	0.54[b]
Libya	163	376	68	83	1.17	0.36
Saudi Arabia	1391	5682	3517	1171	4.92	1.46
UAE	160	1118	87	25	3.72	0.10

Notes:
[a] Aid was also provided in 1980 by Iraq and Qatar; the total aid of six countries
was $9.5 billion.
[b] At WDI income level of $23.5 billion, this amounts to 0.72 percent; 0.54 is DAC
estimate.
Source: OECD, *Development Co-Operation* (1990) (DAC Report); *World Devel-*
opment Report (1982).

4   Potential gains from economic cooperation

In considering regional integration, the first thought is to consider an FTA or customs union (CU).[31] Whether such arrangements improve economic welfare depends on a number of factors outlined by de Melo, Panagariya and Rodrik (1992, Chapter 6 in this volume). However, it is clear that the major goods and services trade of the Middle East will continue to be with the outside world, with energy and other raw material exports predominating for the foreseeable future. Further, the region is not especially coherent in terms of its likely external trade patterns. With the opening of the former USSR, countries in the east of the region are likely to develop their trade to the east; the countries in the Northern ME will be more oriented to Europe.

There are already important regional trading arrangements among some of the countries in the region, most notably the GCC (formally, the Cooperation Council for the Arab States of the Gulf).[32] Other sets of arrangements can easily be envisaged, for instance a free trade zone among Israel, the West Bank and Gaza, and Jordan – and for that matter, with Syria, Lebanon, and Egypt, too, if the peace talks make progress. Even without an FTA, the Israeli economy would benefit from the lifting of the embargo on trade, and the benefits would extend also to its neighbours; progress here, too, depends on the peace talks.

Tempting as it is to trace out FTAs on the map, it is important to recognise that there have been many failed political and economic unions and groupings in the Middle East, and that most regional trading groups have failed. Agreements to set up regional trade areas have typically included four elements: the removal of barriers to trade within the region; the creation of a common external tariff (CET); the development of methods for allocating new industries to the different countries of the region; and the removal of constraints on factor mobility (de la Torre and Kelly, 1992). De la Torre and Kelly conclude that agreements that leave tariff reductions to be negotiated item by item, rather than to be implemented according to a pre-set schedule, rarely succeed. They report also that attempts to implement an industrial policy through a regional trading arrangement have not succeeded.

As this historical record, as well as the NAFTA and Community cases show, negotiating a workable FTA is a long and complex process, demanding of the time and effort of policymakers. The potential economic benefits of these arrangements in the context of the Middle East arise more from political than direct economic benefits: given a predicted trade pattern which is mainly with the outside (the region) world, the direct gains from enlarged intra-regional goods and services trade would probably be relatively small. Nonetheless, both politically and economically, the gains associated with improved economic relations could be enormous: if the fifteen countries of the region were trading freely among themselves, it would certainly be a different world politically, one in which the current hostilities had been severely muted. The beginnings of peace in the Middle East would not only allow trade to develop, but would also bring a massive peace dividend, equal to at least the 10 percent of the area's GDP by which military spending now exceeds the international average.

Those interested both in bringing peace to the region and improving the well-being of its inhabitants must work towards eventually free and open trading and economic relations wihin the region. However, given current hostilities, and the history of past failures, it would not make sense to start trying to improve regional economic relations by negotiating preferential trade arrangements. Rather, attempt to improve and develop economic relations among the countries of the region should start from collaboration *in functional areas*, encouraging officials and private citizens of the different countries of the region to work together on subjects of mutual interest, leading gradually to more general economic relations. This was the model followed in Europe after World War II, where the ECSC and the European Payments Union (EPU) preceded the creation of the Common Market in 1959.

Collaboration is possible in several areas. The most important is water management, which is a matter of agreeing on pricing as well as on the management and development of water sources. Regional communications and transport infrastructure needs further development. Power grids could be tied together, taking advantage of differing peak hours in different countries. Scholarly exchanges could be developed. The tourist industry could be developed jointly in the Northern ME. A Middle Eastern Development Bank will be discussed below.

There is also room for collaboration in other areas. Most urgently, countries need to agree on a set of rules or code of conduct for the employment of migrant labour. Similarly, potential recipients of foreign direct investment should agree on rules to protect investors, as well as to limit the concessions offered to them. If intra-regional aid continues, it should be made conditional on economic reforms in the recipient countries.

Given probable future trade patterns in goods and services, which will be largely outside the Middle East, and the reform and reconstruction needs outlined in section 2 above, states in the region should now focus their trade reform efforts on liberalising their countries' trade and payments regimes, and increasing the efficiency of their own economies, with the aim of encouraging trade in general, rather than intra-regional trade in particular. This can be done at the same time as functional cooperation begins to develop, and without affecting current regional trading arrangements.

5   The Middle Eastern Bank for Reconstruction and Development (MEBRD)

While important opportunities exist for economic collaboration among Middle Eastern countries, they lack a framework in which to pursue them. There are of course many cooperative organisations among the Arab countries of the region, as well as the OPEC Fund and other Arab aid agencies. But there is no regional organisation containing all the countries of the region including Israel. Nor is there any record of sustained collaboration among the countries of the region. They have to begin to learn to cooperate, just as the Europeans did over forty years ago.

Given existing rivalries, cooperation will develop best with the participation of external powers. The natural organisation is a MEBRD. The MEBRD's name describes its functions. It should help reconstruct the war-ravaged economies of the Middle East, and help develop a regional infrastructure. It could be the forum in which other matters of mutual concern – such as water usage, and capital and labour flows – are discussed. If its member countries can collaborate within the context of the MEBRD, then it could serve as the basis for an expansion of trade and enhanced collaboration in other areas.

Like the World Bank, the MEBRD should have a regular development banking function, borrowing in the international capital markets and lending at market terms to its higher-income borrowing members. It should also manage a special fund that lends on concessional terms to the poorest countries in the region. This Middle East Fund would be the equivalent of the International Development Association (IDA).

The Bank itself would be financed through capital contributions by member countries. All countries that hope to bring peace to the region should contribute: if the effort is to be serious, at least the G-7 countries should join. There is a special role for Europe and especially Japan, which has been taking an increasing interest in the region recently. Countries in the region that want to borrow from the MEBRD would have to become members. Countries that are not part of the region as defined in this chapter – such as the Maghreb countries – might want to join as potential borrowers. However, the borrowing membership will have to be limited if the Bank is to serve as a forum in which the problems of the Middle Eastern countries (as defined in Table 13.1) take centre stage.

As in the World Bank and the IMF, voting power would be proportional to contributions. Only a small portion of the contribution would have to be paid in, the remainder serving as a guarantee. Contributions to the Middle East Fund need not be in the same proportions as to the Bank. The richer countries of the region would be expected to play a major role in the Fund, which would be supplemented by contributions from other countries with an interest in bringing stability to the region.

Many difficult issues have to be settled before the MEBRD can become a reality. Here are some questions and answers.

- How should the Bank start, given the conflicts in the region? The Bank should not be hostage to those conflicts. Rather, non-regional members should convene a planning meeting to which they invite all countries in the region, and any other countries that are interested. A charter for the new Bank can be developed quickly, using the precedent of the EBRD and other regional banks.
- How large will the MEBRD be? The Bank cannot be large enough to play a major role in the reconstruction of Iraq if long-term peace comes. It should be large enough to play a major role in Lebanon. Like the EBRD it can start small, say at $10 billion, and then build up its capital if it establishes itself successfully.
- How will the MEBRD interact with the IMF and the IBRD? At the beginning it will rely heavily on those institutions for intellectual and operational support. It will also want to cofinance with them.
- How will the Bank deal with the Palestinians? The Bank should be able to deal with and lend to organisations in the Occupied Territories, and should have provision for future membership of a Palestinian entity or state that emerges in the peace process.
- How should Israeli membership be handled? Israel should be part of the initial membership. The role it plays in the Bank will in practice depend on the rate of progress in Arab–Israeli peace talks.
- Who should manage the Bank? Residents of the region should play a larger role in management than their share of capital, and the Bank should plan to increase their role over time. It is important, however, that the industrialised countries take an important part at the beginning, and that the MEBRD should be built up to the highest professional standards.
- Why should countries funnel concessional assistance through the Middle East Fund? After all, Gulf countries have their own bilateral development programmes. First, non-Gulf countries will also want to contribute to the Fund. Second, by using the Fund, donors make sure that their aid is well used, in accord with economic considerations and

requirements. Third, since its directorate will include representatives of both borrowing and lending countries, the Fund provides a preferable method for the collective provision of aid by the richer Gulf countries than would be possible in a series of bilateral arrangements.

- Why yet another international bureaucracy? What's wrong with the World Bank? There is nothing wrong with the World Bank. There are two reasons for a separate institution: most importantly, to help the countries in the region learn to work cooperatively; and by setting up a separate institution, to enable the contributing countries to make a well-defined financial contribution to strengthening the peace process and the peace.
- Given the tensions in the area, isn't the notion of a cooperative venture hopelessly unrealistic? Perhaps. And perhaps not all the countries that should join will join at the beginning. But the Middle East is not condemned to war forever. Peace should have its chance.
- Is this not merely an external imposition, a remnant of colonialism? That depends on how the organisation works. The shareholders should encourage participation in the organisation and staff by residents of the Middle East, and should be working towards creating an organisation that is eventually run by Middle Easterners for the benefit of the nations in the area.
- Finally, why should the West, suffering from aid fatigue, beset by demands from Eastern Europe, contribute yet more money? There are compelling humanitarian reasons to try to bring peace to the Middle East. But even the most hardened practitioner of *Realpolitik* should recognise the need to change the prevailing destructive tendencies and risks at work within the region – and should recognise that this is best done by working towards cooperation among the countries of the Middle East.

6   Concluding comments

It is only realistic to recognise that the chances for broad-scale regional cooperation in the Middle East are limited by the extent of regional conflicts, and by the extent of trade in goods. Nonetheless, there are important economic complementarities within the region, for instance, between the availability of labour in the Northern ME and capital in the Southern ME, and between Israel and other economies; by overlooking labour flows, it is easy to underestimate the existing degree of interdependence of the Arab states within the region. But there are large potential gains from increased integration and cooperation that are unlikely to be reaped until the region becomes more peaceful and less torn by conflict.

The prime source of improved economic performance in the short run will be the vigorous pursuit by each economy of its own stabilisation and adjustment programmes. As the threat of war diminishes, reduced military spending could provide a large flow of resources to help finance needed human and physical capital investments.

The countries of the region have not learned to cooperate within the region itself. That is one of the reasons to set up an MEBRD, whose assigned tasks will be to finance reconstruction and infrastructure projects. Its more important function is to serve as the locus in which enhanced collaboration among the countries of the region can gradually develop.

NOTES

Department of Economics, MIT, and Research Associate, NBER. This chapter was first presented at the World Bank's Conference on 'Regional Integration', Washington, DC (2–3 April 1992). I am grateful for comments and suggestions by Abdullah Al-Mulla, Fawzi Al-Sultan, Richard Baldwin, Jaime de Melo, Ishac Diwan, Enzo Grilli, Leonard Hausman, Arvind Panagariya, Dani Rodrik, Nemat Shafik and Elias Tuma, none of whom necessarily agrees with the contents of the chapter. I have also benefited from comments and extraordinary assistance with data by Francis Ng of the World Bank.

1 The two Yemens have been merged in all data presented in this chapter.

2 In so doing, I omit countries that are sometimes included in the area, namely Sudan, Turkey, and countries of the Arab Maghreb Union other than Libya – Algeria, Mauritania, Morocco, and Tunisia. These countries are included in the region as defined by Waterbury (1978). I differ from Waterbury also in explicitly including Israel.

3 El Naggar (1987) divides the Arab countries in this group into the oil exporters, the middle-income countries, and the low-income countries. Yemen is the only country in the Middle East as defined here that he includes in the low-income countries. The North–South distinction corresponds closely to El Naggar's oil exporter and other categories, with the exceptions of Libya and Yemen.

4 Although this chapter relies heavily on data, the reader should be warned that the *caveat emptor* rule applies. There are certainly inconsistencies and implausibilities in some of the data presented here; when alternative sources gave different information, I relied on World Bank data unless there was good reason not to.

5 This aggregate is heavily influenced by the World Bank's estimate that *per capita* income in Iran in 1989 was $2530, and the UNDP's estimate of Iraqi income as $3020. In general, the data have to be treated as at best broadly indicative rather than strictly accurate. In some cases, there are large differences between World Bank and UNDP data that should be similar: for instance, measures of *per capita* real income growth are presented for 1965–89 by the IBRD, and for 1965–88 by the UNDP in the HDI. For Kuwait, HDR shows *per capita* income declining less than 1 percent per annum, whereas the

WDR reports an annual decline of 4 percent. Wherever possible in Table 13.1, I have used World Bank data; when those are missing I turn to other sources.

6 In 1980, the income of the six main oil-producing countries – Iran, Iraq, Libya, Saudi Arabia, Kuwait and UAE – was \$330 billion, compared with \$390 billion in 1989. Adjusting for inflation, this is a 22 percent real decline; adjusting for population growth, the decline in *per capita* real income was 43 percent over the period.

7 Sadowski (1991) presents similar data.

8 I use the NAFTA example rather than EFTA (European Free-Trade Area) because the former is currently in the news. EFTA, which has a longer history of actual rather than potential achievement, is in some respects a better model.

9 For a review of some of the existing regional arrangements among Arab countries in the Middle East and North Africa, and analysis of the role of factor as well as goods mobility, see Shafik (1992).

10 Remittance payments are part of exports, not transfers.

11 The source, HDR, does not document the original source of these data; they are described as 'Expenditure, whether by defence or other departments, on the maintenance of military forces, including the purchase of military supplies and equipment, construction, recruiting, training, and military aid programmes' (p. 195).

12 It is necessary here to repeat the data warning: the line between manufacturing and other industrial activity is difficult to draw.

13 I draw in this section on information in the World Bank's *Trends in Developing Economies*, Sadowski (1991), and papers forthcoming in Fischer, Rodrik and Tuma (1992).

14 Shafik (1992) argues that mobility of both labour and capital within the region would enhance stability, by giving all factor-exporting countries an interest in the prosperity and stability of the counterpart factor-receiving countries.

15 See Bisat and Hammour (1992).

16 Since some of the firms that serve the Middle East have moved to Athens and Rome rather than the Middle East, some might return if Beirut were restored.

17 For a critical view of the nature of the economic relations between the Occupied Territories and Israel, see Hamed and Shaban (1992).

18 See Awartani (1992) for an argument that supports a more open economy. One strand of Israeli opinion would like to reduce labour flows between Israel and the Occupied Territories for Israeli societal reasons.

19 Amin (1987) points to the need to redirect the educational system away from producing large numbers of individuals with skills that are not needed in the market.

20 However, the constituencies for change have not yet clearly emerged.

21 Shafik (1992) presents aggregate data for the Middle East (excluding Israel) that show intra-regional trade at 5–7 percent of total trade between 1985 and 1990.

22 The '2' in the heading of the first column adjusts for the fact that total trade is the sum of exports and imports.

23 The high share of intra-regional trade for Bahrain may reflect large re-exports of oil products from other Gulf countries.

24 Differing conventions with respect to freight and insurance, and misdeclarations, must account for some of the discrepancies. There are nonetheless impressive differences. For instance, UAE reports trade with Saudi Arabia as \$61.8 million; the corresponding Saudi number is \$213.4 million.

25 In the past, Syria has also been a major trader within the region.
26 The categories are: food and live animals; beverages and tobacco; crude materials excluding fuels; mineral fuels, etc.; animal, vegetable oil, fat; chemicals; basic manufactures; machines and transport equipment; miscellaneous manufactured goods; and other.
27 Bahrain, Kuwait, Oman, Qatar, Saudi Arabia and UAE.
28 These statements are based on data in Shafik (1992) Table 5.
29 Imports of labour to the recipient country come not only from the Middle East but also from the Maghreb, Turkey, Sudan and Asia.
30 The categorisation of Palestinians in the data may affect this estimate.
31 In a CU, a CET is collected and divided up among the member countries.
32 See de la Torre and Kelly (1992) for an informative review of regional trading arrangements, including discussion of the GCC.

REFERENCES

Amin, G. (1987) 'Adjustment and Development: The Case of Egypt', in S. El-Naggar (ed.), *Adjustment Policies and Development Strategies in the Arab World*, Washington, DC: IMF.

Awartani, H. (1992) 'Palestinian–Israeli Economic Relations: Is Cooperation Possible?', forthcoming in Fischer, Rodrik and Tuma (eds) (1992).

Bisat, A. and M. Hammour (1992) 'Economic Prospects for a Post-War Lebanon', forthcoming in Fischer, Rodrik and Tuma (eds) (1992).

Choucri, N. (1983) 'Asians in the Arab World: Labour Migration and Public Policy', Cambridge, Mass.: MIT Press (mimeo).

Diwan, I. and N. Papandreou (1992) 'The Peace Process and Economic Reforms in the Middle East', forthcoming in Fischer, Rodrik and Tuma (eds) (1992).

El-Erian, M. and S. El-Naggar (1992) 'The Economic Implications of a Comprehensive Peace in the Middle East', forthcoming in Fischer, Rodrik and Tuma (eds) (1992).

El Mallakh, R. (1978) 'Prospects for Economic Growth and Regional Cooperation', in J. Waterbury and R. El-Mallakh, *The Middle East in the Coming Decade*, New York: McGraw-Hill.

El Naggar, S. (1987) *Adjustment Policies and Development Strategies in the Arab World*, Washington, DC: IMF.

Fischer, S., D. Rodrik and E. Tuma (1992) *The Economics of Middle East Peace*, Cambridge, Mass.: MIT Press.

Hamed, O. and R. Shaban (1992) 'One-Sided Customs and Monetary Union: The Case of the West Bank and Gaza Strip under Israeli Occupation', forthcoming in Fischer, Rodrik and Tuma (eds) (1992).

Handoussa, H. and N. Shafik (1992) 'The Economics of Peace: The Egyptian Case', forthcoming in Fischer, Rodrik and Tuma (eds) (1992).

Hilan, R. (1992) 'The Effects on Economic Development in Syria of a Just and Long-Lasting Peace', forthcoming in Fischer, Rodrik and Tuma (eds) (1992).

Kleiman, E. (1992) 'Some Basic Problems of the Economic Relationships between Israel and the West Bank and Gaza', forthcoming in Fischer, Rodrik and Tuma (eds) (1992).

Krugman, P. and M. Obstfeld (1991) *International Economics*, New York: Harper-Collins.

Melo, J. de, A. Panagariya and D. Rodrik (1992) 'The New Regionalism: A Country Perspective', Chapter 6 in this volume.

Richard, A. and J. Waterbury (1990) *A Political Economy of the Middle East*, Boulder, Col.: Westview Press.

Sadowski, Y. (1991) 'Economic Crisis in the Arab World: Catalyst for Conflict', Washington, DC: Overseas Development Council, Policy Focus, **5**.

Shafik, N. (1992) 'Has Labor Migration Promoted Economic Integration in the Middle East?', Washington, DC: World Bank (mimeo).

Summers, R. and A. Heston (1991) 'The Penn World Tables (Mark 5): An Expanded Set of International Comparisons, 1950–1988', *Quarterly Journal of Economics*, **106(2)** (May), pp. 327–68.

Torre, A. de la and M.R. Kelly (1992) 'Regional Trade Arrangements', *IMF Occasional Paper*, **93** (March).

Waterbury, J. (1978) 'The Middle East and the New World Economic Order', in J. Waterbury and R. El-Mallakh, *The Middle East in the Coming Decade*, New York: McGraw-Hill.

Discussion

RICHARD BALDWIN

Chapter 13 is a brave study of an extremely difficult topic. I feel none of us would have had an easy time writing a paper on economic integration of a region in which non-economic concerns play such an important role. Indeed I felt that even an economist as capable and as seasoned as Fischer had a hard time of it. For instance, the first eight pages of the study is devoted to definitions. It is not until p. 426 that the author addresses the topic of the chapter directly. There he states, 'there is no realistic prospect of Middle East-wide regional integration on either the NAFTA or EC models in the near future. More limited moves towards economic cooperation in the region can be envisaged'. I will focus most of my comments on this statement. I realise that politics is the greatest impetus for Middle East economic integration, so that much of my comment is tangential to the main purpose of the chapter. Nevertheless, since I am a trade economist who firmly believes in following comparative advantage, and I have no particular knowledge of Middle Eastern politics, I limit my comments to the economics of Middle Eastern economic integration.

I think no one would disagree with Fischer's basic conclusion that a

Middle East-wide trade bloc is unlikely to form in the near future. In fact, I cannot even think what it would look like. I do, however, have a name for it: the Middle East Trade Opportunity Organisation, which would be known as ME-TOO. I suggest this somewhat flippant title since I think it captures the idea that much of the discussion about forming regional blocs all around the world is misguided. It is true that the European Community, and to a lesser extent the North American nations seem to have done well from regional integration. The sad truth, though, is that the cases of preferential trading areas that have failed far outnumber those that have succeeded. Here I am thinking of the various free-trade areas (FTAs) in Latin America, the Caribbean, and Africa. The recent surge of interest in trading blocs among developing nations stems mostly from a fear of being left out, a 'me too' attitude.

Moreover, I do not think we should be disappointed that the Middle East is unlikely to form its own preferential trading area. Such attempts could divert policymakers' attention from the most important changes necessary to promoting growth – ensuring a stable monetary environment, clear-cut property rights, a well-functioning infrastructure including basic education and a pro-private entrepreneurship attitude. On the trade side, it is far more important for these countries to open up to trade and investment relations with the industrialised world.

My last point is a more general one. I would posit that it is a stylised fact that South–South preferential trading arrangements do not work. They get signed with a great flourish of brotherhood and unity, but almost as soon as the ink of the headlines dries, the deals begin to be ignored. My point is that this fits in well with the notion that policy is endogenous to economy pressures. In the real world, trade policy is based mostly on mercantilist principles (leaving aside foreign policy considerations which clearly are Fischer's main concern). Policymakers view their own liberalisation as a cost, or concession, that must be incurred in order to obtain greater access for domestic firms to export markets. Looking at trade policy through the mercantilist prism, one immediately sees that South–South arrangements do not work since Southern exporters are not very interested in selling to other Southern markets.

ENZO GRILLI

Chapter 13 analyses trade and factor flows in the Middle East region and concludes that, however desirable, prospects for economic integration among the countries in this region are poor. It advocates instead cooperation initiatives, limited to some specific sectors such as water management and regional development banking. The chapter takes, at least implicitly, a functionalist approach – let's begin with modest initiatives of cooperation; these will help foster peace and take the cooperation process to a higher level; integration may come later. The experience of western Europe after World War II is used as a source of guidance for this piecemeal approach to economic (and political) cooperation.

I fully agree with Fischer on the limited prospects for economic integration in the region. This is a very fragmented and fragile region, both economically and politically. It is full of tensions and contradictions, and the political divisions are too well known to be recounted here. Economically, the main division is between: (a) the small (population-wise) 'rentier' countries of the Gulf, where consumption levels and consumption patterns are those of rich countries and production structures are still largely based on the exploitation of non-renewable natural resources; these are basically the high-income oil-exporting countries, and (b) the medium-to-large countries of the region, many of which produce and export some oil, but whose oil revenue is not enough to push incomes and consumption levels beyond those of middle-income developing countries, and whose production structures are still underdeveloped. In the former group consumers demand goods that neither domestic producers nor other producers in the region can supply. Investment goods and skill-intensive services demanded in these countries can also be supplied only by advanced industrial economies. This is why the trade of the high-income countries of the southern Middle East, with respect to both exports and imports, is mostly with the rich industrial countries and not with the poorer and less industrial countries of the region. Only their demand for labour-intensive and skill-specific services – a function of both high income and low populations – can be met by labour flows from their population-rich and lower-income northern neighbours. Thus, trade in goods is very limited within the region, while labour factor trade is very large, both in absolute terms and relative to trade in goods.

Capital, the other factor of production abundant in the first group and scarce in the second, could constitute an important intra-regional flow and permit over time the creation of the wherewithal of economic integration: communication infrastructure throughout the region and manufacturing capacity in the labour-rich countries of the northern Middle East. But this has not happened in the past, not even in the heyday of OPEC. The capital-surplus countries are either capital-investment shy, having a strong preference for keeping their wealth in financial assets, or do not find it secure to either lend for the financing of regional infrastructure – for example, through the various regional cooperative institutions already set up for this purpose – or to invest directly in plant, machinery, and equipment in the labour-rich countries of the region. Security of regional investments, and especially of direct investments, and freedom of profit repatriation must not be perceived as very high.

In these circumstances, beginning the integration process with trade liberalisation among the countries of the region and discrimination against the rest – the customs union (CU) way – makes little sense. I fully agree with Fischer here. The economies of these countries are too competitive and there is too little trade, actual or even potential, among them. The countries with actual excess demand for imports do not require the goods in actual excess supply within the region (the exceptions here are Israel and in part Egypt). It would, therefore, make more sense to start with helping to create integration in factor markets, with emphasis on capital mobility. However, this may not be an easy task as past experience has shown that liberalisation of trade in goods usually precedes integration of capital and labour markets. It is the development of strong trade relations that creates the conditions for the opening up and consolidating of capital flows. Here one must perhaps recall as a possible reason the characterisation of investors made not too long ago by Luigi Einaudi – they have hearts of lambs, legs of hares, and memory of elephants. Another reason is perhaps political. The trust on which strong capital flows – credit and investment – are built does not exist in the region and cannot be easily built. Or can it?

Chapter 13 recognises that regional integration in the EC–NAFTA mode is not feasible within the region, but goes on to say that limited free-trade arrangements among a subset of countries could be possible. But where? Certainly not among the small oil-exporting countries of the Gulf. There is little that they can produce for each other efficiently. Among the large, population-rich countries of the Northern Middle East? I doubt it. Their economies are too strongly competitive. Without Israel in their midst, the possibility of interindustry trade among them would seem to be minimal for many years to come. Intra-industry trade is even a more remote prospect. Even simple free-trade areas (FTAs) are hard to keep going if trade flows do not develop and consolidate the union. Discrimination against the rest of the world would also be very inefficient in this region and its immediate benefits to the member countries would become exhausted very quickly.

The chapter further argues that cooperation in building infrastructure and in managing water resources, for example, could be something to start with. In addition, a regional development bank (MEBRD) could be created to help, among other things, with reconstruction in the region. These more limited, functional cooperation projects would certainly be useful, if they turned out to be feasible. Past experience shows that even the sharing of specific resources such as water on effective regional banking require political trust among neighbouring countries in order to develop. One could argue, as the chapter at least implicitly does, that functionalism worked in Western Europe after World War II. Cooperation in specific sectors such as coal and steel helped to create political trust between two former enemies – France and Germany. This is quite true. But does the same logic apply in the Middle East? In Europe by the time the Coal and Steel Community (ECSC) was set up, peace between Germany and France, and between Italy and France, had already been reached and Germany and Italy had again become democracies. Neither peace, nor democracy – the handmaiden of peace – are yet widely and solidly present in the Middle East.

In conclusion, though I agree with the analysis of the chapter, I am left with a continued sense of pessimism regarding the proposals it contains: with respect both to regional integration in the Middle East, and to the steps for enhanced economic cooperation among its constituent countries. When a mind of the calibre of Stanley Fischer focuses on a search of this type and comes up with such a limited range of cooperation possibilities, things must be really tough. This is perhaps the pessimism of reason. But aside from reason there is in us a *'raison du coeur'*, as Pascal would have called it, which tells us that we surely must continue in our efforts to help peace and economic progress in this tormented region. Both are too important to be left to economic and political reasoning alone.

Round Table Discussion

RICHARD N. COOPER

Larry Summers is said to have said that he favours all of the 'laterals' – unilateral, bilateral, plurilateral, multilateral. I associate myself with that position, provided it leads to more liberal trade.

Jacob Viner's celebrated distinction over forty years ago between trade creation and trade diversion has been mentioned several times in this volume. What has not been mentioned is the motivation that led Viner to that distinction – namely his puzzlement, in the age-old debate between free trade and protectionism, that both adversaries could agree on the desirability of customs unions (CUs) or free-trade areas (FTAs). How can that be? Two groups who seemed to disagree on everything concerning trade policy agreed on this point. Out of that conundrum came Viner's distinction between trade diversion and trade creation, and his conclusion that the two groups had different emphases in mind in favouring CUs. The point is that motivation and details are all important.

Thus the key question is not multilateralism versus regionalism, but what is the motivation underlying the particular proposal at hand, and what are the all-important details. There is plenty of room for regionalism in a framework that requires the right details. The multilateral framework that we have, which it seems to me is a reasonably good one, sets the ground rules under which bilateral or trilateral or regional arrangements can go forward consistently with the multilateral orientation of the general framework.

What are those rules? I share Bob Hudec's view here. It is true that a skilful analytical economist can find a set of rules which could result in a discriminatory trading arrangement that is superior to a trading arrangement which meets the criteria established by GATT Article XXIV. But those rules would involve a formula that depends in a complicated way on the elasticities of substitution between products originating in different countries. Those elasticities are not directly observable, and would therefore have to be estimated using techniques that are not unimpeachable. So the estimates are bound to be controversial, and therefore subject to political manipulation. GATT Article XXIV lays down two perfectly sensible, if not perfect, principles: a CU or an FTA has to cover substantially all the (merchandise) trade between the two partners, so that they cannot limit it to commodities that will emphasise trade diversion; and as far as third countries are concerned the new level of protection

453

should not on balance exceed the level that prevailed before the formation of the arrangement.

These seem to me desirable principles. It is worth mentioning explicitly that they apply only to merchandise trade (and services intimately related to merchandise trade). Many international transactions do not involve such trade, and we do not yet have agreed principles. I will return to that issue, because I believe part of the case for less-than-global trading arrangements lies in the area of services.

Let me pose a question which I suppose many officials of the World Bank are occasionally posed: if you were advising a particular developing country that was considering joining a discriminatory trading arrangement, what would be your stance? In general, my stance would be one of extreme scepticism. Scepticism does not mean opposition in all circumstances; as noted above, the details are critically important. But the world has demonstrated during the past four decades that a developing country that has a clear view of its objectives and a good handle on the instruments of policy can thrive in a non-discriminatory, multilateral framework. It is difficult to believe that such countries, or others, could have done better in the more limited trading arrangements that are likely to emerge from the diplomatic/political process. If one looks at actual proposals – I am making a sweeping generalisation, in the interests of economy – most of them can be traced to foreign ministries or political leaders who are looking for symbolic forms of cooperation. They make their statements, sign their agreements, and then turn them over to ministers of economy or ministers of trade and industry to work out the practical details. Those ministers have not been given much opportunity to think seriously about the proposals or to consult their advisers on them, and in any case they rarely get the political support when it comes to making decisions that are thought to damage the economic interests of important groups.

The best strategy is to focus the country's policies on the world market, and to focus its diplomatic efforts on keeping the world market open. That means especially targeting the United States, the European Community, and Japan. It should give heavy weight to education, but not guarantee college graduates a government job. In particular, it should not be seduced by promises of what we would recognise as trade diversion. In the end, most such blandishments will work out to our country's disadvantage, even if only by diverting its attentions and efforts from more important issues. That proposition is no less true if the blandishments come from the United States or the European Community. Morocco, for instance, has been dislocated by the Community on several occasions: every time the European Community changes policies, Morocco has to adjust. Morocco would be better off today, in my judgement, if it had adopted a more globally-oriented trade policy in the 1960s and not put such heavy weight on developing special relations with the European Community – even though it could be expected to trade extensively with the European Community because of proximity.

Mexico's motivations in desiring an FTA with the United States seem to me not to fall in this category. As I understand it, the Mexican government has two principal reasons for wanting an FTA. The first is to foster and to lock in through international commitments a set of liberal trade policies that the current government has adopted unilaterally, to make credible to the business community that they cannot be easily reversed by subsequent administrations. The second is to lock the United States into a set of procedures that are more predictable for Mexican exporters with respect to the whole range of 'safeguards' – antidumping and antisubsidy procedures in particular. These are both quite respectable motivations, even from a multilateral perspective.

We tend to think of regional arrangements – as the name itself suggests – in terms of geographically contiguous entities. But there is no compelling reason why they should be so limited. Particularly in today's world of low transport costs, other reasons for bilateral or plurilateral trading arrangements may be more compelling than physical proximity. They offer a vehicle for achieving conditional most favoured nation (MFN) status. There are now over 100 contracting parties to the GATT, with highly diverse preferences and circumstances. That is too many to agree on much of anything. As we look ahead, truly multilateral negotiations may well impede rather than foster liberalisation of international transactions.

The impediment arises from the fact that with unconditional MFN many countries are tempted to become free-riders on the process, without contributing to it. Because of the wide diversity of preferences and circumstances, efforts to bring many countries into the negotiation will necessarily greatly narrow the agreed result. At the same time, as has been mentioned elsewhere in this volume, the growth of world trade has been such over the past four decades that there are no longer players so dominant that they are willing to accept numerous free-riders.

A solution to this problem is to revert to conditional MFN – that is to say, the formation of clubs, with club rules and open membership. Any country willing to adhere to the club rules can join, but no country is obliged to join. Membership entails both rights and responsibilities. We got our feet wet during the Tokyo Round with the government procurement code. Governments had widely different reservation positions and the risk under unconditional MFN was that there would be no agreement. The resulting code covered only the signatories, and even then a side agreement was necessary because not all the signatories could agree on telecommunications procurement. GATT coverage of government procurement is highly circumscribed, so the code offered a way to make some progress.

A comparable situation may exist for many services, especially those where the right of establishment is important for doing international business. Countries have radically different views on the desirability of allowing the establishment of foreign business. One may reasonably wonder why countries that do not have a problem with foreign business should be held up by those that do.

So we may face a practical choice in some areas. Do we have clubs with limited (but open) membership, sharing rights and responsibilities? Or do we try to impose unconditional MFN on new areas, and risk no progress because of the problem of free-riders? In some areas unconditional MFN may work, because some parties are sufficiently interested to go ahead despite lack of universal participation in new commitments; but in other areas that will not be the case. Plurilateral arrangements, not confined to geographically contiguous countries, offer a path for moving forward. In Chapters 8 and 9 it was pointed out that conditional MFN with tariffs led to a mess – complex, multicolumn tariff schedules, and a preoccupation with geographical arbitrage. That is correct. It might also lead to a mess ultimately in the area of services. But it might not, since the structure of the market is quite different. In any case, I would favour going through the dynamics, do such liberalisation as we can, and clean up the mess later if it turns out to be a mess.

I will make a final observation. With a note of regret, Krugman in Chapter 3 observed that economists' arguments on the merits of free trade had little to do with trade liberalisation over the last forty or sixty years. An underlying mercantilism, with a concern for export promotion, drove the process as the language of tariff 'concessions' in multilateral trade negotiations suggests.

I have a somewhat different perception. Krugman is correct in characterising the politics of the process. But, to give it a different twist, I like to think that skilful politicians, in the best sense of the term, recognised the merits of the economists' ideas and then figured how best to implement them through a political process that gives emphasis to production, jobs, and exports. No doubt reality is a combination of the two views. But I believe Krugman has underrated the potency of solid economic reasoning in framing trade policy over the past half century or more. It is no longer respectable to be an unqualified protectionist, as Herbert Hoover still was when he died. He never conceded his mistake in signing the Smoot–Hawley Tariff Act. That position would be difficult to defend today, and that marks some success in the march of ideas. So the influence of solid economic reasoning on public policy should not be dismissed so easily.

W. MAX CORDEN

What are the interests of developing countries in regional integration relative to alternatives, and what advice should the World bank give them? These seem to me the central issues on which one should focus here. I think that three of the chapters in this volume – those by Foroutan on Africa (Chapter 8), by Nogués and Quintanilla on Latin America (Chapter 9), and by Whalley on NAFTA (Chapter 11) – have shed a great deal of light on these two questions. I agree with the conclusions in all these chapters.

We have to consider two kinds of integration. First there is integration among groups, or possibly pairs, of developing countries, and the second is integration of particular developing countries with a large developed country or bloc, the 'hub-spoke' case.

1   Free trade areas (FTAs) among developing countries

The plain fact is that such FTAs (or preferential areas) would not make a great deal of difference, and have not in the past. The evidence is in Foroutan's and Nogués and Quintanilla's chapters. It is far better for Argentina to go for the world market – i.e., to liberalise unilaterally and in a non-discriminatory fashion, as she has been doing – than just to go for the Brazilian market. Brazil has the largest economy in the Third World, and yet it is smaller than Canada's (as measured by the dollar value of GDP). And this applies even more to Brazil: the world market is a lot more worthwhile for Brazil than even for Argentina plus Paraguay. It is obviously true for African countries. Given high protection against imports from outside, there will indeed be some opportunities for economies of scale in protected industries to be reaped through freeing trade with competitive developing economies. But this approach is thoroughly second best, and I would expect the gains to be very modest.

Unless protectionist barriers relative to the outside world were actually raised, I would not be worried about trade diversion resulting from moves towards such regional FTAs. But I would be worried about a diversion of interest. The recent trend towards trade liberalisation in so many countries – a dramatic and highly favourable development – must not be slowed up or discouraged by any push for regionalism. Freeing trade regionally is no substitute for opening up to the world – for going for the world market in exporting. Freeing trade (more or less) with everyone is much better. Another danger is that regionalism provides new life for protectionists, the establishment of CUs among developing countries providing a basis for high protection against imports from outside the union.

Of course, an FTA need not be protectionist. A country could liberalise relative to the world at large, and then, in addition, it could form an FTA with a neighbour, with whom the degree of liberalisation would be absolutely complete and more firmly committed than the country's wider liberalisation. One cannot really object to that. I would ignore possibilities of Vinerian trade diversion and place more emphasis on the marginally favourable effect of commitment to permanent liberalisation of trade with the neighbour. In addition, as Foroutan has noted, there is certainly scope for government activity and regulation integration.

Before leaving this topic, I have a footnote comment. It is sometimes suggested that it must surely be desirable to expand the size of countries – i.e., of their economies. It seems obvious that really small economies are not viable: after all, we don't suggest breaking up Belgium into fifty parts. But this argument ignores the trade-diversion possibility, which depends on the level of the external tariff or the tightness of restrictions on imports from outside. If Bombay were an independent economic entity and imposed high protection against imports from everywhere, including India, it would no doubt be worse off. But suppose it went free trade, or near-free trade, following the Singapore road? Has not Bombay lost by being part of the Indian customs and import restrictions union?

2   Integration with developed countries

I come now to the currently most fashionable kind of integration, namely that between developed and developing countries. We have already the long-established example of association of various developing countries with the European Community, the many proposals for more such associations, and the inclusion of the southern countries (Spain, Portugal, Greece) in the Community itself. And now, the big issue is a possible North American Free-Trade Area (NAFTA), to include Mexico and, even more radically, there is the Enterprise for the Americas Initiative (EAI) which suggests the possibility of more such 'hub-and-spoke' cases. On the other hand, it is worth underlining the conclusion from Saxonhouse's Chapter 12 that – contrary to much popular belief and many assertions – there is no such thing as a regional bloc in East Asia, and trade within East Asia appears to be quite well explained by a factor endowment-based gravity model. Japan is a hub, but not one resulting from deliberate discriminatory policies but resulting rather from the size and characteristics of its total trade.

What is the interest of a country like Mexico? The first interest should be in maintaining and expanding its trade liberalisation to the world as a whole. As has been often remarked, one advantage of forming an FTA with the United States would be that at least a part – an important part – of Mexico's trade liberalisation would be locked-in institutionally. The second – equally important – interest is in locking-in its access to the US market (the 'safe haven' argument) and even opening up this market further. Whalley's discussion of CUSTA in Chapter 11 – which is a trade agreement rather than an FTA – is a little chastening about what can be achieved. If the United States insists on all sorts of safeguards, on the right to impose antidumping duties, and so on, one must be a little sceptical about how 'safe' the haven can be made. A third interest is in avoiding, or at least minimising, trade diversion. Whalley refers to adverse exclusionary arrangements, no doubt directed against Japan. The broader danger is that the United States will compel Mexico to impose restrictions on imports from Japan and elsewhere that match the United States' own restrictions, so as to avoid trade deflection – i.e., the direct or indirect import of goods from outside into the United States via Mexico if the latter is less protectionist. The main point is that NAFTA should aim to be an FTA – a true FTA – but should not become a CU, since the latter would lead to Mexico's trade restrictions on imports from outside being determined in Washington, DC.

Two final points. First, while there may be benefits from a country like Mexico or Morocco making a trade agreement with the United States or the Community that ensures long-term free entry into a vast market, for many developing countries – all the countries of South, South East and East Asia and many countries of Africa – the regional road is not an option. For them, there is only the option of multilateral free or freer trade – i.e., GATT and the Uruguay Round. Only an adequate multilateral system can provide the 'safe haven'. At the moment this is also true of most Latin American countries. Conceivably most of Africa can end up associated with the Community and most or all of Latin America with the United States – but it is hard to believe (and not necessarily desirable) that Japan would fulfil a similar role in Asia.

This thought leads into the second point. One can discuss many second-best possibilities, and one can be 'politically realistic' and proclaim GATT dead, regionalism the way of the future, and so on – but it seems to me that one cannot get away from the need of developing countries to have available an open world market for their exports, present and prospective, and to be assured that success will not immediately encounter protectionist reactions (antidumping duties, safeguard measures, pressure to impose so-called 'voluntary' export restraints

(VERs), and the rest). Obtaining long-term guaranteed fully-free entry, without qualifications, into the United States or the Community would, indeed, be quite an impressive substitute, but apart from not being available for most – or even any – developing countries, it would still be thoroughly second best. Since protectionism exists and is universal, across countries and over time, it is indeed 'realistic' to accept it. But it can be reduced, or its growth checked, and that, happily, has also happened many times, including recently in many important developing countries. That is also 'realistic'.

RUDIGER DORNBUSCH

Let me try and make a simple case of why regionalism is an important additional strategy, additional, of course, to all the other things we do. But, first, where do I stand?

I certainly think that GATT is wonderful – has been, is, and will be and that it is pointless to say that we have to choose between GATT and the rest. GATT is a treaty, GATT is there; anything that is done in the course of a regional agreement that is incompatible, GATT will either have to find compensation, or not go forward. In that sense, such a choice is a red herring. Next, GATT is a good thing. In the context of regionalism it offers a well-described set of rules that makes regional trade zones actually interesting arrangements, rather than primarily limited opportunistic views with adverse side effects. Last, is there any fear that the GATT is dead? Lester Thurow, always in search of the limelight, used this phrase and was effective in getting attention. But surely that is not correct. GATT is not dying – it is resting. It is resting in the sense that, unfortunately, the Uruguay Round did offer an agenda that was too large by throwing agriculture in. And we are at a stage where the poker play is on to see the 'end of the world' or Uruguay Round and the bad news is that people have used the 'end of the world' for the last five years in this context, and they cease frightening people. My suspicion is that the Uruguay Round will go to Commission, that the widely-agreed and good things will go forward quickly, and that agriculture unfortunately will have to wait for a more opportune moment. So GATT is alive and well, and I certainly do not side with the people that say GATT is the general agreement to talk and talk. We have had good results.

Now, having GATT – demonstrably a good institution – why do we need more? Here, the first thing is to say 'history'. History is on the side of other mechanisms that also pursue the issue of freer trade: I say 'also' without trying to say more or less, on the side, above or below. Germany, every thirty years, used to make war on France; and that is not done any more. Where does that come from? It comes from the fact – and this is a point that Triffin has made, and once one hears it one appreciates it – that integration was forced on Germany and France under the Marshall Plan starting with the discriminatory European Payments Union (EPU), into the Common Market and now into a European space, and hopefully soon, into something that has Poland in it too, so that they too are safe from Germany. Who has any doubt that Triffin's reflection must carry some weight and perhaps more than the 'welfare triangle'. Perhaps there was discrimination; in fact, we know it was a conscious US decision to make Europe strong against Communism by allowing them a head start of ten years – a very conscious choice and, no doubt, an extremely successful one, of which we just have harvested the tail end. So here is one example of history. The second one is: does anyone doubt that it will be utterly desirable that South Africa engage in very open preferential trade with its neighbours, and the sooner the better? Surely, that has to be true. Surely, the more they trade with each other, the less there is an attempt to go back to very dark prospects for the region, and for peace in the region. And the same has to go for Eastern Europe. There is an open world trading system there, but if that's all Poland gets, Poland is not going to do very well. And on $1 an hour now, and fifty cents soon, who wants to see how that region moves politically? So again I am inclined to say that the triangle isn't all – but that does not mean we have a 'free for all' in trade policy and that any argument is good enough. But occasionally if it seems that a trade arrangement is an important initiative to advance a broader arrangement of integration that diffuses a historically very difficult situation – Germany and France, Germany and Poland, Eastern Europe – let's have a bit of trade integration ahead of world free trade.

The second reason to be concerned about regional arrangements and see something positive in them is to say that we have pockets of closedness that the GATT process has not in fact removed. I am not saying that the GATT process should have removed them, or that this is a failing of that process; I am just observing that GATT notwithstanding, there are still pockets. And the first is that developing countries have high protectionist barriers: we know about this because we are celebrating the cases where it's going away. If there are mechanisms to eliminate these more rapidly, then of course, we should want that. Unilateral liberalisation presents a problem because it means the terms of trade deteriorate; plurilateral may be better for the terms of trade, certainly for the balance of payments. So the less developed country (LDC) issue is the first. The second one is that Japan is completely closed, at least by comparison with any other industrialised country – an import penetration of 3.5 percent unchanged for thirty years and a ratio of non-oil imports to GNP that has a falling trend over the last thirty years, and today is lower than it was in 1955. Germany, which has the same problem on resources, of course, has a rising trend. You might say that, of course, Germany is in the neighbourhood of other countries and Japan is not. But then you have to argue that that is true only for Japanese imports and not for Japanese exports. So, LDC closedness and Japan are the two major issues of the world trade system in respect to openness; the third, of course, is the persistence, and even the growth, of hard core protection in developed countries, in the United States quite obviously textiles, glassware, and footwear. That needs an answer, too and, of course, the GATT process has been the mechanism for achieving massive liberalisation over the past forty years. It is not, I think, the area where GATT is most effective right now. In fact, it isn't the area that is primarily targeted in the current GATT negotiations. Why? Because there isn't really any interest on a multilateral level to engage in political risks at home for sacrificing those areas. That is, of course, when the argument goes much closer, when you can say that the same people who want to trade with Mexico are, in fact, the people who come across the border to produce footwear in the United States as illegal aliens and wouldn't it be a good idea to have them stay at home and import the shoes straight?

What is there on the other side? What would developing countries say to the argument? They would say that industries where they have a strong interest in market access are areas of hard core protection, and that the GATT process somehow has not managed to attack them. That special arrangements are the rule and becoming more and more special and perhaps less and less rewarding and that, therefore, perhaps the right direction is to use regional approaches to soften up the area. Once that has happened, once the special interest is weakened because the competition is already on their back, that's the wonderful moment where you actually can go multilateral.

That takes me to the final aspect of why I favour regionalism in this context. You induce the dynamics of free trade because the more of the areas that used to be totally untouchable are already open to competition in a regional arrangement, the less protectionist you need to be. Of course, I say that with a little bit of care because the other argument might be that any time you have already made the bad sacrifices to your new brothers, then you will be inclined to raise the external obstacles more. But raising the external obstacles is very difficult under GATT, and this is not what has happened in Europe.

Lastly, I add a broader agenda that tends to have more of a hearing in a regional context. In the context of US–Mexico, on the agenda now are environmental issues. I think it is inconceivable now to reach agreements in the GATT of the level of ambition and specificity including border issues that one will get with Mexico. There are labour standard issues that it may be outright unproductive to deal with on a GATT level that are being pursued in discussions with Mexico. There is also the push for modernisation in Mexico that is being handled very aggressively by joint committees from the respective labour departments revealing intelligent practices with which one might monitor accident rates in firms. The level of specificity and the depths to which the special agendas are carried and the back and forth of the concessions that are possible in a regional setting, and I am talking about a bilateral one, so far, are really impressive, and it would be a pity to forego those simply because with 105 in a room with far more diverse conditions and objectives that would be hard to achieve.

There are risks. One is that external restrictions in the regional arrangements come in through the rules of origin and that they become industrial policy. The second issue that is equally important is that Japan has to move ahead because the urge for protectionism comes directly from the perception that nobody can get into the Japanese market. It does not come from Mexico because you can sell there. It doesn't come from China because you can sell there. It comes from the fact that nobody can sell in Japan. Not Europe. Not the United States. Certainly not poor little Russia where all cars have square wheels.

So I come back to the question: should we have regionalism, and the answer is yes. Not as a cynical trade-diverting machine, but rather as an agenda to carry far ahead some objectives, and as you do that find that you can actually bear free trade on a much larger scale. Second, that the free-trade discussions in the United States have shown that there is a lot of enthusiasm for freer trade, a surprising amount in fact, but that the discussion also highlights where it aches, and that is Japan.

I conclude by saying that I do not believe that in my professional life I have seen a year where there was more enthusiasm for free trade of some form than now. And that means GATT, by all accounts, has served us well because otherwise an institution that has promoted freer trade would be indicted for getting the wrong results; it suggests that modernisation is getting a good name. While the pendulum is on that side, we should try and lock in a lot of free trade because it will not stay there forever.

Index